THE BLACKWELL HANDBOOK OF CROSS-CULTURAL MANAGEMENT

Handbooks in Management

Published

Donald L. Sexton and Hans Landström
The Blackwell Handbook of Entrepreneurship

Edwin A. Locke
The Blackwell Handbook of Principles of Organizational Behavior

Martin J. Gannon and Karen L. Newman
The Blackwell Handbook of Cross-Cultural Management

Forthcoming

Michael A. Hitt, R. Edward Freeman and Jeffrey S. Harrison
The Blackwell Handbook of Strategic Management

Robert E. Cole, Barrie G. Dale and Noriako Kano
The Blackwell Handbook of Total Quality Management

Randall S. Schuler and Paul Sparrow
The Blackwell Handbook of International and Comparative Human Resource Management

BPP Professional Education
32-34 Colmore Circus
Birmingham B4 6BN
Phone: 0121 345 9843

THE BLACKWELL HANDBOOK OF CROSS-CULTURAL MANAGEMENT

Edited by

MARTIN J. GANNON AND KAREN L. NEWMAN

Copyright © Blackwell Publishers Ltd 2002

Editorial apparatus and arrangement copyright © Martin J. Gannon and Karen L. Newman 2002

The moral right of Martin J. Gannon and Karen L. Newman to be identified as authors of the editorial material has been asserted in accordance with the Copyright, Designs and Patents Act 1988.

First published 2002

2 4 6 8 10 9 7 5 3 1

Blackwell Publishers Ltd
108 Cowley Road
Oxford OX4 1JF
UK

Blackwell Publishers Inc.
350 Main Street
Malden, MA 02148
USA

British Library Cataloguing in Publication Data

A CIP catalogue record for this book is available from the British Library.

Library of Congress Cataloging-in-Publication Data

The Blackwell handbook of cross-cultural management / edited by Martin
J. Gannon and Karen L. Newman.
        p.   cm. — (Handbooks in management)
Includes bibliographical references and index.
    ISBN 0-631-21430-5
    1. International business enterprises—Management—Social aspects. 2.
Management—Cross-cultural studies. 3. Corporate
culture—Cross-cultural studies. I. Gannon,
Martin J. II. Newman, Karen
L. III. Title. IV. Series.
  HD62.4 .B58 2002
  658′.049—dc21

                                                                    00-011796

Typeset in 10 on 12 pt Baskerville by Ace Filmsetting Ltd, Frome, Somerset

This book is printed on acid-free paper.

Contents

Figures

Tables

Contributors

Nancy J. Adler is a Professor of Management at McGill University, Montreal. Dr Adler consults with global companies and government organizations on projects in Europe, North and South America, and the Middle East. She researches in strategic international human resource management, world leadership, and global women leaders. She has written more than 100 articles and produced the film, *A Portable Life*. Her books include: *International dimensions of organizational behavior*, *Women in management worldwide*, and *Competitive frontiers: Women managers in a global economy*. Professor Adler is a Fellow of both the Academy of Management and the Academy of International Business.

Paul Almeida is an Assistant Professor of International Strategy at the McDonough School of Business, Georgetown University. Professor Almeida studies the inter- and intra-organizational transfer of knowledge in the semiconductor, biotechnology, and software industries. His research has been published in *Management Science*, *Strategic Management Journal*, and *Small Business Economics*, as well as in several scholarly books. Paul Almeida teaches courses in the field of knowledge management, international business, and strategy to MBAs and executives. His Ph.D. is from the Wharton School of the University of Pennsylvania and he has previously worked as an engineer and management consultant.

Pino G. Audia is an Assistant Professor of Organizational Behavior at London Business School. His research focuses on the role of performance as a regulator of organizational behavior, organizational learning, industrial clusters and the emergence of new firms, and cross-cultural management. His work has appeared in such journals as *Academy of Management Journal*, *American Journal of Sociology*, *Organization Science*, and *Journal of Applied Psychology*. He received his Ph.D. from the University of Maryland (USA) and his MBA from Bocconi University (Italy).

Paul Beamish is Associate Dean (Research), Professor of International Business, and Nortel Networks Director of the Asian Management Institute, Ivey Business School,

University of Western Ontario. He was Editor-in-Chief of the *Journal of International Business Studies (JIBS)*, 1993–7. He is the author or co-author of 27 books and over 70 articles or contributed chapters. He researches in international management, strategic management, and especially joint ventures and alliances. His articles have appeared in *Academy of Management Review, Strategic Management Journal, JIBS, Academy of Management Executive*, and many other journals. He has received best research awards from the Academy of Management, Academy of International Business, and the Administrative Sciences Association of Canada.

Robert J. Bies is Associate Professor of Management at the McDonough School of Business, Georgetown University. Professor Bies received his BA and MBA degrees from the University of Washington, and his Ph.D. from Stanford University. His research interests include organizational (in)justice, revenge in the workplace, trust and distrust dynamics, and the delivery of bad news. His work has been published in *Academy of Management Journal, Academy of Management Review, Journal of Applied Psychology, Journal of Management, Research in Organizational Behavior, Research on Negotiation in Organizations, Organization Science*, and *Organizational Behavior and Human Decision Processes*.

Michael Harris Bond has managed to function with delight and adequate effectiveness in three cultural systems other than the Anglo-Canadian variant of his Toronto birthplace: Californian, Japanese, and Hong Kongese. During these residencies he has cooperated productively with host nationals as well as colleagues from a variety of other cultural backgrounds. Being intellectually reflective, he continually wonders how persons are socialized to manage well both within and across different cultural systems. The present state of his understanding is best reflected in *Social psychology across cultures*, a text co-written with his English collaborator, Peter B. Smith.

Chris Brewster joined Cranfield School of Management in 1985. He has substantial experience in trade unions, government, specialist journals, personnel management, and consultancy. As well as teaching, Professor Brewster speaks regularly at international conferences and has acted as a consultant to UK and international organizations, mainly in the areas of personnel policies (his Ph.D. subject) and management training. He has written several books and many articles, and is Director of the School's Centre for Strategic Trade Union Management and Centre for HRM, conducting comparative research programs across the world.

John B. Cullen is Professor of Management at Washington State University. He has also taught on the faculties of the University of Nebraska, University of Rhode Island, Waseda and Keio Universities in Japan (as a Fulbright lecturer), and the Catholic University of Lille. Professor Cullen is the author or co-author of four books and over 50 articles, which have appeared in journals such as *Administrative Science Quarterly, Journal of International Business Studies*, and *Academy of Management Journal*. He currently serves on the editorial board of *Advances in International Comparative Management Journal*.

P. Christopher Earley is the Randall L. Tobias Chair of Global Leadership, Kelley School of Business, Indiana University. He received his Ph.D. from the University of

Illinois. He researches in cross-cultural and international aspects of organizational behavior such as the relationship of cultural values to workgroup dynamics, the role of face and social structure in organizations, and motivation across cultures. Recent publications include *Face, harmony and social structure: An analysis of behavior in organizations* and *The transplanted executive: Managing in different cultures* (with Miriam Erez). He is also editor of *Group and Organization Management* and former associate editor of *Academy of Management Review*.

William Egelhoff is an Associate Professor of Management Systems at Fordham University's Graduate School of Business. Before this he was on the faculty at New York University. He received his Ph.D. and MBA from Columbia University and his interests center around strategy and organizational design in multinational corporations. He has published articles in journals including *Administrative Science Quarterly, Strategic Management Journal,* and *Journal of International Business Studies.* He is author of a book, *Organizing the multinational enterprise: An information processing perspective,* and editor of a new book, *Transforming international organizations.*

Richard H. Franke is a Professor of Management and International Business. As a Ph.D. student of Bass and Barrett at Rochester, with an NAS research fellowship in Yugoslavia (where he met Hofstede in 1972), he began cross-cultural studies of health, crime, and economy. A 1991 *Strategic Management Journal* article with Hofstede and Bond strengthened their earlier findings of national culture's economic influence. Present work extends multivariate findings to 51 nations up to the end of the twentieth century, and seeks to build conceptual models explaining economic performance differences. It provides an expansive data base for cross-cultural research.

Martin J. Gannon (Ph.D., Columbia University) is Professor of Management and Director of the Center for Global Business, Robert H. Smith School of Business, University of Maryland, where he teaches in the areas of international management and behavior and business strategy. Professor Gannon is the author or co-author of 80 articles and 14 books, including *Dynamics of competitive strategy, Managing without traditional methods: International innovations in human resource management,* and *Ethical dimensions of international management.* His interrelated books include *Understanding global cultures: Cultural metaphors for 23 nations* (second edition), *Cultural metaphors: Readings, research, translations, and commentary,* and *Working across cultures: Applications and exercises.* Professor Gannon has been Senior Fulbright Research Professor at the Center for the Study of Work and Higher Education in Germany and the John F. Kennedy/Fulbright Professor at Thammasat University in Bangkok, and has served as a visiting professor at several Asian and European universities. He has also been a consultant to many companies and government agencies. Currently he is the external consultant to GEICO Insurance Company on its senior management training program and the University of Maryland Academic Director of the Northrop Grumman Certificate Program in International Management and Compliance Training (IMPACT).

Michele J. Gelfand is an Assistant Professor of Organizational Psychology at the University of Maryland. Her research examines cultural influences on negotiation and justice, workplace diversity, and sexual harassment in organizations. Her publications have appeared in *The handbook of industrial and organizational psychology*, the *Journal of Applied Psychology*, the *Journal of Personality and Social Psychology*, *Organizational Behavior and Human Decision Processes*, and the *Journal of Cross-Cultural Psychology*, among others. She is now working on a book on cross-cultural OB with Miriam Erez. Michele received her BA from Colgate University and her Ph.D. from the University of Illinois.

Robert Grant is a Professor of Strategy at the McDonough School of Business, Georgetown University. Professor Grant specializes in business and corporate strategy. His current research focuses on organizational capability and knowledge management, diversification strategies, and strategic organizational change in the energy sector. His recent books include *Contemporary strategy analysis*, widely used in MBA programs in Europe and North America, and *Restructuring and strategic change in the oil industry*. He is a member of the editorial board of *Strategic Management Journal* and *Strategy & Leadership*. He has consulted with companies such as Northern Telecom Inc., ENI, American Express, and AMOCO Corp.

Jerald Greenberg (Ph.D., Wayne State University), is Abromowitz Professor of Business Ethics and Professor of Management and Organizational Behavior at Ohio State University. Dr Greenberg has written over 130 publications, specializing in organizational justice. He has lectured extensively on this topic. His publications include *Advances in organizational justice* (with Copranzano), *The quest for justice on the job*, *Justice in social relations* (with Bierhoff and Cohen), and *Equity and justice in social behavior* (with Cohen). He is a Fellow of both the American Psychological Association and the American Psychological Society. Among his professional honors are: a Fulbright Fellowship, the New Concept Award and the Best Paper Award from the Academy of Management.

Louis Hébert (Ph.D., Western Ontario) is Associate Professor of Strategy at the Ecole des Hautes Etudes Commerciales (HEC) de Montréal. He co-wrote this chapter while a Visiting Professor of General Management at the Richard Ivey School of Business. His research interests focus on the management of joint ventures and strategic alliances. Several of his writings have earned him awards, including 1999 *Journal of International Business Studies* Decade Award for a paper on the control and performance of IJVs. Dr Hébert has taught in strategic management and international business in various degree and executive programs in North America and Europe.

Geert Hofstede is Fellow of the Institute for Research on Intercultural Cooperation (IRIC), and of the Center for Economic Research, both at Tilburg University, the Netherlands. He is Professor Emeritus of Organizational Anthropology and International Management (Maastricht). He holds an M.Sc. (Delft) and a Ph.D. (Groningen). He also worked in industry and founded the Personnel Research Department of IBM Europe. He taught at IMD, Switzerland; INSEAD, France; EIASM, Belgium: and IIASA, Austria. His best-known books are *Culture's consequences*, and *Cultures and organizations: Software of the mind*. He has lectured at universities and consulted for institutions and companies around the world.

Jean L. Johnson is Associate Professor of Marketing at Washington State University. Her research includes partnering capabilities development in and management of interfirm relationships, and the management of international strategic alliances. Dr Johnson's research appears in titles such as the *Journal of Marketing*, *Journal of International Business Studies*, *Journal of the Academy of Marketing Science*, and *International Journal of Research in Marketing*. She serves on the editorial boards of the *Journal of Marketing* and the *Journal of the Academy of Marketing Science*, and reviews for others. Dr Johnson spent several years in advertising, and has lived, taught, and researched in France and Japan.

Colin J. Jones is Senior Lecturer in Accounting and Finance at the University of Hull Business School. He worked in industry and commerce as a management consultant before commencing his academic career. Colin has extensive teaching experience, particularly at senior executive management level. His research interests and publications initially related to issues in management accounting and control, but have since extended to other areas of management, particularly in South East Asia. He is currently working on research issues with a cultural focus in the region.

Torsten M. Kühlman is Chair of Human Resource Management at the University of Bayreuth. He holds a doctorate in business administration from the University of Erlangen–Nürnberg and teaches courses in international human resource management and organizational behavior. His research interests focus on overseas assignments, entrepreneurship in China, and interorganizational trust. He serves as a reviewer of *Ergonomics*, *Journal of Occupational and Organizational Psychology*, *Management International Review*, *Zeitschrift für Arbeits- und Organisationpsychologie*, and *Journal of Applied Psychology*.

Marty Laubach is a doctoral student in sociology at Indiana University. He returned to academe after an 18-year career in data processing which included management positions both in the public and private sectors. His primary research interest involves the effects of subjective interpretations of experience on social behaviors, which has generated papers on topics as diverse as a measurement for informal stratification of the workplace (i.e. formal administrative organization) and the social effects of psychism (i.e. religious altered states of consciousness).

Richard Mead is Director of Asian Business Studies at the School of Oriental and African Studies, University of London. Previously he taught at the Sasin Graduate Institute of Business Administration, Thailand. He has nearly 30 years' experience in teaching and researching in communications and management, including periods in Sierra Leone, Libya, Saudi Arabia, Iran, Malaysia, and the United States at the Kellogg School. He is Director of Arts Interlink (arts management consultants) and is currently preparing a third edition of *International management* for Blackwell.

Mark E. Mendenhall holds the J. Burton Frierson Chair of Excellence in Business Leadership at the University of Tennessee. Prior to this he held the Ludwig Erhard Stiftungsproffessor Endowed Chair at the University of Bayreuth and was a visiting professor at the Europa Institute, University of Saarland. He has published numerous books and articles on expatriate management and other international human resource management issues. He is active in the Academy of Management, and is past president of its International Division. His other research and consulting interests are in the areas of leadership and organizational change, the non-linear dynamics of organizational systems, and Japanese organizational behavior.

Karen L. Newman was named Dean at the University of Richmond in 1999. Before joining the University of Richmond, Dean Newman served on the faculty of Georgetown University's McDonough School of Business for 15 years, where she was Associate Dean for Graduate Business Programs from 1993 to 1996. Newman also was a visiting professor at the Czech Management Center in 1997 and 1998, and at the Melbourne Business School periodically between 1991 and 1996. She served on the faculty of Georgetown's Management Development Program for Central and East European Executives from 1991 to 1993 and as Academic Director of that program in 1993. Dean Newman is the author, along with Stanley D. Nollen, of the book, *Managing radical organizational change*. In this work she uses in-depth longitudinal cases from six Central European firms to understand how companies adapt to radical change in their institutional environments. Her 2000 article in the *Academy of Management Review* elaborates a formal theoretical model about radical institutional-level change, organizational learning, and adaptive organizational change. She is the author or co-author of over 40 scholarly articles or book chapters on topics such as organizational change, workplace commitment, cross-cultural management practices, and organizational careers. Dean Newman earned her Ph.D. in behavioral sciences and an MBA from the University of Chicago's Graduate School of Business. She gained a BS degree with honors in economics from Purdue University.

Joyce S. Osland is Associate Professor of Organizational Behavior at the University of Portland, Oregon. She lived and worked overseas in seven countries for 14 years, primarily in West Africa and Latin America, as a manager, researcher, consultant, and professor. Dr Osland's current research and consulting interests include expatriates, cultural sense making, Latin American management, and global leadership. In addition to various articles, she is author of *The adventure of working abroad: Hero tales from the global frontier*, and co-author of *Organizational behavior: An experiential approach*, and *The organizational behavior reader*.

Mike W. Peng (Ph.D., University of Washington) is an Assistant Professor of Management at Ohio State University. His work concentrates on international strategy. He has written two books, *Behind the success and failure of U.S. export intermediaries* and *Business strategies in transition economies*. His research has been published in the *Academy of Management Executive*, *Academy of Management Journal*, *Academy of Management Review*, *Journal of International Business Studies*, and *Journal of Management Studies*, among others. He currently serves on the editorial board of the *Journal of International Business Studies* and *Asia Pacific Journal of Management*.

Mark F. Peterson (Ph.D., University of Michigan) is a Professor of Management and International Business at Florida Atlantic University. His principal interests are in the way managers make sense of work situations and the implications of culture and international relations for the way organizations should be managed.

Anupama Phene is Assistant Professor of Strategy at the David Eccles School of Business, University of Utah. She received her Ph.D. in international management from the University of Texas. Her research primarily focuses on firm strategy in a multinational context, evolution of firms and subsidiaries, and development of firm capabilities in knowledge creation and transfer.

Diana C. Robertson is Associate Professor of Organization and Management at the Golzueta Business School, Emory University. She received her Ph.D. from UCLA and was previously on the faculties of the Wharton School, University of Pennsylvania, and London Business School. Her specialization is business ethics and she has published articles in *Organization Science, Business Ethics Quarterly, Sloan Management Review, Journal of Business Ethics, Human Relations,* and *Journal of International Business Studies.*

Carlos J. Sánchez-Runde (Ph.D., University of Oregon) is an Assistant Professor of Human Resource Management at IESE, University of Navarra, Barcelona. His primary interests are in international HRM and cross-cultural management. He has taught in North and South America and Europe, and has written a book and several papers in strategic HRM and organizational behavior. He has also consulted for organizations like Andersen Consulting, Bayer, the Bertelsman Group, and Seat–Volkswagen.

Peter B. Smith is Professor of Social Psychology at the University of Sussex. He is the author or co-author of six books, including the recent *Social psychology across cultures,* with Michael Bond, and also some 90 other publications in social and organizational psychology. Since the mid-1980s he has collaborated with Mark Peterson in researching a model of leadership based upon the concept of event management in more than 40 nations. He is currently studying effective handling of relations between managers from different cultures, sampling joint ventures and multinationals in China, Belarus, the UK, and Netherlands. He also edits the *Journal of Cross-Cultural Psychology.*

Günther K. Stahl is Assistant Professor of Human Resource Management and Leadership at the University of Bayreuth, from which he holds a doctorate in business administration. He has published books and articles in the field of leadership development, cross-cultural management, and international human resource management, particularly the management of expatriates. He has conducted research projects in Japan and the United States, and his current research interests include careers in multinational corporations, trust within and between organizations, and integration processes in mergers and acquisitions. He has also done consulting work for various organizations.

Richard M. Steers is the Kazumitsu Shiomi Professor of Management, Lundquist College of Business, University of Oregon. He holds a BA from Whittier College, an MBA from the University of Southern California, and a Ph.D. from the University of California, Irvine. He researches in leadership and motivation in organizations, and in cross-cultural management. He is the author or co-author of 20 academic books and over 70 articles. Recent books include *Made in Korea: Chung ju yung and the rise of Hyundai,* and *Korean enterprise: The quest for globalization.* Professor Steers is a fellow and past president of the Academy of Management and a fellow of both the American Psychological Society and the Society of Industrial and Organizational Psychology. He has served on the editorial boards of a number of journals including *Administrative Science Quarterly*, *Academy of Management Journal*, *Academy of Management Review*, and the *Journal of World Business*.

Svenja Tams is a doctoral candidate in organizational behavior at London Business School and is on the adjunct faculty at the London School of Economics. She received an M.Sc. in information management from the London School of Economics. Her current research interests include the formation of self-efficacy, the interaction between task context and self-management, learning competencies, and working in international business environments.

Harry C. Triandis is Professor Emeritus at the University of Illinois. Recent books are *Culture and social behavior* and *Individualism and collectivism*. He was the general editor of the six-volume *Handbook of cross-cultural psychology* and also edited volume 4 of the *Handbook of industrial organizational psychology*. Professor Triandis has published more than 80 chapters in books and over 100 articles and monographs in journals. He is past president of five psychological associations, has lectured in more than 40 countries on all inhabited continents, and has received one honorary doctorate and several awards from psychological associations.

Preface

Almost all academic and professional fields have handbooks highlighting major perspectives, research on them, and the manner in which the perspectives and research can be applied to real-world problems. Ironically, the field of management, which has been so popular in recent years that management gurus are given prominent attention in magazines and the media in general, has been derelict. This is particularly true in the area of cross-cultural management, which seems paradoxical in that globalization confirms the necessity of such analyses. There is only one previous Handbook in the area of cross-cultural and international management, and it focuses on research and research methods (see Punnett and Shenkar, 1996). The current Handbook seeks to emphasize research, but it also attempts to integrate or at least to highlight the major theoretical perspectives in the field of management as they apply to the cross-cultural area and the major problems and issues within this field.

In addition, this Handbook explicitly seeks to demonstrate how the theoretical perspectives and research findings can be applied to actual situations and organizations. Further, the parts of the book reflect an underlying model of management extending from the influence of national cultures on managerial and employee behavior and then logically and sequentially including: strategy, structure, and inter-organizational relationships; human resources; motivation, rewards, and leadership behavior; interpersonal processes; and corporate culture and values.

All of these ideas are more fully presented in the introduction and in the introductions to parts of the Handbook. We decided to write these introductions for several reasons, including the complexity of the material, the need to show relationships between the chapters in each part, and the desire to identify additional and promising areas of research.

To complete such an ambitious agenda, we approached the major cutting-edge authors in the cross-cultural area to write chapters for the Handbook. Some of them were initially reluctant to participate given their busy schedules, but the explanation offered above was sufficient to convince them of the utility of the project. Like us, they recognized the need for such a Handbook and helped to bring it to fruition. Because each comes at the issues from his or her own perspective, the chapters vary in focus, style, and length. We encouraged authors to approach their chapter in their own way, resulting in rich variety across the chapters.

We have consciously attempted to provide perspectives that are frequently viewed as relatively independent from one another. Thus several contributors are cross-cultural psychologists. Others are sociologists and still others are economists. Integrating these perspectives with management perspectives proved to be challenging. In the end, however, we feel that the results more than justified the effort.

We welcome your comments, good and bad, about the book. Our e-mail addresses are:

mgannon@rhsmith.umd.edu; knewman@richmond.edu

Editors' Introduction

When we were asked to edit the first *Handbook of Cross-Cultural Management*, we were excited about undertaking such an ambitious project. Before we could even think about emphasizing the "cross-cultural" in management, however, we needed to define more precisely the term "management," or at least to narrow our perspective so that this broadly expansive term might have meaning in and of itself and within the cross-cultural area. We immediately rejected the approach of a simple definition, as this would greatly restrict our vision and force us to ignore critical areas of importance.

At that point we were attracted to the ideological struggles that in the past have helped to shape the field of management. These struggles usually take the form of direct contrasts, for example, the statistical/quantitative/economic perspective on management issues and problems versus the behavioral perspective. At a very general level, such an approach may be justified. For example, the subfield "human resource management" can reasonably be portrayed in terms of three eras: The traditional era during which narrow personnel functions were emphasized while theory was given minimal attention (until about 1950); the human resources era during which behavioral theories such as theory X and theory Y framed the approaches that managers used to solve problems (1950–75); and the economics era, during which transaction costs economics reframed the approaches to human resources in terms of minimizing the transaction costs or the costs of doing business (1975–90) (see Gannon, Flood, and Paauwe, 1999). Even this solution, however, left much to be desired. For example, "pay for performance" sounds as if it were derived directly from transaction cost economics, but in fact its origins can be found in Adams's equity theory, which is a behavioral theory (Adams, 1965). Thus, at the level of issues and problems, using such broad contrasts to structure and frame this Handbook would be very problematic.

We then began to identify criteria by means of which we could structure this Handbook and its various parts. It immediately became apparent that specific disciplines were studying management issues and problems as if they had little if any relationship to one another. For instance, the voluminous and important work of cross-cultural psychologists is minimally cited by management researchers who study similar problems but from an economics perspective. Thus we decided to include as many important perspectives on management issues as would be feasible within the scope of a Handbook.

Next, we began to organize the parts of the book in terms of the classic issues that managers face. Part I begins with two prominent cross-cultural frameworks within which management takes place, one developed by Geert Hofstede (1980) and the other by Harry Triandis (Triandis and Gelfand, 1998). Their work has been used by a very large number of cross-cultural management researchers and theorists, and it seemed fitting that the reader be exposed to both their most significant and most recent work, especially since these theorists provide an excellent description of the environmental context of cross-cultural management.

Part II then focuses on the key relationships among business strategy, the organizational structures that are appropriate for achieving them, and the inter-organizational alliances and relationships that are dramatically magnified within a cross-cultural environment. In this part the authors relate strategy to appropriate structures, contrast the relative influence of institutions such as laws and culture on actual behavior, examine the relative effectiveness of specific cooperative strategies that firms develop cross-culturally, and look at the manner in which knowledge (both explicit and tacit) is acquired through cross-cultural alliances.

After management has evaluated the broader cross-cultural context or environment in which it must operate and examined the relationships among the macro issues of strategy, structures, and inter-organizational relationships, it must devote attention to managing the human resources within the new and complex arrangements. This is the task of part III. To understand this task, it is helpful to examine human resource practices in multinational companies (chapter 7). It is also helpful to look at the relative efficacy of goal setting and feedback in the appraisal process in different nations. That is, what works in one nation or setting may be a disaster in another (chapter 8). In chapter 9 the authors focus their attention on a truly unique cross-cultural activity, that is, how can a firm use expatriate assignments as a method of employee development? This is an arresting issue, as early studies in the 1970s indicated that such assignments were problematic much more often than not, and even today managers return from such challenging assignments only to be assigned to positions with lower responsibility than they exercised abroad or even before they went abroad. More perniciously, what they learned abroad is sometimes viewed as counter-productive to narrow domestic concerns.

Part IV of the book continues with a focus on micro issues and problems, but the focus switches from human resource management to organizational behavior. That is, how can management lead subordinates effectively when operating in cultures other than their own? More specifically, how can managers motivate and reward subordinates in such a way that their management systems and approaches do not violate basic cultural norms and, in the process, lead to unanticipated negative consequences? The concluding chapter in this part examines the issue of women leaders in the global economy and whether the female style of managing or a fusion of the male and female styles of managing will be more successful than the traditional male style in this changed environment.

In part V the emphasis on organizational behavior continues, but the focus is now on interpersonal processes or relationships between individuals and groups. These interpersonal processes include group dynamics, cross-cultural communication, and negotiation and conflict management between individuals and groups.

All of the topics in the previous parts of the book – business strategy and its relationship with organizational structure and inter-organizational alliances, managing human resources, leading in such a way that subordinates are rewarded properly and become motivated and satisfied, and managing interpersonal processes so that smooth group dynamics and cross-cultural communications lead to successful negotiations and conflict management – tend to shape the values and corporate culture that provide the lens through which managers understand cross-cultural issues and problems. In part VI there is a probing analysis of such values, and it emphasizes concepts of justice and fairness across cultures, trust in cross-cultural relationships, and business ethics across cultures.

Thus parts and chapters of this Handbook logically flow into one another in terms of the major concerns and areas of management. There is an implicit systems feedback loop in the model, since organizational culture and values obviously influence business strategy, the starting point within the cross-cultural context. Unlike a simple definition of management, this perspective allows the reader to see the issues and problems facing managers within a dynamic and systematic context. For example, it is not only strategy and structure that need to fit together appropriately, but also all of the other macro and micro aspects of organizations described above. See figure I.1 for our cross-cultural model of management used to structure this book.

Once we had structured the book, we sought out theorists and researchers whose work is known for its cutting-edge quality. We also attempted to involve researchers from a number of nations so as to avoid an ethnocentric bias, and to include a balanced group of well-known and promising researchers. In doing so, we were ineluctably and happily

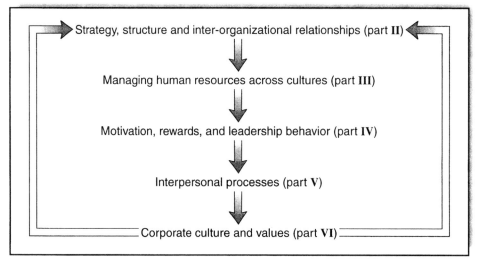

Frameworks for cross-cultural management (part I)

Strategy, structure and inter-organizational relationships (part **II**)

Managing human resources across cultures (part **III**)

Motivation, rewards, and leadership behavior (part **IV**)

Interpersonal processes (part **V**)

Corporate culture and values (part **VI**)

FIGURE I.1 The cross-cultural model of management used to structure this handbook

locking ourselves into a distinctive approach. That is, we wanted to shine as many critical theoretical lights on cross-cultural management as possible. Thus, unlike the "eras of management" approach that would have narrowed our perspective, we actively encouraged our authors to present and, if appropriate, test various theories but within a cross-cultural context.

Our authors responded enthusiastically, and hence the number of important theories that are emphasized in one way or another in this Handbook is impressive. These include such specific theoretical perspectives as transaction costs economics, social exchange theory, metaphor theory, social comparison and equity theory, relative deprivation theory, and information processing theory. The exploration of such a large and diverse number of theoretical perspectives and theories has reinforced the point that theories and issues/problems, similar to business strategy and organizational structure, should be matched. Having the appropriate theory to explain a specific phenomenon or problem or issue is far more helpful than taking an ideological and inflexible position, particularly in an area as complex as cross-cultural management. To cite but one example, Bies and Greenberg go far beyond the cross-cultural dimension of individualism-collectivism to explain the reactions both in the United States and Indonesia to the issue of paying wages in Indonesia that would be substandard in the United States (see chapter 16).

As this discussion suggests, this Handbook is designed for various types of readers. Managers can glean insights into the major cross-cultural issues and problems that they face and use the perspectives in their daily work, for example, employing metaphors in negotiations and conflict management and varying the kinds of interpersonal communications to fit the cultures in which they operate (see chapters 14 and 15). Researchers and doctoral students can explore the chapters presenting new data and testing specific theories and use them as avenues for their own research streams or as ways of gaining new insight. Also, MBA students can begin to see the complexity of issues that they will face as managers within a cross-cultural context. Even policy-makers should find the Handbook of interest in such areas as developing codes of conduct across nations and ways of framing cooperative rather than antagonistic strategies involving various companies and government agencies.

This Handbook, however, represents only a starting point for evaluating management issues cross-culturally. Such issues are neither unique nor distinctive within the cross-cultural environment, but all of them reflect traditional management concerns. As globalization proceeds, we can expect that the number of issues and problems will increase, and the need for new and different theoretical perspectives will correspondingly rise. This Handbook has helped to address this problem by covering a great amount of theoretical territory in a parsimonious manner. But the problem, by its very nature, will continue to confront future generations seeking to make sense of the complex world of cross-cultural relations.

Part I

FRAMEWORKS FOR CROSS-CULTURAL MANAGEMENT

Introduction

Chapter 1 provides an overview of the book and presents the cross-cultural model of management underlying the book's structure. In chapter 1, the authors – Franke, Hofstede, and Bond – employ the well-known five-dimensional framework of national cultures with which they are closely associated in their analysis. The original Hofstede study based on a survey of 117,000 managers, supervisors, and employees at IBM yielded four dimensions of national culture (individualism/collectivism, masculinity/femininity or assertiveness, uncertainty avoidance, and power distance). Later, a second independent but Hofstede-focused study yielded another dimension, time orientation or the degree to which a nation's citizens were willing to sacrifice short-term gains for long-term benefits (see The Chinese Connection, 1987; Hofstede and Bond, 1988).

In this chapter the authors focus on the relationship between national culture using these five dimensions, economic prosperity, and economic growth in a new data analysis of 51 nations in two time periods, 1960–80 and 1980–98. As in their earlier works, the authors conclude that culture matters for many reasons, one of which is that it is predictive of both national economic wealth and economic rates of growth. They also empirically demonstrate that the cultural factors or dimensions leading to economic growth vary in different time periods. This conclusion has been echoed in a prominent symposium on economic growth (see Harrison and Huntington, 2000).

Harry Triandis has taken the Hofstede research in a new and exciting direction, as he explains in chapter 2. He focuses primarily on the Hofstede dimensions of individualism/collectivism and power distance. He has shown that there are four generic types of individualism and collectivism, both of which can be either horizontal (low power distance) or vertical (high power distance). It is possible and helpful to describe specific types of individualism and collectivism within nations and ethnic groups, but first we need to identify the generic type characteristic of a nation or ethnic group (for specific types, see Gannon and Associates, 2001).

Like Hofstede, Triandis is very careful to specify the unit of analysis, as his four generic types refer to the nation and not every individual in it. He then focuses on the individual and points out that a person can be either allocentric (collectivistic) or idiocentric (individualistic). Conflicts arise when there is a difference between the values of the individual and the nation or ethnic group.

Alan Fiske (1992) has independently constructed a system very similar to Triandis's formulation, both at the national/ethnic cultural level and the individual level. One important point that he makes is that it is very difficult for individuals to cognitively focus on others in cultural interactions, and that they tend to simplify reality by employing the four types of statistical scales. We can apply these scales to the Triandis framework in the following way: horizontal collectivism (nominal scale); vertical collectivism (ordinal data); horizontal individualism (interval data); and vertical individualism (ratio data).

But Triandis does much more in this very readable *tour de force*. He expands the concept of a cultural dimension into a cultural syndrome or a shared pattern of beliefs, attitudes, self-definitions, norms, roles, and values organized around a theme. Such syndromes include individualism, collectivism, complexity, tightness of rules, and so forth. He also describes the basic attributes of culture, discusses individualism and collectivism from a historical perspective and treats a wide range of topics such as goal setting and morality. In the concluding section of the chapter Triandis provides guidelines and suggestions to management on these and related issues.

1

National Culture and Economic Growth

RICHARD H. FRANKE, GEERT HOFSTEDE, AND
MICHAEL HARRIS BOND

Questions linking national culture, workplace culture, and national economic performance have been at the forefront of research during the last half of the twentieth century.
Two very different research traditions, one initiated by McClelland (1961) and the
other by Hofstede (1980) addressed the relationship between individual personality,
culture, and economic growth. Though each posited different mechanisms, both concluded that certain characteristics of national culture were associated with economic
growth. In this chapter, we extend this line of inquiry, building explicitly on the
Hofstede research tradition. We first review the literature on national culture and
economic growth. Then we examine economic growth in 51 countries between 1960
and 1980 and also between 1980 and 1998 as a function of national cultural values. We
draw the conclusion that national culture does contribute to economic growth, but that
the relationships shift over time, depending upon the effect of technological break-
throughs. In general, we find that cultures with a long-term orientation are more likely
to grow more rapidly during the periods under consideration than countries with other
national cultural values.

THE HOFSTEDE TRADITION

Geert Hofstede (1980) introduced his now classic dimensions of national culture research
based on data from one multinational firm (IBM). Hofstede analyzed a data base of
survey scores of over 117,000 IBM employees in over 70 nations, collected between 1967
and 1973; his first analysis covered 40 of these nations. The cultural dimensions derived
from the research include power distance (perception of inequality and authoritarian
behavior, and lack of subordinate interest in participation), uncertainty avoidance (anxiety at work, concern over instability, and rule-oriented inflexibility when faced with new
or ambiguous circumstances), individualism (a focus on self rather than group), and
masculinity (an assertive or competitive orientation and gender-role sensitivity). The
primary contribution of Hofstede's initial work was to develop, describe, and validate the

four dimensions of culture. His analysis included the relationship between national culture and past economic growth.

The economic growth analysis in Hofstede's (1980) figure 7.10 showed significant relationships of economic growth with individualism and uncertainty avoidance between 1960 and 1970 among wealthier nations. (Among poorer countries, Franke, Mento, and Brooks (1985) found some degree of political stability was required for Hofstede's cultural measures to influence economic performance.) Contrary to what might be assumed, the less individualistic and less flexible nations grew most rapidly. However, the more individualistic and more flexible nations tended to be richer already. In other words, the correlation between national culture and economic growth came from countries "on the move" rather than countries already among the wealthiest.

A second study (Hofstede and Bond, 1988) used the four cultural measures from the instrument developed for IBM by Hofstede and a Chinese Value Survey measure developed by Michael Bond and his colleagues in China (The Chinese Culture Connection, 1987). This fifth cultural dimension, rooted in Eastern rather than Western culture, was labeled Confucian work dynamism. It is a subset of Confucian values that encourages a persistent and thrifty long-term orientation of personal responsibility and self-respect that is "hierarchically dynamic," and transcends family and social conservatism, as opposed to other equally Confucian values that are oriented toward the past and present (The Chinese Culture Connection, 1987: 150; Bond, 1997). Hofstede (1991) applied the descriptor, "long-term orientation" versus short-term orientation, as a broad label for this complex factor of culture that also is found in countries not exposed directly to Confucian teaching. National averages for long-term orientation measures collected from over 2,000 university students in 22 countries between 1983 and 1985 were reported by Bond and colleagues in the Chinese Culture Connection (1987).

Hofstede and Bond (1988) found that countries with higher long-term orientation grew more rapidly than other countries between 1965 and 1985. Since Confucian values are not likely to have been recent developments caused by rapid economic development, the authors assumed that they were more likely to be a cause rather than an effect of economic growth.

In a third study, possible effects of the five cultural indices on national economic growth were examined more systematically over two economic growth periods by Franke, Hofstede, and Bond (1991). This article made explicit allowance for economic convergence, included replication, and measured economic growth following upon or concurrent with time of measuring cultural indices. For the sample of 18 separate nations with both Western and Eastern measures of culture available, regression models for growth of per capita gross domestic product between 1965 and 1980 and between 1980 and 1987 showed that national value culture accounted for between 70 percent and 80 percent of the differences in economic growth rates (which ranged from less than zero to more than 10 percent per year). Regression results for both periods included significant effects of individualism and Confucian work dynamism or long-term orientation as explanatory variables. Similar to the first study by Hofstede (1980a), the impact of individualism was negative. And, consistent with the work of Hofstede and Bond (1988), the effect of long-term orientation was positive for economic growth.

Another analysis by Franke (1992b) elaborated upon the previous models and added four additional nations. He tested inter-sample reliability and stability over time for national measures of individualism and power distance, using data gathered from alumni of a series of mid-career seminars for European professionals by Hoppe (1990) in 1983 and 1984, more than a decade after Hofstede's surveys of IBM technical and clerical employees. He included data from a set of 62 nations (Franke, 1974) regarding population size, political and civil freedoms, communist versus noncommunist political systems, industrial democracy, and childrearing measures of achievement motivation and control motivation. Further analysis using Hoppe's (1998) adjustments for professional characteristics of the samples shows stability coefficients for the original four variables used by Hofstede that ranged from 0.80 to 0.94, suggesting endurance over time of these national measures.

Correlational analysis showed that measures of individualism and power distance were broadly representative and stable over time, exhibiting significant relationships across nations even when using samples taken from different populations at a different time. Regression results in Franke (1992a, 1992b) were similar to those of Franke, Hofstede, and Bond (1991), supporting the finding that cultures with lower individualism and higher long-term orientation experienced more rapid economic growth. These two factors explained almost 70 percent of the variance in economic growth for the period of 1965 to 1990. Less important as explanatory variables were political freedom (positive), control motivation in childhood (positive), and industrial democracy (positive). Interestingly, as shown by Franke (1974) for earlier time periods, achievement motivation in childhood was negatively related to economic growth, contrary to the McClelland hypothesis.

In sum, the extant body of knowledge about national culture and economic growth acknowledges but does not elaborate upon possible strategies for multinational enterprises operating in a variety of cultures (cf. Barkema and Vermeulen, 1997), or upon what may be the more important issue of human actualization in a world in which democracy and middle-class standards of living are becoming widespread. Evaluating only economic development, there is a clear picture from empirical evidence. With some variety in the samples of nations (ranging from 12 to 52 for certain variables and categories of nations) and over timespans of 7 to 25 years between 1960 and 1990, the major results are that individualism is negatively related to economic growth and that long-term orientation is positively related to economic growth. Interestingly, the United States is preeminent in individualism and is the seventh lowest of 22 nations in long-term orientation. The US was also third from the bottom in economic growth over 1965 to 1980 and eighth from the bottom over 1980 to 1987 among the 18 nations of Franke, Hofstede, and Bond (1991), and fourth from the bottom over 1965 to1990 among the 12 big rich nations of the world (Franke, 1992b). High economic status (GNP per capita) at the beginning of a growth period tends to limit the possibility of high growth rates. In other words, the results described above apply to developing and transforming economies, not to more fully developed economies. Insofar as economic growth is a national goal, these results can provide guidelines for site determination for foreign operations, economic forecasting, and national and international policy-making.

Even though there is strong evidence that culture matters for economic performance in developing countries, there are concerns regarding these results which should be addressed, and which may prove useful in sharpening and extending our findings. Yeh and Lawrence (1995) and Gray (1996) provided both quantitative and context criticism regarding the Franke, Hofstede, and Bond (1991) study. First, Yeh and Lawrence (1995) found the data for one of the 18 nations in the primary sample to be suspect: Since (West) Pakistan and Bangladesh (East Pakistan) were a single nation from 1947 to 1971, with mostly Muslim populations, "one would expect the two countries to have somewhat similar cultural environments" (p. 659). This is a weak argument in view of the different histories, geographical locations, and languages of the two territories and the fact that the artificial association of Pakistan and Bangladesh lasted 24 years only and was ended by a civil war. In Hofstede (1991) the long-term orientation score for Bangladesh is 40, as opposed to Pakistan's value of 0, the lowest for any nation. (There are no Bangladeshi data for the remaining four cultural variables.) If these data are removed, the correlation between the two independent variables of individualism and long-term orientation increases from −0.46 to −0.70, moving from a modest indication of multicollinearity to a significant concern over it (cf. Franke, 1980: fn. 9). Even with these data excluded, there still is some support for the model (between 1980 and 1987). Nevertheless, Yeh and Lawrence's criticism encourages further exploration.

Gray (1996) also questioned the samples as well as the interpretations of Franke, Hofstede, and Bond (1991). In his section 4 and appendix, he removed five East Asian nations that were high in long-term orientation and high also in future-oriented governmental policies, and also removed the United States, since its unique role as world hegemon required self-sacrificing military, economic, and financial actions by its government. Then he reanalyzed our data for a reduced sample of 12 nations, finding, similarly to Yeh and Lawrence, that individualism and long-term orientation do not both survive as independent variables in regression models. In this case, reduction of sample size and reduction of range restrict the multivariate results obtained in the larger and more representative study by Franke, Hofstede, and Bond (1991).

Finally, Yeh and Lawrence (1995: 663–7), and also Gray (1996), stated that our cultural indices are insufficient for a real understanding of what drives economic growth. Additional cultural variables such as "Protestant work ethic" and "entrepreneurial spirit" (Yeh and Lawrence 1995: 663) may be important, and other factors such as capital formation, savings, technological progress, and governmental policy should be considered. Both commentaries call for understanding rather than just explaining differences in economic performance.

DATA AND METHODS

The best response to both Yeh and Lawrence's question regarding the admissibility of Pakistani data and Gray's question regarding dependence upon five East Asian nations and the United States in a small sample is to expand the sample. That way, a few individual nations will not be influential outliers yielding distorted results. Regarding the third question of adding to understanding and usefulness, building upon prior studies and upon the expanded quantitative results, we seek to provide context, and at least some plausible mechanisms of modern economic growth, to aid in understanding past performance differences and to provide a basis for forecasting and improving future performance. But complete understanding will be elusive, with much remaining for further investigation.

Since the Franke, Hofstede, and Bond (1991) sample of 18 nations is small, empirical results might be influenced by the presence or absence of one or two nations. Data for the original four Hofstede dimensions are available for over 50 nations, but the fifth measure – long-term orientation – limits the common sample to 18. Even when four additional nations with long-term orientation data are added (from Hofstede, 1991), a joint sample of 22 individual nations still is sensitive to outlier influence.

Helpfully, in his dissertation, Read (1993: 40) evaluated "three potential proxies for long-term orientation – marginal propensity to save (MPS), gross domestic saving rate for 1980 (GDS80) and the arithmetic average of these measures (SAV)." According to Read, these are "all theoretically appealing proxies because of the important thrift component in long term orientation." Empirically, Read found for the 22 nations having long-term orientation measures, the correlations between long-term orientation and each of the three economic behavior indices were "striking," and the strongest correlation was between long-term orientation and the composite index. For a sample of 21 distinct nations with data for all five cultural indices, we obtain a correlation of 0.564 ($p < 0.01$). We therefore used the following regression equation to estimate long-term orientation for the nations without direct indicators: LTO = 5.337 + 1.535 SAV.

Data for empirical analysis are from 51 nations. National culture dimensions are taken from Hofstede (1980a, 1983, 1993, 1997a). Long-term orientation is taken from The Chinese Culture Connection (1987) where possible, and estimated from Read (1993) for countries without a direct measure. The dependent variable, economic growth, is measured as growth in gross domestic product per capita in percent per year. We also control for economic wealth achieved, measured as gross national product per capita (in 1998 dollars) in 1960 and 1980. Both economic measures are calculated from the World Bank's *World Development Report* 1980 (tables 2 and 17), 1995 (tables 2 and 25), and 1999/2000 (tables 1, 3, and 11), and also data for Iran from *WDR*: 1982 (table 2), for Ecuador from Hagen and Hawrylyshyn (1969: table 10B) and *Statistical Yearbook of the United Nations*: 1981 (table 30), and for Taiwan from Taiwan *Statistical Data Book*: 1999.

We analyze the effect of national culture on economic growth in two time periods, 1960–1980 and 1980–1998, controlling for national wealth at the beginning of each period. This analysis allows us to overcome the problems associated with already being a wealthy country and roughly allows us to examine growth stemming from globalization and the computer technology revolution separately from growth based on the post-World War II industrial order.

RESULTS

Table 1.1 shows zero-order correlations among the variables. As expected, individualism is positively related to national wealth and power distance is negatively related to national wealth in both years. At the same time, in the 1960–1980 period, power distance and long-term orientation are positively related to growth while individualism is negatively related to growth, consistent with previous research. For the period 1980 to 1998, the relationship between economic growth and power distance declines from 0.41 to 0.15, the relationship between individualism and growth declines from −0.55 to −0.37, while the relationship between uncertainty avoidance and growth changes from 0.11 to −0.23.

TABLE 1.1 Zero-order correlations among variables

	National culture					National wealth		Economic growth	
	PDI	UAI	IDV	MAS	LTO	GNP ca. 60	GNP ca. 80	1960–1980	1980–1998
PDI									
UAI	0.25								
IDV	-0.65**	-0.33*							
MAS	0.07	-0.01	0.05						
LTO	0.14	-0.08	-0.28*	0.02					
GNP ca. 60	-0.63**	-0.22	0.73**	0.06	-0.16				
GNP ca. 80	-0.62**	-0.21	0.73**	0.06	0.16	0.94**			
Growth 60–80	0.41**	0.11	-0.55**	-0.01	0.46**	-0.50**	-0.33*		
Growth 80–98	0.15	-0.23	-0.37**	-0.12	0.57**	-0.36**	-0.31*	0.49**	
Mean	56.7	65.8	43.9	49.2	45.0	5139.65	9597.94	5.14	3.38
SD	22.5	24.7	25.7	18.3	22.9	5291.42	8652.34	1.85	2.19
N = 51									

Pearson correlation coefficient, for 51 nations except as noted. *p ≤ 0.05m, **p ≤ 0.01, two-tailed.

TABLE 1.2 Results of multiple regression analysis

Standardized regression coefficients economic growth

	1960–1980 model				1980–1998 model			
	I	II	III	IV	I	II	III	IV
Initial GNPc	− 0.50**†	−0.24***†	−0.24†	−0.23	−0.31†	−0.25†	−0.21†	−0.26†
Individualism		−0.28†	−0.28†	−0.26†		−0.04	−0.17	−0.23
Long-term orientation		0.34*†	0.34***†	0.34***†		0.54***†	0.48***†	0.49***†
Uncertainty avoidance			0.00	−0.01			−0.29***†	−0.28***†
Power distance				0.05				−0.16
Masculinity				0.01				−0.09
F	16.32	11.85	8.70	5.59	5.26	10.52	10.32	7.29
P	<0.001	<0.001	0.001	0.001	0.03	<0.001	<0.001	<0.001
Adjusted R^2	0.24	0.39	0.38	0.36	0.08	0.36	0.43	0.43
R^2 change		0.18	0.00	0.002		0.30	0.07	0.03
P		0.002	n.s.	n.s.		0.001	0.02	>0.1

† $p \leq 0.10$ one-tailed test; *† $p \leq 0.05$ one-tailed test; **† $p \leq 0.01$ one tailed test; for 1980–98, stepwise regression using the same procedure as Franke, Hofstede, and Bond (1991) (without initial GNP *ca.*) yields a model with a significant negative individualism effect.

Results of a block multiple regression analysis are shown in table 1.2. In this type of multiple regression variables are entered one block at a time to test for significant addition to the explained variance, R^2. We controlled for GNP per capita in 1960 for growth from 1960 to 1980 and GNP per capita in 1980 for growth from 1980 to 1998. The control variable was entered first. Individualism and long-term orientation were entered second because of fairly consistent findings in previous research. Uncertainty avoidance was entered third because of its changing relationship with growth. The remaining culture variables were entered last.

In 1960 to 1980, our results replicate those reported earlier. Individualism (negatively) and long-term orientation (positively) are significant correlates of economic growth, controlling for national wealth at the beginning of the period. The two cultural variables contribute significantly to the variance explained while power distance, masculinity and uncertainty avoidance do not contribute to the variance explained in economic growth. In the latter period, we see a different pattern of relationships. Uncertainty avoidance becomes a significant negative factor in the economic growth regression equation and contributes significantly to variance explained even when individualism and long-term orientation are in the equation. In fact, the effect of individualism becomes much smaller and statistically insignificant in the 1980–98 period when initial GNPc is controlled, while the effect of long-term orientation becomes stronger. In all models, it appears that national culture accounts for about 40 percent of the variance in economic growth, but the configuration of effects changes. These results suggest a new engine for economic growth in the twenty-first century, further emphasizing the influence of national culture.

CONCLUSIONS

From the beginning, Hofstede and Bond painted culture's consequences and connections with broad brush strokes. They provided paradigmatic descriptions of cultural values and described their manifestations. Initial publications were followed by articles, books, and chapters in which they and their colleagues amplified and applied the findings of the 1980s. This body of work builds upon and uses for validation and application a wealth of studies that explore culture. Scholars from antiquity to the present have tried to discern how cultural specifics influence the affairs of citizens. To connect the bare bones of numbers and correlations and regressions to the flesh of social description and the breadth of human behavior, Hofstede, Bond, and associates have incorporated the findings of many scholars into their studies.

In seeking to understand differences in economic growth exhibited by different countries, Franke, Hofstede, and Bond (1991: 165) noted that consideration of culture has become important as empirical studies of more tangible factors such as education, population growth, nutrition, capital investment, and technological innovation fail to explain differences in economic growth. Porter's (1990) influential analysis of "competitive advantage of nations" is incomplete without systematic consideration of national cultural characteristics. Subsequent analysis by Armstrong and Collopy (1996) of Porter's (1980) key concept of competitiveness treated it as an aspect of corporate culture. Armstrong and Collopy demonstrated empirically that it has deleterious effects upon large firms' long-term performance and even upon their survival, rather than the benefits proposed by Porter. Culture is worthy of serious consideration, for business organizations as well as for nations, as we try to understand economic growth and performance.

According to neoclassical economic theory, capital investment is a key determinant of economic growth. Yet a number of empirical studies have found investment not necessarily beneficial to economic growth and profitability (e.g., Solow, 1957, 1958; Clark, 1961; Franke, 1979; Denison, 1980; Buzzell and Gale, 1987: ch. 7; World Bank, 1996; Franke, 1999). On the other hand, Read (1993) showed that long-term orientation in national culture is associated with higher savings rates, and savings commonly are invested. If long-term orientation is related to growth but investment is not, then the positive aspects of long-term orientation are not due to their indirect effect on investment (though we did not include capital investment in this study). Making a similar point and using Hofstede's (1980) subsample of 19 rich nations, Franke, Mento, and Brooks (1985) found strong and significant negative associations of national investment ratios during the 1970s with national individualism. While individualism had a significant negative relationship with economic growth between 1970 and 1980, there was not the expected positive impact of investment that neoclassical theory would suggest.

Earlier analyses of political and industrial democracy (Franke, 1992a, and 1992b) showed that both aspects of democracy benefit economic growth. These studies also found that individualism is related positively to political and civil democracy but negatively to industrial democracy. The cultural measure of individualism showed such a strong negative effect on economic growth that it outweighed the benefits of political freedom. On the other hand, industrial democracy (for which data for only 14 nations were available) was more prevalent in nations with lower individualism values simply because low individualism makes cooperative activity easier. Industrial democracy's benefits were of the same or even greater magnitude as the detrimental effects of individualism. The difficulty of working collaboratively in high individualism countries versus the need for work in teams in large, complex organizations may provide one of the answers as to why individualism does not contribute to national economic growth (cf. Franke, 1997, on industrial democracy, and Triandis, 1995, on social loafing).

The technological change now under way with the maturing of the cybernetics revolution makes an additional Hofstede cultural index economically important. Until the 1980s, and contrary to common perception, there existed a "productivity paradox," as expressed by Solow's (1987: 36) comment that "you can see the computer age everywhere but in the productivity statistics." A number of quantitative analyses have demonstrated that increased use of computer and information technology did not result in better economic performance (cf. Franke, 1987b; Brynjolfsson, 1993; Attewell, 1994; Oliner and Sichel, 1994; Landauer, 1995). Only well after 1980 do those who have embraced information technology seem to begin reaping economic rewards (Brynjolfsson and Hitt, 1998). Given that changes in technology are rapid and promise to continue, organizations and nations whose populations adjust more readily are more likely to be successful. Ability to deal with uncertainty thus becomes an economically beneficial quality, and inability to do so a detriment. In keeping with this mechanism, our regression models show that uncertainty avoidance was not an important factor in economic growth during the earlier time period, but for 1980 to 1998 had a significant negative effect on growth. As shown by Shane (1995), innovative roles in organizations may be less legitimate in uncertainty-avoiding societies. Johnson and Lenartowicz (1999: 347) provide a second mechanism for uncertainty avoidance's deleterious effects, show-ing "a strong correspondence between weak uncertainty avoidance and economic freedom." In the atmosphere of economic freedom, which is culturally-based with both customary and codified elements, companies can carry out business more or less as they see fit, which allows their adaptation to changing conditions. The lower a nation's uncertainty avoidance and the higher its economic freedom, the more able an organization is to implement technological change. For nations, economic freedom relates positively to economic growth (Franke and Sagafi-nejad, 1999).

The present study is a reevaluation and extension of the 1991 article by Franke, Hofstede, and Bond. Several concerns of those who commented on earlier work have been addressed. The sample size has been increased by estimating long-term orientation for countries without direct measures and the time period analyzed has been extended and bifurcated. Most importantly, we have controlled for starting wealth to estimate the effects of national culture on economic growth, thus remov-ing the ceiling effect for already wealthy countries. The results remain remarkably stable for the early period. Individualism – concentration on one's own interests and welfare – is strongly positively associated with wealth (GNP per capita) and also strongly negatively associated with economic growth. Long-term orientation is positively related to growth. These findings replicate earlier results. Another per-haps more interesting result in this research made possible by extending analysis another 18 years to 1998, is the emergence of uncertainty avoidance as an inhibitor of economic growth and the less important role played by individualism. With computer and information technology becoming an important part of economic activity, anxious and inflexible workers are unable to make the most of the new tools.

Measures of culture are helpful in explaining performance differences. Further replication of these findings is needed at the national level, within corporations and business units, and even at the individual level. Assuming that effects of cultural traits are durable across different levels of aggregation and also assuming that economic growth continues to be a goal, intervention strategies that will make the most of national culture can be suggested.

For example, Yeh and Lawrence (1995: 663) point out that "Hofstede's measure of individualism appears to reflect . . . a selfish, short-term side . . . where the individual is primarily interested in having a job that provides satisfaction in the present" (also see Gray, 1996: 287). Perhaps this description, consistent with Hofstede's own commentary (1980: ch. 5, 1997: ch. 3), explains lower economic growth rates of already-wealthy nations, as well-fed and comfortable individuals are unwilling to sacrifice their standard of living for others and for the future. Shane (1992) demonstrates that nations' rates of inventiveness are explained by the level of cultural individualism. If individualism and inventiveness are linked but indi-vidualism is detrimental to economic growth, then it follows that inventiveness does not help a nation to grow. Why does inventiveness not pay off in more rapid growth?

An investigation of prior periods of high inventiveness would be helpful in providing answers. Perhaps an earlier "revolution" should be studied, such as that in Britain beginning about 1775 (cf. comparison of the current and previous revolutions by Franke, 1987, and McClelland's, 1961: 139, evidence for rising achievement motivation in England preceding and during the Industrial Revolution). High levels of inventiveness precipitated and sustained the Industrial Revolution, and resulted in the now-rich nations becoming rich. At the beginning of the new millennium, we might be at the threshold of another period of substantial pay-off from inventiveness. After decades of investment in the individualistic and entrepreneurial development of information technologies, there are signs that economic benefits are accruing. Nations that are high in inventiveness and individualism, such as the United States, Britain, and the Netherlands, currently are blossoming in the "new economy," while some developed but less individualistic nations such as Japan are struggling. We can only speculate that once the "revolution" is over and individualistic workers settle down to enjoy their share of the newly created riches, economic growth again will be slower in nations with high individualism.

More interpersonally collaborative and long-term cultures have been particularly successful economically during the first thirty or forty years after World War II. Since around the 1980s, another cultural value – that of flexibility and adaptability – has been shown to benefit economic growth. Individualism may be a detriment to collaboration for economic growth, but may benefit economic performance in spurts as highly individualistic nations invent more, which in turn refuels the economic engines. This may require patterns of cultural adaptation not yet known.

As the twenty-first century progresses, conditions similar to those in Britain early in the nineteenth century and in the United States and Western Europe late in the nineteenth century seem likely to prevail. Rapidly increasing productivity will create exceptional wealth. Hopefully, the citizens of the new century will have learned from the difficulties that accompanied rapid changes of values, social system, and economies in previous centuries. If the increase in wealth continues and if wealth is distributed broadly enough to ensure political stability, a lack of scarcity may enable us to look beyond economics to achieve new and worthy goals.

2

Generic Individualism and Collectivism

HARRY C. TRIANDIS

Culture is a shared meaning system, found among those who speak a particular language dialect, during a specific historic period, and in a definable geographic region (Triandis, 1994a). It functions to improve the adaptation of members of the culture to a particular ecology, and it includes the knowledge that people need to have in order to function effectively in their social environment. Much of culture is reflected in the products of the mind, such as language, myth, art, kinship, norms, values, and in shared meanings about interpersonal behavior (Keesing, 1981). Some elements of culture are objective (e.g., tools) and some are subjective (e.g., beliefs, attitudes). Shared patterns of elements of subjective culture constitute cultural syndromes (Triandis, 1996). Individualism and collectivism are such syndromes. There are many more cultural syndromes.

A cultural syndrome is a *shared* pattern of beliefs, attitudes, self-definitions, norms, roles, and values organized around a theme. If we present such elements of subjective culture to groups of people who speak a particular language, and ask them to make a judgment (e.g., is this value important?), if they make this judgment as a group very quickly, say in less than 2 seconds, and if 90 percent of the groups that we study do the same, then we know that the judgment is widely shared, and thus it is an element of culture (Triandis, Bontempo, Leung, and Hui, 1990). If many of these elements are organized around a theme, such as the importance of the individual (individualism) or the collective (collectivism) then we have identified a cultural syndrome.

Cultural differences are best conceptualized as different patterns of sampling information found in the environment (Triandis, 1989). In collectivist cultures (most traditional cultures, most Asian and Latin American cultures) people are more likely to sample the collective self and to think of themselves as interdependent with their groups (family, co-workers, tribe, co-religionists, country, etc.) than to sample the individual self and see themselves as autonomous individuals who are independent of their groups (Markus and Kitayama, 1991); they are more likely to give priority to the goals of their in-group than to their personal goals (Triandis, 1990b); they are more likely to use in-group norms to shape their behavior than personal attitudes (Abrams, Ando, and Hinkle, 1998; Suh, Diener, Oishi, and Triandis, 1998); they are more likely to conceive of social relationships as communal (Mills and Clark, 1982) than in exchange theory terms (Triandis, 1995a). Collectivist cultures have languages that do not require the use of "I" and "you" (Kashima and Kashima, 1998). In Japanese there are several words for "I" and several words for "you" but their use depends on the relationship between the speaker and the other person. In short, there is no "I" by itself; the "I" depends on the relationship.

The sampling of the individual self is very common in North Western Europe, North America (except in Mexico), Australia and New Zealand. These cultures tend to be individualist. In such cultures the self is conceived as independent of in-groups, personal goals are given priority, attitudes determine much of social behavior, and interpersonal relationships are well accounted by exchange theory. Individualist cultures have languages that require the use of "I" and "you" (Kashima and Kashima, 1998). English is a good example. It would be difficult to write a letter in English without the use of these words. Individualists are very positive about "me" and "we" while collectivists are sometimes ambivalent about "me" but very positive about "we" (Hetts, Sakuma, and Pelham, 1999). Nathan, Marsella, Horvath, and Coolidge (1999) had Japanese, Japanese–American, and European–American samples rate the concepts "individual," "self" and "group" on scales such as good–bad, weak–strong, and fast–slow. The Japanese sample rated "individual" weaker and faster than the other samples. They rated "self" faster; and "group" stronger and slower than the other samples. Szalay (1993) found that Americans make almost twice as many associations to the word "individual" than do Russians, while Russians make almost three times as many associations to the word "people" as do Americans.

A difference between collectivist and individualist selves is reflected in the way people answer the Twenty Statements Test, which requires that they complete 20 statements that begin with "I am . . ." Triandis, McCusker and Hui (1990) reported that Western samples made very few sentence completions that had social content (the mode of Illinois students was zero!). By contrast, about half the sentence completions of East Asians have social content. Ma and Schoeneman (1995) found that American college students averaged 12 percent social content when responding to this task. Kenyan university students in Nairobi averaged 17 percent; Kenyans employed in Nairobi 58 percent; Masai Kenyans 80 percent; and Samburu Kenyans 84 percent. Similar results were reported by Dhawan, Roseman, Naidu, Thapa, and Rettek (1995) based on data from India and the USA. Altocchi and Altocchi (1995) found Cook Islanders acculturated to New Zealand had little social content when responding to the Twenty Statements Test. On the other hand, Cook Islanders who had not gone to New Zealand had very substantial amounts of social content in their responses to this test.

The sampling of collectivist or individual selves depends on both the situation and the personality of the actor.

CULTURAL SYNDROMES

Individualism and collectivism are two cultural syndromes, out of an unknown number of such syndromes. Some examples of cultural syndromes are as follows:

- ◆ *Complexity:* Some cultures (hunters and gatherers) are relatively simple, and other cultures (information societies) are relatively complex. The organizing theme of the syndrome is complexity. For example, in complex societies one finds subgroups with different beliefs, attitudes, etc. while in simple societies individuals are in considerable agreement about their beliefs and attitudes. In fact, cultural uniformity and conformity are higher in simple than in complex societies. Simple cultures have few jobs; if we take into account specialties, such as urologist and general practitioner, complex cultures have a quarter of a million different jobs (see *Dictionary of occupational titles*). The size of settlements is one of the best ways to index cultural complexity (Chick, 1997).

♦ *Tightness*: In some cultures there are many rules, norms, and ideas about what is correct behavior in different kinds of situations; in other cultures there are fewer rules and norms. In the former cultures also, people become quite upset when others do not follow the norms of the society, and may even kill those who do not behave as is expected, while in the latter cultures people are tolerant of deviations from normative behaviors. Thus, conformity is high in tight cultures. In Thailand, which is a loose culture, the expression "mai bin rai" (never mind) is used frequently. In Japan, which is a tight culture, people are sometimes criticized for minor deviations from norms, such as having too much sun tan, or having curly hair (Kidder, 1992). Most Japanese live in fear that they will not act properly (Iwao, 1993).

Tightness is more likely when the culture is relatively isolated from other cultures, so that consensus about what is proper behavior can develop. It is also more likely that tightness will occur in situations where people are highly interdependent (when a person deviates from norms it hurts the relationship) and where there is a high population density (high density requires norms so that people will not hurt each other; also when the other deviates one notices it).

When cultures are at the intersections of great cultures (e.g., Thailand is at the intersection of China and India) contradictory norms may be found, and people cannot be too strict in imposing norms. Also, when the population density is low, it may not even be known that a person who is miles away has behaved improperly. Cosmopolitan cities are loose, except when they have ethnic enclaves which can be very tight, while small communities are relatively tight.

♦ *Individualism and collectivism*: Triandis (1994a) has suggested that individualism emerges in societies that are both complex and loose; collectivism in societies that are both simple and tight. For example, theocracies or monasteries are both tight and relatively poor; Hollywood stars live in a culture that is both complex and loose. This speculation has not been tested rigorously, but the data seem to hang together reasonably well so that it may be the case that, for instance, Japan that is now quite complex is less collectivist than the Japan of the nineteenth century. In fact, reports of nineteenth-century travelers to Japan (see Edgerton, 1985) mentioned hundreds of rules for how to laugh, sit, etc. which apparently no longer operate in modern Japan.

Bond and Smith (1996) did a meta-analysis of studies of conformity and found that collectivist cultures were higher in conformity than individualist cultures. This is what we would expect if tightness and collectivism are closely linked. Similarly, Radford, Mann, Ohta, and Nakane (1991) compared Japanese and Australians and found that the Japanese were influenced by others more when they made decisions than was the case for Australians.

♦ *Vertical and horizontal cultures*: Vertical cultures accept hierarchy as a given. People are different from each other. Hierarchy is a natural state. Those at the top "naturally" have more power and privileges than those of the bottom of the hierarchy. Horizontal cultures accept equality as a given. People are basically similar, and if one is to divide any resource it should be done equally.

◆ *Active–passive cultures*: In active cultures individuals try to change the environment to fit them; in passive cultures people change themselves to fit into the environment. The active are more competitive, action-oriented, and emphasize self-fulfillment; the passive are more cooperative, emphasize the experience of living, and are especially concerned with getting along with others. In general, individualist cultures are more active than collectivist cultures, though the relationship between the two cultural syndromes is probably weak.

◆ *Universalism–particularism*: In universalist cultures people try to treat others on the basis of universal criteria (e.g., all competent persons regardless of who they are in sex, age, race, etc. are acceptable employees); in particularist cultures people treat others on the basis of who the other person is (e.g., I know Joe Blow and he is a good person, so he will be a good employee). In general, individualists are more universalist and collectivists are particularists.

◆ *Diffuse–specific*: Diffuse cultures respond to the environment in a holistic manner (e.g., I do not like your report means I do not like you). Specific cultures discriminate different aspects of the stimulus complex (e.g., I do not like your report says nothing about how much I like you). Collectivists are often more diffuse; individualists are often more specific.

◆ *Ascription–achievement*: People can judge others on the basis of ascribed attributes, such as sex, race, family membership, etc. These are attributes people are born with. By contrast, people might judge others in terms of achieved attributes, such as skill, publications, awards. In general collectivists give ascribed attributes more weight than achieved attributes, while individualists emphasize achieved more than ascribed attributes, though people in all cultures use both kinds of attributes.

◆ *Instrumental–expressive*: People can sample more heavily attributes that are instrumental (e.g., get the job done) or expressive (e.g., enjoy the social relationship). In general individualists are more instrumental and collectivists are more expressive. When Latin Americans meet a friend in the street they are likely to stop and chat, even when they have an appointment. So, they are likely to arrive late for the appointment. The importance of the social relationship eclipses the importance of the instrumental relationship.

◆ *Emotional expression or suppresssion*: People may express their emotions freely, no matter what the consequences, or they may control the expression of emotion. Collectivists around the Mediterranean are quite expressive, while collectivists in East Asia are quite controlling. Individualists are intermediate between these two groups in their emotional expression. For example, Stephan, Stephan, and Cabezas de Vargas (1996) tested the hypothesis that people in collectivist cultures would feel less comfortable expressing negative emotions than people in individualist cultures, and found strong support for that hypothesis.

One can identify many more syndromes, such as those reflected in the Kluckhon and Strodtbeck (1961) value orientations, the culture of honor (Nisbett and Cohen, 1996), and others. This introduction is sufficient for our purposes.

BASIC ATTRIBUTES OF CULTURES

Cultures differ in the way people sample information. As they sample information of a particular type, the behavior that is appropriate for that information gets to be automatic, so that people do not even think about how they are supposed to behave. For example, Americans do not think about driving to the left. Driving to the right is automatic. Cultures include myriads of such automatic behaviors, which reflect standard operating procedures and unstated assumptions, about the way the world is. Members of cultures believe that their ways of thinking are obviously correct, and need not be discussed. Thus, when the Iraqis say that they will not accept a member of an inspection team who is American, they reveal their collectivism: all Americans are the same, and all of them are obviously against us. When the United Nations says that an inspector's nationality is irrelevant, it uses an individualistic assumption. People are different. Americans who work for the United Nations are not necessarily like the Americans who make decisions in Washington. When the Iraqis accept the decisions of their dictator without debate, they reveal that they have a vertical society, where it is "obvious" that whoever has power has the unchallenged right to make decisions. When people in democratic societies give one vote to each citizen they reveal their horizontality: each person is as good or wise as any other.

Perhaps the most interesting aspect about culture is that basic assumptions are not questioned. They influence thinking, emotions, and actions without people noticing that they do. For instance, our Western theories have an individualistic bias, and theories that explain the same phenomena generated in collectivist cultures have a collectivist bias (Triandis, 1995). The last thing we can detect is our own biases!

The theoretical scheme that uses cultural syndromes argues that these syndromes constitute the parameters of any general theory about the way culture influences people. The theory specifies that particular phenomena that have a specific form in cultures that are high on one of these syndromes have a different form in cultures that are low on that syndrome.

This chapter will review the major theoretical notions about collectivism and individualism, mention how they relate to important behaviors that are of general interest, and then summarize how they affect organizational behaviors that have implications for managers.

CULTURE AND BEHAVIOR

The link between culture and behavior is not at all direct. Behavior reflects both behavioral intentions and habits (Triandis, 1980). Habits are automatic behaviors that respond to stimulus configurations without conscious analysis. Driving to the right is a habit for most Americans. However, when the behavior has not occurred in the past, so that it did not have a chance to become automatic (automaticity requires many, sometimes hundreds of repetitions), then information must be processed. Behavioral intentions to do something are more likely when the thought of the behavior is associated with positive emotions (I like to do that), when others approve of the behavior (I should do that), when the self-concept is consistent with the behavior (I am the kind of person who does that), and when the perceived consequences of the behavior are positive (if I do that I will get a positive outcome). The constructs that correspond to these four sentences are *affect*, *norms*, *self-concept*, and *perceived consequences*.

Cultures weigh these variables differently. In individualistic cultures affect is given a large weight; in collectivist cultures norms are given a large weight. More recent work has added the variable of perceived control (Ajzen, 1991), i.e. the extent the individual feels able to do the behavior. This construct is linked to self-efficacy (I can do it) which has developed into a major theory of behavioral prediction (Bandura, 1991). It obviously is included in the self-concept. Collectivist cultures often have lower self-efficacy about behaviors that are new, while individualist cultures often seek new behaviors. In short, culture is associated with behavior indirectly, by influencing the weight of variables that predict behavior rather than by influencing the behavior directly.

However, even if behavioral intentions and habits predict a particular behavior it may not take place because the situation does not provide suitable *facilitating conditions*. For instance, one may be in the habit of eating some food, and like that food, but the food is not available. Clearly, situations are extremely relevant. Thus, the Triandis model (1980) specifies that the probability of a behavior (P) is a function of Habits (H) and Intentions (I) multiplied by Facilitating Conditions (F), which can have a value of zero, thus bring P to a value of zero. In short, $P = (w1\ H + w2\ I)^* F$, where the weights $w1 + w2 = 1.00$. With a new behavior $w2$ is 1 and $w1$ is zero. With an automatic behavior, $w1 = 1.00$ and $w2 = 0.00$.

Recent work by Kasprzyk, Montano and Fishbein (1998) has shown that an integrated behavior model that has much in common with the Triandis model does a good job of predicting behavior. The model also includes perceived control of the behavior and facilitating conditions for the behavior.

Note that this conception has much in common with the argument that cultures sample different information, with different probabilities. It tells us that in individualist cultures people are especially likely to sample information about affect (do I like this?); in collectivist cultures people are especially likely to sample information about norms (does my group say that I must do this?).

A NOTE ABOUT LEVELS OF ANALYSIS

The terms used for cultural syndromes above refer to phenomena at the cultural level. It is important to keep the levels of analysis (cultural, individual) clear, because sometimes a phenomenon that takes one form at the cultural level takes a different form at the individual level of analysis. For example, Hui, Yee and Eastman (1995) found that job satisfaction was *positively* related to individualism at the cultural level, and *negatively* related to the personality equivalent of individualism in data collected in Hong Kong at the individual level. A possible interpretation is that in individualistic cultures people are more affluent (Hofstede, 1980a), and also more job mobile, so that they change jobs (the average American changes nine times during a lifetime), and keep changing until they find a satisfying occupation. The more affluent and individualist the culture the more satisfied they will be with their work. In collectivist cultures such as Hong Kong, individuals are expected to be especially concerned with interpersonal relationships. Those who are *idiocentric* (the personality equivalent of individualism) in Hong Kong, pay too much attention to the task and not enough to interpersonal relationships, and thus tend to be rejected by their co-workers. Being rejected by co-workers is bound to reduce a person's job satisfaction.

Furthermore, there is evidence (Triandis, Bontempo, Villareal, Asai and Lucca, 1988) that individuals who are *allocentric* (behave like collectivists do) receive more and a better quality of social support. Obviously, receiving a lot of social support from co-workers should be related to job satisfaction.

We must also stress that the within culture variance of allocentrism is likely to be greater than the between cultures variance of allocentrism. While there is no direct evidence on that point, a study by Minturn and Lambert (1964) that examined the behaviors of mothers in six very small, *homogeneous* cultures found that for different kinds of behaviors the between cultures variance in behaviors was between 5 and 47 percent while the within culture variance was always larger than 50 percent. Given that these cultures were extremely homogeneous, there is no reason to think that the situation would be different for allocentrism in complex cultures.

Besides, Realo, Allik, and Vadi (1997) working in Estonia, found major differences in collectivism, depending on the location of the people they sampled (e.g., small island versus city), their role, age, and so on. Thus, when we state that a culture is high or low on a syndrome we mean that "on the average" it is likely to be high or low.

THE CONSTRUCTS IN HISTORY

The constructs of individualism and collectivism have been used by political philosophers for three hundred years (see Triandis, 1995a, chapter 2), and by social scientists for about a century. The French sociologist Durkheim (original 1893; translation, 1949) distinguished *mechanical* solidarity (similar to collectivism) and *organic* solidarity (similar to individualism). The first term referred to relationships that are based on common bonds and obligations; the latter term referred to relationships that are contractual. Similarly, the terms *Gemeinschaft* (community) and *Gesellschaft* (society) in sociology, or relational versus individualistic value orientation in anthropology, have been used for some time. There is evidence that individualism emerged in England around the twelfth century (see Triandis, 1995a: chapter 2), though some have argued that it was already present among the ancient Greeks (Skoyles, 1998).

Hofstede (1980a) worked with the responses of IBM employees (117,000 protocols) covering a wide variety of occupations and demographic variables in 66 countries. He summed the responses of the subjects from each country to several value items and conducted a factor analysis of the mean responses based on a sample size of 40 (the number of countries that had enough employees to provide stable means). He identified four factors in his study and called one of them collectivism–individualism. Power distance, which corresponds to verticality, is highly correlated with collectivism. The two other factors, masculinity–femininity and uncertainty avoidance, have received relatively little attention in the social science literature.

Others, such as Bond (1988) working with the values of college students in 21 countries, have found similar factor-analytic results. Triandis et al. (1986) replicated some of Hofstede's results related to individualism and collectivism with 15 samples from different parts of the world.

Systematic empirical work at the individual level identified several psychological processes that correspond to these two cultural syndromes (Hui and Triandis, 1986; Hui, 1988; Triandis, Leung, Villareal, and Clack, 1985; Triandis, Bontempo, Betancourt, Bond, Leung, Brenes, Georgas, Hui, Marin, Setiadi, Sinha, Verma, Spangenberg, Touzard, and de Montmolloin, 1986; Triandis et al., 1988). Specifically, individualism is often related to competition, self-reliance, emotional distance from in-groups, and hedonism; collectivism is often related to high family integrity (e.g., children should not leave home until they get married; parents should live with their children until they die), small distance from in-groups (e.g., feeling honored when an in-group member is honored), and high sociability and interdependence. Later work has shown that self-reliance is also very high among collectivists, but it has a different meaning: While individualists think of self reliance as "being able to do my own thing" collectivists think of self-reliance as "not being a burden on my in-group."

The measurement of tendencies toward individualism and collectivism has used a varity of methods (Hui, 1988; Matsumoto, Weissman, Preston, Brown, and Kupperbusch, 1997; Oyserman, Rhee, Uleman, and Lee, 1996; Realo, Allik, and Vadi, 1997; Singelis, 1994; Singelis, Triandis, Bhawuk and Gelfand, 1995; Triandis, Chen and Chan, 1998; Triandis and Gelfand, 1998; Wagner, 1995; Wagner and Moch, 1986; Yamaguchi, 1994). An examination of the methods that have been used to measure these constructs (appendix in Triandis, 1995a and 1996) shows that more than 20 methods have been used, and while the methods are correlated they often defined separate factors in factor analyses (e.g., Triandis and Gelfand, 1998; Wagner, 1995).

In this chapter we present the most recent conceptualization of these constructs, a review of some of the most recent studies on this topic, and we discuss some applications of the theory of individualism and collectivism to managerial behavior. Useful reviews of the construct have also been provided by Kagitcibasi (1997) and Earley and Gibson (1998).

THEORY

Triandis (1995a) proposed that collectivism and individualism be conceptualized as polythetic constructs. Just as in zoology one or two attributes are used to define a phylum, and additional attributes, in different combinations, define a large number of species, here the defining attributes tell us that we are dealing with collectivism or individualism, and several additional culture-specific attributes define different kinds of collectivism or individualism. For example, both the kibbutz and most East Asian cultures have predominant collectivist elements, but there are major differences among these kinds of collectivism. That is, they constitute different species of collectivism.

The following four defining attributes may be the universal dimensions of the constructs of individualism and collectivism:

1 *Definition of the self:* Collectivists view the self as interdependent with others, which is accompanied by sharing of resources, in a manner similar to what happens in

families. Individualists view the self as autonomous and independent from groups; decisions regarding whether or not to share resources are made individually (Markus and Kitayama, 1991; Reykowski, 1994). In addition, individualists use *individuals* as the units of analysis of social behavior whereas collectivists use *groups*. Individualists are concerned mostly with their own success; collectivists are more concerned with the success of their groups. Interdependence has been measured by Gudykunst, Matsumoto, Ting-Toomey, Nishida and Karimi (1994), and Singelis (1994). In interpersonal situations individualists sample personal attributes, such as personality, ability, attitude; collectivists sample relationships, roles, norms.

2 *Structure of goals*: For collectivists, individual goals are usually compatible with in-group goals, whereas for individualists individual goals are often not correlated with in-group goals (Triandis, 1988, 1990b; Schwartz 1990, 1992, 1994; Wagner and Moch, 1986). When individual and group goals are not compatible, collectivists give priority to in-group goals and individualists give priority to personal goals. Yamaguchi (1994) developed a scale that measures emphasis on collective or individual goals. Thus, individualists sample mostly their personal goals, and pay little attention to in-group goals; collectivists sample in-group goals and pay little attention to personal goals.

3 *Emphasis on norms versus attitudes*: The determinants of social behavior among collectivists are equally (1) norms, duties, and obligations, and (2) attitudes, and personal needs, whereas among individualists the determinants are primarily attitudes, personal needs, perceived rights, and contracts (Bontempo and Rivero, 1992; Davidson, Jaccard, Triandis, Morales, and Diaz-Guerrero, 1976; Miller, 1994). When predicting behavioral intentions from attitudes and norms, across a sample of different behaviors, the beta weights of collectivists are about equal for norms and attitudes while the beta weights of individualists are much higher for attitudes than for norms (Trafimow and Finlay, 1996). Norms are used especially when people are accountable to their in-groups. Accountability increases the tendency of collectivists to cooperate and of individualists to compete (Gelfand and Realo, 1999). Collectivists see less of a link between attitudes and behavior than do individualists (Kashima, Siegel, Tanaka, and Kashima, 1992). Furthermore, well-being for collectivists depends on fitting in and having good relationships with the in-group which requires close attention to the norms of the in-group, while for individualists it depends on satisfaction with the self, and the emotions associated with self-satisfaction (Suh, Diener, Oishi, and Triandis, 1998). Thus, individualists sample mostly personal emotions, while collectivists sample mostly norms, obligations, duties.

4 *Emphasis on relatedness versus rationality*: Collectivists emphasize unconditional relatedness whereas individualists emphasize rationality. Relatedness refers to giving priority to relationships and taking into account the needs of others, even when such relationships are not advantageous to the individual. Rationality refers to the careful computation of the costs and benefits of relationships (Kim, 1994; Kim, Triandis, Kagitcibasi, Choi and Yoon, 1994). This parallels the distinction between communal and exchange relationships (Mills and Clark, 1982). Clark, Ouellette, Powell, and Milberg (1987) provided a scale that measures this aspect. Thus individualists sample the profit and loss of relationships, while collectivists sample the needs of others and the loyalty associated with the relationship.

Multimethod measurements of these four facets of collectivism and individualism (Triandis, Chan, Bhawuk, Iwao, and Sinha, 1995; Triandis and Gelfand, 1998) show correlations that range between zero and 0.70, with a mode at about 0.40 (the *N*s of these studies were more than 100, thus this modal value is highly significant).

In horizontal cultures there is a tradition of equality, as happens in ideologies such as that of the Israeli kibbutz. In such cultures people see each other as virtually interchangeable. For example, in many of the original kibbutzim every adult took the parental role toward every child, and everyone cleaned dishes on a rotating schedule. Thus, here the information that is sampled is primarily that of equality, one person one vote, and the like. If resources are to be distributed this must be done equally.

By contrast, vertical societies assume that people are different from each other, and hierarchy is a given. The strongest case is that of India, where differences in skin color are related to the caste ideology. This aspect of the Indian culture makes it explicit that differences among people are to be emphasized. It is interesting that though the secular government of India has abolished the caste system, and the Indian constitution does not recognize it, villagers, who constitute about 70 percent of the population of India, can become extremely violent (sometimes causing death) against those who dare to cross the caste lines (e.g., a man from one caste eloping with a woman of another caste). It seems that the constitution, which was the product of an enlightened elite, does not mesh well with the original culture. Thus, here the information that is sampled is about hierarchy, obedience, respect, subordination or superordination, giving orders, criticizing, depending on the situation.

Traditional Chinese culture was also vertical. During a famine people got food according to a pecking order; the oldest males were served first, and the youngest females received it last. In Muslim cultures also, while there is an emphasis on the horizontal dimension among males who worship, there is a vertical emphasis in male–female relationships.

When we cross the cultural syndromes of collectivism and individualism with the cultural syndromes of vertical and horizontal relationships we obtain a typology of four kinds of cultures: horizontal individualists, such as Australia or Sweden, vertical individualists, such as the US corporations where being "the best" is emphasized, horizontal collectivists, such as the kibbutz, and vertical collectivists, such as India or China.

In horizontal individualism people do their own thing but they do not compete. They do not want to be better than others, just to be unique. In vertical individualist cultures some people want to be the "best" and win in competitions. Inequality is seen as "natural." If the CEO earns 400 times as much as the entry level worker, that is just "fine." In horizontal collectivism people merge with members of their in-group, but are more or less equal to them; in vertical collectivism people are highly interdependent with their in-group, but they recognize that in-group authorities have the "right answers."

Kabanoff (1997: 689) classified France, Belgium, Italy, and Spain in the vertical individualism category, the US, Canada, UK, Australia, and the Netherlands in the horizontal individualism category, Austria, Israel, Denmark, Finland, Germany, and Sweden in the horizontal collectivism, and Venezuela, Mexico, Singapore, Greece, Philippines, Brazil, Thailand, and Japan in the vertical collectivism category. I do not agree with all these judgments, which suggests that there is an urgent need to determine empirically how these countries ought to be classified.

Vertical relations are most common in societies that are high in Hofstede's (1980a) power distance; horizontal relations are most common in societies that are low in power distance.

It should be noted here that all cultures are vertical to some degree (e.g., even in Sweden the men hold most of the important positions), and even in the most vertical cultures, horizontal relationships are developed across hierarchies (e.g., in India children of different castes play together, or while walking to a shrine people treat everyone alike). The essential point is that vertical or horizontal, collectivist or individualist cognitions become salient depending on the situation. Also, there is a tendency for the vertical collectivist and the horizontal individualist cultures to be more numerous than the other two patterns. For example, the percentage of women in various legislative bodies varies from about 40 percent in Scandinavia to close to zero in extremely collectivist cultures. When men and women are seen as having different statuses that reflects a vertical culture.

Horizontal versus vertical collectivism

Horizontal collectivism includes a sense of oneness with members of the in-group and social cohesiveness. It corresponds to defining attributes (1) and (4) above. Vertical collectivism includes a sense of serving the in-group and sacrificing for the benefit of the in-group, doing one's duty, and behaving as expected of a good member of the in-group. Indians (with their great concern for status, see Triandis, 1972) emphasize a different self. Until they become old and are allowed to withdraw from life's duties, they have many family obligations and are quite interdependent. Thus vertical collectivism is the dominant cultural pattern in India. But some older Indians become detached from groups, and in that case they will be individualists. Thus, the situation (age) is relevant in telling us whether a person is likely to be allocentric or idiocentric.

Kim, Triandis, Kagitcibasi, Choi, and Yoon (1994) described collectivism by focusing exclusively on the horizontal variety. They emphasized the collectivists' concern for the collective welfare, harmony, self-cultivation, interdependence, succorance, nurturance, common fate, and social obligation. Since this is the less common species of collectivism we need to shift our attention to the vertical variety.

The theoretical value added by the typology of vertical and horizontal collectivism (and individualism) becomes salient when one notes that Kim et al. disregarded the vertical aspect of collectivism because of their singular focus on the horizontal aspects of collectivism. Had they considered the vertical aspects of collectivism, they would have observed that many collectivists subordinate their needs, goals, and aspirations to the requirements of the collective. In some cases the requirements of the in-group are oppressive, but people are socialized to "put up" with them. Recent research (e.g., Triandis and Gelfand, 1998) has shown that authoritarianism is somewhat related to vertical but not to horizontal collectivism.

Data from Sweden (Daun, 1991) suggest that the Swedes tend to be "same self," horizontal individualists. Their individualism is shown by their extreme self-reliance, and avoidance of long-term relationships with non-kin. According to Daun many people in Sweden insist on paying for a cigarette on the spot, if they ask for one; the elderly do not live with their children; living by oneself is highly valued; if one is to stay over night at a friend's house one takes one's own sheets; there is very high voluntarism; 87 percent of Swedes indicated that they like to live "as I please."

Their same self is shown by the high value they place on modesty. Specifically, in comparable polls, high social status is desired by only 2 percent of the population versus 7 percent of the Americans and 25 percent of the Germans; personal success is problematic, and eccentrics are strongly rejected. According to a Swedish friend, there is a much valued concept in Swedish, *Jaentelagen*, that essentially means "avoid sticking out."

Swedes do not like being unique, which contrasts with other kinds of individualists, who want to be distinguished, unique. Middle- and upper-class Americans, for instance, are offended if an experimenter suggests to them that they are "just average" (Weldon, 1984; Markus and Kitayama, 1991). We might conclude that many Americans are vertical or "different self" individualists, accepting inequality. While in most social settings they emphasize equality (e.g., use of first names), in economic (e.g., in corporations) and political settings (rejection of the use of taxes to redistribute income) they accept inequalities.

Australians are largely horizontal individualists. They are self-reliant and obtained high scores on individualism in Hofstede's (1980a) survey, but they do not like people who stick out. Feather (1994) has developed a scale that measures the inclination of subjects to bring down "tall poppies" and has shown that Australians are rather high on this attitude, though there are complexities, such as whether the tall poppies are good or bad, that must be taken into account (Feather, 1994). He argues that those with low self-esteem are especially likely to want to see the fall of high achievers. Brislin (1993) reports that professionals from other countries, who travel to Australia to give workshops, are warned that in these workshops they will spend a third of the time defending their credentials.

It could be argued that affluence is shifting most rich cultures toward individualism. Affluence has the consequence of making people independent of their groups. At the same time, independence from groups means less consultation with in-group members, and more risk taking in economic activities, and this pattern, some of the time, is successful and results in more affluence. Thus, affluence and individualism are reciprocally related. For example, we see in Singapore, which is 76 percent a Chinese culture that has the sixth highest national product per capita in the world, that they passed a law that requires individuals to take care of their aged parents. Such laws were not necessary when "filial piety" was strong in Chinese society, but they are needed now because of the affluence. As interpersonal competition increases, individualist societies are becoming more vertical. The rich are different from the poor, both within and across countries. When we compare the income of the top and bottom 20 percent we see that the USA used to have a ratio of 7 and now it has a ratio of 9. Similarly, in most industrial democracies there is an increase in this ratio, except for Sweden where the ratio has been steady at 3.

When resources are limited (e.g., there is only one desirable job available) those who aspire to get that job are likely to become vertical. They will exaggerate their positive attributes, boast, and become very emotional if they do not get the job.

Individualism is often associated with "equality" but also with "competition." Roesch, Carlo, Knight, Koller, and Dos Santos (submitted) studied Anglo-American and Brazilian children. They found that the older the American child the more competitive it was;

the older the Brazilian child the more cooperative it was. In short, as children acquire culture, they behave in ways that are consistent with the culture. Competition is consistent with the individualistic culture of the United States.

PERSONALITY AND SITUATION

Any typology is an oversimplification. Each individual is likely to use some combination of horizontal or vertical, individualistic or collectivist cognitive elements when defining particular social situations. All individuals have access to all four kinds of cognitions, and will sample them depending on the situation. Thus, when the in-group is under threat most individualists will activate collectivist cognitions. When the individual is alone individualist cognitions are more likely. Trafimow, Triandis, and Goto (1991) found that instructing individuals, randomly assigned to this condition, to think for two minutes about what makes them the same as their family and friends results in behaviors that are collectivist. Instructing them to think of what makes them different from their family and friends results in behaviors that are individualist.

In social situations in which harmony, cooperation, and having fun are stressed there is an emphasis on equality, hence on horizontal relationships. Inequality creates stresses, envy, resentment. On the other hand, situations that stress competition, or require subordination of the goals of most people to the goals of an authority, result in vertical relations. Limited resources are more likely to result in vertical than in horizontal relationships.

Lay, Fairlie, Jackson, Ricci, Eisenberg, Sato, Teeaeaer, and Melamud (1998) found a relationship between allocentrism and depression. People who experienced a lot of hassles were more depressed. This relationship was stronger in the case of those who were low in allocentrism than those who were high in allocentrism.

The evidence that humans sample both collectivist and individualist cognitions can be seen in certain studies. Triandis and Gelfand (1998) used scenarios, in multiple choice format, with each option reflecting one of the four patterns mentioned above (HI, HC, VI, VC). The Illinois sample emphasized HI across different situations, but also used the other three patterns. Verma and Triandis (1998) found that an Indian sample used HI 24 percent of the time, HC 28, VI 23, and VC 25 percent of the time, which contrasted with an Illinois sample that used HI 38, HC 26, VI 23, and VC 13 percent of the time. The samples were large, so a 2 percent difference is statistically highly significant. Clearly the large differences were on HI (Americans higher than the Indians) and VC (Indians higher than Americans). In that study, which also presented data from Australia, Japan, Hong Kong, Korea, Greece, Germany, and the Netherlands, Germany had the most individualistic profile (HI = 43, HC = 27, VI = 20, VC = 10) while Hong Kong had the most collectivist profile (HI = 25, HC = 36, VI = 20, VC = 19). These data indicate that all four types of cognitions are available. The situation shifts the probability that one type of cognition or another will be sampled. It is important to pay attention to these findings. People are not "individualist" or "collectivist." They are both or either, in some mixture, depending on the situation.

Relationship between VI, VC, HI, and HC and Behavioral Intentions

It is useful to note the relationship between the typology discussed above and the seven factors reflecting behavioral intentions that were associated with individualism and collectivism, identified by Triandis and colleagues. In a study of Illinois students, Triandis and Gelfand (1998) measured the emphases on the horizontal and vertical individualism and collectivism aspects and independently the tendencies toward competition, hedonism, self-reliance, emotional distance from in-groups, sociability, interdependence, and family integrity. They found that among horizontal individualists the main emphases were on self-reliance and hedonism, and they did not emphasize sociability. Vertical individualists also emphasized self-reliance and hedonism, but in addition they stressed competition; and they were quite low on family integrity and interdependence. Horizontal collectivists were high on family integrity and sociability, but very low on emotional distance from in-groups and on self-reliance. Finally, vertical collectivists were high on family integrity and sociability, and low on emotional distance from in-groups and also on competition. Thus, the two kinds of individualism as well as the two kinds of collectivism have many elements in common, but also elements that contrast them. In general, what is common among the elements of the two cultural patterns is more important than what is different.

Oishi, Schimmack, Diner, and Suh (1998) measured both the VI, HI, VC and HC constructs and the Schwartz (1994) values. They found high ($p < 0.01$) positive correlations between VI and power, achievement and negative correlations with self-direction, universalism and benevolence. HI was highly negatively correlated with power, and benevolence but positively correlated with achievement and self-direction. VC was highly positively correlated with tradition and conformity and negatively correlated with self-direction. Finally, HC was highly positively correlated with benevolence and negatively correlated with power. Thus, each construct has both similarities and differences with the other constructs with which it shares an aspect. The main differences between VI and HI is on self-direction (HI > VI) and power (VI > HI); between VI and VC on achievement (VI > VC); between VI and HC on power (VI > HC) and benevolence (HC > VI); between HI and VC on self-direction (HI > VC), tradition (VC > HI) and conformity (VC > HI); between HI and HC benevolence (HC > HI); between VC and HC tradition (VC > HC) and conformity (VC > HC).

Culture provides implicit theories of social behavior that act like a "computer program" controlling the actions of individuals.

Prevalence of Individualism and Collectivism

Individualism is found in affluent societies (Hofstede, 1980a), especially where there are several normative systems (as happens at the intersection of major cultures, or in some urban (Freeman, submitted), multicultural, cosmopolitan societies), in which case the *individual* has to decide whether to act according to one or another normative system. It is also high among the upper classes and professionals in any society (Freeman, submitted; Kohn, 1969; Marshall, 1997; Peters, 1997; Reddy and Gibbons, 1995), among those who migrated (Gerganov, Dilova, Petkova, and Paspalanova, 1996) or were socially mobile, and among those who have been most exposed to the US-made mass media. Marshall (1997) found that social class was a stronger contrast on individualism than the difference between the cultures of Indonesia and New Zealand.

Collectivism is found in minority groups in the USA (Gaines et al., 1997; Woodell, 1989), in societies that are relatively homogeneous (so that in-group norms can be widely accepted), where population density and job interdependence are high (because they require the development and adherence to many rules of behavior), among members of the society who are relatively old (Noricks et al., 1987) and who are members of large families (because it is not possible for every member to do his or her own thing), and in groups that are quite religious (Triandis and Singelis, 1998).

With respect to the importance of age, Schwartz and Bardi (submitted) reported that a comparison of teachers and students from some 50 nations shows that the teachers are higher than the students on security, tradition, and conformity values, and lower than the students on hedonism, stimulation, and self-direction. Thus it is clear that collectivism is higher among teachers than among students. This suggests that age may increase collectivism.

SOME GENERAL TENDENCIES OF IDIOCENTRICS AND ALLOCENTRICS

Situation–disposition interaction

It is useful to assume that idiocentric and allocentric cognitions are like "tools" that are selected to shape a person's behavior, *depending on the situation.* When an individual is faced with a social situation, the situation "calls forth" one of the four patterns we have been discussing. Situations sometimes are very clear about the appropriateness of a pattern and at other times they are very unclear and ambiguous.

The same situation can elicit different behaviors from people in individualist and collectivist cultures. For example, suppose the situation is that a person wants to take a trip that will inconvenience many other people. The modal pattern of vertical collectivism will activate themes of duties that cannot be performed during the trip and the individual may decide not to take the trip; the horizontal collectivism pattern may activate themes of social support that s/he will not be able to give during the trip, and that again may cancel the trip. But both kinds of individualists will suppress such themes and feel sufficiently emotionally detached from their in-group to be able to take the trip. Thus, in this kind of ambiguous situation, the behavior of members of a culture will "match" the modal pattern of that culture. In other words, there is a strong situation–disposition interaction. Collectivists will not behave in a collectivist way in all situations but only in most; and individualists will behave as collectivists do in a number of situations.

An interesting study by Chatman and Barsade (1995) randomly assigned participants who were either allocentric or idiocentric to simulated cultures that were collectivist or individualist. Allocentrics assigned to a collectivist culture were the most cooperative

(5.61); when assigned to an individualist culture they were low in cooperation (4.75); idiocentrics assigned to the collectivist situation were cooperative (5.02), but when they were assigned to the individualist situation they were low in cooperation (4.77). Thus, it is clear that the situation is a powerful factor determining the level of cooperation.

A similar point is made in a study done in Japan by Caudill and Scarr (1962). They used the scenarios from the Kluckhohn and Strodtbeck questionnaire that measured collaterality (paying attention to peers), linearity (paying attention to those in authority) and individualism (paying attention to own internal needs and views). The scenarios described different situations, and Japanese samples were asked to indicate what they and most people in their culture would do in those situations. The results showed that each situation produced its own pattern and that the situation was the major determinant of the responses of the Japanese participants.

However, the important point to remember is that people who frequently use a particular cultural pattern, e.g., vertical collectivism, are most comfortable doing what that pattern implies. They develop beliefs, attitudes, and select norms and values that fit that pattern; they often behave according to that pattern, and thus develop habits (automatic behaviors carried out without thinking) that are consistent with that pattern. Kitayama (1999) calls such automatic behaviors *cultural affordances,* and he argues that they not only influence the individual's behavior, but also shape the culture, so that the person changes the culture and the culture changes the person. When people are in a new social situation, to the extent that this is possible, they will try to use that habitual behavior pattern. In short, they have developed a "structure of habits" (Triandis, 1980) that fits the cultural pattern, and like the man who has a hammer and tries to do all jobs by using it, will try to use that habitual behavior in most situations. So for instance, allocentrics, even in individualistic cultures, will try to make relationships more intimate; idiocentrics, even in collectivist cultures, will be more likely to use individual goals to determine their behavior.

Certain factors increase the probability that the collectivist cognitive system will be activated. This is most likely to happen when:

1 the individual knows that most other people in the particular situation are collectivists, which makes the norm that one must act as a collectivist salient,
2 the individual is in a collective, e.g., the work group is defined as a family,
3 the situation emphasizes what people have in common, e.g., common goals,
4 the situation emphasizes that people are in the same collective (e.g., the use of the same uniforms), and
5 the task is cooperative.

Certain factors increase the probability that the individualistic cognitive system will be activated. This is most likely to happen when:

1 others in the situation are and behave like individualists, which makes individualist norms more salient,
2 the situation makes the person focus on what makes him or her different, e.g., the person is dressed very differently from the rest of the group, and
3 the task is competitive.

The attributions that people make

A major source of misunderstandings in human relationships occurs when two individuals do not perceive similar causes for a specific behavior. For example, an employee is late for work and perceives that the lateness is due to having missed the bus, while his supervisor perceives the lateness as due to the employee "being lazy." In this example, the employee and the boss are making non-isomorphic attributions (Triandis, 1975). That means that the same behavior is seen as having very different causes, and hence very different meanings.

Collectivists tend to attribute events to situations and causes external to the individual more frequently than do individualists (Choi, Nisbett, and Norenzayan, 1999); individualists attribute events to internal individual causes more frequently than do collectivists (Al-Zahrani and Kaplowitz, 1993; Morris and Peng, 1994; Na and Loftus, 1998; Newman, 1993). As a result, individualists make the "fundamental attribution error," of over-stressing internal relative to external causes of behavior, more frequently than collectivists (Smith and Bond, 1994).

Iyengar, Lepper, and Ross (in press) reported a study in which European–Americans (EA), Asian–Americans (AA) and Japanese (J) made attributions concerning the behavior of themselves and others. When they reported about their own behavior in all cultures they used the "it depends on the situation" response (on a 0 to 7 scale). Specifically, the EAs had a mean of 4.2, the AAs a mean of 4.8, and the Js a mean of 5.8. When they judged the behavior of an "enemy" they all used this attribution much less (means for EA 2.4, AA 2.8 and J 1.0, respectively). But when they judged the behavior of a "friend" the EAs had a mean of 2.6 (almost the same as the judgment of the "enemy") the AAs used the neutral point of the scale, and the Js had a mean of 4.2. Thus, these judgments reflect the distance between self and all others in the case of the EA, and the closeness of friend and self and the large distance from enemy in the case of the Japanese. The AA were intermediate in their judgments.

Collectivists also tend to change themselves to fit in rather than try to change the environment, while individualists try to change the environment rather than change themselves (Diaz-Guerrero, 1979; Weisz, Rothbaum, and Blackburn, 1984). This is associated with more internal control by Westerners and more external control by East Asians. However, we must emphasize that if an East Asian shows much internal control the behavior would be counter-normative, and would create resentment (Sastry and Ross, 1998).

Collectivists do not use the performance equals ability *times* effort formulation which is common among individualists (Singh, 1981). They use a performance equals ability *plus* effort formulation. In short, since the individualists see performance as a personal quality, if the person has no ability *or* expends no effort they see no performance; the collectivists see performance as a group quality, and thus it is possible to succeed if one member of the group has ability and other members expend much effort.

Self-enhancement versus self-criticism

In Eastern collectivism there is a tendency toward self-criticism, while in individualistic cultures self-enhancement is more common (Kitayama, Markus, Matsumoto, and

Norasakkunkit, 1997). When Americans are asked how they compare to others on some valuable quality they see themselves as much better than average (Markus and Kitayama, 1991). Since it is not possible, mathematically, for everybody to be better than average, there is self-enhancement in the USA. The self-enhancement generalizes to enhancement of their family. Heine and Lehman (1997) found that Japanese students evaluated a family member *less* positively than did Canadian students. In a second study the same pattern was observed for the evaluation of the universities of these students. In short, the pattern that is observed about the self also occurs when the person's group is evaluated. Heine (1998) suggests that the central motive of Japanese is self-improvement. That is, they worry that they will not be as good as the in-group wants them to be. They see a large self–ideal discrepancy. By contrast, the central motive of Americans is self-enhancement, that is they are worried about not being better than most members of the in-group. North Americans persist significantly longer on a task following success feedback, whereas Japanese persist significantly longer following failure feedback.

Hetts, Sakuma, and Pelham (1999) used both direct (explicit) measures of the self-concept, such as questionnaires, and indirect (implicit) measures, based on reaction times. Japanese who live in the US have explicit self-concepts that are similar to the self-concepts of Americans, but Japanese in Japan have lower explicit self-esteem than Japanese in the US. In the West people are taught to become what they can be and toot their own horn. In East Asia self-enhancement is less direct, and involves an emphasis on the virtues of the group, and because the group has positive qualities one has positive qualities as a member of the group. As Japanese children mature they view self-enhancement statements with disdain. They argue that the "talented falcon hides his claws." Yet when they are assessed implicitly, they do show self-enhancement. In short, it appears that modesty is the proper behavior, but the implicit self-esteem does reflect self-enhancement.

When collective identities are activated, the salient features of the self-concept are those shared with other members of the in-group (Brewer and Gardner, 1996). In that case the best way to feel good about oneself is to feel good about one's in-group.

In Kitayama et al. (1997) Americans chose a greater number of situations of success than failure as relevant to their self-esteem, while Japanese chose a greater number of failure than success situations as relevant to their self-esteem. Furthermore, Americans increased their self-esteem more in success situations than did Japanese in such situations. Moreover, Japanese self-esteem was more vulnerable in the case of failure than American self-esteem. Thus, we can expect that an American subordinate will have a more positive self-esteem than a Japanese subordinate, and the former will be dissatisfied with average supervisory ratings to a greater extent than the latter. Brockner and Chen (1996) found that high self-esteem functions to protect the self from negative feedback among individualists but not among collectivists.

Goal setting

The goals of collectivists are role relevant (e.g., I must insist that my subordinates do this, because I am their supervisor), while those of individualists are personal need-based (e.g., I must insist that they do this so that I will feel self-respect).

In general, the goals of collectivists are long term, since they see themselves as parts of a chain that includes ancestors (e.g., past employees) and descendants (e.g., future employees). In general, the goals of individualists are short term (e.g., get a good quarterly report). Also, social loafing, i.e., doing less than what one is capable of doing when one's performance is not observable, is less likely among collectivists working with in-group members than among individualists (Earley, 1989; Wagner, 1992).

The more heterogeneous or affluent the population the more likely it is that the goals of individuals and groups will not be compatible, and individuals might do their own thing, ignoring the group.

An important goal of collectivists is to fulfill their duties and obligations. Triandis (1995) pointed out that collectivists usually have few in-groups, while individualists have many. Thus, the social obligations of collectivists are quite focused, while those of individualists are fluid and may be converted to obligations to the larger society rather than to specific in-groups. Consistent with this observation, Oyserman, Sakamoto, and Lauffer (1998) found that collectivism increased obligation to the in-group when identity was made salient (i.e., when in-group membership was important); individualism coupled with low collectivism dampened social obligation; however, people who were high in both individualism and collectivism were found to have increased obligations to the larger society.

Motivation

The motive structure of collectivists reflects receptivity to others, adjustment to the needs of others, and restraint of own needs and desires. The basic motive structure of individualists reflects their internal needs, rights and capacities, including the ability to withstand social pressures (Markus and Kitayama, 1991). Erez (1997) suggests that when people select goals, in horizontal individualist cultures they use goals that maximize their personal involvement, while in vertical individualist cultures they will tolerate assigned goals. Horizontal collectivist cultures will use group-goals, while vertical collectivist cultures will accept without discussion assigned group-goals. Thus it is verticality that leads to acceptance of assigned goals. Of course, since collectivism and power distance are highly correlated (Hofstede, 1980a) collectivists will generally also accept assigned goals. In this context, it is interesting to note the study by Sethi-Iyengar (1998). She found that children of European–American backgrounds were more motivated when they had a choice and showed less motivation when the choice was made for them by authority figures or peers. Conversely, Asian–American children were less motivated when given a personal choice, while having choices made for them by trusted authority figures and peers actually produced the highest levels of intrinsic motivation and performance. Specifically, as reported in Iyengar and Lepper (1999), working with 11-year-olds, they found greater performance among collectivists if the task had been chosen by their mother than if it had been chosen by themselves. The generalization can be made that, in the case of collectivists, if an in-group member chooses the task it is just as satisfying and motivating as it is if they themselves chose the task.

Achievement motivation is socially oriented among collectivists, and individually oriented among individualists. Yu and Yang (1994) developed separate scales for these two kinds of motivation, and showed that these scales are uncorrelated among collectivists.

Among vertical collectivists, the welfare of the in-group is of the highest importance, even if the individual members must suffer. In East Asian cultures individuals are expected to value education and self-improvement, obey rules, practice discipline, and respect authority. These values lead to diligence and achievement that will please the in-group. Collectivists will tend to be high in socially oriented achievement. One of the typical items of the socially oriented achievement scale is: "A major goal in my life is to work hard, to achieve something which will make my parents feel proud of me." Those who score high in socially oriented motivation prefer jobs that provide extensive family benefits to jobs that are enjoyable but do not provide such benefits.

The application of some of these points to the work place is clear: Horizontal cultures will favor small salary differentials, while vertical cultures will tolerate large salary differentials. Collectivists will be motivated by goals that are widely accepted by the in-group, even when they did not have much say in how the goals were developed. Individualists will be more motivated if they had a hand in shaping the goals. In evaluating these points, however, it must be remembered that each human is likely to be both allocentric and idiocentric, and the situation is likely to be the determining factor concerning which goals will be most salient.

Social exchanges

Exchanges have a different character among collectivists and individualists. Triandis (1990b) argued that collectivists "play relationships by ear" and do not expect a clear plan about what is going to happen; individualists are more likely to spell things out: "If I give you this, you will give me that." Second, the time perspective of collectivists is longer. "If I give you something today, you may reciprocate in two years." Third, collectivists do not insist that exchanges be of strictly equal value and of the same resource (Foa and Foa, 1974) (e.g., "If I invite you, I expect a letter of recommendation"); individualists are more careful to make their exchanges of equal value and of the same type of resource (e.g., "If I invite you, I expect to be invited back"). Fourth, collectivists regulate their exchanges through empathy (Kitayama, 1993) while individualists regulate them on the basis of the assumption that people have stable internal preferences, and people ought to be given a chance to choose. In entertaining, individualists are likely to provide many choices: "Do you want this or that?" Collectivists know much about their guests and are most likely to provide them with what they like: "Here is what I know you want."

In horizontal cultures exchanges tend to be symmetrical while in vertical cultures they can be quite asymmetrical. For example in the use of language, horizontals are likely to use *tu* (French) or *du* (German) to each other, while verticals are likely to use *tu* (or *du*) in one direction and *vous* (or *Sie*) in the other direction.

Collectivists are more likely to be cooperative when other persons are cooperative, while individualists are less cooperative, especially in an individualistic environment (Chatman and Barsade, 1995).

What is being exchanged is subject to variation across cultures. In middle-class Turkey, for instance, Kagitcibasi (1990) found that strong and frequent emotional exchanges existed, but there were not many economic exchanges. In lower-class samples, however, she found that there was a sharing of economic resources, since if that did not happen some members of the in-group would go hungry.

The exchange of compliments is very common in individualist cultures, and functions to increase self-esteem, and to "oil" relationships with relative strangers. By contrast, collectivists interact most frequently with intimates and are more likely to exchange criticisms. Kitayama (1996) asked both Japanese and American respondents to report when they last said something good to someone. The modal response of Americans was "a day ago." The modal response of Japanese was "four days ago."

Collectivists expect social situations to be pleasant and to have few negative elements. Triandis, Marin, Lisansky and Betancourt (1984) examining data from Hispanic and non-Hispanic samples, found that the Hispanics, relative to the non-Hispanics, anticipated higher probabilities of positive behaviors and lower probabilities of negative behaviors occurring in social situations. They called this the *simpatia* cultural script. A person who wants to be "simpatico" (likeable, agreeable, pleasant, attractive, non-critical) would behave that way.

Allocentrics in most cultures tend to be more sensitive to social rejection, lower in uniqueness, and higher in affiliation than idiocentrics. These data were collected in Japan, Korea and the USA (Yamaguchi, Kuhlman, and Sugimori, 1995). Allocentrics are also more likely to feel embarrassed (Singelis and Sharkey, 1995). Research by Moskowitz, Suh, and Desaulniers (1994) suggests that idiocentrics are more dominant and allocentrics more agreeable.

Bases for exchanges

There are three bases that have been investigated in most studies: equity (to each according to contribution), equality, and need (to each according to need). The more horizontal the culture the more likely it is that equality will be used in exchanges.

The general finding is that when allocating in equal-status situations, collectivists exchanging with in-group members pay more attention to equality and need, but when exchanging with out-group members they use equity. On the other hand, individualists use equity in most exchanges. Leung (1997) reviewed several empirical studies, and concluded that in general, in equal status situations, equality is preferred in collectivist and equity in individualist cultures. Equality is associated with solidarity, harmony, and cohesion, so it fits the values of collectivists. On the other hand, equity is compatible with productivity, competition, and self-gain, so it fits the values of individualists. Some collectivists even show a generosity rule when exchanging with in-group members; that is, they use equality even when their input or contribution is clearly higher than the contribution of other members. However, in the case of Chinese participants the generosity rule applied only when the reward to be divided was fixed. When the reward was unlimited there was a departure from the equality norm among both Chinese and US participants. In addition, when participants were given a supervisory role so that harmony was not too important among those who were exchanging, regardless of culture they used the equity rule (Hui, Triandis, and Yee, 1991).

Comparisons of Sweden and the USA showed that the Swedes followed the equality norm, more than the need norm, and least often the equity norm (Tornblum, Jonsson, and Foa, 1985). Chen, Chen, and Meindl (in preparation) extrapolated from these observations and suggested that in individualist cultures equity-based reward allocation will be positively correlated with cooperation in both short and long term work relationships. In collectivist cultures equity-based allocations will be positively correlated to cooperation in short term relations but equality-based systems will be positively related to cooperation in long term work relations. These are very promising hypotheses that should be tested.

Rewards

Erez (1997) suggests that the principle of equality will be used more in horizontal cultures and equity more in vertical cultures. In the case of horizontal individualist cultures profit sharing, gain sharing, low salary differentials and fringe benefits will be stressed. Employees will often be paid according to demographic attributes, such as number of family members. In the case of vertical individualist cultures employees will receive individual incentives and high salary differentials will be common. In horizontal collectivist cultures equality of distribution of organizational rewards will be common. In the case of vertical collectivism those at the top will be paid much better than those at the bottom, but group based rewards may be used.

Behavior settings

Collectivists belong to groups as a matter of right, by birth or marriage, while individualists often have to earn their membership in a group. The result is that collectivists rarely develop skills for entering new groups, while individualists are more likely to have such skills. While many collectivists have difficulty getting into and out of a new group, many individualists have few such difficulties (Cohen, 1991). Collectivists usually establish intimate and long-term relationships (Verma, 1992). Individualists usually establish non-intimate and short-term relationships.

Thus, a manager from a collectivist culture that visits an individualist culture may be surprised by the friendliness of the reception, and disappointed that no intimate relationships are established. Conversely, a manager from an individualist culture assigned to a collectivist culture will find establishing contacts most difficult. An intermediary is often necessary to introduce him to his hosts and facilitate the establishment of a contact. But once the contact is established it can develop into a deep friendship in a way that is rare in individualist cultures.

Recreation

The typical collectivist recreation group (1) has stable membership, (2) is relatively large (more than three people), and (3) meets frequently. For example, Korean skiers often ski in groups; American skiers generally ski alone (Brandt, 1974). Choi (1996) found that individuals in collectivist cultures are more likely to engage in joint activities with family members and friends, while individuals in individualistic cultures are more likely to engage in activities alone.

The typical individualist recreation group (1) has variable membership, (2) is often small (two or three people) or very large, and (3) meets infrequently. The cocktail party, after all, was invented by individualists! The corresponding pattern for collectivists is the stable group that may add a few members in one or another social setting. In short, again, individualists see the individual and collectivists the group as the basic units of social organization. In vertical cultures individuals are more likely to pay attention to status cues than in horizontal societies. For example, in India, even a difference of one day in the age of two persons may be used as the cue for the "younger" person to show respect to the "older" person, while in the USA even large differences in age are ignored.

Communication

Collectivists use indirect and face saving communications more than individualists (Holtgraves, 1997). This means that e-mail will be less satisfying to collectivists, since they will not have access to the context (gestures, eye contact, body placement, distance between bodies). Horizontal individualists will e-mail individuals more than groups, while vertical collectivists will e-mail groups more than individuals. Horizontals will send their communications in any direction, while verticals will do so mostly vertically.

Horizontal collectivists share information very widely, while vertical collectivists limit the information they send to only some "important" people. Vertical collectivists can be abusive in their communications to low-status individuals. Bad news is sent to the top less often by vertical collectivists than horizontal collectivists.

Lin (1997) points out that ambiguity in communication can be very helpful in a vertical collectivist culture such as China, where clarity may result in sanctions. One cannot point out to an official that he is not correct. The Chinese, he indicates, admire people who are frank, such as Judge Bao (p. 369), but do not emulate them.

In short, East Asian collectivists are expected to "read the other's mind" during communication, so that communication is quite indirect, and depends on hints, gestures, level and tone of voice, body orientation, use of the eyes, and distance between the bodies. Many individualists say what's in their mind even if the consequence is that the relationship is hurt. As a result Chen, Chen, and Meindl (in progress) extrapolate that face-to-face communication will evoke higher levels of cooperation in collectivist than in individualist cultures, while mediated partial communication (e.g., via electronic, paper means) will evoke higher levels of cooperation in individualist than in collectivist cultures.

Collectivists are more likely to say: "When you need to use my equipment, if I am not using it go ahead and use it." Individualists are more likely to require that their colleague ask for their permission before using the equipment.

During communication, collectivists use "we"; individualists use "I" a lot. In vertical cultures the very use of words is different depending on whether a lower-status person talks to a higher-status person or vice versa. Such differences in word-use are not so frequent in horizontal cultures. In fact, the languages used by collectivists do not require the use of "I" and "you" while the languages used by individualists do (Kashima and Kashima, 1998).

In Japan, as well as among many Native Americans, silence is acceptable. In fact, Japanese women employees think that a silent male is going to be economically successful and will be a good provider and husband. Silence is embarrassing to individualists while it is a sign of strength for some collectivists (Iwao, 1993).

Morality

Morality among collectivists is more contextual and the supreme value is the welfare of the collective. Ma (1988) has provided a Chinese perspective on moral judgment which is different from the individualistic perspective of Kohlberg (1981).

Lying is an acceptable behavior in collectivist cultures, if it saves face or helps the in-group. There are traditional ways of lying that are understood as "correct behavior."

Trilling (1972) makes the point that when people have a strong sense that they themselves determine who they want to be, as is characteristic of individualists, they are more likely to seek sincerity and authenticity than when they feel swept by traditions and obligations, as is more characteristic of collectivists.

Triandis et al. (2001) used a scenario in which the participants were told that they represented a corporation in a negotiation with another company, for a lucrative contract. There was a competitor company that had more capacity than the participant's own company. If the negotiators claimed that they had more capacity than they really had they would have a good chance of getting the contract, but if they admitted that they had less capacity than the competitor company they would probably not get the contract. A number of dependent variables were used, such as what capacity would the participants claim to have. Data were obtained from about 200 students from each of four cultures that are more or less collectivist (Japan, Korea, Hong Kong, and Greece) and from each of four cultures that are more or less individualist (Australia, Germany, Netherlands, and USA). At the cultural level of analysis the data supported the hypothesis that the collectivists would claim that they have a larger capacity than was the case. The percentages of the samples who told the truth were highest in the USA, and lower in some of the collectivist cultures. However, at the individual level of analysis (i.e., analyses within culture) the vertical idiocentrics lied more often than the allocentrics. This was interpreted to be due to the greater competitiveness of the vertical idiocentrics. They just had to get the contract.

Many observers have emphasized the importance of face in collectivist cultures (Hu, 1944; Ho, 1976). A moral person behaves as his/her role is specified by in-group members and society. If the individual deviates from such ideal behavior, there is loss of face, not only for the individual, but also for the whole in-group. In many collectivist cultures morality consists of doing what the in-group expects. When interacting with the out-group it is "moral" to exploit and deceive. In other words, morality is not applicable to all but only to some members of one's social environment.

JOB-RELATED INFLUENCES OF INDIVIDUALISM AND COLLECTIVISM ON BEHAVIOR

In general, individualist cultures will use individual training, responsibility, feedback, problem-solving, performance appraisals, and rewards, while collectivist cultures will use group training (e.g., Bandura, 1996), and group responsibility, feedback, problem-solving, performance appraisals, and rewards. Also, vertical cultures will emphasize that people are different, so that it is fine for them to receive different amounts of training, reward, feedback, and so on, while horizontal cultures will emphasize that people are similar, and so they should receive equal amounts of training, reward, and the like.

Match of organizational and national culture

When there is a match between organizational and national culture, the human relations practices of the organization are likely to be accepted; but when there is a poor match, e.g., a horizontal individualist organizational culture in a vertical collectivist national culture or vice versa, there is a strong possibility that such a mis-match will hinder the acceptance and implementation of human resource practices, such as career planning, appraisal and compensation systems, and selection and socialization (Schneider, 1988).

Collectivists will work best when working with in-group members, and then they will not free-ride or show social loafing (Earley, 1989, 1993). If they work with out-group members they do free-ride and show social loafing. Individualists will generally be most effective when working alone.

Employee selection

Universalistic human resources practices (e.g., selection on the basis of test scores) will be rare in collectivist cultures, while particularistic practices (e.g., selection on the basis of recommendations of in-group members) will be more common. Triandis and Vassiliou (1972) predicted, from subjective culture data, that Greeks and Americans would differ in the way they make employee decisions. Specifically, they predicted that in reaching employee decisions, Greeks will give more weight to the recommendations of friends and relatives than will Americans, and Americans will give more weight to the recommendations of neighbors and unknown persons than will Greeks. When files of prospective employees were presented to Americans working in Greece and to Athenian employers, the predictions were supported.

Lawler and Bae (1998) examined the "males only," "females only," "no gender language" and "equal opportunity" advertisements placed by Thai subsidiaries of Western and Japanese multinationals in newspapers. The level of collectivism of the parent company of the multinational was associated with a high probability of using a "males only" advertisement, while the individualism of the company was related to the probability of using a "no gender language" advertisement. Also, countries high in individualism had laws that prohibited discrimination in employment, but that was not the case in countries high in collectivism. Ozawa, Crosby, and Crosby (1996) found that their Japanese sample was more collectivist and also endorsed affirmative action to a greater degree than their American sample. It would appear that American individualism results in people feeling some discomfort with categorical social arrangements.

In individualist cultures employers may not have as much choice of personnel because in those cultures many people seek to become self-employed, and are more likely to avoid staying in large enterprises (Gerganov et al., 1996).

Job design

Erez (1997) suggests that enriching individual jobs will be the goals of managers in horizontal individualist cultures, and placing individual jobs in a hierarchy of authority and responsibility will be the goals of vertical individualist managers. Horizontal collectivist managers will emphasize autonomous work groups, self-managed teams and quality circles, while vertical collectivist cultures will emphasize team work controlled by top management teams, but will also use quality circles. House, Wright, and Aditya (1997) review some literature suggesting that role stress is higher in vertical collectivist than in other kinds of cultures. Job assignments will be made to groups in collectivist cultures and to individuals in individualist cultures.

Supervisor–subordinate relations

Collectivists often control the expression of unpleasant emotions in the presence of other people, so as not to disturb the relationship. For example, Stephan, Stephan, and de Vargas (1996) found strong support for the proposition that people in collectivist cultures feel less comfortable expressing negative emotions than people in individualist cultures. The data came from Costa Rica and the US.

Collectivists accept a critical supervisor more than do individualists (Leung, Su, and Morris, submitted). Specifically, compared to Americans, in this study, Chinese participants regarded criticism from superiors to be more acceptable and were less negative about the supervisor. However, they were also more likely to perceive their status to be damaged, were less likely to accept the criticism's content, and became more demoralized after the criticism, especially when the criticism came from a high-status superior. Moskowitz et al. (1994) found that idiocentrics were more dominant and less agreeable than allocentrics when interacting with a supervisee; their behavior pattern was reversed when interacting with a boss.

Employee evaluation

Idiocentrics have a better opinion of themselves than do most people. That is because of the self-enhancement bias that was described earlier. Allocentrics often have a modesty bias, so they sometimes see themselves as less competent than other people do. The result is that in employee evaluation situations idiocentrics often are disappointed and feel that their supervisor is biased against them and unfair. Allocentrics are more likely to see themselves the way their supervisor sees them.

If the evaluation results in the employee being laid off, the impact of this action is likely to be smaller in collectivist cultures where the employee can expect help from the in-group than in individualist cultures where the employee cannot expect much support from the in-group. Similarly, the effects of unemployment are more severe in the individualistic North of Italy than in the collectivist South of Italy (Martella and Maass, submitted). In that study unemployment lowered life satisfaction, self-esteem, and happiness, but the effect was stronger in the North than in the South.

Conflict resolution

Trubinsky, Ting-Toomey, and Lin (1991) compared Taiwan and US respondents, and found that in conflict situations the former were more likely than the latter to use obliging, avoiding, integrating, and compromising styles of conflict resolution, as opposed to a confrontational style. Similarly, Ohbuchi and Takahashi (1994) studied 94 Japanese and 98 American students and asked them to report on recent conflicts they had experienced. They collected 476 episodes, which they submitted to a content analysis. They found that the Japanese were much more likely than the Americans to avoid conflicts. The Japanese were motivated to preserve the relationship. The findings were interpreted as being consistent with theoretical notions about collectivism (Triandis, 1989) and interdependence (Markus and Kitayama, 1991). Similarly, Triandis et al. (1988) found that Japanese participants indicated that they avoided conflict in more situations than American participants. Gabrielidis, Stephan, Ybarra, Dos Santos-Pearson, and Villareal (1997) found that collectivists (Mexicans) displayed more concern for others (used accommodation and collaboration) than individualists (Americans). Pearson and Stephan (1998) reported that Brazilians were more collectivist than Americans and expressed more concern for the outcomes of others than did Americans, while Americans focused on their own outcomes. Brazilians, as expected from theory, made more of a distinction between in-group and out-group in their negotiations than did Americans.

Leadership

Good leaders among collectivists are warm, supportive, and production-oriented (Misumi, 1985). Being nurturing first and then demanding of production is the right way to lead in India (Sinha, 1980, 1996). Paternalism is accepted by 80 percent of the Japanese, 51 percent of representative American samples, and by around 65 percent in samples from middle-European countries (Hayashi, 1992).

The ideal leader in horizontal cultures would be a resourceful democrat; the ideal leader in vertical cultures would be the benevolent autocrat. Promotions from within will be more common in horizontal cultures and leader appointments from the outside or a high-status group will be more common in vertical cultures. In horizontal cultures leadership may rotate, and leaders treat subordinates as equals. In vertical cultures leadership reflects the cultural hierarchy (i.e., upper class or caste results in leadership even when the individual does not merit the position). Individualist leaders deal with individuals, while collectivist leaders deal with groups. The distance between leader and followers is small in the horizontal and larger in the vertical cultures.

Erez (1997) suggests that decision making will be individual, and leaders will delegate authority in horizontal individualist cultures, while decisions will be centralized and top–down in vertical individualist cultures. In horizontal collectivist cultures there will be much group participation, while in vertical collectivist cultures decisions will be top–down, and centralized.

House et al. (1997) reviewed literature that indicates that in horizontal individualist cultures managers and employees pay considerable attention to their own experience, while in vertical collectivist cultures they pay attention to formal rules.

House et al. (1997) suggest that authoritarian leadership is more acceptable in vertical collectivist than in other kinds of cultures. Collectivism has been found associated with a high value on group maintenance, paternalism, in-group loyalty and harmony, treatment of in-group members with dignity, face saving among in-group members, and non-confrontational and peaceful resolution of conflict. Individualists, in many studies reviewed by House et al. (1997), prefer individual to group-based compensation practices and exhibit greater tendency to take risks.

Training

Since collectivists are more attached and loyal to their organization they often receive more training than individualists who are likely to change jobs and work for a competitor organization. Also, horizontals are more likely to receive training than verticals, since the latter are expected to be supervised closely, while the former are supposed to be on their own, so they need to know better how to perform their tasks without help.

Cross-cultural training

A major concern is how to train expatriates that must work in another culture. When collectivists and individualists come into contact, those who are bicultural (have lived much time in another culture) are high in *both* individualism and collectivism, while Western samples tend to be high only on individualism and Eastern samples tend to be high only on collectivism (Yamada and Singelis, 1999). Thus, the bicultural individuals will require less training. Bicultural competence also can reduce depression, if the person is high in allocentrism. Lay et al. (1998) found that high bicultural competence reduced depression among allocentrics, while low bicultural competence increased depression among allocentrics. This makes sense, because allocentrics want to relate to others and if they are not competent in relating to the members of the culture they are visiting they are likely to become depressed.

Much training is required when there is a large cultural distance between the culture of the trainees and the culture of the place they are assigned to (Phalet and Hagendoorn, 1996). One way to measure culture distance, based on Hofstede's (1980a) data, was presented by Zeitling (1996). He used cluster analysis and various graphic procedures. Japan is quite distant from most cultures, so that one can expect this assignment to be among the more difficult. By contrast, assignments of Americans to the Scandinavian countries should be relatively easy. Americans should find it easy to work in the UK, Australia, or New Zealand. On the other hand, they are likely to find an assignment to Yugoslavia, Portugal, Thailand, or Taiwan to be a considerable challenge. The greater the cultural distance, the greater the culture shock is likely to be.

Also, when there is a large discrepancy between the personality of the visitor and the hosts, adjustment is more difficult and depression is more likely (Ward and Chang, 1997).

Phalet and Hagendoorn also reported that Turkish workers in Belgium were helped by their collectivism to adjust and be effective. Also, social inequality reinforced collectivism, and cultural distance lowered the achievement of these migrants.

When individualists move to a collectivist culture they experience certain kinds of difficulties that can be overcome if they are properly trained. Triandis, Brislin, and Hui (1988) advised them to pay attention to the group membership of the people they interact with more than is necessary in their own culture. They should expect more differences in the behavior of collectivists when they interact with in-group and out-group members than is found in their own culture. They should expect more emphasis in saving the other person's face, even if that means telling a lie.

Conversely, collectivists moving to an individualist culture should pay less attention to group memberships and more attention to the idiosyncrasies of the individuals they are interacting with. They should avoid lying, and can feel free to express themselves without worrying too much about saving the other person's face. Training materials called culture assimilators (Fiedler, Mitchell, and Triandis, 1971) are helpful in increasing the comfort of the traveler. Bhawuk (1998) showed that a culture assimilator that uses individualism–collectivism theory to explain why particular behaviors are more appropriate in one than in another culture, is more effective than assimilators that do not use this theory.

Organizational commitment

Triandis (1995) summarizes evidence that suggests that individualists are more socially mobile, and are skilled in entering and leaving new groups. This is especially true for vertical individualists when they perceive that joining the new group will advance their status. On the other hand, collectivists prefer more intimate interactions, with stable in-groups. It would follow from this argument that organizational commitment should be higher among collectivists, who may not leave the corporation even when they are not especially satisfied with their job, because they do not want to abandon their friends. Wasti (1999) examined organizational commitment in Turkey, a collectivist culture. She found strong evidence that even among dissatisfied employees leaving the organization was undesirable.

Lay et al. (1998) reported that allocentrics are more attached to their in-groups. Chen, Brockner, and Katz (submitted) examined how people reacted when their in-groups were successful or unsuccessful and when they themselves were successful or unsuccessful. Upon learning that they performed well but their in-group performed poorly, Americans were less likely than Chinese to show in-group favoritism. The willingness of collectivists to forgive imperfect behavior by others is similar to the *amae* pattern found in Japan. According to Yamaguchi (1998), *amae* means that one is willing to accept the other person even when the other person has behaved inappropriately.

CONCLUSION

In this chapter I presented the conceptualization of horizontal and vertical collectivism and individualism, and reviewed the impact of these cultural syndromes on social behavior in general, and on job-related behaviors in particular.

In evaluating the cultural patterns (see Triandis, 1995) we can stress that there are both desirable and undesirable consequences of these cultural syndromes. Other things being equal (e.g., affluence), collectivism is desirable for family stability and health, but from a civic point of view it can be undesirable (higher probability of war, ethnic cleansing). Horizontality is related to social cohesion and satisfaction with one's status in life. Verticality is functional when decisions must be taken quickly with little debate, and when individual goals must be sacrificed to achieve group goals. Individualism is desirable because it is associated with optimism, well-being, high self-esteem, human rights, and peace between states, but it can be associated with high levels of delinquency and crime within countries.

Much future research is needed for the discovery and wide adoption of cultural patterns that utilize the best elements of each of these cultural patterns.

Part II

Strategy, Structure, and Inter-Organizational Relationships

Introduction

Cross-cultural issues in strategy, structure, and inter-organizational relationships became dominant research topics during the 1990s. The fall of communism in Eastern Europe and the rapid pace of change in technology, globalization, and the Internet all contributed to heightened interest in the effects of culture on firms' strategies.

This part contains four excellent chapters covering a range of issues from institutional context (Peng) to culture and alliances (Almeida, Grant, and Phene; Hébert and Beamish) to intra-firm strategy to structure (Egelhoff). Each chapter includes a comprehensive literature review and a research agenda, either implied or explicit, for the future.

Mike Peng leads off with a discussion of the effect of the institutional context on a firm's strategy in "Cultures, Institutions, and Strategic Choices: Toward an Institutional Perspective on Business Strategy." He entices us with a thoughtful review of differences among firm strategies that might be caused by differences in the institutional context of firms – the laws, regulations, systems, and norms that provide the context for business. His own research on business strategy and growth in emerging economies richly informs his review. He examines four emerging streams of research to support his argument that differences in business strategy are due, in part, to differences in the institutional framework within which firms operate. First, he examines the relationship between manufacturers and their suppliers in Japan, noting that the close, cooperative relationship observed is consistent with Japanese institutional arrangements (e.g. *keiretsu*) that rely upon cooperation and that discourage opportunism. Second, he analyzes the effect of the institutional context by examining Chinese entrepreneurs in China and the US, together with Caucasian entrepreneurs in the US. He finds evidence of the effect of differing institutional context because the US-based entrepreneurs, both Chinese–American and Caucasian, differ in their entrepreneurial behavior from Chinese entrepreneurs in China. By including Chinese–American entrepreneurs in the study he is able to compare the effects of institutional context with the effects of national culture, finding the former to be stronger than the latter. He notes that a stable institutional context tends to minimize the effect of national culture while unstable institutional contexts allow the effects of national culture to affect business practices substantially.

Next, he reviews the literature on diversification strategies in different countries, noting again that the institutional context of firms may influence diversification and the financial benefits of diversification. His last section on growth strategies in transition economies similarly entices us with the possibility that institutional context affects growth strategy.

This chapter provides a rich foundation for future research on the effect of institutions on firm strategy. Many of Peng's conclusions are based on non-systematic but intriguing observations. Most of the research cited is quite recent, suggesting a field of research that is just emerging. Peng's chapter, informed by his other empirical and conceptual work, suggests many research opportunities. It is a must for anyone doing research on the effect of institutional context on business strategy.

Almeida, Grant, and Phene's chapter 4, "Knowledge Acquisition through Alliances: Opportunities and Challenges," is another conceptual piece in which the authors make the case for an effect of cultural differences on knowledge acquisition at three levels of culture: the country, the region, and the firm. These authors argue that a firm's home country culture and institutions influence companies' strategies, structures, and systems, consistent with Peng's view. They contend that cultural differences affect both the propensity to form alliances and the ability to learn from them. Greater cultural distance between two countries increases firms' motivation to learn from their partner but also makes it more difficult to learn. Some cultures have a greater propensity to have learning as a goal for an alliance (e.g. Japan) while others are more interested in market access (US).

Regional culture, similarly, affects the way in which business is conducted and therefore the propensity for and goals of alliance formation. The authors use the difference between Silicon Valley and Route 128 in the Boston area to illustrate their point. Regional differences in norms and values are reflected in the companies' cultures and strategies in the two regions. Finally, corporate culture affects the propensity for alliance formation, the goals held for the alliance, and the likelihood of alliance success. Almeida et al. cite research suggesting that inter-organizational differences in culture are a bigger cause of alliance failure than national cultural differences, a problem fairly readily overcome by forming alliances with former partners rather than new partners. As with Peng's work, Almeida et al. set the stage for significant empirical research concerning cultural effects on inter-organizational learning.

Hébert and Beamish examine cross-national and domestic joint ventures in chapter 5 ("Cooperative Strategies between Firms: International Joint Ventures"). They suggest that JV structure with respect to parent company control and JV autonomy will affect the JV's performance and that these effects will be different for domestic JVs as compared to international JVs. By integrating both transaction cost analysis and social exchange theory, Hébert and Beamish present a much more comprehensive conceptual framework for investigation: one that accounts not only for the economic factors associated with JV control but also with issues of trust and mutual forbearance, consistent with Almeida et al.

This is the only empirical chapter in this part. Hébert and Beamish's results are enticing and suggest ample opportunity for future research. While they hypothesize that shared control and JV autonomy would be positively related to performance, their results are mixed. Similarly, the strength of these relationships in international JVs, as compared to domestic JVs, is mixed. Researchers in this field will find the literature review and hypothesis development sections of the chapter invaluable. Empirical results are typical of those in the field, suggesting much work remains in the field before we have a full understanding of the relationships among control, autonomy, and performance in domestic and international joint ventures.

Egelhoff reviews existing approaches to the issue of strategy and structure fit in multinational corporations (MNCs) in chapter 6 ("The Importance of the Strategy–Structure Relationship in MNCs"). He notes fairly consistent support since the 1970s for strategy–structure relationships that describe what MNCs do, but little consistent support for the effect of good strategy–structure fit on firm performance. He goes on to develop a new theory that might account for the observed lack of relationship between fit and performance, suggesting that we study organizations' specific behaviors and their fit with specific elements in the competitive environment rather than strategy and structure more globally. Egelhoff develops a conceptual framework in which he examines modes of coordination, using an information-processing framework to conceptualize the relationship between strategy and structure. In particular, he argues that fit will be good when the information-processing requirements of strategy (and by implication, the competitive environment) match the information-processing capacity of the firm's structure.

The purpose of a firm's structure and processes is to help the firm implement a strategy that is appropriate to the demands of the competitive environment, including its cultural context. By applying the information-processing perspective to four typical MNC structures (Stopford and Wells, 1972), he shows how decision making and information flow will differ in each. He structures the bulk of his chapter around the Stopford and Wells typology. Most of his discussion is centered on coordination mechanisms in each type, though he spends some time discussing the implications of different structures on employee motivation as well. He uses the pharmaceutical industry to illustrate his approach to the strategy–structure fit. His careful explication of coordination mechanism in each of the four types of MNC structures is but one example of the type of research that this chapter can spawn. Numerous other organizational behaviors can be analyzed in this framework, yielding a rich description of the strategy–structure relationship in MNCs. With rich descriptions in hand, careful empirical work at the appropriate level of detail can be undertaken to re-examine the fit–performance relationship. Egelhoff's chapter establishes a broad and important research agenda for scholars and practitioners alike.

Future research might integrate the perspectives offered in the Peng and Almeida et al. chapters with Egelhoff's work. Peng argues that company strategies vary by institutional context and Almeida et al. remind us that firms are imprinted with distinguishable characteristics, based on their home country's culture and institutions. Presumably, these factors would affect both the strategies and structures selected by MNCs. How does the imprinting factor affect Egelhoff's work? Does home country modify the strategy–structure relationship or the fit–performance relationship? These questions and others emerge from chapters in this part.

Hébert and Beamish and Almeida et al. both point out that alliances fail at a high rate. Each examines different reasons for failure, Almeida et al. in the inherent difficulty of the alliance owing to cultural differences and Hébert and Beamish in the way in which the alliance is structured. Integrating these two perspectives allows us to specify what control and autonomy configurations facilitate inter-organizational learning and how specific differences in culture might moderate the control–performance relationship.

3

Cultures, Institutions, and Strategic Choices: Toward an Institutional Perspective on Business Strategy

Mike W. Peng

This chapter focuses on a key question: Why do strategies of firms from different countries differ? This is the first among the five most fundamental questions in strategic management. Moving from an intuitive answer based on national cultural differences, researchers' attention has increasingly focused on the underlying institutional frameworks that drive strategic choices. Drawing from research on business strategies in non-Western economies, this chapter outlines the emergence of an institution-based view of business strategy which sheds light on why firms differ, reviews four streams of research in a broad range of strategies and countries published mostly in the 1990s, and critiques and extends some of the current work by suggesting a number of future research directions.

Why do strategies of firms from different countries differ? This is the very first question among the five most fundamental questions in strategic management raised by Rumelt, Schendel, and Teece (1994: 564). The other four questions are: (1) How do firms behave? (2) How are strategy outcomes affected by strategy processes? (3) What determines the scope of the firm? and (4) What determines the international success and failure of firms? Rumelt and colleagues (1994: 570) maintain that while there are other questions to ask, "they all relate in one way or another" to these five fundamental questions.

This chapter focuses on the question of why firms differ. Since the diversity of firm strategies around the world can arise as the result of many possible forces internal or external to the organization, this question engenders a wide variety of disparate answers from economists (Nelson, 1991) and sociologists (Carroll, 1993). An intuitive response to this question is that because strategies are formulated and implemented by top managers who are influenced by their different national cultures, firm strategies naturally differ. This culturalist perspective, while insightful, has to confront a second puzzle: that is, holding industry constant, why sometimes strategies of firms from culturally proximate countries are different, while during other times strategies of organizations from culturally different countries are similar? Notable examples in the literature include (1) the differences in governance and investment strategies among firms in Canada, France, Germany, Great Britain, and the United States, despite their cultural link (Gedajlovic and Shapiro, 1998; Thomas and Waring, 1999), and (2) the similarities in growth strategies during the economic transition in Eastern Europe and China, in spite of their lack of cultural similarities (Peng, 2000; Peng and Heath, 1996). How to explain this phenomenon?

A number of scholars have argued that in addition to culture, a firm also needs to take into account wider influences from sources such as the state and society when making strategic choices (DiMaggio and Powell, 1991; Oliver, 1997; Scott, 1995). These influences certainly include culture, but are broader than the typical notion of "national culture" exemplified by Hofstede's (1980, 1991) work. Consisting of rules, norms, values, and taken-for-granted assumptions about what constitutes appropriate or acceptable economic behavior, these influences are broadly considered as *institutional* frameworks (North, 1990). This new perspective, consequently, can be called an *institution-based* view of business strategy (Oliver, 1997).

Since no firm can be immune from institutional frameworks in which it is embedded (Barber, 1995; Dacin, Ventresca, and Beal, 1999; Granovetter, 1985), there is hardly any dispute that institutions matter. In order to make further theoretical progress, researchers must "tackle the harder and more interesting issues of how they matter, under what circumstances, to what extent, and in what ways" (Powell, 1996: 297). This chapter, consequently, has three objectives. First, the broad contour of the new, institution-based view of business strategy is outlined. Second, I review the recent international management literature to assess the progress made in the direction Powell (1996) called for. Specifically, I highlight recent research, mostly published in the 1990s, on business strategies in *non-Western* economies. Given that most existing research takes place in the West, a focus on non-Western economies allows us "to vary institutional contexts"; otherwise, "it is difficult if not impossible to discern the effects of institutions on social structures and behaviors if all our cases are embedded in the same or very similar ones" (Scott, 1995: 146). The four substantive areas reviewed are: (1) supplier strategies in Japan, (2) Chinese entrepreneurship in multiple countries, (3) diversification strategies in emerging economies such as Chile, India, and Korea, and (4) growth strategies in transition economies such as China and Russia. Finally, current research is critiqued and directions for future research are suggested.

CULTURES VERSUS INSTITUTIONS

Since both cross-cultural researchers and institutional theorists have used the term "culture" liberally, it is useful to set the terms straight. Hofstede (1991: 5) defines culture as "the collective programming of the mind which distinguishes the members of one group or category of people from another." Although he acknowledges that culture can manifest itself not only at the national level, but also at the macro, regional level and micro, organizational level, his influential work has primarily focused on national-level cultures, and has been widely followed.

On the other hand, institutional theorists with an economics or sociology background do not define culture directly. Instead, they focus on "institutions," which include "culture." For example, sociologists DiMaggio and Powell (1991: 8, added emphasis) write that "The new institutionalism . . . comprises an interest in institutions as independent variables, and a turn towards cognitive and *cultural* explanations." According to economist North (1990: 3), institutions are "the rules of the game in a society or, more formally, are the humanly devised constraints that shape human interaction." Similarly, sociologist Scott (1995: 33) defines institutions as "cognitive, normative, and regulative structures and activities that provide stability and meaning to social behavior." Consequently, an "institutional framework" is defined by Davis and North (1971: 6) as "the set of fundamental political, social, and legal ground rules that establishes the basis for production, exchange, and distribution."

Institutional theorists suggest that "institutions" include laws, regulations, norms, values, as well as "cultures." This implies that "institution" is a broader construct than "culture." While their conceptualization of "culture" does not necessarily preclude national culture, it typically focuses on the rules and practices at the organization or industry level, and *not* on the national level (DiMaggio, 1997; Dacin et al., 1999). Therefore, when reading the work of institutional theorists, especially those with a sociology background, it is important to note their level of analysis when they discuss "culture." Since our purpose is to review the work focusing on business strategy, delineating the conceptual differences between multiple definitions of "culture" is beyond the scope of this chapter. When the term "culture" is used here, I refer to "national culture" simply as "a matter of expediency" (Hofstede, 1991: 12).

FORMAL AND INFORMAL INSTITUTIONAL CONSTRAINTS

Institutional frameworks interact with organizations by signaling which choices are acceptable and supportable. As a result, institutions help reduce uncertainty for organizations as they interact with each other. Institutional frameworks are made up of both formal and informal constraints (North, 1990). *Formal* constraints include political rules, judicial decisions, and economic contracts. *Informal* constraints, on the other hand, include socially sanctioned norms of behavior, which are embedded in culture and ideology (Scott, 1995). North (1990) suggests that in situations where formal constraints fail, informal constraints will come into play to reduce uncertainty and provide constancy to organizations. These insights have important implications for the development of an institution-based view of business strategy (Peng, 2000).

AN INSTITUTION-BASED VIEW OF BUSINESS STRATEGY

Strategies are about choices. Therefore, an analysis of business strategy needs to "recognize the exercise of choice by organizational decision makers" (Child, 1972: 10). Given the influence of institutional frameworks on firm behavior, any strategic choice that firms make is inherently affected by the formal and informal constraints of a given institutional framework (North, 1990; Oliver, 1991, 1997). Viewed from such a perspective, much of the strategy literature, which largely focuses on Western firms, does not discuss the specific relationship between strategic choices and institutional frameworks. To be sure,

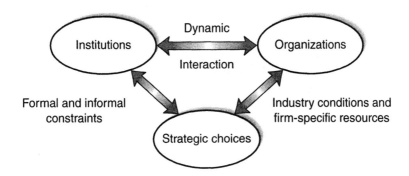

FIGURE 3.1 Institutions, organizations, and strategic choices
Source: Peng (2000)

the influence of the "environment" has long been featured in the literature (Aldrich, 1979; Lawrence and Lorsch, 1969; Pfeffer and Salancik, 1978). However, what has dominated this research is a "task environment" view, which focuses on economic variables such as market demand and technological change. Until recently, scholars have rarely looked beyond the task environment to explore the interaction among institutions, organizations, and strategic choices (Scott, 1995). Instead, a market-based institutional framework has been taken for granted.

Such an omission is unfortunate, because it is precisely the institutional frameworks in developed economies that prompt Western firms to choose certain strategies and constrain them from choosing others (Peng and Heath, 1996). "Today," wrote Child (1997: 54), "we are much more conscious of" the importance of the relationships between organizations and institutions. Treating institutions as independent variables, an institution-based view on corporate strategy, therefore, focuses on the dynamic interaction between institutions and organizations, and considers strategic choices as the outcome of such an interaction (figure 3.1). Specifically, strategic choices are not only driven by industry conditions and firm-specific resources that traditional strategy research emphasizes (Barney, 1991; Porter, 1980), but are also a reflection of the formal and informal constraints of a particular institutional framework that decision makers confront (Oliver, 1997; Scott, 1995).

By the 1990s, more and more scholars had come to realize that institutions matter (DiMaggio and Powell, 1991; Scott, 1995), and that strategy research cannot just focus on industry conditions and firm resources (Khanna and Palepu, 1997; Peng, 2000; Thomas and Waring, 1999).[1] While taking institutions seriously is only a first step, working out the analytic logic of their influence is the second, and explicating the underlying mechanisms comes next (Williamson, 1985, 1991). This chapter can be considered as a part of this broad intellectual movement in search of a better understanding of the relationship among institutions, organizations, and strategic choices. Next, we turn to four areas of recent international management research in a variety of non-Western economies to illustrate how the institution-based view has evolved and developed.

Supplier Strategies in Japan

While most strategy research focuses on Western firms, recently, it has become virtually "impossible to discuss the matter of business strategy long without the issue of Japanese economic organization surfacing" (Williamson, 1991: 87). Of particular concern to strategy researchers is the *keiretsu* networks, the webs of interfirm relations that envelop many Japanese firms (Gerlach, 1992). Specifically, within such a network, independent suppliers seem to be willing to site their factories close to major manufacturers such as Toyota and Honda, in the absence of a long-term contract. Such a high degree of asset specificity creates economic value by reducing delivery time and costs. However, according to research in the West (Williamson, 1975, 1985), such a high degree of asset specificity is likely to result in high transaction costs, because the value of suppliers' location-specific assets will depreciate considerably when they no longer have a contract with manufacturers and/or when suppliers want to deliver to other manufacturers located elsewhere. Consequently, suppliers are predicted to be unwilling to site their factories in a vulnerable location, and manufacturers often need to engage in costly vertical integration. In contrast to such thinking, Japanese firms seem to have an unlikely combination, namely, high asset specificity and low transaction costs, thus presenting a puzzle to researchers (Dyer, 1997).

One answer to solve the puzzle is to invoke the difference in national cultures between Japan and Western countries such as the United States (Dore, 1987). A high propensity to cooperate is believed to be rooted in the Japanese culture, and, consequently, a high degree of interfirm cooperation is more likely. Beyond this simplistic culturalist perspective, more recent work has increasingly focused on the institutional frameworks in which Japanese firms are embedded (Hill, 1995). Specifically, while Japan has developed a set of formal legal frameworks based on the American model in the postwar decades, they are not used extensively. Instead, Japanese firms tend to place a greater emphasis on informal constraints, such as consensus- and trust-building instead of formal contracts. In other words, "the informal constraints of Japanese society do a *relatively* better job of holding opportunism in check than those of many Western societies," resulting in both a high degree of specialization and low transaction costs (Hill, 1995: 129, original emphasis). The upshot is that major manufacturers such as Toyota and Honda can avoid costly vertical integration typically found in Western automobile companies, while still benefiting from cooperation with suppliers (Womack, Jones, and Roos, 1990).

Although research on Japanese supplier strategies has demonstrated that interfirm strategies can be organized differently and still generate competitive advantage (Dyer and Singh, 1998), this work is a *weak* test of the institutional perspective. This is because the national cultures between Japan and Western countries are so different that it is difficult to distinguish the impact of institutional influences independent of national cultural influences. The next section reviews some recent work that takes on such a challenge.

Chinese Entrepreneurship in Multiple Countries

A strong test of the institutional perspective needs to demonstrate that institutions matter independent of national cultures. Such work has only begun recently. Most research in this area starts with a cross-cultural perspective, that is, comparing and contrasting the impact of different national cultures on firm behavior. For example, the dramatic contrasts between Chinese[2] and American cultures have attracted a number of cross-cultural studies which report significant differences (Chen, 1995; Earley, 1993; Holt, 1997). However, critics argue that many *cross-cultural* studies do not accomplish their objective; rather, they end up being *cross-national* studies that reflect the impact of environmental factors such as different formal and informal institutional frameworks in various countries (Farh, Earley, and Lin, 1997: 441; Kelley and Worthley, 1981: 164; Tan and Peng, 1999: 3). Therefore, they suggest that it is difficult to conclude whether the observed differences between subjects in two different countries are due to cross-cultural or cross-national differences (Tan and Peng, 1999: 3). Due to such "confusion concerning the roles of cultural and national context" (Earley and Singh, 1995: 337), there is a long-standing debate on whether cultural or national differences drive managerial differences.

Improving upon previous designs, McGrath and colleagues (1992) introduce a third sample from Taiwan. Similarly, Ralston and colleagues (1992) and Tse and associates (1988) bring in a third sample from Hong Kong. Subjects in Taiwan and Hong Kong are assumed to share the cultural roots with their counterparts in mainland China, and operate in a different, market economy. However, since Taiwan and Hong Kong represent a third national environment, employing these samples, although representing substantial progress, is still unable to allow researchers to isolate the role of national institutions that is independent of the cultural effect, or vice versa (Shenkar and Ronen, 1987).

Attempting to fill such a gap, my colleague and I employed a rigorous, quasi-experimental design to better isolate the role of cultural and national differences (Tan and Peng, 1999). It is widely known that the Chinese are an entrepreneurial people, as evidenced by the wealth they generate throughout Southeast Asia and now increasingly in North America and Western Europe (Fukuyama, 1996; Kao, 1993; Seagrave, 1995). However, entrepreneurial activities in mainland China were kept at a minimum during the Maoist period until the 1970s. Since then, the emergence of entrepreneurship in mainland China seems to indicate that it is the development of market-supporting institutions, both formal and informal, that gives birth to a new wave of entrepreneurship (Peng, 2000: 6, 2001). We test this proposition by focusing on entrepreneurs who have founded new businesses. Specifically, we draw on three samples, namely, mainland Chinese, Chinese–Americans, and Caucasian–Americans. These samples represent two distinctive national environments (the People's Republic of China versus the United States) and two different cultures (Chinese versus American). We measure the differences in entrepreneurs' perception of the environment and their strategic orientations. Two competing hypotheses are generated. First, if the *national* institutional effect predominates, then Chinese–American and Caucasian–American entrepreneurs would show similar patterns of response compared with those of mainland Chinese entrepreneurs. Conversely, if the *cultural* effect predominates, then mainland Chinese and Chinese–American entrepreneurs would show similar patterns of response when compared with those of their Caucasian–American counterparts (Tan and Peng, 1999).

The introduction of the Chinese–American sample "bridges" the two national samples. On one hand, these entrepreneurs compete with their Caucasian–American counterparts in the same national environment (Waldinger, Aldrich, and Ward, 1990). On the other hand, Chinese–American entrepreneurs have been found to maintain significant cultural similarities with counterparts in their former homeland (Fukuyama, 1996). Under the joint impact of cultural and environmental influence, the response of Chinese–American entrepreneurs, therefore, cannot be predicted *a priori* in a single direction, and has to be entertained in two competing hypotheses.

Our empirical results lend strong support for the institutional perspective (Peng, 2001; Tan and Peng, 1999). Specifically, Chinese–American and Caucasian–American entrepreneurs tend to share more similarities in terms of their environmental perceptions and strategic orientations when compared with their counterparts in mainland China. Despite a presumed cultural link between mainland Chinese and Chinese–American samples, these two groups differ significantly on many dimensions. These results, therefore, provide some preliminary evidence suggesting that it is institutions, rather than national cultures, that drive entrepreneurship. Given that the institutional environments between mainland China and the United States are radically different, our findings are hardly surprising. More work may need to concentrate on "partially similar" cases (Shenkar and von Glinow, 1994), such as by comparing and contrasting firm strategies in different emerging economies, which we now turn to.

DIVERSIFICATION STRATEGIES IN EMERGING ECONOMIES

As a loosely defined term coined at the outset of the 1990s, "emerging economies" commonly refer to a number of countries in Asia (China, Hong Kong, India, Southeast Asia, South Korea, and Taiwan), Central and Eastern Europe (the Czech Republic, Hungary, Poland, and Russia), and Latin America (Argentina, Brazil, Chile, Colombia, Mexico, and Venezuela) (*Economist*, 1998: 94). Interestingly, diversification strategies throughout these economies share certain similarities that are at odds with what has generally been found in the West.

Since the 1970s, research in the West suggests that, on average, firms with a higher level of diversification are less profitable than firms with a lower level of diversification (reviewed by Hoskisson and Hitt, 1990; Montgomery, 1994). What seems to hurt performance the most is a strategy of conglomerate (or unrelated) diversification. Consequently, unrelated conglomerates have largely become a thing of the past in major developed economies, especially the United States, by the 1980s and 1990s (Davis, Diekmann, and Tinsley, 1994).[3] In contrast, highly diversified conglomerates, often called "business groups," have often been found extensively in emerging economies (Granovetter, 1994; Khanna and Palepu, 1997; Powell and Smith-Doerr, 1994). These countries include Chile (Khanna and Palepu, 1999), Hong Kong (Au, Peng, and Wang, 2000; Redding, 1990), India (Ghemawat and Khanna, 1998), South Korea (Hamilton and Biggart, 1988; Ungson, Steers, and Park, 1997), and Taiwan (Hamilton and Feenstra, 1995), to name a few. More recently, diversified "enterprise groups" (Keister, 1998; Peng, 1997) and "financial industrial groups" (Johnson, 1997) have also emerged in China and Russia, respectively.

Seen through a Western lens, the persistence and emergence of these diversified conglomerates throughout emerging economies seems puzzling (Granovetter, 1994). A culturalist perspective would suggest that the national cultures of these emerging economies may foster such culturally important practices. The validity of this view, however, is questionable in light of significant cultural differences among this diverse group of countries spanning multiple continents. Another perspective suggests that as a highly institutionalized organizational form due to historical reasons, these conglomerates persist in such "backward" countries with little performance benefits. A stronger proposition, often embraced by Western media and advisors to governments in emerging economies, is that these conglomerates actually destroy value and therefore should be dismantled (*Business Week*, 1999a). Rigorous evidence supporting this proposition, however, is rare. Preliminary findings actually suggest that in contrast to the conventional wisdom in the West, there seem to be discernible performance *benefits* associated with conglomerates in emerging economies, as Khanna and Palepu (2000) find in India. These findings thus confront researchers: How to reconcile the striking differences in diversification strategies from developed and emerging economies?

The answer seems to lie in the institutional perspective with a focus on the underlying formal and informal institutional frameworks permeating these countries (Peng and Lee, 2000). While emerging economies are hardly uniform, their formal institutions tend to fall short to varying degrees in providing support for low transaction-cost business operations in three critical areas: (1) a credible legal framework, (2) a stable political structure, and (3) functioning strategic factor markets (Khanna and Palepu, 1997; Peng and Heath, 1996).

In emerging economies, because of the weaknesses of formal institutions, "informal constraints rise to play a *larger* role in regulating economic exchanges in these countries during the transition" (Peng and Heath, 1996: 504, added emphasis). The main informal constraints come from three sources. First, the *interpersonal* relations among executives serve as a focal point for valuable managerial networking. Although managers all over the world devote a considerable amount of time and energy to cultivate interpersonal ties (Mintzberg, 1973), managers in emerging economies, due to a lack of publicly available, reliable information about market opportunities, perhaps "rely more heavily on the cultivation of personal relationships to cope with the exigencies of their situation" (Child, 1994: 150). By engaging in reciprocal, preferential, and mutually supportive action, managers in diversified conglomerates, who often share the same family, clan, and/or education background, are able to reduce uncertainty in their decision making.

Second, *external* connections linking these executives and key stakeholders, especially government officials, are also a crucial part of the informal institutional constraints in emerging economies (Boddewyn and Brewer, 1994; Oliver, 1997). Given the need to co-opt sources of environmental uncertainty (Pfeffer and Salancik, 1978), it is not surprising that managers maintain a "disproportionately greater contact" with government officials (Child, 1994: 154). Recent work by Peng and Luo (2000) found that in China, connections with officials appear to be more important than ties with other managers in terms of their impact on firm performance. Bribes, gifts, and other corrupt practices may be part of working with the bureaucracy. But that is not the whole story. In many cases, educating officials is more important than exchanging favors (Khanna and Palepu, 1997). Conglomerates can leverage their government contacts, and present to officials a united front of the interests of diverse industries and businesses represented by a single group, thus minimizing the risk of overloading the bureaucracy (Peng and Lee, 2000).

Finally, the *reputation* of conglomerates serves as an informal but strong signaling device to reduce uncertainty for customers and investors. In consumer markets throughout emerging economies, independent consumer information organizations are rare, and government watchdog agencies are ineffective. Moreover, consumers have little redress mechanisms if a product or service does not deliver on its promise (Khanna and Palepu, 1997). As a result, consumers are reluctant to trust new brands. Conversely, since established brands wield tremendous power, conglomerates with a quality reputation can leverage their names to enter new industries, including unrelated ones.

When attracting financial investors, the reputation of diversified conglomerates thus becomes a valuable, unique, and hard-to-imitate competitive advantage (Barney, 1991). It is interesting to note that in contrast to the United States, where Internet business is dominated by start-ups such as Amazon.com which raised significant capital, Internet services in emerging economies are predominately provided by established conglomerates such as Hong Kong's Wharf and Singapore's Sembcorp, which can more easily raise external financing and provide internal funding (*Business Week*, 1999b). Such an ability to raise capital, as well as to internally allocate capital, compensates for a crucial void in the development of financial markets. In addition to financial investors, foreign direct investors are also more likely to be attracted to established conglomerates than to unknown independent firms in emerging economies. Again, the reputation and prestige of these groups saves on search costs for foreign investors, which can be tremendous given the lack of information and the steep learning curve in these countries (Luo and Peng, 1999).

Overall, informal constraints offer some constancy and predictability in the absence of well-developed formal market-supporting institutions. Specifically, diversified conglomerates are able to compensate for the lack of formal institutional constraints by performing basic functions by themselves, such as allocating capital, obtaining market information, and enforcing contracts. In contrast, in developed economies, specialized organizations (e.g., stock exchanges, market research firms, law firms, and the courts) as part of the formal institutions will handle these responsibilities, thus nullifying the need to support these costly activities within the firm.

Taken together, research on diversification strategies in emerging economies not only highlights the explanatory power of the institutional perspective, but also reminds us of the institutional embeddedness of the recent findings of diversification research in developed economies (Peng and Lee, 2000). It is important to note that the negative relationship between conglomerate diversification and performance was actually not found during an earlier era in the West (Hubbard and Palia, 1999; Matsusaka, 1993; Morck, Shleifer, and Vishny, 1990). Instead, financial markets' response to unrelated acquisitions was *positive* in the 1960s. These findings thus document "a dramatic reversal in [US] investor sentiment toward diversification – positive in the 1960s, neutral in the 1970s, and negative in the 1980s" (Matsusaka, 1993: 358). In the 1960s, external capital markets were less developed in terms of firm-specific information disclosure than in later decades. For example, relative to the current period, there was less access by the public to databases, analyst reports, and other sources of information that could reduce transaction costs between external investors and firms. As a result, conglomerates in the United States at that time were perceived *ex ante* by external capital markets to have an advantage in their abilities to allocate capital internally, a logic very similar to the favorable reaction of external markets to conglomerates in emerging markets now. In short, the institutional perspective highlights the historical specificity of a particular relationship between diversification and performance, which may not hold true longitudinally.

GROWTH STRATEGIES IN TRANSITION ECONOMIES

Before the current economic transition, firms in socialist countries in Eastern Europe, the former Soviet Union, and China were not interested in growth. A fascinating aspect of the transition process is that firms there are now compelled to grow to be more competitive in the emerging ocean of market competition, thus presenting strategy researchers with a previously unencountered question: How do firms in transition economies achieve growth? (Peng and Heath, 1996).

Existing research on the growth of the firm suggests that there are typically three strategies for growth, namely, generic expansion, mergers and acquisitions, and/or networks and alliances (Penrose, 1959; Williamson, 1975, 1985). Work on firm growth in transition economies highlights the institutional prerequisites that support each of these three growth strategies. Specifically, generic expansion calls for a staff of capable managers. Mergers and acquisitions require functioning strategic factor markets. Developing networks and alliances need to build trust and mutual understanding (Peng and Heath, 1996). While the institutional frameworks supporting the first two growth strategies are formal ones, those for the last strategy are of an informal nature based on interpersonal relationships (Peng, 2000).

Empirical work has been initiated in China, first through a qualitative phase building on three longitudinal case studies conducted over a seven-year period (Peng, 1997). This work has recently moved to a quantitative phase (Peng and Luo, 2000). Several interesting findings emerge. First, generic expansion, based on firms' own resources, is typically infeasible initially, because of the lack of certain critical resources at most firms. Second, handicapped by both a lack of capital and a lack of formal strategic factor markets, nor can most firms hope, at least initially, to acquire necessary resources through mergers and acquisitions. Many so-called mergers have been mandated by the government in an effort to bail out ailing state-owned firms. Third, an informal, network-based growth strategy is typically favored by a variety of firms. They usually rely on developing inter-organizational networks by tapping into the complementary resources at partner firms in order to jointly pursue growth opportunities (Peng, 1997). Specifically, state-owned firms like to team up with foreign firms and private firms in order to access financial capital, advanced technology, and entrepreneurial energy (Shenkar and Li, 1999). Non-state firms are interested in obtaining some political support from the government by collaborating with state-owned firms. Foreign firms tap into the capabilities of domestic partners in order to navigate the uncertain waters of transition economies (Brouthers and Bamossy, 1997; Luo and Peng, 1999; Yan and Gray, 1994). Finally, micro, interpersonal ties among managers at multiple firms are translated into macro, inter-organizational relations leading to better firm performance – in short, a *micro–macro* link (Peng and Luo, 2000).

Given that strategic choices are inherently affected by managers' national cultures

(Hofstede, 1991), it is not surprising that Chinese managers, who have a widely noted cultural propensity to rely on informal ties, resort to personal connections to achieve organizational goals. However, Boisot and Child (1996), Peng (1997, 2000), and Peng and Heath (1996) argue that, in addition to cultural influences, institutional imperatives during the transition may further necessitate the extensive reliance on personalized exchange relationships. Such an institutional interpretation is borne out by similar findings from transition economies throughout Central and Eastern Europe (Grabher and Stark, 1997). These countries include Bulgaria (Davis, 1996), the Czech Republic (Soulsby and Clark, 1995), Hungary (Rona-Tas, 1994; Stark, 1996; Whitley et al., 1996), and Russia (Buck, Filatotchev, and Wright, 1998; Burawaoy and Krotov, 1992; Davis, Patterson, and Grazin, 1996; Peng, Buck, and Filatotchev, 1999; Puffer, 1994; Sedaitis, 1998). Note that in these countries there is little influence of the Chinese (or Asian) culture which puts a premium on interpersonal ties. Nevertheless, the emergence of a network-based strategy, which "blurs" existing organizational boundaries and creates "recombinant property" (Stark, 1996), has been widely reported. For example, managerial ties in post-1989 Hungary are found to be more "relational" and similar to "Asian" practices than arms' length, "Anglo-Saxon" practices (Whitley et al., 1996: 409). It is evident that despite the cultural differences, similar institutional imperatives during the transition must have played an important role in leading to similar growth strategies throughout transition economies (Peng, 2000).

While initial studies find that growth strategies in transition economies converge on a network- and alliance-based strategy, it is important to caution that this is a *dominant* strategy, which should not be confused as the *only* strategy (Peng and Heath, 1996: 517). A network-based strategy is not without its problems. The first is the lack of codification of information, routines, and capabilities. The second is the lack of a formal organizational basis; often, members "do not operate as unified groups" (Johnson, 1997: 341). Decision making in these networks tends to be case by case, with extensive negotiations and bargaining among members. These loosely structured, largely informal networks are based on trust, reputation, and mutual understanding, which, unfortunately, can be exploited if there are divergent economic interests and/or when the enforcement mechanism is weak (Peng, 2000: 64). As a result, there is a recent move throughout different transition economies to establish large, fully incorporated enterprises and business groups with a unified command structure and a number of subsidiaries, as opposed to loosely connected network members. Examples include the push for a "modern enterprise system" in China (Peng, 1997) and for "financial industrial groups" in Russia (Johnson, 1997). Some of these groups, such as the Chinese "red chips," have ventured abroad with some success (Au, Peng, and Wang, 2000).

Consequently, these activities increasingly call for a strategy of mergers and acquisitions to achieve growth (Peng, Luo, and Sun, 1999). Such a need, in turn, has fueled the urgency to strengthen the formal institutional constraints, namely, to establish an adequate legal framework to allow for such market-based transactions (Frye, 1997). In other words, the failure of *formal* institutional frameworks has led to the reliance on *informal* constraints, which results in a network-based strategy. Furthermore, the problems of such a strategy call for strengthening *formal* institutions, and therefore, the dynamic interaction between institutions and organizations comes full circle (figure 3.1). Specifically, it evolves precisely in a manner described by North (1990: 5) in that strategic choices made by organizations are influenced by the institutional framework, and "in turn, they influence how the institutional framework evolves."

CONTRIBUTIONS, CRITIQUES, AND EXTENSIONS

Contributions

While a short chapter is certainly unable to do justice to such a vast and expanding literature, it is evident that significant progress has been made since the 1990s. At least two major contributions emerge. First, international management research on non-Western economies has answered the very first fundamental question in strategy on "why firm strategies differ" identified by Rumelt and colleagues (1994), through developing and extending an institution-based view of business strategy. Note that this new perspective does not imply a rejection of existing work based on competition- and resource-based views (Barney, 1991; Porter, 1980). Instead, it supplements and enriches mainstream strategy research by drawing attention to the often overlooked importance of institutions, both formal and informal (North, 1990; Oliver, 1997), which are broader than the traditional notion of national cultural differences. Not only does existing strategy research focus largely on the West, so does most institutional work. As a result, the importance of institutions fades into the background, which is generally ignored by most strategy researchers. A focus on non-Western economies is therefore theoretically important because it allows us to highlight the importance of institutional forces (Scott, 1995: 146). In other words, non-Western economies have become "viable research laboratories" (Shenkar and von Glinow, 1994: 56). Such work, I believe, has provided the *strongest* support to the institution-based view, because research in developed economies, where the "rules of the game" are taken for granted, has had a difficult time partialing out the institutional effect on firm strategy and performance that is independent of economic and cultural effects (e.g., Palmer, Jennings, and Zhou, 1993). Research on non-Western economies, on the other hand, has not only clearly demonstrated that institutions matter, but has also made significant progress to take on the challenge suggested by Powell (1996: 297) to specify the *nature* of such a link in terms of "how they matter, under what circumstances, to what extent, and in what ways."

In addition to advancing strategy research, institution-based research on business strategies in non-Western economies also contributes to institutional theory by demonstrating the benefits of integrating with economics-oriented research. Some institutional theorists suggest that the "new institutionalism . . . comprises a *rejection* of rational-actor models" often found in economics-based research (DiMaggio and Powell, 1991: 8, added emphasis). While such a perspective may be insightful when studying educational institutions and public bureaucracies, where institutional research initially rose, recent work argues against pitting "strategic and institutional," "substantive and symbolic," and "economic and social" factors against each other (Powell, 1996: 295). When institutional theory moves away from schools and bureaucracies to assert its influence in the arena of efficiency-driven business organizations, a focus on efficiency outcomes, with some integration with economics-based research, becomes necessary (Dacin et al., 1999; Oliver, 1997; Scott, 1995). Otherwise, the usefulness of institutional theory, which may be still in its adolescence (Scott, 1987), in explaining performance-oriented organizational phenomena such as business strategy is limited. In the long run, efficiency outcomes may be the "*result* of the institutionalization of economic expectations of organizational actors" (Martinez and Dacin, 1999: 79, original emphasis). In other words, economic and institutional processes come hand-in-hand in driving strategic choices.

In our particular case, traditional institutional analyses would suggest that certain strategies (e.g., supplier relations in Japan, conglomerate diversification in emerging economies) persist simply because such a practice is widely adopted (or institutionalized), independent of evidence that it "works." Such a perspective, however, is difficult to accommodate in the emerging evidence suggesting the existence of concrete performance benefits associated with these strategies. At this conjuncture, an integrative approach incorporating both the institutional and economic perspectives would be sensible. The challenge for researchers is to uncover the underlying mechanisms that relate institutions to organizational strategies, and then to link them with firm performance, along the lines suggested by Khanna and Palepu (2000) and Peng and Luo (2000).

Critiques and extensions

Originating in the 1970s (Davis and North, 1971; Meyer and Rowan, 1977; Williamson, 1975), the new institutionalism in the social sciences was still in its adolescence by the 1980s (Scott, 1987), and its application to strategic management is a more recent development (Oliver, 1997) – note that virtually all key references reviewed in the four substantive sections are published in the 1990s (and beyond). As a result, there are a number of important problems that existing research has yet to address.

Perhaps foremost is the need for more theoretical development in order to answer the question first raised by Coase (1937): "What is the nature of the firm?" A lot of existing work on "firm" strategies does not agree on what exactly a firm is. A firm in the West has relatively clear boundaries characterized by authoritative control by top management (Williamson, 1975, 1985). A firm, especially the large conglomerate, in many non-Western economies tends to have "blurring" boundaries permeated by personal connections, partial ownerships, and board interlocks. Such a firm is often called a "business group" (Granovetter, 1994). Even though members of a group may remain autonomous (and some may be publicly traded as separate entities), the group is viewed as "a community" (Powell and Smith-Doerr, 1994: 388). However, the difficulty in defining firm (or group) boundaries has not only led to empirical problems when measuring their strategy, size, and performance, but also resulted in a conceptual debate on whether these organizations qualify as "firms."

Specifically, Hamilton and Feenstra (1995: 58) argue that the narrowly defined Coasian firm with clear boundaries "does not have the same empirical and conceptual significance throughout the world but, rather, is a prominent feature ... only in modern Western societies." While research on *keiretsu* conglomerates (or networks) from another developed economy, Japan, has forced strategy researchers to raise the validity of our conceptualization of the firm based on the Western model (Gerlach, 1992), more recent work on emerging economies finds that these conglomerates dominate the organizational landscape in many countries (Ghemawat and Khanna, 1998; Peng and Heath, 1996). A traditional answer is to suggest that these organizations are "outliers" operating under a different set of logic, and that the field can afford to ignore them and develop "grand" theories (mostly focusing on Western economies). However, in light of the growing importance of emerging economies (let alone the Japanese economy) and their increased integration with the global economy, such an answer becomes indefensible, if we as a field ever endeavor to approach a *global* science of organizations (Peng and Heath, 1996). While delineating the essence of this debate is beyond the scope of this chapter, future conceptual progress on what constitutes a "firm" is clearly needed when carrying out strategy research in both Western and non-Western economies.

Second, most existing research is of a static nature, that is, scholars propose and test *linear* directions, such as both close supplier relations and conglomerate diversification lead to better performance. The *dynamic* aspects of the complex relationships among institutions, organizations, and strategic choices have rarely been explored. For example, supplier relations that are too close may introduce rigidities in product designs, resulting in a loss of much-needed flexibility. It is not known, however, how close the relationship with suppliers is. In terms of conglomerates in emerging economies, after all, they confront the same problems that plague those in the West: The more activities a firm engages in, the harder it is for the head office to coordinate, control, and invest properly in different member units. Therefore, "how much scope is too much" remains to be explored, because it is evident that beyond a point of inflection, further diversification will only backfire (Peng and Lee, 2000). As a start, my colleague and I in a recent study document the diminishing (but still positive) benefits of organizational learning by foreign firms in a transition economy (Luo and Peng, 1999). In future research and practice, the need to identify such a point of inflection in highly dynamic and uncertain institutional environments remains a major challenge.

Third, how national cultures, interacting with institutional frameworks, affect strategic choices needs to be explored in more depth. Will strategies in non-Western economies converge on Western models? Given that individual managers making strategic decisions are influenced by their own national cultures (Hofstede, 1991), convergence is not likely to be the case, at least in the short term. On the other hand, work by Ralston and colleagues (1997) suggests that complete divergence is also not feasible in today's increasingly integrated global economy. By implication, what seems more likely is "crossvergence," in that strategies in non-Western economies will continue to be different from those observed in the West, while, beyond some point of inflection discussed above, gradually moving toward more "similar" strategies, as market-supporting institutions are developed. Currently, we know very little about how these cultural processes manifest themselves in strategic choices, and therefore, need to pay attention to these processes in future research.

Finally, given the dramatic boom–bust economic cycle throughout the global economy (e.g., the Japanese crisis since the early 1990s, the Asian crisis in 1997, the Russian crash and Latin American crisis in 1998), how strategies should be crafted and implemented during different phases of the economic cycle needs to be better understood. For example, despite the idea that conglomerates diversify in order to reduce their overall volatility over the entire economic cycle (Montgomery, 1994), empirical research in the West has actually documented that the performance of conglomerates is more volatile than that of non-conglomerate firms (Hill, 1983). Specifically, relative to their non-conglomerate counterparts, conglomerate performance improves more significantly during the upswing, but deteriorates more rapidly during the downswing. Whether similar dynamics are played out in non-Western economies is currently unknown and deserves serious attention from strategy researchers.

CONCLUSION

This chapter started with a seemingly simple question on why firm strategies differ. Moving from an intuitive answer based on national cultural differences, researchers' attention has increasingly focused on the underlying institutional frameworks that drive strategic choices. Since "frame-breaking experiences only come from examining and comprehending organizations operating in other places and other times" (Scott, 1995: 151), business strategies in non-Western economies have attracted significant attention. Drawing from recent international management research on business strategies in non-Western economies, this chapter has outlined the emergence of an institution-based view of business strategy, reviewed four streams of research in a broad range of countries, and critiqued and extended some of the current work. Overall, research in this area has increasingly appeared in leading journals, thus starting to disseminate this knowledge and assert its influence in the mainstream literature. To be sure, the studies reviewed in this chapter, mostly published in the 1990s, are just the entering wedges into the complex and dynamic relationships among institutions, organizations, and strategic choices, and certainly not the final words on them. Companies' strategic moves and our learning about them are not likely to stop soon. One thing for sure is that the importance of institutional influences on business strategies will be increasingly appreciated in the new millennium, thus necessitating more attention from researchers, practitioners, as well as policy makers around the world.

NOTES

1 Boddewyn (1999: 11) made a similar comment on the nature of international management research: "International management research is a 'total' project that cannot be limited to considering only traditional firm and industry variables loosely related to selected environmental factors."
2 The term "Chinese" is used here in a historical and global sense, when I refer to the far-flung international Chinese community. The term "mainland Chinese" will be used when discussing entrepreneurs and firms in the People's Republic of China.
3 Outside the United States, unrelated conglomerates have been found in certain developed economies, such as France (Encaoua and Jacquemin, 1982), Japan (Gerlach, 1992), and Sweden (Collin, 1998).

4

Knowledge Acquisition through Alliances: Opportunities and Challenges

PAUL ALMEIDA, ROBERT GRANT, AND ANUPAMA PHENE

INTRODUCTION

Knowledge has long played an important role in the theory of the firm. The emerging resource-based view of the firm focuses on knowledge as a key competitive asset and recognizes knowledge as the basis of firm growth (Grant and Baden Fuller, 1995). Kogut (1993) suggests that knowledge is not just a cornerstone of competitive advantage but the basis for sustainable advantage since it cannot be easily transferred or replicated. Firms that are adept at the development, transfer, and exploitation of knowledge are therefore most likely to succeed.

An organization cannot, however, develop within its boundaries all the critical knowledge needed to prosper and grow (Dussauge, Garrette, and Mitchell, 1998; Coase, 1937). Technological dynamism, reflected in an environment punctuated by competence-destroying technologies, has forced firms to maintain a wide range of technological knowledge and skills (Tushman and Anderson, 1986). Very few firms can develop this wide range of knowledge internally (Lane, Lyles, and Salk, 1998; D'Aveni, 1994). A major contribution to a firm's knowledge base must come from outside sources. In a classic study of 17 R&D laboratories, Allen and Cohen (1969) found that vendors, "unpaid outside consultants" and informal contacts with government bodies and universities are important sources of knowledge used in research. Research of major product and process innovations at Du Pont between 1920 and 1950 by Mueller (1966) showed that the original knowledge sources of the most critical inventions were outside the firm. In fact, suppliers, buyers, universities, consultants, government agencies, and competitors all serve as sources of vital knowledge and expertise (Jewkes, Sawyers, and Stillerman, 1958). Access to a broader knowledge base through external learning increases the flexibility of the firm, critical in a dynamic environment (Grant, 1996). The resource-based view of the firm, which originally focused on the role of internal capabilities, has now been extended to include resources that span firm boundaries – often embedded in interfirm relationships (Dyer and Singh, 1998).

In one of the seminal articles in strategic management, Hamel and Prahalad (1989) suggest an avenue for accessing external knowledge is through alliances. The article suggests that international collaborative agreements, in particular, present firms with the opportunity to develop complementary capabilities. Thus cross-national (and cross-cultural) alliances are important learning tools. The explosive growth of strategic alliances over the years, especially in high-technology industries such as semiconductors and commercial aircraft supports the view of the increasing importance of collaborative agreements in accessing external knowledge (Dyer and Singh, 1998; Mowery, Oxley, and Silverman, 1996; Contractor and Lorange, 1988). In a globalizing world, firms are increasingly faced with numerous pressures – higher costs of production of knowledge, increased risks associated with innovation and shorter product life cycles – alliances offer firms an incentive to share the risks and costs associated with knowledge creation. International strategic alliances in particular enable firms to source knowledge embedded in different national contexts. Cross-cultural learning permits firms to tap into foreign systems of innovation and gives firms access to a wider range of solutions to technological problems (Bartholomew, 1997).

Though alliances, knowledge transfer, and culture have independently attracted increasing attention, there is little research that examines the three concepts simultaneously and interactively. This chapter focuses on the influence of culture (and cultural differences) on the process of knowledge transfer through alliances.[1] We develop a model to show that culture is relevant to alliance formation and success at three levels of analysis – the country, the region, and the firm. We argue that the motivation and incentives to form alliances and the ability to learn from alliances are strongly influenced by cultural context. Though knowledge transfer through collaboration is influenced by national and regional culture, ultimately it is firm culture that most impacts the success of knowledge transfer.

CROSS-CULTURAL KNOWLEDGE TRANSFER

Alternative Institutional Mechanisms

The production and diffusion of knowledge is often spatially bounded. Research has shown that knowledge is sticky – it does not flow *easily or quickly* across plants within a firm (Szulanski, 1996), across locations (von Hippel, 1988), and across regions or countries (Almeida, 1996). Why does knowledge remain contained within firms, regions, and countries? Why is the transfer of knowledge across institutions and countries difficult? The answer to these questions lies both in the nature of knowledge and the nature of institutions. Knowledge is often tacit; as Polanyi (1966) put it, "we know more than we can tell." Tacit knowledge is, by nature, difficult to identify and transfer and requires "rich" mechanisms to facilitate its flow (Daft and Lengl, 1986). Firms, regions, and countries often embody within them communities, with common practices, norms, values, and codes. This common culture permits rich and frequent interaction between its members and the smooth flow of knowledge within its borders. While a common culture permits interaction and thus the flow of knowledge within a country (or firm), cultural differences across countries restrict the flow of knowledge across their borders.

We examine the relative merits of three institutional forms – the firm, the market and the alliance in facilitating cross-border (and cross-cultural) knowledge flows.

To exploit or access knowledge across country borders, a firm could choose between two alternative mechanisms – foreign direct investment (extending the firm's boundaries across borders) or the market (using arm's length transactions to buy or sell knowledge). The transactions costs approach suggests that markets for knowledge often fail due to asset specificity, opportunism, and the difficulty in determining the value of knowledge. Firms take the internalization route in international expansion as a result of this market failure. The knowledge-based view of the firm suggests that the critical advantage of the firm over the market is that the firm provides a rich social context and a set of higher-level organizing principles, for collaborative economic activity (Kogut and Zander, 1996). Thus firms are superior because they provide a common social context for the cross-cultural flow of knowledge.

Markets and firms are, however, not the only institutions for organizing cross-border economic activity. Collaborative interfirm relationships or alliances, whether viewed as market-hierarchy hybrids, or distinct organizational forms based upon relational contracts, are alternatives to markets and hierarchies. Alliances avoid many of the transactions costs associated with market contracts for knowledge. Alliances are likely to be superior to markets in terms of their ability to provide a framework for multi-period rather than single-period games, and their capacity to overcome problems of opportunism through investments in trust and mutual exchanges of hostages.

In addition, because alliances do not involve irreversible investments in routines, institutional structures, and other organization-specific competencies, they may also be able to achieve much greater flexibility than is available to the firm. However, it is this very absence of investment in common language, social norms, organizational routines, and institutionalized modes of decision making that limits a partner's ability to engage in inter-organizational knowledge transfer. In supporting higher organizing principles and the knowledge transfer they permit, alliances are inevitably inferior to firms. This is empirically supported in Almeida, Grant, and Song's (1998) study of cross-border transfer of knowledge, which found evidence of the multinational corporation's superior effectiveness in transferring knowledge than either alliances or pure market relationships. This does not imply that direct investment will always be preferred to international strategic alliances in transferring knowledge assets. Grant and Baden-Fuller (1995) show that, when excess capacity in knowledge resources arises because of a mis-match between a firm's knowledge domain and its product domain, when uncertainty exists as to the future input–output relationships between knowledge and products, and when early-mover advantages are present, then the advantages of alliances are likely to offset their disadvantages. Thus alliances will always remain an important institutional mechanism for the cross-border transfer of knowledge.

ALLIANCES AND KNOWLEDGE TRANSFER

The idea of acquiring knowledge through the formation of alliances has attracted the attention of both empiricists and theoreticians in strategic management. Much of the research relating alliances to knowledge transfer deals with: (1) the potential of firms to learn through alliances and (2) the capability of firms to accomplish successful knowledge transfer (whether for learning or exploitation). Studies dealing with these issues often look at the context in which successful knowledge transfer takes place.

Hamel (1991) classifies the determinants of the learning process in alliances as, motivation or desire to learn on the part of the allying partners, and the capacity of a partner to learn (presented by complementarity of capabilities and receptivity). The issue of opportunity or motivation to learn through alliances is a common one in the strategy literature. Teece (1992) suggests that strategic alliances are an important source of external knowledge especially in the international context. The global environment contains a diversity of knowledge, embedded in national systems of innovation. Since firms face disadvantages regarding the lack of local knowledge relating to social, political and economic conditions in foreign markets (Beamish, 1994), alliances can be a way of accessing diverse knowledge. Often, alliances are a necessity for cross-border knowledge transfer, since some kinds of firm specific and location specific knowledge, such as firm capabilities in negotiating with local government, labor force, competence with local market access, may be accessed only by partnering with local firms (Makino and Delios, 1996). Chang (1995) shows firms can gain this country-specific knowledge through experience in the host country or from other firms through the formation of alliances. Firms can source not just country specific expertise but firm specific technologies, and the associated skills and capabilities from alliance partners (Hamel et al., 1989; Powell and Brantley, 1992; Mody, 1993). In addition to the learning motive, alliances provide firms with the opportunity to transfer and exploit knowledge in new locations. International alliances offer firms an incentive to transfer technology and know-how across firm and country boundaries (Mjoen and Tallman, 1997).

The capability of a firm through an alliance has been variously defined in the literature as absorptive capacity (Levinthal, 1992),[2] learning effectiveness (Inkpen, 1998) and receptivity (Hamel, 1991). This capacity to learn has been indicated by a firm's investment in research and development; relatedness or overlap of knowledge bases of the partners; the diversity of the technological portfolio of the firm; and the stock of knowledge connections or interfirm routines available to the firm (Almeida and Rosenkopf, 2000). Few studies have actually measured the success of firms in learning through strategic alliances. An exception is the Mowery, Oxley, and Silverman (1996) study which showed through the examination of patent data, that after the formation of an alliance, partnering firms grew technologically closer, indicating knowledge transfer through collaboration. Gulati (1996) indicates that the capability of firms to learn from alliances is affected by cultural distance – US firms learnt less in alliances with non-US firms. The governance structure of the alliance is also a significant determinant of the ability to learn. Alliances, which more closely resemble a hierarchy (rather than a market), performed better at inter-organizational learning (Oxley, 1997), especially in the transfer of complex capabilities (Kogut, 1988).

The motivation and ability to learn from partners of course depends on the characteristics of the partnering firms. The incentive and ability to learn depend on the openness (Hamel, 1991) or protectiveness of partners to prevent leakage of core competencies (Inkpen, 1998). Given that firms differ in their openness and their knowledge sets, partner choice (Delios and Makino, 1996) and trust (Aulakh, Kotabe, and Sahay, 1996) are important dimensions that determine the incentive to gain knowledge through alliances. The characteristics of the knowledge being transferred also determine the incentive to learn. The tacitness and complexity of knowledge, as well as causal ambiguity make knowledge acquisition from a partner more difficult and reduce the incentives for learning (Simonin, 1999; Reed and DeFillipi, 1990). The intent of partners to learn is also country dependent. Typically Japanese firms show greater interest in learning from alliances and from external sources in general (Mansfield, 1988).

The above discussion highlights a number of factors that influence the knowledge transfer (whether related to learning or exploitation) process within alliances. Knowledge creation, transfer and exploitation occur in the context of a community and are embedded in social systems (Powell et al., 1996; Granovetter, 1985). This context in which knowledge transfer takes place is created by economic, social, political and cultural factors. We focus on the role played by culture and argue that the influence of culture on the transfer of knowledge within alliances is multi-dimensional and more complex than hitherto investigated. In the next section, we develop a model to capture the dimensions along which culture and cultural differences affect knowledge transfer in alliances.

ALLIANCES, KNOWLEDGE AND THE ROLE OF CULTURE

We consider the role culture plays in influencing knowledge transfer through alliances at three levels of analysis – the country level, the regional level and the firm level. Previous studies on the role of culture in alliances have largely focused on national cultural distance between the alliance partners and its consequences for the performance of the alliance.[3] Our model (figure 4.1) recognizes that the culture exists and impacts knowledge transfer at three different levels, and suggests that, though country and regional culture play direct and indirect roles, firm culture is the primary influence on interfirm knowledge transfer in alliances. The model indicates that culture, and the institutional context to which it is related, impacts knowledge transfer through alliances in two ways. First, culture effects the likelihood of alliance formation by providing firms with differential *motivations and incentives* to establish alliances. Second, culture and cross-cultural differences have an impact on the *ability* of firms to transfer knowledge through alliances. Thus the model implies that culture has a significant effect on interfirm knowledge transfer through alliances, driving partners' motivation, incentives, and ability to learn.

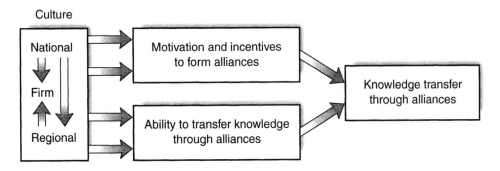

FIGURE 4.1 Alliance and knowledge transfer: the role of culture

We consider, below, three levels of culture that influence interorganizational learning – national, regional and organizational – and examine how each one shapes the knowledge transfer process in inter-firm collaborations.

NATIONAL CULTURE

National culture and institutions act independently and interactively to influence the way business is conducted in a country. Porter's (1990b) "diamond" illustrates how a combination of country specific factors act together to influence firm behavior and thus country competitiveness. The success of Japan in the fax industry serves as a good example of the influence of national culture and the institutional environment on firm behavior and success (Enright, 1993). The cultural propensity of Japanese individuals and businesses for written documentation, the complexity of the Japanese script, the need for small fax machines to accommodate limited office space, and the communication-intensive management style of Japanese firms combined to create a predictive and sophisticated demand for fax machines. Japanese firms responded to these local cultural and economic conditions, and developed the technology and capabilities to serve this unique domestic demand, and later exploited this country-based knowledge and expertise abroad. Thus national culture played an important role in influencing firm behavior and success.

The study of the Japanese fax industry illustrates how national culture influences the organizational culture, strategy, and capabilities of the nation's firms. Chandler (1990) and Kogut (1992) suggest that firms carry with them the influences of their home country. These influences include organization culture, practices, systems, and structure which are developed in the context of their home country environment and are "imprinted" on these firms, subsequently influencing their actions abroad. Tallman (1991) finds empirical support for this view in his study of the foreign automobile firms in the US. He finds distinct differences between Japanese and European firms and concludes that international firms and their strategies are shaped by country of origin. Thus organizational culture of a firm is heavily influenced by the national culture of the country of origin (see figure 4.1).

National culture can act both as an obstacle to cross-country learning and as an incentive for the same. First, national culture plays a role in influencing the *incentives* or motivation to learn from other countries. Hamel, Doz, and Prahalad (1989), in their seminal article on alliances and learning, suggested that while Japanese firms were motivated to form alliances in order to learn from their partners, American firms were usually motivated by other goals such as market access.[4] The intent to learn from alliance partners on the part of Japanese firms was a shared country-based norm and was an important part of their international strategy. Hence the degree to which alliances are viewed as learning tools will vary across firms and is dependent on the firm's country of origin.

The differences in culture between countries can increase the *incentives* or the motivation to learn, especially through cross-border alliances. Studies have shown that knowledge is localized and countries develop expertise in unique fields (Almeida, 1996; Cantwell and Immarino, 1998). If knowledge is inextricably bound to a local context, it may be best accessed through a partner embedded in this context.[5] Further cultural differences between countries may inhibit a firm from successfully learning through the establishment of wholly owned subsidiaries making alliances an important mechanism of learning. Fladmoe-Lindquist and Jacque (1995) suggest that firms use low-cost governance structures to overcome the disadvantage of cultural distance. Empirical studies provide some support for this view. The greater the cultural distance between the home and host country, the greater is the likelihood that a firm will choose a cooperative mode of entry (such as an alliance) rather than equity ownership (Kogut and Singh, 1988; Gatignon and Anderson, 1986). Thus greater cultural distance appears to increase the propensity for alliance formation.

Cultural distance may advance a firm's motivation to learn, but it also limits the ability of alliance partners to learn from each other. Countries have specific institutional environments that vary in the extent to which they foster goodwill, trust and cooperation between economic entities (Hill, 1995). Dyer (1996) supports this view, showing that the Japanese cultural and industrial environment enables its firms to generate relational rents through cooperative alliances. Conditions for alliance formation and learning may be less conducive in other countries.

Numerous studies have suggested cultural conflicts limit sharing of information and learning across countries and firms (Fiol and Lyles, 1985; Parkhe, 1993; Salk, 1992). Madhok (1997) theorizes that when allied firms have significantly different cultures, the partners possess routines and procedures which are incompatible, and these result in an inability to absorb and exploit know-how efficiently. These differences in modes of learning arising from cultural differences are evidenced in Appleyard's (1996) survey of employees of semiconductor companies. The study indicated differences in patterns of learning across nationalities – Japanese employees rely on public channels of learning while US employees depended on private channels. The obstacles presented by national cultural distance to interfirm learning through alliances are especially significant when the transfer of tacit knowledge is necessary. Hedlund and Nonaka (1993) point out that the processes of knowledge creation in firms are culturally embedded. For instance, Western firms place their primary emphasis on knowledge creation at the individual level and upon the management of explicit knowledge at the group and organizational levels. Japanese firms, by contrast, are far more committed to the movement of knowledge within and between several levels – the individual, group, organizational, and inter-organizational level. National patterns of knowledge management evidenced by firms, can lead to differences in the learning abilities of each partner, limiting knowledge acquisition across cultures. Thus our model suggests that though cultural distance increases the incentive to learn from a partner, it simultaneously decreases the ability of the partners to learn.

REGIONAL CULTURE

Though countries have been the traditional focus of studies on culture and technology development, increasingly industrial regions are looked upon as the crucibles of knowledge and economic development. The existence of geographically clustered firms is hardly new and the phenomenon of localized informational flows through social networking within geographic areas has been observed historically as well as internationally

(Almeida and Kogut, 1999). Localized knowledge sharing was as common between firms in the steel industry in nineteenth-century England (Allen, 1983) as in today's regional clusters in Italy (Piore and Sabel, 1984; Pyke, Becattini, and Sengenberger, 1990) and Baden-Württemberg in Germany (Herrigel, 1993).

Most successful regional networks share common characteristics as regards informal relationships between firms and knowledge transfer across member organizations. Regions also reflect national ways of organizing as well as country-based values and beliefs. However, most regions possess a unique cultural environment for firms conducting business within them. Saxenian's (1994) description of two prominent high-technology regions in the US – Boston 128 and Silicon Valley – provides an excellent insight into the widely differing regional cultures. While Silicon Valley is characterized by entrepreneurship and both formal and informal knowledge sharing between firms, the Boston 128 region has few informal or formal relationships between firms and is dominated primarily by large firms. While the Silicon Valley culture accepted the reality of knowledge transfer across firms through human mobility, the Boston 128 culture dictated firms relied on secrecy – there was little localized knowledge sharing between firms. Finally, the culture and history of Silicon Valley facilitated the formation of numerous alliances among firms located in the region; collaborations were infrequent among firms in the Boston 128 corridor.

The contrast between Boston 128 and Silicon Valley illustrates that regional culture can differentially influence both the tendency of alliance formation among firms and also the likelihood that these alliances will result in knowledge transfer. Regions, like countries, imprint on "member" organizations certain norms and unique ways of doing business. Regional culture thus influences firm behavior and culture and therefore the extent of knowledge transfer through alliances.

ORGANIZATIONAL CULTURE

Organizational culture plays an important role in facilitating the flow of knowledge within organizations but it can often serve as an impediment for knowledge transfer across alliance partners. Though organizations are influenced by national and regional culture, they develop varied cultures through their unique histories and strategies. These cultural differences may often retard the ability of alliance partners to facilitate knowledge transfer across their boundaries.

The interplay between organizational culture and national culture and their effect on learning is well illustrated by the NUMMI[6] alliance between General Motors and Nissan. Both firms hoped to learn from their alliance partners. As is typical in Japanese organizations, Toyota's valuable knowledge involved their systems and practices – these were deeply embedded in their organization context and therefore were difficult to observe and duplicate. General Motors' ability to access knowledge from Toyota was slow and limited. The knowledge that Toyota sought from General Motors was more codified and transparent (again reflecting the national context). This allowed Toyota to more easily access their American partner's knowledge (Inkpen, 1998).

The incompatibility of corporate cultures is one of the most important reasons why alliances fail. Cyert and Goodman (1997), analyzed differences in motivation, process, and research objectives between universities and firms to explain why alliances between them failed. These differences, which hindered alliance success, manifest themselves in divergent goals, time orientations, languages, and assumptions, creating a very different cultural context for each partner. This divergence in culture and motivations hindered the ease of communication and knowledge transfer for the alliance partners. It is not surprising that Simonin (1999) finds that organizational culture is a bigger and more enduring obstacle to alliance success compared to national culture.

However, cultural differences between firms need not provide an enduring obstacle to knowledge transfer. Meschi's (1997) findings indicated all cultural differences between partners recede over time. One device to overcome incompatibility of interfirm culture is to build on alliances with existing partners. Gulati (1995) demonstrated that the social context (and shared understanding) resulting from prior alliances between two partners, leads to increased alliance formation in the future. This result suggests that as alliance partners work together, they establish inter-organizational routines and greater cultural alignment, and this results in a greater ability to learn from each other. Thus firms can overcome cross-cultural challenges and improve their ability to learn from alliances, through experience.

CONCLUSION

The model, discussed above, regarding the role of culture and its impact on knowledge transfer through alliances, highlights some issues of relevance to practitioners and researchers.

Country and regional cultures (and their differences) impact the *motivation* and *incentives* to form alliances and benefit from knowledge transfer through alliances. First, the motivation to form alliances (that facilitate learning) is influenced by country (and region) specific cultural and industrial norms and expectations regarding interfirm collaborations. Second, country differences also impact the perceived incentives of learning from alliances. Differences in institutions and culture across countries also lead to variations in the resources and capabilities of firms located in these countries. Inter-country variations in expertise suggest incentives to potentially benefit from the transfer of knowledge – by using alliances to simultaneously exploit complementary capabilities (arising from country differences) and by using alliances to learn. Thus country and regional differences increase the incentive and motivation to form alliances and benefit from knowledge transfer through them.

In contrast to the *motivation* and *incentive* to benefit from cultural differences through alliances, the *ability* to gain knowledge from alliances is not enhanced but rather impeded by country, regional, and firm cultural differences. Cultural differences hinder the development of trust and increase the costs of communication essential for the transfer of the more tacit forms of knowledge. Cultural differences between collaborating organizations may not only inhibit the efficacy of more formal modes of knowledge transfer (e.g. e-mail, shared databases etc.) but more critically, may limit the use of informal mechanisms of knowledge transfer (e.g. face-to-face conversations, impromptu conversations). Thus while cultural differences across regions and countries can be expected to increase the number of learning-oriented alliances, they may decrease the utility of these alliances by restricting the actual learning taking place.

Though *country-level* cultural differences have often been the main focus of studies dealing with culture and economic action, we suggest that ultimately *interfirm* cultural differences are the primary influence on the ability of firms to use alliances as mechanisms of knowledge transfer. Alliances, after all, are planned, developed and implemented by individuals and groups acting within firm specific constraints and contexts. A firm's culture is, of course, influenced by its history and its experiences in the country and region in which it is embedded. However, an organization's leadership, strategy and structure strongly impact the cultural norms and beliefs within the organization. Thus for collaborating organizations the challenge of dealing with cultural differences should be focused primarily upon differences in the organizational culture of partnering firms. Thus regardless of national cultural differences or similarities of their countries of origin, firms with similar organizational cultures are likely to more successfully learn through an alliance than firms with more dissimilar organizational cultures.

The above observations suggest a point of caution to managers involved in the formation and implementation of alliances. National differences in culture are more observable and analyzable than firm specific cultural differences. To the extent that firm culture reflects the national cultural context, decisions on alliance attractiveness and effectiveness based on broad national cultural pictures may be sufficient. But in an increasingly global world, multinational firms develop their own cultural identity that reflects their experiences in multiple locations and their strategy over time. The "new" multinational corporation may possess a culture which may not reflect any one given country or region. The challenge in assessing a firm's culture and its impact on alliance formation and learning is more challenging in this case.

A common theme in both scholarly research and the popular press is the low rate of success for most alliances. The above analysis offers a possible reason for these findings. Country and regional cultural differences, which suggest a positive incentive and motivation for learning through alliances, are easily identifiable and observable up front. However, firm-level cultural differences which impede the success of an alliance are not as easily identifiable and often reveal themselves only after the implementation of an alliance. This imbalance in observability and timing of the culture-related pros and cons of alliance formation, may lead to an inaccurate assessment of the costs and benefits of alliance formation, leading to the formation of alliances that may be difficult to effectively implement.

Finally, this analysis suggests that since alliances are by definition between two firms, and since the critical cultural differences are at the firm level, every alliance is essentially cross-cultural in nature. By realistically approaching the challenges of knowledge transfer across cultures, whether in domestic or international alliances, managers can increase the probabilities of alliance success.

NOTES

1 This chapter interprets culture as commonly held values, beliefs and practices within a unit of analysis, which impact economic action.

2 Cohen and Levinthal's concept of absorptive capacity of course refers to the capacity to recognize and incorporate useful external knowledge through any mechanism

3 One exception is the Levinson & Asahi (1995) study which considers four levels of culture that affect inter-organizational learning, national, organizational, occupational, and small group.

4 It is interesting to note that the authors pointed to these country-based differences in motivation, even though most of the US and Japanese firms discussed in the article were international firms with a presence in many countries.

5 The embeddedness of information in cultures varies, information in "Oriental" cultures is more context bound than information in "Occidental" cultures (Benedict, 1946).

6 The New United Motor Manufacturing Inc. (NUMMI) joint venture was formed in 1984, between General Motors and Toyota.

5

Cooperative Strategies between Firms: International Joint Ventures

LOUIS HÉBERT AND PAUL BEAMISH

The objective of this chapter is to cast some light on the relationship linking the control structures used in joint ventures (JVs) to the performance of the organizations involved. Using elements of social exchange theory (SET) and transaction cost analysis (TCA), it compares the direction and strength of this relationship in international and domestic JVs, and thereby examines the moderating effect of the international nature of JVs. Using a sample of Canadian-based JVs, hypotheses are discussed and tested. Results suggest the impact of control structures on JV performance is contingent on the dimensions of control and autonomy, and on the international versus domestic nature of JVs.

With the increasing strategic importance and frequency of joint ventures (JVs), the effective management of these shared equity and decision-making arrangements involving two or more firms (the parents) has achieved significant importance. Despite their competitive and strategic benefits, JVs often encounter performance problems (Anderson, 1990). By their inherent nature, the presence of two or more parents represents a potentially significant source of complexity, often making these ventures difficult and laborious to manage (Killing, 1983). In coping with this complexity, the control structure in place in a JV has been considered to be a critical determinant of these ventures' performance (Killing, 1983; Schaan, 1983; Beamish, 1988). Control structures refer to the pattern according to which management responsibilities are distributed first between partner firms, and second, between the JV and the parent firms. The first dimension can be defined as the division of control, or as the extent of control sharing between parent firms; the second as the autonomy of a JV.

With limited empirical evidence and conflicting results, prior research provides little understanding of the relationship between control structures and the performance of JVs. In this context, this paper attempts to answer three main questions: (1) What are the control structures, in terms of control sharing and autonomy, used in JVs?; (2) How do these control structures affect the performance of JVs?; and (3) Do these structures affect international and domestic JVs differently? In this study, a JV is considered to be international (IJV), where at least one of the parent firms is headquartered outside the venture's country of operation. A JV is considered domestic (DJV) when the parents and the JV are headquartered in the same country.

JV Control and Performance: A Review of Prior Research

First raised by West (1959), the issue of the control of JVs has been receiving greater attention in recent years. Control is a critical element because it represents a firm's ability to coordinate its activities, to implement its strategy and to ensure that its JV is managed in ways consistent with its interests and objectives. In JVs, the exercise of effective control may prove to be a difficult task since firms cannot solely rely on their ownership position. By definition, they also agree to relinquish some control. For these reasons, several researchers have examined both the exercise of control and how this control affected the performance of JVs.

In their review of the literature, Geringer and Hébert (1989) suggested that research efforts have largely examined different dimensions of JV control, a situation reflecting the complex nature of this concept. They distinguished three dimensions of control: the *mechanisms* used to exercise control; the *extent* of control exercised – measured either by a parent's managerial control over decision making of the JV or its equity share; and the *focus* of control, i.e., the specific activities over which control is exercised. This framework revealed a clear bias toward the *extent* of control being the most commonly used and studied dimension of control (see table 5.1). Other dimensions have received irregular and unsystematic attention. Very few studies adopted a perspective of control that integrated different dimensions.

Research on the extent of control can be separated according to the construct of control. In the first stream, control is defined in terms of a parent firm's influence over the JV decision making. For instance, in exploring how decision making responsibilities were divided among parent firms and IJV managers, Killing (1982) identified different types of control structures used by parent firms. Specifically, he distinguished dominant partner JVs (where only one parent plays an active role in JV decisions) from shared management JVs (where both parents play an active role) and independent ventures (where JV management enjoys significant autonomy). The second stream defined control in terms of equity. This perspective acknowledged the importance firms attribute to their ownership stake to achieve effective control over a JV. Besides ownership, as shown by Schaan (1983) and Kumar and Seth (1998), a variety of control mechanisms are available to firms. Yet, their use is often perceived to be dependent on or complementary to a parent firm's equity share. A partner's equity has also been found to be correlated, although not always perfectly, with its effective managerial control (Lecraw, 1984; Hébert, 1994).

Despite this difference in the construct of control, these streams share some commonalities. In particular, they both perceived a parent's control position as a reflection of its parent firms' bargaining power and resource contribution (Blodgett, 1991; Yan and Gray, 1994). Control is exercised in different degrees over these resources and assets against undesired dissemination and exposure. Both streams also assumed that firms inevitably sought to achieve an overall control over their JVs, rather than targeting

TABLE 5.1 Selected studies on JV control: dimensions of control

Authors	Mechanisms of control	Focus of control	Extent of control	
			Managerial control	Equity control
Behrman 1970	x			
Tomlinson (1970)	x			
Franko (1971)	x			
Friedmann and Beguin (1971)	x			
Stopford and Wells (1972)	x			
Gullander (1976)	x			
Dang (1977)			x	
Rafii (1978)	x			
Janger (1980)			x	
Fagre and Wells (1982)				x
Killing (1982, 1983)			x	
Schaan (1983)	x	x		
Beamish (1984)			x	
Lecraw (1984)		x		x
Geringer (1986)		x	x	
Awadzi (1987)		x		
Blodgett (1987, 1991, 1992)				x
Blumenthal (1988)			x	
Hill (1988)		x	x	
Kogut (1988a)				x
Tillman (1990)			x	
Woodcock and Geringer (1990)				x
Yan and Gray (1994)			x	
Hébert (1994, 1997)		x	x	
Sohn (1994)			x	x
Lee and Beamish (1997)			x	x
Park and Russo (1996)				x
Child, Yan, and Lu (1997)			x	x
Lin, Yu, and Seeto (1997)		x	x	
Ding (1997)			x	
Kumar and Seth (1998)	x			
Makino and Beamish (1998)				x
Bouquet and Hébert (1999)	x			x
Delios and Beamish (1999)				x
Lü and Hébert (1999)				x

specific activities and decisions. Yet, in recognizing the limitations of this perspective, some scholars suggested the existence of a fourth category of control structure, a split control JV, where each parent's control is selective and exercised over distinct dimensions of the venture (Beamish, 1988; Killing, 1988).

Recent efforts reminded us of the shortcoming associated with neglecting the focus and mechanism dimensions of control. For instance, Mjoen and Tallman (1997) showed that firms tended to exercise control over JV activities involving strategically important resources. This specialized control was itself a key determinant of a parent firm's overall control. The presence of split control structures was also supported in JVs where parent firms contribute complementary resources (Lin, Yu, and Setoo, 1997). In turn, Kumar and Seth (1998) investigated factors explaining the use of a variety of control mechanisms besides ownership. They examined mechanisms such as the frequency of contact between parent firm and JV manager, the role and structure of the JV board of directors, the staffing of JV management positions, the design of incentive plans, and the presence of socialization activities for JV managers. Their analyses showed that the number of these mechanisms increased with the strategic interdependence between the JV and its parent. Essentially, their research suggested that in addition to the extent of control exercised by parent firms, the range of mechanisms used reflected their attempt to effectively protect firm-specific assets against undesired dissemination and contracting hazards.

Beyond the exercise of control, scholars have tried to enhance understanding of the relationship between the control and the performance of JVs. In this regard, Beamish (1984) suggested that the control of JVs was "the most common variable discussed in conjunction with performance in the JV literature" (p. 45). This growing body of research can be organized in four groups mostly related to the dimensions of control identified earlier (see table 5.2).

The first group includes studies of JVs that examined different aspects of the formation and management of the ventures, without focusing primarily on the exercise of control. For instance, Tomlinson (1970) is considered to be the first to study the control–performance relationship although he examined the "attitude of parents toward control" rather than control per se. While they do not permit drawing any conclusion on the relationship between JV control and performance, both Tomlinson (1970) and Franko (1971) contributed to the establishment of this relationship as a relevant and valid field of research.

Killing's (1982) pioneering research provides the conceptual and empirical foundations for most of the research that constitutes the "mainstream" of research on JV control and performance. He argued that since the presence of more than one parent constitutes the major source of complexity in a JV, dominant parent JVs will be easier to manage and more successful. Using a convenience sample of 37 IJVs, Killing concluded that dominant partner JVs were preferable to shared management JVs. However, the relationship between dominant control and IJV performance was not statistically significant, while superior levels of performance were observed in independent JVs. In this case, he suggested that the JVs' autonomy was more a result than the cause of their performance.

Despite its commonsensical and conceptual appeal, subsequent studies provided little clear and systematic evidence either supporting or challenging Killing's hypothesis. For instance, Beamish (1984) found that unsatisfactory performance was correlated with the

TABLE 5.2 Selected studies on the control structure–JV performance relationship

	Authors	Type of JVs[a]	Measure of performance	Control–performance relationship
Early studies	Tomlinson (1970)	LDC IJVs	Profitability	Negative correlation
Overall division of control	Franko (1971)	LDC and DC IJVs	Instability	Contingent on MNC parent's strategy
	Janger (1980)	LDC and DC IJVs	Not provided	No relationship, yet supposed as contingent
	Killing (1982)	DC IJVs	Survival and perceptual measure	Dominant control related to performance
	Hill (1988)	DC DJVs and IJVs	Multidimensional scale	No relationhip
	Blumenthal (1988)	DC DJVs and IJVs	Multidimensional scale	No relationship
	Tillman (1990)	LDC IJVs	Multidimensional scale	Foreign control related to conflict and to low performance
				Shared control related to performance
	Yan and Gray (1994)	LDC IJVs	Perceptual measures	Dominant foreign control related to both measures of performance
	Ding (1997)	LDC IJVs	Multidimensional measures of financial and non-financial performance	
Division of equity	Lecraw (1984)	LDC IJVs	Corrected success	Equal division related to low success
	Blodgett (1987, 1992)	DC IJVs	Duration, survival and re-negotiation of JV contract	Equal division related to duration and survival
	Kogut (1988a)	DC DJVs and IJVs	Duration	No relationship
	Woodcock and Geringer (1990)	DC DJVs and IJVs	Survival	Equal division related to survival
	Park and Russo (1996)	DC DJVs and IJVs	Survival as JV	Uneven division related to acquisition by majority parent
	Park and Ungson (1997)	DC DJVs and IJVs	Survival	Equal division marginally related to termination
	Makino and Beamish (1998)	LDC IJVs	Survival and single-item performance measure	Majority ownership related to survival but not to performance
	Lü and Hébert (1999)	LDC IJVs	Survival	Foreign ownership related to survival
Control over specific activities	Schaan (1983)	LDC IJVs	Perceptual measure of satisfaction	Contingent on fit among criteria of success, activities controlled and mechanisms
	Lecraw (1984)	LDC IJVs	See above	Control over critical activities related to performance
	Awadzi (1987)	DC DJVs and IJVs	Composite measure	Dominant control over specific activities related to performance
	Hill (1988)	DC DJVs and IJVs	Multidimensional scale	No relationship
	Hébert (1994, 1997)	DC DJVs and IJVs	Objective and multidimensional scale of performance and satisfaction	Shared operational control related to performance and satisfaction in IJVs

[a] LDC = Less developed country; DC = Developed country; DJV = Domestic joint venture; IJV = International joint venture.

Source: Adapted from Hébert (1994)

foreign parent's dominant control. These results were echoed by Tillman's (1990) study of Japanese–Thai JVs. Extensive control by the Japanese parent resulted in high levels of conflict which in turn had a negative impact on performance. Blumenthal (1988) noted that a parent firm's satisfaction was negatively correlated with high levels of influence by its partner. In a more explicit attempt to test Killing's hypothesis in US–China JVs, Yan and Gray (1994) indicated that shared control was associated with superior performance although the negative impact of dominant foreign control was not detected. In contrast, also in US–China JVs, Ding (1997) observed that foreign dominant control was positively related to both financial and non-financial performance. Lastly, Hill (1988) and Janger (1980) did not find one structure to be more successful than another.

Similar divergences are observed in the large body of research that relied on the equity share of the parents to measure control. In a first group of studies, foreign equity and majority control generally increased JV duration and the chances of survival. Among others, recent efforts showed that foreign control reduced the risk of termination in situations involving technology-intensive assets and when the foreign partner had limited experience in the JV industry (Lü and Hébert, 1999). The opposite view was proposed for developed country JVs. Blodgett (1987, 1992) argued that equal bargaining power between partner firms of a JV would put pressure on both of them to make accommodations to the partnership. Equal bargaining power, reflected in the parent firms' respective equity holdings, would stabilize the venture and ensure its survival. Consistent with this view, Blodgett found that JVs with a relatively equal division of ownership had a significantly higher likelihood of achieving long life than JVs with an unequal division of equity between the parent firms. Blodgett's empirical results also showed that majority/minority JV contracts had a tendency to be renegotiated often. Woodcock and Geringer (1990) also found that JVs with equally divided ownership had higher survival rates than JVs with unequally divided ownership.

The fourth and last group of studies investigated the control exercised over specific activities and decisions of JVs, rather than the overall division of control. Early studies (Schaan, 1983; Lecraw, 1984; Awadzi, 1987) suggested that a parent firm's ability to achieve effective control over some key activities or strategic resources led to higher JV performance. Hébert (1997) confirmed this contention and observed that shared control over operational decisions was a significant factor of performance compared to the control over technological or strategic decisions. In turn, Mjoen and Tallman (1997) also found that a parent's control over strategic resources had a positive effect on its performance assessment. Although the studies did not explicitly examine split control structures, their results provided some evidence supporting the effectiveness of these structures.

The preceding review essentially demonstrated that our understanding of the control–performance relationship in JVs is still limited. With scant evidence and conflicting results and despite considerable research efforts, this relationship remains, at best, inconclusive (Beamish, 1993). This situation could be interpreted as the result of two main factors, the fragmentation and the theoretical foundations of prior research.

First, prior research appears highly fragmented on the basis of the object of study, as well as on the basis of the conceptualization of control and performance outcomes. Specifically, scholars have focused either on a mix of domestic JVs and IJVs, on DC IJVs, on LDC IJVs, or on both DC and LDC IJVs. As demonstrated by Beamish (1985),

LDC IJVs typically have purposes and dynamics quite different from those of DC IJVs. The fragmentation of prior research is also evident in the conceptualization and operationalization of the division of control and performance constructs. Indeed, prior research used two different constructs of control: division of decision making responsibilities and division of equity. The situation is similar for the construct of performance, for which a variety of objective and perceptual measures have been used. Studies focusing on division of equity also tended to rely on objective measures of performance. This fragmentation may explain the limited support for Killing's hypothesis. It also limits the comparability of many studies and the generalizability of their results. Subsequent attempts to study the impact of control on performance require more integrated and comparable approaches. They should also not be limited to the overall division of control but give more explicit attention to the control exercised over specific activities and decisions.

Second, prior research on JV control has been influenced primarily by transaction costs analysis. Consistent with this framework, it focused on the role of control in protecting firm-specific assets against undesired dissemination, contracting hazards, and opportunism. JV control has been presented as an effective response to these concerns and risks. This perspective is observable not only in JV research but also in the entire strategic alliance literature (Gulati, 1998). Nevertheless, this perspective provides an incomplete assessment of control. It does not account for the resource commitments and governance costs associated with the exercise of control. As discussed later, it also overlooks the social embeddedness of JVs as well as the influence of control on the relationship between parent firms, and particularly on the development of trust and mutual forbearance.

Therefore, this chapter presents a model of the control–performance relationship in JVs in order to address the shortcomings of prior research. Focusing on developed country JVs, our framework integrates elements of both transaction cost analysis (TCA) and social exchange theory (SET) in order to provide a more integrative perspective of the efficiency of the exercise of control. It distinguishes domestic and international JVs in order to assess the moderating effect of the type of JV on this relationship.

THEORETICAL FRAMEWORK AND HYPOTHESES

This study's conceptual framework draws both from TCA and SET. TCA has been extensively used to examine the dynamics of JVs (Beamish and Banks, 1987; Hennart, 1988; Kogut, 1988a). This framework helps to identify the source of transaction costs and to specify the governance structure that most efficiently mediates transactions, in order to minimize these costs. In turn, SET has its origins in the works of Thibaut and Kelley (1959) and Blau (1964), mostly on interpersonal relationships. These authors suggested that exchange relationships would emerge and persist if the participants perceive mutual benefits from their interactions. It is also one of the central tenets of SET that greater interdependence and cooperation will result in greater mutual rewards for the partners (Gabarro, 1987). SET has been used extensively in recent years for the study of inter-organizational relationships (e.g., Levinthal and Fichman, 1988), particularly of vertical relationships (e.g., Anderson and Narus, 1984, 1990; Dwyer, Schurr, and Oh, 1987).

SET also constitutes an appropriate framework for the study of JVs since it is consistent with Toyne (1989), who noted that exchange was a valid concept for international business research.

These two theoretical approaches were thought to be complementary with regard to the scope and purpose of the study. Specifically, SET appeared to compensate for conceptual limitations of TCA regarding the concept of transaction and behavioral assumptions. In the context of JVs defined as inter-organizational relationships (IORs), TCA embodies some limitations, as we argued above. Some authors have criticized TCA for its strict economic rationale and its assumptions, which often approximate those of neoclassical economics (Zucker, 1986; Johanson and Mattsson, 1987). For instance, in viewing IORs as discrete, static, and technologically separable exchange transactions, TCA tends to neglect the social context surrounding transactions (Granovetter, 1985; Hill, 1990). Thus, TCA appears in some instances to be inadequate for examining IORs, such as JVs, where firms are involved in repetitive exchange.

In contrast to TCA, SET includes both economic and social aspects in the analysis of relationships (Dwyer, Schurr and Oh, 1987; Johanson and Mattsson, 1987). It views IORs as dynamic and iterative processes shaped by the actions of the partners (Cook, 1977; Van de Ven and Walker, 1984). Furthermore, TCA assumes that economic actors are basically opportunistic (Granovetter, 1985) and that they exhibit "self-interest-seeking with guile" behavior (Williamson, 1975: 26). In this context, only hierarchies can reduce risks of opportunistic behaviors, and thus minimize related transactions costs. Transaction participants are protected from opportunism not by trust or commitment but by a substitute – the institutional arrangement mediating their exchange (Maitland, Bryson, and Van de Ven, 1985). While TCA acknowledges the possibility of trust or commitment in market transactions, these transactions are considered exceptions, and not the usual state of affairs (Williamson and Ouchi, 1981; Williamson, 1985). This behavioral assumption also implies that frequency of transaction is a factor of transaction costs. In contrast, SET will suggest that frequent interactions offer the opportunity to develop cooperation and exchange (Perrow, 1986; Johanson and Mattsson, 1987).

With economists minimizing the role of trust and commitment in IORs (Hirschman, 1982; Lorenz, 1988), TCA may not be adequate to study factors supporting the emergence of trust and commitment. In turn, SET views trust, commitment and conflict as critical components of social exchange processes (e.g., Blau, 1964; Cook, 1977). Moreover, social exchange theorists have given considerable attention to the impact of power on the dynamics of relationships (Blau, 1964; Hallén, Johanson, and Seyed-Mohamed, 1991). As a result, social exchange theory provides an appropriate theoretical base for the analysis of the impact of control on the quality of relationships in JVs, including the development of trust, commitment, and conflicts. In fact, power and control are closely related concepts. Power can be defined as the ability to influence the behavior and output of an entity (Rubin and Brown, 1975). In turn, control can be seen as the actualization of that ability (Provan and Skinner, 1989), or the reflection of a firm's power position (Blodgett, 1991). Many researchers have used these two terms interchangeably (Kelley and Thibaut, 1978; Wilkinson, 1979; Anderson and Narus, 1984). In conclusion, the combination of TCA's focus on efficiency and SET's focus on relationships is expected to provide a more integrative view of the dynamics of JVs.

RESEARCH HYPOTHESES

Control sharing and performance

The conventional perspective of control suggests that the exercise of control is a mechanism to reduce the transaction costs typically associated with JVs. Specifically, goal incongruence as well as coordination between parents can generate substantial transaction costs, associated primarily with opportunistic behavior and asset-specificity (Williamson, 1975, 1985; Ouchi, 1977, 1980). The dissemination of a firm's specific advantage or proprietary technology may also result in transaction costs and reduce the stream of rent associated with the exploitation of its specific advantage. These different transaction costs can limit the potential gains from cooperation and pose serious threats to the venture's performance. Therefore, control is exercised in order to reduce the risks of opportunism and dissemination. It is supposed to enable a firm to minimize the transaction costs that could possibly limit its strategic benefits and destabilize a JV. Killing's (1982) dominant control hypothesis is consistent with this perspective of control. The use of dominant control is expected to reduce the risks of opportunism and dissemination to which a firm is exposed in a JV.

Unfortunately, this perspective does not account for the resource commitment and costs associated with control. Extensive control can generate significant governance and bureaucratic costs that may harm the efficiency of a JV and offset its competitive benefits (Geringer and Hébert, 1989; Ohmae, 1989). It also overlooks the social embeddedness of JVs (Granovetter, 1985). It treats them as discrete independent events and thus neglects the presence of prior relationships and interactions, which can alleviate the risks of opportunism (Gulati, 1995). Specifically, it disregards the possibility of trust between parent firms. Beamish and Banks (1987) suggested that a foundation of mutual trust between JV partners is likely to reduce the risks and costs of opportunism that may decrease the mutual benefits of JVs. In such an organizational context, parent firms are likely to take a longer-term perspective regarding their involvement in a JV and the continuation of the cooperative relationship, rather than merely focusing on obtaining short-term advantages at the expense of their partner and the JV. Similarly, Buckley and Casson (1988) argued that the presence of mutual trust reduced the transaction costs of cooperative ventures.

Within a SET framework, the impact of control structures on the performance of JVs is possible if attention is given to the concept of power and especially to the balance of power in relationships. In a relationship, power results from the possession of resources that the other party needs and from the control over the sources of these resources (Rubin and Brown, 1975). This need or dependence is also a function of the scarcity of these resources (Fagre and Wells, 1982; Lecraw, 1984) and their appropriability (Hamel, Doz, and Prahalad, 1989). Thus, the relative dependence of the partners toward these resources determines their relative power and thereby the balance of power in the relationship. The same association can be made between bargaining power and the division of control structure in JVs (Blodgett, 1991; Gray and Yan, 1992). Shared control could be linked to symmetric bargaining power while dominant control would reveal a power imbalance between parent firms.

Nevertheless, the balance of power between partners has been described as having a significant impact on the dynamics and viability of relationships (Blau, 1964). The presence of asymmetry in the distribution of power has been thought to have a destabilizing effect on a relationship (Burgess and Huston, 1983). In a situation of power imbalance, the high-power party's position encourages it to use its power to its advantage, and thus, at the expense of the other party, in order to gain a greater share of the rewards from the exchange (Cook, 1977; Frazier and Rody, 1991). In contrast, balanced relationships are expected to be more stable since no party enjoys a favorable power differential that would enable it to alter the exchange to its advantage.

As a result, power imbalance is associated with conflict and poor performance. Following attempts by the high-power party to exploit its power position, opportunistic behaviors, decisions without mutual consent, and what may be perceived as abuse of power and inequity, the low-power partner is likely to express dissatisfaction (Anderson and Narus, 1984). These efforts to exploit the dependence of the low-power partner serve to reduce the benefits the low-power partner receives. Complying with the powerful party's decisions or dictates also involves costs, either in taking resisting actions or in relinquishing some of the benefits of the relationship. For similar reasons, the low-power partner is likely to be apprehensive about the stronger party's behavior (Anderson and Weitz, 1989). These apprehensions may weaken the low-power partner's attachment to the relationship and interest in investing in a relationship with limited benefits. They will impede the development of cooperation between partners and thereby their capacity to achieve the objectives pursued within the context of the relationship (Anderson and Narus, 1984; Dwyer, Schurr, and Oh, 1987). Finally, the position of the high-power party is often perceived as aversive and thereby constitutes a source of conflict (Pruitt, 1981). The low-power individual is likely to rationalize actions that may well take the form of opportunistic behaviors (Provan and Skinner, 1989). These actions are likely to result in conflicts and dissatisfaction, and to hinder the relationship.

This line of reasoning can be applied to JV control structures. Building from the notion that parent firms enjoy similar power positions in JVs with extensive control sharing, these JVs should exhibit higher performance. Here, parent firms should also express greater satisfaction. In turn, JVs with little control sharing, where one parent firm dominates, can be expected to demonstrate lower performance. Therefore, the following hypothesis proposing that control sharing between parent firms will have a positive impact on the performance of JVs can be formulated:

H1:   There will be a positive relationship between the extent of control sharing and the performance of JVs.

Autonomy and performance

Killing (1983) and Gray and Yan (1992) argued that the presence of autonomy reduces the inherent complexity associated with the management of a JV. Being simpler to manage, the JV is more likely to perform well. Using a TCA rationale, the presence of extensive autonomy involves limited coordination costs and resource commitment from parent firms. It minimizes governance costs that could constrain the efficiency of the venture and offset its competitive benefits. Furthermore, a JV's autonomy may enhance its flexibility to respond rapidly to changes in its environment. In turn, extensive parent coordination may delay decision making, substantially reduce a JV's responsiveness, and represent important governance and management costs. From a SET perspective, JV autonomy entails limited power and control imbalance, since parent firms have little involvement in their management and activities. This situation restricts the potential for one partner to alter the relationship to its advantage, and may encourage mutual forbearance by the parents (Jarillo, 1988; Larson, 1988). It also reduces the risks of inter-partner conflict due to interference by one or both parent firms (Deloitte, Haskins, and Sells International, 1989; Lynch, 1989). Thus, the following hypothesis proposes a positive influence for autonomy on performance:

> H2:   There will be a positive relationship between the extent of autonomy and the performance of JVs.

International versus domestic JVs

The third hypothesis involves the comparison of IJVs and DJVs. It considers the moderating effect of the type of JV on the control structure–JV performance relationship. The existence of national culture differences in IJVs in addition to differences in organizational culture is thought to involve unique complexity. Different national cultures embody diverse attitudes and values which find their materialization in distinct business cultures and practices (Hofstede, 1980a). For instance, the dynamics of trust, the attitude toward control and the emphasis on learning have been found to vary signifi-cantly among firms from different national cultures (Ohmae, 1989; Hamel, Doz, and Prahalad, 1989; Parkhe, 1992). The presence of parent firms from different countries has been described as a source of disagreement and conflict in IJVs, and a factor in their frequent failure and performance problems (Killing, 1983; Beamish, 1988). Thus, IJVs are expected to exhibit dynamics distinct from DJVs, where parents share the same national culture.

These differences are expected to affect the relationship linking control structures and JV performance. Particularly, the use of control structures with limited control sharing may add to the inherent fragility of IJVs. Being already subject to instability and conflict fueled by cultural differences, limited control sharing may increase the risks of conflict, dissatisfaction and poor performance. In contrast, as argued earlier, extensive control sharing may support the development of trust and cooperation. It may also reduce the risks of conflict and opportunism, and the fragility of IJVs. The positive impact of control sharing will likely be greater in IJVs compared to DJVs, where there are no national culture differences that could impede the development of trust and cooperation and favor conflict. Since cultural similarity is a stabilizing force in DJVs, one could expect that little control sharing would have a less negative impact on JV performance compared to IJVs. Similarly, limited autonomy may increase the risks of conflict, and by extension of poor performance, to a greater extent in IJVs compared to DJVs. In addition, an IJV will likely be in operation in a market different or at a distance from at least one of the parent firms (or both). In this context, extensive coordination by parent firms may result in costly delays in decision making. It may even lead to bad decisions since one of the partners may not have the required expertise or the access to the proper information to deal with the IJV's different environment. It may also limit considerably the IJV's ability to respond to competitive challenges. In sum, the distinct nature of IJVs compared to DJVs should result in control structures affecting the performance of these two types of JVs differently. Consequently, the following hypothesis and sub-hypotheses can be formulated:

H3: The relationship between control structures and performance will be moderated by the international nature of JVs.

H3a: The relationship between control sharing and performance will be stronger in IJVs compared to DJVs.

H3b: The relationship between autonomy and performance will be stronger in IJVs compared to DJVs.

Methods

This research studied two-parent, manufacturing JVs based in Canada. Only DJVs and IJVs, where one of the parents held no more than 75 percent of the JV's equity, were retained. It focused on JVs in operation on January 1, 1985, and those formed since that date, but not after January 1, 1990, in order to obtain a sample containing a mix of terminated and surviving JVs. A listing of jointly owned organizations was obtained from Statistics Canada's CALURA database, supplemented by *Inter-Corporate Ownership (1990)*. After verification and contacting all parent firms, Canadian and foreign, 141 JVs were kept for study. This number is believed to represent a reasonable approximation of the population of qualifying JVs. Data required for hypothesis testing were collected from senior parent firms' managers and general managers of JVs (JVGMs). Data were obtained from 173 informants (response rate: 43 percent) on 93 JVs (66 percent of the qualifying population. See table 5.3).

Measures

Control sharing was measured with a scale similar to Geringer's (1986). Respondents were asked "How was control over each of the following decisions allocated between your firm and your partner?" for 18 categories of decisions and/or activities of the JV. The response scale was a Likert-type five-point scale (1 = "Your firm controls"; 3 = "Shared control between your firm and your partner"; 5 = "Your partner controls"). Autonomy was measured with a similar scale ("How much control over each of the following decisions was allocated between JV managers and the parent firms at the time of the JV formation") for the same decisions and/or activities. The response scale was a Likert-type five-point scale (1 = "Decided totally by parent firms"; 3 = "Shared control by parent and JV managers"; 5 = "Decided totally by JV managers"). JVGMs were asked to assess control sharing and autonomy using adapted questions and response scales; for example, whether one of the parents controlled (1 or 5), or if both parents shared control (3).

Different measures of JV performance were used in order to enhance reliability of results. In accordance with Beamish (1984), JV performance was measured by assessing the parent firms' mutual satisfaction. Using a three-item scale derived from Anderson and Narus (1990), respondents were asked to indicate their agreement on a Likert-type

TABLE 5.3 Control structures in Canada-based JVs

	All JVs (N = 173)	IJVs (N = 128)	DJVs (N = 45)
Operational control[a]			
Hiring/firing non-technical personnel	1.96	1.85	2.07#
Hiring/firing technical personnel	1.96	1.83	1.04
Pricing	2.07	1.94	2.11
Distribution	1.88	1.81	2.07#
Marketing	1.87	1.72	2.04#
Day-to-day management	1.74	1.63	1.93*
Hiring/firing of JV senior managers	2.21	2.03	2.20
Cost control	2.13	2.07	2.02
Manufacturing	1.84	1.80	1.93
Total: operational control	1.96	1.92	2.05
Technological control			
Patents and trademarks	1.79	1.51	2.11***
Technology/engineering of product	1.76	1.64	1.89**
Process technology	1.83	1.76	2.07
R&D	1.97	1.76	2.08#
Total: technological control	1.84	1.70	2.03**
Strategic control			
Hiring/firing JV general manager	2.44	2.38	2.16
Financing of the JV	2.57	2.37	2.69*
Deciding capital expenditures	2.79	2.74	2.78
Location of the JV	2.45	2.31	2.40
Total: strategic control	2.56	2.45	2.51

Significance of the DJVs/IJVs differences: # $p < 0.10$; * $p < 0.05$; ** $p < 0.01$; *** $p < 0.001$.
[a] 1 = one parent firm controls the venture; 2 = one parent firm exercises greater but not complete control; 3 = parent firms share control.
Source: Adapted from Hébert (1994)

five-point scale (−2 = Strongly disagree; 0 = Neither agree nor disagree; + 2 = Strongly agree) with three statements (for example, "My firm and our partner are very content with all aspects of the JV") focusing on satisfaction with the JV, its performance and the relationship between the partners. In addition, business performance was measured with a scale assessing performance versus expectations along 12 dimensions (sales, profitability, market share, costs, JV management, R&D, product and process technology, manufacturing, raw materials, marketing, and distribution). A single-item scale for the overall performance of the JV was also used. In both cases, the response scale was a Likert-type five-point scale (-2 = Below expectations; 0 = Equal to expectations; $+2$ = Above expectations). Two objective measures of performance were used: the survival (0 = No; 1 = Yes) and the duration (in years) of the JV. These objective measures have been found to correlate with perceptual assessments of satisfaction and performance (Geringer and Hébert, 1991).

All analyses were conducted using the software SPSS–X, including assessment of reliability and validity of our constructs, OLS regression and moderated regression analyses. For hypothesis testing and regression analyses, factor scores were computed using varimax rotation when required.

RESULTS

Patterns of control

Initial analyses revealed that the extent to which control was shared or not between parent firms tended to vary considerably across activities and decisions of JVs (see tables 5.4 and 5.5). For instance, control over decisions labeled as strategic appeared to be more shared than others, a situation interpreted as reflecting the shared decision making nature of JVs. These decisions are also frequently involved in veto rights found in typical JV agreements (Killing, 1983; Schaan, 1983). In turn, dominant control by one of the parents appeared to be more frequently exercised over technological activities in comparison to other dimensions. Parent firms' attempts to ensure protection of technological assets may well serve to explain this predominance of dominant control. JVs were also found to have extensive operational autonomy as decisions over these activities appeared to be made mostly by JV managers, rather than by parent firm managers. In turn, JVs had significantly less technological autonomy and strategic autonomy. Decisions related to process and product technology as well as R&D were mostly shared between JV and parent firm managers, while patents and trademarks, capital expenditures, and financing decisions remained under the parents' authority.

Comparison of control structures in IJVs and DJVs revealed the most notable differences concerned technological decisions. Technological control was found to be significantly less shared in IJVs compared to DJVs. Further investigation of the control exercised by local and foreign firms in IJVs showed that technological control was frequently under foreign dominant control (50 percent of all IJVs) and rarely under shared control (15 percent) or local dominant control (35 percent). IJVs were also found to enjoy significantly less technological autonomy than their domestic counterparts, especially for R&D and patents. There were few other significant differences between IJVs and DJVs. Yet, control over day-to-day decisions was significantly more shared in DJVs. In several IJVs, the responsibility for day-to-day management was assumed by the local partner, presumably to reduce the foreign parent's cost associated with managing operations at a distance or in a different country, as well as to speed up decision making for matters requiring daily attention.

TABLE 5.4 Autonomy of Canada-based JVs: IJVs vs. DJVs

	All JVs (N = 173)	IJVs (N = 128)	DJVs (N = 45)
Operational autonomy[a]			
Hiring/firing non-technical personnel	1.87	1.66	2.06
Hiring/firing technical personnel	1.96	1.78	2.13
Pricing	2.56	2.42	2.61
Distribution	2.52	2.36	2.59
Marketing	2.62	2.42	2.71
Day-to-day management	1.96	1.82	2.09
Hiring/firing of JV senior managers	2.82	2.78	3.55**
Cost control	2.31	2.17	2.38
Manufacturing	2.12	2.11	2.21
Total: operational autonomy	2.25	2.21	2.33
Technological autonomy			
Patents and trademarks	3.48	3.68	2.96**
Technology/engineering of product	3.06	3.19	2.76#
Process technology	2.46	2.49	2.36
R&D	2.95	3.13	2.50**
Total: technological autonomy	3.11	3.10	2.64**
Strategic autonomy			
Financing of the JV	3.90	3.92	3.86
Deciding capital expenditures	3.63	3.61	3.63
Location of the JV	3.64	3.69	3.38
Total: strategic autonomy	3.72	3.74	3.63

Significance of the DJVs/IJVs differences: # $p < 0.10$; * $p < 0.05$; ** $p < 0.01$.
[a] 1 = Decided totally by JV managers; 3 = Shared equally by JV and parent managers; 5 = Decided totally by parent firm managers.
Source: Adapted from Hébert (1994)

Control and performance

In our investigation of the relationship between control and performance, our hypotheses were globally supported (see Hébert, 1994, for complete results). Summary results presented on tables 5.5 and 5.6 show that the sharing of operational control had a positive relationship with the three subjective performance variables. In contrast, results for technology and strategic control sharing were not significant. Consequently, hypothesis 1 was partly supported. For autonomy, the empirical support for hypothesis 2 was

TABLE 5.5 Control structures and JV performance: OLS standardized regression coefficients (N = 108)

Dependent variables	Control sharing			
	Operational control	Technological control	Strategic control	R^2
Mutual satisfaction	0.25**	0.03	0.19*	0.07*
	(0.09)	(0.09)	(0.09)	
Business performance	0.47***	−0.07	0.07	0.21***
	(0.08)	(0.08)	(0.08)	
Overall performance	0.34***	−0.09	0.03	0.10**
	(0.09)	(0.09)	(0.09)	
Survival	−0.03	0.13	0.06	0.01
	(0.10)	(0.10)	(0.10)	
Duration	−0.04	−0.10	−0.03	0.00
	(0.10)	(0.10)	(0.10)	

Dependent variables	Autonomy			
	Operational autonomy	Technological autonomy	Strategic autonomy	R^2
Mutual satisfaction	0.22*	−0.17	0.24*	0.11**
	(0.09)	(0.09)	(0.09)	
Business performance	0.20*	−0.20*	0.28*	0.14***
	(0.09)	(0.09)	(0.09)	
Overall performance	0.14	−0.18*	0.20*	0.07*
	(0.09)	(0.09)	(0.09)	
Survival	0.01	0.22*	0.04	0.03
	(0.10)	(0.10)	(0.10)	
Duration	−0.15	0.01	−0.05	0.00
	(0.10)	(0.10)	(0.10)	

Standard errors are in parentheses: * $p < 0.05$; ** $p < 0.01$; *** $p < 0.001$.
Source: Adapted from Hébert (1994)

mixed. Results were in the expected direction between operational and strategic autonomy and the subjective performance variables. However, the relationships linking technological autonomy with business performance and overall performance were found to be negative and significant.

The comparison of DJVs and IJVs revealed some differences in the various relationships. The relationships linking operational control sharing with business and overall performance were significantly stronger in IJVs. Technological control sharing was found to be a significantly more important factor of overall performance in DJVs. In addition, the negative relationships between technological autonomy and performance variables were stronger in IJVs. In sum, these results supported the moderating effect of the

TABLE 5.6 Control structures and performance in DJVs and IJVs: OLS standardized regression coefficients

Dependent variables	Domestic joint ventures (DJVs)[a]				International joint ventures (IJVs)[b]			
	Operational control	Technological control	Strategic control	R^2	Operational control	Technological control	Strategic control	R^2
Mutual satisfaction	−0.06 (0.23)	0.31 (0.23)	0.12 (0.19)	0.03	0.30** (0.11)	−0.05 (0.11)	0.17 (0.11)	0.09*
Business performance	−0.01 (0.23)	0.26 (0.23)	−0.04 (0.19)	0.03	0.54*** (0.10)	−0.07 (0.10)	0.10 (0.10)	0.29***
Overall performance	−0.31 (0.22)	0.44# (0.22)	−0.24 (0.19)	0.10	0.43*** (0.10)	−0.14 (0.10)	0.13 (0.10)	0.22***
Survival	0.28 (0.22)	−0.20 (0.22)	0.37* (0.19)	0.09	0.04 (0.11)	−0.11 (0.11)	0.04 (0.11)	0.00
Duration	−0.03 (0.19)	0.18 (0.19)	0.24 (0.19)	0.03	−0.14 (0.11)	−0.20 (0.11)	−0.04 (0.11)	0.01

Dependent variables	Operational autonomy	Technological autonomy	Strategic autonomy	R^2	Operational autonomy	Technological autonomy	Strategic autonomy	R^2
Mutual satisfaction	0.50* (0.19)	0.25 (0.19)	0.00 (0.17)	0.23*	0.10 (0.11)	−0.26* (0.11)	0.20# (0.11)	0.11**
Business performance	0.11 (0.21)	0.28 (0.21)	−0.00 (0.19)	0.02	0.15 (0.10)	−0.26** (0.10)	0.30** (0.10)	0.20***
Overall performance	0.09 (0.23)	0.26 (0.23)	−0.05 (0.19)	0.01	0.08 (0.10)	−0.26* (0.10)	0.23* (0.10)	0.12**
Survival	0.10 (0.22)	−0.20 (0.22)	0.04 (0.20)	0.01	0.05 (0.11)	0.01 (0.11)	0.21# (0.11)	0.01
Duration	−0.27 (0.20)	0.49* (0.20)	−0.11 (0.19)	0.09	−0.20# (0.11)	0.01 (0.11)	−0.13 (0.11)	0.02

Standard errors are in parentheses. # $p < 0.10$; * $p < 0.05$; ** $p < 0.01$; *** $p < 0.001$.
[a] N = 29; [b] N = 79.

Source: Adapted from Hébert (1994)

TABLE 5.7 Summary of results

Control structures	All JVs	IJVs	DJVs
Sharing of operational control	Satisfaction (+)** Business performance (+)*** Overall performance (+)***	Satisfaction (+)** Business performance (+)*** Overall performance (+)***	Overall performance (+)*
Sharing of technological control	—	Overall performance (−)***	—
Sharing of strategic control	Satisfaction (+)**	—	Survival (+) *
Operational autonomy	Satisfaction (+)* Business performance (+)*	—	Satisfaction (+) *
Technological autonomy	Business performance (−)** Overall performance (−)* Survival (+)*	Satisfaction (−)* Business performance (−)** Overall performance (−)*	—
Strategic autonomy	Satisfaction (+) * Business performance (+)* Overall performance (+)*	Business performance (+)** Overall performance (+)**	Duration (+)*

Source: Adapted from Hébert (1994)

international versus domestic nature of a JV, although this effect was in a different direction than hypothesized for technological control and technological autonomy. Results are summarized in table 5.7. (See Hébert, 1994, for detailed moderated regression results supporting these conclusions.)

DISCUSSION

Essentially, our results supported the existence of a relationship between the control structures and the performance of JVs, although not always in the expected direction. They also suggested that the control structure–performance relationship was contingent on the type of JV and on the focus of control. Explanations for these contingency effects could draw on cultural differences and social knowledge on one hand and on the strategic motivations of JVs on the other hand.

The coexistence of parent firms with different national cultures stressed the critical role the control structure in place in an IJV may play in trust, commitment and inter-partner communication. With cultural differences placing a stress on the relationship between parents, effective communication, mutual trust, and genuine gestures of commitment achieved even greater significance. Perceived as a major commitment- and trust-building mechanism, shared control was associated with several types of behaviors and actions, such as the willingness to make decisions openly, to share information, to seek input from the partner, and to ensure a feeling of involvement in decision making. These actions and behaviors were portrayed as supporting the development of mutual trust and genuine cooperation. Both parent firms' involvement in decision making also served to secure their mutual commitment to major decisions and orientations.

In turn, attempts by any of the parent firms, foreign or local, to exercise dominant control was frequently described as meeting serious resistance from its partner. Local parent firms were generally opposed to their foreign partner exercising dominant control. Typically, they judged the foreign partner's knowledge of the local environment as being too limited to effectively manage the venture. In turn, foreign parents were seldom willing to relinquish complete latitude to their local partner as it could impede the acquisition of knowledge about their local market.

In DJVs, shared control was often seen as the norm: leaving dominant control to their partner would have been perceived as selling off their activities or withdrawing from the business. Sharing control reflected the objective of pooling resources and undertaking cooperation in the domestic arena. Furthermore, a majority of DJVs involved firms from the same industry, or at least firms and managers who knew each other or had been involved in previous business relationships. Essentially, DJVs were thought to involve substantial social knowledge. Consistent with Sohn (1994), this social knowledge could represent an effective social-based control mechanism and reduce a parent firm's dependency on formal and resource-consuming control mechanisms. The absence of national culture differences and this social knowledge reduced the role played by control structures and were thought to explain their limited importance for these ventures' performance. With parent firms from different countries, however, IJVs typically involve less social knowledge. This situation may increase parent firms' need for formal mechanisms to protect their interests and to implement their strategy. Therefore, this social knowledge argument could also explain the greater importance of control for the performance of IJVs.

In addition to playing a different role in IJVs compared to DJVs, control structures used in these ventures were also found to be different. This situation was thought to reflect the distinct strategic motivations underlying their formation. The examination of the parent firms' respective contributions revealed that DJVs exhibited characteristics of "scale" JVs (Hennart, 1988; Kogut, 1988b) where partners belong to the same industry and contribute similar resources. In turn, IJVs were "link" JVs where partners typically contribute complementary resources. They followed the common pattern of a foreign partner providing technology while the local partner contributed marketing/distribution resources. Thus, not only did foreign firms form IJVs to exploit their technological resources on the local market, they also maintained dominant technological control and left limited technological autonomy to their ventures. Therefore, the differences between DJVs and IJVs could be linked to these organizations' distinct strategic dynamics.

The control–performance relationship also appeared to be contingent on the focus of control. Again, the distinct strategic dynamics of IJVs and DJVs may explain these results. The case of IJVs which exhibited higher performance with extensive sharing of operational control and limited technological autonomy is particularly manifest in this regard. The success of these technology-marketing ventures could be related to the effective adaptation and marketing of the technology and its related products in the local market – a function of the integration of the local and foreign partners' respective resources. Therefore, the presence of shared operational control may have permitted the effective integration of the local partner's marketing/distribution resources with the foreign parent's technology/product. Limited technological autonomy and the related continuous technological relationship with parent firms also provided the technological support necessary for the technology's adaptation and to ensure continuous technological development. In contrast, DJVs did not require the same relationship with parent firms since they did not involve similar technological motivations and the integration of complementary resources.

The arguments for a strategy–structure fit

These two contingencies can also be interpreted within a strategy–structure perspective. The importance of studying alliances such as JVs within the context of the parent firms' strategy has been emphasized before (Porter and Fuller, 1986). Subsidiaries can assume distinct strategic roles depending on their competitive environment, their parent firms' strategy and their competencies, and these roles have different organizational requirements (Stopford and Wells, 1972; Bartlett and Ghoshal, 1986, 1995). Particularly, Geringer and Hébert (1989) proposed that JV performance was a function of the fit between the parent firms' strategy, the IJV strategy, and the parameters of control. Our findings were thought to exemplify Geringer and Hébert's (1989) proposition. The formation of DJVs and IJVs indeed involved distinct strategic motivations, and these motivations were associated with unique patterns of control. The success of IJVs and the effective implementation of the parent firms' strategy were linked to their ability to establish structures consistent with their strategic motivations and which provided effective integration of their respective resource contributions.

CONCLUSION

This chapter has attempted to provide additional insight into the control–JV performance relationship. Empirical evidence supported the existence of this relationship, yet left a much different picture of the control structure–JV performance relationship. Rather than the global and direct relationship proposed in the literature, this study suggested that this relationship was complex and exposed to several contingencies. For instance, it was shown to be contingent on the type of JV and the focus of control. These contingencies may explain the limited evidence and conflicting results found in previous research. The study also showed that control and autonomy were not monolithic concepts and that different patterns of control and autonomy were used for different activities of JVs. The identification of these dimensions represents an empirically grounded basis for examining control structures in JVs. Finally, the above results allowed the assessment of this relationship's strength. They showed that while of limited consequence for the performance of DJVs, the division of control for operational decisions was a significant factor of performance in IJVs.

The results obtained may have some important implications for both the research on, and the management of, JVs. This study's results underline the importance of not limiting investigation to the overall control structure of JVs. It appears critical, for a thorough understanding of control in JVs, to devote attention to the focus of control and to its division over specific single functions and group of activities. These results also demonstrate the need for distinguishing between IJVs and DJVs in future research and specifically, for not combining them in research samples. The unique dynamics of developed country JVs compared to less developed country JVs have often been discussed (e.g., Beamish, 1985). Nevertheless, the particular character and dynamics of developed country IJVs, arising from the presence of parents with different national cultures and resource contributions, should be taken into consideration in the examination of key elements of JVs such as their control structure. Firms currently involved or contemplating involvement in JVs should also account for these types of distinctive dynamics and strategic motivations. As pointed out by Bartlett and Ghoshal (1995), efforts to devise an effective control structure should focus on permitting an effective integration of the partner firms' competencies rather than on forcing a strict equality between them.

6

The Importance of the Strategy–Structure Relationship in MNCs

William Egelhoff

The importance of fitting a company's organizational structure to its strategy was initially highlighted by Chandler (1962). His work subsequently spurred a series of studies of strategy and structure in domestic firms (Pavan, 1972; Channon, 1973; Rumelt, 1974; Dyas and Thanheiser, 1976), and in multinational corporations (MNCs) (Stopford and Wells, 1972; Franko, 1973; Daniels, Pitts, and Tretter, 1984, 1985; Egelhoff, 1982, 1988a). These and other studies described a reasonably consistent and seemingly important set of fits between MNC strategy and MNC structure. The primary advantages associated with such strategy–structure models of the MNC include: (1) a clear specifying of when one type of structure is superior to another, and (2) the identification of those elements of strategy which are most important to a firm's structure. Taken together, these characteristics made strategy–structure models attractive guidelines for evaluating and designing a firm's structure and considering the implications of changes in firm strategy.

Since the 1980s, however, scholarly interest in traditional strategy–structure theory has waned. Instead, there has been a growing interest in non-structural and more informal approaches to organizing international firms. The dominant models here have been transnational (Bartlett and Ghoshal, 1989) and heterarchical (Hedlund, 1986) models of MNC organizational design. These new models assign little power or meaning to formal organizational structure (or its relationship to strategy). They basically argue that structure (and its fit with strategy) is too rigid and inflexible a mechanism to cope with the high levels of unpredictable change that today's MNCs face. Instead of formal hierarchical structure, they favor organizing MNCs with more of a non-hierarchical network design. The latter relies more heavily on ad hoc relationships and informal communications to coordinate a firm's operations. Such ad hoc behavior is primarily motivated and provided with commonality of purpose through shared vision. While the actual extent to which formal structure can or should be replaced by a network design is usually left vague, most discussions of transnational or heterarchical models of MNC organizational design leave one with the impression that the role of formal structure can be greatly reduced, if not eliminated. And, if structure becomes unimportant as a coordinating and motivating mechanism, then its fit with strategy also becomes unimportant. This is the challenge that the new network models of MNC organizational design pose to traditional strategy–structure theory.

This chapter takes the above challenge as a starting point and attempts to define what the role of the strategy–structure relationship is (or should be) in today's MNC. The defense and improvement of existing theory is crucial to the scientific underpinning of a field. Without it, a field is in danger of simply becoming an arena for developing new fads. Management research in business schools is sometimes regarded as such by other faculties of a university. Unfortunately, such thinking cannot summarily be dismissed. Using the present case as an example, it is almost impossible to find published articles that seek to defend or further improve strategy–structure theory, once articles about the new network theories of the MNC begin to appear in earnest. Nor can one find much attempt to objectively evaluate or reconcile the opposing theories. Network theories of the MNC were introduced and further developed with a strong normative overtone, that either ignored existing theory or treated it as a straw-man. The lack of serious comparison and debate between old and new theories weakens the scientific underpinnings of international management as a scholarly field.

The next section of this chapter summarizes existing strategy–structure theory and evaluates its appropriateness for today's MNCs. Subsequent sections attempt to further conceptualize the strategy–structure relationship in ways that allow it to be extended and integrated with network models of the MNC. The chapter concludes with an applied example using the pharmaceutical industry, and recommendations for future research.

EXISTING RESEARCH AND THEORY ON THE STRATEGY–STRUCTURE RELATIONSHIP IN MNCs

The earliest and best-known model of strategy and structure in MNCs stems from the Stopford and Wells (1972) study of 187 US MNCs. According to this model, an MNC's organizational structure needs to fit two important aspects of international strategy: the relative size of foreign sales and the degree of foreign product diversity (see figure 6.1). The interaction of these two contingency variables specifies four different strategic domains, each of which is associated with a different type of structure. Low foreign sales and low foreign product diversity are associated with having one international division separate from but equal to other divisions (international division structure), low foreign sales and high product diversity with a worldwide product division structure, high foreign sales and low foreign product diversity with a geographical region structure, and high foreign sales and high foreign product diversity with matrix or mixed structures.

Subsequent studies have both confirmed and challenged parts of the Stopford and Wells model. Franko's (1973) study of 60 European MNCs confirmed the fits of the Stopford and Wells model, with one major exception. European MNCs tended not to use the international division structure. Instead, when foreign sales and product diversity were relatively low, they tended to have foreign operations report directly to the parent CEO (referred to as a mother–daughter or direct report structure). As foreign sales and product diversity increased, they too followed the strategy–structure relationships specified by the Stopford and Wells model.

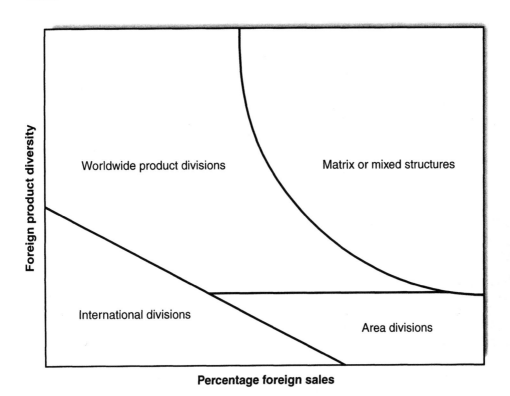

FIGURE 6.1 The Stopford and Wells model showing the relationship between strategy and structure in multinational corporations

Bartlett's (1979) case studies of ten US MNCs with international division structures found that this structure could successfully handle high levels of foreign sales and foreign product diversity. This contradicted the strategic domain specified by the Stopford and Wells model. Davidson and Haspeslagh's (1982) study of strategy and structure in 57 US MNCs also supported a wider strategic domain for the international division structure. A later study of 93 US MNCs by Daniels, Pitts, and Tretter (1984, 1985) generally confirmed the relationships of the Stopford and Wells model, except they found that when foreign sales are relatively small, MNCs tended to use a product division structure instead of an international division structure.

Egelhoff (1982, 1988a) subsequently studied strategy and structure in 50 MNCs (24 US, 26 European). He used an information-processing perspective (Galbraith, 1973) to specify fit relationships between MNC structure and eight aspects of international strategy, including size of foreign sales and degree of foreign product diversity from the Stopford and Wells model. He added product modification differences among subsidiaries, degree of product change, size of foreign manufacturing, number of foreign subsidiaries, extent of outside ownership, and extent of foreign acquisitions. The key strategy–structure fits identified by this study are shown in figure 6.2. These results support many of the relationships of the Stopford and Wells model, as they relate to size

Types of structure

Elements of strategy	Functional divisions	International divisions	Geographical regions	Product divisions
Foreign product diversity	Low foreign product diversity			High foreign product diversity
Product modification differences between subsidiaries	Low product modification differences between subsidiaries			
Product change				High rate of product change
Size of foreign operations		Relatively small foreign operations	Relatively large foreign operations	Relatively large foreign operations
Size of foreign manufacturing			High level of foreign manufacturing	
Number of foreign subsidiaries	Few foreign subsidiaries	Low to moderate number of foreign subsidiaries	Large number of foreign subsidiaries	Large number of foreign subsidiaries
Extent of outside ownership in foreign subsidiaries	Low level of outside ownership in foreign subsidiaries			
Extent of foreign acquisitions	Few foreign acquisitions			

FIGURE 6.2 Important fits between elements of strategy and types of organizational structure
Source: Reprinted from "Strategy and structure in multinational corporations: An information-process approach" by William G. Egelhoff, published in *Administrative Science Quarterly*, Volume 27 Number 3 by permission of *Administrative Science Quarterly*. Copyright 1982 Cornell University

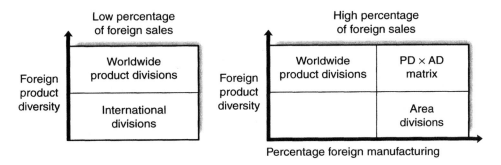

FIGURE 6.3 Revised model showing the relationship between strategy and structure in multinational corporations

Source: Reprinted from "Strategy and structure in multinational corporations: A revision of the Stopford and Wells model" by William G. Egelhoff, published in *Strategic Management Journal*, Volume 9, 1988. Copyright John Wiley & Sons Limited. Reproduced with permission

of foreign sales and degree of foreign product diversity. In several areas, however, Egelhoff's study modified and extended the Stopford and Wells model. It specified a very constrained strategic domain for the worldwide functional division structure (five fits are identified in figure 6.2), which was not included in the Stopford and Wells model. And, it discovered the importance of a new variable, the size of foreign manufacturing. This variable helped to further specify the boundaries between the strategic domains of a worldwide product division structure, a geographical region structure, and a matrix structure. Figure 6.3 shows this revision to the Stopford and Wells model. All three structures tend to be associated with high foreign sales. When foreign product diversity is high and foreign manufacturing is low, this specifies the strategic domain of a worldwide product division structure. When the reverse is the case (low foreign product diversity and high foreign manufacturing), a geographical region structure is specified. And, when both foreign product diversity and foreign manufacturing are high, a product division × geographical region matrix structure is required.

In a later study, Habib and Victor (1991) also used an information-processing perspective to study strategy–structure fit in 144 US manufacturing and service MNCs. The study confined itself to examining foreign sales and foreign product diversity as the relevant aspects of strategy, and tended to retest and confirm the key relationships of the Stopford and Wells model. Interestingly, it found no significant differences between manufacturing and service MNCs in terms of strategy–structure relationships, thus extending the Stopford and Wells model to cover service MNCs.

The above studies largely define existing strategy–structure theory as it relates to MNCs. Perhaps the most impressive aspect of this theory is the relatively consistent empirical support found for many of the strategy–structure fits. A recent study of strategy and structure in German MNCs reveals that most of the fits are still apparent in today's firms (Wolf and Egelhoff, 1999). The pervasiveness of such strategy–structure fit across nationalities and time suggests that it might be a fundamental condition for firm survival and organizational performance, and, indeed, during its heyday, this was often how it was described (Miles and Snow, 1984). But, interestingly, empirical attempts to link fit to firm performance (typically financial performance) are unconvincing. While this is regarded as a serious problem by some, I have argued: (1) that finding independently hypothesized strategy–structure fits in a sample of surviving and growing (i.e., successful) firms constitutes support for the hypothesized fit and its logic, and (2) that the linkage between specific aspects of organizational design and measures of financial performance is problematic for several reasons. Chief among these is the fact that it is unlikely there is any single operational fit that contributes in a consistently strong way to some broad measure of organizational performance (such as profitability or return on investment). We assume that overall fit relates strongly to overall performance, but cannot measure fit or its relationship to performance at this level (Egelhoff, 1988b: 265–8).

In my opinion, the primary shortcoming of strategy–structure theory is not the failure to link differing levels of fit to differing levels of organizational performance. In fact, I doubt that this is the best way to either justify or improve strategy–structure theory. Instead, I believe the route to both of the above lies through better conceptualizing the underlying meaning and implications of strategy–structure fit and misfit. Existing theory largely has an empirical tone rather than a conceptual tone. It primarily describes a number of directly observed fits between strategy and structure, based on a series of survey studies. But why a fit is good and contributes to organizational performance is largely absent from the theory. While there are some eclectic explanations accompanying the fits, most strategy–structure models lack a general or abstract logic that might be used to hypothesize such fits independent of their empirical discovery. This lack of a deeper conceptual understanding severely limits the value of most existing strategy–structure theory, for it gives such theory a static or historical perspective (i.e., it can't be applied to new or different situations that haven't been directly studied).

It is important to notice that all MNCs, even those with a good deal of network organization, tend to have some kind of formal structure at the macro level where the parent–subsidiary relationship exists. And, it would appear that firms take this structure and its fit with strategy seriously. When competitive environments and strategies change, firms frequently restructure. And, such structural change is generally accompanied by company statements that a firm is restructuring in order to better implement or execute its strategy. A recent study of German firms found that structural change has increased in recent years and that it generally supports the fits contained in existing strategy–structure theory (Wolf, 1999). Thus, firm behavior tends to support the argument that strategy–structure fit is still regarded as relevant to firm survival and performance.

But, this is not necessarily a compelling argument for the relevance of strategy–structure fit. Most human beings still have appendices, even though the appendix no longer contributes to the survival and performance of the human organism. Is formal organizational structure and its fit with strategy a similar kind of vestigial property of organizations, that has largely lost its purpose? Existing strategy–structure theory and research largely fail to address this question. But such failure doesn't resolve the question in favor of the critics of strategy–structure theory. Their arguments are largely based on the limitations of existing strategy–structure theory, and not on any new empirical evidence or conceptual argument that structure and its fit with strategy are unrelated to firm survival and performance. Resolving this issue will require either new empirical evidence or new conceptualization. It is the latter approach that this chapter will pursue.

Further Conceptualizing the Strategy–Structure Relationship

It is important to observe that strategy and structure are not the most basic concepts that explain the survival and performance of firms in competitive environments. As figure 6.4 shows, both are intervening concepts that lie between the characteristics of a firm's competitive environment and the organizational behaviors emitted by a firm. For example, one characteristic of a competitive environment might be whether customers want technologically superior global products or differentiated national products. Organizational behavior, which largely consists of the decisions and actions taken by a firm, can either fit or misfit this environmental characteristic. If customers primarily want a technologically superior global product (like a microprocessor), a firm that decides to decentralize product development and proceeds to develop different national versions of a microprocessor will probably not succeed. There is a misfit between an important environmental characteristic and the behavior of the organization. As an intervening and higher-level concept, strategy selects and enacts the key characteristics of a firm's environment. It identifies the various environmental requirements that the firm intends to address, and further generalizes about how the firm will address them. Similarly, organizational structure shapes and influences a firm's organizational behavior so that it too reflects some higher-level purpose and focus. Viewed this way, fitting strategy and structure on one level helps to align a myriad of individual organizational behaviors with a specific set of environmental requirements at a lower level.

Such higher-level intervening concepts are most useful when environments are complex and organizations are large. A two- or three-person firm competing in a simple environment doesn't need a formal structure or strategy to align the small number of organizational behaviors with the obvious demands of the environment. But, as firms become large, the potential combinations of organizational behavior a firm can emit become infinite. And, as environments become complex, the range of environmental demands a firm might potentially address also becomes great. Under these conditions, aligning one with the other is extremely problematic without the aid of some higher-level intervening concepts like structure and strategy.

As figure 6.4 also indicates, it is not the fit between strategy and structure that directly influences organizational performance, even though this is what research has attempted to test. Rather, it is the fit between the actual organizational behaviors of a firm and the characteristics of its competitive environment that leads to organizational performance and the natural selection of the firm for survival or failure. In this case, the fit between strategy and structure is used as a proxy for the fit between the underlying characteristics of the competitive environment and organizational behaviors. Existing theory concentrates on the empirically discovered fits between strategy and structure shown above the dashed line in figure 6.4. What is needed to improve such theory is to conceptually understand how structure shapes and influences a firm's organizational behaviors and how these behaviors relate to (fit or misfit) the characteristics of the firm's environment. In other words, existing strategy–structure theory needs to be further conceptualized in terms of the underlying concepts and relationships shown below the dashed line. The following two subsections attempt to describe how structure shapes and influences

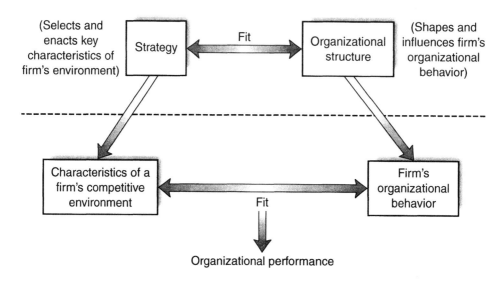

FIGURE 6.4 A model showing the role played by strategy and structure as higher-level, intervening concepts

coordination and motivation in MNCs. Both are crucial aspects of organizational behavior, and together they probably capture most of the impact organizational structure has on organizational behavior.

The implications of structure for coordination

The primary conceptual framework which has been used to describe the coordinating potential of MNC structure has been an information-processing perspective (Egelhoff, 1982, 1988b, 1991; Habib and Victor, 1991). With this perspective, the organization is viewed as an information-processing system, and information processing between organizational subunits is considered an important aspect of organizational behavior and performance. Each of the various types of structure is seen as facilitating certain types of information processing between the subunits of the organization, while at the same time restraining other types of information processing.

   The elements of a firm's strategy, on the other hand, are seen as posing different requirements for information processing between the subunits of an MNC. If strategies can be described in terms of the kind and amount of information processing required to implement them, then one can create a general framework for hypothesizing and measuring fit between structure and strategy. There is good fit between structure and strategy when the information-processing requirements of a firm's strategy are satisfied by the information-processing capacities of its structure. This information-processing model of international strategy and structure has been specified in some detail in Egelhoff (1982, 1988b, 1991), and the present chapter first summarizes and then builds off this earlier conceptualization. As shown in figure 6.5, Egelhoff identifies four dimensions of information processing in MNCs and uses these to measure and describe the information-processing capacities of the different types of international structure.

The *purpose and perspective of information processing* can be defined in terms of whether it is primarily strategic or primarily tactical. Tactical information processing deals with the large volume of relatively routine day-to-day problems and situations confronting an organization. The decision-making perspective required to handle these situations tends to be relatively narrow, and it usually exists at the middle and lower levels of management. Strategic information processing attempts to deal with a much smaller volume of relatively nonroutine, and usually more important, problems and situations. These problems deal with the fundamental position of the organization in its environment and usually involve changing this position. Thus, strategic information processing has a different purpose and requires a different perspective than tactical information processing. It addresses higher-level organizational goals, is broader in scope, and usually has a longer time horizon. This perspective tends to exist at the higher levels of an organization's hierarchy.

Research suggests that different levels of an organization's hierarchy tend to process different kinds of information and have different purposes for processing information. The association of tactical and strategic perspectives with different levels of an organization presupposes that some kind of hierarchy exists in most MNCs. Recent literature suggests that MNCs may be becoming less hierarchical (Hedlund, 1986; Bartlett and Ghoshal, 1989). To the extent that an MNC is less hierarchically organized, it becomes more difficult to generalize about where strategic and tactical perspectives exist in an organization.

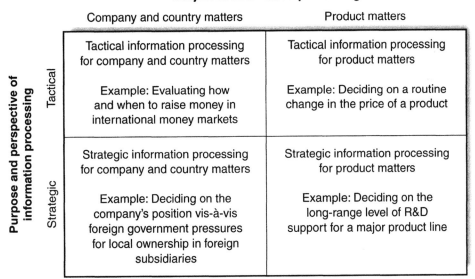

FIGURE 6.5 Four types of information processing

Source: Reprinted from "Strategy and structure in multinational corporations: An information-processing approach" by William G. Egelhoff, published in *Administrative Science Quarterly*, Volume 27 Number 3 by permission of *Administrative Science Quarterly*. Copyright 1982 Cornell University

The framework also reflects the *subject or content of information processing* and distinguishes between information processing for product matters (product and process technology, market information) and information processing for company and country matters (finance, tax, legal, government relations, human resources). Subject knowledge or specialization tends to vary horizontally across organizations. Different organizational structures tend to cluster it into different subunits. Using these distinctions, four types of information processing are developed, as shown in figure 6.5. The four types are generally not substitutes for each other, since they tend to address different problem areas that require different types of knowledge and different perspectives of the organization and its goals.

The above set of information-processing dimensions helps to distinguish where in an organization different kinds of knowledge and different kinds of decision-making capability lie. It identifies which parts of an organization need to be linked together in order to solve a given problem or address a specific decision-making situation. In other words, these dimensions are useful for measuring and understanding the influence of different types of structure on information processing.

Egelhoff (1982) used this conceptual framework to analyze the information-processing capacities of the four types of macro-structure commonly used by MNCs: worldwide functional divisions, international divisions, geographical regions, and worldwide product divisions. This approach uses relative organizational distance (or closeness) through the formal organizational structure to define where communication will be facilitated and where it will be hindered between organizational subunits. In addition to organizational distance (which specifies the interconnection among subunits), macro-structure also influences what type of information (measured in terms of subject) and what type of processing (measured in terms of purpose and perspective) can occur between interconnected subunits. Horizontal differentiation (or specialization) largely determines in which subunits certain types of knowledge reside, just as vertical differentiation largely determines at what levels tactical and strategic perspectives of the business can be taken. How parent headquarters (HQ) and foreign subsidiaries are differentiated and which subunits are directly linked through the hierarchy largely determines how much of each of the four types of information processing a structure will provide. These amounts or capacities are summarized in table 6.1.

A worldwide functional division structure means that the functional activities in a foreign subsidiary report directly to their respective functional divisions in the parent. Since none of the functional subunits could operate as a separate business, the formulation of business strategy requires a cross-functional perspective. In a functional division company a cross-functional or general management perspective only exists at one level, at the top of the parent HQ. Subunits in foreign subsidiaries cannot participate in or make direct inputs to the strategy-formulation process, for nearly all information processing within a subsidiary or between it and the parent takes place within a functional area. Consequently, this structure provides almost no strategic information-processing capacity between foreign subsidiaries and the parent. The centralization of strategic information processing means that processing capacity is limited (only a few people at one level of the parent are involved) and it is difficult for new information about the environment to enter the process. The functional structure should facilitate tactical information processing between the parent and foreign subsidi-

TABLE 6.1 Type and level of information processing capacity provided by different types of structure

| | Level of information-processing capacity | | | |
| | For company and country matters | | For product matters | |
	Tactical	Strategic	Tactical	Strategic
Functional divisions	High[a]	Low	High[a]	Low
International divisions	High[b]	High[b]	Low	Low
Geographical regions	High[c]	High[c]	High[c]	High[c]
Product divisions	Low	Low	High	High

[a] Only within a functional area. Low across functions; [b] only between subsidiary and international divisions; [c] only between subsidiary and regional headquarters.
Source: Reprinted from "Strategy and structure in multinational corporations: An information-processing approach" by William G. Egelhoff, published in *Administrative Science Quarterly*, Volume 27 Number 3 (September 1982) by permission of *Administrative Science Quarterly*. Copyright 1982 Cornell University

aries as long as the processing can take place within a functional area. Tactical information processing across functions, however, will be low, since the structure does not facilitate communication between divisions at either the subsidiary level or the tactical levels of the parent.

With an international division structure, all foreign subsidiaries report to an international division that is separate from the domestic operations. This structure tends to facilitate information processing between the parent and foreign subsidiaries, while at the same time it hinders information processing at the parent level between the international division and the domestic operations. Product knowledge tends to be centered in the domestic divisions, while knowledge about such company and country matters as international finance and foreign political conditions is centered in the international division. Consequently, parent–subsidiary information-processing capacity is relatively high for company and country matters and relatively low for product matters. There is a general management or strategic apex at both the subsidiary and international division levels. Thus, strategic as well as tactical information processing can take place between a subsidiary and the international division, but it will center around company and country matters rather than product matters.

A geographical region structure divides the world into regions, each with its own HQ. Each HQ is responsible for all of the company's products and business within its geographical area. The regional HQ is the center of the company's knowledge about company and country matters within the region. Most regional HQs also contain either product or functional staffs to provide coordination for product matters across subsidiaries in the region. There is a general management or strategic apex at both the subsidiary and regional HQ levels. As a result, this structure facilitates a high level of all four types of information processing between a subsidiary and its regional HQ. The information-processing capacity between a foreign subsidiary and domestic operations or a subsidiary in another region is low. The only mechanism for coordinating across regions is the corporate HQ.

A worldwide product division structure extends the responsibilities of the domestic product divisions to cover their product lines on a worldwide basis. Under this structure, there is a tendency to centralize product-related decision making at both the strategic and tactical levels in the parent product groups and decentralize all non-product decision making to the foreign subsidiaries. Consequently, the capacity for processing information between the parent and foreign subsidiaries for company and country matters tends to be low, since much of it has been decentralized to the local subsidiary level and parent management has a product orientation. Product-related tactical and strategic information-processing capacities, on the other hand, tend to be high. The foreign product divisions in the subsidiaries are connected to the centers of product knowledge in the parent. For each product line, there is a strategic apex at both the subsidiary and parent product-division levels. The conceptual framework discussed here and its underlying logic was empirically supported by Egelhoff (1982).

The above information-processing perspective of structure has largely focused on organizational distance (or closeness) through the formal hierarchy as its key concept. This perspective probably needs to be broadened to include cognitive distance – the distance between the thoughtworlds (Dougherty, 1992) of two or more subunits. Subunits that are cognitively distant (their perspectives of the same task or situation are different) will experience more difficulty processing information than subunits that are cognitively close (share a common understanding of the task or situation). Cognitive distance especially hinders the exchange of tacit knowledge or information between subunits. Physical distance between subunits can also influence their capacity to process information. Although this is not directly a characteristic of structure, certain structures imply physical distances. An international division structure implies physical distance between foreign and domestic operations. A geographical region structure implies physical distance between geographical regions. Physical distance tends to hinder informal coordination between subunits. The subsequent application of these concepts to an example will attempt to reflect cognitive and physical distance as well as the concept of organizational distance, which is traditional to an information-processing theory of structure.

The implications of structure for motivation

While structure has frequently been linked to coordination, its influence on motivation has largely been ignored. This chapter will use expectancy theory, probably the most general and influential motivational theory in the area of management, to explore the potential influence of structure on motivation. Expectancy theory views the motivation to engage in a given behavior as a function of the goals that people identify with and their expectancies about the paths that link this behavior to their goals (Vroom, 1964). While it is not surprising that different subunits in a company have different goals (e.g., R&D and marketing), it is more interesting to observe that their goals for the same common, interdependent task or activity can also differ. For example, both R&D and marketing are involved in new product development. People in the R&D subunit of a company may see the primary goal as discovering a truly superior technology, so that the company can dominate the product category over the long term. At the same time, people in the marketing subunit may see the primary goal as getting a new model into the market before the end of the year, in order to pre-empt competitors. And, not only can goals for the same task vary, the expectancies and paths that people see linking various behaviors to these goals can also vary. R&D people may believe that focused research over a certain period of time has a high probability of yielding a significant technological advantage, which will result in the company dominating the product category. The marketing people may be skeptical of this path, but strongly believe that being first to market (even without a significant technological advantage) will discourage competitors from making serious marketing commitments, which will result in the company dominating the product category. This simple example supports two very different, and probably inconsistent, types of product development behavior. Structure enters this picture because it grouped people into separate R&D and marketing subunits, and thereby assigned each group different goals and expectancies. Since these differences in goals and expectancies motivate different behaviors, structure (via motivation) can also have a major influence on the organizational behaviors emitted by a firm.

This approach to linking structure to organizational behavior is not as focused or elaborated as the previous information-processing model which focuses on the implications of structure for coordination. But, if employed selectively, it can perhaps be used to explore the influence of structure on other critical behaviors that lie outside of coordination. While structure undoubtedly influences (motivates) vast amounts of organizational behavior, most of this is uninteresting. In order to avoid becoming lost in this morass, we will attempt to apply this framework to the critical behaviors associated with a narrowly defined topic. This attempt to apply a motivation perspective to structure adds a more exploratory bent to the otherwise incremental extension of strategy–structure theory proposed in the previous subsection.

THE PHARMACEUTICAL INDUSTRY: AN APPLIED EXAMPLE

This section will attempt to extend existing strategy–structure theory by describing how each of the four MNC structures shapes the coordination and motivation of critical behaviors in an international pharmaceutical company. The specific task to be considered is technology development, an important and complex activity in such firms. The objective is to better understand the strategy–structure relationship by viewing its influence at the level of organizational behavior.

Worldwide functional division structure

Under a worldwide functional division structure, all foreign and domestic R&D will report in to the same global R&D HQ. Technology planning, resource allocation, and budgeting will follow this authority structure, and in the process they will drive a lot of tactical, product-related information processing between the central R&D HQ and foreign R&D subunits. The need to periodically monitor and control performance against these plans and budgets will generate additional rounds of such information processing. This coordination occurs within the global R&D division, and foreign R&D subunits will tend not to coordinate any of this with local marketing or manufacturing subunits, even when they share the same physical site. Instead, marketing and manufacturing planning and controlling will also result in largely vertical global information flows within each of these functional areas.

Because technology development needs to be coordinated with both marketing and manufacturing, it is useful to consider how this occurs. Since there is no natural alignment between a foreign research laboratory and the activities of the local marketing subsidiary under a worldwide functional division structure, marketing and R&D will primarily be coordinated at the worldwide HQ level. Here globally aggregated marketing requirements can be reconciled with R&D capabilities and plans. It is difficult for technology development activities to respond to local market requirements that differ from the global requirements. This structure essentially denies the strategic significance of such local requirements and even blocks them at a tactical level from reaching bench-level R&D personnel who might otherwise respond to them.

While manufacturing and R&D will also be coordinated at the worldwide HQ level, there is a further requirement to transfer new technology from R&D to specific foreign manufacturing sites. Since new product technology is highly codified, it transfers relatively easily. Transferring the process technology required to manufacture the new pharmaceutical compounds is a more difficult problem. Typically, the process technology development group of a pharmaceutical company resides in the parent country, close to the largest new product development laboratory. Both formal and informal coordination will occur between these two R&D subunits. They are organizationally and physically close, although cognitively, process technology development groups lie somewhere between the thoughtworlds of the product technology development group (with a more basic research orientation) and the manufacturing engineers (with a more applied orientation). Historically, companies would transfer the new process technology to a domestic plant first, so that physical closeness could facilitate informal coordination during this difficult transfer of new technology across functions. After the new technology was successfully scaled up and debugged in a manufacturing environment, it could be more readily transferred to foreign plants.

Increasingly, however, global competition is forcing companies to manufacture a new compound at a dedicated plant, and this frequently requires the initial movement of new technology directly to a foreign site. The functional structure does not fit this kind of cross functional transfer of uncertain knowledge, and companies frequently try to compensate for it by using other non-structural means of facilitating this coordination (high levels of horizontal information processing, including frequent visits and temporary transfers of personnel). Still, because it goes against the natural information-processing capabilities of the structure, this remains one of the most difficult coordination problems for many pharmaceutical companies.

Informal coordination under this structure tends to occur within functional divisions. It is usually high within an R&D site, where there is organizational, cognitive, and physical closeness. All of these facilitate familiarity and informal coordination. While organizational and cognitive closeness also tend to exist between subunits in the R&D division, physical distance in international companies hinders informal coordination. The resources available for travel, personnel transfers, and electronic communication influence the extent to which informal coordination occurs between dispersed subunits in an R&D division. But, the most salient influence here is the absence of informal coordination between R&D and other functional areas. Only at the worldwide HQ level is there organizational and physical closeness, and some reduction in cognitive distance, if members of the top management team share a more common vision regarding technology development than lower levels of the organization.

Thus, the overall fit a worldwide functional division company needs with its environment is to minimize requirements for cross-functional coordination, and especially requirements for such coordination at tactical levels of the organization. Strategies that emphasize fundamental technological uniqueness and lengthy technology development processes tend to define such an environment. Here most of the uncertainty and the resultant requirements for tactical coordination tend to occur within the R&D function. Coordination with marketing is largely strategic (evaluating potentials, establishing priorities, and deciding on the research agenda). Coordination with manufacturing is also largely strategic (largely involving capacity planning), aside from the need to directly transfer new process technology to manufacturing. By focusing so much of the coordinating and information-processing capacity of the organization within individual functions (and sacrificing more cross-functional information processing), this structure clearly favors strategies that rest on advantages that can be created by a single function.

While a pharmaceutical company may possess a strong sales force in certain countries and low cost or flexible manufacturing capabilities, the most highly valued advantage is undoubtedly the capability to discover and further develop new chemical compounds that possess certain kinds of efficacy. And this process largely occurs within the R&D function, independent of the rest of the company. In fact, some pharmaceutical companies have been successful, without possessing any marketing or manufacturing strengths. The independence of these functional strengths is such that companies can readily access them through such arm's-length mechanisms as licensing and strategic alliances. The kind of cross-functional coordination provided by internal organization is not a necessity and, in many cases, doesn't appear to add that much value to a pharmaceutical firm. Strategies and environments that reflect these characteristics tend to fit a worldwide functional division structure.

In addition to coordination, the other aspect of organizational behavior most shaped by structure is motivation. In the example of the pharmaceutical company, the values and goals of the three functional areas vary considerably, and this motivates different concerns and organizational behaviors when it comes to technology development. The R&D area is primarily concerned with building and perfecting its technical capabilities and doing competent, thorough research. It typically seeks to find some significant and unique solution to a problem. This is how the R&D area attempts to create competitive advantage from technology development.

The marketing area, on the other hand, has as its primary goal being first to market with a new product. It, therefore, wants to shorten the product and process technology development cycles as much as possible. While it too seeks products that have some differentiating advantage over competitors' products, this is frequently something less than the significant and unique solution that motivates researchers. As a result, marketing frequently argues for curtailing the time that a project is with R&D and presses for quicker transfers of new technology. This is how the marketing area attempts to insure that the advantages available from new technology development are realized and exploited by the company.

The interests and organizational behavior of the manufacturing area tend to lie between the two extremes of the R&D and marketing areas. They are also more specific and limited in scope. The primary concern of the manufacturing area is to develop an appropriate and debugged manufacturing process technology that can be easily scaled up and reliably run in the plant. As a result, manufacturing typically wants a development process that is complete enough, and where there is sufficient coordination between R&D and manufacturing, that the above occurs.

Thus, a worldwide functional division structure leads to different kinds of motivation and organizational behavior in the three functional areas. Even when considering the same subject, technology development, the goals and concerns of the functional areas are quite different. So are the expectancies of the different areas with regard to which organizational behaviors lead to the desired performances and outcomes associated with new technology development. These differences are great, primarily because the areas are so disconnected. And, most of this disconnection stems from the structure of the organization. Only at the strategic level does the worldwide functional structure facilitate some broad reconciliation of these different motivations and organizational behaviors. At the tactical levels of the organization they largely remain separated and different. As with coordination, this pattern of differing motivations fits strategies and environments that don't require the simultaneous interaction of the three functional areas. In the case of pharmaceuticals, the three areas sequentially contribute to the value added process (R&D develops a new product, manufacturing succeeds in manufacturing it, and marketing sells it). In pharmaceuticals, there is generally minimal overlap or simultaneity in this process, and this fits the low cross-functional coordination and different functional motivations associated with a worldwide functional division structure.

International division structure

Under an international division structure, all foreign operations (including any R&D or technology development) report in to country managers, who, in turn, report in to an international division HQ. The integration of foreign subsidiaries with each other and with parent country domestic operations occurs through this HQ. Since an international division structure tends to be associated with relatively small foreign operations, most formal R&D tends to reside in the parent country, where it primarily develops new technology for the needs of the parent country. To the extent that foreign technology development occurs, it is aimed at satisfying local country needs that differ from those of the parent country.

Under this structure, any technology development going on in a foreign subsidiary is fully coordinated with the other functional subunits of the subsidiary, principally marketing and manufacturing. In a pharmaceutical company, a local product development group would probably not attempt to develop a completely new drug for the local market (this capability and activity would probably be confined to the parent country). But it might well spend its time reformulating and modifying drugs that the parent company has developed or licensed so that they fit the unique needs of the local market (a different dosage or strength, a different method of delivery). Both formal and informal coordination between product development and marketing are high, since there is both physical and organizational closeness (both subunits report to the subsidiary general manager).

And even cognitive distance will be much closer than in the functional division structure, since here the product development group will identify with satisfying local market needs instead of more basic research objectives.

There might also be some process technology development activity in the subsidiary. Its focus would be on improving existing manufacturing processes and bringing in and modifying new process technology from other sites in the company. This group would have good formal and informal coordination with the local product development group and local manufacturing. Once again, there is physical and organizational closeness, and cognitive differences are not great. All of these subunits share the same goal of adapting and manufacturing products for the local market, and it is unlikely there will be major differences in understanding how to do this.

The level of coordination between subsidiaries can vary widely under an international division structure. Generally, for product-related matters like technology development, a high level of coordination is not directly facilitated by the structure. The strong local coordination discussed above tends to focus each subsidiary's behavior on its own national market, and this generally leads to differences between subsidiaries. If the international division HQ identifies opportunities to leverage technology development across subsidiaries, it may act to coordinate this activity. For example, it may attempt to monitor the various national needs for reformulating certain drugs and coordinate this work across the subsidiaries in order to eliminate duplication. In this instance, the HQ would have reduced the organizational distance between the subsidiaries for product technology development by setting up an HQ function to oversee this activity or set of organizational behaviors. Generally an international division HQ can't do this around too many activities, since it reduces the level of autonomy and coordination available within subsidiaries, and this will be resisted by country managers.

The level of coordination between foreign subsidiaries and technology development subunits in the domestic part of the company is extremely low. They are separated by physical and organizational distance, and even considerable cognitive distance. The latter, because domestic technology development is focused solely on the home market, which is often quite different from international markets in terms of technology requirements. This leads to domestic technology development subunits ignoring and being generally ignorant of international technology requirements, and international technology development subunits being rather autonomous and frequently taking the initiative to acquire their own new technology.

Thus, an international division structure best fits a strategy and competitive environment where the technology requirements of the company's international markets are different and less sophisticated than the requirements of the parent country market. Under such circumstances, there is no need for parent country technology subunits to learn anything from international operations. Furthermore, any technology that is transferred from the parent to international operations will tend to be mature, which means it will be well understood and relatively easy to transfer. Aside from exports, the international division structure would not support transferring leading edge technology between the parent's domestic technology development subunits and international operations. This generally contains more tacit knowledge and knowledge that is not fully debugged, and these require higher levels of informal coordination. The international division structure clearly supports technology development that varies from country to country and derives most of its value from fitting local country needs. The high level of cross-functional information processing that takes place between R&D, marketing, and manufacturing within a subsidiary, is the great advantage of this structure. This means that subsidiary strategies can be readily altered to fit changes in local environments. An example of a pharmaceutical strategy that relies on this would be one based on strong local proprietary brands of common drugs rather than leading edge prescription drugs. Here subsidiary technology development efforts would typically be directed at modifying technology, in close coordination with subsidiary marketing and manufacturing personnel, to exploit local market opportunities.

In terms of motivation, an international division structure will generally lead to different technology development goals and different expectancies about how to attain these goals at the subsidiary level. Similarly, the goals and expectancies of the parent's domestic technology development activities will tend to differ from those of the foreign subsidiaries. Under this structure, goals and expectancies are shaped more by the experiences and environment of the immediate organization than they are by the experiences and environment of the wider organization. This will motivate technology development behaviors that are locally oriented and not necessarily synergistic across the company. If for some reason the goals and expectancies related to technology development are similar across subsidiaries and with parent country operations, the international division structure is probably inappropriate. It will not naturally provide the integration that this situation invites. Consistent with the previous discussion, a consideration of motivation further fits the international division structure to strategies that primarily rest on local adaptation, with minimal synergy across countries.

Geographical region structure

Under a geographical region structure, all of a company's activities within a geographical region report in to the region's HQ. In most cases, these activities are first organized into national subsidiaries, which then report in to a regional HQ. Some activities, like R&D, might report direct to a regional head of R&D, or jointly to a subsidiary general manager and a regional head of R&D (under a matrix reporting relationship). In some cases, R&D might even be concentrated at a single regional site, with responsibility to support the national subsidiaries in the region. All of these configurations of technology development are consistent with a geographical region structure.

While coordination will vary some across these different configurations, there will generally be good coordination across technology development efforts within a region. There is organizational and some degree of physical closeness, and both facilitate formal and informal coordination between R&D subunits in the region and also coordination with regional marketing and manufacturing subunits. The greater the organizational and physical concentration of technology development within a region (a single regional center being the extreme case), the easier it will be to coordinate technology development within the region and, potentially, with technology development occurring in other regions. However, greater regional concentration hinders coordination between technology development and national marketing and manufacturing subunits. On the other hand, when technology development in a region is entirely dispersed to national subsidiaries, coordination with national marketing and manufacturing is facilitated while coordination at the regional level and between regions is hindered. But overall, a geographical region structure encourages such coordinating behaviors as the establishment of regional technology councils and integrated technology planning across subsidiaries.

A salient characteristic of the geographical region structure is poor coordination between regions. They are organizationally and physically distant, and this hinders both formal and informal coordination between regions. Since strategy, including technology strategy, is largely developed at the regional level, the only basis for integrating technology development across regions is by mutual agreement or some non-structural intervention by the parent HQ. Both of these tend to be rare, so most technology development has a regional rather than a global focus.

It is difficult to conceive of a technology development strategy for pharmaceuticals that fits a geographical region structure. The basic development of most prescription drugs has a global orientation, while the formulation and modification of branded, over-the-counter drugs to fit local markets tends to have a national focus. If there were more regional similarities in development requirements, a regional structure would fit, but current requirements appear to be largely global or national. If European integration were to produce similar requirements across countries (as it has for the registration of new drugs), it might ultimately encourage using a regional structure to manage the activities and behaviors that address these requirements. Other activities, such as those that develop new prescription drugs and those that formulate new versions of over-the-counter drugs, might be organized with structures that respectively have a global and a national focus. Such attempts to fit structure to a variety of different technology development strategies within a firm requires either a mixed structure (where different structures exist for different parts of the organization) or more vertical levels of structure (with different structures at different levels).

In terms of motivation, a geographical region structure in Europe might lead to such technology development goals as developing a well coordinated European testing and registration process for new drugs, and trying to modify and place existing drugs into as many of the region's national markets as possible. At the same time, it would probably hinder the region's participation in developing drugs that might be of considerable interest to other regions, but won't be manufactured or heavily marketed in Europe. Thus, a regional structure focuses behavior on regional goals at the expense of global or national goals. For this reason, it will probably only be selectively used by pharmaceutical companies to coordinate and motivate certain activities and behaviors.

Worldwide product division structure

Under a worldwide product division structure, foreign and domestic R&D subunits will report in to several different product division HQs. In some cases R&D sites may report in directly to the product division HQ, while in other cases they may first report to national product companies which then report to the worldwide product division HQ. In the first case, where all R&D sites report directly to a head of R&D within a worldwide product division HQ, both organizational and cognitive distances will be small within a product division. Consequently, there will tend to be good formal and informal coordination across R&D sites in a product division. Coordination with marketing and manufacturing, however, will largely occur at the product division HQ level. This tends to give technology development a global focus.

When the second case prevails and R&D activities report to national product companies, coordination among R&D sites can vary widely. While there is the potential for effective coordination across R&D sites within each product division, leadership from the product division HQ will generally be required for this to occur. This leadership reduces the organizational distance that has been created by having local R&D sites report through national product companies. Under this configuration, coordination between R&D and marketing and manufacturing at the national product company level is greatly increased, and technology development tends to have a national focus.

While technology development is coordinated within each product division, coordination between product divisions will tend to be poor. The divisions are organizationally distant and, if their technologies are very different, substantial cognitive distances can also exist. In the event that technologies are similar, a firm might want to encourage coordination of technology development across product divisions. Although cognitive distances may be small, it is unlikely that effective informal coordination will emerge, since organizational distance and the lack of formal coordination tend to leave individuals in different product divisions unfamiliar with each other and with no basis for initiating contact. A firm desiring such coordination under these circumstances would either have to add a functional matrix structure to formally connect R&D subunits across product divisions, or employ some non-structural information-processing mechanisms to achieve this coordination.

A worldwide product division structure best fits a strategy that has significant technological differences between product lines. In pharmaceuticals, this might involve prescription drugs, over-the-counter drugs, and veterinary products. Here technology development requirements differ between product lines, and the need for coordination largely lies within a product line. The poor coordination provided by this structure between product divisions is not a handicap. In this case the subject of information processing varies from one product division to the next, and the nature and style of information processing also varies. In the prescription drug division the coordination of technology development probably has a global focus, while in the over-the-counter drug division it may have a national focus. The worldwide product division structure can accommodate this kind of difference between business level strategies.

In terms of motivation, goals and expectancies about what behaviors contribute to their attainment are likely to vary significantly between product divisions that face different technological requirements. These differences in technology requirements, goals, and expectancies are very apparent between a prescription drug product division and an over-the-counter product division. They further impede information processing between product divisions, but facilitate the simultaneous implementation of several different business strategies within a company. If technology requirements are similar across product divisions, it might be advisable to remove technology development from the product division structure and organize it as a global function.

The above example illustrates the very different behavioral implications of the different types of MNC structure. Understanding structure at the level of formal and informal organizational behavior, and appreciating the fits and misfits that occur between this behavior and the critical characteristics of a firm's environment leads to a deeper and more conceptual understanding of the strategy–structure relationship.

Conclusion

In this chapter I have tried to further conceptualize the strategy–structure relationship in MNCs. By evaluating the implications of structure at the level of organizational behavior, one can see that formal organizational structure and its relationship to strategy is still important to the organizational functioning and performance of MNCs. Critics of this view have generally argued that formal structure is too blunt a mechanism for designing coordination, that the strategy–structure model leads to an overly mechanical view of how organizations function. And this may be true, if one employs the simple view of formal structure that is typically presented in strategy–structure research articles. But the strategy–structure relationship is more than some consistent associations between a structure and various elements of strategy. In large, complex organizations like MNCs, formal structure has significant implications for coordination and motivation. It shapes and influences large amounts of organizational behavior. This neither contradicts nor is contradicted by recent views of network behavior in organizations. In fact, at the level of organization behavior the two views can be combined and reconciled.

The strategy–structure perspective doesn't (or shouldn't) say that coordination only occurs through formal structure or hierarchy. As the costs of informal communication go down in organizations (including MNCs), this kind of coordination is likely to increase. Along with this there may be a reduction in formal communiqués and formal meetings. One may tend to see the former as evidence of a network organization developing and the latter as evidence of a decline in the use of formal organization. But one needs to be careful in how one conceptualizes this growing network of informal communication.

Proponents of a network view of organizations are generally vague in specifying what causes or shapes networks. Most often they assume that such networks are "all channel networks," where every subunit or person is directly connected to every other subunit or person in the network or organization. This kind of network clearly cuts across any divisions created by formal structure, and structure becomes irrelevant to communication and coordination.

In contrast to the above assumption, this chapter suggests that informal networks in MNCs are strongly influenced by formal structure and that they are likely to be partial or incomplete networks rather than all channel networks. By specifying organizational, cognitive, and physical distances between subunits of individuals, formal structure influences the type of informal communication networks that arise in an organization. As illustrated by the above applied example, one would expect that the configuration of informal communication networks surrounding technology development will vary significantly across different types of structure. Thus, the influence of formal structure goes well beyond its direct influence on formal communication. The need to fit strategy and structure is still important, even when network coordination and informal communication increase.

In order to reconcile traditional strategy–structure views of the MNC with network perspectives, however, models of the strategy–structure relationship need to be extended to include more of the behavioral implications of structure. This is an important task for the field to undertake. The potential to extend strategy–structure theory through additional empirical research is limited, unless deeper conceptualization precedes and underlies such research. From the other side, network models of the MNC are very incomplete if they ignore the influence of formal structure on organizational networks. If strategy–structure theory is not extended and reconciled with network models of the MNC, the field will largely replace the former with the latter, instead of integrating and cumulating relevant knowledge.

Part III

MANAGING HUMAN RESOURCES
ACROSS CULTURES

INTRODUCTION

We examine cross-cultural issues in human resource management in this section. The opening chapter by Chris Brewster, "Human Resource Practices in Multinational Companies," sets the stage with a broad review of some of the key issues in international human resource management (IHRM) and a research agenda. Brewster identifies several IHRM areas that have not been well researched, including IHRM in not-for-profit and non-government organizations; IHRM in small and medium-sized companies; IHRM and knowledge management; IHRM that does not involve US companies; and the broad area of differentiation versus integration of HRM practices. The bulk of the chapter addresses the last issue, differentiation and integration. Brewster points out a number of dimensions along which differentiation versus integration as strategic responses will vary, among them the structure of international operations; the MNE's home country; the availability of technology; the strength of institutions in host countries; and the MNE's experience of managing international operations. He comes to the conclusion that there is much we do not yet know about how IHRM practices vary across countries and enterprises. He goes on to highlight the notion of dualities (Evans and Doz, 1992) in which both integration and differentiation are accomplished simultaneously rather than one being the opposite of the other.

Brewster's discussion of the role of IHRM in knowledge transfer is important because so much tacit knowledge resides within human resources. If knowledge transfer is inefficient or ineffective, the enterprise is less competitive. When knowledge transfer must account for differences in culture and expectations, a difficult task becomes even more difficult. Brewster nicely points out that this is a critical area for future research.

The second chapter in this part, by Audia and Tams ("Goal Setting, Performance Appraisal, and Feedback across Cultures") is another comprehensive review of the literature. The authors examine numerous studies in some depth in the areas of goal setting, feedback, and performance appraisal, finding that culture tends to moderate the relationship between each of these and performance or satisfaction. They note that the

lack of research on performance appraisal across cultures is probably due to the fact
that performance appraisal itself violates cultural norms in some countries. Audia and
Tams interpret the extant research and develop a comprehensive research agenda going
forward. They note that the best and most comprehensive extant research has been
done in the area of cultural moderators of the relationship between goal setting and
various outcome variables (e.g., performance and goal commitment). Therefore the most
important work yet to be done is on the topics of feedback and performance appraisal,
with the obvious caveat that performance appraisal itself is counter-cultural in many
regions.

This chapter is an excellent review of the cross-cultural literature on goal setting,
feedback, and performance appraisal. The authors do an admirable job delineating an
appropriate research agenda for the future.

The last chapter in this part, by Mendenhall, Kühlmann, Stahl, and Osland ("Employee Development and Expatriate Assignments") is a comprehensive and coherent
review of expatriate adjustment research from many literatures. Its greatest value, apart
from the sheer catalog of research on the topic, is in integrating disparate literatures that
have developed in parallel. By informing one perspective with others, the authors
develop new understandings and a more complete theory of expatriate adjustment. The
authors identify four types of models – learning, stress and coping, developmental, and
personality – organizing their review under these four broad headings. They then
develop a very compelling discussion concerning the gaps in both theory and in empirical
research in the field, identifying ample opportunity for future scholarship. In particular,
they suggest that work is needed in clarifying the dependent variable(s) of interest; the
longitudinal process of acculturation; and the US-based ethnocentric bias of much of the
research.

The authors close with a practical discussion of international staffing and development
practices in MNCs and the need for better decision making concerning expatriate
assignments. This section of the chapter dovetails nicely with the Brewster chapter in that
the authors discuss the global vs. local issue implicitly. It also complements the Audia and
Tams chapter by covering hiring and development where Audia and Tams cover
performance appraisal and feedback. Finally, the authors bring the discussion back to
one dependent variable of interest – performance on the job. They discuss ways in which
MNCs can improve expatriate managers' performance through support on the job and
in their family lives.

These authors bring years of sophisticated research on the subject to this chapter.
Their review of the literature and explication of research agendas is first rate – a worthy
resource for researchers in the field.

These chapters are consistent with those in part II insofar as they identify the
institutions of a culture as a potential determinant of HRM practices and a moderator of
the relationship between HRM practices and outcomes. The Audia and Tams chapter
presents a compelling dilemma in cross-culture research. How do we research a phenomenon that is, itself, counter-cultural? How would we meaningfully research the role of
face-saving in US companies? Why would we want to? Face-saving is not culturally
central in the US. It is not recognized as a major employee motivator or important
consideration in HR practices. Research on goal setting in some non-US cultures would
have similar challenges. One important question raised by these chapters is, to what

extent can micro organizational practices be implemented uniformly and studied systematically? To what extent should they be implemented uniformly? We have evidence that HRM practices widely accepted in the US such as individual merit pay actually detract from work unit performance in countries whose cultures do not support meritocracy (e.g. Newman and Nollen, 1996). The authors in this part present us with intriguing possibilities about both the opportunities and the challenges of cross-cultural research in HRM.

7

Human Resource Practices in Multinational Companies

Chris Brewster

It is a truism to point out that the world is becoming more international. This applies to our technology, our travel, our economies, and our communications – if not always obviously to our understanding. In the economic sphere, foreign direct investment stock was worth over three trillion US dollars well before the end of the twentieth century and its growth in the final decade was more than twice that of national capital formation. The annual value of worldwide cross-border acquisitions and mergers increased every year of that final decade, reaching not only record totals, but a record rate of growth according to KPMG Corporate Finance. And this internationalization of production is, compared to the internationalization of the sale of goods and services, only a small part of the total amount of international trade. Furthermore, these economic measures of the internationalization of the economy ignore or underestimate the effects of the public sector and non-profit sector in internationalization. In the last few decades there has been an enormous growth in the influence of cross-border institutions such as the European Union (EU), NATFA and ASEAN; and in the influence of non-governmental organizations extending from churches and charities to scientific and sporting bodies.

In all these international organizations or multinational enterprises[1] (MNEs) human resource management (HRM) is a key to success; for the vast majority of organizations, the cost of the people who do the work is the largest single item of operating costs that can be controlled and adapted to circumstances. Increasingly, in the modern world the capabilities and the knowledge incorporated in an organization's human resources are *the* key to success. On both the cost and benefit sides of the equation, human resource management is crucial to the survival, performance and success of the enterprise. For international organizations, the additional complications of dealing with multicultural assumptions about the way people should be managed become important contributors to the chances of that success.

This chapter assesses our understanding of international HRM (IHRM). It argues that, as currently conceived, the subject ignores some of the recent developments in internationalization and that a new definition of IHRM is required. The chapter builds on critiques of existing studies, an exploration of the crucial issue of differentiation and integration, and the possibilities provided by the concept of knowledge management. Some practical examples of the options in terms of differentiation and integration in IHRM lead to a final section in which both a definition of IHRM incorporating these issues is proposed and a future research agenda is outlined.

UNDERSTANDING INTERNATIONAL HUMAN RESOURCE MANAGEMENT

Cultural differences and the need for cultural awareness come into the HRM literature through two routes: comparative human resource management and IHRM. The distinction between the two has been clearly made by Boxall (1995). *Comparative* human resource management explores the extent to which HRM differs between different countries (or occasionally between different areas within a country or different regions of the world such as North America, the Pacific Rim states, and Europe (Brewster and Larsen, 2000). *International* HRM, the subject of this chapter, examines the way in which international organizations manage their human resources in the different national contexts in which they operate. The international context adds extra complexity to the management of people beyond that found in a purely national setting. The organization managing people in different institutional, legal, and cultural circumstances has to be aware not only of what is allowed and not allowed in the different nations and regions of the world, but also of what makes for cost-effective management practices. The literature is replete with examples of home country practices that may be allowed in other countries, but which depress rather than improve productivity and effectiveness. Organizations addressing IHRM, therefore, have to deal not just with a variety of practices, but also with a range of policy and even strategy issues.

As a starting point, Schuler et al. (1993) offer an integrative framework for the study and understanding of strategic international human resource management (SIHRM). This goes beyond theories of strategic human resource management based in the domestic context and incorporates features unique to the international context (see also Sundaram and Black, 1992; Adler and Bartholomew, 1992). They define SIHRM as:

> human resource management issues, functions and policies and practices that result from the strategic activities of multinational enterprises and that impact on the international concerns and goals of those enterprises. (Schuler et al., 1993: 720)

These authors argue that the key determinant of effectiveness for MNEs is the extent to which their various operating units across the world balance two competing requirements. First, there is the need to be differentiated, to allow for the impact of local institutions and cultures on the effective operation of the organization. Simultaneously, there is a need to be integrated, controlled and coordinated so as to provide economies of scale and international learning (see also Punnett and Ricks, 1992; Ghoshal, 1987; Galbraith, 1987). This issue is developed further below, after the implications of the current approaches to IHRM have been examined.

It has been argued that existing definitions of IHRM tend to be limited and fail to distinguish the international aspect clearly enough. A more useful categorization might be "strategic HRM in MNEs" (de Cieri and Dowling, 1999: 307). Following these authors, we can identify a variety of theoretical perspectives which contribute to IHRM: institutionalism; resource dependency; transaction costs; strategic choice; behavioralism; and the resource-based theory of the firm. Much of this theorizing, and much of the original research on this topic, reflects a predominant North American influence, even though one of the originating texts in the field of IHRM was European (Torbiörn, 1982). This highlights an important issue in IHRM research in general: the hegemony of the USA. Because of the extensive influence of US multinationals and the power of the US academic tradition in defining the nature of research into HRM in general (Brewster, 1999), US researchers have had a defining influence on research into IHRM.

By far the largest amount of research into the topic is conducted in the USA and focused on US MNEs, and the US texts have tended to "set the agenda." This is changing as researchers recognize that international organizational experiences elsewhere predate even the establishment of the USA. There are now ever greater numbers of countries with substantial international organizations; and ever more internationally operating organizations which are not based in the USA. In some parts of the world, such as the Arab states and the Pacific region, the influence of locally based MNEs is becoming crucially important. And, of course, the EU experiment adds a different flavor to the concept of internationalization. One of the key missions of the EU, the dismantling of the barriers to the international movement of goods, labor and capital within Europe, has led to a substantial increase in cross-border trade in a region which was already well down that road. It is, therefore, unsurprising to note the extensive growth in the amount of research into IHRM now being conducted in Europe (Brewster and Scullion, 1997; Brewster and Harris, 1999).

However, our understanding of IHRM has not developed in line with the growth in practice. There is still much room for better understanding of successful HRM practices in an international context, as many researchers have argued (see, for example, Pucik, 1984; Dowling and Schuler, 1990; Laurent, 1986; Evans et al., 1989; Evans and Lorange, 1994; Hossain and Davis, 1989; Nedd et al., 1989; Shaw et al. 1990; Mendenhall and Oddou, 1991; Weber and Festing, 1991; Dowling et al., 1994; Scherm, 1995; Boxall, 1995). While it is recognized that the international HRM issues that have been researched are of practical importance to human resource managers, this work has been criticized as focusing too narrowly on functional activities and as lacking appropriate theoretical structures. (Kochan et al., 1992; Evans et al., 1989; Dowling and Schuler, 1990). The essence of their critique is that the current literature in IHRM defines the field too narrowly and is influenced by a discussion of concepts and issues with little backing in systematic research. Hence, they argue that a new field of IHRM studies should be built round a broader set of questions.

The majority of studies in IHRM have traditionally focused on expatriation: the cross-border assignments of employees that last for a significant period of time (see chapter 9). For many organizations and many commentators IHRM and expatriate management are virtually synonymous. This is understandable since expatriates are among the most expensive human resources in any internationally operating organization and they are almost invariably in crucial positions for the organization. They have, and their management involves, issues and problems that go beyond those of most other employees. And yet we know less about expatriates and the management of expatriates than we do about other employees. This expensive and critical group is often far from being well managed.

IHRM, however, covers a far broader spectrum than the management of expatriates. It involves the worldwide management of people. Several researchers have proposed detailed models of how IHRM fits into the overall globalization strategy of organizations (see, e.g., Heenan and Perlmutter, 1979; Adler and Ghadar, 1990; Doz and Prahalad, 1986; Milliman, von Glinow, and Nathan, 1991; Rozenzweig and Nohria, 1994; Schuler, Dowling, and de Cieri, 1993). The location of operations and the choices of how to staff them are critical issues for all international organizations. The complexity of HR decisions in the international sphere and the broad scope of its influence go far beyond the issue of expatriation, to an overall concern for managing people effectively on a global scale.

Arguably, the subject as defined heretofore tends to miss some key issues which are increasingly relevant as the degree and range of forms of globalization become ever greater. First, the literature has tended to overlook the most international organizations of all: the not-for-profit sector. This includes two general groups: the inter-governmental organizations (IGOs) and the international non-governmental organizations (NGOs). The former group will include bodies such as the United Nations and its 23 constituent agencies; the World Bank and the various international banks established and owned by differing combinations of national governments; the Organization for Economic Cooperation and Development; the North Atlantic Treaty Organization; the European Union and its varied agencies; and a plethora of others. The number, range, and scope of such organizations is extensive and is expanding rapidly. An even more rapid expansion is occurring amongst the NGOs. International churches, charities, trade union federations, bodies such as the International Standards Organization and international scientific associations, now operate in every country in the world and have more or less extensive international operations.

Many of these NGOs have the longest histories of internationalism found among any organizations. The Roman Catholic church, for example, might not use modern management terminology, but an argument could easily be made that it has been managing its human resources internationally for almost two thousand years. International activities by government diplomats have been conducted for over a thousand years in the case of some countries. Furthermore, the international NGOs are a significant engine of internationalism and are amongst the most international organizations in the world. Many of them have no "home base" country; employ people from more than a hundred countries; operate in several different official and, sometimes, unofficial, languages; and have to cope with genuinely multi-cultural workforces. However, they form something of an un-researched "black box" which does not appear in the IHRM literature.

The second area of internationalism ignored in much of the literature involves the increasing cross-border activities of small and medium-sized enterprises. In Europe, particularly, where many of the barriers to establishing operations and locating staff in other countries have been dismantled, there are now large numbers of organizations with only a handful or a few dozens of employees that nevertheless operate in a number of different countries (Matlay, 1997). The other major development in this area has been the development of e-business which has opened up international operations in many different areas (Coviello and Munro, 1997; Karagozoglu and Lindell, 1998). The internationalization of small and medium-sized enterprises and the consequent employment of staff in different countries have also tended to be below the visibility line as far as the IHRM literature is concerned.

DIFFERENTIATION AND INTEGRATION

There are other areas where the literature has been lacking: the management of international tasks through the use of agency, partner, or subcontracted workers; the increasing development of international business travel as a means of managing international operations; and the slow but steady extension of telecommunications mechanisms and teleconferencing as a way of coordinating activities (Brewster and Scullion, 1997). There is a need for an understanding of IHRM which covers all of these largely unexplored topics.

Such an understanding, if it is to be helpful for analytical purposes rather than just pointing to types of organization or process which have been neglected, needs to be built upon a core analytical concept. This chapter follows authorities such as Schuler et al. (1993); Punnett and Ricks (1992); Ghoshal (1987); and Galbraith (1987) in focusing on the tension between *differentiation and integration*, sometimes referred to as the "global *vs* local" dilemma as a defining characteristic of the international perspective on HRM. This understanding may need to be developed beyond this somewhat simplistic dichotomy (see below), but it encapsulates a number of key questions for all organizations operating internationally:

- ◆ What freedom does an international organization have in regard to imposing its own approaches to HRM on its operations throughout the world?
- ◆ How can an international organization aware of the need to be sympathetic to local cultures still ensure that it gains optimum value from its internationalism?
- ◆ What is the relationship between the strength of organizational culture and national cultures?

This section of this chapter focuses on this key issue, that is fundamentally linked to the discussions of national culture elsewhere in this book. It explores the somewhat simplistic nature of the dichotomy between differentiation and integration, examines the antecedents of decisions which tend to one or other end of the spectrum and then applies the concept to IHRM.

Current approaches to IHRM may tend towards different ends of the differentiation/ integration spectrum but few commentators, and even fewer practitioners, would argue that the issue is anything other than central to IHRM. Easy answers do not exist: the consultants' advice to "think global and act local" is a meaningless mantra when it is applied to practice. The issue still has to be teased out both theoretically and empirically. In all cases, sensitivity to which aspects of business practices in any particular country are emic (i.e. culture-specific aspects of concepts or behavior) and etic (i.e. culture common aspects) is regarded as essential to a strategic choice of HR levers. The question of the balance of emphasis between the national cultures and the organizational culture remains.

The choice of differentiated or integrated IHRM is an important one for the MNE. It will affect costs significantly: differentiated HRM can be less costly because there is less centralizing work for HQ, less monitoring, less international transfer of employees. However, it will lead to a looser and less integrated organization with much less learning across borders, as noted below. An integrated strategy will allow for standardization and international learning, but may be more costly.

Of course, presenting this choice as a dichotomy, whilst of analytical value, may not capture all the possibilities. Many international organizations are now divisionalized, with each division operating as a business unit and quite possibly following different strategies from those followed by other divisions within the same organization. Writers such as Hedlund, 1986; Bennis, 1992; Ghoshal and Bartlett, 1990; and Lorange and Roos, 1992, have highlighted the growth of complex dependency networks, federalization, global strategic alliances and loose coupled linkages, all of which confirm the variety of possibilities.

The dichotomy between integration and differentiation may therefore be too simplistic. Organizations may need to operate simultaneously at both ends of the spectrum. Evans and colleagues have termed this phenomenon "duality." The notion of "dualities" has been argued as being at the core of complex organizations, particularly applied to building an international competence (Evans and Doz, 1992; Evans and Genadry, 1999). Elsewhere these dualities have been termed dilemmas (Hampden-Turner, 1990), or dialectics (Mitroff and Linstone, 1993). Evans and his colleagues argue that HRM is a critically important tool for building dualistic properties into the firm. In terms of HRM, the key mechanism through which this can happen is layering, which involves building new capabilities and qualities into the organization's culture while reinforcing its past cultural strengths. An additional perspective would address the issues of building on the local cultures whilst generating and exploiting the economies of scale and compound learning that can arise from international integration. Organizations that are deeply layered often operate more informally than can be seen from an examination of rules, hierarchies, or management processes. Layering often occurs through the long-term development of key managers and professionals who are recruited for careers rather than short-term jobs and therefore the HRM functions of recruitment and selection, development, retention and reward management are vital regulators of this process.

Furthermore, however complex a view of the differentiation/integration dichotomy is taken, the debate is not necessarily resolved for any organization on a consistent basis. There may well be differences between functions with, for example, R&D being centralized or carried out in an International division whilst selling is localized (Forsgren and Pahlberg, 1992). Several researchers (Rosenzweig and Nohria, 1994; Kobayashi, 1982; DiMaggio and Powell, 1983) argue that although this tension between the pressures for internal consistency and local isomorphism affects all the organization's functions, it is in HRM that there will be the greatest tendency to adhere closely to local practices.

Despite the complexities which are subsumed by the differentiation/integration dichotomy, for most organizations it continues to have resonance; and for our purposes here it is a useful analytical tool, since it relates directly to issues of national culture vs. organizational culture. The importance of the differentiation/integration debate here is that differentiation tends to assume that national cultures are so strong that the organization will be most successful when it takes careful account of them, whilst integration assumes that a coherent and cohesive corporate culture is the source of advantage.

The tension between *differentiation* and *integration* results from the influence on IHRM of a wide variety of exogenous and endogenous factors. Exogenous factors include industry characteristics such as type of business and technology available, the nature of competitors, the extent of change and country/regional characteristics such as political, economic and socio-cultural conditions and legal requirements. Endogenous factors include the structure of international operations, the international orientation of the organization's headquarters, the competitive strategy being used, and the MNE's experience in managing international operations. Authorities such as Astley and Van de Ven (1983) have pointed out that organizational theorists vary in the degree to which they emphasize one end or the other of this scale.

These are more than academic concerns. For the organization, the many factors which influence the choice of "global vs. local" HR practices and policies means that there is a myriad ways in which dysfunctional or ineffective decisions can be taken; and perhaps a recognition that, in this immensely complex area, there may be no "right solutions." Rather, the organization may find an ongoing need to pay careful attention to organizational policies, and to be prepared continually to review them.

Various factors can be identified from the literature as being important in determining the extent of internal consistency or local isomorphism. These will include issues such as the sector, the market, resource flows, embeddedness in the local environment, organizational origin, and local environment. This list moves from those items that are, as it were, technical, to those which have a greater cultural resonance.

Thus, following Porter (1986), we would expect sectoral differences. There will, for example, be variation between the operations of private employment agencies tightly connected with local markets even when they are part of a global chain, and the internationally operating pharmaceutical industry. We would expect differences between the way retail banking and merchant banking operate in terms of their affinity to local practice. Where proximity to the market is a critical factor, there will be a pressure towards local autonomy (Dunning, 1993). A related issue concerns the nature of the industry, with greater local isomorphism in a multi-domestic industry as opposed to a global industry (Porter, 1986; Prahalad and Doz, 1987; Bartlett and Ghoshal, 1989b).

A second factor in determining the extent of internal consistency or local isomorphism is the strength of the flow of resources such as capital, information and people between the parent and the affiliate. Conglomerates, where the different businesses are in effect unconnected, are unlikely to have common management systems (Marginson et al., 1993). By contrast, where there are continual and critical transfers between headquarters and the subsidiaries or, in cross-border manufacturing, between the subsidiaries, then the need to maintain consistency becomes dominant.

A third factor concerns the degree to which an affiliate is embedded in the local environment. This refers to its method of founding and its age, as well as its size, its dependence on local inputs, and the degree of influence exerted on it from local institutions. Many organizations have operations that have been long established in a foreign country, are tied in to local networks of suppliers and outlets and are linked with local government. Locals there are often surprised to discover that they are not locally owned. It is unsurprising that in such circumstances, internationalization by acquisition often involves the acquiring company being limited in the degree to which it can impose common systems (Edwards et al., 1993; Newman and Nollen, 1998). Integration of HRM on greenfield sites of international organizations tends to be greater (Brooke and Remmers, 1970; Hamill, 1983; Bartlett and Ghoshal, 1989b).

Other factors, closer to the cultural issues that are the focus of this book, help to determine the extent of differentiation, including the parent organization's orientation to control (Dunning, 1993). Different organizations prefer different degrees of central control. There is also a country of origin factor in play here: some countries have a preference for uncertainty avoidance which is reflected in the organizations based in and originating from those countries (Hofstede, 1984). For example, Japanese companies and US companies are more likely than others to have close control from headquarters over their foreign operations (Bomers and Peterson, 1977; Hamill, 1983).

A linked factor relates to the differences between home and host country. These differences may be either institutional or cultural. The power of local educational, financial, legal, labor market, and political systems remains extensive, so that policies which ignore these issues would be futile (Whitley, 1992). Thus, certain kinds of operation may well be substantially influenced by local legislation or other local regulations (Rozenzweig and Nohria, 1994). The stronger the institutional framework, the fewer options the global company may have to impose their own approaches (Milkman, 1992; Gooderham et al., 1999). These approaches may also be shaped by strong local conventions, or by local cultures. Where these are clear and unequivocal, then the room for maneuver of the MNE is obviously restricted. The fact that the anti-union US company Toys-R-Us was forced to recognize trade unions before it could open in Sweden is a good example. Where the local cultures are less clear, more tolerant, or simply unfocused, then the MNE has more scope to import practices if it so wishes.

A further factor relates to the characteristics of the parent, including such elements as the home country culture and the degree of cultural distance from the local culture. Arguably, a high degree of distance between cultures might lead to more attempts to impose internal consistency as headquarters feels less comfortable with the possibilities of unknown approaches.

Evans and Lorange (1989) argue that in geocentric or global companies corporate culture is especially important. The social control mechanisms provided by corporate culture attempt to override, or to compensate for, the peculiarities of national culture. In this sense, the corporate culture is the glue that holds the organization together. Many of the processes which contribute to the development of this global corporate culture are HRM processes: corporate-wide training programmes, international transfer of employees, networking through both formal and informal meetings, etc. (Evans et al., 1989; Edstrom and Galbraith, 1977). Doz and Prahalad (1986) argued that what they call "subtle management processes" can assist in the maintenance of internal consistency: internal communication, corporate troubleshooting, corporate jamborees, and opportunities for global networking, have the effect of encouraging a global orientation.

Others, however, are more cautious. Laurent (1986), viewed the ability of even a strong corporate culture to overcome national cultures as "illusionary." His research among respondents from different European countries in one company found that the national cultures remained powerful. Within the organization there are subcultures and countercultures, there is abuse of rhetoric, and in the international organization, the power of the national cultures of the host territories. There will often be significant tensions where the corporate culture and the national cultures meet.

The dichotomy applied to IHRM

Attempts have been made to examine organizational stances on these issues of differentiation and integration in IHRM. An early, and influential, approach to linking these strategies to the attitudes and values of top management at headquarters was made by Heenan and Perlmutter (1979). They classified the options as ethnocentric, polycentric, regiocentric, and geocentric; and outlined how organizations could adapt their HRM approaches and practices to fit the external environment in which the firm operates, and its strategic intent. Ethnocentric organizations are those in which power is concentrated in the home country's headquarters; polycentric and regiocentric organizations are those in which power is delegated to and exercised by the subsidiaries at national or regional level; and geocentric organizations are those in which power is shared between the headquarters and the local subsidiaries with managers cooperating with each other in integrated operations.

Adler and Ghadar (1990) used this framework to suggest that organizations will need to follow very different IHRM policies and practices according to the relevant stage of international corporate evolution, which they identify as: domestic, international, multinational, and global. Evans and Lorange (1989), also using Perlmutter's categories for shaping HRM policy, identified two "logics": product-market logic and social-cultural logic. Under the product-market logic, different types of managers are needed for the various phases of the product lifecycle. Categories of managers are also split into "corporate," "divisional," and "business unit" levels, with different duties attributed to each category. Using the social-cultural logic, these authors suggest two alternative strategies for dealing with cultural and social diversity. The first strategy is labeled the global approach (Perlmutter's ethnocentrism or geocentrism) in which the company's own specific culture predominates and HRM is relatively centralized and standardized. Under the second strategy, the polycentric approach, responsibility for human resource management is decentralized and devolved to the subsidiaries.

Kobrin (1994) attempts to operationalize and test relationships between a geocentric managerial mindset, geographic scope and the structural and strategic characteristics of firms and industries. The Perlmutter (1969) definition of a geocentric mindset or strategy is contrasted with a multinational strategy, defined as a continuum. MNEs whose strategy is multidomestic or nationally responsive are at the multinational end of the continuum, while MNEs which are integrated transnationally are at the other, geocentric, end. Kobrin argues that a geocentric mindset is not necessarily always linked to a transnationally integrated strategy and/or a global organizational structure. He puts forward a tentative hypothesis that the need to transmit knowledge and information through the global network may lead, through increased interpersonal interaction, to organizational geocentrism in terms of attitudes and IHRM policies.

The Perlmutter categories have been critiqued on the grounds that they imply an evolution from earlier to later categories which may not be the case; that they imply, without evidence, that the earlier stages are less appropriate or effective; and that they give equal weight to the various categories when in practice the vast majority of organizations are clearly ethnocentric (Mayrhofer and Brewster, 1996). However, they remain a source of valuable theoretical analysis.

KNOWLEDGE MANAGEMENT AND TRANSFER

These attempts to encapsulate potential approaches to IHRM have not generally taken account of the more recent work on knowledge transfer within international organizations. The focus on knowledge transfer is a relatively new way of viewing HRM within MNEs. Of the three elements transferred within international organizations (product, capital, and knowledge), knowledge is the one most closely related to human resources: it is people who have the knowledge which is applied and transferred in the activities developed by the organization (Itami, 1987).

Knowledge has been defined as a recipe that specifies how to carry out activities. It may refer to input processes, such as purchasing skills, throughput processes like product design, or output processes such as marketing knowhow. Knowledge differs from information, which is simply a statement of facts (Kogut and Zander, 1993).

Knowledge can be distinguished as context specific vs. context generalizable; present vs. future focused; tacit vs. explicit; individual vs. collective; higher level vs. lower level; and generic vs. specific. These categories can be applied to IHRM.

The *context specific vs. context generalizable* variable, as applied to MNEs, is directly related to the fact that internationalization exposes the company to multiple markets in which different knowledge can be applied and can develop. Depending on its usefulness outside the location where it is developed, knowledge can be context specific or context generalizable. If it is confined to its place of origin, it is context specific. If it is effective in different countries, it is context generalizable (Taylor et al., 1996).

The distinction between *present vs. future focused* is encapsulated in the approach (see *Strategic Management Journal*, special issue 1996) whereby the organization focuses on internal analysis in order to identify, protect, and develop knowledge so as to attain a competitive advantage. This strategy is dictated by the organization's own knowledge. This firm-specific knowledge provides the company with a competitive advantage not just in the present, but also in the future (Dunning, 1980; Tallman and Fladmoe-Linquish, 1994). In addition to providing an opportunity to derive additional rents from existing knowledge, internationalization provides learning opportunities through exposure of the company to new cultures, ideas, experiences, etc., which can be used to create new expertise that complements and leverages its current knowledge.

The *tacit vs. explicit* distinction follows Polanyi (1962) who distinguished between them on the basis of the observation that "we can know more than we can tell." Explicit knowledge can be codified (expressed in words and numbers), and easily communicated and shared in the form of hard data, manuals, codified procedures, or universal principles. This knowledge can be readily transferred around the world, by information technology or telecommunications, but represents only the tip of the iceberg of the entire body of knowledge. Much, perhaps most, of our practical knowledge is of a tacit nature. Tacit knowledge is deeply rooted in the individual's experience and is only revealed through its application. Because it is not easily visible and expressible, it is difficult to communicate or to share with others. This explains, for example, the academically disparaged but widely practised training methods involved in "following the experienced employee" and the more recent, and more respectable, attention paid in the HRM literature to "mentoring."

Know-how can be *individual vs. collective* (Spender, 1996). Collective knowledge is associated with capabilities: what a group of people working together is capable of doing. According to Grant (1996b), collective knowledge is the outcome of knowledge integration: it is the product of the coordinated efforts of many individual specialists who possess different, but complementary, skills. Of course, both collective and individual knowledge can be explicit or tacit. Relevant examples of explicit collective knowledge (and hence a type of knowledge that can be objectified), are the established human resource practices (i.e. performance appraisal procedures, selection methods, etc.). On the contrary, the organization's culture is an example of tacit collective knowledge. It is something which is manifested in the practice of an organization, but which cannot be objectified.

The distinction between individual and collective knowledge is only the first step in an approximation of the knowledge structure in organizations. According to Grant (1995), knowledge is organized in a hierarchical structure: *higher level vs. lower level*. Some knowledge is very concrete and involves performing a certain task, whereas other knowledge is the integration of different types of expertise. Within the firm, specialized knowledge relating to individual tasks is integrated into broader functional knowledge: marketing knowledge, manufacturing knowledge, human resources knowledge, and the like. At the highest level of integration is knowledge that requires the integration of different types of functional expertise. For example, new product development knowledge usually requires the integration of many individual specialists in R&D, marketing, manufacturing, finance, and human resources. As a rule, in the most international of MNEs lower-level knowledge will be developed at local level and may only be applicable in that site or country. However, many MNEs do attempt to harness lower-level knowledge by extensive internal benchmarking operations. Higher-level knowledge will be developed at the headquarters or international level and the task then becomes one of assessing and arranging the extent to which it makes sense to transfer it.

Finally, here, and importantly for knowledge (as a firm's resource) to be a source of a sustainable competitive advantage, it has to be imperfectly mobile (Barney, 1991). Therefore we need to distinguish between *generic vs. specific knowledge*. Specific knowledge is less mobile than generic knowledge (Milgrom and Roberts, 1992). Generic knowledge is knowledge that can be applied in a wide variety of organizations (i.e. accounting expertise). On the contrary, specific knowledge has a high internal value but is of little value to third parties. An example of this type of knowledge is an employee who knows a digit of the code that opens the safe. This information is highly valuable when combined with the knowledge of other employees, but its value diminishes outside the organization. As a result, the person who possesses this knowledge will lose most of his or her relevant value upon abandoning the organization.

The knowledge transfer approach helps to explain some typical features of IHRM. Expatriates, employees on international assignments, have obvious potential for use as a knowledge transfer mechanism (Bonache and Brewster, forthcoming). International conferences of an MNE's staff in particular areas of the world, frequently traveling executives, teleconferencing and similar approaches can achieve some of the same effects in terms of knowledge transfer. Such mechanisms go some way to explaining why, in an era of ever more widespread, powerful, and cheaper information technology, there is an increasing reliance on expatriates (Scullion and Brewster, 1997). They also help to explain why, in spite of the fact that the success of assignments depends on factors other than technical competencies, expatriate selection tends to emphasize this criterion above all (Tung, 1981; Mendenhall and Oddou, 1985; Björkman and Gertsen, 1993). And the desire of the MNE to transfer knowledge also helps to explain why the basic source of expatriate recruitment is still located in the home country operation of the company itself (Torbiörn, 1982; Naumann, 1992; Mayrhofer and Brewster, 1996). Knowledge transfer is also part of the answer to the puzzle as to why expatriates are used even in markets where there is plenty of skilled labor (Boyacilliger, 1990). As Penrose states (1959), the capabilities of the company's management personnel necessarily establish a limit on company expansion in any given period of time.

The development of information and communication technology (ICT) will raise questions about both international transfers and international traveling. Video-conferencing is much cheaper than having people travel around the world, and undoubtedly there will in the future be more video-conferencing and more use of e-mail etc. This is where the distinction between explicit and tacit knowledge comes into play. Our understanding of negotiating skills, for example, tells us that it is more difficult to say "No" face to face than it is by fax or e-mail. In these circumstances, international travel by the sellers makes a lot of sense. And we all know that teamwork is better fostered by meetings than by even the best video-conferencing. Explicit knowledge can be transferred by a wide range of other mechanisms. The widespread use of mail and telephone, company reports and visits is now increasingly supplemented by real-time information technology (Suutari and Brewster, 1998). Given that expatriates and international travelers are very costly and difficult to manage, and that it is difficult to measure their contribution or value, there will be a pressure to use these much cheaper mechanisms wherever possible. Where, however, the organization is leveraging tacit knowledge, these expensive mechanisms will continue to be used.

Like other theories, the knowledge transfer approach to IHRM is explicitly a partial explanation of the international allocation of human resources and their transfer around the organizational system. As such, it is complementary to other theories. Other theorists, for example, have shown that international assignments are a mechanism for integrating local units (Edstrom and Galbraith, 1977). Or they put forward theories which explain how allowing very culturally distant subsidiaries a greater degree of local sensibility can be a mechanism for developing resource capabilities (Boyacilliger, 1990; Nohria and Ghoshal, 1994) and may be the result of bargaining rather than rationality (Forsgren et al., 1995). The knowledge transfer theory complements attempts to identify other variables that may influence the way the organization manages its human resources in the different countries, such as the company's stage of development and level of internationalization (Adler and Ghadar, 1990), or the company's international orientation (Perlmutter, 1969; Kobrin, 1994). Before attempting to link these notions to the concept of differentiation/integration, and outline the kinds of research that might develop from this wider approach to IHRM, it is worth examining some examples of the kinds of ways in which the differentiation/integration dichotomy is worked through in practice.

Choices In IHRM

The point has already been made that different management functions may have different degrees of differentiation within one MNE, with HRM generally being one of the most differentiated. Furthermore, within HRM some practices (pay, conditions, holidays, retirement arrangements, participation, and consultation) will be more constrained, and issues such as management development, less constrained. (Rosenzweig and Nohria (1984) see the order in which six key practices will most closely resemble local practices as: (1) time off, (2) benefits, (3) gender composition, (4) training, (5) executive bonus, and (6) participation.)

Many international organizations struggle with the issue of which elements of their human resource policies and practices can be centralized and which decentralized. This is linked to the ongoing debate in the literature about the extent to which MNEs bring new HRM practices into a country, in comparison to the extent to which they adapt their own practices to those of the local environment. Arguably, ethnocentric organizations are more likely to be HRM innovators in the foreign locations (Marginson et al., 1993) while polycentric organizations are more likely to adapt to the local environment (Evans and Lorange, 1989; Marginson, 1994). In practice, of course, there is always an interplay between the two and both factors apply to some degree; the question is one of degree. There is now considerable evidence that in HRM, MNEs will bring in new practices but are in general likely to conform to national practice (see, e.g.: DiMaggio and Powell, 1983; Maurice, Sellier, and Silvestre, 1986; Due, Madsen, and Jensen, 1991; Rosenzweig and Nohria, 1994; Hollingsworth and Boyer, 1997; Cleveland et al., 1999; Brewster, Morley, and Mayrhofer, 2000).

In this context, a key question underlying human resource practices in multinational enterprises is identifying what should be decided for the organization as a whole and what should be decided locally. At the extremes the arguments are clear: pay levels for locally recruited and employed staff are determined locally; management development systems for those selected as future organizational leaders should be worldwide.

Relevant pay rates within the local community will be unknown to specialists at the headquarters of the organization. They can only make such decisions by drawing on and then second-guessing the local specialists – a dysfunctional waste of resources. Paying people the same salaries wherever they work makes little sense in a world where living standards vary considerably between countries, though international intergovernmental organizations such as the United Nations are close to that position. Other MNEs may have levels of pay which vary considerably, but nonetheless develop worldwide policies, for example that the top quartile always include a performance related salary element, etc.).

On the other hand, the organization needs to retain the right to promote and encourage its best and brightest, beyond the local unit if necessary, wherever they are found. An organizational objective, common to many MNEs, of drawing on the very best talent available irrespective of country of origin, requires that the management development systems have some cross-border coherence. Identifying the best people in each country will be of maximum benefit if there is some way of comparing these individuals across countries. Here, too, reality is not as simple as this statement implies. For example, one very successful international bank, Citicorp, has a uniform system throughout the world. The company argues that this facilitates identification of the best wherever they are in the world: and its results would seem to suggest that they are good at it. Another, equally successful international bank, and a direct competitor, Hong Kong and Shanghai Banking Corporation, has different systems in different regions and countries, and compares leading individuals after they have been identified by these different systems. This company argues that the different cultural environments in which it operates mean that imposing a worldwide system would mean missing people who may not be brought forward by a uniform, and therefore probably culturally biased, system. And this company too has good people coming through at the senior levels.

Between these extremes there is much uncertainty and significant problems arise. A few examples will suffice to highlight the problems. Should there be a local performance assessment system, so that performance can be related to the local pay scales and take account of local cultures; or should the performance assessment system be international, so that it can identify likely future leaders wherever they are found in the organization? And, should the organization communicate with its employees individually or through trade union or representative structures?

Taking performance appraisal first, we have enough knowledge of the effects of culture to know that there is no easy answer to this question. The US-style performance appraisal process assumes that employees will work jointly with their boss to set targets, to assess their own performance, to comment on the extent to which their boss has helped them with achieving their targets – or made things more difficult for them. It also assumes that they will do much of this through a face-to-face interview. It is not likely that such performance appraisal systems will operate in the same way in many Eastern societies, where open responses to seniors are discouraged, where challenging the boss's expectations of what is possible would be seen as insubordination, where admitting faults amounts to a loss of face and where, for example, the idea of criticizing the boss's work in front of that boss would be seen as some sort of organizational suicide.

The organization will seek to ensure the objectives which appraisal is seen as meeting: encouraging improved performance, assessing career options and identifying training needs. But how to do this? The more the organization attempts to enforce a worldwide system, the more likely it is that managers will bend the system to their local requirements. Often this will involve exaggerated or incomplete reports or even reporting back on interviews that never in fact took place. Hence, what appears to be exactly comparable data may be very misleading. The more the organization is responsive to these cultural issues the less likely it is to have information which it can use to assess people across national boundaries.

The question of communication channels is complicated by national institutions. In Europe, for example, employers are required to recognize trade unions for collective bargaining in different circumstances in different countries: when certain thresholds (usually the existence of one or a certain number of union members among employees) are reached; when employees request it; or, exceptionally, when unions win ballots. In many European countries employers are required to establish and pay for employee representation committees which may have extensive powers, including, for example, the right to review appointments or to be consulted prior to major investment decisions. Of course, national laws and institutions are a reflection of and a support to national cultural values.

MNEs, therefore, have a series of decisions to make. Will they deal with the trade unions? Will they refuse to? Will they check the legislation carefully and do the minimum necessary to comply with the legislation? Or will they embrace the law and the purposes behind it on the grounds that such behavior will show them as a good citizen and that other MNEs in that country have been successful whilst adopting the local employment systems in full? Or will they allow individual countries (and, by extension, individual country management teams) to make their own decisions? What, in short, is to be the balance between the central organizational control and local country autonomy?

These examples show the power of the notion of differentiation/integration as one means of understanding IHRM, but the point has been made above that most definitions of IHRM do not refer directly to particular concepts and that new ideas such as knowledge transfer are often not included either.

CONCLUSION

We may therefore need to re-examine the definitions of IHRM, particularly in order to ensure a more consistent analysis of the approaches that international organizations are struggling with or developing. By defining IHRM as, for example, "the strategic, policy, and practical issues related to how MNEs of any type or size manage their human resources, including their approaches to balancing issues of differentiation and integration whilst enhancing the flow of knowledge transfer within the organization," we can focus on a potentially new research agenda.

Elements of this research agenda would include work on such matters as:

- IHRM in small and medium sized enterprises;
- IHRM in not-for-profit international organizations;
- the way that different organizations in similar circumstances attempt to balance the value of differentiation and national cultures in creating new knowledge; with the value of integration and the power of the overall organizational culture in enabling transfer of knowledge;
- alternatives to expatriation (frequent traveling executives, organizational conferences, teleconferencing, etc.) as a mechanism for knowledge transfer and integration;
- the effects of different HRM practices in different national cultures;
- IHRM and knowledge transfer in less standard organizational forms (joint ventures, partnerships, alliances, etc.).

The dualities identified by Evans and Doz (1992) and Evans and Genadry (1999) are a reflection of the complications involved in managing HRM generally and the extra level of complexity added by internationalism. The key paradox noted in this chapter, between the need for the organization to have HRM policies responsive to local national cultural demands and simultaneously to have the benefits of internationalization and economies of scale through leveraging organization-wide knowledge transfer, is a classic example of this complexity. There are unlikely to be exact or final answers to the questions raised by IHRM. However, the resolution of the paradox may lie in the learning process. The knowledge transfer perspective is useful in highlighting the fact that an advantage enjoyed by MNEs is their ability to learn from the range of ways of handling human resources available from the different cultures in which they operate. There are few organizations that would claim they have resolved the problems of ensuring that the messages concerning

HRM have been comprehensively transferred from headquarters to the subsidiary countries, and even fewer that would claim that the two-way learning process is effective. In sum, there is much to be done before we can ensure that the dual requirements of differentiation and integration are well understood and can be managed effectively in international human resource management, so that knowledge transfer can be leveraged effectively.

NOTE

1 One small, but important, point here concerns terminology. This chapter refers to multinational enterprises (MNEs) rather than multinational corporations (MNCs), since many of the points made here, and much of the discussion about the impact of cultures on these international organizations, will apply at least as strongly to the not-for-profit sector as to private organizations. Anyone who has spent time walking down the (usually lengthy!) corridors of any of the UN agencies, or the (usually less impressively appointed) corridors of the international charities, will understand that it is here that organizations are at their most multicultural. The research focus on the private sector has tended to ignore this crucial and growing aspect of internationalization.

8

Goal Setting, Performance Appraisal, and Feedback across Cultures

Pino G. Audia and Svenja Tams

Since the 1980s we have witnessed significant improvements in our understanding of goal setting, feedback, and performance appraisal – three critical processes in the regulation of behavior in organizations (Locke and Latham, 1990; Kluger and DeNisi, 1996; Ilgen, Barnes-Farrell, and McKellin, 1993). In this chapter we review research on these three processes across cultures. Early cross-cultural research was motivated primarily by a concern that managerial techniques and theoretical models developed in North America would not apply abroad (Hoftstede, 1980b). While we do not ignore this concern, we are also interested in discovering whether research across cultures has helped to enrich and refine existing theoretical models. Indeed, one important issue in theory development is identifying links between contextual variables, such as culture-related variables, and the central processes of a model.

In our review we adopt a wide definition of culture as the human-made part of the environment comprising objective elements – tools, roads, and appliances – and subjective elements – categories, associations, beliefs, attitudes, norms, roles, and values (Triandis, 1994b: 111). Virtually all research relevant to our review focuses on various subjective elements of culture. Our first step was to search the Social Sciences Citation Index for the period 1992 to 1999 and to review abstracts of articles from journals publishing research on organizational psychology and international management on the three topics of goal setting, feedback, and performance appraisal. Based on that initial search and a review of cross-cultural research by Erez and Earley (1993), we extended our search to articles published since the mid-1980s. Although we were primarily interested in cross-cultural research, we included descriptive accounts and single country studies if these provided a valuable contribution. First, we review research relevant to goal setting, feedback, and performance appraisal. Then, we conclude by outlining directions for future research in each area.

GOAL SETTING

The central tenet of goal theory is that specific, challenging goals lead to higher task performance than vague, "do your best" goals (Locke and Latham, 1990). The theory specifies four mechanisms that mediate the goal–performance relationship – direction, effort, persistence, and task strategies. It then identifies several variables that act as moderators, weakening or strengthening the goal–performance relationship. Among the most critical moderators are ability, goal commitment, and feedback. Low levels of any of these three factors weaken the positive effect of specific, challenging goals on task performance. Although the main focus of the theory is the effect of goals on performance, it examines also the factors affecting goal choice. These include factors affecting perceived performance capability – such as self-efficacy, ability, and past performance – and those affecting perceived desirability – such as group norms, mood, and values. Our review reveals that studies across cultures concerned mainly two issues relevant to goal theory: the influence of cultural values on goal commitment and goal choice.

Goal commitment

In a field experiment with two samples of workers from England and the United States, Earley (1986) examined the effect of two types of task-related information on performance, goal acceptance, and self-efficacy. He found that workers in England who received information from their shop steward performed better than those who received information from their supervisors. English workers' goal acceptance was also increased when they received information concerning the meaning of the job from shop stewards. In contrast, workers in the US responded equally well to information from both types of sources. Earley interpreted these findings as indicative of the British industrial environment being characterized by a high degree of power distance between labor and management. He concluded that the difference between English and American workers in goal acceptance was due to the greater trustworthiness and credibility English workers attributed to their in-group representative.

This first clue that cultural differences may affect goal commitment was subject to closer scrutiny in a study by Erez (1986). However, her study directed attention to the effect of different ways of setting goals. More precisely, Erez studied the effect of participative, delegative, and assigned goals across three Israeli sub-cultures: (1) the private sector – guided by utilitarian goals with no explicit policy of employee participation; (2) the Histadrut, which is the federation of most unions in Israel; and (3) the kibbutz sector – known for its strong collectivistic values. Performance differed significantly across the three sectors and was highest when goals were set without participation in the private sector, by a representative in the Histadrut, and through group participation in the kibbutz. Thus, these findings provide additional evidence that culture moderates goal commitment and, more specifically, that the effectiveness of group participation in goal setting over assigned goals is amplified among people with collectivistic values.

In a third study, Erez and Earley (1987) compared goal commitment and performance of US, Israeli–urban, and Israeli–kibbutz subjects. Again, the experimental study used three levels of participation (assigned, representative, and participative). The results show that performance of the Israeli students was significantly lower when goals were assigned to them than when goals were participatively set. In addition, Israeli students who were assigned goals performed significantly lower than their American counterparts. However, there were no significant differences between the Israeli and the American students when goals were participatively set. In essence, American subjects showed indifference to different levels of participation whereas Israeli students reacted adversely to the non-participatively assigned goals. Thus, this study lends further support to the moderating effect of culture.

Goal choice

Examinations of values and goal preferences are not uncommon in cross-cultural research. For example, Niles (1998) compared goals and means of achievement of individualistically oriented Australians and collectivistically oriented Sri Lankans. In contrast to the stronger collectivistic orientation towards family and social responsibility of Sri Lankans, Australians' achievement orientation was directed towards individualistic goals. Whereas both groups preferred individual achievement as a means of strengthening the work ethic and ranked external powerful influence similarly, family influence was among the most important achievement means for Sri Lankans compared to Australians who considered social support as more important.

Beyond their descriptive nature, studies linking culture and goal preferences may have significant practical implications for managing organizations located in a variety of cultural zones. Earley (1989) has shown that group members with collectivistic values are less likely to loaf than group members with individualistic values. He has also demonstrated that social loafing rarely occurs in collectivistic cultures like China but occurs more often in individualistic cultures like the United States. Earley suggests that the reason social loafing does not occur among collectivists is that they place group goals ahead of their own interests.

Consistent with this interpretation is a study by Erez and Somech (1996), which provides some indirect evidence of the effect of culturally based conceptions of the self on goal choice. Their experimental study of Israeli kibbutz members and managers from an urban area examines the effects of culture (independent and interdependent self-concept), goal-setting (difficult individual goal, difficult group goal, and do-your-best goal), and task phase (individual, pooled team, pooled task with communications, and pooled task with communications and economic incentive) on performance. Across both subcultures, the presence of specific and difficult goals, whether individual or group, reduced process loss from social loafing. However, people with an interdependent self-concept did not engage in social loafing even when they were not given group goals. Again, the most plausible explanation of this finding is that people with interdependent selves might have autonomously set group goals because they value contributing to the group.

Summary

The research by Erez (1986) and Erez and Earley (1987) provides some converging evidence that non-participative goal setting is less effective in cultures characterized by collectivistic values and low power distance. Importantly, rather than showing the inadequacy of goal theory, this cross-cultural evidence has actually helped to spur further theoretical developments. Drawing in part on this evidence, Locke, Latham, and Erez (1988) proposed a model of goal commitment, which significantly extended goal theory. Among other factors affecting the level of goal commitment, their model identifies variables that are highly variable across cultures such as authority and peer pressure. Thanks to this formulation it is now possible to integrate the role of culture in goal theory through its effect on some of these factors. For example, authority figures may increase goal commitment by assigning goals. But this effect is likely to be weaker in low power distance cultures characterized by lower deference to authority (i.e., low power distance), like Israel.

Although the relationship between culture and goal choice has received much less attention, two studies by Earley (1989) and Erez and Somech (1996) on social loafing suggest its importance. Both studies seem to indicate that this important organizational phenomenon is less likely to occur in collectivist cultures because collectivists naturally set for themselves group goals which act as an antidote to social loafing.

Feedback

Feedback, defined as any information from the task, others and the self about the outcome of task performance, complements goal setting since it provides information about the appropriateness or correctness of goal directed behavior (Ilgen, Fisher, and Taylor, 1979). Goals mediate the cognitive appraisal of feedback by determining its relevance and valence. Feedback itself provides people with knowledge about results without which they have difficulties in setting reasonable goals and appropriately adjusting effort, direction, and task strategies (Locke and Latham, 1990).

However, the feedback process is not limited to goal-relevant aspects. The feedback model guiding most empirical research is still that originally developed by Ilgen, Fisher, and Taylor (1979). Their model distinguishes several stages in the feedback process: perception, acceptance, desire to respond, intended response, and response. They identify characteristics of the source, characteristics of the message, and characteristics of the recipient as the most prominent factors affecting these stages. Perhaps the most important addition to this model came from a series of studies by Ashford and colleagues (e.g., Ashford and Cummings, 1983; Ashford, 1989) that shifted our understanding of feedback recipients from passive receivers to active seekers of feedback. Our review reveals that studies of feedback across cultures concerned mainly differences in how people respond to feedback and feedback-seeking behavior.

Responses to feedback

A study by Earley (1986) found that workers in England had greater trust in task-related information that was conveyed by shop stewards than by supervisors. In contrast, American workers made no difference between both sources of information. Although no individual-level measures of power distance were available, the findings seem to indicate that the greater social distance and distrust between workers and supervisors in the English industrial relations environment affected negatively feedback acceptance. In a subsequent study, Earley and Stubblebine (1989) compared the effect of positive feedback on performance between two samples of American and English workers. The American sample was characterized by a lower average power distance and a higher degree of uncertainty avoidance than the English sample. Both samples did not differ on the collectivism–individualism dimension. Positive feedback had a greater impact on performance of American than English workers. This provides some additional evidence that the cultural characteristics of power distance and uncertainty avoidance may moderate the effect of feedback on performance.

These findings remain limited to the effects of task-related information and positive feedback. Some indirect evidence on the moderating effect of culture on negative feedback acceptance comes from a cross-national study of responses to verbal insults (Bond, Wan, Leung, and Giacalone, 1985). Since the study does not report the content of the insult, it is hard to establish whether the insult could be seen as a form of negative feedback. Consequently, we interpret the findings of this study only as suggestive of possible relationships between culture and feedback acceptance. Chinese and American students were presented with a scenario describing the case of a business meeting involving the company president and members of two departments. The verbal insult was delivered either by a high-status source to a low-status target or vice versa. While Americans showed no significant differences across conditions in their responses to insults, Chinese perceived the insult from the high-status, in-group person as less illegitimate. Stronger collectivism and higher power distance among Chinese may make them also more receptive to negative feedback coming from in-group members, particularly those with high status.

Additional evidence on the effect of cultural values on responses to feedback comes from a study by McFarland and Buehler (1995) which examined responses to comparative feedback among North American students with different cultural heritages. The frog-pond effect – i.e. feeling better about oneself when performing highly relative to an unsuccessful peer group rather than when performing poorly in a successful group – was more pronounced among participants high in individualism, low in private collective esteem, and low on a positive perception of their social group. North American students with Asian, African, or Indian cultural backgrounds who were classified as collectivists, high in private collective esteem, and with a positive perception of their social group were less influenced by that type of feedback. The authors concluded that comparative feedback has different effects depending on the psychological closeness to one's comparison group. With increasing salience of collective identity, the group's overall performance is assimilated into one's self-identity in such a way that a superior peer group performance may compensate for low individual performance.

A study by Earley, Gibson, and Chen (1999) across three nations examined how individualism and collectivism affected people's responses to individual and group feedback. Their sample includes managers from one individualistic and two collectivistic cultures – American and Czech and Chinese, respectively. While individual feedback affected self-efficacy and individual-based performance beliefs and satisfaction for both individualists and collectivists, group feedback affected self-efficacy for collectivists but not for individualists. While lending support to the moderating role of culture in the feedback process, this study undermines the simplistic notion that individualists focus mainly on individual-based feedback and collectivists focus mainly on group-based feedback. Instead, it suggests a more complicated picture in which a collectivist's sense of self is based on personal as well as group-based information.

Finally, Brockner and Chen (1996) investigated whether culture moderates the well-established positive relationship between self-esteem and self-protection in response to negative feedback. More precisely, since that relationship was obtained in North America, a culture characterized by an independent construal of the self, their main hypothesis was that the link between self-esteem and self-protection would be weaker in cultures where people hold an interdependent self-construal of the self. Their study used a US sample and a People's Republic of China sample. Instead of limiting their analysis to a cross-national comparison, Brockner and Chen examined also the direct effect of individual self-conceptions. Essentially, their study confirms the positive relationship between self-esteem and self-protection in response to negative feedback for the US sample as a whole and shows that only the subset of participants from the PRC with more independent self-construal exhibited the same positive relationship. Importantly, the between-culture differences were attributable to self-construal since culture was no longer significant when self-construal was added. Thus, in addition to demonstrating that culture moderates the effect of self-esteem on people's responses to negative feedback, this study shows also the mediating effect of individual self-conceptions. As Brockner and Chen (1996: 613) observe, cultural background affects people's self-conceptions which in turn influence the impact of self-related variables on their cognition, affect, and motivation.

Feedback seeking behavior

Two studies shed some light on how culture may affect feedback seeking behaviors. Bailey, Chen, and Dou (1997) surveyed professional students in the US, Japan, and China and found clear differences in the feedback seeking behavior of Americans and Japanese. Japanese were more likely to seek failure feedback than Americans. Americans were more likely to desire success feedback. Chinese were likely to seek both success and failure feedback. Existing research suggests that ego-protection concerns and impression management influence the choice of the feedback seeking strategy (Northcraft and Ashford, 1990; Ashford and Tsui, 1991; Ashford and Northcraft, 1992; Morrison and Bies, 1991). The avoidance of failure feedback among Americans can be explained by individualists' greater concern for ego-protection. In contrast, stronger impression management concerns exist for individuals high in collectivism-orientation. The strong collectivistic norms and a concern for group harmony in Japanese culture may explain why Japanese may consider inappropriate the seeking of success feedback indicating individual excellence. The unexpected striving for success feedback among traditionally collectivist Chinese has been explained by the recent introduction of individual performance appraisal systems in the economy (Bailey et al., 1997) but warrants further study.

Since the amount of research in this domain is limited, we report results of a laboratory study and a survey both using US samples that address indirectly the influence of collectivistic and individualistic norms on feedback seeking. Lee (1997) examined the relationship between help-seeking behavior, individualistic-collectivistic norms, gender, and status. Like feedback seeking, help seeking is proactive behavior enacted to gain specific resources. The main difference between the two concepts lies in the fact that help seeking is focused toward solving specific problems, while feedback seeking behaviors are relevant even when no problems exist. For this reason help seeking is probably closest to seeking feedback when one is not performing well. In any case, we report these findings only as suggestive of potential relationships between culturally relevant norms and feedback seeking behaviors.

Although help seeking was higher in the equal-status condition than in the unequal-status condition, results were not statistically significant. There was no difference in help-seeking frequency between individualistic and collectivistic norm conditions which were operationalized through the use of rewards based on individual performance and group performance. However, males with collective norms sought more help than those with individualistic norms. Women did not differ in help seeking across both norms. Results of the survey show that there was more help seeking from equal-status others than from unequal-status others. Help seeking did not differ across the individualism and collectivism norm conditions but males sought more help than women in collective norms. Again, these findings were obtained using two culturally homogeneous samples. Moreover, the two studies did not measure cultural values at the individual level. Nonetheless, this evidence suggests that power distance and collectivism–individualism may affect the extent to which people engage in feedback-seeking behaviors across cultures.

Summary

At least four studies show some evidence that Hofstede's cultural dimensions affect people's receptiveness to feedback. Greater power distance seems to cause lower trust in the source which, in turn, causes lower acceptance of the feedback information (Earley, 1986). People high in collectivism and power distance seem also more receptive to harsh feedback when it comes from in-group, high-status members (Bond et al., 1985). Collectivists are also less receptive to the "frog pond effect" whereby people feel better when doing better in comparison to a poorly performing group than when doing poorly in comparison to a highly performing group (McFarland and Buehler, 1995). Finally, individualists are also less affected than collectivists by group feedback (Earley, Gibson, and Chen, 1999).

Notably, one study focused not on cultural dimensions but on how people conceive the self across cultures (Brockner and Chen, 1996; but see also Erez and Somech, 1996). Different self-construals affected people's response to feedback. Specifically, people with an interdependent self-concept and high self-esteem displayed less self-protection in response to negative feedback than people with an independent self and high self-esteem. Although we find only one cross-national study of feedback seeking, it reveals striking and unexpected differences which merit further investigation. While Americans were found to prefer success feedback while avoiding negative feedback and Japanese found to prefer negative feedback while avoiding success feedback, Chinese sought both success and failure feedback. Finally, a study of help seeking suggests potential relationships between power distance and collectivism–individualism and feedback seeking.

PERFORMANCE APPRAISAL

Research on performance appraisal focuses on the rater and the cognitive processes that may bias performance evaluations (Feldman, 1981; DeNisi, Cafferty, and Meglino, 1984; DeNisi and Williams, 1990). Summarizing other developments in the area of performance appraisal, Wexley and Klimosky (1994) noted that the content of appraisal has shifted from evaluations of ratee competencies to evaluations of outcomes and behavior. Moreover, increasingly attention has been given to how the characteristics of the manager–subordinate interaction affect appraisal. These include the quality of the dyadic relationship such as the in-group–out-group relationship, perceived similarities, perceptual congruence, closeness of supervision, race and sex differences, openness in communications to one another, and the managerial attribution process. Other factors affecting the performance appraisal process are the choice of the rater which may be based on characteristics such as rater competence and organizational position, features of the formal feedback interview including participation and self-review, and, finally, the use of appraisal information for promotion. More recently, research has examined the role of performance appraisal and impression management strategies in performance appraisal (e.g., Crant and Bateman, 1993; Taylor et al., 1995).

Although cross-cultural and international management scholars have cautioned against the inappropriate transfer of Western management techniques to other cultures (Adler, 1986; Erez and Earley, 1993; Hofstede, 1980b), we note a lack of empirical studies that examine the effectiveness of performance appraisal systems from a cross-cultural perspective. In the first part of this section, we review relevant empirical research. Our review includes one study examining the effect of collectivism-orientation on performance appraisal (Ramamoorthy and Carroll, 1998) and two studies on reward allocation (Chen, 1995; Chen, Meindl, and Hunt, 1997). In the second part of this section, we discuss research that suggests a relationship between cultural differences in communication styles and effectiveness of performance appraisal systems.

Performance appraisal systems

The focus on economic efficiency and market orientation has led to the introduction of merit-based promotion systems in former and reformed communist countries. There is, however, evidence indicating that cultural values cause deviation from Western models of performance appraisal. In China, for example, the Confucian tradition emphasizes hierarchical values which are often in conflict with not only the espoused collectivist values promoted by the communist system but also the recommended participative style of performance appraisal (Gu, 1990). Findings from a comparative study of HR practices in the USA, the People's Republic of China and Taiwan by Huo and Von Glinow (1995) suggest that due to the high power distance in China, managers tend to be reluctant to use two-way communications and counseling in performance appraisal. Also, participation by the employee and peer evaluation tend to be absent in performance appraisal.

Evidence for a stronger resistance to formal performance appraisal among collectivists has been presented by Ramamoorthy and Carroll (1998). They measured individualism and collectivism-orientation in their survey of 342 US students with some work experience. They obtained measures of competitiveness, solitary work preference, self-reliance, primacy of group interests, and supremacy of group goals. Specific dimensions of collectivistic orientation were related to aspects of the performance appraisal process. Competitiveness was related negatively to participation in goal setting. Supremacy of group goals, lower self-reliance and lower solitary work preference were related negatively to the desire for feedback. Supremacy of group goals and of group interest were related negatively to a desire for due process in appraisal discussions. The authors interpreted these findings as suggesting a lower preference for formal appraisal systems among collectivists.

Performance appraisal has multiple functions of which the setting of measurable goals and evaluation of results is only one. In addition, it provides the basis for long-term coaching and resource allocation. In this respect, two studies by Chen and colleagues indicated that employees from the US and the People's Republic of China use different criteria for reward allocation. In the first study, US and Chinese employees were asked to assume the role of a newly appointed president who had to evaluate the appropriateness of seven allocation rules for material, socio-emotional, and mixed rewards. Chen (1995) found that Chinese respondents preferred differential allocation rules (i.e., performance, rank, seniority, and job-related needs) for both material and socio-emotional rewards. In contrast, US employees preferred egalitarian (i.e., group equality, personal needs, and individual equality) rules for socio-emotional rewards and differential rules based on performance ratings for material rewards. The second study was similar. Chinese employees role-played a newly appointed president who had to evaluate the appropriateness of seven allocation rules and match these with seven reward types (Chen, Meindl, and Hunt, 1997). In addition, the degree of vertical and horizontal collectivism of individuals in the all-Chinese sample was measured (see Triandis, this volume). Vertical collectivism was positively related to support for reward allocation reform, which suggests a preference for formal appraisal among this group. Cultural values were stronger predictors of resistance to a particular reward allocation form rather than its endorsement. While vertical collectivism was negatively related to egalitarian preferences, horizontal collectivism was negatively related to differential preferences. Together these two studies suggest that cultural variables affect people's preferences among different performance appraisal systems.

The lack of cross-cultural studies testing the validity of the prevalent cognitive model of performance appraisals may be due in part to the fact that, unlike goal and feedback processes, the performance appraisal process as conceived in North America often violates basic cultural assumptions in other nations. The assumption underlying the North American performance appraisal process is that the setting and evaluation of performance goals facilitates the development of employees and serves as the basis for reward allocation. However, these functions of performance appraisal may be in conflict with the preferred communication style in many non-Western countries. For example, accounts of researchers from China, Russia, and India suggest limitations in the implementation of performance appraisal in these countries. The ambiguity characterizing communications among Chinese people and the modesty with regards to one's own ability (Lin, 1997) challenge a prerequisite of Western-style performance appraisal. The avoidance of open communication has been explained by the interest in self-protection from arbitrary abuse by those in power. According to Confucian philosophy, taking-the-middle-way means saying half of what one thinks. Ambiguity has become a cultural standard that allows respectful communication and is a sign of politeness toward those with more authority or seniority. Moreover, those with more power have no interest in revealing too much to their subordinates.

Based on a comparison of Russian and US managers, Elenkov (1998) argued that the reliance on political influence combined with lower individualism scores among Russians makes them less susceptible to direct feedback and goal setting. Instead, it is argued that performance feedback should be conveyed through an intermediary. In a review of research on management practice in India, Sinha (1994) attributed the lack of recent research on performance appraisal in India to the fact that Indian culture emphasizes relationships and loyalty over performance and efficiency. It does not encourage evaluating other people in terms of objective standards. Nandakumar (1985) observed that appraisers are easily swayed by appraisees' attempts to influence them. The appraisal system allows ambiguity and evaluation that is based more heavily on personal liking rather than performance. Customs clash with merit-based evaluation since recruitment serves obligations to family ties and promotions are based on seniority. A person and his or her performance are not separated and negative appraisal is perceived by employees as a sign of distrust on the side of the supervisor. As a consequence, appraisals tend to be framed in a positive way and there is little recognition for the value of corrective performance feedback (Sinha, 1997).

CONCLUSION

Clearly the major finding of our review of cross-cultural studies of performance appraisal is the lack of findings given the paucity of research on this topic. Perhaps the lack of cross-cultural studies using the prevalent cognitive models of performance appraisals may be due to the strong Western-based cultural-specificity of such models. Furthermore, the lack of research in this area may reflect the limited implementation of Western-type performance appraisal systems across cultures. This result seems consistent with the strong effects of culture on preferences for different performance appraisal systems emerging from the three studies included in our review.

Directions for future research

Leaving aside for a moment the content implications of the studies reviewed here, we note that cross-cultural investigations of behavior in organizations have become increasingly more sophisticated. We see a shift from the simplistic objective of discovering cross-national differences to a desire to understand the theoretical mechanisms explaining the moderating role of culture at the individual level. At the low end of this sophistication scale are cross-national studies that identify the influence of culture by simply comparing samples of subjects across nations. Typically, such studies provide post-hoc interpretations of cross-national differences invoking variations in Hofstede's cultural dimensions. At the high end of the sophistication scale are studies that seek to establish and explain relationships between cultural values (e.g., Earley, 1989) or, more recently, culturally based self-conceptions (e.g., Brockner and Chen, 1996; Erez and Somech, 1996) and behavioral outcomes. Such studies have begun to specify some of the theoretical mechanisms explaining the moderating role of culture. In our view, the contribution of contemporary cross-cultural research lies more in stimulating theory development than in simply testing the external validity of North American theories. In particular, this emphasis has raised our understanding of the effect of cultural variables both across nations and within the same nation (Brockner and Chen, 1996; McFarland and Buehler, 1995).

Going back to the content implications, our review suggests that the contributions made by cross-cultural research to the three areas of study vary dramatically. Cross-cultural research on goal setting obtained the highest return on effort. By clarifying the link between cultural variation and the effects of participation in goal setting, that research contributed to extending goal theory so as to include variables that are directly influenced by culture. However, the high impact of cross-cultural research on goal setting is the exception. Several studies have clarified the moderating role of culture on responses to feedback but the feedback literature has been relatively slow in integrating such cross-cultural evidence. This is probably explained by the fact that those studies, though relevant to the feedback process, were primarily concerned with other issues. Facing a different problem, research on performance appraisal has been plagued by a lack of attention to cross-cultural implications. Our review seems to suggest that one reason for such lack of attention is that, unlike theories of goal setting and feedback process, current models of performance appraisal are so imbued with North American values that they are not considered a reasonable object of investigation in many cultures.

Taking a closer look at each area, we now sketch some potential avenues for future research. As indicated above, currently goal theory specifies several variables that affect goal commitment. Future research could investigate how culture moderates the effect of these variables on goal commitment. For example, peer pressure is expected to affect positively goal commitment. However, this effect is likely to vary across cultures characterized by independent and interdependent self-conceptions because these affect how people acquire and process information. People with an independent self are less likely than their counterparts to seek and consider pressure cues coming from peers.

Another direction for future cross-cultural research on goal setting lies in exploring the link between cultural values and goal choice. For example, Triandis and Bhawuk (1997) propose that the dimensions of relatedness, interdependence and ranking, influence the choice of goals. They combine aspects of collectivism-individualism with horizontal (same self) and vertical (different self) orientation in a two-by-two typology and suggest a series of propositions relating cultural values to goals (see Triandis, this volume). In their view, collectivists will tend to have group goals that sacrifice group members' individual goals. However, whereas horizontal collectivists will expect all group members to share goals and to favor socially oriented achievement, vertical collectivists will expect group members to accept differences of goals among people. On the other hand, individualists are guided by individual preference rather than in-group goals. But while horizontal individualists will expect each group member to have unique goals, vertical individualists will expect some group members to select goals that will put other group members at a disadvantage.

In addition to exploring the effects of different conceptions of the self and cultural values, cross-cultural research might also examine the role of different self-regulatory modes. Oettingen (1997) suggests that cultures differ in the way they influence people to think about the future and that such cultural differences affect the kind of goals people set for themselves. Traditional societies direct action through ritual and myths. People tend to set distal goals but fail to decompose such goals in a series of proximal goals. This result is due to their inability to contrast a desired end state with the current reality. Conversely, modern societies guide individuals to create expectations and set goals through reflection on their history of personal success. In such societies self-regulation results from expectations based on the mental contrasting of positive images about the future with reflections on the current reality. Thus, people are capable of setting distal goals as well as proximal goals.

For future cross-cultural research on feedback, promising opportunities lie in using the independent vs. interdependent self-construal model proposed by Markus and Kitayama (1991). Their model provides rich and clear theoretical linkages between culturally based conceptions of the self and important processes such as acquisition and processing of information, and emotional and efficacy responses to performance feedback. Another promising research direction is the investigation of the effects of cultural differences between source and recipient. Such research could help integrate the rich literature on communication across cultures with the feedback literature. For example, one could investigate how the combination "collectivist feedback source" – "individualist feedback recipient" and its opposite affect the communication process.

Finally, future research on performance appraisal needs to stretch beyond examining the relevance of Western management practices to other cultures. Triandis and Bhawuk (1997), for example, suggested that performance appraisal may be neglected in collectivistic cultures if it conflicts with a preference for group harmony. In fact, in addition to characterizing interpersonal interaction in a social system, the concept of harmony incorporates regulatory and exchange principles. Likewise, the cultural dimension of shame versus guilt (Earley, 1997a) may also affect compatibility with the Western model of performance appraisal. Guilt and personal responsibility are emphasized in the Protestant ethic that permeates Western economic organization (Weber, 1958) and provide the foundation from which Western models of performance appraisal evolved. In guilt-based or more Westernized cultures, formal performance appraisal represents the organizational system of exchange regulation where both employee and manager agree on mutual obligations related to effort, compensation, and professional development. By contrast, in a shame-based culture, the individual may experience less control over the appraisal process and perceive formal appraisal solely as an organizational means to attribute negative consequences.

Fiske's conceptualization of social exchange rules may help researchers to verify the cultural relativity of different performance appraisal systems. Fiske (1990, 1992) suggests four different models of social exchange by which cultures structure the motivation, planning, evaluation and other aspects of social life that are similar to the Triandis framework (Triandis and Bhawuk, 1997). In communal sharing, people are treated as equivalent. In authority ranking, rules of exchange are based on hierarchical positions. In equality matching, people focus on imbalances in social exchange. Market pricing as the dominant rule in Western society is based on calculation of cost–benefit ratios. Using Fiske's typology, future research could investigate whether certain cultures that are incompatible with the Western formal appraisal system adopt alternative appraisal systems closer to their values. For example, cultures characterized by group harmony might adopt a performance appraisal system compatible with communal sharing rules of exchange.

In conclusion, our review suggests wide scope for further cross-cultural research that promises to advance our understanding of goal setting, feedback, and performance appraisal across cultures. Besides telling us whether we should transfer work practices across cultures, this research has the potential to expand current theoretical models of organizational behavior.

9

Employee Development and Expatriate Assignments

MARK E. MENDENHALL, TORSTEN M. KÜHLMANN,
GÜNTHER K. STAHL, AND JOYCE S. OSLAND

The expatriate adjustment research literature has grown enormously since the late 1970s, and the trend seems to be continuing unabated as the field moves into the new millennium. Thus, it seems both timely and prudent to pause and take stock of the nature of this growth and the implications that it holds for future research and practice in the field.

Those scholars who began conducting research on expatriate adjustment in the late 1970s and early 1980s (especially those in the field of human resource management and organizational behavior), find themselves, ironically, in a new, vastly different professional culture. They are no longer pioneers, but part of a worldwide cadre of scholars who are actively engaged in conducting research in the area of expatriate adjustment and international human resource management. However, despite this progress, challenges remain in the field.

It is an unfortunate fact that it is not uncommon for scholars who study expatriation from a human resource management perspective to be unaware of expatriate research that is being done by someone in another discipline, and vice versa. Scholars who research expatriate issues from the disciplines of anthropology, communication, human resource management, psychology, and sociology have few common journals in which to publish their findings and models; thus, scholars find homes for their research papers in the journals that reside in their major fields. This contributes to an unfortunate condition of the "right hand not knowing what the left hand is doing," since it is rare for scholars to seek out and read journals that are outside of their fields.

The field may technically be *multi*-disciplinary in nature, but it is not yet truly *inter*-disciplinary; the research findings that reside in separate disciplines remain, for the most part, in publication "silos" that do not lend themselves to integration between disciplines. Some scholars have informally discussed the necessity of a comprehensive review of the expatriate adjustment literature so that a collective sense regarding "what we know and what we don't know" about the phenomenon of expatriation can be developed. There seems to be a need for the important findings, theories, and patterns of knowledge about expatriation and repatriation to be warehoused in one place, so that scholars from a variety of disciplines can access the totality of information that is extant.

The purpose of this chapter is to take a first step in beginning to bridge this "awareness gap" in the field. We will attempt to concisely examine the theoretical literature of expatriate adjustment, and will then broadly summarize the general empirical findings in relationship to the field's theories. Additionally, this chapter will attempt to link the literature review to issues of application and practice, a dimension that has been lacking in previous review efforts.

Toward a Typology of Expatriate Adjustment Models

The initial context for theory-building efforts in the field, and the main motivation behind early theory-building efforts generally centered on the need to organize independent variables that atheoretical, empirical studies found were linked to various measures of expatriate adjustment. Using this approach as a foundation, over time theorists began to develop more conceptually and logically elaborate models based on theoretical assumptions.

In order to compare and contrast the various theories/models, a rough typology of models was developed, based upon the classification typologies of Kühlmann (1995a) and Stahl (1998); in this chapter we classify the theoretical models in the field in the broad categories of: (1) learning models; (2) stress-coping models; (3) developmental models; and (4) personality-based models. Some models in the field are "theoretical hybrids" that draw from multiple theoretical perspectives; these will be discussed within the categories to which we believe each one conceptually best fits. Also, the literature of cross-cultural communication theory will not be reviewed; though much of it arguably deals with some aspects of expatriate adjustment, it does not do so from the specific perspective of the expatriate, and often does not relate its constructs and findings to broader issues of adjustment. For an introduction to this literature, please see Samovar and Porter (1991).

Learning models

Some scholars who worked in the theory-development domain in the area of expatriate adjustment in the 1970s and early 1980s relied heavily upon extant psychological learning theories as foundations for their own model development efforts (David, 1971, 1972, 1976; Dinges, 1983; Guthrie, 1975, 1981). They made the assumption that since expatriate adjustment had to do with learning new skills and techniques of adaptation, it was logical to use constructs from learning theories in the field of psychology as foundational constructs for their own models.

Guthrie (1975) summarized these views when he stated that there were parallels between expatriates living overseas and extinction-produced aggression, changes in reinforcers, changes in secondary reinforcers, accidental reinforcement, and the reinforcement of novel behavior, and held that "it may be fruitful to look upon a second culture as a massive change in reinforcement contingencies" (1975: 112). The work of these scholars did not produce full-blown theories per se, but their research was grounded in the traditional propositions of behaviorism, albeit applied to the realm of expatriate adjustment. Their research approach laid the groundwork for later scholars' more comprehensive theory building efforts.

As the influence of Skinnerian behaviorism waned in psychological circles, neo-behaviorist theories, such as social learning theory (Bandura, 1977) emerged and the ideas inherent in these new models were applied by some scholars in the field to the problem of expatriate adjustment.

Bochner argued that "the major task facing a sojourner is not to adjust to a new culture, but to learn its salient characteristics". He focused on attempting to understand the processes of social skill acquisition within a new culture. He believed that focusing on adjustment issues tended to bias the researcher to view expatriate adjustment as some-thing that existed within the personality of the expatriate; that is, if the expatriate experienced failures overseas, such scholars deduced that the failure was probably due to some underlying pathology (Furnham and Bochner, 1982).

Bochner (1981) extended the social skills model of Argyle and Kendon (1967) to the study of expatriate adjustment. This model makes the assumption that socially unskilled people have simply not learned, for a variety of reasons, the social interaction norms of their home culture. The model, originally developed to explain socially unskilled behavior within a single culture envisions social interaction as a performance, and that difficulties arise when the actors cannot maintain a successful performance. Socially unskilled people manifest poor performance in being able to express their attitudes and emotions, exhibit proper body language, understand gazing patterns, carry out ritualized interpersonal routines (such as greeting others), and properly display assertion in social settings (Furnham and Bochner, 1982).

Furnham and Bochner (1982) argued that the above problems mirror those of expatriates, and thus asserted that the social skills model was a useful one for the study of expatriation. They also argued that the model has the benefit of not being tied to "hypothetical intrapsychic events . . . which are used as explanatory principles (Bochner, Lin, and McLeod, 1980) . . . [rather] its conclusions rest on information about how particular groups experience specific situations in particular host societies" (Furnham and Bochner, 1982: 167). Testable hypotheses can be derived from the model's primary proposition, namely, that the lack of requisite social skills determines the degree of culture shock experienced by an expatriate (Furnham and Bochner, 1982).

Black and Mendenhall (1990), and in another article with Gary Oddou (Black, Mendenhall, and Oddou, 1991), applied social learning theory (Bandura, 1977) to the study of expatriate adjustment. Like Bochner and Furnham, they argued that adjustment required that expatriates learn new roles, rules, and norms of social interaction. Extend-ing Bandura's ideas of social learning theory, they held that most new behaviors during an international assignment are acquired through observational–imitative learning. Ma-jor adjustment problems occur "because there is a high ratio of feedback to the individuals that they are exhibiting inappropriate behaviors relative to the new and appropriate behaviors they have learned, coupled with a low utilization of modeled and observed behaviors which are appropriate in the new culture" (Black and Mendenhall, 1991: 237).

Using principles inherent in social learning theory (attention, retention, reproduction, incentives, and expectancies), they argued that learning novel cross-cultural skills re-quired certain levels of rigor in training content, symbolic, and participative modeling processes, and training methods linked to these variables, and developed a theory-based, contingency framework for conceptualizing and designing cross-cultural training programs based on these ideas. In 1991, with Gary Oddou, they developed a more comprehensive framework of cross-cultural adjustment. In the development of this model, they reviewed the US domestic relocation literature and derived a domestic model from it; next, they reviewed the cross-cultural adjustment literature and developed a model from it. They combined these models into an integrative, comprehensive one of "international adjustment" and derived 19 propositions from this model, which in turn could each generate multiple research hypotheses. This model is a hybrid, in that it includes dimensions that come from the personality/trait literature, relocation/transition literature, and sense-making literature to name a few. An overarching theme, however, is that the rules and values of a new culture must be learned in order for adjustment to take place, which places their hybrid example perhaps most at home in the "learning models" category. Other theoretical contributions of this model include the notion of anticipatory adjustment, a multi-dimensional view of degree of adjustment, the inclusion of mode of adjustment as an influence on expatriate adjustment, and a clearer depiction of the dynamics and importance of task performance on the adjustment process (Black et al., 1991).

Nicholson, Stepina, and Hochwarter (1990), using ideas from cognitive psychology, proposed a social information-processing model of expatriate adjustment. While other learning-oriented scholars discussed the cognitive learning of new cultural norms by expatriates, these scholars attempted to delineate more carefully how such a process takes place. Nicholson et al. (1990) argued that people need new information for understanding another culture. Otherwise, they use their own culture information and scripts. These internal schematic scripts are our learned expectations as to what to do in such situations.

The model links the dynamics associated with these schematic scripts and relates them to the process of expatriation: selection through repatriation through subsequent promotion and assignment. It delineates positive and negative cognitive behavioral patterns associated with differing assignment outcomes. They argue that training should provide basic distilled conceptual patterns of schematic frameworks for social information processing in unfamiliar settings. Thus, in their view, the purpose of training is to provide a cognitive structural framework for understanding situations in the other culture and to assist expatriates in the development of a repertoire of cognitive and behavior schema and responses.

In general, the field of expatriate adjustment suffers from a paucity of research whose goal is to test specific theories. Much of the empirical research in the field is atheoretical or only tangentially theoretical in nature. The theories above that have seen the most emphasis in terms of theory-testing have been the social skills model and the Black, Mendenhall, and Oddou model. Nevertheless, the number of studies that have investigated these theories by testing their hypotheses is quite minimal.

Empirical studies that lend support directly to the social skills model have been conducted by Argyle, Furnham, and Graham (1981), and Furnham and Bochner (1982). However, numerous studies that did not specifically test the social skills model, yet whose findings corroborate it, can be mustered in its support (see Furnham and Bochner, 1982). Similarly, a number of studies can be marshaled to support the Black et al. (1991) model of international adjustment (Black, 1988; Black, 1990; Black and Gregersen, 1991a, 1991b; Black and Porter, 1991; Black and Stephens, 1989) and the number of other studies that corroborate, but do not explicitly test parts of the theory, are numerous as well (see Black et al., 1999; Selmer and Shiu, 1999).

An interesting implication of all of the learning-based cross-cultural adjustment theories is that the key to adjustment is for expatriates to learn the ways of the new culture to which they are assigned. A growing body of research has shown that cross-cultural skills training can be effective in facilitating adjustment to a foreign culture and in improving work performance abroad (Befus, 1988; Bhagat and Prien, 1996; Black and Mendenhall, 1990; Deshpande and Viswesvaran, 1992; Earley, 1987; Kealey and Protheroe, 1996), thus partially substantiating the claims of the above theorists, albeit in a roundabout way.

Stress-coping models

Based on the premise that the very act of living and working in a foreign culture can cause massive stress, a number of scholars have applied psychological stress-coping models to the study of expatriate adjustment (e.g., Befus, 1988; Barna, 1983; Coyle, 1988; Dyal and Dyal, 1981; Kühlmann, 1995a; Stahl, 1998; Walton, 1992; Weaver, 1986; Weissman and Furnham, 1987). Befus (1988), after reviewing the plethora of theories regarding the etiology of "culture shock," concluded that the feelings of anxiety, confusion, and disruption that often accompany culture shock may be most aptly described as individual reactions to stress. Unlike Oberg (1960) who defined culture shock as an illness, Befus views it as a normal stress reaction under conditions of uncertainty, information overload, and loss of control.

> Culture shock is an adjustment reaction syndrome caused by cumulative, multiple, and interactive stress in the intellectual, behavioral, emotional, and physiological levels of a person recently relocated to an unfamiliar culture, and is characterized by a variety of symptoms of psychological distress. (1988: 387)

Scholars normally limit culture shock to the initial period of transition and adjustment to a foreign culture; however, it can be argued that the dysfunctional behavior that expatriates frequently exhibit throughout their overseas assignment is also, at least, partly caused by acculturative stress.

In some of the early attempts to evaluate life changes as they relate to acculturative stress, scholars applied models and findings of the "Critical Life Event" research program to cross-cultural adjustment (Barna, 1983; Dyal and Dyal, 1981; Roskies, Iida-Miranda and Strobel, 1977; Spradley and Phillips, 1972). This view of the acculturative experience holds that any life change, whether positive or negative, is intrinsically stressful, in that it produces disequilibrium and requires adaptive reactions (see Ward, 1996, for a review of this line of research).

While there are many conceptual and methodological problems associated with the Critical Life Event approach, its application to the field of expatriation proved to be useful in quantifying the potential stress of living and working abroad. For example, Coyle (1988) used the Social Readjustment Rating Scale developed by Holmes and Rahe (1967) to demonstrate that the amount of change associated with moving to another country can be a potential 355 units – a score that, according to the author, reflects a 90 percent possibility of health breakdown if a person does not adapt quickly to the changes involved in relocation. However, few empirical studies using the Critical Life Event approach have thus far been reported in the field of sojourner adjustment, and correlations between the amount of life-change associated with relocation and physical or mental health were usually found to be weak (e.g., Roskies et al., 1977).

A more promising but related approach to the study of expatriate adjustment focuses on the chronic role strains that may result in continuing stress overseas (Dyal and Dyal, 1981). Role-theory approaches emphasize the fact that expatriate managers face various competing demands that make their role a very difficult one (e.g., of adjusting to the local cultural environment and, at the same time, maintaining a trusting relationship with the home office). As early as 1973, Yun noted that

> it is almost impossible for the managers to avoid role conflicts, since their role is built in such a way that it is easily vulnerable to potential conflicts ... The expatriate manager is a sandwich-man being trapped in between his own and foreign cultures, his own and host governments, and his office and his family. (1973: 105–6)

Yun (1973), Rahim (1983), and Torbiörn (1985) uncovered in their models the major relations between expatriate managers and different stakeholders in the home and host country, and demonstrated that expatriates must act as a connecting link between the various groups – a task that can create a chronic, intrapersonal conflict situation. Black, Mendenhall, and Oddou (1991), in their model of international adjustment, proposed that a high amount of role conflict and role ambiguity may have detrimental effects on the adjustment and effectiveness of expatriate managers.

Empirical findings support the basic premises underlying these models. Zeira and his colleagues (Harari and Zeira, 1974; Zeira, 1975; Zeira and Banai, 1984; Zeira and Harari, 1979) have demonstrated that the role set of expatriate managers is very complex because expatriates and their various stakeholders in the host and home country often have conflicting expectations of each other. A recent study found that role conflicts are among the most frequent and severe problems that expatriate managers encounter in their overseas assignments. They are also those problems that expatriates find most difficult to cope with – even more difficult than problems resulting from cross-cultural differences in managerial systems, work organization, and communication patterns (Stahl, 1998, 1999).

Findings of other studies indicate that role conflict and role ambiguity reduce adjustment, satisfaction, commitment to the parent company, and increase intent to leave the assignment early, while role clarity and role discretion positively affect criteria of adjustment and effectiveness of expatriate managers (Black, 1988; Black and Gregersen, 1990; Black and Gregersen, 1991; Gregersen and Black, 1992; Naumann, 1993).

While Critical Life Event and Role Theory approaches focus on the various stimuli, loads, or pressures that expatriates encounter overseas, other stress models emphasize the physiological reactions due to relocation. Barna (1983) applied Selye's (1974) stage model of the General Adaptation Syndrome to describe and explain the phases of expatriate adjustment: (1) the alarm reaction stage; (2) the stage of resistance; and (3) the stage of exhaustion. Barna hypothesized that the intense and prolonged physiological activation that is characteristic of individuals who are trying to adjust (or trying to resist adjustment) to an unfamiliar environment produces the symptoms of culture shock. Barna noted that,

> after several months of sustained excitation, reserve energy supplies become depleted, the person's "resistance is down" (the exhaustion stage of the General Adaptation Syndrome), and he or she consciously or unconsciously starts using protective mechanisms. These could be the perceptual or behavioral changes mentioned so often in the culture-shock literature. (1983: 29)

Barna's analysis also points to the dilemma that the most functional behaviors for cross-cultural adjustment, such as getting to know host nationals by joining their activities, learning the foreign language, exploring the unfamiliar surroundings, etc., are also those that are likely to bring about stress. Consequently, the effective management of stress, not stress avoidance, should be the goal of expatriate training. According to Barna, learning to recognize when one is under stress, arranging for privacy when one needs to relax, and taking a positive attitude towards events that cause stress are effective ways to prevent overstress (Barna, 1983).

Stress-coping approaches attempt to overcome the one-sided stimulus and response models that have dominated the early research on acculturative stress. Lazarus (Lazarus, 1980; Lazarus and Folkman, 1984), the leading scholar in research on stress and coping, emphasizes the fact that stress does not depend on the objective situation but upon how the individual subjectively evaluates the situation. *Coping* is defined as "efforts, both action-oriented and intrapsychic, to manage (i.e., master, tolerate, reduce, minimize) environmental and internal demands, and conflicts among them, which tax or exceed a person's resources" (Lazarus and Launier, 1978: 311). In contrast to much of the earlier research in the area of expatriate adjustment that relied upon psychological stress models, the coping paradigm suggests that expatriates are not passive agents over whom events unfold. Rather, managers in an international assignment are able to draw from a large repertoire of coping strategies, both open and intrapsychic, to regulate stressful emotions, bring situational problems under their control, and be proactive agents of change (Feldman and Thomas, 1992; Kühlmann, 1995a; Stahl, 1998; Tung, 1998).

The models of Ward (1996), Aycan (1997), and Kühlmann (1995a) draw heavily on the stress-coping model of Lazarus. Ward (1996) presented a model of the acculturation process that distinguishes between psychological and socio-cultural adjustment and in-cludes individual, situational, and societal predictors of adjustment. The model considers culture contact as a major life event that is characterized by stress, disorientation, and learning deficits and requires cognitive appraisal of the situation and behavioral, cogni-tive, and affective responses for stress management. Ward's model, however, is silent about how exactly individuals cope with the strains of living and working in a foreign culture.

Aycan's (1997) process model of expatriate acculturation partly fills this gap by including individual coping strategies as determinants of adjustment and performance. The model suggests that expatriate managers, depending on their appraisal of the foreign environment, employ a variety of coping processes, including search for social support and temporary withdrawal to "stability zones." Kühlmann (1995a) proposed a compre-hensive typology of strategies that individuals use in coping with the strains of living and working in a foreign culture. According to the model, the strategies that expatriates use in coping with the problems encountered overseas range from the very problem-focused to the very symptom-focused, from action-oriented to intrapsychic, and from person-oriented to situation-oriented behavior.

Stress-coping approaches have only relatively recently stimulated empirical research in the field of expatriate adjustment. Several studies found that coping is not a "one-strategy-for-each-person phenomenon" (Brislin, 1981: 277), as early research on expatriate adjustment suggested; on the contrary, it was shown that expatriate managers are able to draw from a large repertoire of coping strategies, both open and intrapsychic, to manage situational problems in their international assignments (Feldman and Thomas, 1992; Feldman and Tompson, 1993; Stahl, 1998; Tung, 1998). However, the findings of these studies also indicate that coping strategies of expatriate managers, albeit sometimes helpful in reducing the strains of living and working overseas, are often only moderately successful or even counter-productive in dealing with the problems encountered in an international assignment.

Other findings suggest that certain coping dispositions, that is, relatively stable behavioral tendencies in dealing with stressful encounters, discriminate between effective and ineffective expatriate managers; for example, cross-culturally effective expatriates have a stronger tendency towards planful problem-solving behavior, culture learning, relationship building, and conflict resolution, but a weaker disposition towards ethnocentrism, resignation, and withdrawal from the local culture (Stahl, 1998). Finally, research within the stress-coping framework produced evidence that stress-inoculation training can be effective in facilitating adjustment to a foreign culture (Befus, 1988; Walton, 1992).

Developmental models

Adler (1975, 1987) proposed a five-stage model of the transitional experience in a foreign culture, which he describes as an alternative view of culture shock. The stages are: contact–disintegration–reintegration–autonomy–independence. They represent movement from a state of low self- and cultural awareness to a state of high self- and cultural awareness. Another refinement of the culture shock model (Black and Mendenhall, 1991; Oberg, 1960; Ward, Okura, Kennedy, and Kojima, 1998), is Gudykunst and Kim's (Gudykunst and Kim, 1992; Kim, 1988, 1989; Kim and Ruben, 1988) "stress–adaptation–growth model of cross-cultural adaptation." Their model is based on the assumption that individuals are homeostatic and undertake adaptive activities only when environmental challenges threaten their internal equilibrium. This process, they argue, leads to cross-cultural adjustment and personal growth.

> Temporary disintegration is . . . the very basis for subsequent internal transformation and growth. When the environment continues to threaten internal conditions, individuals by necessity continue to strive to meet the challenge through their adaptive activities of acting on the environment as well as responding to it . . . This uniquely human adaptive capacity is reflected in increased knowledge, attitudes, and behavioral capacities. (Gudykunst and Kim, 1992: 251)

Both the Adler and Gudykunst and Kim models assume that contact with another culture causes individuals to psychologically disintegrate, regroup, and then attain a higher level of development and maturation. The stress–adaptation–growth model, with its emphasis upon recurring environmental demands for adaptation and growth, moves away from a linear conceptualization of stages that begin when expatriates enter another culture and end when they are fully adapted. As Pedersen noted, "Transformation occurs through a series of degeneration and regeneration events or crises in a nonregular and erratic movement of change. Part of this process is conscious and other parts more unconscious as the visitor seeks greater success in the host environment" (1995: 4).

This emphasis upon success, termed intercultural competence, is figural in Bennett's (1986, 1993) model of intercultural sensitivity. Created to help cross-cultural educators and trainers diagnose a learner's stage of development in dealing with cultural difference, this personal growth model was derived from extant intercultural communication theory as well as extensive practical experience. Bennett's model is represented by "a continuum of increasing sophistication in dealing with cultural difference, moving from ethnocentrism through stages of greater recognition and acceptance of difference, here termed 'ethnorelativism'" (1986: 2). The three ethnocentric stages are: denial, defense, and minimization; the three ethnorelative stages are acceptance, adaptation, and integration. Bennett and Hammer (Hammer, 1999) have developed an instrument to measure these stages of intercultural sensitivity; unfortunately, to date, none of the other personal growth theories have been operationalized to this degree.

Like Bennett, Osland (1995) formulated a phenomenological model based upon both theory and practical experience. In one of the few expatriate studies involving grounded theory and qualitative research, Osland analyzed the stories of returned expatriates and articulated a transformational model that describes the subjective experience of expatriates. She contends that the metaphor of the hero's adventure myth (Campbell, 1968) is a framework that captures the essence of the overseas experience for many expatriates and highlights the transformation that often occurs in the cross-cultural context. Like mythical heroes, many expatriates pass through these stages: "The Call to Adventure," "Crossing the First Threshold," "The Magical Friend" (cultural mentor), "The Road of Trials" (including the paradoxes inherent in life abroad), "The Ultimate Boon" (transformation), and "The Return." The hero's adventure metaphor makes no pretense of assigning time markers to each stage, because personal transformation is an unpredictable and nonlinear process (Mendenhall, 1999). Osland's model goes beyond adjustment, a more frequent focus in expatriate research, to underscore the importance of the broader concept of personal transformation.

All of these models assume that the cross-cultural experience can result in positive personal growth. Although the cross-cultural context is particularly fertile ground for personal development and transformation, however, not all expatriates take advantage of the opportunity for personal growth. Osland (in press) hypothesizes that some of the factors that influence this propensity are: reason for going overseas, personality, attitude, intercultural sensitivity, desire for personal growth, and motivation to succeed at work and become acculturated.

Research indicates that the strains of adjusting to a foreign culture may lay the groundwork for subsequent skill acquisition and personality development (Kealey, 1989; Ratiu, 1983; Ruben and Kealey, 1979). Kealey and Ruben (1983), based on empirical findings, argued that the persons who will ultimately be the most effective in adjusting to a foreign culture can be expected to undergo the most intense culture shock during transition. Apparently, "there is simply no way to derive the benefits of growth without the concomitant experiences of stress" (Kim and Ruben, 1988: 308).

Many expatriates consider personal growth and acquisition of cross-cultural skills as an important – perhaps the most important – outcome of their international assignments (Adler, 1981; Osland, 1995; Thomas, 1995). All but one of the expatriates in a qualitative study reported changing overseas and could readily identify how they had changed (Osland, 1995). However, cross-cultural contact through expatriation does not "automatically" result in better understanding, reduced stereotypes, higher empathy and improved cross-cultural skills, as is shown by tests of Amir's (1969) "contact hypothesis" (Amir, 1976; Brislin, 1981; Bochner, 1982).

Personality-based models/approaches

Historically one of the most prominent issues, which has been discussed in the field of expatriate research was the categorization of successful expatriates via their personality characteristics. The underlying concern was practical. Identifying the attitudes, traits, and skills that predict success as an expatriate would improve selection procedures as well as training practices. Since the 1960s a growing body of anecdotal, prescriptive, and research literature has focused on describing what it takes to be successful during an overseas assignment. Divergent lists of potential prerequisites for expatriate success have been generated. However, they lack comparability concerning terminology, conceptualization of success, bases for the deduction of characteristics, and configuration of samples (Spitzberg, 1989).

Kealey and Ruben (1983) conducted a thorough literature review on predictors of overseas success that had been published through 1981. Drawing on studies of Peace Corps volunteers, overseas businessmen, technical experts, and military personnel, they found evidence for a high degree of consensus among a set of predictors which include empathy, flexibility, tolerance, respect, interest in local culture, and technical skills. Although the results suggest the existence of a general "overseas type," who successfully copes with the challenges of an overseas assignment irrespective of country of sojourn, local culture, task, and organization characteristics, Kealey and Ruben (1983) declared that the relative contribution of any specific trait will depend on the environment and the task confronting the expatriate.

In a more recent appraisal of the search for personality characteristics, which predict overseas success, Kealey (1996) concluded, that the "research continues to replicate previous findings and thus confirms the validity of a set of general traits and skills needed to be successful in another culture" (1996: 84). Based upon the current state of research dealing with predictors of cross-cultural success of sojourner groups like foreign students, expatriate managers, and development workers, Kealey proposed the concept of the "model cross-cultural collaborator." This ideal type can be described by three categories of non-technical skills, all which are relevant to predicting success in an overseas assignment: (1) adaptation skills (e.g., flexibility, stress tolerance), (2) cross-cultural skills (e.g., realism, cultural sensitivity), and (3) partnership skills (e.g., openness to others, professional commitment).

This profile of skills is recommended as a guide to the selection process of international assignees as it summarizes the consensual findings of empirical research on personality characteristics needed for achieving overseas success. Nevertheless, the author continues to stress that the general profile has to be weighted according to the demands of the position, the organization, the host country, etc. (Kealey, 1996).

Two other attempts to organize the multitude of potential predictors of expatriate success in broader categories have been undertaken by Mendenhall and Oddou (1985), and Brislin (1981). Their comprehensive efforts to categorize the hodgepodge list of personality-based overseas success predictors resulted in a three- and a six-dimensional solution respectively, which show – despite their different terminologies – a consensus on the personality characteristics that can be accepted as valid predictors of overseas success.

In contrast to these inductive categorizations of personality-based predictors, Ones and Viswesvaran (1997) utilized the Five Factor Model of Personality (Big Five) from Costa and McCrae (1992) as an organizing framework. The majority of the personality variables that have been related to the success of expatriates can be conceptually linked, with high levels of interrater agreement, to the Big Five dimensions: emotional stability, extraversion, openness to experience, agreeableness, and conscientiousness. The largest number of personality-based determinants of overseas success fit into the "openness to experience" factor.

Ones and Viswesvaran (1997) demonstrated the theoretical fruitfulness of their approach by proposing and explaining specific relationships between Big Five factors and aspects of overseas job performance; however, these relationships require confirmation by future research studies. Another theoretically unresolved issue, the interaction of personality variables and situation characteristics in the process of overseas adjustment and performance, has gained comparatively less attention.

Brislin (1981) was one of the first authors who went a step beyond the traditional enumeration of personality-based predictors and vague references to moderating situational factors. In addition to the above-mentioned structure of personality factors predicting expatriate success, he examined the situations that may influence expatriates' adjustment and job performance. The 15 situational characteristics considered by Brislin include, among others, the time constraints of an overseas assignment, the complexity of tasks, and the presence of a role model. In spite of the detailed examination of potential influences from the expatriate's environment, specific interactive relationships between the person and situation factors outlined in his model have not yet been adequately delineated.

Kealey (1989) argued that personal as well as situational factors are relevant in explaining and predicting expatriate success. Personality characteristics and situational variables interact in the production of expatriate behavior and success. The person-specific perception, interpretation, and evaluation of the same overseas setting mediate this interaction. Some hybrid models of expatriate effectiveness (e.g., Black et al., 1991) elaborate the sets of person and situation variables by listing personality characteristics, task variables, organization characteristics, and national culture dimensions which are supposed to contribute to the expatriate's success. But such efforts have yielded a paucity of propositions that specify the dynamics and effects of interactions within and between the sets of success antecedents.

To date, only a small number of studies have focused on exploring *empirically* what it takes to be a successful expatriate. Most of the research continues to be predominantly cross-sectional in nature and to use self-report data obtained from interviews, surveys, and supervisor/human resource manager ratings (Dinges and Baldwin, 1996).

In response to criticism that most studies on the success factors of expatriates have been limited to US–international assignees and to one country of destination, Arthur and Bennett (1995) conducted a survey with a sample of more than 300 expatriates from 26 countries who were assigned to 43 countries. The participants had to assess the relative importance of personality characteristics that were perceived to contribute to the expatriate's success. A factor analysis of the responses identified five factors: "job knowledge and motivation," "relational skills," "flexibility/adaptability," "extra-cultural openness," and "family situation." The factor "family situation" ranked highest in the descending order of importance, a result that corroborates other research on international assignments (Black et al., 1999). In a reanalysis of their data, Arthur and Bennett (1997) used Campbell's (1990) theory of job performance as a framework and tested it against four alternative models of international assignee job performance. Results of confirmatory factor analysis indicated that an eight-factor solution showed the best fit to the data. The factors were labeled "flexibility," "family situation," "management/administration," "integrity," "effort," "tolerance," "cross-cultural interest," and "openness."

In addition to identifying the specific underlying dimensions of expatriate success, it is also important to try to assess the effect of success criteria on possible predictors of adjustment as well. Cui and Awa (1992) asked 70 business expatriates in China to rate the importance of 24 personality-based predictors in reference to cross-cultural adjustment and overseas job performance. The results suggest that cross-cultural adjustment and effective job requirements have different predictors and priorities. In adapting to a new culture traits like patience or flexibility play a more dominant role, whereas job performance requires more interpersonal skills (e.g., the ability to establish and maintain social relationships). A rather small number of studies have explored the influences of both personality characteristics and situational variables on the success of international assignments. For example, Kealey (1989) found that personal characteristics are more important in predicting overseas adjustment than situational variables.

In contrast, results of a study by Parker and McEvoy (1993) indicate that overseas work adjustment was mainly affected by organizational variables (e.g., compensation and career opportunities) whereas general living adjustment primarily was a function of person variables. This study investigated a model of intercultural adjustment comprising individual, organizational, and environmental factors by using data from 169 expatriates. Black and Gregersen (1991) similarly investigated the relationships among individual, job, organizational, and non-work predictors and three facets of cross-cultural adjustment. Person and situation characteristics appeared to show a complex pattern of relationship with the dimensions of cross-cultural adjustment.

Stahl (1998) explored the coping strategies of 120 German expatriates who were assigned to Japan and the US. The results show that both countries vary in the problems and conflicts they present for expatriates. Each class of stressful situation requires a specific set of coping activities that can be attributed to such personality traits as "the need to learn," "extraversion," and "empathy." However, the personality characteristics of successful expatriates in different countries and with different jobs showed little variance, a finding that supports the notion of a general overseas type.

FUTURE DIRECTIONS FOR SCHOLARS

In this section we will discuss the gaps that exist, both theoretically and empirically, in the field, and suggest some general strategies that scholars might consider in bridging these gaps.

Problems of operationalization

The dependent variable that has driven the theoretical work of the field has been alternately referred to as acculturation, adjustment, effectiveness, success, or satisfaction. Not only is there a lack of agreement regarding the overlaps and distinctions between these operationalizations, but there has been little, if any, argument by scholars regarding this issue (Thomas, 1998).

Furnham and Bochner (1986) stated that acculturation involves the integration of the foreign and home culture. Expatriate effectiveness is often implicitly based upon this definition of acculturation. However, the constructs of expatriate adjustment, adaptation, and acculturation are concepts that are usually used interchangeably by scholars. Adjustment is often implicitly defined by many scholars as a subjective report of the expatriates' satisfaction with different aspects of their sojourn. This trend began with the work of Lysgaard (1955).

It can be argued that acculturation is a prerequisite for job effectiveness, since it is difficult to imagine an international situation in which an expatriate could succeed without making any attempts to adapt to the local culture. Perhaps there are some types of jobs that require little acculturation and interaction with the host country culture. Acculturation may not automatically lead to effectiveness, but it is assumed by most scholars working in the field that it appears to be a prerequisite in some way for effectiveness to occur.

Many of the theories discussed in this chapter do not explicitly delineate the relationship between expatriate adjustment and subsequent job performance. Regarding the variable of expatriate performance, it is clear from the theoretical literature that there is no consensus in the field regarding a clear definition of this variable. In empirical studies it is generally measured by self-reports due to difficulty of getting superiors' ratings.

In the empirical literature, expatriate success is measured in terms of turnover, adjustment, or task performance (Thomas, 1998), the most frequent measure being turnover. Thus, success is frequently operationalized as intent to remain overseas for the time originally agreed upon by the expatriate and the company. Other turnover-related variables are organizational commitment and job satisfaction (Thomas, 1998).

Wilson and Dalton (1998) operationalize effectiveness as adjustment and job performance. They note the difficulty of constructing a valid measure of expatriate effectiveness since perceptions of effectiveness depend upon the point of view of various actors. Determination of expatriate effectiveness varies depending upon whose perspective is sought and the role played by attributions within the particular organization. A true picture of effectiveness may emerge only when one polls all those involved – the organization, the expatriate, his or her peers, host country and third country co-workers or subordinates, local government representatives, and the client/supplier network, in addition to sources of objective data. From a practical "data-collection standpoint," the use of subjects from a variety of organizations limits the operationalization of effectiveness to expatriate self-reports, the most common measure, and their recollection of the organization's evaluations of their work (Osland, 1990).

The challenge of operationalization of the dependent variable of expatriate effectiveness/success/adjustment/satisfaction is not a new one: Stoner, Aram, and Rubin described it well in 1972 and not much has changed since then:

> The problem of investigating the question of effective overseas performance is complicated by the shortage, in many studies and reports, of a satisfactory – or in some cases any – measure of performance, and by the problems of heterogeneous environments, heterogeneous yet small populations of subjects under study, and the failure to distinguish between chance relationships and those which are statistically significant. (1972: 304)

Paucity of longitudinal studies

Very few longitudinal studies exist in the literature, resulting in all the attendant methodological problems of cross-sectional analysis. However, a few exceptions to this trend exist.

A noteworthy longitudinal study was undertaken by Kealey (1989). Technical advisors of the Canadian International Development Agency were asked to assess several personality traits before their international assignments, and were asked to complete a survey of performance criteria during their sojourn as well. A statistical analysis of "winners" and "losers" identified a few personality characteristics that discriminated between these groups. The resulting profile of the effective technical advisor included characteristics which Kealey and Ruben (1983) and Kealey (1996) also identified as general predictors of expatriate success. Some characteristics that were found to discriminate in Kealey's (1983) longitudinal study were not included in his later development of the concept of the model cross-cultural collaborator.

Martin, Bradford, and Rohrlich (1995) used a modified expectancy violations model on 248 US students. The students described their expectations concerning 13 aspects of overseas living, pre- and post-sojourn. The findings indicated that: (1) sojourners consistently reported that expectations were met or positively violated; (2) fulfillment/violation of expectations was related to location of sojourn and somewhat to gender, but not to prior intercultural experience; and (3) there was a positive relationship between the violation of expectations and the overall evaluation of sojourn experience, supporting the expectancy violations model. Ward and her associates (Ward and Kennedy,1999; Ward et al., 1998), in two longitudinal studies, found that psychological and sociocultural adaptation challenges are generally greater in the early stages of an overseas sojourn and that they decrease over time. This pattern held for a variety of nationalities, with social difficulty decreasing over a year's time after the first few months of stay in the new culture.

The need is simple and concise: more scholars have to begin conducting longitudinal studies. The barriers to this course of action are obvious – money, time, access, and the pressure to publish now, not in the future. Nevertheless, the need remains.

Ethnocentric bias

Most empirical research in the field examines the expatriation process from a one-sided perspective, focusing solely on accounts of expatriate managers. Few empirical studies on expatriation have included the host country perspective. Notable exceptions are the studies of Zeira and his colleagues (e.g., Zeira and Banai, 1984, 1985), and of Sinangil and Ones (1997), who examined factors that host country stakeholders perceive to contribute to expatriate success. Selmer (1997) provides an in-depth view of the cultural context of both Swedes and Chinese and their cross-cultural similarities and differences. His book is a good example of cross-border research regarding what occurs when two diverse groups begin interacting with one another.

In order to avoid this common ethnocentric bias in expatriation research, it will be necessary to include the host country perspective in research designs. Scholars in the field need to do a better job systematically addressing the determinants, processes, and outcomes of expatriate effectiveness from a host country perspective. Such an approach causes complexity in the life of the social scientist—one must find multiple, new sample groups and wrestle with extricating the data from them in a way that preserves the validity of the data. However, until more scholars pursue this route, our understanding of the phenomenon will remain limited.

Further examination of paradoxes

The empirical research in the field of expatriation has produced a number of contradictory – or even paradoxical – findings that require further examination. For example, the variable of "culture novelty" (Black et al., 1991) refers to the notion that host countries that are culturally distant from the home country are harder to adjust to than less alien environments. Alternatively referred to as "cultural distance" (Stening, 1979), "cultural toughness" (Mendenhall and Oddou, 1985), and "culture barriers" (Torbiörn, 1987), the theoretical evidence intuitively and logically suggests that culture novelty is a determinant of expatriate adjustment. However, there is only mixed empirical support for the "culture novelty hypothesis."

While some studies support the culture novelty hypothesis (Black and Stephens, 1989; Furnham and Bochner, 1982; Parker and McEvoy, 1993; Stroh, Dennis, and Cramer, 1994; Torbiörn, 1982; Ward and Kennedy, 1992), other findings did not support the culture novelty hypothesis (Black and Gregersen, 1991; Janssens, 1995; Kealey, 1989; Parker and McEvoy, 1993; Selmer, in press; Takeuchi and Hannon, 1996). These contradictory findings suggest the need for further exploration of the mechanisms through which culture novelty influences the degree and the mode of expatriate adjustment (Thomas, 1998).

It has often been argued that previous experience in a foreign country will facilitate adjustment to a new expatriate environment (e.g., Brewster and Pickard, 1994; Church, 1982; Engelhard and Hein, 1996), and empirical studies have in fact found a positive relationship between previous overseas work experience and cross-cultural adjustment (Black, 1988; Parker and McEvoy, 1993). However, findings of a larger number of studies indicate that previous experience abroad does not affect, or can even negatively affect, expatriate adjustment and effectiveness (Black and Gregersen, 1991; Cui and Awa,

1992; Dunbar, 1992; Kumar and Steinmann, 1988; Pinder and Das, 1979; Stahl, 1998). Thus, the relationship between previous international experience and adjustment in a foreign assignment may be more complex than formerly thought. For example, in a study of technical advisors posted to developing countries, Kealey (1989) found that individuals with more experience abroad showed higher levels of satisfaction and higher self-ratings of effectiveness. However, Kealey also found in this study that previous experience did not correlate with job effectiveness as rated by peers or researchers. Altogether, the results of empirical studies indicate that "learning the ropes" in a foreign posting is a process that must begin anew after each assignment – a finding that seems to contradict common sense and, if validated, would have profound implications with respect to the human resource development function of international job assignments.

Empirical investigations on the effectiveness of cross-cultural training point to another interesting paradox. While research has generally produced strong empirical support for a positive relationship between pre-departure training and different criteria of adjustment (Bhagat and Prien, 1996; Bird, Heinbuch, Dunbar, and McNulty, 1993; Black and Mendenhall, 1990; Deshpande and Viswesvaran, 1992; Earley, 1987; Kealey and Protheroe, 1996), some studies found that cross-cultural training inhibited adjustment to a foreign culture (Black and Gregersen, 1991; Gregersen and Black, 1992). Gregersen and Black (1992) speculate that "the negative relationship may be a function of too little training, a false sense of security, or inaccurate information derived from it" (1992: 84).

Quantitative bias

To summarize the preceding section, empirical research in the field has produced a number of contradictory findings that require further examination of the processes through which expatriates adjust to living and working in a foreign culture. However, it seems unlikely that adjustment processes can be easily unearthed via the standardized survey questionnaires that empirical studies on expatriation have almost exclusively relied on in the past. Qualitative methodologies, such as in-depth interviews, naturalistic case studies, participant observation, and participant observation need to be employed in order to provide alternative data (Church, 1982; Kühlmann, 1995a; Mendenhall, 1999). If this is done, some of the aforementioned paradoxes may be dissolved. For example, qualitative interview data in a recent study on expatriation (Stahl, 1998) suggested that the unexpected negative relationship between previous overseas experience and cross-cultural adjustment that was found in a sample of German expatriates in Japan and the US was caused by a relatively high number of "corporate gypsies" who had already been posted to several other countries before their current assignment and who simply "refused" to adjust to yet another foreign culture. There are several examples of qualitative expatriate studies, some of which also employ quantitative methods and triangulation (Adler, 1987; Briody and Chrisman, 1991; Napier and Taylor, 1995; Osland, 1995; Selmer, 1997).

The need for model testing

Another serious gap in the field is the lack of model testing. Research on expatriation since the late 1970s shows that most of the empirical work in the field has been anecdotal or atheoretical in nature. The various models that have been developed to describe and explain the adjustment process in an expatriate assignment have not been adequately tested, and it is not uncommon that scholars develop new models without testing or building on previous models. This is unfortunate because the models that have been reported in this chapter not only integrate and organize the extant empirical findings in the field but also allow for the formulation of new, testable hypotheses. For example, Black, Mendenhall, and Oddou (1991) derived 19 testable propositions from their model of expatriate adjustment. These propositions include the relationship between variables such as individual skills and attitudes, HRM practices, aspects of the role set of expatriate managers, and various dimensions of cross-cultural adjustment. However, the number of empirical studies that have examined the postulated relationships is still limited. The same holds true for other models in the field such as those of Aycan (1997), Ones and Viswesvaran (1997), Parker and McEvoy (1993), and Ward (1996), whose propositions and hypotheses have not yet, or have only partially, been tested.

Alternative models and alternative paradigms

Mendenhall (1999) discussed the need to employ alternative paradigms in the study of expatriation in order to view the phenomenon from a more complete perspective. Traditionally, the scholars who have studied this field have employed research methodologies that have been created from the assumptions of logical positivism (Landis and Wasilewski, 1999; Mendenhall, 1999). He suggests that studying expatriation from the perspective of such paradigms as non-linear dynamics and hermeneutics, in addition to that of logical positivism, will provide a more comprehensive understanding of the phenomenon (Mendenhall and Macomber, 1997; Mendenhall, Macomber, Gregersen, and Cutright, 1998).

Scholars should also remember that expatriation is not a unique phenomenon of the late twentieth century. What can be learned – both good and ill – from the years of experience that many churches have gained from sending missionaries abroad? What did the merchants of the East India Company report about their intercultural encounters? How did the British Civil Service prepare its assignees for India? Perhaps there may be important insights to be gained by studying expatriate adjustment through the lenses of historical research methods.

It may also be fruitful if scholars were to consider creating contingency models that would delineate the impact of different environments and overseas tasks on the development of expatriates with specific personality backgrounds. There is an astonishing paucity of empirical research on the consequences of an overseas assignment in terms of competence building and personality development. Not every problem the expatriate encounters is culture-bound. Many problems have to do with parent–host company relations, family situations, climatology (e.g., sunlight deprivation), etc. It may be possible that current theoretical models of the expatriation process may concentrate too heavily on the issue of adjustment to the foreign culture.

To summarize, it is evident that despite the volume of research (both theoretical and empirical) on expatriate adjustment that has accumulated since the 1970s, the vistas for future research are open and invite further exploration. A great deal of the current work is prescriptive and lacks a sound empirical base. The empirical studies that have been conducted are often atheoretical in nature and do not explicitly test existing models. Many of the extant theoretical models are heavily influenced by the disciplinary affiliation of researchers and their country of origin; thus, the research in this field remains overall ethnocentric and monodisciplinary. To overcome these deficiencies more inter-disciplinary as well as international collaboration will be important. Such a collaboration would provide deeper insights into the dynamics of expatriation and would more thoroughly validate applications from such research for practitioners, who must deal with the complexities and strains associated with living and working overseas.

APPLYING THE MODELS TO IHRM FUNCTIONS

Great strides have been made over the past decades in the design of instruments to assist HR professionals in the selection, training, career planning, and reintegration of expatriates. Unfortunately, the progress that has been made in the acquisition of knowledge and the design of techniques necessary to improve the management of expatriates has not been paralleled by a similar improvement in IHRM policies and practices of MNCs. The following sections examine current IHRM practices as well as innovative approaches to expatriate management.

Recruitment and selection of expatriates

The effective recruitment of human resources in MNCs is a complex function that involves a number of staffing issues: executive nationality staffing policies, predictors of cross-cultural effectiveness, equal employment opportunity, recruitment of host-country nationals, etc. (Dowling, Welch, and Schuler, 1999). In most cases there are only a small number of candidates to choose from for an international assignment due to the specialized requirements of the job and the availability of personnel who are capable and willing to work abroad for an extended period of time. In particular, the widely held belief that career opportunities are better for those who stay at home where the decisions are made, i.e. at head office, makes it difficult for MNCs to recruit able managers for an overseas posting (Gertsen, 1990; Hamill, 1989; Tung, 1988).

This problem is further intensified by the fact that the goals that are usually associated with an international assignment, such as coordination and control, transfer of knowhow, and development of informal information networks (Edström and Galbraith, 1977; Tung and Miller, 1990), require recruitment of managers with an intimate knowledge of the company. This need for internal recruitment narrows the pool of candidates for an expatriate assignment. As a consequence, "the man chosen is often simply the man who happened to be there" (Torbiörn, 1982: 51).

A shortage of candidates may partly explain why international staffing practices hardly ever resemble the sophisticated selection processes proposed in the literature. A recent study conducted by Arthur Andersen Inc. (1999) found that only 26 percent of the surveyed companies had a strategic international staffing plan, and less than 15 percent had specific international assignment selection criteria and processes in place. The findings of another survey show that 94 percent of US companies hold line management responsible for assessing the suitability of international candidates, and 96 percent rate the technical requirements of a job as the most important selection criteria for international assignments (National Foreign Trade Council; see Swaak, 1995).

Although the roles of line management and of the HR function in international staffing processes vary across countries and industries (Black et al., 1999; Brewster, 1991), results of other surveys also indicate that MNCs base selection decisions for international assignments primarily on candidates' technical knowledge and past performance in the home country. This practice does not seem to have changed much since the 1970s, and it appears to be invariant across MNCs in different countries (Baker and Ivancevich, 1971; Baliga and Baker, 1985; Brewster, 1991; Gertsen, 1990; Hamill, 1989; Ivancevich, 1969; Marx, 1996; Miller, 1973; Tung, 1982; Wirth, 1992).

The international staffing problem is further intensified by the fact that most companies lack effective methods for selecting managers for overseas postings. The findings of several surveys show that US, European, and Japanese MNCs tend to rely on unstructured interviews and references from superiors when making international staffing decisions (Gertsen, 1990; Stahl, 1998; Swaak, 1995; Tung, 1982; Wirth, 1992). These instruments have been criticized for their low validity in predicting performance even within the domestic environment; as a basis for international selection decisions, their results may be totally misleading. Yet, the systematic utilization of selection procedures with higher predictive validity, such as biographical data questionnaires, structured interviews, and assessment centers, is virtually non-existent in MNCs. A study conducted by the National Foreign Trade Council (see Swaak, 1995) found that only 18 percent of the surveyed companies used structured interviews, 6 percent used psychological testing, and 2 percent had a formal assessment center. Black, Gregersen, and Mendenhall (1992), after reviewing current international selection practices, conclude that, "unfortunately, the short-term approach of most multinational firms leads them to rely on a limited set of criteria (technical skills) and the least reliable and valid selection methods" (1992: 72).

In summary, it appears that international selection processes vary little from those used for domestic assignments. In placing a heavy emphasis on technical qualification and past performance in the home country, HR professionals and line executives who are responsible for international selection decisions ignore the fact that success in a domestic operation does not necessarily guarantee a manager's effectiveness in a foreign environment. As has been mentioned in this chapter, empirical research has clearly demonstrated that extra-professional factors, such as interpersonal skills, communication competence, adaptability, and certain perceptual predispositions, are critical to the success of managers in an international assignment.

Improving international selection decisions

How can international selection decisions be improved? Effective methodologies to assist managers in the decision-making process have been discussed by several authors (e.g., Black et al., 1999; Kealey, 1996; Ronen, 1986; Tung, 1981). Kealey (1996: 100) suggests an integrated screening and selection system that includes three phases or components:

1 establishing the profile of skills and knowledge;
2 planning and implementing the selection procedures;
3 training and monitoring the overseas performance.

In selecting from a pool of candidates for an international assignment, individual qualifications have to be matched with the job requirements, cultural constraints, and the host organization environment. As Torbiörn (1982) has noted, "selection will be based on the candidates' own qualifications and merits, but these should always be viewed in light of what the overseas assignment will demand in each specific case" (1982: 46). It is obvious that positions such as chief executive officer or marketing manager of a foreign operation require more contact with the local community than others; without the ability to adjust to the foreign culture and to establish trusting relationships with host nationals, managers in such positions will not be able to achieve the various goals associated with their assignments. In contrast, managers occupying positions that require less interaction with the local community, such as financial analysts or technical "troubleshooters," may be able to perform successfully on their jobs without adjusting to the foreign culture and establishing close contacts with host nationals (Ronen, 1986; Tung, 1981). These examples illustrate that it is necessary to undertake a careful analysis of the job, organization, and host culture first, and then establish and prioritize the selection criteria according to the demands of the particular position.

After the demands of an overseas position have been identified, individual data must be collected that allow for the prediction of success or failure. While factors such as technical qualification and past performance in the home country can be easily evaluated by superior appraisals, as stated earlier in this chapter, the criteria that are predictive of success in an international assignment are difficult to measure. Nevertheless, some progress has been made over the past decade in the design of screening and selection techniques for overseas assignments (Black et al., 1999; Brown, 1987; Deller, 1997, 1999; Gertsen, 1990; Kealey, 1996; Kühlmann and Stahl, 1998; Ronen, 1986; Spreitzer, McCall, and Mahoney, 1997; Stahl, 1998, 2001). Specific instruments that have been developed for the selection of expatriates include:

- personality tests;
- biographical data questionnaires;
- structured interviews;
- behavioral assessment techniques.

The validity of these methods to predict the success of expatriate managers is still unknown. However, since instruments such as unstructured interviews or personality tests have proved to be of little use in evaluating the skills required for effective performance in an overseas assignment, the most promising avenue for improving international selection processes probably lies in the utilization of behavioral assessment techniques (Black et al., 1992; Gertsen, 1990; Mendenhall, Dunbar, and Oddou, 1987). Kealey (1996) summarized the benefits of behavioral assessment techniques when he noted that "the best predictor of behavior is behavior. What people say and what people do are often inconsistent" (1996: 97).

Before concluding the section on expatriate recruitment, two important issues deserve further attention. First, in order to avoid an ethnocentric bias in the selection of expatriates, it seems necessary to include the host country perspective in the decision process as well (Ronen, 1986; Sinangil and Ones, 1997; Zeira and Banai, 1985). Since in some cases, at least, the expectations of local stakeholders may differ from those of the corporate headquarters, selection criteria for an international assignment have to be compatible with the expectations of the host environment. Zeira and Banai (1984, 1985) advocate an "open-system approach" to the selection of expatriate managers that includes criteria such as cultural empathy, tactfulness, tolerance, and the ability to withstand pressures of conformity to the corporate headquarters' expectations when such pressures conflict with legitimate expectations of the host country organization. "This broadening of the spectrum would make it possible for MNCs to base the selection of their international executives on the expectations of the real environment in which EMs [expatriate managers] operate and with which they must cope" (Zeira and Banai, 1985: 37).

Another overlooked feature in the international selection process is the adaptability and support of the family. Although research has clearly demonstrated the importance of the family, particularly the spouse, to the success of an international assignment (Adler, 1997; Black and Stephens, 1989; Pellico and Stroh, 1997; Shaffer and Harrison, 1998; Torbiörn, 1982; Tung, 1981), the family is usually not included in the selection process. According to Brewster (1991), only 16 percent of European companies conduct interviews with the potential expatriate and spouse as part of the international screening process. Gertsen (1990) found that less than 10 percent of the surveyed companies interviewed the spouse because HR managers thought this was interfering with the employee's private life. However, Wirth (1992), in a survey of HR professionals in German MNCs, found that more and more spouses expect to be part of the selection process for an international assignment. If treated as a job counseling session, and if combined with a realistic preview of the living conditions overseas, potential expatriates and their families will probably benefit from such interviews, as long as they are conducted in a professional manner by well-trained HR managers (Black et al., 1999; Sieveking, Anchor, and Marston, 1981).

Training and development of expatriates

As expatriate assignments play an increasingly critical role in the execution of international business strategies and the development of global managers, the effective training of expatriates is of strategic importance to the overall success of MNCs. Despite the importance of expatriate assignments and the high costs associated with them, the findings of several surveys show that most companies provide either inadequate pre-departure preparation or no formal training at all (Baliga and Baker, 1985; Brewster, 1991; Forster, 1997; Gertsen, 1990; Marx, 1996; Stahl, 1998; Torbiörn, 1982; Tung, 1981, 1982; Tung and Arthur Andersen Inc., 1997; Wirth, 1992). While MNCs are generally helpful in arranging transport, housing, etc., and in preparing assignees for the requirements of their job, few expatriates are offered comprehensive training programs designed to enhance their understanding of the foreign culture and to improve cross-cultural skills.

Tung (1982) found evidence that European and Japanese MNCs were somewhat more conscious of the importance of cross-cultural training than US companies. However, a more recent survey of HR managers of European MNCs found that only 40 percent of the companies offered some kind of pre-departure preparation; of these companies, only half included an element of cultural orientation in their programs (Brewster, 1991). The picture looks even gloomier if expatriates are surveyed instead of HR managers who may, in some cases at least, tend to report inflated figures (Stahl, 1998).

In general, companies that do offer cross-cultural training programs provide preparation that is not comprehensive in nature. Most programs emphasize area orientation briefings and language acquisition but provide little training of cross-cultural skills (Dowling et al., 1994; Hiltrop and Janssens, 1990; Mendenhall et al., 1987). Also, the duration of most cross-cultural training programs is relatively short considering the amount of knowledge and skills that is needed in order to succeed in an international assignment – the majority of programs take one week or less (Baliga and Baker, 1985; Brewster, 1991). Besides, companies tend to not provide much follow-up training once the expatriate manager has been posted abroad (Mendenhall, 1999; Osland and Bird, in press). Finally, the spouses of expatriates are usually left out of whatever type of preparation is provided by the company (Black and Gregersen, 1991; De Cieri, Dowling, and Taylor, 1991; Torbiörn, 1982). For example, Black and Stephens (1989) found that over 90 percent of the firms in their study offered no pre-departure training for spouses.

In summary, then, little appears to be provided in the way of pre-departure preparation and in-country training for expatriate managers and their families. The main reasons of MNCs for not offering comprehensive training programs are (Baumgarten, 1995; Gertsen, 1990; Kühlmann, 2001; Mendenhall et al., 1987; Ronen, 1989; Tung, 1981):

♦ the belief that cross-cultural training programs are not effective or relevant;
♦ trainee dissatisfaction with training programs;
♦ time constraints prior to an international assignment;
♦ the trend toward employing local nationals in foreign subsidiaries;
♦ the costs involved in providing cross-cultural training;
♦ no perceived need for cross-cultural training on the part of top management.

The reluctance to provide comprehensive training for expatriate managers is akin to the general failure on the part of MNCs to commit efforts and resources to the development of global leadership skills. Based on the results of a survey of US *Fortune* 500 firms, Gregersen, Morrison, and Black (1998) found that most companies lack the quantity and quality of global leaders they need: 85 percent do not think they have an adequate number of globally competent executives, and 67 percent believe that their existing leaders need additional knowledge and skills before they meet needed capabilities. In spite of this, 92 percent of the firms report that they do *not* have comprehensive systems for developing global executives. Other studies have also found that MNCs frequently fail to bridge the gap between existing management resources and those necessary for meeting the challenges of a global business world (Arthur Andersen Inc., 1999; Edström and Lorange, 1984; Forster, 1997; Kopp, 1994; Tung and Miller, 1990).

Improving expatriate training and development

A growing body of research has shown that cross-cultural training can be effective in sensitizing individuals to cultural issues, in facilitating adjustment to a foreign culture, in improving work performance abroad, and in helping employees to develop a global mindset (Albert, 1983; Bhagat and Prien, 1996; Bird et al., 1993; Black and Mendenhall,

1990; Brewster and Pickard, 1994; Cushner and Landis, 1996; Deshpande and Viswesvaran, 1992; Earley, 1987; Kealey and Protheroe, 1996; Podsiadlowski and Spieß, 1996; Tung, 1982).

The methodologies available for training and development of expatriate managers can be classified into four categories on the basis of the approaches used and the content of the training (Gudykunst, Guzley, and Hammer, 1996; Gudykunst and Hammer, 1983):

1 *Didactic culture-general training*: Academic lectures on the influence of culture on behavior; cultural self-awareness training; culture-general assimilators.
2 *Experiential culture-general training*: Cross-cultural communication workshops; self-assessments; assignments to micro-cultures.
3 *Didactic culture-specific training*: Area orientation briefings; analysis of case studies; intercultural sensitizer training.
4 *Experiential culture-specific training*: Culture-specific simulations and role-plays; bi-cultural communication workshops; field trips in the host country.

Numerous kinds of training programs exist within each of these four categories (see Baumgarten, 1995; Bhawuk, 1990; Black and Mendenhall, 1990, 1991; Brislin, Landis, and Brandt, 1983; Gudykunst et al., 1996; Helmolt and Müller, 1993; Pusch, 1994; Ronen, 1989; Thomas, 1995) that can be differentiated according to degree of content rigor and participant involvement. Black and Mendenhall (1990) hypothesized that the required level of rigor of cross-cultural training depends upon the situational factors of the international assignment. In general, the greater the novelty of the host culture, the higher the degree of interaction with host nationals, and the greater the novelty of the job to be carried out, the more rigorous and participative the training method should be (Black and Mendenhall, 1990; Black et al., 1999).

How can the quality of expatriate training be improved? First, it seems necessary that cross-cultural training programs utilize multilevel approaches to stimulate learning processes in the cognitive, affective, and behavioral area. In addition to purely didactical or analytical approaches, a comprehensive training program should also include elements that foster experiential learning, such as role plays, negotiation simulations, and field experiences (Baumgarten, 1995; Kühlmann, 1995b; Mendenhall et al., 1987).

Second, it seems important that training is not seen as a one-shot remedy just prior to departure. Pre-departure programs can equip the expatriate with the basic knowledge and skills to "survive," but training has to be continued during the overseas assignment to help the expatriate cope with the difficulties encountered (Black et al., 1999; Grove and Torbiörn, 1985; Mendenhall and Stahl, 2000).

Third, since the success of an expatriate assignment depends not only on the expatriate himself/herself but also on the local people he/she has to work with, companies should train the host-country staff for cross-cultural interaction as well (Baumgarten, 1995; Dowling et al., 1994; Vance and Smith-Ring, 1994).

Fourth, some empirical studies show that a realistic job preview increases overall adjustment and overseas job performance (Feldman and Tompson, 1993; Stroh, Dennis, and Cramer, 1994). Providing the expatriate with accurate job expectations and a clear sense of what he/she is "getting into" seems to aid the adjustment process, and can easily be added as an element of expatriate training programs. Finally, as spouses often face more serious adjustment difficulties than the expatriates themselves do, they also have to be included in the training (Adler, 1997; Briody and Chrisman, 1991; De Cieri et al., 1991; Harvey, 1985; Osland, 1995).

Even a comprehensive cross-cultural training program such as the one described above is not likely to be effective unless it is part of an integrated international human resource development system. Since most of the determinants of expatriate success lie in the area of abilities, attitudes, and personality traits, they require development over an extended period of time (Baumgarten, 1995; Mendenhall, 2001). Companies need to identify the potential of managers for an international assignment early on in their careers and select those for development who have the required talent. Such an integrated, long-term approach to the career planning, selection, and development of expatriate managers is best viewed within the framework of global leadership development.

Within this framework, international transfers are viewed as maybe the most powerful strategy for developing global leaders (Adler and Bartholomew, 1992; Evans, Lank, and Farquhar, 1990; Gregersen et al., 1998; Mendenhall, 1999; Yeung and Ready, 1995). Consequently, the careful selection and training of expatriates is not only seen as a prerequisite for successfully accomplishing the task goals of an international assignment but also as a means for developing the human resources that are necessary for meeting the challenges of a global business world.

Ongoing support of expatriates and their families

In overseas assignments, expatriates and their families have to find ways to cope with the changes that the new job and foreign environment require. Even a thorough preparation for the assignment cannot entirely protect expatriates from adjustment troubles, confusion due to unexpected behavior, the experience of unpredictability, and the feeling of abandonment and isolation. International assignments often involve role conflicts between family and career or between home-country expectations and host-country job demands. It takes expatriates up to 12 months to feel comfortable in the new position abroad and in the foreign environment (Tung, 1998). Within this critical time frame the performance and well-being of expatriates (and their families) are affected (Black and Mendenhall, 1991; Church, 1982; Grove and Torbiörn, 1985). This suggests that MNCs should offer support to expatriates and their families not only in the preparation phase but also during the actual time abroad.

The main reasons why MNCs provide their expatriates with ongoing support are to (Fontaine, 1996; Schröder, 1995): (1) improve job performance, (2) support adjustment to the new living conditions and cultural environment, and (3) help maintain contact with the home country. The last two goals are valid for both expatriates and their families.

Improving job performance

Expatriates face the challenge that their style of working or managing varies from what the host-country colleagues are used to. To adjust the expatriates' behavior to their new work environment, companies provide skills-oriented support. Common practices include the following (Debrus, 1995; Fontaine, 1996; Harris and Moran, 1991): job training by predecessor from the home or host country; nomination of a mentor for the expatriate in the host company; continuing language education or performance appraisals during the assignment; and in-country coaching.

Performance appraisals have special significance, as their purpose is not only to increase performance in ongoing assignments but also to form the information base for career decisions after the return to the home country. But the appraisal systems used for expatriates by MNCs show several shortcomings – for example (Gregersen, Black, and Hite, 1995; Black, Gregersen, and Mendenhall, 1992; Harvey, 1997):

◆ The performance criteria do not incorporate the strategic goals of the assignment and the specific purposes for the appraisal (evaluation, development, compensation etc.).
◆ Performance criteria and standards are not tailored to the local context of the foreign assignment. Few MNCs take contextual influences (economic conditions, legal constraints, employee qualification etc.) into consideration when appraising the expatriate's performance.
◆ Expatriate appraisals tend to include a smaller number of raters than domestic appraisals. For the most part only local supervisors are involved, who may not be familiar with the unique aspects of international assignments.
◆ The majority of MNCs do not conduct expatriate performance appraisal more than once a year.

Harvey (1997) put together a comprehensive model of important issues that need to be taken into consideration when developing a performance appraisal system for expatriates. The model incorporates the purpose of the appraisal, the position characteristics, the environmental context of the ratee's performance, rater and ratee characteristics, the assessment criteria, and the process of appraisal itself. A more recent model by Tahvanainen (1998) depends upon the interaction of the following variables: nature of the job, organizational structure, standard performance management system, style and skills of the manager and employee, top management support, size of the company unit and maturity level of the company operations in the host country. She developed her contextual model of expatriate performance management based upon her analysis of the practices of 99 international companies operating in Finland, and upon her case study of Nokia Telecommunications. In these studies she found no significant differences in how the performance of expatriates and domestic employees is managed.

Adjustment to the living conditions and the cultural environment

The bulk of support instruments have traditionally focused on helping expatriates and their families to cope with the difficulties of living in foreign surroundings. A variety of instruments are being used:

◆ relocation service (assistance with passport, banking, tax, moving, and housing arrangements);
◆ designing an adequate salary including cost-of-living allowances, tax-equalization, take-over of rent payments etc.;
◆ easing access to social networks (clubs, charities);
◆ intercultural orientation and training during the assignment;

- ◆ spousal assistance for dual-career couples;
- ◆ counseling in personal or job-related crises.

More and more MNCs realize that the spouse plays an important role in the decision to accept an international assignment and for its success (Black and Stephens, 1989; Birdseye and Hill, 1995; Nicholson and Imaizumi, 1993, Black and Gregersen, 1991; Shaffer and Harrison, 1998). Moreover spouses suffer from more intense and prolonged adaptation difficulties than the assignees (Bird and Dunbar, 1991; Black et al., 1999; Black and Stephens, 1989; Briody and Chrisman, 1991; Brewster and Scullion, 1997; Torbiörn, 1982). As the number of dual-career couples continues to grow, MNCs not only have to develop programs that help spouses settle in a foreign environment but also have to address the professional concerns of spouses with pre-move employment status (Stephens and Black, 1991, De Cieri, Dowling, and Taylor, 1991). According to a survey undertaken by Pellico and Stroh (1997), corporate spousal assistance programs include providing help to obtain a work permit and find a position, career counseling, and assistance through attending courses to maintain or improve career-related skills.

MAINTAINING RELATIONSHIPS WITH THE HOME COUNTRY

An overseas assignment has a defined end. Expatriates will need and want to go home. Therefore, assignees as well as their families have to maintain their private and professional relationships within the home country. Staying in contact with the home country involves some extra effort due to the long time without face-to-face contact. Family ties and friendships fade away and the expatriate becomes forgotten in the home company while being abroad.

Therefore MNCs offer various services to foster existing relationship between expatriates and their home country/company. Commonly provided support includes (Wirth, 1992; Kendall, 1981; Blocklyn, 1989):

- ◆ mailing of professional journals and newspapers;
- ◆ information on personal and organizational changes within the home company;
- ◆ visits from HR managers;
- ◆ participation in continuing education programs in the home country;
- ◆ sponsorship of home leaves;
- ◆ nomination of a mentor within the home company.

The phrase "Out of sight, out of mind" describes the most important concern among expatriates (Adler, 1997; Horsch, 1995; Tung, 1988). Therefore, the nomination of a mentor in the home company is of specific relevance. A mentor who previously has worked in the host country and is familiar with the expatriate's job can reduce uncertainty by offering information and introducing the expatriates to colleagues in the host country. The mentor is the person of contact for all questions related to the parent company and keeps the expatriate informed about changes and developments while he and his family are overseas. Ideally, the mentor is a senior-level manager who has the connections and influence to find a suitable job for the returnee. In addition a mentor has to make sure that the expatriate's needs are taken into consideration in personnel decisions and that an adequate position is designed and kept free for him/her upon return. Actually, few companies provide a mentor to their outgoing expatriates (Black et al., 1999; Marx, 1996; Wirth, 1992).

Most MNCs provide support of some sort. However, the number and type of support activities varies across companies. Determining the appropriate organizational assistance for assignees and their families in adjusting to working and living abroad appears to be a subject that requires future research. Besides company assistance, social support is of great help for expatriates and their partners, although it may not be readily available for them in a new environment. Family members, friends, and co-workers can offer a variety of supports, not commonly provided by an expatriate's company (Adelman, 1988; Fontaine, 1996): guidance in all aspects of living abroad, validation of identity, reinforcement of confidence, feeling of being understood, senses of familiarity, intimacy. Therefore, MNCs should not only help to establish relationships with supporting groups of home-country and host-country nationals but also offer training to expatriates on how to build up social support on their own.

Repatriation

Coming home after an overseas assignment is often at least as stressful as adjustment to the conditions of working and living abroad (Martin, 1984; Adler, 1997). The reasons are manifold. Although many expatriates are guaranteed a continued employment after the completion of the assignment, the re-entry level and salary remains unspecified (Marx, 1996; Tung, 1997b; Price Waterhouse, 1997). As career advancement is a key motivation for accepting a foreign assignment, worries about the career development are common (Baughn, 1995; Gomez-Mejia and Balkin, 1987). Other frequently cited concerns for repatriates include the feeling that the company does not value their overseas experience and newly acquired skills, reduced job discretion, and difficulties to adapt to unexpected changes the home office and the home country have undergone during the stay-abroad course of the overseas assignment (Adler, 1997c; Black, Gregersen, and Mendenhall, 1992; Hammer, Hart, and Rogan, 1998). In addition to the problems expatriates themselves are experiencing, other family members may be grappling with readjustment difficulties.

Problems with re-entry lead to substantial dissatisfaction and turnover among repatriates during the first years after repatriation (Harvey, 1989; Stroh, Gregersen, and Black, 1998; Price Waterhouse, 1997). Finding suitable positions for repatriates is a significant problem for MNCs, that has been exacerbated by the recent trends of downsizing, delayering, and outsourcing of operations in domestic companies. As a consequence, MNCs are facing an increasing reluctance among candidates to accept international assignments. While there is increasing recognition of the importance of selection and development of international assignees among MNCs, there is little consideration of the problematic nature of their repatriation (The Conference Board, 1996; Caligiuri and Lazarova, 2001). The following tactics have been proposed to prevent repatriation problems:

◆ *Realistic re-entry preview:* Already when selecting an expatriate it is important to create realistic expectations upon repatriation. Explaining to the expatriate what to expect upon return makes it possible for him to develop ways to deal with the problems foreseen (Black, 1992; Caligiuri and Lazarova, 2001).

♦ *Preferential treatment of repatriates in job decisions*: Some companies have implemented the policy that in case of multiple applicants for one position former expatriates are given precedence. Thus the company shows, visibly, that international experience is valued.

♦ *Career planning*: Future career steps, along with developmental needs, are already discussed with the employee before his or her return. Yet repatriation programs offered by MNCs typically do not include long-term career planning (The Conference Board, 1996; Marx, 1996) but are confined to a general guaranty for future employment.

♦ *Limiting duration of assignments*: The average assignment length is between three and five years. A limitation to this timeframe prevents the employee's expertise from becoming obsolete and reduces the risk that the expatriate adopts standards and values of the host country that are different from the ones valid in the home country.

The most common measure to cope with work-related problems of repatriation *after* return is to offer a reorientation program. Immediately after return the repatriate is provided with information about the changes in the company, such as personnel, products, strategies, and organizational structure.

Just as the professional transition back into the parent company can cause problems, so too can the readjustment to a non-work environment and social relations in the home country. Gradually MNCs are starting to help repatriates fit back into their home country. Repatriates and their families are increasingly being offered professional assistance and counseling on the experience of returning home and how to adjust back to social lifestyle, status, or housing (Sussman, 1986). Given the increasing number of dual-career couples many MNCs provide support for returning spouses of expatriates to obtain employment upon return. Repatriation procedures for spouses include career counseling as well as financial assistance to reimburse costs related to job search (Pellico and Stroh, 1997).

Utilizing overseas experience

Expatriates have acquired detailed knowledge about the global marketplace and have enhanced cross-cultural skills that are critical for managing MNCs. The difficult transition to the new job in the home country is made easier by giving expatriates recognition, by letting them function as a mentor, or by giving them the opportunity to share their knowledge and experience through training sessions. On the other hand the company can create the perception within the organization that an overseas assignment is valued. Returnees whose international experience is made use of and who are recognized by colleagues achieve more and are happier (Adler, 1981).

The approaches to repatriation as addressed in the previous section are intended to augment the transition from the overseas assignment back to working and living in the home country. They simply put all expatriates into a single category, which is typically based upon two assumptions. First, expatriates and their skills will truly be needed back home within the MNC. Second, all expatriates are looking for long-term careers within MNCs (Caligiuri and Lazarova, 2001). Yet, these assumptions may not apply to all expatriates. Especially, when the main goal of an assignment is not to develop global skills but, rather, to fill a technical or managerial gap in the host country, MNCs need to consider whether the expatriate's skills, gained during the overseas assignment, are needed within the company. If not, expatriates should be given a realistic preview prior to their assignment. Their turnover upon repatriation can be considered functional. MNCs should also expect some "natural" turnover.

Even a good repatriation program will not be able to retain all returnees because there will always be some who will find better career opportunities in companies other than the one that sent them abroad. Given that international experience is an asset in today's job market, it is not surprising that some repatriates are willing to change companies after completion of their international assignment. Thus, repatriation programs have to be integrated into the broader strategic international assignment process.

CONCLUSION

This review has been lengthy out of necessity, for the literature in this field has burgeoned since the 1970s. The pioneering stage in the evolution of the field of expatriate adjustment is over. Yet many scholars act as if they are pioneers – they conduct atheoretical empirical studies, devise theories that seem to overlap significantly with already extant theories, and see this domain as a small, emerging piece of the wider IHRM field. Yet, as this review indicates, it is not a time to build a foundation; rather, it is time to build *upon* the foundation of the extant literature. We hope that this chapter will aid all who work in this field to: (1) see the many vistas of opportunities in this field for the creation of new theories that are not simply spin-offs of existing theories; (2) carefully and thoughtfully add to the empirical findings of the field in a strategic rather than a scatter-shot way; and (3) extend the knowledge of the field into other areas of management via multidisciplinary integration and creative collaboration. Finally, we also hope that this review shows practitioners that there is a solid theoretical and empirical foundation upon which to design more effective IHRM programs, policies, and practices.

Part IV

MOTIVATION, REWARDS, AND
LEADERSHIP BEHAVIOR

INTRODUCTION

In previous parts authors elucidated frameworks for studying cross-cultural management and differences in strategy, structure, and human resource management that might be attributable to culture. In this part the authors move to the micro level of human behavior at work. We begin with a comprehensive review of differences in personal values, work motivation, and job attitudes by Steers and Sánchez-Runde ("Culture, Motivation, and Work Behavior"). Steers and Sánchez-Runde present a compelling review of the literature, highlighting the many gaps in our knowledge about the role of culture in workplace behavior.

Their chapter begins with an in-depth examination of several streams of research, beginning with cross-cultural studies of personal values, then moving to a review of Hofstede's and Triandis's work on national culture (see also Editors' Introduction and part I). Where studies of personal values identified differences across cultures in individual values, both Hofstede and Triandis focus on cultural values and how they are manifested in workplace structures and processes. Steers and Sánchez-Runde go on to highlight the effect of cultural bias in research. This section of the chapter is very useful as researchers struggle to minimize the unconscious effects of their own culture on their scholarship. The authors cite several studies that, though influential in the field, are plagued by a pro-Western bias.

One of the great benefits in this chapter is its in-depth coverage of certain topics. The authors' treatment of achievement motivation is an excellent case in point. They summarize the basic findings from McClelland, then go on to an elegant review and discussion of the cross-cultural evidence concerning achievement motivation, include enough detail to encourage the reader to investigate the topic in more depth.

The chapter continues with a discussion of rewards and the applicability of different reward schemes in different cultures. The authors highlight a significant number of good studies that demonstrate clearly that reward schemes that may work well in one culture do not have the desired effect in other cultures.

The real value-added in this chapter is found in the authors' development and discussion of a culture-based model of motivation. The model offers an integration of over 100 studies and a research agenda going forward. Its comprehensiveness makes it difficult to test in total, but it suggests any number of research directions for scholars. Interestingly, the model itself may be culture-bound. It represents linear relationships very much in the Western research tradition. The next chapter by Smith and Peterson suggests that our cultural background influences the models we use and test. The Steers and Sánchez-Runde model is logical and linear – a comfort to Western researchers but perhaps not capable of capturing phenomena in other cultures. But then it is only fair to ask, is any model capable of capturing phenomena universally across cultures? Probably not.

The Smith and Peterson chapter (11), "Cross-Cultural Leadership", is weighted toward a new synthesis and way of thinking about leadership rather than toward a comprehensive literature review. The authors point out that several reviews of cross-cultural leadership have been completed since the 1990s. These authors build on the extant reviews rather than conduct their own.

They identify four ways of thinking about cross-cultural leadership: models developed in the US and applied elsewhere; models developed outside the US and applied in the US; leadership of cross-cultural teams; and strategic leadership in multinational organizations. In examining the extant literature briefly, they identify gaps in knowledge about cross-cultural leadership toward which we can direct our research focus.

Their point of departure is a model of leadership as a process of social interpretation. Behaviors that are construed by followers to be leadership in one culture may be construed as something else entirely in another culture. Leadership is distributed differently within a work group in one culture compared to another culture. Attributions about appropriate leadership behavior vary by culture, though their descriptors (e.g., decisiveness, fairness) may be the same. Their "event management" model of leadership has been tested cross-culturally and they find differences by culture in the extent to which different resources (such as peers, superiors, subordinates, experience, training, and company rules) are used for interpreting and reacting to ambiguous events.

Smith and Peterson describe Misumi's "PM leadership" theory in their review of work that originated outside the US. This theory of leadership suggests that: measures of leader behavior should be developed to fit each research situation and leaders who exhibit leadership with both P (performance) and M (maintenance of interpersonal relationships) do so in a holistic, interwoven way, consistent with the high context nature of Japanese society. In other words, the theory itself has characteristics of the culture in which it was developed and Misumi's suggested ways of studying the phenomenon are specific to the Japanese culture, even though the two dimensions of leadership are familiar to Western scholars.

Smith and Peterson conclude by suggesting two areas for additional work. First, while US-based theories of leadership have been instrumental in knowledge creation about leadership, we need more non-US theories of leadership because concepts that are important in the US may not be universally important. Second, research on local variations in leadership rather than the search for global, universally effective leadership behaviors is needed. The nuance of effective leadership within a culture is found by examining leadership within a culture, then understanding and appreciating the meaning attached to behavior in that culture. While great strides have been made in understanding cross-cultural leadership, much work remains.

The last chapter in this part is by Nancy Adler ("Women Joining Men as Global Leaders in the New Economy"). Adler is well known for her work on women managers across cultures. This chapter, unlike others in the book, is a rich analysis of male and female leaders and leadership. Rather than a literature review leading to research questions, Adler builds a model that includes organizational evolution and evolution in leadership, moving from homogeneous organizational cultures and all-male leadership to diverse, multi-faceted organizational cultures that benefit from diverse leadership.

Adler suggests four different approaches to gender differences in leadership, models that assume men's "typical" style is superior, models that assume no differences between men and women, models that assume women's "typical" style is superior to men's, and models that appreciate and incorporate both male and female "typical" leadership strengths. Adler makes the argument effectively that global, networked, non-hierarchical organizations benefit from appreciating and incorporating the differences between men and women in leadership as well as the differences among culturally diverse employees. She argues that effective organizations will no longer try to fit all employees into a single leadership mold. Effective organizations will assign leaders to positions based on the skills the leader can bring to the position. Very effective organizations will leverage diversity to create innovation and competitive advantage.

The articles in this part are outstanding in different ways. Steers and Sánchez-Runde treat us to a heroic review of the literature on cross-cultural motivation and work behavior, developing a comprehensive model to guide future research. Smith and Peterson stimulate our thinking with their sense-making model of leadership, focusing their attention on very recent work on global leadership, some of which is not yet published. Adler paints a vivid picture of the benefits of cultural and gender diversity in top management as a source of competitive advantage. Each chapter is different. Each is compelling. Each reminds us that the search for universal truths about leadership and motivation across cultures is likely to be futile.

10

Culture, Motivation, and Work Behavior

Richard M. Steers and Carlos J. Sánchez-Runde

Almost 2,500 years ago, the Chinese philosopher Confucius observed that all people are basically the same; it is only their habits that are different. Almost four hundred years ago, the French mathematician Blaise Pascal noted that things believed to be true in one country are often believed to be false in another. And much more recently, the Honda Motor Company co-founder Takeo Fujisawa concluded that Japanese and American managers are 95 percent the same, but differ in all important respects. Confucius, Pascal, and Fujisawa, coming from very diverse cultures and different centuries, all understood what has too frequently eluded contemporary social scientists: national culture does make a difference in determining how we think and how we behave. This is equally true in our personal lives and our work lives. Unfortunately, however, too many investigations have ignored even the most rudimentary cross-national differences while studying work and organizations (Adler, 1983; Child, 1981; Roberts and Boyacilliger, 1984; Steers, 1989). All too often, it has been assumed, incorrectly, that relationships found between variables in one culture will likely transcend other cultures. As French sociologist Michael Crozier (1964: 210) observed in his classic study of bureaucratic organizations, managers have long understood that organization structures, attitudes, and behaviors differ across cultures "but contemporary social scientists have seldom been concerned with such comparisons."

THE CULTURAL ENIGMA

It is easy to understand why researchers often avoid cross-cultural variables in management research. Culture is not an easy variable to define or measure. Data collection is often difficult and expensive. Translation problems complicate measurement and analysis. Personal biases, however unintentional, frequently cloud both the choice of a research topic and the interpretation of results. Causal relationships are problematic. Intercultural sensitivities often impose self-censorship on dialog and debate. And everything takes more time than was originally planned. As a result, serious study of the relationship between culture and behavior presents researchers with a complex puzzle or enigma that is not easily understood. Even so, being difficult, expensive, complex, imprecise, sensitive, time-consuming, and risky does not justify ignoring what is clearly one of the most important variables in the study of human behavior in organizations.

Fortunately, the omission of cultural variables in the study of management has been increasingly redressed since the 1990s such that today there exists a reasonably solid research literature focusing on several aspects of work and organizations. Many of our early theories of organizations and management practice, once thought to be largely universalistic, are now confirmed to be culture-bound. For example, recent empirical studies have demonstrated that cultural variations can have a significant influence on such phenomena as work values, equity perceptions, achievement motivation, causal attributions, social loafing, and job attitudes, to name a few. This is not to say that this literature is anywhere near complete; it is not. However, it is fair to say that recently we have witnessed an increasing interest in the serious study of cross-cultural issues as they relate to managing people in organizations.

Today, most contemporary management scholars realize that cultural differences can have a profound impact on work motivation and job attitudes. What remains elusive, however, is a solid understanding of how or why culture influences fundamental motivational processes. There is something about the concept of culture as it relates to organizational dynamics and management practice that makes it "difficult to identify," "fuzzy," "complex and multifaceted," and "amorphous" (Hall, 1992; Trice and Beyer, 1993; Baligh, 1994; Brislin, 1993). As anthropologist Edward T. Hall (1992: 210) observed: "I have come to the conclusion that the analysis of culture could be likened to the task of identifying mushrooms. Because of the nature of the mushrooms, no two experts describe them in precisely the same way, which creates a problem for the rest of us when we are trying to decide whether the specimen in our hands is edible." As a result, partial models with little empirical support have sometimes been offered as substitutes for science in the belief that a naïve theory is preferable to no theory at all. Thus, we are sometimes left with findings that certain actions may differ across national boundaries, but can only speculate concerning the underlying reasons behind such actions. For instance, recognizing that managers in different countries behave differently when confronting the same challenge is important for understanding management practices, but it is only the beginning of the journey for understanding social dynamics in the workplace.

The purpose of this chapter is to help redress this limitation by systematically reviewing our current knowledge base concerning the relationship between culture and work motivation, and then organizing these findings in such a way that improved modeling of this relationship becomes possible. As a starting point for this examination, we will follow Triandis' (1972, 1995) definition of *culture* as a collectivity of people who share a common language, historical period, and geographic location, as well as possessing shared beliefs, norms, roles, values, and attitudes.

This review is divided into several sections. First, cross-cultural influences on *personal values* are reviewed as they relate to work behavior. This is followed by a review of the research on culture and *work motivation*. Next, the role of culture in the formulation of *job attitudes* is examined. Following this three-part review, an attempt is made to integrate available empirical findings towards the development of a culture-based model of moti-

vation and work behavior. Finally, by way of conclusion, several methodological considerations are discussed as they relate to future research on this topic.

CROSS-CULTURAL INFLUENCES ON PERSONAL VALUES AND WORK

Values reflect individual beliefs about desirable end states or modes of conduct for
pursuing desirable end states (Rokeach, 1973). As such, they serve a useful function by
providing individuals with guidelines or standards for determining their own behavior
and for evaluating the behavior of others. While interest in personal values dates from
the early work of Lewin (1935) and Allport (1937), the systematic study of values in the
workplace began in earnest only since about the 1960s. Within the workplace, key
questions emerge concerning how personal values influence employee willingness and
preparedness to contribute towards the attainment of organizational goals. From a cross-
cultural perspective, further questions emerge concerning how variations across cultures
may or may not affect employee behavior in the workplace, as well as what managers
might do to accommodate such variations where they are found to exist. For example,
values concerning the relative importance of individualism vs. collectivism can influence
the manner in which employees work together. As noted by Markus and Kitayama
(1991), many Americans tend to assert their individuality and revel in their differences,
while many Japanese tend to emphasize harmonious interdependence with others and
shun the spotlight. Such values can represent an important influence on work-related
behaviors.

Approaches to the cross-cultural study of personal values in the workplace vary
depending upon the underlying assumptions made about their nature. The early work of
England and his colleagues employed a survey-based inventory of values in different
regions of the world by extending the seminal work of Rokeach. A second approach,
based on identifying value differences across national cultures, can be seen in the work of
Hofstede, Triandis, and Schwartz. A third approach has stressed the need to study values
principally from a non-Western vantage point in the belief that Western researchers
unintentionally insert their own cultural biases into the models and measures they use to
study non-Western cultures. An example of this third approach can be seen in the work
on Confucian dynamism by Bond and his associates. Each perspective is reviewed here.

Personal values studies

Work-related values have been studied systematically from a cross-cultural perspective
since the mid-1960s (Guth and Tagiuri, 1965; England, 1975). Subsequent researchers
have built upon these initial efforts to the point that today we have a reasonably clear
conception of how work-related values can influence behavior across cultures. While
Guth and Tagiuri focused their attention on the relationship between managerial values
in different cultures and corporate strategy formulation, England and his colleagues
focused more directly on the impact of managerial values on employee behavior at work.

Based on his initial research, England developed the Personal Values Questionnaire
(PVQ), which measures 66 personal values held by managers in different countries

(England, 1975; Davis and Rasool, 1988). These values were then clustered into several dimensions for further analysis. England found significant differences in the personal values among managers in the five countries he studied: Australia, Japan, Korea, India, and the United States. American managers tended to be high in pragmatism, achievement-orientation, and a demand for competence. They placed a high value on profit maximization, organizational efficiency, and productivity. Japanese and Korean managers also valued pragmatism, competence, and achievement, but emphasized organizational growth instead of profit maximization. Indian managers stressed a moralistic orientation, a desire for stability instead of change, and the importance of status, dignity, prestige, and compliance with organizational directives. Finally, Australian managers emphasized both a moralistic and humanistic orientation, an emphasis on both growth and profit maximization, a high value on loyalty and trust, and a low emphasis on individual achievement, success, competition, and risk.

The initial work by England and his colleagues formed the basis for a subsequent international study of managerial values called the Meaning of Work Project (MOW International Research Team, 1987). This study sought to identify the underlying meanings that individuals and groups attach to work in the following industrialized nations: Belgium, Germany, Holland, Israel, Japan, United Kingdom, United States, and Yugoslavia. Three dimensions were used in the study: (1) work centrality, defined in terms of the relative importance of work for employees; (2) work goals, defined as the relative importance of 11 work goals and values sought and preferred by employees; and (3) societal norms about working, which compared beliefs about work as an entitlement or an obligation. Differences were then compared across nations. For example, Japan was found to have a higher number of workers for whom work was their central life interest, compared to both Americans and Germans who placed a higher value on leisure and social interaction. A high proportion of Americans saw work as a duty, an obligation that must be met. Japanese workers showed less interest in individual economic outcomes from work than most Europeans and Americans (England and Quintanilla, 1989).

A separate systematic effort by an international research team to codify work values as they are influenced by national boundaries was conducted by Elizur, Borg, Hunt, and Beck (1991). Their research led to the development of the Work Values Questionnaire (WVQ), which identifies 24 values, including achievement, status, job interest, meaningful work, independence, recognition, supervisory support, pay, and benefits. They surveyed eight countries (China, Germany, Holland, Hungary, Israel, Korea, Taiwan, and the United States) and found interesting commonalties as well as differences across nationalities (see figure 10.1). Achievement was considered as the most important work value in China, Taiwan, Korea, and Israel, second most important in Holland, Hungary, and the US, and ninth in Germany. Job interest was ranked first in Germany, Holland, the US, second in Taiwan and Israel, third in Korea, seventh in Hungary, and eighth in China. Personal growth, recognition, esteem, advancement, and use of one's abilities ranked high for all nationalities except Germany and Hungary. By contrast, Germany and Hungary ranked having the support of both co-workers and supervisors as very high. Perhaps the major contribution of this study beyond the survey data is the creation of a well-designed research instrument for future use in the study of work-related values across cultures.

Additional country-specific studies, most notably comparing American and Japanese

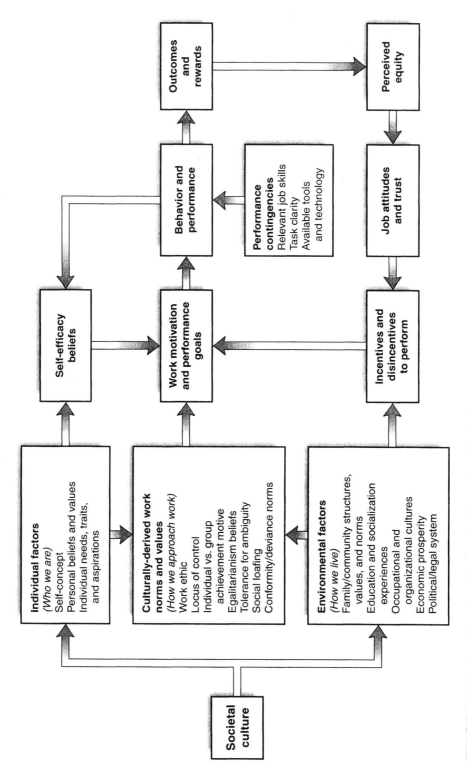

FIGURE 10.1 A culture-based model of motivation and work behavior

managers, have expanded our knowledge in this area. Hopkins, Lo, Peterson, and Seo (1977) found Japanese managers to be significantly more fatalistic and more authoritarian than their American counterparts. Likewise, Hayashi, Harnett, and Cummings (1973) found Japanese managers to be more conciliatory and risk-oriented than Americans. Yamagishi and Yamagishi (1994) found that Americans are more trusting in other people in general, consider reputation more important, and consider themselves to be honest and fair, while Japanese see greater utility in dealing with others through personal relations. These findings are consistent with England's earlier findings (e.g., England and Koike, 1970). Other studies by Vogel (1963) and Lincoln and Kalleberg (1990) found Japanese managers to be consistently harder workers than their Western counterparts.

Work values were also investigated in a series of studies of Korean employees by Steers and his associates (Steers, Shin, and Ungson, 1989; Koch, Nam, and Steers, 1995; Ungson, Steers, and Park, 1997; and Steers, 1999). Results were compared with the work values found in other Asian cultures, as well as in Western cultures. Several findings from these studies are relevant here. First, like the Vogel and Lincoln and Kalleberg studies among the Japanese, Steers et al. (1989) found that Korean workers and managers exhibit a very strong work ethic. In interviews, Korean workers took pride in claiming that they worked even harder than the Japanese did. Supporting evidence for this can be seen in a 1994 study of average work hours in various countries where it was found that Korean workers on average worked longer hours and took fewer vacation days than workers in Thailand, Hong Kong, Taiwan, Singapore, India, Japan, and Indonesia (Steers, 1999). In this study, Indonesians worked the shortest number of hours per year, while Indians took the largest number of vacation days each year. Beyond long working hours, the Korean corporate culture was found to be typically characterized by a strong Confucian belief in absolute loyalty to the company, adherence to the will of superiors, a strong belief in paternalism, seniority as a prominent factor in promotion, group-oriented achievement instead of individual achievement, the importance of preserving group harmony even at the expense of individual fairness, and a heavy reliance on personal relationships in business relations instead of legal contracts.

National culture models

Geert Hofstede's landmark study of national cultures helps to define the psychological landscape for researchers attempting to understand cultural differences in the workplace (Hofstede, 1980a, 1991). Based on his survey of 117,000 managers, supervisors, and employees working for IBM in 40 different countries, Hofstede posited that there are central tendencies within various cultures that can be identified and compared. He initially identified four dimensions: power distance, individualism–collectivism, uncertainty avoidance or acceptance of risk, and "masculinity–femininity" or assertiveness. A fifth dimension, Confucian dynamism, was added later through the efforts of Michael Bond and his associates (see below).

While a more thorough examination of Hofstede's work can be found elsewhere in this volume, suffice it to say here that his model of national cultures adds conceptual richness to the study of work-related values and employee motivation. This is particularly true with respect to the individualism–collectivism dimension that has received the most research attention. To the extent that American workers hold strong individualistic values, for example, managers can design incentive systems that appeal to this value. Likewise, to the extent that Japanese workers adhere to more collectivist values and norms, these firms can design incentive and reward systems to reflect this reality. However, in more heterogeneous societies such as the United States, we would expect greater divergence from these central tendencies. Thus, as noted by Lawler (1992), many American firms have been moving towards a "cafeteria model" of compensation that allows employees greater discretion in selecting potential rewards. In Japan, by contrast, where there is less heterogeneity on such values, cafeteria pay plans may prove ineffective. Indeed, they may cause considerable damage to an organization's work culture to the extent that they cause jealousy and dissension among group members.

While Hofstede's work has been criticized for making extensive generalizations concerning the characteristics of various cultures, he does not argue against the existence of individual differences within specific cultures. There are obviously individualistic Japanese and collectivistic Americans, for example. Instead, he asserts logically that each culture manifests certain identifiable central tendencies that can be used in a general way to differentiate across national boundaries. In this regard, it is interesting to observe that while a number of management researchers criticize Hofstede's work on both theoretical and empirical grounds, many of these same individuals make extensive use of his model in their studies of work attitudes and behavior across cultures.

Related research addressing the dimension of individualism–collectivism can be found in the work of Triandis (1972, 1995), reviewed elsewhere in this volume. Triandis significantly broadened our understanding of the individualism–collectivism dimension in at least two ways. First, he more clearly differentiated between individuals high in individualism and individuals high in collectivism. He notes that individualists: (1) stress personal goals over group goals; (2) maintain cognitions centered around their personal preferences, needs, rights, and contacts; and (3) emphasize rational analyses of the advantages and disadvantages of these relationships. By contrast, collectivists tend to: (1) emphasize group goals over personal goals; (2) maintain cognitions centered around group norms and obligations; and (3) emphasize relationships as a moral imperative. Triandis also emphasized that both individualism and collectivism can be practiced vertically, reflecting an emphasis on hierarchy and inequality, and horizontally, reflecting an emphasis on equality (see chapter 2 for details).

Building on the work of Hofstede and Triandis, Schwartz (1994; Smith and Schwartz, 1997) provided an alternative model of culture-level value dimensions. Schwartz began his analysis by specifying how societies try to resolve three interrelated problems: (1) relations between individuals and groups; (2) assuring responsible social behavior; and (3) the role of humankind in the natural and social world. From here, he initiated a major empirical study of values in 42 cultural groups in 38 countries. In contrast to Hofstede's four (and later five) cultural value dimensions, Schwartz identified seven: conservatism, intellectual autonomy, affective autonomy, hierarchy, mastery, egalitarian commitment, and harmony. Based on these findings, he argued that the cultural adaptations that evolve in an effort to resolve the three societal problems reside in a specific set of values he calls "value types." Three value types are identified: (1) conservatism vs. autonomy, reflecting beliefs that people find meaning either in membership in a collectivity or within themselves as individuals; (2) hierarchy vs. egalitarianism, reflecting beliefs that people within a society are either necessarily unequal and behave best under some hierarchical form or are moral equals who share basic interests as human beings; and (3) mastery vs. harmony, reflecting beliefs that people should either seek to control the natural and social world or preserve nature and fit harmoniously into it. This model and its accompanying research instrument provide a promising new approach to the study of values across cultures.

Non-Western approaches

A major criticism of many of the extant studies of work-related values is that they were designed in the West using Western theoretical concepts. As such, they may have a tendency to overlook or ignore culturally based values from other regions of the globe that either do not exist or are not readily identifiable in the Western consciousness. They also seem to view other cultures using Western constructs as the acceptable standard of evaluation.

An example of this tendency can be seen in the work of Inkeles (1977; Inkeles and Smith, 1974). Through a series of studies focusing on Chile, Bangladesh, India, Israel, and Nigeria, Inkeles sought to explain how cultures are transformed from "traditional" to "modern" societies. Modern individuals were defined as being highly independent and autonomous when making personal decisions, open-minded and flexible in approaching new experiences, and informed about political affairs. By contrast, traditional individuals were characterized as exhibiting interpersonal distrust, hostility towards government, lack of innovation, fatalism, a limited world view, and low empathy (Inkeles, 1977). Based on this model, Orpen (1978) surveyed South African blacks and dichotomized them into modern and traditional groups. Members of the modern group were found to be more accepting of the Protestant work ethic ideal, had higher job satisfaction, and placed greater emphasis on intrinsic work values than members of the traditional group.

The problem with such studies lies in determining who is in the best position to define and measure the principal constructs under study (e.g., modern vs. traditional). In point of fact, it is typically the Western researchers who use Western cognitive templates for purposes of definition and analysis. But even if this was accepted as standard practice, perceptual biases and distortions still creep into the analyses. For example, if modern societies are indeed characterized by a high level of individual independence and autonomy of action and a low level of fatalism, how would one describe contemporary Japanese society? And if modern societies are characterized by a high trust in government and a limited worldview, how would one describe contemporary American society? Obviously, when such underlying assumptions permeate the research process, they tend to distort our perceptual biases by leading to studies and results that ultimately reinforce our stereotypes.

Another example of possible Western bias can be seen in the southern African concept of *ubuntu*. Ubuntu is perhaps best described as a clan value that requires members to serve the needs of other group members even at their own expense (Steers, Bischoff, and Higgins, 1992). It is communal in the sense that it requires people to share what they have when someone else is in need, regardless of who worked to acquire it. As such, it is a manifestation of *horizontal* collectivism (see Triandis' chapter 2 in this volume). It is a clan obligation that overrides any sense of ownership or concerns over inequity in input–

output ratios. If your neighbor needs food, for example, it is your responsibility to feed him, even if you are also poor. This concept has no Western equivalent, except possibly compassion. When white Afrikaners began settling in South Africa to operate farms, factories, and mines, they quickly discovered that the incentive systems that they offered the local black population failed to have the desired effect. These systems were based on European values of individual achievement and competition, and failed to recognize the communal values inherent in many tribal cultures.

Another non-Western value that has received attention recently is Confucian dynamism (Bond, 1987; Bond and Kwang, 1986; Hofstede and Bond, 1988; Ralston, Gustafson, Cheung, and Terpstra, 1993). This value is based on the work of Michael Bond and his associates, who sought to measure value orientations from an Eastern, specifically Chinese, perspective. Based on their research in 23 countries, they developed an instrument called the Chinese Values Survey (CVS). A pivotal part of the instrument was a scale, called Confucian dynamism, designed to reflect the basic values and precepts articulated by Confucius and his followers. This value reflects the extent of one's relative preference for a long-term or short-term orientation in life. A long-term orientation includes a belief in such values as persistence, ordering relationships by status and observing this order, thrift, and having a sense of shame. A short-term orientation consists of values characterized by stability and personal steadiness, saving face, respect for tradition, and reciprocation of greetings, favors, and gifts. Bond chose to label the scale as "Confucian" since most values at both ends of the scale are derived from Confucian teachings. However, the values clustering at one end of the pole are more future-oriented and dynamic (perseverance and thrift), while the values clustering at the opposite pole are more static and focus on the past and present (stability and respect for tradition). As with most value scales, there is no intended correct position. Bond went on to examine the relationship between those who approached life in a more dynamic and future-oriented fashion and found it related to individual and national achievement.

A good example of how Confucian dynamism works can be found in Gordon Redding's (1990) classic study of overseas Chinese. It is estimated that overseas Chinese command a collective gross national product approaching $300 billion, far exceeding the GNP of Australia. This has been accomplished by ignoring almost all of the characteristics of "modern" management that have been accepted in the West. Redding found that Chinese entrepreneurs shared similar values regardless of where they lived or worked. They preferred economic endeavors in which significant gains could be made with little manpower, such as commodity trading or real estate. They maintained a low profile and were extremely cost-conscious, reflecting traditional Confucian values. They tended to create small, family-run firms that specialized in a narrow product range (in contrast to Japanese or Koreans) and cooperated with other small firms for essential services through personal networks. Decision-making was highly centralized in one dominant family member (who was frequently female, in contrast to Japan and Korea), and other family members were often given new ventures or products to try their skills on. Throughout, everything was based on family membership and, if someone was not a family member, he or she was forever an outsider.

In summary, the available research literature on culture and personal values consistently demonstrates a strong and significant relationship. This is true regardless of whether Western or non-Western templates are used for either conceptualization or empirical research. As a result, it seems highly advisable to include the role of cultural differences in any future modeling efforts, as well as managerial actions, that involve one's self-concept, individual beliefs and values, and individual traits and aspiration levels. These individual factors, in turn, have been shown to be closely related to self-efficacy, work norms and values, and ultimately work motivation (Bandura, 1996).

CROSS-CULTURAL INFLUENCES ON MOTIVATION AND PERFORMANCE

While personal beliefs and values are clearly a determinant of subsequent work motivation, other factors also contribute, including: (1) individual need strengths; (2) cognitions, goals, and perceived equity; (3) incentives, rewards, and reinforcement; and (4) individual beliefs and social norms concerning levels of required effort. The role of culture on each of these four factors will be examined in turn.

Manifest needs and work behavior

Need theories of motivation date from the seminal works of Henry Murray (1938) and Abraham Maslow (1954). Both of these researchers argued that individuals are largely motivated by various needs that serve to guide behavior. When manifest, such needs focus individual drive towards endeavors aimed at satisfying these needs. Murray believed that people are motivated by perhaps two dozen needs (e.g., achievement, affiliation, autonomy, and dominance) that become manifest or latent depending upon circumstances. By contrast, Maslow suggested that needs are pursued by individuals in a sequential or hierarchical fashion from basic deficiency needs (physiological, safety, and belongingness) to growth needs (self-esteem, and self-actualization). The original works of Murray and Maslow were later adapted to the workplace by McClelland (1961) and Alderfer (1972), respectively. McClelland (1961) focused his efforts on the three needs of achievement, affiliation, and dominance (referred to as need for power), while Alderfer's (1972) ERG theory simplified Maslow's five needs into three somewhat broader ones: existence, relatedness, and growth.

An early cross-cultural application of Maslow's need hierarchy model to the workplace was completed by Haire, Ghiselli, and Porter (1961), who found systematic differences in managerial need strengths across cultures. Later studies found the need hierarchy structure proposed by Maslow to be similar, but clearly not identical, in such countries as Peru, India, Mexico, and the Middle East (Badawy, 1979; Buera and Glueck, 1979; Jaggi, 1979; Stephens, Kedia, and Ezell, 1979; Reitz, 1975). Subsequently, Hofstede (1980b) argued persuasively that Maslow's need hierarchy is not universally applicable across cultures due to variations in country values. Evidence from Blunt and Jones (1992) supports this conclusion.

While Maslow's model of motivation has received some attention in other cultures, greater efforts have been directed towards applying the Murray/McClelland model, especially as it pertains to the need for achievement.. The basic thesis underlying much of McClelland's work is a hypothesized relationship between aggregate levels of achievement motivation and subsequent economic growth among nations. According to this reasoning, as achievement motivation levels rise within a nation, so too does the extent of entrepreneurial behavior and economic development (McClelland and Winter, 1969). As a result, McClelland argued for the development of large-scale national training efforts in achievement motivation for underdeveloped countries.

McClelland's basic thesis, while disarmingly simple, has generated considerable controversy in the research literature as it relates to the basis of work motivation across cultures. To begin with, the projective test typically used to measure achievement (Thematic Apperception Test) is itself controversial, with a number of studies questioning its validity and reliability (e.g., Iwawaki and Lynn, 1972). Beyond this, several studies suggest that the relationship between achievement motivation and subsequent success on a national level is far more complex than first suggested. Iwawaki and Lynn (1972), for example, found national achievement motivation levels between Japan and Great Britain to be roughly identical, even though Japan's economic growth rate far exceeded Britain's. McCarthy, Puffer, and Shekshnia (1993) found similar results when comparing Russian and American entrepreneurs. However, Krus and Rysberg (1976) found that entrepreneurs from highly diverse cultures (in this case East Europeans compared to Americans) can also have significantly different levels of achievement motivation. And Salili's (1979) study of Iranian men and women suggests that gender may also influence achievement motivation. Here it was found that Iranian women had achievement motivation scores that more closely resembled their American female counterparts than their Iranian male counterparts.

Based on their comprehensive review of this subject, Bhagat and McQuaid (1982: 669) concluded that achievement motivation patterns will likely "arise in different cultural contexts in different forms, stimulated by different situational cues and may be channeled toward accomplishing different types of goals." Thus, DeVos (1968) found that Indians and Chinese frequently achieve considerable economic success outside their native cultures, even though their native cultures have traditionally been seen as being low in achievement motivation. And Maehr (1977; Maehr and Nichols, 1980) suggested that achievement should not be conceptualized or evaluated exclusively in terms of economic success. While economic or academic success may be normative indicators of achievement in the West, other variables, such as family success or success in personal relationships, may be more salient indicators elsewhere in the world. Based on a series of cross-cultural studies, Heckhausen (1971) concluded that a major limitation of McClelland's theory was its lack of differentiation between the affective orientations of fear of success and fear of failure. Both of these sentiments tend to be more prevalent in non-Western societies than Western ones.

Finally, several studies have questioned the original concept of achievement motivation as an individual effort instead of a collective one. DeVos and Mizushima (1973), for example, suggest that a major aspect of achievement motivation in Japan involves a need to belong and cooperate with others, thereby linking the need for affiliation to the need for achievement much more closely than is typically found in the West. Yu and Yang (1994) make the same argument for Korea. And, as noted elsewhere, the existence of a group achievement motive throughout much of East Asia is a pre-eminent driving force in many work environments, while individual achievement is neither valued nor rewarded. Indeed, it is frequently punished (Abegglen and Stalk, 1985; Steers et al., 1989).

Support for this position comes from a study by Sagie, Elizur, and Yamauchi (1996).

They studied managers in five countries (Holland, Hungary, Israel, Japan, and the US) to test the universality of achievement motivation theory. Their findings led them to conclude that achievement motivation is perhaps best conceptualized as consisting of three facets (behavioral modality, type of confrontation, and time perspective) and that different cultures will excel in each of the various facets. In general, achievement motivation was found to be highest for the more individualistic American sample and lowest for the more collectivist Hungarian and Japanese samples. However, the study also concluded that a clear distinction needs to be made between individual and collective achievement motivation to reflect cultural variations.

While considerable progress has been made concerning the role of need theories of motivation in different cultural settings, a major omission must also be noted. Specifically, the vast majority of the cross-cultural research on needs focused on higher-order needs (e.g., achievement or self-actualization) and frequently ignored lower-order needs. In this regard, it must be remembered that much of the world's working population, particularly in the less industrialized nations, remains of necessity focused on trying to meet the more basic lower-order needs like safety and security. Studies by Blunt (1976) and Jones (1988) found, for example, that Kenyan and Malawi managers both attached the greatest importance to security needs, not higher-order needs. And Elenkov (1998) found Russian managers stress security and belongingness needs as opposed to higher-order needs. Moreover, even within more industrialized nations, large working populations similarly remain focused on meeting lower-order needs. It may be only the fortunate few who have a realistic opportunity to pursue self-actualization or genuine achievement in the workplace.

Cognition, motivation, and performance

Cognitive approaches to motivation remain a dominant force in the study of organizational behavior (Mitchell, 1997; Steers, Porter, and Bigley, 1996). Included here are such theories as equity theory (Adams, 1965), goal-setting theory (Locke and Latham, 1990), and expectancy/valence theory (Vroom, 1964; Porter and Lawler, 1968). These theories are based largely on the assumption that people tend to make reasoned choices about their behaviors and that these choices influence, and are influenced by, job-related outcomes and work attitudes. While the majority of cognitive theories, as well as much of the empirical work relating to them, derive from American efforts, a number of studies have also been conducted to test the external validity of these models outside the United States.

Equity theory focuses on the motivational consequences that result when individuals believe they are being treated either fairly or unfairly in terms of the rewards and outcomes they receive (Adams, 1965; Mowday, 1996). The determination of equity is based, not on objective reality, but on the individual's perception of how his or her ratio of inputs to outcomes compares to the same ratio for a valued colleague. Accordingly, when an individual thinks that he or she is receiving less money for the same work than the referent other, the person would likely seek some remedy to return to a state of perceived equity. Remedies could include a work slowdown, filing a grievance, seeking alternative employment, etc. It is also possible for the individual to find remedy by changing his or her referent other, perhaps by rationalizing why the other person actually deserved more pay. By the same token, the theory asserts somewhat more controversially that when individuals feel over-compensated, they will likely increase their work efforts, again to achieve a balanced state compared to their referent other.

Considerable research supports the fundamental equity principle in Western workgroups, particularly as it relates to conditions of underpayment. However, when the theory is applied elsewhere, results tend to be more problematic. Yuchtman (1972), for example, studied equity perceptions among managers and non-managers in an Israeli kibbutz production unit and found that, contrary to initial predictions, managers felt less satisfied than workers. He explained this finding by suggesting that in the egalitarian work environment managers may feel that they are being under-compensated vis-à-vis their value and effort on behalf of the organization. Results were interpreted as supporting the theory.

However, other international researchers have suggested that the equity principle may be somewhat culture bound (Hofstede, 1980b). Notably in Asia and the Middle East, examples abound concerning individuals who apparently readily accept a clearly recognizable state of inequity in order to preserve their view of societal harmony. For example, men and women frequently receive different pay for doing precisely the same work in countries like Japan and Korea (Abegglen and Stalk, 1985; Chung, Lee, and Jung, 1997). One might think that equity theory would predict that a state of inequity would result for female employees, leading to inequity resolution strategies such as those mentioned above. Yet, in many instances, no such perceived inequitable state has been found, thereby calling the theory into question. A plausible explanation here may be that women workers view other women as their referent other, not men (Steers et al., 1992). As a result, so long as all women are treated the same, a state of perceived equity could exist. This is not to say that such women feel "equal"; rather, compared to their female reference group they are receiving what others receive. A state of equity – if not equality – exists. Kim, Park, and Suzuki (1990) lend credence to this explanation in their study of equity perceptions in Japan, Korea, and the US. Their results led them to conclude, "the most important general conclusion emerging from our study is that the equity norm is generalizable across countries. It appeared in all three countries" (1990: 195).

A second prominent cognitive theory of motivation that has received considerable attention in the West is goal-setting theory. Goal-setting models focus on how individuals respond to the existence of specific goals, as well as the manner in which such goals are determined (e.g., level of participation in goal-setting, goal difficulty, goal specificity, etc.). Considerable evidence supports the conclusion that many employees perform at higher levels when given specific and challenging goals in which they had some part in setting (Locke and Latham, 1990). Despite the large number of US studies on this subject, few studies have been conducted in other cultures (Erez, 1986). Most of these focused on the influence of employee participation and were conducted either at a societal level, focusing on participative and collectivistic values (Ronen and Shenkar, 1985), or on organizational level practices and their impact on job attitudes (Haire, Ghiselli, and Porter, 1966; Heller and Wilpert, 1981). Locke and Schweiger (1979) also note that participation in the determination of work goals in Europe is institutionalized by law and anchored in political systems that stress egalitarian values. Such is not the case in the US.

However, a few studies have examined goal-setting effects at the individual level of analysis across cultures. French, Israel, and As (1960) were perhaps the first research team to compare participation in goal determination in the workplace. In contrast to previous findings among American workers, French et al. found that Norwegian workers shunned direct participation and preferred to have their union representatives work with management to determine work goals. It was argued that in Norway such individual participation would have been seen as being inconsistent with their prevailing philosophy of participation through union representatives. More recently, Earley (1986) found that, again in contrast to the US, British workers placed more trust in their union stewards than their foremen, and therefore responded more favorably to a goal-setting program sponsored by the stewards than by management. Earley concluded that the transferability of management techniques such as participation in goal setting across cultural settings may be affected by prevailing work norms. To test this proposition, Erez and Earley (1987) studied American and Israeli subjects and found that participative strategies led to higher levels of goal acceptance and performance than the assigned strategy in both cultures. Culture did not moderate the effects of goal-setting strategies or goal acceptance, but it did appear to moderate the effects of strategy on performance for extremely difficult goals. For both samples, acceptance was significantly lower in the assigned than in the participative goal-setting conditions. However, only in the Israeli sample was acceptance highly related to performance under assigned goals.

Both the equity and goal-setting principles can be found in the integrated expectancy/valence theory of work motivation (Vroom, 1964; Porter and Lawler, 1968). This theory postulates that motivation is largely influenced by a multiplicative combination of one's belief that effort will lead to performance, that performance will lead to certain outcomes, and the value placed on these outcomes by the individual. Thus, if an employee believes that if she works hard she will succeed on a task, and that if she succeeds her boss will in fact reward her, and that if the rewards to be received are valuable to her, she will likely be motivated to perform. On the other hand, if any one of these three components is not present, her motivation level will fall precipitously. The second part of the theory uses the equity principle to examine the relationship between performance and satisfaction. This model predicts that subsequent job satisfaction is determined by employee perceptions concerning the equity or fairness of the rewards received as a result of performance. High performance followed by high rewards should lead to high satisfaction, while high performance followed by low rewards should lead to low satisfaction.

Unfortunately, while expectancy/valence theory lends itself conceptually to rich cross-cultural comparisons, it remains difficult to operationalize for purposes of empirical study. Eden (1975) applied it to a sample of workers in an Israeli kibbutz and found some support for the theory. Matsui and Terai (1979) also found expectancy/valence theory could be applied successfully in Japan. However, a key assumption of this model is that employees have considerable control over the means of performance, the outcomes they will work for, and their manager's ability to successfully identify and administer desired rewards. Unfortunately, all three of these variables can vary significantly by culture. While Americans tend to believe they have considerable control over their environment, people in many other countries do not. Workers in Muslim cultures, for example, tend to manifest a strong external locus of control and believe that much of what happens is beyond their control. One could argue, therefore, that expectancies work best in helping to explain worker behavior in those countries that tend to emphasize an internal locus of control.

Another caution concerning the applicability of Western motivation theories in general to other cultures involves the role of attributions in the process of individual judgment. Attribution theory was largely developed in the US, based on laboratory experiments using predominantly white college undergraduates (Kelley, 1973; Weiner, 1980). This theory focuses on how individuals attempt to understand and interpret events that occur around them. One aspect of this theory which has been repeatedly demonstrated in American studies is the self-serving bias, which asserts that in a group situation a leader will tend to attribute group success to himself and group failure to others. Hence, a manager might conclude that his work team succeeded because of his leadership skills. Alternatively, this same manager may conclude that his team failed because of group negligence and despite his best efforts. Recent evidence by Nam (1991), however, suggests that this process may be influenced by cultural differences. In a comparison of Koreans and Americans, Nam found support for the self-serving bias among his American sample but not in his Korean sample. Following Confucian tradition, Korean leaders accepted responsibility for group failure and attributed group success to the abilities of the group members – just the opposite of the Americans. Clearly, work motivation theories, regardless of their theoretical foundations, must account for cultural variations before any assertions can be made concerning their external validity across national boundaries.

Incentives, rewards, and reinforcement

A third important category of work motivation research focuses on how incentives, rewards, and reinforcements influence performance and work behavior. Theoretical justification for this research can be found in both cognitive theories and reinforcement theories, including social learning theory, behavior modification, and behavioral management theory (Bandura, 1986, 1996a; Luthans and Kreitner, 1985). Critical to much of this research is the role played by self-efficacy in helping determine behavior. Bandura (1986) has argued that incentives and reinforcements can be particularly meaningful if the employees have a high self-efficacy; that is, if they genuinely believe they have the capacity to succeed. Self-efficacy is important because it helps individuals focus their attention on task, commit to challenging goals, and seek greater feedback on task effort (Kanfer and Ackerman, 1996; Locke and Latham, 1990; Tsui and Ashford, 1994).

Considerable research indicates that culture often plays a significant role in determining who gets rewarded and how. Huo and Steers (1993) observed that culture can influence the effectiveness of an incentive system in at least three ways: (1) what is considered important or valuable by workers; (2) how motivation and performance problems are analyzed; and (3) what possible solutions to motivational problems lie in the feasible set for managers to select from. Thus, while many American firms prefer merit-based reward systems as the best way to motivate employees, companies in less individualistic cultures like Japan, Korea, and Taiwan frequently reject such approaches as being too disruptive of the corporate culture and traditional values (Milliman, Nason, von Glinow, Hou, and Kim, 1995).

Moreover, the specific rewards that employees seek from the job can vary across cultures. As Adler (1986) points out, some cultures emphasize security, while others emphasize harmony and congenial interpersonal relationships, and still others emphasize individual status and respect. For example, a study by Sirota and Greenwood (1971) examined employees of a large multinational electrical equipment manufacturer operating in 40 countries around the world and found important similarities as well as differences in what rewards employees wanted in exchange for good performance. Interestingly, in all countries, the most important rewards that were sought involved recognition and achievement. Second in importance were improvements in the immediate work environment and employment conditions such as pay and work hours. Beyond this, however, a number of differences emerged in terms of preferred rewards. Some countries, like England and the United States, placed a low value on job security compared to workers in many nations, while French and Italian workers placed a high value on security and good fringe benefits and a low value on challenging work. Scandinavian workers de-emphasized "getting ahead" and instead stressed greater concern for others on the job and for personal freedom and autonomy. Germans placed high on security, fringe benefits, and "getting ahead," while Japanese ranked low on personal advancement and high on having good working conditions and a congenial work environment.

Kanungo and Wright (1983) found similar results in their four-country study of outcome preferences among managers from Canada, France, Japan, and the United Kingdom. This study focused on the relative preferences expressed by the managers for three types of job outcomes: organizationally mediated (e.g., earnings, fringe benefits, promotion opportunities), interpersonally mediated (e.g., respect and recognition, technically competent supervision), and internally mediated (e.g., responsibility and independence, achievement). Results showed that the British managers strongly preferred internally mediated (or intrinsic) job outcomes, while their French counterparts preferred organizationally mediated (or extrinsic) outcomes. The British managers also placed a higher value on receiving respect and recognition, while the French placed more emphasis on the quality of technical supervision. Canadian managers of British heritage resembled their British counterparts in terms of outcome preferences, while Canadians of French heritage did not closely resemble their French counterparts. Finally, the Japanese were found to be more similar to the British and Canadians in their outcome preferences than to the French. Overall, the greatest cultural divergence in this study was found to be between the British and French.

Merit pay systems that are common in the US attempt to link compensation directly to corporate financial performance, thereby stressing equity. Other cultures believe compensation should be based on group membership or group effort, thereby stressing equality (Erez and Earley, 1993; Pennings, 1993). This issue requires an assessment of distributive justice across cultures, especially as it relates to individualism or collectivism. One example of this can be seen in an effort by an American multinational corporation to institute an individually based bonus system for its sales representatives in a Danish subsidiary (Schneider, Wittenberg-Cox, and Hansen, 1991). The sales force under study rejected the proposal because it favored one group over another. The Danish employees felt that all employees should receive the same amount of bonus instead of a given percent of one's salary, reflecting a strong sense of egalitarianism.

Similarly, a study of Indonesian oil workers found that individually-based incentive systems created more controversy than results (Vance, McClaine, Boje, and Stage, 1992). As one HR manager commented: "Indonesians manage their culture by a group process, and everybody is linked together as a team. Distributing money differently amongst the team did not go over that well; so, we've come to the conclusion that pay for performance is not suitable for Indonesia" (323). Similar results were reported in studies comparing Americans with Chinese (Bond, Leung, and Wan, 1982; Leung and Bond, 1984; Miller, Giacobbe-Miller, and Zhang, 1998), with Russians (Elenkov, 1998), and with Indians (Berman, Murphy-Berman, and Singh, 1985). In all three cases, Americans expressed greater preference than their counterparts for rewards to be based on performance instead of equality or need.

Chen aptly (1995) points out that in studies of individualism and collectivism as they relate to issues of reward equity and distributive justice, consideration must be given to the types of rewards available to the employees. As predicted in his study of American and Chinese managers, Chen found that Americans preferred reward systems that allocated material rewards based on equity but allocated socio-emotional rewards based on equality. In contrast, Chinese managers preferred both material and socio-emotional rewards to be allocated based on equity. Chen's finding with respect to material rewards supports the earlier finding by Kim, Park, and Suzuki (1990) in Japan and Korea. Chen explained his findings by differentiating between vertical and horizontal collectivism in organizations. Evidence was found in Chen, Meindl, and Hunt (1997) to support the hypothesis that the new-found support for performance-based rewards in China may be explained by the existence of vertical collectivism. Horizontal collectivism, on the other hand, works against the equity principle. It was suggested that "collectivists are capable of adopting differential distributive logic as long as such logic is believed to be beneficial to collective survival and prosperity" (1997: 64). Another factor that may help explain this seemingly counterintuitive finding regarding a Chinese preference for equity over equality may lie in the nature of the Chinese sample, which consisted mainly of younger workers, with an average age of 34. (The subjects in the Kim et al. study were also young.) Thus, part of this change in views towards equity-based rewards may represent a shift in employee values – especially among the young – as a result of the surge in China's new quasi-market economy. Evidence consistent with this argument was found by Saywell (1999).

In this regard, it is interesting to note that the bases for some incentive systems have evolved over time in response to political and economic changes. China is frequently cited as an example of a country that is attempting to blend quasi-capitalistic economic reforms with a reasonably static socialist political state. On the economic front, China's economy has demonstrated considerable growth as entrepreneurs are increasingly allowed to initiate their own enterprises largely free from government control. And within existing and former state-owned enterprises, some movement can be seen towards what is called a reform model of incentives and motivation. Child (1994; see also Tung, 1991a) makes a distinction between the traditional Chinese incentive model in which egalitarianism is stressed and rewards tend to be based on age, loyalty, and gender, and the new reform model in which merit and achievement receive greater emphasis and rewards tend to be based on qualifications, training, level of responsibility, and performance. Child and Tung both point out, however, that rhetoric in support of the reform model far surpasses actual implementation.

In Japan, meanwhile, efforts to introduce Western-style merit-pay systems frequently led to an increase in overall labor costs (Sanger, 1993). Since the companies that adopted the merit-based reward system could not simultaneously reduce the pay of less productive workers for fear of causing them to lose face and disturb group harmony (*wa*), everyone's salary tended to increase. Conceptual justification for these results is offered by Milliman, Nason, Gallagher, Huo, von Glinow, and Lowe (1998). Similar results concerning the manner in which culture can influence reward systems, as well as other personnel practices, emerged from a study among banking employees in Korea (Nam, 1995). The two Korean banks were owned and operated as joint ventures with banks in other countries, one from Japan and one from the US. In the American joint venture, US personnel policies dominated management practice in the Korean bank, while in the Japanese joint venture, a blend of Japanese and Korean HRM policies prevailed. Employees in the joint venture with the Japanese bank were found to be significantly more committed to the organization than employees in the American joint venture. Moreover, the Japanese-affiliated bank also demonstrated significantly higher financial performance.

On the other hand, Welsh, Luthans, and Sommer (1993) argued that some Western incentives might work in post-communist societies. They compared three common Western incentive systems to determine their effectiveness among Russian textile factory workers: (1) tying valued extrinsic rewards to good performance; (2) administering praise and recognition for good performance; and (3) using participative techniques to involve workers in decisions affecting how their jobs were performed. Welsh et al. found that both extrinsic rewards and positive reinforcement – both considered behavioral management techniques – led to significantly enhanced job performance, while participative techniques had little impact on job behavior. The authors concluded that behavioral management techniques could represent a useful motivational tool in the post-communist culture under study. However, the researchers also suggested that the Russian employees might have been overly skeptical about the genuineness of the participatory techniques used in the study.

Cultural differences concerning uncertainty, risk, and control can also affect employee preferences for fixed versus variable compensation. As Pennings (1993) found, for example, more risk-oriented American managers were frequently prepared to convert 100 percent of their pay to variable compensation, while more risk-averse European managers would seldom commit more than 10 percent of their pay to variable compensation. Similarly, cultural variations can influence employee preferences for financial or non-financial incentives. Thus, Schneider and Barsoux (1997) note that Swedes will typically prefer additional time off for superior performance instead of additional income (due in part to their high tax rates), while if given a choice Japanese workers would prefer financial incentives (with a distinct preference for group-based incentives). Japanese workers tend to take only about half of their 16-day holiday entitlement (compared to 35 days in France and Germany) because taking all the time available may show a lack of commitment to the group. Japanese workers who take their full vacations or refuse to work overtime are frequently labeled *wagamama* (selfish). As a result, *karoshi* (death by overwork) is a serious concern in Japan (*Sunday Times*, December 11, 1993), while Swedes see taking time off as part of an inherent right to a healthy and happy life.

Free riders and social loafing

A key concern of high performance work teams is maximizing the collective contribution of group members toward the attainment of challenging goals (Lawler, 1992). In a competitive global economy, such collective action becomes a strategic advantage that can differentiate winners from losers. As such, the tendency of select group members to restrict output in the belief that others will take up the slack represents a serious impediment to organizational effectiveness. Free riders and social loafing as social phenomena have been scrutinized in a small but important set of studies (Latane, Williams, and Harkins, 1979). In this regard, Olson (1971) notes that individuals may loaf in a group setting because they assume that the actions of others will ensure the attainment of the collective good, thereby freeing them up to redirect their individual efforts towards the attainment of additional personal gains. This perspective is consistent with agency theory of motivated behavior (Jensen and Meckling, 1976).

Social loafing can only be successful when individual behavior can be hidden behind group behavior. To accomplish this, group norms must support, or at least tolerate, a high level of individualism. It is therefore not surprising that such behavior tends to be more prevalent in organizations in America and Western Europe than in East Asia (Earley 1989, 1993; George, 1992). Matsui, Kakuyama, and Onglatco (1987) found, for example, that Japanese workers performed better in groups than alone. Gabrenya, Latane, and Wang (1983, 1985) found similar results in a Taiwanese study. Earley (1989) specifically tested this hypothesis among Chinese and American managers and found that individualistic–collectivist beliefs moderated the tendency towards social loafing. Specifically, he found that more social loafing occurred in the individualistic American group than in the more collectivist Chinese group.

Building on these results, Earley (1993, 1997a) posited that while individualists would consistently perform better when working individually rather than in a group, collectivists would perform better either when working in an in-group as opposed to in an out-group condition or working individually. Since the basis of collectivism is rooted in allegiance to the group, such individuals would only exhibit this allegiance and subsequent effort when working with members with whom they have had a long and mutually supportive relationship. Working in groups where members were relative strangers would not engender the same cohesiveness or motivational pattern. Earley (1993) tested this hypothesis using a sample of US, Chinese, and Israeli managers. Results supported the hypothesis. Collectivists anticipated receiving more rewards and felt more efficacious, both alone and as group members, and thus performed better, while working in an in-group situation than while working in either an out-group situation or working alone. Individualists, on the other hand, anticipated receiving more rewards and felt more efficacious, and thus performed better, when working alone than while working in either an in-group or out-group situation.

In conclusion, cultural differences have a strong influence on work motivation. Culture can influence individual need strengths, cognitive processes governing effort determination, interpretations of and responses to various forms of incentives, and output restriction mechanisms such as social loafing. What is perhaps surprising here is not so much the magnitude of this influence, but its breadth. Based on available findings, cultural differences seem to permeate many aspects of both the decision to participate and the decision to produce, the two fundamental decisions facing organizational members (March and Simon, 1968). In view of these findings, it is surprising how few studies of work motivation have intentionally incorporated cultural variables into either their models or their research designs.

CROSS-CULTURAL INFLUENCES ON JOB ATTITUDES

Following the work of Allport (1939) and Triandis (1971), an *attitude* can be defined as a predisposition to respond in a favorable or unfavorable way to objects or persons in one's environment. In point of fact, attitudes represent a hypothetical construct since they are not observable and can only be inferred from self-reports and subsequent behaviors. They are generally thought to be unidimensional in nature, ranging from very favorable to very unfavorable. And they are believed to be related to subsequent behavior. Attitudes are thought to consist of three interrelated components: (1) a cognitive component, focusing on the beliefs and thoughts a person has about another person or object; (2) an affective component, focusing on a person's feelings towards a person or object; and (3) an intentional component, focusing on the behavioral intentions a person has with respect to a person or object.

The importance of job attitudes in the workplace has been the subject of intensive examination since the early work of Brayfield and Crockett (1955). These studies have generally focused on one of three attitudes: job satisfaction (Locke, 1976; Porter and Lawler, 1968), job involvement (Lodahl and Kejner, 1965), and organizational commitment (Mowday, Porter, and Steers, 1982). However, while considerable research has focused on this subject within a single-country frame of reference (most notably the US), efforts to look at attitudes cross-culturally have been somewhat sparse. And as noted by Bhagat and McQuaid (1982), and in contrast to studies of work motivation, many of the early studies of cross-cultural influences on job attitudes were atheoretical in nature and somewhat simplistic in design. These studies examined bilateral relationships between job attitudes and specific outcome variables, such as performance or absenteeism in two different cultures. Hypotheses were frequently derived with little concern for extant theories underlying job attitudes and with little in-depth knowledge of the cultures under study.

In one study, for example, Kraut and Ronen (1975) examined various facets of job satisfaction in a large multinational corporation with locations in five countries. Results indicated that country of origin was a better predictor of job performance than any of the facets of satisfaction. While an intriguing finding, little effort was made to consider the potential role of cultural variations in influencing such findings. In another study, Slocum (1971) found that the Mexican hourly workers exhibited greater job satisfaction than their American counterparts. Culture was identified as the reason for the significant differences, although little effort was made to examine why culture should make a difference. Moreover, the study did not explore economic or work environmental factors that could also help explain the findings.

Several studies examined the relationship between locus of control and job attitudes across cultures. Runyon (1973), for example, initially suggested that the relationship between locus of control and job involvement was culture-bound. However, a subsequent investigation by Reitz and Jewell (1979) questioned this finding in a study of skilled and unskilled workers in Japan, Mexico, Thailand, Turkey, Yugoslavia, and the United States. Results showed that in all six highly divergent countries workers with an internal locus of control were more involved with their jobs than those with an external locus of control. This finding, while significant for both genders, was stronger among men. Reitz and Jewell concluded that locus of control is, in fact, not culture-bound. A recent study by Spector, Cooper, Sanchez, and Sparks (in press) offers the first comprehensive look at the impact of locus of control across cultures. Spector et al. found evidence of a consistent positive relationship between internal locus of control and several measures of work-related well-being, including job satisfaction, in their study of 5,000 managers in 24 nations. Locus of control was also found to be positively related to individualism, as would be predicted by theory.

In a major study of job attitudes and management practices among over 8,000 workers in 106 factories in Japan and the US, Lincoln and Kalleberg (1990) concluded that Japanese workers were less satisfied but more committed than their American counter-parts. The researchers explained this difference through an in-depth examination of both Japanese societal culture and corporate culture. For example, the age and seniority-grading system (*nenko*) prevalent in Japanese firms reinforces a family-like relationship between workers and companies; it shows concern for employee welfare. This, in turn, is reciprocated by workers in the form of stronger commitment to the organization, even if the jobs themselves are distasteful. By contrast, in the transitory culture that permeates many US firms, less mutual concern exists between employers and employees. Employees frequently feel more like contract workers than members of the firm. As a result, lower commitment levels are reflected. (Whether this strong commitment exhibited by Japanese workers will continue in the face of an increasing emphasis on performance-based pay raises and promotions and more limited lifetime employment remains to be seen.) The prevalence of after-work socializing among Japanese workers (*tsukiai*) was also cited as another way for workers to reinforce their friendship ties and trust levels among themselves, thereby further solidifying their ties with the companies. Again, this contrasts sharply with the typical American practice of running for the parking lot or subway at the close of work.

In addition, Lincoln and Kalleberg argued that the differential job satisfaction levels between Japanese and American workers may occur because American culture stresses being upbeat and cheerful and putting the best possible face on events. By contrast, Japanese frequently bias their assessments in the opposite direction towards the self-critical and self-effacing. As such, using Western questionnaires to ask questions about job satisfaction may prompt workers in the two cultures to respond in opposite ways, with one group over-estimating their satisfaction levels and the other under-estimating them.

Aggregate work attitudes can change significantly over time as the result of structural changes in the political or economic environment. For example, Shin and Kim (1994) found that general job attitudes among Korean industrial workers declined sharply following the violent labor turmoil that erupted throughout that country in the late 1980s. Specifically, worker attitudes toward their supervisors and their companies declined (from 77 percent holding positive attitudes toward their supervisors and 91 percent holding positive attitudes toward their companies to 41 percent and 65 percent, respectively), as did their willingness to follow supervisory directions (from 94 percent to

59 percent). The rise of unionization and the ensuing labor disputes, largely sanctioned by the government, served to weaken the traditional psychological ties and obligations between workers and companies with a resulting decline in job satisfaction and commitment.

In summary, cultural differences appear to have a significant influence on attitude formation, as well as on the consequences of attitudes once formed. This conclusion supports Triandis's (1971) signal work on this topic and, again, has clear and important implications for both researchers and managers interested in how individuals and groups respond to events and actions in the workplace. Attitudes and accompanying trust levels influence the manner in which employees perceive and respond to reward systems. This, in turn, influences subsequent work motivation and performance. Thus, as suggested earlier by Porter and Lawler (1968), the consequences of job attitudes are ignored by managers at their own (and their organization's) peril.

A Culture-Based Model of Motivation and Work Behavior

This review of over 120 studies on the role of culture in motivation and work behavior logically raises the question of how we can make sense out of these disparate findings. Clearly not all of the findings fit into a mosaic that is easy to interpret. Earlier efforts by Kanungo and Wright (1983) and Ronen (1986) to map these fundamental processes stimulated considerable thought and investigation. As a result, additional research evidence is now available to guide further model-building efforts. Based on this research, we propose a model of how culture influences personal values, motivation, and work behavior as a possible guide to future research in this area (see figure 10.1).

As a point of departure, our model recognizes that cultural differences represent a fundamental contextual variable that influences both individual and environmental characteristics. Culture provides the stage upon which life events transpire. *Individual factors* that can be influenced by cultural variations include the development of one's self-concept, personal values and beliefs, individual needs, traits, and aspirations (Rokeach, 1973; Markus and Kitayama, 1991; Earley, 1989, 1997b). *Environmental factors* that can be influenced by culture include family and community structures, values and norms, education and socialization experiences, occupational and organizational cultures, the status of economic development, and the political and legal system (Hofstede, 1980a, 1980b; Triandis, 1972; Schwartz, 1994). Some cultures emphasize hard work and sacrifice, while others highlight social relationships and enjoyment. Some stress individual achievement, while others stress group achievement. Some favor communal rewards while others prefer individual rewards. Culture also influences the beliefs and values of one's family and friends; younger members of a society learn what to believe in and what to strive for at least in part from older generations. Educational institutions are significantly influenced by culture, as are organizational and occupational values.

As a result of these individual and environmental characteristics, people enter the workplace already imbued with a set of *culturally derived work norms and values* about what constitutes acceptable or fair working conditions, what they wish to gain in exchange for their labor, how hard they intend to work, and how they view their career. Included in this group of culturally derived work norms and values are the general strength and quality of the employee work ethic, individual vs. group achievement norms, proclivity towards egalitarianism, tolerance for ambiguity, social loafing or free rider, and norms concerning conformity and deviance from group wishes (Triandis, 1972; Hofstede, 1980a; Earley, 1989; Elizur et al., 1991). Locus of control also seems important here in view of evidence that some societies tend to emphasize taking control of the future (internal locus), while others tend to believe that the future is beyond their control (external locus) (Reitz and Jewell, 1979).

However, culturally based influences on work norms and values are not universal. Even in the most collectivistic societies, individual differences exist, although the magnitude of variation may differ by culture. Professionals tend to expect more from the workplace in terms of status, rewards, and freedom of action than most blue-collar workers in both Japan and the United States, for example. Moreover, some cultures attempt to minimize status and reward differences between occupational groupings (e.g., Sweden), while others tend to enhance them (e.g., Korea). Individual and group assessments of equity, or what is deemed to be fair and just, seem to underlie this process across cultures (Kim et al., 1990).

In addition, culture influences to some degree one's *self-efficacy beliefs* through education and socialization experiences, as well as the level of *incentives and disincentives* that are offered to employees in exchange for their labor (Earley, 1997b; Pennings, 1993; Chen, 1995; Bandura, 1996a; Kanfer and Ackerman, 1996). As we might expect, incentives and disincentives are frequently influenced by such factors as education level, occupation, corporate personnel practices, level of economic prosperity, group norms, and the political and legal system in which people work.

In turn, *work motivation and employee performance goals* are heavily influenced by three factors: (1) culturally derived work norms and values; (2) self-efficacy beliefs; and (3) rewards, incentives, and disincentives that result from performance. Work norms and values are important because they help determine the nature and quality of work effort, whether effort is to be based on the individual or group, beliefs about the equity and equality of incentives, and levels of work-related uncertainty that can be tolerated on the job (Earley, 1989). Self-efficacy is important because it determines one's confidence to put forth effort on the job (Bandura, 1996b; Early, 1997b). In this regard, Erez and Earley (1993) have proposed a model that specifically addresses the relationship between culture, the self-concept, and work behavior. Finally, intrinsic and extrinsic rewards of various types are important because they provide both the incentives and disincentives to perform. Expectations concerning possible rewards represent a powerful force for employee motivation, although the magnitude and type of such incentives may vary across cultures (Porter and Lawler, 1968; Locke and Latham, 1990; Welsh et al., 1993). For example, considerable research indicates that in many Western societies pay-for-performance compensation systems can significantly help to raise productivity (Lawler, 1992). In other cultures, however, merit-based systems frequently fail due to egalitarian norms (Child, 1994; Milliman et al., 1998).

Corporate-based incentives can also have the effect of creating disincentives to perform, largely through the intervention of group norms. Social phenomena such as social loafing and sanctions governing levels of output frequently serve to restrict the impact of incentives on performance (Earley, 1989). In some cases, employees are pressured by colleagues not to break group-determined production quotas, despite incentives to do so. In other cases, employees are legitimately concerned about working themselves out of a job if they perform at high levels.

Following from the research on cognitive theories of motivation, we would expect work motivation to strongly influence subsequent *work behavior and performance* (Vroom, 1964; Porter and Lawler, 1968; Steers, Porter, and Bigley, 1996; Mitchell, 1997). It is important to note here that individual, group, and organizational goal setting – particularly when these goals are specific, accepted, and moderately difficult – clearly plays a role in motivated behavior by focusing employee effort towards readily identifiable targets of performance (Locke and Latham, 1990).

However, employee motivation alone is insufficient to guarantee high performance. In addition, employees must possess several *performance contingencies*. These include having relevant personal abilities and job skills, a clear understanding of the requirements of the task, and the appropriate tools and technology to complete task assignments efficiently. To a large extent, these factors are determined by available educational opportunities, on-the-job training, supervisory competence, and the company's or country's ability to secure relevant job technology to support employee efforts. Obviously, the acquisition of some of these performance contingencies is influenced by cultural factors, although this is not shown in figure 10.1 for space considerations.

As a result of subsequent job performance, employees receive a variety of *outcomes and rewards*. These can be extrinsic or intrinsic in nature. The manner in which employees interpret these consequences will largely influence their *perceived equity*, as well as the nature and quality of their resulting *job attitudes*. To the extent that employees believe that the rewards they receive are fair and just, we would expect them to develop more positive work attitudes, as well as increased confidence and trust in management to be fair. To the extent that the resulting rewards and outcomes are seen by employees as unfair or inequitable, we would expect them to develop more negative attitudes, as well as increased distrust of the future actions of management (Porter and Lawler, 1968). The nature and quality of both job attitudes and employee trust then clearly feed back to influence how employees view future incentives offered by their employer, thereby influencing subsequent work motivation and performance goals. Moreover, when employee performance levels are high, we would also expect self-efficacy beliefs to be reinforced, thereby increasing or at least preserving subsequent motivational levels. We would expect the opposite impact on self-efficacy and subsequent motivation when employee performance levels are low.

This model of the effects of culture on work motivation and subsequent performance is based on the current cognitive theories on work motivation, as well as on available research findings on the effects of cultural differences on attitudes and behavior. It represents an attempt to put such findings in perspective in a manner that is useful for both researchers and managers. However, this is a research model; it remains to be systematically tested in its own right. This must be the province of future research efforts.

CONCLUSION

Since the 1990s there has been a significant increase in both the quantity and quality of research concerning the role of cultural differences in work motivation and job attitudes. Recent studies on culture and motivation exhibit better theoretical grounding, more rigorous research designs, improved measures, and more sophisticated data analytic techniques. For instance, the use of multiple methods for data collection can be seen in studies by both Heller and Wilpert (1981) and Chew and Putti (1995). And among the few studies that incorporated a quasi-longitudinal design, Hofstede's (1980a) classic work stands out. Recent studies also employ more rigorous measures (Elizur et al., 1991; Bond, 1987) and better study designs (Earley, 1989; Lincoln and Kalleberg, 1990; Vijver and Leung, 1997).

As a result, we now have a reasonable body of evidence from which to draw some initial conclusions. Perhaps most importantly, evidence of the significant ways in which cultural differences can influence work values, motivation, and job attitudes is now irrefutable. No longer can researchers ignore or trivialize the significance of culture in future studies on work behavior. This conclusion necessitates a reexamination of many of our current theories of both work attitudes and behavior, as well as management theories in general, to incorporate cultural factors as a more central conceptual variable. An attempt has been made here to consider the role of culture as it specifically relates to work motivation and performance. However, more research and conceptualization along these lines would be of considerable benefit to the field. In view of the increasing globalization of markets, services, and manufacturing, ignoring cultural factors in corporate decision-making and action can have significant adverse economic repercussions for companies and countries alike. It is therefore hoped that this review will stimulate future endeavors by both researchers and managers to better understand the global realities of the workplace.

Despite recent progress, however, the field can still do better. Several specific concerns relating to research on work motivation should be noted. Many of these criticisms of the management research literature in general also apply to the research on managerial values and work motivation. For example, while progress has been made in creating multinational research teams as one means of reducing national and cultural biases, the same cannot be said for creating multidisciplinary teams. In our view, much could be gained from incorporating the views of management scholars along with various social scientists, including psychologists, sociologists, economists, and anthropologists, in serious studies of the motivational basis of employee behavior and performance. Seldom is such cooperation seen.

The field of cross-cultural motivation requires a significant increase in rigorous, comprehensive, and theory-based studies that further our *systematic* understanding – and predictability – of behavioral phenomena in organizations around the world. Most of the studies in this domain focus on testing one small piece of one theory, ignoring a larger set of variables and relationships that in reality can frequently influence both attitudes and behavior. Seldom do we see the logic or preparation that can be found in Lincoln and Kalleberg's (1990) study of Japanese and

American employees or Earley's (1989; 1997b) study of social loafing in China and the US. These studies are theory-driven, technically accurate, and logical in their choice of samples. Moreover, comparative studies of the relative predictive powers of competing motivational models in and across cultures are seldom found in the literature, making progress in the important area highly problematic. In this regard, the study by Welsh et al. (1993) comparing three Western incentive systems among Russian workers may represent a model for others to emulate. Finally, in addition to cross-cultural studies, more in-depth single-country studies focusing specifically on how culture actually influences attitudes and behavior would be helpful.

In addition, the general failure to select samples that represent strategically different cultures for purposes of theory building has plagued cross-cultural research from its inception. All too frequently, we see samples of convenience that appear to be selected prior to any consideration of study variables or even theory. Indeed, some have referred to this problem as "vacation empiricism" (Steers et al., 1992), and it hardly constitutes sound research. Instead, it represents a significant hurdle to further progress in the field. A good example of theory-driven strategic sampling combined with the use of a rigorous research instrument can be seen in the comparative work values study by Elizur et al. (1991). In short, what is needed is more theory-based sampling, not sampling-based theory.

It is also possible that some of the data we currently have on cultures are highly selective. Most of the field research reported here was conducted in work organizations, which routinely try to recruit and retain the best people available. As such, the people under study are generally likely to be more literate and better educated than the norm for a given society, and may not be representative of society as a whole. Conclusions based on such samples must be interpreted with caution.

Finally, more attention needs to be focused on the nature and quality of the research instruments under study. With the notable exception of Bond's (1987) Confucian dynamism scale, most variables under study in this field derive from Western thought and consciousness. For example, why do we study job attitudes instead of face? Why do we study individual competitiveness instead of group harmony? Indeed, many research instruments employ Western concepts that do not even have direct conceptual equivalents in some other cultures (e.g., job satisfaction). Other Western concepts frequently used in questionnaires do not convey identical meanings across cultures (e.g., reward equity). Translation problems in research instruments are also rampant, even when there is conceptual equivalency. Perhaps greater use of ethnographic methods would allow local employees to help identify those variables that are central areas of concern for purposes of study.

In sum, considerable progress has been made on this topic, and the role of cultural differences in work behavior is now better understood. However, despite this progress, we are left with the conclusion that serious efforts are still required to build on these current findings in an effort to extrapolate more of the essence of culture as a predictive study variable. We remain largely mired in the realm of knowing *what* and, to some extent, knowing *how*. What would be particularly useful at this point for the study of cross-cultural management would be expanding our understanding of *why*.

NOTE

The authors wish to thank Nancy Adler, Greg Bigley, Chris Brewster, Chris Earley, Ida Kutschera, Fred Luthans, Richard Mowday, Lyman W. Porter, James Terborg, Harry Triandis, and the two handbook editors for their valuable comments and assistance on earlier drafts of this chapter. We also wish to express our appreciation to the US Department of Education, IESE, and the University of Oregon for their support and encouragement throughout this project.

11

Cross-Cultural Leadership

PETER B. SMITH AND MARK F. PETERSON

Most people would agree that leadership, particularly at upper echelons, is a crucial element in the success of international businesses and other types of multinational organizations. The topic has been much studied and extensive reviews can be found of the existing research literature, including several that cover research about leadership across cultures. Bass (1990) devotes a chapter to cross-cultural leadership themes in research through the 1980s. Several subsequent detailed reviews bring us very close to the present (Dorfman, 1996; House, Wright, and Aditya, 1997; Peterson and Hunt, 1997). Rather than duplicate these reviews, our goal here will be to direct attention to their contributions and to address issues that were either outside their scope or that have arisen only very recently.

In writing a chapter about cross-cultural leadership, we recognize that different authors use the label "cross-cultural" in various ways. For present purposes, we will distinguish four strands of meaning. First, the phrases "cross-cultural leadership" and "international leadership" are often used to encompass studies which have taken theories of leadership developed within the United States and tested their predictive validity in other parts of the world. Second, authors from the United States often also refer to models of leadership developed and tested in countries other than the United States under the heading "cross-cultural." Third, there are studies that focus upon leadership of work teams whose composition *is* actually multicultural. Given the multicultural nature of the workforce in many of the leading industrial nations of the world, it could be argued that most studies of leadership, both within and outside the USA, fall into this category. However, most such studies do not focus upon specifically cultural aspects of the relations between leaders and those with whom they work. Finally, the study of leadership is brought into the international strategy and overall international management literature through the emphasis that transformational and charismatic leadership theorists have placed on how senior executives can shape entire organizations. Strategic leadership of multinational organizations is often referred to by US authors as "global leadership."

THREE RECENT REVIEWS

Traditional leadership themes

Dorfman (1996) picks up the cross-cultural theme of earlier reviews by Bass (1990), Smith and Peterson (1988), and Bhagat et al. (1990). He notes the significance of leadership issues for global management and the need to deal scientifically with the problem of how culture affects leadership. His review is structured around themes that have been significant in US leadership research — trait theories, behavioral theories, contingency theories, participation, charisma, and transformational leadership. He establishes the potential relevance of cultural issues to each of these themes, and then describes approaches to culture based on values and social information processing. The bulk of this review covers single-nation studies done outside the USA, as well as comparative studies which take an international perspective.

The most significant contribution of Dorfman's review lies in the links it provides between domestic US theories and tests of those theories outside of the USA. In his treatment of the behavioral approach, for example, Dorfman covers studies that have translated traditional leadership behavior measures and administered them in other languages. Considerate, supportive leaders are largely preferred throughout the world. Reactions to task-oriented leadership appear to be more complex. Dorfman also lays the ground for some of his own later research (discussed below) by surveying early studies of performance-contingent social rewards and punishments. Finally, he includes a review of leadership in different parts of the world and a description of some developing projects, including the GLOBE and the event management projects, which have developed further since his review and hence are both described below.

Major multiple country studies

House, Wright, and Aditya (1997) review cross-cultural leadership with the purpose of developing a new international study of leadership, the GLOBE project. In contrast to Dorfman's focus on international links to main themes in US research, House et al. place more emphasis on the smaller number of large-scale multiple-country leadership studies. Much of their review deals with concepts of culture, the methods needed to study culture, and the pros and cons of different schemes for identifying culture dimensions. These issues are explored elsewhere in the present Handbook.

Specifically within the leadership field, they begin by noting the two earliest multiple country projects: a study of managerial needs (Haire, Ghiselli, and Porter, 1966) and a study of managers in training exercises (Bass, Burger, Doktor, and Barrett, 1979). House et al. then identify a further 15 multiple-country studies published between 1989 and 1996. These include studies of cultural differences in leadership prototypes or preferences, leader behavior patterns, follower responses to leader behavior, and the origins and qualifications of people appointed as leaders.

House et al. then review issues that may have implications for leadership. Religion, elites, historical leaders, the modernization process, and the functional demands on leaders are seen as combining to produce a tension between opposing forces toward convergence and continuing cultural distinctiveness in leadership throughout the world.

The upshot is that the degree of convergence in various aspects of leadership becomes an interesting empirical question. They conclude that there may be some cultural universals in basic leadership constructs alongside some more culturally contingent specific expressions of them. They formulate three summary propositions:

- The *cultural congruence* proposition: "cultural forces affect the kind of leader behavior that is usually accepted, enacted, and effective within a collectivity" (p. 589).
- The *cultural difference* proposition: "increased task performance of followers, organizations, and institutions in societies will be induced by the introduction of selected values, techniques and behavior patterns that are different from those commonly valued in the society" (p. 591).
- The *near universality of leader behaviors* proposition: "some leader behaviors are universally or nearly universally accepted and effective" (p. 591).

House et al. conclude by presenting a complex integrative model, to be used in the GLOBE project. We will discuss this when we turn to that project.

Basic questions

Peterson and Hunt (1997) pose four fundamental questions about international research into leadership. These questions provide a basis for linking the topics covered in a special issue of *Leadership Quarterly* (Hunt and Peterson, 1997). First, is leadership a universal idea? They conclude that there is a universal necessity for something that resembles what people in English-speaking societies would recognize as leadership, although the specifics vary by society and by setting. Second, should universal leadership constructs be sought, or should we look for radically unique aspects of leadership in different societies? They conclude that at least within organizational settings, sufficient similarity is apparent to make it worthwhile to compare the relationship of similar aspects of leadership to similar sorts of outcomes in various parts of the world. Third, should leadership be studied scientifically? They conclude that it should, and that despite the incompleteness of highly structured methods, a great deal can continue to be learned through the systematic application of experimental, survey, and ethnographic methods. Fourth, does the concept of leadership have a technological/modern US bias? They conclude that it does, but that this bias is consistent with the choice by many groups of people throughout the world to organize themselves for production work into large-scale organizations.

The Peterson and Hunt paper brings us to the intended contribution of the present chapter. Their review complements those by Dorfman and House et al. by providing an orienting perspective towards basic issues in the field. We will build on these reviews by first explaining our own viewpoint. We will then turn to recent studies based on US theory applied abroad, take another look at research originating outside the USA, and finally consider leadership within multicultural settings and multinational corporations.

ESTABLISHING A VIEWPOINT

Our perspective on leadership is focused upon the process of social interpretation. We see organization members, whether they are leaders or not, as encountering a continuous stream of events in their surroundings and striving to make sense of them and to influence the meaning that others give to them.

We can illustrate this process by considering what occurs during the writing of this chapter. The "events" to which we as authors seek to give meaning include relatively concrete ones like the set of published writings by others as well as more diffuse ones such as the current state of the cross-cultural leadership field. We make sense of these events by drawing from a variety of sources of meaning or alternative ways of understanding and looking at what we experience. In writing the chapter, each of us is drawing from his own experience. We are also anticipating and responding to the views of the literature expressed by others. Furthermore, we anticipate probable reactions and actually solicit reactions from relevant colleagues. This process of giving meaning to the writing process also requires that we draw on norms as to what a handbook chapter should be, from the views we have inferred and that have been expressed by the editors, and from publication agreements. In the ordinary sense, it is we who are writing this chapter (and norms suggest that we should accept full responsibility for all its blemishes or possible strengths), but our reasoning suggests that we are not entirely independent actors. We are also focal points through which information, debates, ideas, and values that are influencing the field of organization studies are being brought to bear on the topic of cross-cultural leadership.

This kind of reasoning produces quite a strong conclusion – all people at all times are in similarly ambiguous situations. Everyone seeks to make sense of events as part of a larger context through which events are given meaning. Those individuals that we choose to identify as leaders are a special category of people who draw from multiple sources in order to influence the meanings given to organizational events and thereby to influence choices and actions. The same applies to ourselves in our present role of authors. We seek to persuade you to think about the giving of meaning by leaders and the influence on them of meanings deriving from others as "event management."

In taking this viewpoint, we acknowledge the cultural background from which we come, but we try to avoid some of the shortcomings we recognize to be typical of our background. North American and many other Western cultures have been characterized as relatively individualistic (Hofstede, 1980; Schwartz, 1994; Smith, Trompenaars, and Dugan, 1996; Triandis, 1990). One characteristic that has been noted among persons within individualistic cultures is that they (or we) tend to interpret the actions of those around them in terms of individual traits, qualities, or styles of behavior. The role of social context or the actions of others in determining the behaviour of an individual is given much less attention.

Others have argued effectively that an author's cultural background will influence the theories he or she formulates (Erez, 1990; Hofstede, 1993). We can extend this argument by suggesting that the cultural milieu within which theories are formulated affect what will be published, read, and used in a particular society. This proposition is well-illustrated by the types of leadership theories which have attracted most support within North America. The focus has been very much upon the qualities and behaviors of effective leaders and only late in the development of US leadership theory have a few scholars forcefully drawn attention to the excessive emphasis upon leaders as individuals and the need to better recognize the influence of social context upon the performance of work teams or organizations (Kerr and Jermier, 1978; Meindl et al., 1985). Even today, our sense is that the US academic ideal remains to search for a small number of behaviors by powerful individual leaders that dramatically shape the activities of all other organization members. This ideal is also reflected in the types of US theories that have been tested abroad.

In contrast, cross-cultural psychologists portray members of the more collectivist nations of the world as giving much greater attention to social context. Leaders, like other members of these cultures, are not so much seen by themselves or others as an entity apart from their immediate social context. Their role is more permanent, more integral to the social fabric. Persons working with a leader are likely to act in ways which are not caused by the specific acts or qualities of their leader, but simply because the leader occupies a specified leadership role. As part of the maintenance of overtly harmonious leader–follower relationships, all manner of positive qualities may be attributed to the leader. Some caution is therefore required before inferring that because the subordinate describes the superior's behavior in positive terms in such a society, the subordinate's performance will be enhanced in the same way that we would expect from US research. Within the collectivist context, a simple unidirectional causal chain is even less likely to give a good explanation of what is going on than is the case in the USA. As Meindl et al. (1985), Lord and Maher (1991), and others have noted even within the US context, positive qualities may be attributed to leaders whose organizations are experiencing success, even where there is no evidence that the success is caused by the leader. This type of attribution is likely to be more frequent in collectivist cultures, because of the stronger and more permanent links between leaders and their teams.

A second finding has emerged from a number of areas of investigation in cross-cultural psychology. A useful distinction can be made between *general* and *specific* aspects of social behaviors. This is illustrated within the field of leadership by aspects of Misumi's (1985) theory, treated below; the distinction has been incorporated into other more recent studies (House et al., 1999). Misumi proposes that there are certain general or universal functions which effective leaders must either fulfill themselves or see that they are fulfilled by other means. However, the way in which these functions are to be fulfilled in a given social context will vary, depending upon the meanings which are placed upon particular behaviors within that context. So, if one seeks to establish universal generalizations about leadership processes, one should design measures whose content is broad and general. On the other hand, if one seeks to understand cultural differences in the meaning given to particular leader actions, one should design measures whose content focuses upon rather specific behaviors (Smith et al., 1989).

Our interest is in avoiding an individualistic bias. Our belief that while there are general leadership functions, the meaning of specific actions is culturally contingent; this shapes our view of the cross-cultural leadership field. In surveying the existing literature, the extent to which research recognizes the embeddedness of a leader in a larger context and takes account of the interdependencies between specific leader actions and the different meanings that are given to them in particular contexts will determine the value of the research. Studies which do both these things have greater potential, both for advancing cross-cultural understanding of leadership and for practical intervention purposes.

US Theories Tested Abroad

The great bulk of cross-cultural studies of leadership fall within this category. Many leadership theories that developed in the USA and were later tested abroad have been covered in the prior reviews discussed above. We focus here on four lines of theory that continue to be actively pursued at the present time. One is the theory of transformational leadership. The second is the GLOBE project, which has been built around several theoretical perspectives, most notably the concept of "value-based" leadership. The third is the theory of performance-contingent leadership, and the last is the event management theory as applied to leadership.

Transformational leadership

Although the theory of transformational leadership has roots outside the USA in Weber's (1924/1947) theory of the routinization of charisma, it has become a central theme in recent US leadership research. The impetus for this came from a set of articles and books by House (1977), Burns (1978), and Bass (1985), exploring the leadership process. Subsequent US interest broadened to consider how leaders can influence organizational cultures (Ashkanasy, Wilderom, and Peterson, 2000). At least part of this interest was triggered by a desire to incorporate into US organizations the cooperative qualities viewed as typical of organizations in collectivist cultures.

Bass (1985) proposed that where there exists between superior and subordinates a shared or transforming vision of what is to be accomplished, subordinate performance will be greater. This hypothesis has been tested within samples in more than 20 nations (Bass and Avolio, 1993; Bass, 1997). His Multifactor Leader Questionnaire (MLQ) has undergone a number of revisions but has been used, in translated versions, in the same series of unmodified forms in all countries. Results are uniformly found to support the transformational hypothesis. In most studies, the ratings of leader effectiveness are completed by the same sample of subordinates who characterize the leader's transformational style. This provides no independent verification of the relation between leader style and leader performance. However some studies do also include independent data sources. For instance, Steyrer and Mende (1994) found that in a sample of 120 Austrian bank branches, those branches whose managers were rated by their subordinates as transformational subsequently increased market share.

Bass (1997) accepts that his measure of transformational style is formulated in a relatively general manner, and acknowledges that within differing cultural contexts a leader might need to act in quite different ways in order to be perceived as transformational. For instance, he suggests that within a collectivist culture a leader might need to act in an autocratic or directive manner, while in an individualistic culture a more democratic or participative style would be required. If it is true that this type of substantial difference does exist in the behaviors required in order to be judged transformational, that may explain why the factor structures obtained from MLQ data from different nations have varied widely (Dorfman, 1996).

The GLOBE project

A similar conception of effective leadership underlies the more recent, and more extensive, GLOBE project (Den Hartog, House, Hanges, Dorfman, Ruiz-Quintanilla, and 134 coauthors, 1999; House, Hanges, Ruiz-Quintanilla, Dorfman, Javidan, Dickson, Gupta, and 170 coauthors, in press; House, Wright, and Aditya, 1997). Leadership is defined in GLOBE as "Ability to influence, motivate and enable others to contribute to success of their organization" (House et al., in press: xx). Sampling managers from three industries within 61 nations, GLOBE seeks to integrate implicit leadership theory, the value/belief theory of culture, implicit motivation theory research, and a structural contingency theory of organizations. Reports of the project to date seek to determine the extent to which "value-based" leadership is universally effective.

House and colleagues' formulation of value-based leadership resembles his earlier emphasis on charisma, and Bass's description of transformational style. They have in common the notion that effective leadership is not simply a matter of an exchange of rewards for effort, but that leader and subordinate have a shared and emotionally charged sense of purpose. The GLOBE project has included also an array of other measurements which will make it possible to determine whether the extent of support for the overall hypothesis can be accounted for by variations in different dimensions of cultural values and by variations in organizational practices. Data on respondents' prototypes of effective leadership will also make it possible to determine the specific qualities which are associated with value-based leadership in a given nation's sample.

Full results of this very large-scale project are not yet available. However, similar to Bass's findings, value-based leadership is found to be strongly favored in most if not all samples. Operationally, value-based leadership is defined as positive endorsement of the following leader traits and qualities: enthusiastic, positive, encouraging, morale booster, motive arouser, confidence builder, dynamic, convincing, visionary, inspirational, decisive, performance-oriented, with high integrity. Analyses are not yet published which would shed light on what a leader in a given culture would need to do to be perceived in this highly positive manner.

The GLOBE project evokes implicit leadership theory as a basis for investigating what sorts of leadership people around the world find most and least helpful. The GLOBE project researchers use implicit leadership theory rather differently from how it has usually been understood. Traditionally, implicit leadership theory has dealt with those aspects of leadership-related cognition of which respondents are least aware. The original studies provided respondents with cues about both leader behavior and group performance and then looked to see if cues indicating high or low performance distorted perceptions of behavior (Lord et al., 1978). Some subsequent studies have interpreted the factor structure of leadership questionnaires as a way to access the implicit theories that respondents from different cultures hold about leadership (Ah Chong and Thomas, 1997).

The GLOBE project applies implicit leadership theory quite differently. It first defines leadership, then presents respondents with a set of leadership attributes and behaviors to which they give one of seven Likert-scaled responses ranging from "substantially impedes" to "substantially facilitates" leadership. This phrasing is reminiscent of earlier studies of explicitly expressed leadership ideals and attitudes. The GLOBE project then draws on Lord and Maher's (1991) hypothesis that leadership is inferred when the actions observed in a person match a "prototype" of leadership held by the observer. Those behaviors that are rated as most facilitative are taken as defining these leadership prototypes. House et al. (1999) report 22 items for which country scores show a mean of 5 ("slightly facilitates" effective leadership) or higher in 95 percent of the countries studied. These items include 13 such as "trustworthy," "plans ahead," "encouraging," "decisive," and "excellence-oriented" that come from subscales of a second-order charismatic/value-based leadership factor. The remaining 9 universally endorsed items such as "dependable," "effective bargainer," and "communicative" represent subscales from a second-order team-oriented leadership factor.

Den Hartog et al. (1999) describe country differences in the enactment of charismatic/value-based leadership using qualitative analyses of leadership in different countries. They note that charisma and visionary leadership are viewed as risky in Mexico, among other countries, and among political leaders in India. Perhaps the risk is associated with popular skepticism about whether the "integrity" ideal that is integral to espoused ideals in the GLOBE conception of charismatic/value-based leadership is ever being genuinely realized. They also note that the means of communicating a vision can be quite culturally contingent, ranging from use of exceptional public oratory in the USA, to persistently and quietly demonstrating exemplary personal service by people like Mother Teresa, and to engaging in quiet politicking in China. Similarly, the typical charismatic quality of showing concern for individuals may be culturally variable, ranging from a relatively limited acknowledgment and accommodation to subordinates' personal situations in some countries to a quite active involvement in their personal lives in others. However, once a person has established high status, the data indicate that communicating egalitarianism is a useful part of charismatic leadership in many nations.

The GLOBE Project scholars plan further analyses of the relationship of leadership preferences, particularly preference for charismatic or value-based leadership, to various outcomes. They are also interested in how national and organizational contingencies affect leadership ideals and correlates. Publications from this very large project will no doubt continue to appear for some years.

Performance-contingent leadership

A third project derived from existing US theory has employed the more traditional concepts of reward and punishment. Subordinates of managers in electronics assembly plants in USA, Mexico, Taiwan, Korea, and Japan characterized their superiors in terms of their reliance on contingent and non-contingent rewards and punishments (Dorfman, Howell, Hibino, et al., 1997). Ratings were also made on scales for charisma, directiveness, and participation. Leaders who made rewards contingent on performance were positively evaluated in all five nations, whereas on the other scales the results varied between samples. Thus, for this project too, the most general measure was the one which showed a result favoring the universality of leader effectiveness, with the more specific scales giving less consistent results. This international project, however, reports results only for contingent and non-contingent rewards, not for contingent and non-contingent punishments. A related study found enough cultural variability in the way that non-contingent punishment is viewed to suggest that the factor structure and hence the meaning of contingent and non-contingent punishment may not generalize readily (Peng and Peterson, 1998).

Event management

The final project to be considered in this section originated from the account of leader "event management" first formulated by Smith and Peterson (1988) and subsequently developed more fully (Peterson, 1998b; Peterson and Smith, 2000). It too must be considered as based upon US theory, although as will be seen, considerable attempts were made to develop a model of leadership which did not have implicit within it the cultural preconceptions which are widespread within individualist nations. The event-management model of leadership moves away from the individualist emphasis on portraying leaders as the source of a one-way influence process. In place of this, leaders are seen as contending with a series of potentially ambiguous events. Surrounding them is a network of persons and impersonal sources of information, each of which may be used as a source of guidance in interpreting events, and each of whom may also be influenced by the leader. The model thus incorporates some of the elements of reciprocal influence thought to be characteristic of relations within more collectivist cultures.

All events at work are not equally ambiguous, and many can be quickly assigned to a category which has been handled frequently before. Others may require extensive guidance from or negotiation with a variety of sources. In a preliminary study, the model was tested by identifying eight moderately frequent work events, and eight sources of guidance on which leaders were thought to rely with some frequency. These included one's own experience and training, superiors, peers, subordinates, and specialists, as well as more impersonal sources, such as formal rules, informal organizational norms, and "beliefs which are widespread in one's nation as to what is right." Managers in China reported more reliance on formal rules, while managers from the UK and USA relied more on their own experience and training (Smith, Peterson, and Wang, 1996).

In a second study, nine events specific to the context of local government in the USA and Japan were studied (Peterson, Elliott, Bliese, and Radford, 1996). These included events that differed in their importance, uncertainty, and the resources most directly involved. Ten sources of meaning including people in various roles (e.g., superiors, subordinates), impersonal sources (like unwritten rules), and external sources (like regulatory boards) were considered. Reliance on sources was found to vary both by event and by nation. So, leaders are relied upon to handle some situations more than others, and the situations in which people make the most use of leaders also varies by country.

More extensive sampling has shown that, like the projects described above, the event management project also detects a universal. In every one of 29 nations sampled, leaders in middle-management positions reported relying on their own experience and training more than on any of the other sources of guidance (Smith and Peterson, 1995). However, these data can also be analyzed in ways which can identify differences between cultures as well as the universals. By ranking how strongly each source of guidance is used relative to reliance on the same source in other nations, more interesting patterns are revealed. For example, the degree of leaders' reliance on their own experience and training is strongly correlated with Hofstede's scores for the individualism of the nations sampled

(Smith, Peterson, and 13 coauthors, 1994). Leaders in individualist nations also report being more guided by subordinates than those elsewhere.

These results indicate some consistent differences in the average behaviors of leaders within different nations. Individual-level studies have also been conducted of the relationship between sources of meaning that managers report using and their self-evaluations of how well the events are handled. Smith, Peterson, and Misumi (1994) compared evaluations of event management by members of electronics assembly teams in the UK, USA, and Japan. The sources of guidance rated as effective differed between nations. A further study used samples of managers from six nations in Central and Eastern Europe, and found substantial divergence in leaders' own evaluations of what was effective. For instance, in Hungary and the Czech Republic reliance on one's own experience was seen as effective, whereas in Romania reliance on widespread beliefs was favored for several events (Smith et al., 2000). Thus, there is preliminary evidence that this way of studying relations between leaders and their work teams cannot only detect national differences between specific ways of handling events, but also picks up cultural differences in what is perceived to be effective.

The four lines of research we have described under the general heading of "US theories tested abroad" have some commonalities that mark recent developments in such research. Recent work within each line consists of much more than a simple replication of something found in the USA. The process of translation, backtranslation, evaluating metric equivalence, and collecting data from meaningful samples scattered around the globe has always been difficult, so difficult in fact that large-scale international projects are quite infrequent. Recent projects, though, have struggled to overcome the Americanness of their theoretical origins. The GLOBE project included a substantial effort to design new survey items rather than simply taking and adapting earlier US surveys. It also included a substantial qualitative element that has potential to pick up local nuances. The Dorfman et al. study (1997) follows an earlier tradition by translating surveys designed in the USA, but it documents the uniquenesses of context that helps explain quantitative results, and allows scaling metrics to vary by country to better pick up areas of comparability and incomparability. The event management projects draw from theory outside the leadership field and use measures tapping issues noted as relevant by collaborators in countries quite different from those of the project's coordinators. Criticism of the Americanness of theory is at least beginning to be replaced by examples of projects that find ways to limit the downside of research that has been influenced by single nation perspectives.

NON-US THEORIES

Few theories of leadership formulated by researchers outside the USA have become widely known. Furthermore, it is by no means self-evident what is a "non-US" theory. The distinction among the autocratic, democratic, and *laissez-faire* social climates that condition the effects of leader behavior came from a German, Kurt Lewin, who had concerns about his home country and was interested in contrasting it with the United States (Lewin et al., 1939). Does the influence of this research on subsequent US theory make it German? We think not, but it does draw attention to the global history of social science. Most non-US leadership researchers, including those whose work is discussed below, have had extensive contact with US researchers and their theories resemble in some respects certain North American formulations. This resemblance could be due to functional universals in leadership, or to the way that the social constructions favored by US academics have become globally instutionalized. Nonetheless, the distinction between US and non-US leadership theory is worth making, because it provides an opportunity to assess the extent to which there is or is not a global convergence in conceptualizations of leadership.

PM theory

The best-known non-US theory is that formulated by Misumi (1985) in Japan over the past forty or fifty years. Misumi's work was stimulated by contacts with Lewin before World War II and was substantially influenced by US experimental social psychology and survey methodology. In order to take some of the emotional connotations out of Lewin's leadership concepts and make them more scientific, Misumi identified two functions which effective leaders in any situation will need either to provide directly or to insure that they are provided in some other fashion. These are described as the Performance function (known as "P") and the Maintenance function, (known as "M"). The P function has to do with task accomplishment, while the M function has to do with the maintenance of good working relations among those who are engaged on the task. Misumi's PM theory thus has a superficial similarity to early US theories of leader style, such as the Ohio State studies. However, there are two key differences between these two lines of research. First, Misumi argues that the ways in which leadership functions are to be filled must vary from one situation to another. For instance, in one study he found an important aspect of effective P leadership in Japanese local government to be whether or not leaders exploit their position for personal gain by asking subordinates to do personal favors such as working on their boss's home (Misumi, 1985). Quite different survey forms with different specific dimensions falling in the P and M categories were designed not only for leaders in such fields as banking, manufacturing, transportation, and shipbuilding, but also for leaders at different hierarchical levels in local governments (Misumi and Peterson, 1985). In contrast, while some US leadership researchers designed survey forms tailored to specific industries (for example, different forms for education, the military, and manufacturing), the predominant tendency has been to create a single set of constructs and measures designed for any and all leadership settings. In contrast, Misumi argues that measures of leadership functions need to be developed anew within each substantially different setting in which leadership is studied.

The second way in which PM theory is distinctive is that Misumi postulates that the exercise of the P and the M functions are not independent, but complement one another. In other words, the effectiveness of a leader who places substantial emphasis on both the P and M functions is said to be greater than could be predicted by simply summing the known effects of a leader who is high on P and one who is high on M. House (1987) insightfully describes the theory as "all things in moderation" leadership. Misumi argues that assessing a statistical interaction term is not the right way to get at this combination for a number of reasons. This interaction is said to occur only where both P and M functions are moderately high, and hence is not necessarily detectable as the type of interaction which would emerge from hypothesis testing using ANOVA. In Misumi's view, charismatic or transformational leadership that is based on tying the follower's view of what is good for them personally to their view of what is good for task accomplishment is a *specific* form of PM leadership. To US scholars, charismatic or transformational leadership are distinct leadership dimensions whose content can be specified, unlike Misumi's P and M functions.

Both of the ways in which PM theory differs from US leader style theories can be seen as consistent with characteristic US and Japanese approaches to problem-solving. Americans often favor the analysis of situations into a series of separate elements, whose independent effects on one another can then be assessed. Japanese tend more often to stress the ways in which elements of a situation are interwoven with one another and must be evaluated holistically (Hampden-Turner and Trompenaars, 1993). The work of both Misumi and the Michigan leadership researchers derived from the heritage of Kurt Lewin. Consistent with Japanese holistic thinking, Misumi maintained the contextual and configurational themes of Lewin's field theory while the Michigan researchers followed US practice by dissecting the themes and transforming them into dimensions. Misumi also relied on experimental data when seeking to establish causal relationships, whereas the pragmatism that moved US leadership research from early laboratory studies to the field emphasis of later years led most researchers in the troublesome direction of trying to infer causality from correlations within survey data.

PM theory has been tested in a very wide range of Japanese organizations by Misumi and his associates (Misumi and Peterson, 1985). Leaders high on both P and M have been shown to be most effective, in terms of both subjective evaluations by subordinates and objective assessments, such as lower accident rates and higher productivity. Studies have been conducted using tightly-controlled laboratory settings as well as in extensive field studies in large organizations.

A small number of studies have been reported that test aspects of PM theory outside Japan. Smith, Misumi, Tayeb, Peterson, and Bond (1989) tested the hypothesis that different specific behaviors were associated with high scores on a particular set of P and M measures designed for electronics assembly plants in different parts of the world. Supervisors in Japan, Hong Kong, the UK, and USA were studied. The questionnaire asked about very specific aspects of the supervisors' behavior, such as when they arrived at work, whether they ate lunch with their work team, how often they spoke to work team members and so forth. The sharpest distinction between P and M was found among US respondents. At the other three sites, behaviors which were seen as related to one leadership function were often seen as having some implications also for the other function. Furthermore, some behaviors which were positively correlated with high P or M at one site were negatively correlated with that function at other sites. The study thus supported Misumi's view that leader behaviors have no objective and generalized meaning: they acquire meaning through the context in which they occur.

Despite variability in the specific content of leader functions, PM theory asserts that valid measures of the P and M functions will be associated with effective leadership in all settings. Smith, Peterson, Misumi, and Bond (1992) found some support for this within their four-nation sample of electronics assembly plants. Peterson, Smith, and Tayeb (1993) compared factor structures and found that P and M could predict subordinate attitudes and work performance in the USA, UK, and Japan. Ah Chong and Thomas

(1997) found that measures of P and M predicted work performance among Pakeha (white) and Pacific Islander New Zealanders. Casimir and Keats (1996) tested PM theory among Anglo and Chinese Australians. High P, high M leaders were preferred, but Chinese followers' reactions were more influenced by variations in work context than were Anglos, as the reasoning above would lead one to expect. Peterson, Maiya, and Herried (1994) developed related PM measures suited to several specific US settings. They too found a common pattern of more positive attitudes under leadership where P and M were both high, but not the kind of precise ordering of leadership types that has been well documented by laboratory research in Japan. Attempts to use PM leadership theory in the People's Republic of China indicated that a dimension tapping ideologically appropriate, ethical behavior should be added (Peterson, 1988a). Although the prediction that high PM leaders will be effective has thus been supported in a number of countries, this way of reporting results tends to obscure Misumi's assertion that the specific dimensions representing basic P and M functions and the specific behaviors which fulfill them effectively will vary in every context.

NT theory

A second non-US leadership theory is that formulated in India by Sinha (1980, 1995). Sinha's NT theory also postulates two key dimensions of effective leader behavior, those which are concerned with Nurturance and Task. Sinha observed that within the relatively hierarchical context of India, leaders often emphasize task aspects of leadership and neglect any form of nurturant or supportive behaviors. Indeed, some studies show that autocratic supervision is preferred by subordinates in India. However, Sinha's research revealed that Indian leaders in a range of organizations were in fact more effective when they were able to foster greater participation by subordinates. This was accomplished through a gradual process of nurturing subordinates toward the taking of greater responsibility. Thus for Sinha, in a way that resembles the Misumi model, the preferred style of leadership is one in which Nurturant and Task behaviors are simultaneously provided, thereby providing a type of distinctively paternalistic leadership.

NT theory has not been directly tested outside India. However, some studies reported from other relatively collectivist nations have yielded supportive results. For instance, Ayman and Chemers (1983) found paternalistic supervision effective in Iran. Their questionnaire measure of paternalism included items such as "a good supervisor should be like a good father." Items which have this degree of specific content are likely to be evaluated in different ways within different cultural contexts. However, if discussion is focused at the more general level of leadership functions favored by Misumi, there is a considerable convergence of opinions in recent years. Jaeger and Kanungo (1990) propose that the need for both hierarchy and participation indicates that the preferred leader style in organizations in collectivist nations would be charismatic or transformational. A leader who could successfully identify a vision of organizational purpose and achieve endorsement of it by those within the organization could both retain a high degree of power and enlist willing participation.

More specifically, Sagie (1997), from Israel, has presented what he calls a "tight–loose" model of leadership. He discusses the cultural and organizational contexts in which it is possible for a leader to both maintain a tight control and encourage participation.

However, drawing on our earlier discussion of the ways in which leader behaviors are interpreted in different contexts, we may expect these proposals to receive general support only if they are tested using measures formulated in rather general ways. If the measures refer to more specific aspects of leadership we shall find that tight–loose leadership is more effective within the cultural contexts where leaders are able to integrate control and participation. The extensive studies of both Sinha and Misumi provide indications of how this can be accomplished in India and in Japan.

Other recent single-nation formulations

Pelled and Xin (1997) emphasize the view that responses to leaders in collectivist cultures will rest on their role or position as much as on what they actually do. Their position is supported by a study in a Mexican *maquiladora*. The positive effects of high leader–follower similarity on organizational attachment were mediated by complex interactions with age and with gender. El-Hayek and Keats (1999) found Lebanese Australian organization leaders to be motivated by collective motives such as status, recognition, and responsibility, compared to Anglo-Australian leaders who gave more weight to individualistic motives such as financial gain and promotion.

Tjosvold, Hui, and Law (1997) obtained critical incident ratings from 66 Hong Kong managers. Path analysis indicated that constructive controversy between leaders and those with whom they worked was strongly linked to cooperation and less linked to competition than earlier US results had shown. Sun and Bond (1999) surveyed upward and downward influence tactics used by 219 mainland Chinese managers. Factors named Contingent Control and Gentle Persuasion were identified. Consistent with the theme of the present review, they argued that at a general level these factors are consistent with those identified by Western researchers, but many of the specific items making up the factors were different. Rao, Hashimoto, and Rao (1997) also studied influence tactics, but focused on Japanese managers. They found some tactics similar to those reported from the USA, but some additional distinctive tactics, including after-hours socializing and emphasizing benefits to the company rather than to the individual.

None of these five diverse recent studies links directly to the leadership theories discussed above, but all yielded findings showing some of the distinctive attributes of leadership within more collectivist cultures that the earlier literature would lead us to expect.

INTERCULTURAL STUDIES

Given the growing frequency of work teams composed of persons from differing cultural backgrounds, it is regrettable that so much of the existing literature refers to leadership within monocultural contexts. Studies are required of the degree to which leaders adapt their behavior to the cultural expectations of those with whom they work, and of the effectiveness with which this is accomplished. The effectiveness of both multinational corporations and joint-venture organizations will be dependent on how well this is done. Den Hartog and Verburg (1997) drew from a theory of the use of rhetoric by charismatic leaders (Shamir, Arthur, and House, 1994) to analyze the discourse used in speeches by chief executives of three multinational corporations. Speeches given by Anita Roddick of Body Shop expressed her vision of "one best way" of running an organization and made no references to diversity. Jan Timmers of Philips laid great emphasis on the existence of diversity across hierarchical levels and across nations and stressed the importance of listening to the views of employees and customers locally. The discourse used by Matthew Barrett of the Bank of Montreal was intermediate between the other two CEOs. Each of these organizations has achieved substantial success since the 1990s, but this type of analysis cannot indicate what has been the contribution to this success of differing types of CEO discourse, nor how individual employees have reacted to these presentations.

Almost all of the more specific studies have looked at the interface between North American managers and those from China and Japan. The importance of this interface was underlined in an early study by Black and Porter (1991). They found that while eight of twelve dimensions of managerial behavior correlated significantly with appraisal results among US managers working in Los Angeles, only one of these dimensions showed a significant relationship with appraisals among US managers working in Hong Kong. Hui and Graen (1997) compare the Chinese practice of *guanxi* (doing mutual favors in the context of long-lasting family or friendship-based relations) with Graen's earlier US-based model of an LMX relationship between superiors and subordinates. They conclude that if US managers are to be effective in China, they need to establish relations which transcend the Western boundary between work and non-work relations. Interestingly, a recent survey of Hong Kong and US managers by Tsui (1998) showed that a substantial proportion of her US respondents were also able to identify *guanxi*-type relationships which had aided their careers.

Smith, Wang, and Leung (1997) surveyed 134 Chinese managers who were working directly with non-Chinese managers in joint-venture hotels. A series of problem events were identified. Respondents were then asked how much they relied on various ways of handling these problems and how effective was each way of doing so. Greatest difficulty was found with Japanese superiors and least with superiors from Hong Kong and Taiwan. In relating to Western managers, direct communication was rated as most effective, but indirectness and more traditional Chinese behaviors were reported as more frequently used.

Graen and Wakabayashi (1994) describe the heavy input of resources that was required to achieve a gradual transfer of more team-oriented leadership styles from Japanese to US supervisors working in Japanese plants in the USA. In another study of a US plant, Peterson, Peng, and Smith (1999) found differences in US subordinates' response to Japanese and American supervisors. There were initial indications that pressure from Japanese supervisors was more acceptable than from American supervisors. However, the effects changed over time, as working relations in the plant stabilized and the number of Japanese supervisors declined. Rao and Hashimoto (1996) surveyed 202 Japanese managers in Canada who had both Canadian and Japanese subordinates. They reported giving more reasons and using more sanctions when dealing with Canadian subordinates. Presumably this occurred through the need to make explicit what would have been more implicit in communication with the Japanese subordinates.

The studies so far available thus indicate that leaders' relations with those around them are affected by cultural differences. There are indications that some leaders are able to adapt their behavior, especially where training is provided, but very little evidence as to how often these changes are accomplished or how effective they are.

GLOBAL LEADERSHIP

The analysis of the specific skills of leadership within multinationals is in its infancy. It requires that we apply to multinational corporations the sort of rational planning theory characteristic of organization strategy analysis, charismatic and transformational leadership theory, and understandings of the way that contexts define meanings. These literatures are not yet being well integrated.

One line of theory about challenges facing leaders of multinational corporations (MNCs) comes from the Harvard tradition of drawing from cases of large companies. Bartlett and Ghoshal (1998) suggest that the global leadership responsibilities of an MNC manager depend on which of four main responsibilities the person holds. Rather than leadership behavior style, this work is reminiscent of Mintzberg's (1973) analysis of leadership in terms of managerial roles. For a manager with global responsibilities for a product or business, the challenges are to provide a global product strategy, coordinating allocation of resources to fit the product strategy, and coordinating resources flows (e.g., components) across countries. The role of a manager with global responsibilities for a particular function is to scan for innovations throughout the world relevant to that function, to disseminate these innovations within the company, and to creatively promote use of new ideas without the support of hierarchical authority or financial control. A geographic subsidiary manager is responsible for providing the MNC with expert information about the manager's own geographic area, to be an advocate for this area, and to implement corporate strategy as it applies to that area. Bartlett and Ghoshal argue that top-level corporate managers of MNCs need to provide overall corporate strategic direction, use personal control rather than just financial control to find ways of making optimal global use of innovations from any part of the MNC, and actively update and reconsider even basic corporate mission and strategy. This line of work is steeped in a distinctive approach to strategy and is not yet well integrated into other potentially related literatures, particularly those about charismatic and transformational leadership.

Most other empirical studies of global leadership consist of opinion surveys asking senior executives their opinions as to the qualities required in present and future multinational chief executives. For instance, Korn-Ferry International (n.d.) obtained responses from 160 MNCs, and found relatively similar opinions from their US, European, and Asian respondents. Opinions were that future leadership will be more team-based, require more "feminine" qualities and be more customer-focused.

Gregersen, Morrison, and Black (1998) base their recommendations to multinational executives about the qualities a global leader should have and how these qualities should be developed on a series of interviews and questionnaires with representatives of firms from Europe, North America, and Asia. The view they take is that such respondents are in a good position to diagnose and articulate the qualities of effective global leaders. The authors suggest that global leaders have unbridled inquisitiveness, that they possess personal character traits of emotionally connecting with people from diverse backgrounds and having uncompromising integrity, that they can handle both the duality between the need for more information and the need to act under uncertainty as well as the duality between local responsiveness and global consistency, and that they have both business and organizational savvy. The process of developing global leaders is said to require assessing talent, providing travel experiences that do not insulate managers from the local culture, providing experiences working with multicultural teams, arranging training programs with an appropriate participant mix, appropriate contents, and action learning components, and providing overseas assignments. Their research, typical of similar work, is heavily prescriptive and relies on the ability of executive informants to handle the complex task of accurately determining what really does promote effectiveness of various sorts. Most typically, the leadership literature has been reluctant to accept executives' diagnoses of what constitutes effective leadership. Leadership ideals have rarely been taken at face value as indicating what in fact does contribute to effective leadership. Similarly, research about the actual effects of the sorts of global leadership principles coming from consultancy-based projects remains to be conducted.

Strategic management of the largest organizations often rests not on an individual leader but on leadership by top management teams (Hambrick and Mason, 1984). Elron (1997) applies this perspective to multinationals by studying top management teams within subsidiaries of 22 US multinationals. Consistent with the literature on multicultural teams, she finds that the cultural heterogeneity of these teams stimulates issue-based conflict but also contributes positively to subsidiary performance.

The GLOBE project among others is currently suggesting the global applicability of a charismatic style of leadership. However, Den Hartog et al. (in press) note the possibility that even the contributions elicited by charismatic leaders can create problems. It is often assumed that organizations which contribute effectively in the marketplace without harming their employees are also contributing constructively to society. In parts of the world where national economies are small or in a process of becoming more market-oriented, this assumption is less viable. Many countries with smaller economies are still struggling to develop leadership systems where organization success does not compete with national success. In large nations, the appointment of a person with significant management skills to work for a multinational rather than for the government is of little concern: others can fill the vacant role. In a small country, the choice is more consequential since the labor market for senior managers is more limited. Similarly, the actions of a multinational operating in a small African or Caribbean nation can create considerable disruption to the local economy. The task for leaders in such situations is not only to create organizational success, but to contribute to the success of the local society. Certainly, the same holds to a degree in the United States and Western Europe, but the significance of this issue is greater in situations where multinationals have relatively strong resources compared to local governments.

Global leaders who think only of their organization's priorities may also be tempted by short-term advantage to exploit current difficulties in regulating international trade after the manner of the largely unregulated nineteenth-century industrialists. Our analysis suggests that the best protection from such hazards is for leaders to draw meaning from multiple sources rather than from themselves alone and to recognize that the people whom they seek to influence are also drawing meaning from multiple sources. The problem for researchers remains one of understanding how effective leaders can best acquire such perspectives, and how to caution the more charismatic type of global leader against the overly individualistic view that would result in the pursuit of what are really only personal or narrowly organizational aims.

CONCLUSION

Researchers into cross-cultural leadership are increasingly addressing questions that have long needed to be addressed, but much remains to be done if the field is to provide useful guidance to managers working throughout the world. Although an overemphasis on testing theories developed in the USA remains a limitation, the testing of such theories outside the USA is certainly quite a bit preferable to assuming that they apply without even testing them. Even this type of research is increasingly seeking to create valid ways of representing US theory rather than simply translating US surveys. While more research influenced by non-US themes is certainly needed, the field can continue to advance by carefully checking the local applicability of any theory or measure. Projects such as those of Misumi and Sinha provide examples of how one might proceed to develop research derived from ideas important in particular countries.

Relying on theory from one country in trying to understand another creates two problems well known in cross-cultural psychology. First, it risks imposing concepts in settings where they have little meaning. An aspect of leadership that is critical in one part of the world may have little consequence elsewhere. Within leadership research, this may not be too great a problem. For example, leader actions oriented toward goal achievement and toward maintaining team morale may well be universal, perhaps even inherent in the nature of work groups. The difficulty has been knowing what specifics represent these concepts in different societies.

The second problem is one of neglecting locally important aspects of leadership. This cannot be addressed by the testing of US findings abroad. An overemphasis on individual leaders who guide a set of followers can only be counterbalanced by research into the way that leaders fit into a larger role set and an even broader range of sources of meaning. Key members of the role set and particular important sources of meaning, such as norms, tacit understandings, rules and laws, are best identified within local cultures and incorporated into local leadership models. Results from this type of research can also open up topics neglected within Western nations. Tsui's work provides an example by showing how *guanxi*-like phenomena also operate in the USA. Perhaps the US taboo against what are thought of as cronyism and nepotism has encouraged US researchers to look elsewhere. Rao et al.'s work suggests another interesting possibility that communicating organizational benefits to subordinates might be a neglected aspect of Misumi's performance-oriented leadership. The successful application of an in-group, out-group distinction to leadership in Japan and China by Graen and his colleagues has also stimulated thought about the importance of in-groups and out-groups in relation to leaders in the USA.

Some progress is thus evident in the internationalizing of leadership research, and hence in the growth of a conception of leadership which is not itself culture-bound. We can expect this process to continue, to the extent that research projects become increasing bilateral and to the extent that local validation of measures becomes the norm rather than the exception.

12

Women Joining Men as Global Leaders in the New Economy

Nancy J. Adler

"For all practical purposes, all business today is global" (Mitroff, 1987: ix). As management scholar Ian Mitroff (1987: ix) aptly observes, "Those individual businesses, firms, industries, and whole societies that clearly understand the new rules of doing business in a world economy will prosper; those that do not will perish." "Global competition has forced executives to recognize that if they and their organizations are to survive, let alone prosper, they will have to learn to manage and to think very differently" (Mitroff, 1987: x).

WOMEN: INCREASINGLY IMPORTANT AS GLOBAL LEADERS

How prepared are multinational enterprises to recognize that their global competitiveness depends on including the most talented people in the world on their executive teams, women as well as men? Based on history, the answer would appear to be, "Not very." Women today hold less than 3 percent of the most senior management positions in major corporations in the United States (Wellington, 1996) and less than 2 percent of all senior management positions in Europe (Dwyer, Johnston, and Lowry, 1996). In countries such as Italy, the proportion of women executives falls to a paltry 0.1 percent (Dwyer et al., 1996; see also International Labor Office, 1997).

Can companies – or countries – afford to continue their historic pattern of male-dominated leadership? As global competition intensifies, the opportunity cost of such traditional patterns escalates. Most leaders know their companies can no longer afford to ignore potential talent "simply because it's wearing a skirt" or because it holds a different passport (Fisher, 1992). Whether or not they have chosen to act on it, CEOs recognize that in a global economy, "Meritocracy – letting talent rise to the top regardless of where it is found and whether it is male or female – has become essential to business success" (Kanter, 1994: 89).

Careful observation reveals a rapidly increasing number of countries and companies moving away from the historic men-only pattern of senior leadership. For example, of the 44 women who have served in their country's highest political leadership position – either as president or prime minister – over 60 percent have come into office since the 1990s, and all but six are the first woman their country has ever selected.[1] Similarly, among the current women CEOs leading major companies, almost all are the first woman whom their particular company has ever selected.[2] The question is no longer, "Is the pattern changing?" but rather, "How is it changing? And how will companies take advantage of the change?"

GLOBAL LEADERSHIP: THE CHALLENGES OF FOCUSING ON WOMEN

As companies increasingly select their executives from among the best women and men worldwide, rather than restricting candidates for senior positions almost exclusively to men – as has been done so often in the past – an inevitable question arises: How different are women executives, if at all, from their male counterparts? Advocates of the two seemingly opposite positions – "Women and men executives are exactly the same" and "Women and men are distinctly different" – often tenaciously adhere to their own point of view and respond incredulously or even with hostility to proponents of perspectives other than their own. Not surprisingly, this crucial similar-or-different dilemma surfaces frequently within multinational enterprises and organizations. Given the paucity of research on global women leaders, existing studies cannot, as yet, resolve the dilemma (Osland, Snyder, and Hunter, 1998; Powell, 1999; Yeager, 1999).[3]

Given the inherent ambiguity, global executives and leadership scholars need to understand the similarity-versus-difference controversy in such a way that it facilitates, rather than undermines, organizational effectiveness (Thomas and Ely, 1996). The first step toward such a constructive reframing is to recognize that, whether similar or different, increasing the number of women in the executive ranks will increase competitiveness. Why? Because whether women executives lead in similar or different ways to male executives, drawing from both groups increases the pool of potential talent. As basic statistics make clear, if you draw from a larger population, on average, you will select better leaders.

Given the transparent advantage inherent in drawing from a larger pool of candidates – one that includes both women and men – why do so many people, and companies, continue to get sidetracked by the similar-versus-different controversy? The explanation lies in the fact that the controversy cannot be discussed, let alone resolved, by simply answering a single question. Rather, as highlighted in table 12.1, the assumptions one makes relative to three distinct, albeit related, issues define both the confusion and the complexity. The first question is, "Do women lead in similar ways to men?" The second related question is, "If women and men lead differently, whose leadership style is more effective?" And third, if women and men differ, "Do the differences in leadership style advantage or disadvantage the organization's overall effectiveness and competitiveness?"

Inherent in the three questions, and adding to the complexity of any global leadership initiative, is the confusion caused by some people appreciating difference simply as "difference" while others judge it as reflecting either inferiority or superiority. As shown in table 12.1, the three questions differ markedly on this appreciation-versus-judgment

TABLE 12.1 Global leadership: the nature of the questions

Fundamental questions	Type of question	Treatment of difference	Underlying dilemma
Do women lead in similar ways to men?	Descriptive	Appreciative of difference	Similiarity vs. difference
Do men or women lead more effectively?	Evaluative	Judgmental	Superiority vs. inferiority
Is diversity an advantage or a disadvantage to the organization	Evaluative	Judgmental	Advantage vs. disadvantage

Source: Adler, N. (forthcoming). Advances in global leadership: The women's global leadership forum. In W. H. Mobley and M. McCall (eds), *Advances in global leadership*, Vol. 2. New York: JAI Press

spectrum. The first question, "Do women lead in similar ways to men?" is strictly descriptive; it simply asks if one observes differences in the ways women and men lead. Such differences are not judged to be either good or bad. Unlike the second and third questions, the first question is appreciative (i.e., descriptive), not evaluative. In contrast, both the second and third questions – "If women and men differ, whose leadership style is more effective?" and "Are male/female differences an advantage or a disadvantage to the organization?" – are evaluative. Depending on their perspective, people judge either men's or women's ways of leading to be superior. Similarly, depending on one's perspective, differences in leadership styles are judged to be either good or bad for the organization.

Although in most organizations one perspective dominates, the full range of the similar-versus-different, superior-versus-inferior, and advantage-versus-disadvantage assumptions is believed, expressed, and, all too often, argued about. It is important, therefore, to understand how the various arguments influence global companies' attempts to achieve a more balanced representation of male and female executives from all regions of the world and, more importantly, how they influence overall organizational functioning.

ALTERNATIVE APPROACHES: UNDERSTANDING HOW ORGANIZATIONS VIEW DIFFERENCE

As highlighted in table 12.2, alternative attitudes toward difference – as expressed in people's responses to the three questions – lead to four very different approaches to increasing the number of women in leadership positions and to valuing, or not valuing, their potentially unique contributions to the organization.[4] As will be discussed, the four approaches are:

- identifying with men's leadership styles;
- denying differences;

TABLE 12.2 Global leadership: approaches to difference

Approaches	Identifying with men	Denying differences	Identifying with women	Creating synergy
Assumptions				
Do women lead in similar ways to men?	Different	Similar	Different	Different
Do men or women lead more effectively?	Men	Neither	Women	Neither
Is diversity an advantage or a disadvantage to the organization?	Disadvantage	Disadvantage	Disadvantage	Advantage
What is valued?	Conformity to men's ways	Culture of sameness	Conformity to women's ways	Leveraging diversity
Cross-cultural equivalent	Ethnocentric (pro-men)	Parochial	Ethnocentric (pro-women)	Cultural synergistic

Source: Adler, N. (forthcoming). Advances in global leadership: The women's global leadership forum. In W. H. Mobley and M. McCall (eds), *Advances in global leadership*, Vol. 2. New York: JAI Press

- identifying with women's leadership styles; and
- creating synergy – leveraging women's and men's leadership styles.

In the first and third approaches, people acknowledge differences, but see them as negative. The first approach assumes men's ways of leading are better while the third approach assumes women's ways are better. By contrast, in the second approach, people deny the possibility of differences. The fourth approach acknowledges differences without judging either men's or women's leadership styles to be superior. While organizations can adopt any of the four approaches, the synergy approach, by integrating and leveraging women's and men's unique styles into complementary approaches, is most conducive to sustained, long-term global effectiveness (Adler, 1997c; Thomas and Ely, 1996). Each of the four approaches, with its respective underlying assumptions, is described below.

IDENTIFYING WITH MEN'S LEADERSHIP STYLES

The first approach views men and women as distinctly different and judges men's styles of leading to be superior to those of women. Men are seen as displaying characteristics that have historically allowed them to lead effectively, including having:

an ability [to act in an] ... impersonal, self-interested, efficient, hierarchical, tough minded, and assertive [manner]; an interest in taking charge, control, and domination; a capacity to ignore personal and emotional considerations in order to succeed; a proclivity to rely on standardized or "objective" codes for judgment and evaluation of others; and a heroic orientation toward task accomplishment. (Fondas, 1997: 184, based on Brod and Kaufman, 1994; Gilligan, 1982; Glennon, 1979; Grace, 1995; Kanter, 1977; and Seidler, 1994)

Whereas the most common descriptions of men – as aggressive, independent, unemotional, objective, dominant, active, competitive, logical, worldly, skilled in business, adventurous, self-confident, and ambitious – support the image of men as leaders, especially in the United States, the descriptions that have traditionally been used for women – as talkative, gentle, tactful, religious, quiet, empathetic, aesthetic, submissive, and expressive – have consistently undermined the image of women as leaders (Ashmore, Del Boca, and Wohlers, 1986; Broverman et al., 1972; Harriman, 1996; and Williams and Bennett, 1975). Although the specific characteristics vary somewhat from organization to organization, and culture to culture, the overall pattern in this first approach is for organizations to identify success with men's, rather than women's, ways of leading.

Identifying with the masculine echoes the same cultural dynamic as classic ethnocentrism; in male/female terms, such ethnocentrism might be labeled male chauvinism. Whereas women are recognized as differing from men, all such differences are judged to be detrimental to women's ability to lead, and therefore to the organization's potential performance. From this perspective, it is inconceivable that women's unique approaches to leading might benefit the organization. Both men and women, therefore, attempt to minimize the differences between their own approaches and the male norm. Seeing men's ways as superior, women attempt to think like, act like, and lead like their most successful male colleagues. Similarly, men who see women's approaches as counterproductive attempt to minimize the differences by coaching high-potential women to act like men, and complimenting them when they succeed. Women who identify with men generally believe that the organization will only promote them into executive positions if they lead in exactly the same ways as the most successful men. Such women admit that, in general, women differ from men, but see themselves as the exception. They see themselves as fitting men's typical pattern, not that of the majority of women (see Hampden-Turner, 1993). Similar to many of their male colleagues, these women see the typical female pattern as incompatible with executive success.

Comments characteristic of identifying with the masculine include, for example, derisively describing meetings of executive women as "a coffee klatch" or "the girls' knitting club," and cautioning colleagues that such meetings will probably turn into "bitch sessions." Such comments as "How could this meeting be important if only women executives are attending?" and "Men make better bosses" reflect the assumed superiority of men. Each comment expresses the belief that women differ from men and that the difference will not help companies enhance their performance. The historic pattern of promoting primarily men into organizations' most senior leadership positions reflects companies' overall tendency to value men's ways of leading above those of women. Surveys documenting that most women believe that they need to *develop-a-style-that-men-are-comfortable-with* reveal women's pervasive assumption that they have to adapt to the male norm to succeed (Adler, Brody, and Osland, 2000, 2001 in press; Wellington, 1996). From this perspective, women's conformity with the male pattern is neither surprising nor illogical.

DENYING DIFFERENCES

The second approach to dealing with both cultural and male/female differences is denial – choosing to assume that no salient differences exist. In this approach, rather than judging women's leadership styles to be inferior (as is done in the first approach) or superior (as is done in the third approach), both men and women simply assume that there is only one way to lead. From this perspective, talking about a men's or women's style of leading is meaningless, as is any consideration of diversity's value to the organization.

On a cultural level, denial is most similar to parochialism: "Because I am most familiar with my own culture, I believe that it is the only culture." Because all of us are most familiar with men leading, many people simply assume, albeit implicitly, that men's approaches provide the only possible model for success. Women who deny differences generally believe that, as professionals, they are just like the men who have always led major corporations. Men who deny differences often compliment women for managing or leading "just like a man." Denying differences leads to a *culture of sameness*, in how organizations treat their male and female professionals as well as in how they treat people from Asia, Africa, Europe, the Americas, and the Middle East. Given the *culture of sameness*, organizations attempt to foster effectiveness by treating everyone identically.

Examples of men and women denying differences are pervasive, especially in the United States. Perhaps the most visible expression of denial is Americans' use of *politically correct* speech and behavior, in which, among other foci, all recognition of women as women is curtailed as a hedge against potential discrimination. Complimenting a woman on her looks, for example, becomes unacceptable, in part because it explicitly violates the denial-of-difference norms by recognizing that the woman is, in fact, a woman. Women who express resentment at the press for referring to them as women leaders (rather than just as leaders) are exhibiting a form of denial. Similarly, women who reject being invited to events, in part because they are women, are also exhibiting denial. They reject the idea that they differ from their male colleagues in any substantive way that would make it reasonable to hold a special event for women, or to solicit a woman's point of view at a high-level meeting, or for the press to recognize that "she" is not a male leader. Showing characteristic denial, one European woman's response to her CEO's invitation to the company's first women's summit was: "I am happy to attend . . . if I'm being invited because of my business acumen as one of the top 100 people in the company, [and] not simply because I am 'a girl.'" The denial is transparent both in the woman's use of the pejorative term for an adult woman – "a girl" – and in the opposition she creates between the category of "executives seen to have business acumen" and "executives seen as women." Women's implicit, and often reality-based, fear is that being seen as a woman will diminish their perceived stature as a leader. Similarly, male executives who question their organization's plans to design unique recruitment procedures for women, or to institute women's mentoring networks, or to build more flexible work scheduling to meet women's needs deny the possibility that male and female professionals might differ. In all cases, those who deny differences prefer that everyone be treated identically, as if no differences, in fact, existed.

IDENTIFYING WITH WOMEN'S LEADERSHIP STYLES

Similar to the first approach, the third approach accepts that women and men differ. However, unlike the first approach, the third approach judges women's – not men's – leadership styles to be superior, especially for the twenty-first century's more networked, less hierarchical, global organizations. Labeled as the *feminine advantage*, women's greater tendency to use more democratic, inclusive, participative, interactional, and relational styles of leading are cited by many scholars as among the reasons women's styles of leading will bring more value than men's to modern organizations (Fondas, 1997: 259, based on Chodorow 1978; Helgesen 1990; Lippman-Blumen, 1983; Marshall, 1984; and Rosener, 1990, among others).[5] Anthropologist Fisher (1999: xvii), for example, concludes that women have many exceptional faculties for leading, including "a broad contextual view of any issue, a penchant for long-term planning, a gift for networking and negotiating, ... a preference for cooperating, reaching consensus, and leading via egalitarian teams, ... an ability to do and think several things simultaneously, ... emotional sensitivity, ... and a talent with words." Based on the assumptions made in this third approach, all managers – men and women alike – are encouraged to incorporate a more feminine approach into their leadership style.

Echoing the dynamics of the first approach, identifying with women's styles of leading could be seen as a type of reverse chauvinism, and is, in fact, a variant of traditional ethnocentrism. Similar to both the first and second approaches, managers perceive diversity – in this case, deviance from women's ways of leading – as disadvantaging the organization in its ability to compete effectively.

One of the most common work-based expressions of the *feminine advantage* is the belief that women executives can better understand and work with women clients. Similarly, the assumption that women are better able to develop relationships with clients from more relationship-oriented cultures, such as Asians and Latin Americans, highlights the thinking underlying a woman-based approach. In identifying with the feminine, women are seen, and see themselves, as better than men at offering organizations the type of leadership they most need in a global economy.

CREATING SYNERGY: INTEGRATING AND LEVERAGING MEN'S AND WOMEN'S LEADERSHIP STYLES

The fourth approach, similar to the first and third approaches, accepts differences; women and men are not seen as leading identically. However, unlike the prior approaches, it does not judge either women's or men's styles of leading to be superior. Rather, the organization values each style as contributing uniquely and synergistically to the whole. Benefits come primarily from the potential for combining and leveraging men's and women's different styles of leading. Using a synergy approach, the organization benefits not just from combining women's and men's styles of leading, but also those of people from a wide range of cultures and countries.

For organizations to successfully pursue a synergistic approach, they must not only include both women and men in their leadership ranks, but must also ensure that each maintains his or her unique voice. To the extent that one group assimilates the approaches of the other group, synergy becomes impossible. Under the leadership of former Prime Minister Gro Harlem Brundtland, Norway became one of the first countries in the world to achieve a gender-balanced cabinet, and thus the potential for real synergy. Currently led by CEO Andrea Jung, Avon Products has become one of the first major global companies to similarly achieve gender-balance among its most senior leaders.

THE EVOLUTION OF ORGANIZATIONAL CULTURE

Whereas companies' organizational cultures evolve over time – sometimes leading, and at other times lagging, more general societal trends – the evolution is not random. As highlighted in figure 12.1, the most common order of evolution in major companies generally begins with a homogeneous culture with all (or almost all) men in the managerial and executive ranks. As companies begin to hire women managers, usually initially for entry-level positions, they expect the newcomers to fit into the existing male culture; that is, the company expects the newly hired women to identify with the existing male culture. As the number of women and their level in the organization increases, organizations frequently begin to deny differences. In the name of equality and fairness,

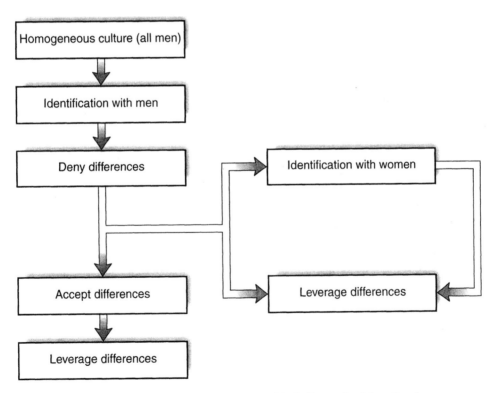

FIGURE 12.1 Evolution of corporate culture: toward including and valuing diversity

they claim not to notice if a manager is male or female, but rather only assess if he or she is productive. Denial gives way to acceptance as organizations begin to recognize that men and women are not identical. Once such acceptance is made explicit, organizations are able to move on to the final phase, leveraging differences. In some organizations, particularly woman-led entrepreneurial start-ups, women's styles of leading are valued for a period of time above those of men.

As summarized in table 12.3, the external societal forces encouraging organizations to favor one approach over the others, and to transition from one approach to the next, have varied over time, as have the strategies organizations use to respond to each successive set of external pressures. The following section describes each evolutionary stage in more detail.

Homogeneous Culture

Historically, the leadership cultures of most companies initially included only men. The global analogy, of course, is the historical dominance of senior executive teams by people from a company's home culture: American companies led by American men, German companies led by German men, and Chinese companies led by Chinese men (see Dorfman, 1996). Such homogeneous cultures are only possible when little or no external or internal pressure exists to force them to change; as was the case prior to the 1960s when organizations felt little need to invite women into their all-male leadership cultures. In such homogeneous cultures, questions of diversity remain irrelevant.

Single-Culture Dominance: Identifying with Men

Beginning in the 1960s, most prominently in the United States, various equal employment opportunity laws were passed and increasingly enforced.[6] In response to these external legal pressures, organizations began recruiting women, primarily into lower-level positions. Such compliance was reactive, not proactive – with most companies viewing recruitment efforts as an aspect of human resource policy, not as strategic initiatives related to the success of the business. Companies simply aimed to increase the number of women sufficiently to avoid external legal sanctions; they did not to seek to gain unique business advantages from the women they hired.

As select women began to be promoted, organizations realized that these female "outsiders" could potentially become leaders. In response, they reasserted the superiority of their historic ways of leading – that is, the ways of the dominant male leadership culture. In essence, organizations invite people from a diversity of backgrounds to join their leadership ranks, while rejecting the notion of diverse leadership styles. Whereas people from various groups may become leaders, they can do so only if they replicate the leadership approaches of the dominant group. As women begin joining the organization, the organization implicitly and explicitly reasserts the superiority of men's ways of leading. The organization's identification with men's ways of leading causes it to select a preponderance of male leaders along with a few, select women, each of whom is valued for leading like a man. To succeed in such cultures, women know that they must become

TABLE 12.3 Evolution of organizational culture: toward a more competitive organizational culture

Organizational culture	Pressure for change		Level of pressure	Male/Female ratio	Level of woman	Primary goal
	External	Internal				
Homogeneous culture	Little or none	Little or none	None	All men	None	None
Identification with men	Legal compliance	Recruitment	Human resources	A few women	Managers	Increase number of women
Denial of differences	Legal compliance	Recruitment	Human resources	Increasing number of women	Managers	Increase number of women
Accept differences	Global competition	Retention	Competitive business strategy	Increasing number of women	Senior managers	Increase numbers and change original culture
Identificaton with women	Global competition	Retention	Competitive business strategy	Mostly women	Leaders	Change original culture
Leverage differences	Intense global competition	Retention	Competitive business strategy	Balanced number of women and men	Leaders	Change original culture

"more male than the men." The few women selected for leadership positions therefore identify more with men than women, and the organization praises them for leading in the style of men. The praise given former Prime Minister Golda Meir, that she was the best man in the Israeli cabinet, echoes this dynamic.

In this period, global companies often select their first non-headquarters-culture executive or board member. To succeed, the cultural "outsider," similar to his female equivalent, often must adopt the thinking and behavioral patterns of the dominant culture, and is praised for having done so. American companies, for example, often chose a Canadian as their first non-US executive, someone who they perceive as being most like them. The search is not for difference, but rather for high-potential people who excel at thinking and behaving in the ways of the historic leadership group.

DENIAL OF DIFFERENCE

As the world moved out of the post-war era, globalization – and with it global competition – replaced equity legislation as the defining external dynamic. Diversity shifted from being an issue of legal compliance to one of competitive strategy. To compete in the new global economy, companies increasingly needed to attract and retain the best and brightest people, men and women. Their goal became to identify excellent performers. Company policies began to shift from recruiting women for lower-level positions, to attempting to recruit, promote, and retain more women for the previously all-male domain of upper-level management and senior leadership. As company policy shifted, asserting that men's ways were best gave way to a denial of difference.

To comply with the law, and to appear to be fair to the newly recruited women, companies attempted to treat women in exactly the same way they treated men. To do otherwise would have rendered the company suspect of prejudice and liable to legal sanction. From a global perspective, companies proudly announced that they would treat all employees the same worldwide. The underlying absurdity of this rigid equality is reflected in one multinational's decision to offer financial assistance to high-potential European managers for gaining a master's degree, a strategy that had worked well in recruiting top candidates in the United States. The company had failed, however, to realize that most Europeans already have access to free, or nearly-free, state-supported education. It was offering to pay for education that was already free; not a particularly effective incentive. The same fallacious logic led companies to offer all employees time off for military service, but not for maternity leave. The pretense, but not the reality, is that there are no differences.

Today, denial of differences among men and women is most evident in the United States in Americans' adherence to "politically correct" vocabulary and behavior that eschews recognition that a particular manager is male or female, or from a specific cultural, religious, or racial group.

Although denial-of-difference strategies were well meant, a disturbing trend emerged: the best and brightest women began leaving companies in record numbers. As became apparent, treating women identically to men was not leading to optimal conditions for women or for companies. In response, companies began designing systems that were more responsive to women's unique work and lifestyles.

ACCEPTING DIFFERENCE

Recurring experiences with actual differences, combined with the unexpectedly high turnover rates among women managers, led many companies, eventually, to accept that everyone is not the same and to appreciate the need to design more responsive systems. Competitive business pressures further motivated such recognition, often eclipsing both the influence of corporate diversity policies and the previous focus on recruitment and retention. Companies began asking – many for the first time – what women's and men's unique skills were, and how such skills could enhance the company's competitive positioning. Without initially accepting that differences existed, companies could not ask these questions.

Based on an appreciation of differences, companies began recognizing that individuals often understand people from their own culture better than do most outsiders. Simultaneously, they recognized that an increasingly large proportion of the personnel making major purchasing decisions for their products and services were women. More than one company concluded that women might therefore be best able to develop the most effective marketing strategies for the firm's female clients. Companies thus began to value women for their ability to understand and work well with female clients. Whether it was women designing cars for women or TV programs for women, companies increasingly asked females to help them succeed in markets dominated by women decision-makers and end-users.

Women executives were no longer being asked to think and act like men, but, rather, for the first time, they were being asked to think like women.

Such employee/client "matching" parallels the approach taken by multinational companies when implementing multidomestic strategies: the German company expanding operations into China chooses to send a managing director who speaks Chinese to Shanghai, the American company decides to send a Korean–American to manage its new Seoul headquarters, and Quebec-based companies choose to send Hispanic–Canadians to service their Latin American markets.[7] Each recognizes and chooses to use the innate cultural abilities of its key employees.

The advantages companies gain at this stage from accepting differences are limited to culture-matching situations; women are valued for their ability to market to women, and the Chinese are valued for their ability to manage operations in China. The matching approach is a cultural-fit strategy, not a strategy that combines or leverages differences into innovative solutions to organizational problems. Using such "fit" strategies, companies value women primarily for their ability to understand other women, not for their ability to integrate their unique perspectives with those of their male colleagues.

LEVERAGING DIFFERENCES

By the end of the century, global competition had intensified to the point where the opportunity cost of both discrimination and blindness had become prohibitive as had the cost of under-utilizing people by relegating them to working primarily "with their own kind." Companies searched for ways to increase their global competitiveness, primarily by out-learning and out-innovating their competitors. Leading companies recognized that the fundamental value of diversity, when well managed, was not gained from "fit" strategies, but, rather, from the increased possibilities for diversity-based learning and innovation. Companies no longer wanted women simply to fit in, nor to work strictly with other women; rather, they needed women to strengthen the company's competitive culture by leveraging their perspective and combining it with that of leading men. Companies chose to include women among their leaders, not simply so they could work with women clients, but so the organization could benefit from diversity by combining women's and men's perspectives into more innovative and effective business strategies. Whereas in the past, the women who fit in – who thought and acted like the majority of the men – were most valued, now companies valued women who thought and acted like themselves. Similarly from a cross-cultural perspective, Chinese executives were no longer valued singularly for their Chinese language skills and knowledge of the Chinese culture, but, rather, for their ability to bring a unique perspective to discussions concerning the company's overall business strategy and tactics. Synergy, combining unique differences into innovative approaches, is the inherent value in diversity.

CONCLUSION

No longer men alone

Over the course of a half century, companies' approaches had shifted, albeit often implicitly, from reactive compliance (meeting legislated requirements for equality) to proactively initiated competitive strategies designed to enhance business success. The focus on females had shifted from recruiting lower-level women – who were expected to fit-in – to hiring, promoting, and retaining very senior-level women – leaders who could change the organization. Evaluation had shifted from quantitative measures – increasing the ratio of women to men to comply with external legal requirements – to qualitative measures – integrating masculine with feminine perspectives to enhance business competitiveness. Expectations had thus shifted from wanting women to "become who they weren't" – men – to encouraging women to "act as who they are" – women.

Is the evolution over? No. Few global companies have reached the stage at which they consistently value diversity, whether cross-cultural or male/female, and can readily leverage it to their advantage. Equally daunting, few women have, as yet, had the opportunity to consistently use all of their strengths in the service of senior-level leadership. The majority of leaders, both male and female, remain constrained within styles of leadership more restricting than those needed for the twenty-first century. Evolution toward more synergistic approaches, by both organizations and individuals, will be enhanced and accelerated by a more open discussion of the nature of diversity and a deeper understanding of the assumptions embedded in our leadership processes.

NOTES

1 For a more in-depth discussion of women political leaders, see Adler's "Global women political leaders: An invisible history, an increasingly important future" (1996), "Global leaders: A dialogue with future history" (1997a), "Did you hear? Global leadership in charity's world" (1998a), and "Societal leadership: The wisdom of peace" (1998b).

2 For a more in depth discussion of global women business leaders, see Adler's "Global leaders: A dialogue with future history" (1997a), "Global leadership: Women leaders" (1997b), "Global leaders: Women of influence" (1999a), "Global entrepreneurs: Women, myths, and history" (1999a), and "Twenty-first century leadership: Reality beyond the myths" (1999c).

3 While few studies have focused on women leaders, especially from a cross-cultural perspective, researchers have studied the differences between women and men in general, and between female and male managers. Although unanimity on the actual existence of differences and their effects has yet to be reached, scholars do agree that male and female managers are perceived differently (Maccoby and Jacklin, 1974). Most US research contends that both men and women describe successful managers as more like men than women (Schein, 1975), with the exception of Schein, Mueller, and Jacobson's follow-up study (1989) in which men, but not women, persisted in sex-typing managers.

4 The four approaches are based on the combined work of Milton and Janet Bennett and Maureen Murdock. The Bennetts developed a six-phase model to explain people's ability to learn about and work effectively with people from other cultures (see M. Bennett, 1993; J. Bennett, 1993; and J. Bennett, 1999). Based on the work of Joseph Campbell, Murdock (1990) developed a multiphase model for understanding women's personal and professional development vis-à-vis the masculine and feminine aspects of their personality.

5 In one of the few cross-cultural studies on leaders, Gibson (1995) found that women in four countries were more likely than men to focus on interaction facilitation than men, who placed more emphasis on goal setting. Several studies from the United States and other countries found that women prefer a more participative style than men (Bayes, 1991; Eagly and Johnson, 1990; Soutar and Savery, 1991).

6 In the United States, sex discrimination in employment has been illegal since the 1960s (see Fagenson and Jackson, 1994). Title VII of the Civil Rights Act of 1964 provides federal protection for women against discrimination in hiring, job assignments, transfers, promotions, and discharges as well as other employment-related decisions (Lee, 1993). The Equal Pay Act of 1963 requires employers to pay women and men equally for the same work. Executive Order 11,246, amended by Executive Orders 11,357 and 12,086, prohibits sex discrimination by recipients of federal contracts exceeding $10,000 and requires employers to create and employ affirmative action policies (Lee, 1993). Based on the difficulty women have had in winning discrimination cases and receiving compensation, the Civil Rights Act of 1991 was passed providing women who file a discrimination charge with the right to have a jury trial and to sue for expanded compensatory and punitive damages (Lee, 1993).

7 Multidomestic strategies focus on each country individually. For a discussion of the range of transnational strategies, see Bartlett and Ghoshal (1989a).

Part V

Interpersonal Processes

INTRODUCTION

For many researchers and practitioners the issues raised in this section are among the most vexing in all of cross-cultural management. When two people from different cultures interact, how much of the quality of the interaction is attributable to cultural differences? When conflict arises, is it due to context or to content? The three chapters in this section address these issues in three unique ways.

Earley and Laubach's chapter (13), "Structural Identity Theory and the Dynamics of Cross-Cultural Work Groups," is a tour de force review of the extant research literature in the area. The authors begin with a review of the group identity and development literatures, then move to the relationship between the individual and the group(s). Individuals derive their identity, in part, from their multiple group memberships and must continually make choices about which identity is paramount in a given interaction. How and when different identities become salient is a focal point of the chapter.

The second section of the chapter is devoted to a review of research on participation, conflict management, collective efficacy, and diversity across cultures, highlighting the importance of national cultural differences in employees' reactions to and performance under different management conditions (see also Newman and Nollen, 1996). The authors then move on to examine cross-cultural teams, reviewing the extensive literature on conflict resolution. (See also chapter 15 by Gelfand and McCusker in this volume.) They note an implicit assumption in the literature that multi-culturalism causes conflict, but the issue of importance is how conflict is managed and whether or not conflict helps or hurts team performance.

One of the most interesting sections of the chapter deals with the effect of diversity of all sorts on team performance and team member satisfaction. The authors present a lively discussion in which the nuances and inconsistencies in the extant research are teased out. National culture is, of course, one source of diversity. The authors reconcile some of the inconsistencies in the literature by suggesting that national culture plays a major role as a filter for identity salience. Because national culture is more like a sociographic characteristic (such as race or gender) than a professional or learned characteristic (such as occupation), national culture is more likely to be closer to the core of one's self-identity and thus more likely to be invoked in more situations. The authors note that conflict in teams based on sociographic characteristics is more likely to be non-constructive and therefore detract from the team's performance, while conflict based on professional or task characteristics is more likely to be constructive and performance-enhancing.

The main contribution of this chapter, in addition to the extensive literature review, is to frame the effects of cross-cultural dynamics in teams in terms of identities, identity construction, and identity salience. Whether cross-cultural differences contribute to team outcomes depends upon the extent to which the identities associated with culture are salient in a given situation, differ across individuals in a given situation, and affect the outcomes of interest in a given situation. Cross-cultural teams, per se, are neither more nor less satisfying or high-performing. The similarities and differences in identities of group members evoked by the task at hand are more likely to explain the effect of cross-cultural team membership on team performance.

The second chapter in this part is written in a very different style. Mead and Jones present their work as an essay on cross-cultural communication ("Cross-Cultural Communication"). Applying two different models of communication in high and low power distance contexts, they illustrate how cross-cultural communication can be problematic, particularly in the rapidly transforming cultures in Asia and Central Europe. The authors identify superior–subordinate relationships as the nexus within which cross-cultural communication issues will emerge and illustrate several task circumstances in which culturally consistent communication may not be appropriate. One example is highly directive communications in high power distance cultures but with tasks that require consultation and problem solving for high performance, as are often found in the rapidly changing organizations in the transforming economies. These authors illustrate concrete ways in which progress at the company level is impeded in some of these economies because the traditional culture and style of communicating is not appropriate to the new world of competition in which the firms find themselves. As the authors conclude, it is ironic and troubling that cross-cultural communication issues receive so little attention as companies around the world change more and more rapidly.

Finally, Gelfand and McCusker take a very novel approach to negotiations and conflict management by elaborating the notion of metaphors as ways of understanding culture and its effects on interpersonal processes ("Metaphor and the Cultural Construction of Negotiation"). They argue that the effects of culture can be understood as an example of social information processing. (See also Smith and Peterson, chapter 11.) National culture is a source of the schemas or mental maps we use for apprehending, processing, and giving meaning to information. In other words, culture is a meaning system.

Metaphors, similarly, are mechanisms by which we transmit knowledge across meaning systems. We think of metaphors within culture as a way to illuminate or explain a phenomenon for which we have little or no direct experience and few if any existing mental maps. Metaphors help us understand new phenomena and help us conceptualize and process new data by drawing parallels with existing mental maps in another domain. Metaphors are learned and embedded in a particular cultural context. They vary across cultures, though their purpose is the same across cultures.

The authors move on to discuss metaphors within negotiations. They note that the use of metaphors is common and that the metaphor chosen defines and limits the discourse of the negotiation. They distinguish between psychological functions of metaphors and social functions of metaphors. Psychological functions frame the nature and understanding of the problem being solved, the scripts available for the negotiation, and the feelings evoked in the negotiation. War metaphors yield different negotiations from sports metaphors. Garden metaphors yield a different process from chess metaphors. Social functions of metaphors help negotiators share a context so that the meaning and use of metaphors between or among the negotiators is consistent. The fact that many metaphors do not translate well across cultures causes obvious problems in negotiation and conflict resolution.

The authors use a vivid example to illustrate the effects of cultural and metaphorical differences in negotiating. They illustrate two metaphors, "negotiation as sport" for the US and "negotiation as household gathering" for Japan. Sports in America involve rules, winning and losing, opposition, strategy, scores, and referees. Sports metaphors work well for and tend to produce distributive negotiations. Team sports can produce integrative negotiations, but refer more to how team members interact rather than how two teams compete against one another. Sports metaphors work well in the US culture with its emphasis on individual achievement and merit-based rewards.

The *ie* or household is a dominant metaphor in Japanese society, dating back centuries. *Ie* is more than family. It represents continuity, control of assets, and has a strong future orientation. Instead of winning and losing, the dominant motivations are continuity, growth, and preservation. "Rules" in the *ie* are every bit as binding as in a sporting event, but unwritten. "Referees" are the father or the eldest son. The *ie* is hierarchical, based on status or longevity, not performance in the latest contest. It is no wonder that Americans and Japanese have so many stories to tell about negotiation failures. With different dominant cultural metaphors used implicitly, the problem to be solved, scripts to be used, and feelings engendered are not even similar.

The authors in this part remind us that cross-cultural issues in interpersonal relations are embedded deeply in national culture and cannot be understood with simplistic or superficial cultural differences. Delving into identities and cultural metaphors is not an easy research task but a necessary one if we are to begin to understand the contribution of culture to interpersonal relations.

13

Structural Identity Theory and the Dynamics of Cross-Cultural Work Groups

P. Christopher Earley and Marty Laubach

The creation of a global village, transnational corporations, internet and similar influences remind us constantly that a science of organizations and management is incomplete without the integration of concepts of culture and self-awareness. It is no longer appropriate to discuss organizational activities and employee actions without incorporating a more complete view of where such activities take place. Not only must we include an immediate social context, but we must deal with the international and cultural aspects of the social world as well. More than ever, understanding of employee action requires knowledge of how action is related to the environment in which it is embedded. Using this general focus, we examine a number of significant issues concerning cultural influences on work groups and teams.

Our emphasis is the extension and elaboration of other reviews concerning work teams evaluated cross-culturally. The interested reader is referred to a number of articles including Mann (1980), Triandis (1994b), Tannenbaum (1980), Earley and Gibson (1998), Granrose and Oskamp (1997), and Ravlin et al. (in press) among others. Our review contains three sections, the first of which is a discussion of traditional approaches to studying teams including the emphasis used in this chapter. In the second section, we use our framework to review literature concerning cultural influences in relation to work teams. Finally, we make a number of recommendations for future research and indicate how our contextual–structural approach extends existing lines of work.

OVERVIEW OF CONCEPTUAL APPROACHES

Given the increasing complexity of organizations, work requires a high degree of interdependence and interaction among employees. This interaction is often relegated to a work group, or team (Earley and Gibson, 1998; Gersick, 1988; Guzzo, 1986; Guzzo and Waters, 1982; Guzzo et al., 1993; Hackman, 1976; McGrath, 1984). People do not work within a social void, rather, they interact and are interdependent upon others as they work and behave in an organization. People work together so as to perform various tasks and simultaneously fulfill social needs. Given the prevalence of work groups in modern organizations, it is clear that they are an essential element in understanding cross-cultural aspects of work and organization. Our lives are organized around many groups such as families, work crews, religious groups, sports teams, etc. Much of what we do for business and pleasure revolves around the group. This is not to imply that all actions occur in a group; many of our actions occur within aggregates rather than natural groups. Groups and teams are psychologically and sociologically distinct from casual aggregates of individuals. Whereas a group has specific qualities involving roles, structure, etc., aggregates simply refer to a collection of individuals who gather for individual purposes and needs (e.g., the audience at a movie). Of course, not all activities are group-based. We perform actions for our individual needs in an individual context such as purchasing a favorite dessert, playing solitaire, watching a movie on television alone, etc. Our focus is on the social context of work-group behavior in which people gather to perform some task or maintain group stability and relations.

In addition, it is useful to define what we mean by a work group or team (we use these two terms interchangeably for this review). McGrath (1984) defines a group as a social aggregate that involves mutual awareness and potential mutual interaction. McGrath distinguishes a group from other types of social aggregates based on three dimensions: size, interdependence, and temporal pattern. He argues that a group includes two or more people while remaining relatively small so that all members can be mutually aware of and potentially interact with one another. Mutual awareness and potential interaction provide at least a minimum degree of interdependence so that members take actions of other group members into account. Interdependence, in turn, implies some degree of continuity over time. In other words, a group is an aggregation of two or more people who are to some degree in dynamic interrelation with one another and it includes such units as families, work groups and social or friendship groups. Turner et al. (1987: 1) describe a group as one that is psychologically meaningful for the members, and to which they relate themselves subjectively for comparisons; group members adopt norms and values from this group. A member of a group accepts membership in this group and it influences the member's attitudes and behavior. They distinguish the group from aggregate using an individual's attachment to the group as a reference group rather than mere membership. However, their definition is not restrictive in size or temporal considerations as is that of McGrath and they even discuss crowd behavior as a manifestation of "group behavior."

Work groups and related dynamics have been addressed from a cultural viewpoint using a limited number of perspectives. The approaches taken by researchers include self-concept theory, social cognition and mental models, and conflict management and group process. Without question, the dominant position used to address the nature of cross-cultural groups has been the application of self-concept theories (Markus and Kitayama, 1991). The two models which have received most attention in self-concept theory are the related frameworks proposed by Tajfel (1982) and Turner (1985). Tajfel (1982) and Tajfel and Turner (1986) proposed a model of self-concept in their Social Identity Theory (SIT). According to this model, an individual's self-evaluations are shaped in part by their group memberships. An individual will develop and foster a positive self-image by accentuating the positive attributes of their in-group and the negative attributes of out-groups. Tajfel's extensive research on intergroup bias often employs a methodology referred to as a minimal group technique in which individuals are assigned to groups on a random basis. His work and that of his colleagues has demonstrated that an individual assigned to a group (again, even on a random basis) will discriminate in favor of his or her in-group.

A related model, proposed and described by Turner (1985) and Turner et al. (1987) called Self Categorization Theory (SCT) can be thought of as a logical extension of basic identity theory. It suggests that people perceive themselves as group members in a hierarchical structure of groups. At the most general level, people distinguish themselves from non-humans; among humans, groups are based on intraclass similarities and interclass differences. Turner et al. assume that individuals are motivated to maintain a positive self-evaluation of self-categories through a comparison of self and other member characteristics with prototypes of the next higher level of categorization. SCT has several interesting features that can be used to describe cultural influences. Turner et al. argue that group formation occurs for several reasons. First, groups can form as a result of spontaneous or emergent social categorizations from the immediate situation. Second, they occur as a result of some preformed, internalized categorization scheme available from cultural sources such as work class, gender, race, etc. Unfortunately, SCT does not provide much information concerning this latter antecedent of group formation and this is the focus of our model. The basic premise that individuals use preformed categories in forming in-groups as well as making judgments about out-groups seems to be crucial in understanding group processes in various cultures.

More recent models of self-concept have been proposed such as Brewer's Optimal Distinctiveness Theory (1993). According to distinctiveness theory, a person's self-concept is regulated as a balance between social integration with others in important reference groups and maintaining a differentiated self. Any group member faces two simultaneous attractions (repulsion): a desire to be integrated with others who provide self-image and a desire to remain unique and a separated self. Brewer's theory argues that people psychologically trade off their individuality needs with team identity needs. Counterbalancing forces may motivate the creation of commonalities among group members and an integrated team culture will serve as the basis of a common identity. A "split" group may balance individual and team identities so that members are not motivated to adjust this balance (Earley and Mosakowski, 2000; Ravlin et al., in press).

A number of other scholars focus on the cognitive aspects of group membership in a cultural as well as domestic context (DiMaggio, 1997; D'Andrade, 1984; Erez and Earley, 1993; Klimoski and Mohammed, 1994; Messick and Mackie, 1989). A focus on cognition emphasizes thought processes and information processing. Cognitive representations of groups consist of complex, hierarchical structures that contain elements such as category labels, attributes, and exemplars. A category representation refers to a category label (e.g., college professor), an abstracted prototype (e.g., list of features such as old and gray, beard, glasses, befuddled), and the projection of these characteristics to the group as a whole (stereotype). For example, a category label such as a "college professor" may have associated with it general prototypes of a professor such as being old and having a gray beard or wearing glasses. Stereotyping occurs if these prototypic characteristics are applied to the general population of college professors.

Klimoski and Mohammed (1994) talk about a "team mental model" as a shared psychological representation of a team's environment constructed to permit sense-making and guide appropriate group action (Elron et al., 1998). When team members perceive shared understandings with other members, the positive affect and propensity to trust generated by such a discovery fuels performance improvement (Klimoski and Moham-med, 1994) and bolsters the group's belief in its capability to perform, often referred to as the level of group efficacy (Bandura, 1997; Gibson, 1999).

Research has been applied to the study of work teams as they develop and evolve as well by Hackman and his colleagues (1976, 1990), McGrath (1984), Gersick (1988), and Guzzo and Waters (1982). Much of this work was focused on the nature of the work group itself including features such as context (e.g., Hackman, 1976), group development (e.g., Gersick, 1988), group potency and perceived efficacy (e.g., Jackson et al., 1995), and group composition effects (e.g., Jackson et al., 1995 book; Hambrick and Mason, 1984; Maznevski, 1994; Tsui, Egan, and O'Reilly, 1992). Much recent work on teams from both a domestic as well as an international context has emphasized the compositional nature of a team from a demographic and cultural diversity perspective (e.g., Cox, Lobel, and McLeod, 1991; Hambrick, Davison, Snell, and Snow, 1998; Maznevski, 1994).

While these perspectives are useful in isolating critical forces involved in individual–group interactions, integrating them into useful analytical models for understanding the dynamics of work groups and teams requires recontextualizing these studies within a framework that includes the effects of organizational structures from which they are created. This framework must recognize the means by which organizational interests and power are distributed and the multiple sources of influence acting in group dynamics.

The traditional framework for groups argues that organizational structure influences the group's environment and task situation because it represents a "structured set of requirements/demands/opportunities/possibilities/constraints" (McGrath, 1984: 16). While this analytical demarcation between the work group and organization is useful in traditional bureaucratic organizational models, it is of limited utility for many contemporary organization forms. Ouchi (1980) and Graham and Organ (1993) describe organizational forms developed around a normative (Kunda, 1992) control and coordination process required for ambiguous and shifting environmental needs. The relative instability of requirements makes McGrath's boundary meaningless and removes the sense of insulation between group and wider organizational dynamics implied in the framework. This perspective oversimplifies the interaction between organizational levels and competing interests and the complications rising from multiple group memberships.

Organizations are formally structured to represent organizational interests and power in member actions. This process operates through the dominant control and coordination procedures, often through some combination of supervision, work rules, and socialization (Edwards, 1979). Work groups are commissioned within this framework of interests and power, and inevitably reproduce or account for such interests and power within their own structure. However, organizational interests are not monolithic. Organizational theorists remind us that organizations are composed of coalitions (Thompson, 1967; Pfeffer and Salancik, 1978; Selznick, 1996) which are continuously negotiating the meanings and importance of tasks. In addition, organizational behaviorists from the time of the Hawthorne study (Roethlisberger and Dickson, [1939] 1967) have recognized the uncontrollable effects of informal organization, which Littler and Salaman (1984: 68) describe as "those patterns and relationships which occur in a systematic manner, . . . which are not prescribed by formal regulation and specification, and indeed might occur in conflict with it." Examples of informal structures include friendship networks, minority group networks whose members look out for each other, (non-union) worker solidarity networks, and informal administrative networks in which an individual's real organizational power may far exceed his or her structural position.

Individuals within a given work group must therefore be recognized as having multiple memberships in groups representing formal functions and strata within the organization, cross-functional and cross-strata groups representing different coalitions, and informal groups representing an intersubjective world of organizational culture, friendship networks, and mutual interest networks. These informal groups may be influenced but not controlled by the formal organizational structure, and may work to forward or to hinder its goals. Work groups that include cross-cultural influences add another set of influences.

Specifying these effects in individual-level analysis remains a problem and at best involves strange juxtapositions of variables. There has been a long tradition for specifying the effects of formal organizational structure by neo-Marxian analysts, who probably have the most experience dealing with issues of position-based power; they see formal organizational structure as a combination of material ownership, supervisory authority, and skill resources (Wright, 1978). However, the effects of national and ethnic culture have only recently been included in models, and consensus seems to have revolved around the use of shared values as the defining concept (Hofstede, 1980a; Triandis, 1980a). The effects of coalitions and informal organizations have a much less established presence in organizational analyses, in part because the theory for these is relatively undeveloped, aside from work on organizational citizen behaviors (Organ, 1990), the various forms of network analyses (e.g., Cook and Whitmeyer, 1992; McPherson, Popielarz, and Drobnic, 1992; Friedkin, 1993), and consent, which Littler and Salaman (1984) theorized as coming directly from actions in the informal organization.

One existing framework that might prove useful in organizing the effects of multiple group memberships at the individual level is Identity Theory (Stryker, 1980, 1987). It holds that behavioral response patterns that are unique to situations involving group membership are organized as identities, so that a person has separate identities as a student, a family member, or as an employee. Identity theory differs from SIT and SCT in that its conception of identities is individual[1] and involves role expectations and behaviors that are accepted and incorporated into the self, as opposed to collective identities based on socially defined categories which involve evaluations to which the person or collective reacts. Stryker's Identity Theory explicitly brought social structural constraints[2] into a symbolic interactionist conception of the self; to distinguish it from social identity theory we will refer to it as "structural identity theory" (see also Thoits and Virshup, 1997). In his theory, separate identities are ordered in a "salience hierarchy" in which highly salient identities are more likely to be evoked in response to a given situation. The salience of an identity is based on the individual's level of commitment to the social networks in which the identity is played out. Stryker defines commitment as "the costs to the person in the form of relationships forgone were she/he no longer to have a given identity and play a role based on that identity in a social network" (Stryker, 1987: 90).

In a work group, employees negotiate between behavioral responses from identities created around role expectations surrounding their position in the formal structure, in a coalition, in an informal structure, or in an ethnic or other cultural group. Workers respond to role-expectations using whichever identity is more salient in any given situation. Situations, for which responses from multiple salient identities conflict, become problematic, and the individual then responds with whichever identity holds a stronger commitment (Stryker, 1987; Burke and Reitzes, 1991). For example, a response based in an ethnic identity hostile to the ethnicity of another member might be tempered by the behavioral response based in a managerial identity to which the individual is more committed. Thus, understanding group dynamics involves discerning and measuring the relative importance of factors that enter into decisions of which identity becomes salient under given conditions.

One factor that this framework specifically recognizes as affecting the relative salience of identities is control and coordination mechanisms used in organizational contexts. Table 13.1 compares organization types from Ouchi (1979) and Graham and Organ (1993) with control methods (Edwards, 1979; Kunda, 1992) that appear dominant. Simple control uses role expectations that evoke identities constructed around subordinate response patterns. All potentially competing identities are effectively "frozen out" by this control method and worker consent is not a consideration. Bureaucratic control evokes identities whose subordinate behavioral responses are constructed around issues of legitimation, equity, and fairness embedded in organizational rules. This control form is susceptible to competition from identities whose behavioral patterns are based in the informal organization; as Littler and Salaman (1984) describe, organizations strike informal deals which, in terms of this framework, reduce the salience of competing identities. Normative control evokes identities whose behavioral patterns are constructed around merged interests within the organization. In this sense, normative control merges identities based in informal organizational groups with identities based in the formal organization. People operating under normative control have high levels of organizational commitment, or in structural identity theoretical terms, have commitment to these merged identities (Burke and Reitzes, 1991).

Another factor that our framework recognizes as influencing the salience of identities is the cultural context of the individual actors, as expressed in their culture-related values. A worker from a collectivist culture would tend to have a higher commitment to an identity that reflects the interests of his or her in-group, regardless of that in-group's relationship with the organizational structure. If the in-group is the organization, as is fostered by "clan-type" organizations (Ouchi, 1980), then the worker will respond to role expectations with the minimal efforts characteristic of normative control. However, if the worker's in-group is not the organization, and especially if its interests are in potential conflict with the organization (e.g. class-based interests), then control methods must present role expectations in a way that favors evoking a subordinate identity over the competing in-group identity. In addition, a cultural value that favors high power-distance relationships can support a worker's commitment to subordinate roles, facilitating the use of simple or bureaucratic control.

This framework serves to contextualize the previous frameworks as a subset of interactions and considerations taking place within work groups. It adds not only competing and potentially more salient behavioral responses to those postulated by SIT and SCT, but also depth to the salience process beyond comparison of stereotyped

TABLE 13.1 Comparison between the Graham and Organ and Ouchi typologies of organizations

Graham and Organ (1993)	Transactional	Social exchange	Covenantal
Motivational paradigm	Expectancy	Equity/fairness	Fealty to values
Degree of inclusiveness	Narrow	Moderate	Holistic
Expected duration	Short-term	Intermediate	Long-term
Culture	Weak	Moderate	Intensive
Cost of exit	Low	Moderate	Substantial
Voice	Low	Moderate	Strong
Commitment	Low	Moderate	High
Ouchi (1979)	*Market*	*Bureaucracy*	*Clan*
Social requirements	Norm of reciprocity	Norm of reciprocity Legitimate authority	Norm of reciprocity Legitimate authority Shared values and beliefs
Information requirements	Price	Rules	Traditions
People treatment	Take anyone No further treatment	Training and monitoring	Intensive screening and socialization
Edwards (1979);[a] Kunda (1992)			
Appropriate workplace control methods	Simple control Technical control	Bureaucratic control	Normative control

[a] This was about the types of workplace control used by management, and gives a nice analysis of Taylorism.
Source: From Graham and Organ (1993: 483) and Ouchi (1979: 838)

sociodemographic characteristics among actors. This contextualization can be seen in a hypothetical example of a work group in which two white Americans are training four Mexicans on technology transferred from a closed plant in the American's home town. The Americans are an engineer and a machine operator who is a union member, and the Mexicans are a supervisor and three trainees. The union member as a focal actor has a wide range of possible behaviors towards the Mexican trainees, from overt to covert hostility, to acquiescence to the situation, to attempts to recruit them for the union. SIT and SCT would analyze his responses in terms of: (1) which set of sociodemographic or organizational categories (for himself and the Mexican trainees) would be possible for the situation; (2) his understandings and sense of relevance for the potential categories; (3)

degree to which the categories' normative imperatives fit the situation; and (4) degree to which the differences between the potential sets of categories are contextually more relevant than the similarities. Of course, this interaction is only one set within the group context. The union member's behavior is potentially constrained by the presence of the American engineer, who may be a minority woman (two more potentially conflicting sociodemographical categories) who, in turn, may have an ambiguous organizational relationship with him by being a professional and presumably aligned with management. Within the work group, the focal actor's behavior is presumably consistent, so whatever categories he selects to guide his own behaviors must somehow blend together to maintain some form of self-consistency. Aside from the stereotypical behaviors based on whatever categories he assigns to himself and others, and Tajfel and Turner's key motives of self-esteem and uncertainty reduction (Thoits and Virshup, 1997), SIT and SCT offer no additional clues for which categories would become salient. The structural identity framework simplifies this analysis by focusing on the possible identities available to the actor and his commitment to each as determined by the consequences of inappropriate performances for each identity – e.g. the loss of job for displays of hostility, the benefits of solidarity for unionizing the new plant, etc. This framework also assumes self-esteem and uncertainty reduction, but specifies uncertainty reduction in terms of consistency and self-preservation with respect to the maze of interests and power demands converging at each task.

With regard to optimal distinctiveness, the same issues of multiple groups and salience contextualizes the process of finding the optimal point at which a work group member balances his or her needs for sameness and individuation. These balance points must be very tentative considering the paradoxical instances in which workers identify with a company but engage in hostile work actions over disputes, then re-identify after the dispute is resolved. These same considerations serve to contextualize cognitive representations and team mental models.

REVIEW OF CROSS-CULTURAL AND INTERNATIONAL TEAMS RESEARCH

In this section, we review the literature pertaining to cross-cultural work on teams. We will include as well a few studies concerning cross-cultural diversity and demography given that these are relevant to our general approach and can be thought of as "cross-cultural" in a broad sense. Given the vastness of this literature, we have broken down the literature by a number of subheadings including decision-making and participation, conflict and negotiation, collective efficacy and performance, and composition and diversity. See also Audia and Tams, this volume.

Decision-making and participation

Collective decision-making and participative decision-making have long histories in work team research. The largest stream of cross-cultural research on group decision-making was stimulated by Lewin's Field Theory (1951). The essence of his approach is that participation in the decision-making process will enhance individuals' acceptance of, and commitment to, a decision. In follow-up work using Lewin's framework, Misumi and his colleagues (e.g., Misumi, 1984; Misumi and Haroaka, 1960; Misumi and Shinohara, 1967) have shown that the group decision method is highly effective in inducing attitude and habit changes for Japanese workers. Misumi found that the participation influence was more effective using natural groups than ad hoc ones. More recent comprehensive reviews of participation have been published by Locke and Schweiger (1979) and Wagner et al. (1997).

Participative management can be formed as a subculture in some of the departments within a given organization (Wagner et al., 1997). For example, French, Kay, and Meyer (1966) examined the effect of participation in the setting of goals as part of a performance appraisal system in the General Electric Company. They found that participation in goal-setting was more effective in a department with a participative climate. Assigned goals were more effective in a department with a non-participative climate, particularly when employees felt threatened by the appraisal process.

Earley (1986) argued that cultural differences explained the differential effectiveness of a goal-setting method that was implemented in the US and England. A goal-setting technique initiated by shop stewards was more effective than one initiated by supervisors in England. No such differences were found in an American sample. Earley concluded that English workers placed greater trust in their stewards than in their supervisors or managers, and it was for this reason that they responded more favorably. Using the proposed framework, we argue that the managerial practice more congruent with cultural norms evoked identities more conducive to meeting the goals. In the English case, identities based in informal relationships with stewards were more salient than formal structural relationships with supervisors. Stewards evoked in-group identities in workers and supervisors evoked out-group identities. Steward-initiated goals became a part of the salient in-group behavioral role-expectations. Supervisor-initiated goals became a part of the behavioral role-expectations of a less salient identity, exerting much less of a behavioral imperative. In the American case, workers give more legitimacy to structural relationships, so probably the identity as subordinate to management was more salient for workers.

Erez and Earley (1987) conducted a cross-cultural study in the US and in Israel to test for the moderating effect of culture on the relationship between participation in goal-setting and performance. The United States is known for its individualistic values and moderate levels of power distance in organizations. In contrast, Israel is known for its collectivistic values and for a low level of power distance (Hofstede, 1980a). In Israel, employee participation programs are institutionalized in the labor relation system. They take the form of work councils in the private and public sectors, and the form of employees' representatives in management in the histadrut sector, which is the general federation of unions, and the employer of about one-quarter of the industry. The highest level of participation is implemented in the kibbutz sector which symbolizes the values of collectivism, group orientation, and egalitarianism. Ultimate decision-making power in the governance of the kibbutz resides with the general assembly of all the kibbutz members (Leviatan and Rosner, 1980).

Participants in this study (Erez and Earley, 1987) were 180 university students, of whom 120 were Israeli (sixty of them were Kibbutz members), and 60 others were Americans. They were all asked to perform a task under one of three goal-setting conditions: group participation, participation through a representative, and no participation. The results demonstrated that performance of the Israeli students was significantly lower when goals were assigned than if goals were participatively set. In addition, Israeli students who were assigned goals performed significantly lower than their American counterparts. There were no differences between the Israeli and the American students when goals were participatively set. This finding clearly demonstrated the moderating effect of culture. The more collectivistic and lower power distance Israeli students reacted adversely to the non-participative assigned goals as compared to the more individualistic and higher power distance American students. A non-participative approach was inconsistent with the cultural norms in Israel, and hence, was negatively interpreted by the self. The results led to the conclusion that the differences between the two countries are not so much in terms of the beneficial effect of participation, as they are in terms of the adverse reaction of individuals to their assigned goals.

Cultural differences may also occur between subcultures within one country, and may lead to a differential effect of participation. Erez (1986) examined the effectiveness of three levels of participation in three industrial sectors within Israel, which represent three different points on a continuum of participative values: (1) the private sector – guided by utilitarian goals with no explicit policy of employee participation; (2) the histadrut, which is the federation of most unions in Israel; and (3) the kibbutz sector – known for its strong collectivistic values, with emphasis on group rather than individual welfare, and on egalitarian rather than utilitarian approaches to profit sharing (Leviatan and Rosner, 1980). The three sectors convey different work environments and provide different opportunities for participation. Results of this study demonstrated that group participation was most effective in the kibbutz sector, participation by a representative was most effective in the histadrut sector, and no-participation was most effective in the private sector. Once again, the contingency approach was supported and direct group participation was found to be most effective in a group-centered collectivistic culture.

The effectiveness of group goals versus individual goals varies across cultures. In Japan the combination of group and individual goals was more effective than individual goals alone (Matsui, Kakuyama, and Onglatco, 1987). However, in individualistic cultures group goals very often result in social loafing and free riding because group members in individualistic cultures do not share responsibility to the same extent as group members in collectivistic cultures (Earley, 1989).

The contingency between participation and culture is clearly exemplified by the participative management techniques in Japan such as quality circles and *ringi-sei* decision-making (Earley and Erez, 1997; Nakane, 1970a). The Japanese set of values is characterized by collectivism, group orientation, and respect for seniority (Hofstede, 1980a; Odaka, 1986; Triandis, 1988). Group orientation conveys the priority given to the continuity and prosperity of the social system. Collectivism is reflected in self-definition as part of groups, subordination of personal goals to group goals, concern for the integrity of the in-group, and intense emotional attachment to the group (Triandis, 1988). This culture nourishes the collective-self, which gains a central role in processing and interpreting information (Triandis, 1989). The core values of the Japanese culture were implemented into the corporate level and have shaped the Japanese management practices. Concern for the continuity of the organization and for the integrity of the group has led to the development of a system of lifetime employment in the larger firms for approximately 25 percent of the total Japanese workforce. The terms "management familism" (Kume, 1985), or "corporate collectivism" (Triandis, 1989) have been used to describe Japanese management, implying that both management and employees have a high level of life-long mutual commitment. Japanese managers attributed their success to the lifetime employment system which enabled them to develop mutual commitment between employees and employers, team work, and group cohesiveness (Erez, 1992). Employees' participation displays the value of corporate collectivism. It takes the form of small group activities, including quality circles on the shopfloor level, and management improvement activities at higher organizational levels.

Quality control circles are small groups in the same workshop that voluntarily and continuously undertake quality control activities, including the control and improvement of the workplace (Onglatco, 1988: 15). In Japan, quality control circles have two main objectives: One is to enhance the company-wide quality level, and the second is to contribute to the employees' self-growth. The QC circles activity in Japan has significantly increased over the years, from about 6,000 circles in 1975 to almost 230,000 circles in 1985 (Onglatco, 1988). QC circles in Japan significantly contributed to the improvement of product quality, enhanced the level of efficiency and of cost reduction, and facilitated innovation. For example, a software company reported a 70 percent reduction of error rate since the implementation of the system, and one of the banks reported a significant relationship between circle activation index and an efficiency index (Onglatco, 1988). QC circles were found to have a significant positive effect on employees' attitudes in Japan, particularly on social understanding, enhanced sense of participation, and fulfillment of higher-order needs.

A more naturalistic form of decision-making for the Japanese work environment is referred to as the *ringi-sei* system (Kerlinger, 1951; Nakane, 1970a; Triandis, 1989). In this consensus system, decisions are made "anonymously" and subordinates and leaders are bound together in obligations and loyalty. Decisions are made according to a bottom-up procedure such that each subordinate authorizes a tentative solution or decision to some problem and proceeds to "clear it" through increasing levels of superiors adjusting the decision according to each level's suggestions. By the time the actual decision must be made, it has been altered and endorsed by all individuals who will be involved in its implementation. This system reflects a strong self-motive of consistency and self-enhancement through group loyalty and commitment. It also reflects a ritualistic style of decision making that reinforces a strong hierarchy within a particular social structure. In contrast, the American approach is to offer two or three alternatives with one recommended alternative. In this way decision-makers have wider discretion.

The Japanese example demonstrates that when the motivational techniques are congruent with the cultural values, they satisfy the self-derived needs and result in a high performance level. In Japan, the collective self was found to be more complex and more dominant than the private self. Therefore, self-enhancement, self-efficacy, and self-consistency are experienced when an individual makes a contribution to the group and gets recognition for his/her contribution. Motivational techniques that facilitate the contribution of the individual to group success tend to be effective. Reciprocally, effective group performance reinforces perceptions of collective efficacy, which further affect group and organizational performance.

Both of these examples can be analyzed using the structure–identity theory in the same way as the English steward example. The cultural conditions which the Israeli students experienced fosters identities which have more collectivist behavior patterns, and are more likely to be evoked than identities with subordinate behavior patterns. But when experimenters set goals for the students, they evoked subordinate identities that were less salient and had less of a behavioral imperative than the identities evoked under conditions in which the goals were set participatively. Still, workers for whom the identity as subordinate to management is stronger would not be as susceptible to competing identities. In addition, the Japanese examples illustrate how organizations use normative control through a highly persuasive involvement with their employees, thus fostering highly salient worker identities in which informal organizational interests are merged with formal organizational interests.

Another stream of research related to decision making and participation is how a team allocates rewards and distributes resources within the team. This research suggests that there are three general rules underlying concepts of distributive justice – equity, equality, and need. Tornblom, Jonssons, and Foa (1985) compared the use of three allocation rules (equity, equality, need) in the United States and Sweden. They showed that the egalitarian emphasis characteristic of Sweden resulted in a higher priority being placed on an equality exchange rule rather than need or equity but that Americans emphasized equity over equality or need. Murphy-Berman, Berman, Singh, Pachuri, and Kumar (1984) examined the allocation rules of need, equity, and equality with respect to positive and negative reward allocations (bonus pay versus pay cuts) in the United States and India. They found that Indian managers preferred a need rule over equality and equity whereas Americans preferred equity over the other two. They concluded that their results may reflect that in India people are less responsive to merit pay because societal status is determined largely by affiliation and caste rather than individual achievement.

Bond, Leung, and Wan (1982) and Leung and Bond (1984) examined reward allocation preferences in Chinese samples. They found that Chinese, who are considered to be collectivistic, use an equality rule in allocating rewards to in-group members more than do Americans (who are guided by individualistic values). More recently, however, Chen (1995) found a reversal of this typical pattern (Chinese preferring equality over equity and Americans preferring equity over equality) in his study of Chinese and American managers. He demonstrated that Chinese managers (People's Republic of China) were more inclined to use an allocation rule based on equity over equality with a heavy emphasis on material over social rewards, possibly because of the move toward a competitive economic system.

Further, individually based incentive systems among Indonesian oil workers created more controversy than results (Vance, McClaine, Goje, and Stage, 1992; see also Steers and Sánchez-Runde, this volume). Indonesians come from a relatively collectivistic culture emphasizing group process with a strong sense of interdependence among people so an individual incentive scheme is perceived as divisive.

A structural identity framework would suggest that the identities being evoked in allocation decisions reflect the salience of different group memberships. Collectivist responses of equal allocations reflect a high salience of an identity based around the group among whose members the allocation is being made. An individualistic response of equity-based allocations suggests three possibilities: a lower salience of the identity based in the group among whose members the rewards are being allocated, a higher salience of identities with other groups for which wealth (especially differentials in wealth) is a status marker, or different socializations for acceptable behavior. A need-based allocation reflects an identity based on recognition and willingness to accept personal consequences to help resolve broader social problems.

A final area is the relatively recent impact of technology on group-related decisions in an international context. Electronic communication can provide useful opportunities if it creates a work environment that provides for enhanced interaction (Warkentin, Sayeed, and Hightower, 1997). The key appears to be the relational links developed among team members. For example, Warkentin et al. studied a worldwide web-based asynchronous computer conference system and found that teams using this communication system could not outperform traditional (face-to-face) teams under otherwise comparable circumstances. Relational links among team members were found to be a significant contributor to the effectiveness of information exchange. Though the virtual and face-to-face teams exhibited similar levels of communication effectiveness, face-to-face team members reported higher levels of satisfaction. In an important study that bridges both the communication theory and multinational organizational theory, Ghoshal, Korine, and Szulanski (1994) found that interpersonal relationships developed through lateral communication mechanisms such as joint work in teams, taskforces, and meetings. The researchers examined subsidiary–headquarters communication and inter-subsidiary communication based on data collected from 164 senior managers working in 14 different national subsidiaries within the consumer electronics division of Matsushita, a Japanese company, and 84 managers working in nine different national subsidiaries of N. V. Philips, the Holland-based competitor of Matsushita. Findings demonstrated that lateral communication mechanisms had significant positive effects on the frequency of both subsidiary–headquarters and inter-subsidiary communication.

Again, these results reflect differences in the processes by which commitment to group–group based identities are made. Symbolic interactionism (Stryker, 2000), the meta-perspective from which Stryker developed the theory, postulates that people construct identities from behaviors learned through the exchange of symbols which, in most cases, involve gestures and words. Developing a set of behavioral responses into an identity around nothing more than words on a screen is theoretically possible but less likely to have the same salience as an identity developed around symbol-rich face-to-face interaction.

Conflict and negotiation

We use this category to capture a number of related streams of research on cross-cultural aspects of work teams.

Difficulties arise in cross-cultural teams caused by cultural interactions occurring on many levels. They may involve threats to a person's social and self-identity, or "face" (Earley, 1997a), or problems in understanding and communicating with others (Tung, 1997). They may lead to workers' diminished commitment to the organization and poor organizational performance (Granrose, 1997), but intercultural contacts can also be associated with successful accommodation (Berry, 1997). When different cultural groups interact, there are several possible models that specify changes in the groups' cultural patterns (Berry, 1997; Granrose, 1997).

Ravlin et al. (in press) emphasize understanding groups from a cultural perspective focusing on the conflict experienced within these groups. They argue that when organizational groups are composed of members of multiple cultures, a primary concern is that conflict between members of different cultural backgrounds will impede group effectiveness. This model examines the influences of belief systems regarding values and status, and the role that acceptance of these beliefs by members of cultural subgroups plays in processes generating latent and manifest conflict within the group. They draw from theories of social information processing, social identity, value congruence, status characteristics, and legitimacy both to develop propositions regarding conflict-related responses in such groups and to hypothesize conditions under which such conflict may either enhance or diminish group effectiveness.

In a related vein, Weldon and Jehn (1995) use conflict as a way of discussing and describing culturally based group dynamics. Jehn (1995) posits that there are two different types of conflict that operate in a group, relational and task-relevant, and that relational conflict has potentially detrimental effects on team dynamics whereas task-relevant conflict can be useful in generating alternative positions and views for a team.

Kirchmeyer and Cohen (1992) examined the effects of constructive conflict on culturally diverse decision-making groups. In a laboratory exercise, 45 four-person groups recorded their recommendations regarding a business problem, and afterward members individually completed a questionnaire on the experience. Ethnic minorities contributed considerably less to decisions than non-minorities did. However, with increasing use of constructive conflict, groups made more valid and important assumptions, and the performance and reactions of ethnic minorities improved at rates either the same as or greater than those of non-minorities. Thus, for managers facing growing ethnic diversity in the workplace, the practices of constructive conflict offer a promising approach to group decision making.

Pelled, Eisenhardt, and Xin (1999) focused on the role of diversity and conflict on work-group performance drawing heavily upon conceptual and empirical work formulated by Jehn (1995). In a study of 45 teams, Pelled et al. found that occupational diversity drove task conflict. However, they also discovered that various other types of diversity drive emotional conflict and had a dysfunctional impact on team outcomes. Both the studies focusing on intranational as well as international team conflict highlight the distinction that we made earlier concerning consent and types of identities. For example, work by Jehn (1995) and Pelled et al. (1999) suggests that certain types of identities (e.g., task or occupation) do not give rise to dysfunctional, interpersonal conflict in teams whereas other sociodemographic types (e.g., gender, race) do. Identities based on task or occupation require different types of role performances than do sociodemographic identities, are performed within the context of a larger social structure, and engender different types of commitment. Identities based in occupations often include socialization for the types of professional conflicts that occur, providing an emotional distance that focuses on productivity. When occupational conflicts occur in a work group, they pit a worker's occupational identity against her or his organizational identity, raising the issue of commitment to each (i.e. the cost of no longer continuing either identity). Considering that in many cases the organizational identity permits the occupational identity to be activated, we argue that conflicts involving occupational identities should be directed toward organizational productivity. Conflicts involving sociodemographic identities are different in that socialization for conflicts involving these identities does not necessarily include considerations for contextual factors such as organizational productivity. These conflicts often engage intense and deep emotions and relate to broader social histories than immediate task interests. Often commitments to sociodemographic identities can supersede commitment to organizationally based identities.

Collective efficacy and performance

Several streams of research demonstrate that group-level phenomena differ from culture to culture. The first of these pertains to collective cognitions known as collective (or group)-efficacy beliefs. Group-efficacy is analogous to self-efficacy at the individual level, defined as "a judgement of one's (or a group's) capability to accomplish a certain level of performance" (Bandura, 1986: 391). People tend to avoid tasks and situations they believe exceed their capabilities. Efficacy judgments promote the choice of situations and tasks with high likelihood of success, and eliminate the choice of tasks that exceed one's capabilities. Self-efficacy has been mainly developed with respect to the individual (Bandura, 1986, 1997). However, a perceived collective efficacy is crucial for what people choose to do as a group, how much effort they put into it, and how persistent they are when facing failures (Gibson, Randel, and Earley, in press; Guzzo et al., 1993; Prussia and Kinicki, 1996; Shamir, 1990). The strength of groups, organizations, and nations lies partly in people's sense of collective efficacy (Bandura, 1986). Bandura (1986, 1997) suggested that individuals hold performance beliefs about the groups to which they belong and that the strength of groups and organizations lies in people's sense of group efficacy that they can solve their problems and improve their lives through concerted effort (Bandura, 1986). Other researchers have verified the hypothesis that group beliefs about capability influence team performance (Campion, Medsker, and Higgs, 1993; Guzzo, Yost, Campbell, and Shea, 1993; Lindsley, Brass, and Thomas, 1995; Shamir, 1990; Zander and Medow, 1963). Although research has focused on the nature of group decisions in organizations, relatively little is known about the nature of these decisions in varying cultural contexts (Mann, 1980).

It is now reasonably well established that judgments of group efficacy have a positive effect on group performance and effectiveness (Bandura, 1997; Guzzo et al., 1993; Shamir, 1990). For example, Campion, Medskar, and Higgs (1993) found that three group effectiveness measures for 80 work groups were correlated with 19 different work-group characteristics drawn from the existing literature on group effectiveness. Of the 19 characteristics, the strongest predictor of effectiveness was the measure of group performance beliefs, or efficacy judgment. Furthermore, the extent to which the groups possessed confidence in their ability was the only characteristic that demonstrated a statistically significant relationship with all effectiveness measures. However, it is not clear how these judgments of group efficacy are influenced by social context. Bandura (1986) suggested that efficacy is, in part, socially constructed, and that such construction may differ as a function of national culture. Just as our culture teaches us what ideals to hold and what beliefs to endorse (Rokeach, 1973), it plays a role in how we construct our efficacy expectations (Bandura, 1986, 1997).

Gibson (1999) argued that group-efficacy effects are complex and moderated by several contingency factors. Findings from two intercultural studies she conducted support the contingency approach. Group efficacy was not related to group effectiveness when: (1) task uncertainty was high; (2) team members worked independently; and (3) collectivism was low. In contrast, when group members knew what was required to perform a task, worked interdependently, and valued collectivism, the relationship between group efficacy and group effectiveness was positive. This evidence for moderators may explain why relationships between group efficacy and group effectiveness have been modest in previous research. Arguably, high task uncertainty, low interdependence, and low collectivism make it difficult for group members to combine and integrate information about past performance, task constraints, or context.

It is not clear how, exactly, collective efficacy is shaped by the social environment and whether it is more likely to develop in certain cultures than others. An analogy between self- and collective efficacy suggests that collective efficacy is shaped both by the history of positive and negative experiences on the group level, as well as by the immediate situation (Shamir, 1990). Thus the relative salience of individual versus collective efficacy might be shaped by both the situation and culture. For example, in group-oriented cultures with a history of effective teamwork, collective efficacy might be higher than in group-oriented cultures with a history of failures.

The nature of personal versus collective efficacy judgments continues to be questioned by researchers. Gibson et al. (in press) examined various conceptualizations of personal and collective efficacy including the view that collective efficacy may best be reflected by an average of individual team members' estimates of a group's capability. However, preliminary findings from their study suggest that there is a slight advantage for prediction in using a measure of collective efficacy based on a single judgment of estimated group capability derived from a group discussion process rather than the aggregation of individuals' personal estimates. To complicate matters, the weights attached to each group member's opinions may vary as a function of cultural background. Earley (1999) found that in high power distance cultures, team members having high status demographic characteristics had an inordinate amount of influence over a group's collective efficacy estimates.

A related stream of research draws upon theories of collective cognition to better understand how the meaning of teamwork varies across national and organizational cultures. Based on interview transcripts with 59 teams across four cultures and six organizations, Gibson and Zellmer-Bruhn (1999) examined teamwork schemata using an iterative process of both inductive and deductive analyses. Categories of teamwork schemata were inductively derived, and then quantified. The four teamwork schemata arrived at through this process were characterized as: (1) family; (2) sports; (3) community; (4) associates; and (5) military. The frequency of occurrence of these schemata across cultures and organizations was then analyzed to deductively test research questions about variance in meaning. Results suggest a variety of themes to describe teamwork.

Shared mental models are the backbone of Klimoski and Mohammed's (1994) approach to the study of teams as well. A "team mental model" (Klimoski and Mohammed, 1994) is a shared psychological representation of a team's environment constructed to permit sense-making and guide appropriate group action (Elron et al., 1998). When team members perceive shared understandings with other members, the positive effect and propensity to trust generated by such a discovery fuels performance improvement (Klimoski and Mohammed, 1994) and bolsters group efficacy (Bandura, 1997).

A specific aspect of performance receiving attention in the cross-cultural literature stems from work by Van Dyne, Graham, and Dienesh's research (1994) on covenantal ties and organizational citizenship behavior. Organizational citizenship behavior, defined as the activities outside one's organizationally defined role, reflects actions of team members both during and outside of work. Van Dyne et al. argue that a number of individual and contextual factors influence citizenship behavior through the mediating role of a covenantal relationship – a personal relationship resulting in action being performed without expectations of reciprocity. Over time, the vitality of the relationship itself becomes an important focus for those who have covenantal ties, and citizenship behavior is a way the relationship is maintained and strengthened. Fiske (1991), Foa and Foa (1976), and Van Dyne, Graham, and Dienesch (1994), among others, suggested that this form of relationship is characteristic of people who have a common family structure, shared history, closely linked outcomes, or closely shared cultural perspectives.

Farh, Earley, and Lin (1997) examined the relevance of cultural context, social contracts and justice for the display of organizational citizenship behavior in several groups of Taiwanese employees. They analyzed the relationship between citizenship behaviors and organizational justice in two studies in a Chinese context, using two cultural characteristics (traditionality and modernity) and one individual (gender) characteristic. Their results suggested that employees who perceive their interactions within an organization as recognized and legitimate are more likely to engage in citizenship behavior. This finding is consistent with Van Dyne et al.'s argument (1994) that if a covenantal relationship exists, citizenship behavior is more likely to occur. For less traditional, or male, Chinese, justice perceptions seem to stimulate citizenship behavior through the formation of a covenantal relationship of employee and organization. However, they argued that traditionalists, or women, are likely to have an expressive tie to their organization based on role expectations in society. These preexisting roles exist, in part, because of *wu-lun*, or the Confucian values people have come to endorse through socialization concerning their role in society. An expressive tie leading to citizenship behavior is not dependent on justice perceptions for traditionalists or women; rather, the tie flows from prior socialization and role expectations. If expressive ties do not already exist by virtue of cultural values, social structure, or gender-based socialization, justice perceptions will be related to citizenship behavior to the extent that they create an attachment between the employee and the organization (Lind and Tyler, 1988).

Farh et al.'s (1997) results were less powerful for the cultural value of modernity. Modernity moderated the relationship between citizenship behavior and the participative facet of procedural justice and distributive justice, as predicted, but few other consistencies were observed. Their results suggest that there is an important limitation to the mediating role of a covenantal tie in the relationship between citizenship behavior and organizational and individual factors, namely, that the nature of social ties within a society influences the display of extra-role employee behavior. Some researchers have argued that organizational influences affect citizenship behavior by creating covenantal ties between employee and employer (Organ, 1990). Farh et al. concluded that traditionalists and Taiwanese women may already have formed a convenantal form of relationship with their organization, and so distributive and procedural justice would not predict engagement in citizenship behavior.

Another area receiving attention in team performance is based on the findings of social motivation (also see Steers and Sánchez-Runde, this volume). Social motivation can be viewed from two perspectives, facilitation and inhibition. Social facilitation is illustrated by work on group presence (Geen and Gange, 1977; Paulus, 1984). The presence of others during performance activates concepts such as self-image and individual competence since these "others" are observing the individual (Erez and Earley, 1993). The result of this social pressure is an increase in arousal that translates into enhanced performance for well-learned behavior but decreased performance in the use of novel behaviors. Essentially, the desire to look good creates an impetus to perform well. From a cultural viewpoint, we might argue that a facilitation effect will depend on members' relative importance of status within the existing social structure (Ting-Toomey and CoCroft, 1994). Thus, an individual coming from a group-oriented culture (e.g., Israeli kibbutz member) may not experience the same level of increased motivation attributable to group presence because of lower novelty.

Another aspect of social motivation refers to losses in performance as a function of group interaction independent of process losses, that is, social loafing (Gabrenya, Latane, and Wang, 1983). A few studies of social loafing have been conducted in cultural contexts other than the United States. For instance, Gabrenya et al. (1983) found loafing existed in a replication with Taiwanese school children of a traditional clapping and shouting task. This result was in contrast to an earlier study by the same authors (1981) who found a *facilitation* effect of group-based performance for Taiwanese and Hong Kong graduate students attending US universities. In their 1983 study, the authors speculated that the loafing effect may have occurred as an artifact of the sound-generation task. They argued that such a task may not have been sensitive to group-oriented cultural differences since the group members were not permitted to communicate with one another, nor did they share a joint sense of purpose. They found support for this alternative hypothesis in a subsequent work although they did not relate their findings to specific aspects of culture but relied solely on national differences in their samples. Matsui, Kakuyama, and Onglatco (1987) looked at the differential impact of individual and group responsibility for work performance (though the study did not examine social loafing). The authors argued that the superiority of group-based to individual-based performance in their study may have been related to the collectivistic background of their subjects (Japanese students). They speculated that the collective orientation of the Japanese may have led to an enhanced sense of camaraderie among group members. Earley (1989) directly tested the hypothesis that social loafing would be moderated by individualistic–collectivistic beliefs using a sample of Chinese and American managerial trainees. His results demonstrated that loafing effects occurred in the individualistic (e.g., primarily the American) but not the collectivistic (e.g., primarily the Chinese) samples. He conducted a follow-up study (Earley, 1993) using samples from the US, Israel, and the PRC using a process model of social loafing. He found that loafing did not occur for collectivists if they worked in the context of an in-group but it did occur if they worked alone or in an out-group. Individualists socially loafed regardless of group membership (in-group or out-group) but they did not loaf in an individual performance condition. Further, Earley found that the effect of interaction of group context (in-group, out-group, individual) and individualism–collectivism on performance (loafing) was mediated by individuals' rewards for performing as well as their individual and group efficacy.

The connection between role performance and identity has been long established.

Burke and Reitzes (1981: 84) defined identities as "meanings attributed to oneself in a role," and asserted that identities are created and maintained through three processes: "naming" or "locating the self in socially recognizable categories," interacting with others based on that identity, and confirming self-conceptions generated by that identity. These interactions entail performance and assessment whether that performance is appropriate for the claimed identity. During identity-based performances, "the self maintains control by altering performances until there is a degree of correspondence between one's identity and the identity that is implied by one's actions interpreted . . . within a common cultural framework" (Burke and Reitzes, 1981: 85). They note that the link between self-conception and behavior comes from a desire to achieve high levels of self-esteem and self-consistency (see also Swann and Reed, 1981). Stryker (1987: 95) suggests that identity salience is linked with a higher sensitivity to environmental cues relating to that identity, suggesting a mechanism by which higher salience improves performance.

This framework suggests that when workers commit to an identity as a team member, they tie self-esteem and self-consistency to role-performances based on that team's performance. This effect would be expected to be strengthened in workers from collectivist cultures, for whom commitment to and salience of group-level identities would be higher than for workers from individualist cultures, for whom individual-based identities would be more salient. Claims of group efficacy, especially those developed in group processes, can be seen as explicitly establishing criteria by which to judge role-performance, placing self-consistency, self-esteem, and the esteem of significant others at particular risk. This effect can be expected to be strengthened by public role-performance as the studies of social motivation continue. With regard to social loafing, workers from collectivist cultures, reflecting their higher-salience group identity, would be expected to work harder for group goals and contexts (at least in-group) than for their lower-salience individual identities, while workers from individualist cultures would improve role-performance in accordance with their higher-salience individual identities.

Finally, as described earlier, these effects can be expected to interact with organizational control methods, such as the normative control used by covenantal (Graham and Organ, 1993) or clan (Ouchi, 1980) type organizations. As the focal group for the identity is widened and individual and organizational interests are merged, the range of behaviors included in role-performances can also be expected to increase, leading to the inclusion of citizenship behaviors.

Composition and diversity

This section reviews a number of key papers concerning the role of composition and diversity in international and cross-cultural research on teams. The breadth of this topic precludes a complete review so the interested reader is referred to books by Cox (1993) and Jackson and colleagues (1995) as well as the early work by Hambrick and Mason (1984) on top management teams and Pfeffer (1983) on organizational demography.

Even a rather quick perusal of this literature suggests a strong "diversity" of research findings concerning the significance of compositional influences on work teams. Several research streams inform the impact of heterogeneity on team effectiveness (Earley and Mosakowski, 2000). The first is organizational demography which uses external observable traits as surrogates for internalized mediating psychological states (Lawrence, 1997).

Demographic research on team composition examines relative differences in observable characteristics such as age or functional background, and finds that team similarity is positively associated with team effectiveness and interpersonal attraction (Hambrick and Mason, 1984; Tsui et al., 1992). Homogeneous team members generally report stronger affinity for their team than heterogeneous team members (Ibarra, 1992). Similarities are not based simply on objective characteristics; rather, they are based on perceived commonalities of team members. This homogeneity leads group members to share expectations of how each member should act, even though actions may be differentiated. Members share expectations and perceptions of group entitativity (Campbell, 1958; Lickel et al., 1998), or the degree to which group members bond into one coherent unit and make only weak attachments within subgroups (Jackson et al., 1995; Lau and Murnighan, 1998).

Recently, an approach suggesting that team information processing is the mechanism whereby team demographics are translated into firm performance has received increased attention. Information processing is defined as a team discussing and coming to a collective understanding of information (Klimoski and Mohammed, 1994). Although collective information processing is a complex phenomenon, it can be reasonably captured by team members' beliefs (Gibson, 1999). Beliefs are defined as remembered cause-and-effect associations learned through experience (Thompson, 1967). Beliefs function as a storage mechanism for team members' knowledge and can be recalled and applied to strategic decisions. The effects of beliefs on outcomes can be captured by two variables: belief integration and belief variety (Ginsberg, 1990; Walsh et al., 1988). In one empirical study of these variables, Corner and Kinicki (1999) found that homogeneity with a team was positively related to belief integration; there was a positive relationship between experience and belief variety, a negative relationship between integration and firm performance, and a positive relationship between belief variety and firm performance. These findings illustrate that mediating mechanisms such as belief integration and belief variety may partially account for the previous pattern of inconsistent results regarding the relationship between top management team (TMT) homogeneity, experience, and firm outcomes.

In contrast, the cultural diversity literature (e.g., Cox, 1993; Cox, Lobel, and McLeod, 1991; Jackson and associates, 1992; Watson, Kumar, and Michaelson, 1993) studies team members' demographic backgrounds, and highlights demographic variables presupposed to relate directly to cultural attributes, values, and perceptions. The benefits of cultural diversity are often attributed to the variety of perspectives, values, skills, and attributes that diverse team members contribute (Maznevski, 1994). Finally, groups research addresses team composition effects (e.g., Hackman, 1976, 1987; McGrath, 1984; Tajfel, 1982; Tajfel and Turner, 1979; Turner, 1985). For example, research on minority influence (e.g., Moscovici, 1976; Nemeth, 1986) demonstrates that small amounts of heterogeneity (e.g., a single, vocal dissenting opinion) can enhance team functioning contingent upon the task. The groups literature suggests the relationship of heterogeneity to performance is mixed and subject to a number of constraints imposed by the work setting (McGrath, 1984; Nemeth, 1986).

Attitude similarity and demographic homogeneity have generally been shown to be positively related to group cohesiveness (Jackson et al., 1995). Demographically similar groups tend to exhibit higher satisfaction, and lower absenteeism and turnover (e.g.,

Jackson, Brett, Sessa, Cooper, Julin, and Peyronnin, 1991). These findings are consistent with the well-established principle that people are attracted to similar others, and the proposition that heterogeneous groups experience more conflict (Jehn, Northcraft, and Neale, 1997). Indeed, research indicates that cultural diversity generates conflict, which in turn reduces the ability of a group to maintain itself over time and to provide satisfying experiences for its members (Earley and Mosakowski, 2000; Ravlin et al., in press).

At the same time, heterogeneity in top management teams has demonstrated some positive effects on performance. For example, organizational demography researchers often use external observable traits as surrogates for internalized mediating psychological states (e.g., Lawrence, 1997; Tsui, Egan, and O'Reilly, 1992). This view has historical roots in the strategic management literature examining firm competitive moves (e.g., Ginsberg and Buchholz, 1990; Hambrick, Cho, and Chen, 1996; Prahalad and Bettis, 1986; Pfeffer, 1983). For example, Hambrick et al. examined a large sample of actions and responses of 32 US airlines over eight years. The top management teams that were diverse, in terms of functional backgrounds, education, and company tenure, exhibited a relatively great propensity for action and both their actions and responses were of substantial magnitude. But they were also slower in their actions and responses and less likely than homogeneous teams to respond to competitors' initiatives. Thus, although heterogeneity is a double-edged sword, its overall net effect on airline performance in terms of market share and profits was positive.

In related research, Duhaime and Schwenk (1985), for example, have shown how cognitive simplification processes may influence acquisition and divestment decisions. Jemison and Sitkin (1986) discussed how obstacles to integration of divergent perspectives may impede acquisition process. Prahalad and Bettis (1986) demonstrated how the dominant logic for conceptualizing the business domain of a firm that is held by the top management team links diversification to performance.

Recent evidence suggests that heterogeneity has advantages, such as unique information and discussion of innovative ideas, that may dissipate over time. Kim (1997) found that laboratory groups with both task and team experience display a larger bias toward discussing common information and achieve lower task performance than groups with only task experience, only team experience, or neither task nor team experience. This evidence supports the notion that experience may represent a necessary but not sufficient condition for groups to reduce bias toward discussing common information. Kim argues that if progress is truly to be made in reducing discussion bias toward discussing common information, it may be that task and/or team experience must be based on feedback that is specific, credible, and diagnostic in order to form accurate and fully developed shared understandings. Elron, Shamir, and Ben-Ari (1998) argue that the strength of multinational teams such as United Nations security forces may be derived from their diversity leading to a unity. They suggest that several influences lead to an integrated culture including a pre-existing shared "military" culture across forces, bureaucratic control structures, integrative goals/missions, shared conditions such as "foreign-ness", the temporary nature of the assignment (anything can be tolerated for a short period), and formal integrating mechanisms (e.g., joint training exercises, cross-cultural training).

Maznevski (1994) proposed a model of cultural diversity in teams focusing on the communication aspects of group interaction. According to her approach, communication acts as an integrating mechanism needed for diverse teams to work in an integrated fashion. She proposed that highly diverse teams lacking integration (derived, in part, through effective within-team communications) would perform worse on a complex task than a team having little diversity. If, however, the diverse team was highly integrated then it will be more effective than a more homogeneous team on a complex task.

Research conducted by Gruenfeld, Thomas-Hunt, and Kim (1998) demonstrated that in freely interacting groups composed of majorities and minorities, statements made by those in the majority are higher in integrative complexity than those of minority-faction or unanimous group members. After participating in group discussion, subjects assigned to majority factions experienced an increase in integrative complexity, while subjects assigned to either minorities or unanimous groups experienced a decrease in integrative complexity. The authors argue that the increase on the part of majority factions is a consequence of minority influence. Minority members act as catalysts for divergent thinking among the majority.

Moghaddam (1997) points out the difficulty of changing organizational or cultural practices, because informal social norms often perpetuate stable interaction patterns despite strenuous official attempts to change them. Granrose (1997) focused specifically on how workers from differing cultural backgrounds can be socialized into effective organizational groups. In discussing the inevitable tension between differentiated treatment of employees and integrating them into a stable and consistent organizational culture, she emphasizes the importance of individual–organizational "fit" in producing organizational commitment and effective performance. Tung (1997a) proposed several skills and competencies needed to deal effectively with diverse work groups and a variety of methods that can help to develop these skills.

A critical point is not team composition per se but the impact that composition has on a team's dynamics. Some insight is gained by looking at a recent study described by Earley and Mosakowski (2000). They argue that team member characteristics influence the emergence of a shared culture in two general ways. First, team members' personal characteristics shape their expectations of appropriate interaction rules, group efficacy beliefs, and group identity. Second, these personal characteristics affect team members' expectations of how other members should act within the team. Thus, a person's demographic background influences her self-construal as a team member and her view of others within the group (Lickel, Hamilton, Wieczorkowska, Lewis, Sherman, and Uhles, 1998; Markus and Kitayama, 1991).

These shared understandings emerging from team interaction have been called alternately a "hybrid culture" (Earley and Mosakowski, 2000), "third culture" (Casmir, 1992), team-based mental models (Klimoski and Mohammed, 1994), or synergy (Adler, 1991). A hybrid team culture refers to an emergent and simplified set of rules and actions, work capability expectations, and member perceptions that individuals within a team develop, share, and enact after mutual interactions. To the extent these rules, expectations, and roles are shared (Rohner, 1987; Shweder and LeVine, 1984), a strong culture exists. These characteristics need not be completely shared among team members just as cultural values are not uniformly shared among societal members (Rohner, 1987), but there may be significant overlap among team members.

Another potential moderator of the impact of team heterogeneity is length of time the team has existed together as a team. This is consistent with Pelled's (1996) model, as well as Elron's (1997) research on top management teams. Elron examined top management teams in international subsidiaries of multinational corporations. She found that cultural heterogeneity within the TMT was positively related to the level of issue-based conflict. Subsequently, issue-based conflict negatively affected TMT performance but had a positive relationship with subsidiary performance. No support was obtained for a negative relationship between cultural heterogeneity and cohesion. Elron argued that one possible explanation is that the negative effects of value dissimilarity on cohesion weaken over time, and in long-term groups like the TMT, become insignificant.

In a similar vein, Keck (1997) found that firms in continually disrupted contexts were more successful when they built teams that stayed together for longer periods but were functionally heterogeneous. This led Keck to argue that in turbulent contexts, cultural differences will be more disruptive than productive for heterogeneous teams. Pelled (1996) developed a model of intervening processes linking demographic diversity to work group outcomes that recognizes both the types of diversity represented in the group (the demographic predictors) and the types of conflict experienced by the group (the intervening processes). She argues, for example, that as the visibility of demographic diversity increases, affective conflict within the group increases. In contrast, as the job-relatedness of demographic diversity increases, substantive conflict will increase.

This notion was supported by Watson, Kumar, and Michaelson (1993). These researchers investigated the impact of cultural diversity on group interaction and group problem solving over time. Their study involved 36 work groups of two types: (1) homogenous – consisting of all white Americans, and (2) heterogeneous – consisting of white Americans, black Americans, Hispanic Americans and foreign nationals. Over the course of four months, these work groups completed four projects. Various aspects of performance, including range of perspectives, number of potential problems identified, generation of multiple alternatives, quality of recommendations, overall performance and group interaction process were measured on a monthly basis. During the first three months, homogeneous groups outperformed the diverse groups on several of the performance measures and reported significantly more effective process than the diverse groups. However, after four months, diverse groups scored significantly higher on range of perspectives and alternatives generated, and both types of groups reported equally effective group processes. Watson et al. (1993) conclude that diversity constrains process and performance among members of newly formed groups; however, limitations can be overcome, and eventually diverse groups can outperform homogeneous groups. By the end of the study, the two kinds of groups became equivalent.

In an organizational setting, Smith et al. (1994) confirmed the link between demography and process in teams. They used data from 53 high-technology firms to test three alternative models of the effects of top management team demography and process on organizational performance: (1) a demography model, in which team demography accounts entirely for performance outcomes, and process has no impact; (2) a process model in which process contributes incrementally and directly to performance outcomes, over and above the team's demography; and (3) an intervening model, in which the effects of the top management team on performance outcomes are due entirely to the effects of its demography on process. Results demonstrated partial support for the intervening model, in which process is a mediator of the relationship between demography and performance, and the process model, in which demography and process variables each affect performance separately.

These results suggest a fourth, more complex model of top management team behavior, with greater emphasis on team social integration. In the Smith et al. study, social integration was related to both return on investment and one year growth in sales. Social integration is a multifaceted phenomenon that reflects the attraction to the team, satisfaction with other members of the group and social interaction among the group members (O'Reilly, Caldwell, and Barnett, 1989: 22). Presumably, management teams that work well together react faster, are more flexible, use superior problems techniques, and are more productive than less integrative teams.

Outside parties within the organization may influence a team by giving the team specific goals or targets for performance. In a multinational team, the role of outside parties is complicated by identifying those "outside" versus "inside." In highly collective cultures, there is a strong sense of "in-group" and "out-group" (Earley and Gibson, 1998; Triandis, 1995a). Individuals from a collectivistic society call for greater emotional dependence on one another than individuals from individualistic societies and their organizations are expected to play a stronger role in their lives. For example, in many Asian cultures, an individual's company is not only expected to provide a salary, medical coverage, and other benefits common to the West, but they provide housing, childcare, education, and even moral and personal counseling as well as political indoctrination.

The structural identity framework we have been proposing suggests that group identity-based self-conceptions are constructed in an interactive process with other group members. Any difficulties in communication or lack of shared meanings of behaviors that arise within heterogeneous groups can impede the processes involved in group or team level identity creation, commitment, and salience. As members develop shared meanings and improve communication, these impedances should diminish over time, a suggestion consistent with findings. Aside from organizational political considerations, many of the negative effects of diversity described in this section come more from the socialization of actors to attribute stereotyped characteristics and behaviors to others in different sociodemographic categories than from any inherent group process. An important qualification to our position is that if group identities are fundamental to self-concept, then the dysfunctional aspect of heterogeneity is not likely to become ameliorated over time. That is, if an identity is highly salient and internalized (Lau and Murnighan, 1998), subgroup differences may continue to act as a basis for intragroup conflict that will continue despite repeated opportunities for team members to interact with one another. As Earley and Mosakowski (2000) argue, these repeated opportunities to interact for teams characterized by a few highly significant "faultlines" (Lau and Murnighan, 1998) may exacerbate rather than ameliorate conflict.

CONCLUSION

Our purpose in this chapter was to review and integrate important studies from the cross-cultural work teams literature. We examined a number of studies from several areas including participation, team conflict, collective efficacy and performance, and diversity. An overall judgment concerning this vast body of work is that the topic of international and cross-cultural teams continues to be of strong and increasing interest among organizational scholars. What appears absent at this point is an integrating theme concerning how member differences along cultural lines might impact work team dynamics. We have suggested a general integrating construct, namely, structural identity theory that incorporates the effects of multiple group influences, including formal and informal organizational structures and culture.

This framework defines identities in terms of the behaviors that allow individuals to respond to role expectations related to their positions within social networks. Cross-cultural work teams are especially seen as arenas in which individual members interact on the basis of their embeddedness in multiple organizational and occupational networks. Team members inevitably hold multiple identities on the basis of formal organizational structure, informal structures such as organizational coalitions, and occupational networks. They possess other identities on the basis of their social networks that are organizationally related but not necessarily sanctioned, such as professional associations, unions, or work-based friendship networks. In addition, they possess identities that reflect personal or wider social considerations such as networks formed through families, religious organizations, or shared sociodemograpic characteristics (e.g. national or ethnic cultures). These socially constructed identities converge within individual team members as salience hierarchies. The dynamics of the team's interactions activate role expectations that relate to these other networks, thus offering these identities a potential to be evoked that corresponds to the member's relative level of commitment to those networks rather than to the team.

This framework suggests that key predictors of group dynamics are the relative commitments team members have to their various identities (i.e. social networks), the nature of the role expectations that are being presented,[3] and the behaviors that those networks socialize as appropriate role performances. If a team member's commitments to organizational networks supersede her commitment to other networks, her responses will be focused on organizational interests. If a worker's commitment to class-based identities supersedes his commitment to the formal organization, and the presentation of organizational expectations evokes the class-based identity over a subordinate identity based on low power position, then his performance will likely be impeded. If a worker is placed in a multiethnic team and her socialized behavior for interethnic role performance is not conducive to communication and cooperation, then her commitment to ethnic networks supersedes her commitment to the team.

Cross-cultural considerations enter into this framework in each of these factors. This framework defines culture as a "shared meaning system ... [in which] members of the same culture ... are likely to interpret and evaluate situations and management practices in a consistent fashion" (Earley and Erez, 1997: 2), and enters behaviors in the form of habits (Triandis, 1994b), taken for granted assumptions (Berger and Luckmann, 1964), and values which shape the criteria on which workers develop and maintain positive representations of their selves. These self-evaluative criteria become the basis of self-regulatory processes by which workers monitor role performance (Swann and Reed, 1981; Burke and Reitzes, 1981; Earley and Erez, 1997). Workers from collectivist cultures, whose sense of self is highly interdependent with networks they define as in-groups, will have less differentiation between (and higher commitment to) identities based around the in-group than identities based on non-in-group networks. If an organizational division is considered in-group, then there will be less differentiation between identities based in formal and informal groups in that division than with identities based in a team with members from other organizational divisions or from outside the organization. Team tasks involving in-group interests will more closely touch the criteria for self-evaluation of collectivist workers, thus focusing team performance. In addition, role expectations presented in terms of group efficacy will meet the criteria that best focus their self-evaluative monitoring. Workers from individualist cultures will have more differentiation between identities, and commitment will be higher for identities based in networks that advance individual interests. Tasks presented in terms of role expectations involving self-efficacy allow them to express unique abilities and will more likely focus their self-evaluative attention, improving performance. In addition, workers from high power distance cultures will more likely respond to management practices that present role expectations in terms of subordinated roles than workers from low power distance cultures, which are more likely to respond to participatory management practices.

In terms of group dynamics, any team must overcome distorted meanings and disjointed work habits based on individual differences that impede group communication and coordination; team members must construct new shared meanings and coordinate habitual behaviors. Cross-cultural teams must also overcome distorted meanings and disjointed work habits resulting from cultural differences. The effort and focus with which members create team identities reflect their relative commitments to: organizational networks that support the team; their socialized responses to individual or group-oriented issues; and directed or participatory presentation of team expectations.

We have used this framework to contextualize interpretations of existing research themes represented in the cross-cultural literature – motivation, conflict, efficacy, diversity. The framework's ability to analyze the effects of multiple groups at the level of the individual, its offering of an analytical tool that can accommodate organizational and cultural influences previously unconsidered, and its ability to reconceptualize existing theories and data recommends it as a potentially unifying framework for research into cross-cultural group dynamics. As a well established theory from sociological social psychology, Stryker's Identity theory has a long history and developed methodology for hypothesis testing (Burke and Tully, 1977; Jackson, 1981; Burke and Reitzes, 1981, 1991; Stryker and Serpe, 1982; Thoits, 1983; Nutterbrock and Freudiger, 1991). It represents the type of cross-fertilization from other substantative areas that can help sustain the vitality of an active research area.

NOTES

1 This is said recognizing that identities are "thoroughly social in conception" (Stryker, personal communication) because they are created and invoked in social contexts, while SIT and SCT only refer to socially defined categories and their conception requires no actual interaction based on, or commitment to, the identity.

2 He maintained the essential symbolic interactionist concept of fluidity and social construction in interactions by rejecting structural determinism and defining structure in probabilistic terms, in which "all possible interactional sequences and all possible outcomes of those interactional sequences are not equiprobable" (Stryker, 1987).

3 In this model, environmental contingencies enter through role expectations, influencing but not always shaping the dynamics.

14

Cross-Cultural Communication

RICHARD MEAD AND COLIN J. JONES

Interpersonal communication across cultures is of central importance, and there is an abundant academic and professional literature on the topic. However, the divergence between this literature and managerial practice is surprisingly wide. For example, when Russia was moving towards capitalism in the early 1990s, the importance of cultural and institutional factors was downplayed by economists and corporations seeking to use Western-style approaches in this "torn" nation, that is, a nation whose leaders were seeking to transform it overnight with minimal regard accorded to historical and cultural factors (Huntington, 1996). In the case of Russia, the few lonely voices arguing for the importance of culture were generally disregarded (see Gannon and Associates, 1994). Similarly, in seeking to explain the Asian crisis of the late 1990s, Western economists and corporations have focused on economic factors and have taken cultural differences largely for granted.

However, cross-cultural research by Triandis and his team indicates the danger of over-generalizing from Western to non-Western systems (see Triandis, this volume). Their work emphasizes the importance of two generic forms of individualism, horizontal and vertical, and two generic forms of collectivism, horizontal and vertical. This formulation represents a combination of Hofstede's dimensions of individualism/collectivism and power distances (small and large) and is generally recognized as a significant refinement of Hofstede's research. In Hofstede's original research on 40 nations, no nation appeared in the quadrant "small power distance/collectivism," but 20 nations were in the quadrant "large power distance/collectivism." In addition, five of the 40 nations were in the "large power distance/individualism" quadrant. Thus a large part of the world is quite different from the Western nations such as Sweden, Finland, Norway, and Denmark that are characterized by small power distances and individualism.

This chapter explores the issues of hierarchical communication patterns and the degree to which such communication patterns impede or facilitate progress during periods of abrupt economic and social upheaval. This chapter deals generally with the implications for cross-cultural communication, and emphasizes the distinction between vertical and horizontal communication patterns. It examines the relationship between culture, communication style, and task; and discusses the implications for economies undergoing rapid change. The basic argument is that rapid economic development influences what tasks are performed and how; and that changes demand modifications in the communication styles appropriate to task relationships. But communication styles are deeply influenced by culture. When culture acts as a conservative influence on communication style, the demands of task and culture come into conflict. We examine the wider cultural implications from this perspective. The chapter argues the case in regard to spoken dialogue, but many of the same points can be applied to other communication forms – most dramatically to the use of electronic media.

Two Models of Communication

Communication style is understood here in terms of relationships between addressor and addressee. We deal with these relationships in terms of models of one-way and two-way styles. Despite their longevity and their failure to account for non-linear and non-verbal factors (paralinguistic factors, "noise" from the situation) the models still provide useful clues as to the participants' experience of control.

The one-way model of communication is as follows:

1 (Addressor) A decides what to communicate;
2 (Addressor) A encodes a message;
3 (Addressor) A transmits the message;
4 (Addressee) B decodes the message;
5 (Addressee) B acknowledges and/or acts upon the message.

Whereas in one-way communication B might merely acknowledge A's message and perhaps act upon a directive, in two-way communication B contributes propositional substance. Thus in two-way communication:

1 (Addressor) A decides what to communicate;
2 (Addressor) A encodes a message;
3 (Addressor) A transmits the message;
4 (Addressee) B decodes the message;
5 (Addressee/addressor) B decides what to communicate in feedback;
6 (Addressee/addressor) B encodes a message;
7 (Addressee/addressor) B transmits a message;
8 (Addressee/addressor) A decodes the message;
9 (Addressee/addressor) A/B acknowledges and/or acts upon the message, or returns to stage 1.

The one-way communication model suggests that A has the power to control B's activities, and B accepts this exercise of control. When A contributes an opinion, B accepts it; where A gives a directive, B executes it. But in two-way communication B feels competent to contribute opinions, information, and even disagreement.

Thus far, the one-way model would appear to typify superior–subordinate dialogue in a relatively high-power or vertical context. Hofstede's (1997) description of the classroom in the high-power-distance culture demonstrates the influence of culture in a situation parallel to that of manager–subordinate relations:

"Students in class speak up only when invited to; teachers are never publicly contradicted or criticized and are treated with deference even outside school ... In such a system the quality of one's learning is virtually exclusively dependent on the excellence of one's teachers" (p. 34).

In such a classroom, it is common for students to accept and take notes during a lecture, even where they suspect the professor is mistaken. The analogy to the work situation is obvious.

Conversely, where power distances are relatively small:

> teachers are supposed to treat the students as basic equals and expect to be treated as equals by the students ... Students make uninvited interventions in class, they are supposed to ask questions when they do not understand something. They argue with teachers, express disagreement and criticisms and show no particular respect to teachers outside school ... Effective learning in such a system depends very much on whether the supposed two-way communication between student and teacher is indeed established. (p. 34)

ADDITIONAL CULTURAL INFLUENCES

Power distance is not the only aspect of culture likely to influence a preference for one communication style over another. Habitual use of the one-way style implies an aversion to conflict. Hofstede notes that in cultures with high needs to avoid uncertainty there is "high stress; subjective feeling of anxiety ... Students [are] comfortable in structured learning situations and concerned with the right answers. Teachers [are] supposed to have all the answers" (p. 125). Collectivism is also a powerful incentive to avoid communicative styles that seem to invite conflict; in the more collectivist cultures "harmony should always be maintained and direct confrontations avoided" (p. 67).

Students moving from one classroom to the other may notice the different implications for individual identity and the power relationship. Japanese students at the end of their program in a top American MBA school described to the first author how, for their initial months, they had been amazed and depressed by the ease with which American students participated in lectures. The Americans asked questions, gave their own examples and even argued with the professor. In Japan, only a student with specialized knowledge or bad manners would behave in this way. How could these Japanese students compete with such brilliant colleagues? Then they began to listen and realized that much of this participation was not significant or insightful. The Americans were using their license to participate as a way of signaling presence, interest, and individual identity.

It had taken these Japanese students several months to realize intellectually that differences in the communication styles of Americans and themselves arose from cultural factors rather than control over content. But this realization did not automatically translate into new behavior. They continued to behave like typical Japanese even when they had begun to identify the cultural dynamics of the situation. This is not surprising. Understanding of cultural difference does not simply equate to acquisition of the "other-culture" values. The "deep" cultural values with which we are concerned here are acquired very early in life, and cannot be easily changed. The conservatism of culture and the conditions under which radical changes do occur is discussed in Mead (1998: ch. 3).

The parallel between classroom and workplace is imprecise particularly in the low power distance case. Other than in extreme cases of student misbehavior, the teacher is expected to prioritize the students' interests. However, the manager is expected to prioritize the organization's needs and in practice he associates his interests with those of the organization. In cases when the interests of the organization and subordinate are in conflict the subordinate loses.

This proviso makes the point that a simple reading of the models may have a very limited application. A range of other factors modify cultural priorities. Obviously, the strength (or weakness) of the participant's personal commitment to the communication may override norms of how he is expected to behave in such circumstances. For example, when the subordinate in a one-way context feels threatened, has more to gain from a successful communication, or more to lose from a failed communication, he is likely to contribute more – even when this contribution transgresses the norms. Perhaps he "answers back" and refuses to accept a decision in his attempt to move from one-way communication. In the same situation, the superior who is not prepared to risk his authority in a confrontation retreats and/or attempts to dominate through a one-way style.

Other factors that modify the equation between culture and communication style are associated with the task.

1 When the task is *simple*, a two-way dialogue may be unnecessary, even when power distances are low and tolerances of conflict are high.
2 When the task is *close-ended*: there is only one way of achieving a satisfactory result.
3 When the task is *routine*, and B has performed the task frequently before, a two-way dialogue may be unnecessary.
4 When the task is *urgent*, the luxury of two-way communication may incur too high a price. For instance, in military maneuvers expert staff are trained to reduce the components of the task to simple routines. Instructions are communicated by one-way styles, which facilitate speed and efficiency. "Prepare to fire . . . fire"; conversation as to whether we should fire now or wait a further few seconds is not appropriate.

When tasks are *complex* and *non-routine*, a two-way communication style may be appropriate even in a cultural context when one-way communication between superordinate and subordinate is more likely to be the workplace norm. Problems arise when the participants fail to recognize the need to modify their habitual styles when communicating with superordinates and subordinates, and fail to recognize the communicative meaning of a modified style.

This brings up the question of how the intended meaning of an utterance is interpreted. No problems occur where there is a precise match between grammatical form and locutionary intent. For example, the manager tells a subordinate "Show me the warehousing budget." Obviously a directive is intended. But no such simple match occurs in the case of the following statement form: "I haven't seen the warehousing budget." And this lack of signaled match raises problems of interpretation and hence of response.

Table 14.1 (simplified from Sinclair, 1980) shows the levels at which this statement might be interpreted: from high as a statement of fact, to low as a directive. Correct interpretation depends on making an accurate reading of contextual clues. These include clues from:

1 the specific task – what interpretation is "rational," given the characteristics of the task;
2 the physical situation. "I haven't seen the warehousing budget" may have different meanings when spoken on the golf course and in the office;
3 non-verbal factors;
4 the participant's psychology;
5 the organizational relationship;
6 the responsibilities associated with each person's rank;
7 the organizational culture;
8 the national culture.

The following case demonstrates how easily a wrong interpretation can be made. Both participants were Thai. The director of a Thai management school was a manager of the traditional hierarchical type of organization. He had embarked upon a new program, to train short-term industrial placements, and asked a trusted Thai subordinate to design the cover of a brochure. This manager listed the information that the cover should convey. When the subordinate submitted his draft a few days later the director commented, "it's very crowded." Apologizing, the subordinate withdrew and spent a week attempting a redesign. Eventually he returned to admit failure. He could not see a way of simplifying without reducing the quantity of information. The director told him that he had wasted the week. "I was making a comment. The fact that the cover looked crowded could not be helped. That is essential information."

The subordinate had applied the sensible rule; when a manager's utterance is ambiguous, try to interpret at the lowest possible level in table 14.1 – as a directive. Only if this interpretation is not appropriate, try the next level up – as a wh-question; and so on. The subordinate had interpreted "it's very crowded" as a directive to produce a new design. All of the clues or stimuli 2–8 above supported or at least did not militate against this incorrect interpretation. What the subordinate had not taken into account was the influence of number 1 above – the task, which was new. The shared lack of experience of both superior and subordinate in marketing this type of program meant that neither was able to offer or evaluate a solution.

TABLE 14.1 Levels at which a statement might be interpreted, from highest to lowest

- A statement of fact, perhaps requiring only acknowledgment, such as: "It's hot today again."
- A yes/no question: "Have you seen the warehousing budget?"
- A wh-question (Who/what/when/where/why/how?): "When is the warehousing department going to present its budget?"
- A directive: "Show me the warehousing budget."

The point applies generally to the problems of adjusting from a one-way to a two-way communicative style. Adjustment to communicative ambiguity may be painful for persons in cross-cultural situations, for example when one participant comes from a relatively high power distance culture and the second from a culture in which power distances are low.

The opportunities for cross-cultural confusion (when the cultures coincide with different ethnic groups) are obvious and do not concern us further here. We are concerned with communicative inefficiencies between sub-cultural groups, when sub-cultural groups bring differing preconceptions to performing a shared task.

Matching Communication Style and Task

Communication style is efficient when it is appropriate to the task. Inefficiencies arise when the task changes and participants attempt to adhere to the previous communication style. Suppose that members of a group have a history of working on a simple, close-ended and routine task. A one-way communication style between supervisor and group members is appropriate to the task. At the bar after work, an altogether different style is appropriate, as the Japanese salarymen so famously exemplify. But suppose that the task changes. For example, a company reengineers and specialist assembly line teams are replaced by mixed-specialism groups responsible for negotiating task design, implementation, and the allocation of materials and quality standards. Now two-way communication, possibly involving a wide number of participants, is appropriate.

When the culture is marked by relatively low power distances, low needs to avoid uncertainty and high individualism, this transition may be welcomed. Indeed, it is implicit in Hammer and Champy's (1993) seminal work on reengineering and subsequent texts, that in the Anglo cultures of the United States and the United Kingdom for example, participation in process design motivates. But this experience of rapid transition to complex, open-ended and non-routine work, and consequent needs for major adjustments in communicative style, may be deeply unsettling in a traditional hierarchical culture whose members associate a one-way style with task-related communications between superordinate and subordinate.

This condition for communicative maladjustment is common in Asian societies which have leapt so spectacularly from agrarian-based economies to the production of high technology. A representative text comments:

> The recent economic changes in Southeast Asia have been astonishing in their speed and scope. In the space of a decade, the economies of Singapore, Thailand, Malaysia and Indonesia have not only been expanded but transformed. Southeast Asia's industrial revolution has been compressed into less than half a generation. (Evans, 1996: 5)

Evans was writing in the final year of the apparent economic miracle. But the sophisticated economic and political analyses made by him and the other contributors to this volume were not equipped to explain the impact at the grassroots level of human interactions. Factors at the macro level are still given most emphasis. The subsequent crisis of 1997–8 is typically characterized as a problem of financial inefficiencies that can be resolved by "international financial reform ... What the global economy needs now is a way to minimize the frequency and intensity of crises" (Blinder, 1999: 53).

This approach assumes relatively short-term causes to the problem. It does not recognize how far the crisis has arisen from non-financial, non-economic factors. We argue that emergent contradictions in the local cultures contributed significantly to the economic crisis, and that these contradictions arise in part from a failure to adjust communicative styles to economic and technological change.

In a traditional enterprise (for instance, a farm, a craft producer, a trader) the boss possessed expert knowledge of operations, and on that basis controlled work-related communications. However, economic development has created new industries and new tasks. These are often complex, open-ended and non-routine, and demand communication styles that are not typical of the old style.

For example, the managers of a company are planning to market a new technology which they hope to develop with a joint-venture partner. No one manager controls all the necessary information. The marketing manager, finance manager, R&D manager, production manager, and HR manager all have expertise, but no one has all the expertise needed in order to achieve an optimum solution. All must participate, and that means all

- ◆ recognize the need for participation;
- ◆ share perceptions of what discourse functions are participatory (for instance, agreement, disagreement, suggestions, opinions, as opposed to a sequence of directions and acceptances of direction);
- ◆ develop skills in communicating and interpreting these functions.

The need for new skills challenges not only communicative competence but perhaps more severely, individual perceptions of self-worth in relation to that of others. This new cosmology cannot be comfortably acquired in hierarchical cultures where power distances are wider than in the United States and the United Kingdom. To take the example above, the experienced CEO and owner of the company needs to adjust more than the junior manager who only recently completed degree training.

The CEO who cannot adjust may well lose the services of the young technologist. Executive mobility rates in Southeast Asian countries are difficult to research, but evidence suggests that they are high; Mead et al.'s pre-crisis 1997 study of 96 middle-level Thai managers found an average tenure of 5.6 years, with a median of only 4.3 years. In comparison, 1989–91 OECD figures for tenure with present employers reported for all employment groups an average of 6.7 years in the United States to 10.9 years in Japan, with tenures in various European countries between the two (*The Economist*, 1993: 21).

The problems are acute because they have arisen in a very short time, namely Evans's (p. 5) "half a generation" in which the Asian industrial revolution has occurred. At least in local subsidiaries of Western multinationals, the 1997 crisis may have exacerbated the problems.

In regard to Thai subsidiaries, Andrews (1999) points out that previously the corporate headquarters of a Western multinational was prepared to tolerate local business practices when the subsidiary was making profits. But now that profits are much reduced and the aura of unstoppable success has gone, these practices are no longer tolerated. Corporate headquarters exerts much tighter control, including control on communications styles within and between units. This implies that, first, corporate headquarters assumes that its communication style is easily acquired by competent local employees, whereas acquisition may be painful. Second, demands for change in these companies are immediate, and may be very stressful.

Below a superficial level, Asian cultures have been unable to adjust adequately to the wave of economic and technological changes that have occurred with such rapidity. A one-way style is inappropriate and inefficient, and the confidence and skills needed to practice a two-way style are often not developed.

Societies that were once relatively homogeneous (such as those in Southeast Asia) are losing their cohesion as social groups increasingly lack a common style for communicating their interests and experiences. These splits are more radical than in their Western counterpart societies, which are more heterogeneous and which have had far longer to accommodate to economic, social, and political change. Whereas the United Kingdom threw off absolutist monarchy in 1649, Thailand only made this break in 1932 – and in this respect was ahead of many of its Asian neighbors. All our experience indicates that cultural values expressed in communication style take far longer to adapt to change than do formal organizational structures.

Generational splits are most obvious. The first author, interviewing applicants for an MBA school, asked one young male if he intended to return to work for the family company after graduating. The applicant replied "No. I already see that my father is making mistakes, but he intends to work for another twenty years. I don't want to spend that time fighting him." In such cases the preferred option is to work for a foreign multinational in order to gain experience, status, and contacts, to start a company of one's own, and perhaps only then to play a major role in the family company.

Members within the same age group are more differentiated than in the past. Those members of the young managerial class who have been educated in the West adapt more easily to the new technologies and economic priorities than do their non-traveled contemporaries. An insightful employer may recognize the differences and even apply them positively.

For example, in 1995 the Bangkok head office of one local bank recruited only Western educated graduates into its international business department, and only local graduates to local lending. The international department was characterized by considerable two-way communication between managers and subordinates, and structures were interpreted relatively flatly. On the other hand, structures in the local lending department were interpreted more hierarchically, on the civil service model. Managers exercised greater overt control of verbal interactions with subordinates. Loyalty to the superior was of greater importance than in the international department, and communications across peer sub-departmental units were fewer.

This meant that those employees with greater experience of Anglo-values were being given opportunities to develop a two-way communication style in relatively flat and flexible structures. But those who lacked this international experience were employed in traditional structures using predominantly a one-way style.

The fact that the differences between the groups were expressed in communication style and implementations of structure has several implications. The wise company that recognizes these differences may reap the rewards of successfully applying different aptitudes in achieving different, more or less complex, goals. Nevertheless, top management must be prepared to manage an increasingly complex culture. The company that fails to recognize increasing cultural heterogeneity in its workforce may be in for trouble.

CONCLUSION

In conclusion, this chapter has emphasized the importance of cultural factors, particularly the degree of power distance, on how members of the culture group adjust to new tasks. It has suggested that cultures in which one-way communication styles traditionally predominated in the workplace are likely to have greater difficulty in adapting to complex and non-routine tasks. This has clear implications for cross-cultural communication, and generally, indicates the shallowness of arguments that national cultures can be or even should be forced into convergence and "globalized."

Many economists and respected commentators have stated openly that they do not know how to control the global economy, and that a global depression may be the greatest threat facing mankind. The examples of crisis in Russia and Asia lend credence to their fear. Formal economic models designed to manage correct local crises will not provide lasting solutions until they are interpreted in terms of the values of the local culture. Finally, given the economists' open admission of continuing concern, it is ironic and troubling that cultural factors still receive low priority in analyzing the problems facing our heterogeneous world community.

15

Metaphor and the Cultural Construction of Negotiation: A Paradigm for Research and Practice

MICHELE J. GELFAND AND CHRISTOPHER McCUSKER

As we enter the new millennium, cross-cultural negotiations are becoming the norm, rather than the exception, involving people at all levels of the organization – from CEOs to customers alike. Yet the increasing need for practical solutions on managing cultural dynamics in negotiation is not matched by the focus on culture in the science of negotiation, which remains primarily a Western enterprise (Pruitt and Carnevale, 1993). The purpose of this chapter is to further advance cultural perspectives in the science of negotiation. Our aims are to review some of the existing research perspectives on the topic, to discuss their strengths and weaknesses, and to provide an alternative and complementary perspective for further research. Specifically, we introduce a *metaphor* perspective on culture and negotiation. Metaphor plays a dual role in that it is both a theoretical mechanism for linking research on culture and negotiation and a practical tool for managing negotiation processes. We offer its theoretical basis, examples of its manifestations in the US and Japan, and descriptions of research issues that arise from studying how negotiation is socially constructed through metaphor. Before discussing culture, we first define negotiation and provide a brief overview of its *sans*-cultural traditions.

NEGOTIATION

Negotiation has been described as a communicative exchange (e.g., Putnam and Poole, 1987) through which participants "define or redefine the terms of their interdependence" (Walton and McKersie, 1965). It is a pervasive form of social interaction that is conducted frequently in formal arenas, such as international relations, industrial relations, and manager–subordinate relations, as well as informal arenas, such as interpersonal relations and marital decision-making (Pruitt and Carnevale, 1993). Although these arenas are quite diverse, there are some common elements of negotiation that are applicable across contexts. Specifically, negotiation situations have at least five core characteristics: (1) parties have, or perceive that they have, a conflict of interest; (2) parties are engaged in communication; (3) compromises are possible; (4) parties can make provisional offers and counter-offers to each other; and (5) parties are temporarily joined together voluntarily, and their outcomes are determined jointly (Chertkoff and Esser, 1976; Cross, 1965; Rubin and Brown, 1975).

Negotiation has been a research priority since the earliest days of social psychology (e.g., Deutsch and Krauss, 1962) and organizational behavior (e.g., Walton and McKersie, 1965). Negotiation research is important for both theoretical and practical reasons. Theory-driven research seeks an understanding of basic processes and outcomes of negotiation, whereas practical research attempts to find ways to help negotiators get better results. Many aspects of negotiation have received attention (see reviews by Carnevale and Pruitt, 1992; Bazerman et al., 2000). Although there is no single all-encompassing theory or method of negotiation, Pruitt and Carnevale (1993) concluded that a dominant paradigm underlies most behavioral research on negotiation. Most of this research places an emphasis on psychological processes. Indeed, one of the main contributions of the dominant paradigm has been the demonstration that negotiation dynamics are influenced by the manner in which negotiators are thinking and feeling.

Within the dominant paradigm there are different research emphases (see Bazerman et al., 2000). For example, research within the cognitive tradition examines negotiation as a form of decision making and focuses on perception and information processing (Bazerman and Carroll, 1987; Bazerman and Neale, 1983; Thompson, 1990). Research within the motivational tradition examines negotiation as a response to social conflict and it focuses on the role of goals and interests (Pruitt, 1981; Pruitt and Carnevale, 1993; Pruitt and Rubin, 1986). In both of these traditions, researchers often make a distinction between what is referred to as *distributive* negotiation structures from those that are *integrative* in nature. In the former, negotiators' interests are diametrically opposed, resulting in the fact that a gain for one party is a loss for the other. However, in integrative structures, while negotiators' interests are opposed, they also have differences in priorities on the issues, resulting in the possibility of tradeoffs. As a result, it is possible to create agreements that are of mutual advantage or win–win.[1] In recent years, there is also an ever-increasing interest in the social context of negotiation (Kramer and Messick, 1995). For example, recent studies analyze issues such as negotiators' relationships, negotiation teams (e.g., Thompson, Peterson, and Kray, 1995), and social norms (e.g., Pruitt and Carnevale, 1993).

Culture is the broadest social context in which negotiations occur (Carnevale, 1995). The importance of culture in negotiation has been increasingly recognized (e.g., Adler, 1986; Faure and Rubin, 1993; Fisher, 1980; Harris and Moran, 1979; Janosik, 1987; Weiss, 1993). Next, we discuss why culture is important in the science of negotiation, and review perspectives on culture and negotiation that do exist.

THE CULTURAL MANDATE

We are living in an era of increasing global intimacy as interdependent relationships among people of different cultures are on the rise. As expressed by Clifford Geertz (*New York Times Magazine*, April 9, 1995, p. 44), thanks to "the deprovincialization of the world, we're going to be in each other's faces more." Since benefits derived from interdependent relationships are greater when conflict is managed constructively (Deutsch, 1973), the practical consequences of culture for interpersonal negotiation must be understood. As such, a behavioral perspective on culture and negotiation is needed for practical reasons.

The theoretical motivation for studying culture and negotiation is also compelling. Research on negotiation should strive to build *universal* laws – those whose validity generalizes across cultural contexts. Universal claims make sense when laws are based on variables that are commonly and similarly experienced by all humans, such as biological factors (e.g., hormones), ecological pressures (e.g., need for shelter), or exposure to elementary social structures (e.g., parent–child relations) (Pepitone and Triandis, 1987).

However, as we have noted, most behavioral research on negotiation has been done in North America and Western Europe, regions of the world identified as relatively individualistic (Hofstede, 1980a). Both personal and environmental factors should be taken into account to understand negotiation behavior (Lewin, 1935). Consistent with individualism, behavioral negotiation theory typically assumes self-interested parties and downplays group aspects of the negotiation environment (Pruitt and Carnevale, 1993). Since culture might impact both behavior of negotiators and assumptions of researchers, a better understanding of each may result from cross-cultural research.

In sum, a provocative area of inquiry lies at the intersection of culture and negotiation for both practical and theoretical reasons. Below we summarize existing research perspectives on culture and negotiation, discuss their strengths and weaknesses, and offer an alternative and complementary perspective based on metaphor.

EXISTING PERSPECTIVES ON CULTURE AND NEGOTIATION

In recent years, there has been increasing attention to the study of culture and negotiation. Emerging perspectives can generally be grouped into three categories: (1) *case study approaches*, which provide in-depth analyses of specific intercultural or intracultural negotiations; (2) *cross-national comparative approaches*, which document differences and similarities in the use of negotiation tactics in different geographic locations; and more recently, (3) *cultural dimension approaches*, which analyze negotiation behavior across cultures according to dimensions of cultural variation (Hofstede, 1980; Schwartz, 1994). While not necessarily inclusive of all possible approaches to the topic, this represents much of the empirical approach to the study of negotiation and culture (see also reviews by Gelfand and Dyer, 2000, and Lytle, Brett, Barsness, Tinsley, and Janssens, 1995). Collectively, these approaches illustrate that culture is an important element of negotiations. As with any theoretical perspective, each gives unique insights into cultural effects in negotiation, and each has strengths and weaknesses, which are discussed below.

The *case study* approach offers a rich, culture-specific (*emic*) perspective on culture and negotiation, and includes specific advice regarding negotiation styles in different cultures. One can find information about negotiating in *China* (Blackman, 1997; Pye 1982), *Japan* (Hawrysh and Zaichkowsky, 1989; March, 1990), *Korea* (Tung, 1991a), *Mexico* (Harris and Moran, 1979), *Russia* (Schecter, 1998; Smith, 1989), *Spain* (Burton, 1994) among others (Acuff, 1997; Salacuse, 1991). Likewise, there are a number of in-depth case studies and archival studies of intercultural negotiations available (Anand, 1981; Cohen, 1991;

Cohen, 1987; Faure and Rubin, 1993; Glenn, Witmeyer, and Stevenson, 1977; Kimura, 1980; Strazar, 1981).

Strengths and weaknesses. Case studies are useful in that they provide holistic accounts of a specific negotiation context, and typically provide information on what to avoid when conducting negotiations in particular cultures. Yet, at the same time, because they home in on different aspects of culture and different aspects of negotiation, they are less useful for building theory across a wide variety of contexts. Since such accounts do not have any common metric, it is difficult to understand what is cultural per se, and how culture operates in negotiation. Moreover, given that such accounts are difficult to generalize, it is difficult to prescribe advice to managers negotiating in multiple cultures. Finally, such accounts are often static, and do not account for cultural change and within-culture differences.

Cross-national comparative approaches are the most common kind of research on this topic. They involve making systematic comparisons between samples of interest drawn from different locations of the world. An inference is made that "culture" amounts to "people from different locations." For example, culture has been defined as "a difference in national heritage and permanent residence of the parties in negotiation" (Graham, 1983: 198). Obtained between-sample differences on negotiation variables then count as evidence that "cultural differences" exist. Considerable evidence suggests that negotiation behavior varies from location to location based on this approach. For example, existing research can be found comparing the tactics and outcomes of Americans with Brazilians and Japanese (e.g., Graham, 1984), Canadians (e.g., Adler, Graham, and Gehrke, 1987), Chinese (e.g., Adler, Brahm, and Graham, 1992), French (e.g., Campbell, Graham, Jolibert, and Meissner, 1988), and Russians (e.g., Graham, Evenko, and Rajan, 1993), among others.

Strengths and weaknesses. This approach has begun to accumulate a diverse pattern of empirical facts, usually taking the form, "People from country X use more Y tactics and achieve more (or fewer) outcomes in negotiation than people in country Z" (Zartman, 1993). Such results demonstrate that culture plays a role in negotiation, and that we cannot necessarily generalize findings from one country to another. Moreover, unlike the previous approach, this research attempts to find a common metric upon which negotiations can be compared. While such differences provide evidence in favor of the claim that culture plays a role in negotiation, this approach has been criticized for its atheoretical orientation (Lytle et al., 1995; Zartman, 1993). For example, Zartman (1993: 17) concludes that culture is "every bit as relevant as breakfast and to much the same extent. Like the particular type of breakfast the negotiators ate, culture is cited primarily for its *negative* effects. Yet even the best understanding of any such effect is *tautological*, its measure *vague*, and its role in the process basically *epiphenomenal.*"

Such concerns arise mostly from the practice of inferring culture from "location of sample," which can lead to inexplicit theorizing about culture, circular causal reasoning, and conclusions that resemble stereotypes. As explained by Zartman (p. 18), "Although conceived as the determinant of personal behavior, culture is a social phenomenon and so is related to a particular society. But it is never clearly established why the given traits inhere in that society. The approach perpetuates stereotypes and self-proving hypotheses . . . African culture (or whoever) is what Africans (or whoever) do, and they do it because they are Africans (or whoever)." Also, this issue extends to the problem of managing cross-cultural negotiations. For instance, what are the managerial consequences of average tendencies of groups of negotiators? One negotiates with another person, not with "Africans, on average."

The third and more recent approach is the *cultural dimensions approach*. Research in this tradition often derives predictions about negotiation behavior and outcomes based on broad *culture-level* dimensions, most notably, individualism–collectivism, power distance, uncertainty avoidance, and/or masculinity–femininity (Brett and Okumura, 1998; Gelfand and Christakopolou, 1999; McCusker, 1994; Natlandsmyr and Rognes, 1995; Tinsley, 1998). This approach offers a much-needed "theoretical" boost to the study of negotiation within the *etic*, comparative tradition by incorporating cultural dimensions into negotiation theory.

For example, Natlandsmyr and Rognes (1995) created two opposing hypotheses based on Hofstede's broad culture value dimensions: Norwegians would have more integrative outcomes than Mexicans based on their low masculinity, weak uncertainty avoidance, and low power distance scores in Hofstede's (1980a) study. Alternatively, based on Hofstede's (1980a) individualism scores, they hypothesized that Mexicans would have more integrative outcomes than Norwegians. Support was found for their first hypothesis, in that Norwegians had more integrative outcomes than Mexicans. Likewise, Tinsley (1998) linked dimensions of culture with negotiators' beliefs about normative conflict models. She found that cultural differences on hierarchical differentiation (acceptance of social inequality, such as Japan), explicit contracting (using formal agreements, such as in Germany), and polychronicity (processing many tasks simultaneously, such as in the US) were related to preferences for using authorities, relying on external regulations, and integrating interests in conflicts, respectively.

Strengths and weaknesses. Research in this tradition represents an advance from previous approaches by shifting the focus from using "location" to infer culture (and merely documenting differences), to making a *priori* predictions from general cultural dimensions, and in some studies, verifying those cultural assumptions with existing measures (e.g., McCusker, 1994). In this respect, we are in a better position to understand some of the reasons for *why* there are differences in negotiation. Nevertheless, a weakness of this approach is that it generally uses *broad* and *distal predictors* (i.e., dimensions of culture) to understand *specific* behavior in negotiations. However, such "historical" concepts are not the best predictors of current actions (Fishbein and Ajzen, 1975). In contrast, actions are determined from contemporaneous psychological states — those that exist at the time the actions are occurring. This is what Lewin called the "life space" or psychological environment produced by the immediate situation. In this view, the past does affect current action, but only insofar as the past shapes the life space of a person at the present.

Indeed, the notion that broad dimensions are not as useful for predicting specific behavior has been illustrated in research on culture in negotiation. For instance, several authors (e.g., Tinsley, 1998) have noted there is much between-country variance in negotiation behavior and outcomes that is not explained by broad cultural dimensions. This suggests that our current traditions do not offer enough insight into how culture operates. Finally, the dimensional approach suffers from an inability to give prescriptive advice for managers. Cultures differ on many dimensions and are complex wholes (Lytle et al., 1995), and as such, advice given based on individual dimensions has the potential to be piecemeal and even conflicting.

SUMMARY

Existing research perspectives have undoubtedly helped us to begin to understand the importance of culture and negotiation, and each has unique strengths and weaknesses, all of which point to the need for new research perspectives. We believe that building on the strengths of each approach is important in advancing other perspectives on culture and negotiation. In particular, studies of culture and negotiation have demonstrated that we need to have a *holistic* account of culture that captures the multidimensional nature of culture (i.e., *the case study approach*). We also need to have a common metric upon which to make comparisons (i.e., *the cross-national comparative approach*), and we need to formulate theory regarding *why* differences arise in negotiation (*cultural dimensions approach*). Yet even further, we argue that we need to have an account of culture that is *proximal* to the negotiation context (is in the here and now), to demonstrate how culture *functions* in the system of negotiation, and demonstrate culture's *utility* for managers.

A METAPHOR PERSPECTIVE ON CULTURE AND NEGOTIATION

Based on the previous discussion, we advance an alternative, yet complementary, perspective on cultural information processing and negotiation, which has its roots in cultural psychology (Bruner, 1990; Shweder and Levine, 1984), linguistics (Lakoff, 1993; Gibbs, 1990; Ortony, 1993), cognitive science (Gentner, 1983) and psychological anthropology (Schwartz, White, and Lutz, 1992). Consistent with a Lewinian perspective, and with existing views in cultural psychology, we argue that culture affects how people "enter into meaning" in the contemporaneous negotiation context. Central to our analysis is the assertion that shared metaphors, or coherent, holistic conceptual meaning systems, which have been developed and cultivated in particular socio-cultural environments, *function* to interpret, structure, and organize social action in negotiations. Below, we discuss the nature of culture as meaning systems, before turning to a discussion of the function of these meanings in negotiation.

CONCEPTUALIZING CULTURE

In conceptualizing culture, we focus on the nature of culture as it exists in the here and now of negotiating. We adapt Geertz's (1973: 89) perspective, which posits that culture consists of "historically transmitted patterns of meanings embodied in symbols, a system of inherited conceptions expressed in symbolic forms by means of which people communicate, perpetuate, and develop knowledge about attitudes toward life."

Meanings fundamentally reflect mappings across conceptual domains, or what has been referred to as *metaphor* (Lakoff, 1987). While we experience them through language, metaphors operate on a conceptual level. The idea that metaphors are more than linguistic devices stems from Reddy (1993), who showed how the "conduit" metaphor conceptualizes the experience of communication. Since then, a growing body of evidence from cognitive science and linguistics supports the contention that metaphors are the basic mechanism through which humans conceptualize experience (Gibbs, 1990; Lakoff, 1987; see also Ortony, 1993).

More specifically, metaphors are coherent conceptual systems in which different domains of experience are put into the same category so that knowledge from one can be used to make sense of the other (Lakoff, 1993). Metaphors can be thought of as sets of conceptual mappings that take place between domains of experience. While humans are capable of a wide array of different conceptual mappings, some are *selectively developed, activated, and perpetuated through participation in social institutions and practices*. As an example, Lakoff (1993: 243) illustrates how most basic concepts, such as time, are based on everyday socio-cultural experiences, and conceptualized through metaphor:

> We have a TIME as MONEY metaphor, shown by expressions like he's wasting time, I have to budget my time, this will save you time; I've invested a lot of time in that; he doesn't use his time profitably. This metaphor came into English use about the time of the industrial revolution, when people started to be paid for work by the amount of time they put in. Thus, the factory led to the institutional pairing of periods of time with amounts of money, which formed the experiential bases of the metaphor. Since then . . . the budgeting of time has spread throughout American culture.

As in the above example, metaphors use information from a well-developed knowledge source domain (i.e., money) to construct a mental model about another target domain (i.e., time). Through cross-domain mappings, the entities associated with money (i.e., budgeting, saving, wasting) are specifically applied to the domain of time.

The cognitive process of making sense of something new based on what is known already has been referred to as *apperception* (James, 1890). Through apperception, sets of ontological correspondences are made between current and past experiences, and an interpreted "pattern of" behavior from a previous social situation becomes a "pattern for" expressing behavior in a current one. Thus, in the previous example, we construct meaning about the concept of time through a well-developed frame of reference, and the experience of time *becomes like* the experience of money. Importantly, it is assumed that this process takes place rapidly, automatically, and largely unconsciously (Lakoff, 1993), and further, once it has taken place, the meanings become indistinguishable from reality itself (Markus et al., 1997).

Apperception and metaphoric mapping are assumed to be natural cognitive processes that are universally applicable to all humans. Yet because metaphoric mappings stem from participation in social institutions and practices, the *content* of metaphoric mappings varies tremendously across socio-cultural contexts. Put simply, exposure to a similar cultural environment leads to shared metaphors (mental sameness) between members of groups. *Mental sameness* refers to intersubjective similarity in perceptions of a cultural environment between members of cultural groups (Malinowski, 1927). Likewise, to the extent that experiences diverge across socio-cultural contexts, metaphoric mappings between individuals will diverge as well. For example, the notion of "time as money" is a shared metaphor in the West, which is based on shared experiences, yet it does not exist in all cultures (Hall, 1984; Lakoff and Johnson, 1980). Thus, while metaphoric mappings are believed to have a universal function (i.e., provide a conceptual scheme for interpretation and expression), and follow a universal process (i.e., the process of apperception), the products of this process, which are the contents of metaphors, should be culture-specific (see also Gannon and Associates, 1994).

Finally, consistent with a Geertzian perspective, although shared conceptual mappings are implicit, they are created, perpetuated, expressed, and institutionalized in various *symbolic forms*, such as language, laws, everyday routines and rituals, artifacts, etc. For example, conceptual mappings of time and money result in the development of language through which we communicate our conceptual mappings. In this respect, language is seen as a tool for "creating, maintaining, and communicating social and psychological realities, rather than merely a representational system" (Miller, 1997, citing Ochs, 1988: 94). Thus, symbols are the shared *explicit* coordinates of metaphoric mappings. Put differently, while conceptual mappings are ontologically subjective (i.e., thoughts are private), cultural symbols are epistemologically objective (i.e., symbols are transmitted between participants and can be directly experienced by more than one participant; see also Searle, 1995).

In sum, culture consists of shared meanings which are structured through cross-domain mappings (i.e., metaphors) that develop through experience, and that are embodied and perpetuated in various symbolic forms. Most basic concepts, such as time, are based on everyday experience, and conceptualized through metaphor (Lakoff and Johnson, 1980). Metaphors are not merely linguistic devices, but rather are a fundamental cognitive process. While this process is likely universal, the content of metaphors is culture-specific.

With this perspective in mind, we now turn to the role of metaphor in the system of negotiation. Just as other concepts and activities are conceptualized through metaphor, we argue that negotiations are conceptualized through metaphoric mappings. However, such metaphoric mappings are not universal – they are conditioned through participation in institutions and practices. That is, based on shared experience, a set of ontological correspondences are made between one domain of experience (such as war, or competitive sports) and the domain of negotiation; they help it create different subjective and social realities of negotiation in different cultures. In the next section, we elaborate on this argument by first discussing the nature and function of metaphor in negotiation, and then discussing examples of metaphors of negotiation in the US and Japan.

THE FUNCTION OF METAPHOR IN NEGOTIATION

Consider the following example of *argument as war*, offered by Lakoff and Johnson (1980: 4):

◆ Your claims are *indefensible*.
◆ He *attacked every weak point* in my argument.
◆ His criticisms were *right on target*.
◆ I *demolished* his argument.
◆ I've *never won* an argument with him.
◆ He *shot down* all of my arguments.

As discussed by Lakoff and Johnson (1980), this example is not merely reflective of a linguistic device, but rather the *experience* of argumentation is conceived of in terms of the domain of war. In this respect, "many of the things we do in arguing are partially structured by the concept of war. Though there is no physical battle, there is a verbal battle, and the structure of an argument – attack, defense, counterattack, etc. reflects this . . . it structures the actions we perform in arguing" (Lakoff and Johnson, 1980: 4).

Importantly, in the previous example, war metaphors do more than merely represent knowledge. They also have directive functions in negotiation. First, metaphors function to *create intentional subjective realities* (Bruner, 1990; Miller, 1997). In other words, metaphors dictate what negotiators should take to be their psychological reality – what does and does not exist (Kashima, 1994). In this respect, we argue that metaphors have a constitutive function in negotiation (cf. Miller, 1997) in that they contain concepts for defining the subjective reality of negotiation. Moreover, such subjective states are intentional in that they guide action. As Kashima (1994) states, "metaphors are not just food for thought, but food for action" (p. 352). The second function is social and concerns negotiation as a form of collective action. Here, we argue that coordinated, organized social action between negotiators is made possible through shared metaphoric mappings and their objective symbolic referents. In this respect, we suggest that metaphors have an *organizing* (Weick, 1979) function in the system of negotiation. Each of these functions is discussed in turn.

Psychological Functions of Metaphor

The first function of metaphors in negotiation is to provide a set of ideas for interpreting the context, or defining the environment, of negotiation. Since negotiation is a form of social activity that exists only through mutual participation, metaphors provide a coherent, conceptual scheme for defining that activity. To use a metaphor, the conceptual content of metaphors can be used to "define the game" that "we" are playing. Metaphors give an answer to the question, "what are *we* doing here?" for individual participants in a contemporaneous social context which are constitutive of the activity. For example, Searle (1995: 27–8) explains how ideas have a "constitutive function" for social activities with the game of chess:

> the rules of chess do not regulate an antecedently existing activity. It is not the case that there were a lot of people pushing bits of wood around on boards, and in order to prevent them from bumping into each other all the time and creating traffic jams, we had to regulate the activity. Rather, the rules of chess create the very possibility of playing chess. The rules are *constitutive* of chess in the sense that playing chess is constituted in part by acting in accord with the rules. Such rules come in systems, and the rules individually, or sometimes the system collectively, characteristically have the form: X counts as Y in context C.

Searle's quote shows how the objective context of chess is virtually meaningless for someone with no knowledge of the game. The board, how the pieces are lined up, the way each piece moves, and so on, are not intrinsic properties of the physical context. Rather, the rules of chess transform those objective features of the context into a meaningful social event. It is the rules themselves, as a system of ideas, which create the very possibility of the game. In addition, for chess to exist as a possibility, two people must similarly hold the belief, "we are playing chess" and have a common understanding of how "we" play. The entire set of actions that "I" can take as an individual chess player depends entirely on the fact that "we are playing chess" has been established as a social reality.

Much like knowing the rules of chess is a prerequisite to playing the game, knowledge of metaphors is a prerequisite to negotiation. In other words, negotiation is an experience that is possible because pre-existing ideas define a meaningful social context. Metaphors create the very possibility of "we are negotiating."

In addition, Searle's quote suggests that constitutive rules, like the ones that define the game of chess or the context of negotiating, come in systems. That is, it is possible to think of metaphoric mappings in terms of a system of ideas that come from a domain of experience and that are useful in making sense of another domain of experience. Systems tend to have a hierarchical structure (Simon, 1962). Lakoff and Johnson (1980) describe this hierarchical feature in terms of "entailments" of metaphor. With respect to negotiation, at the most superordinate level, metaphors are used to define the "we" negotiation situational context. In other words, metaphors provide a basis for answering the question, "*What kind of situation are we experiencing?*" For example, is this context a battle? A family gathering? A game? A dance? Within a particular superordinate metaphor category, there are many possible subsystems of meaning. These can be thought of as metaphoric entailments, or subcategories, of a negotiation context. While an infinite number of subsystems are possible, we analyze three that derive from a logical analysis of social systems (Thelen, 1959; Simon, 1962; McCusker, 2001).

Specifically, the first level of analysis is *problems*. While a context surrounds all aspects of negotiation, problems concern the tasks of negotiation. At the level of problems, the kind of question answered by metaphors is, "*What kind of task are we doing in this situation?* For example, are we conducting a performance contest to see who will win (entailed by a game context)? In laboratory studies of negotiation, participants are given instructions about problems, yet in real life metaphors contain such instructions. Indeed, research has shown that definitions of negotiation tasks can be construed differently (e.g., Bazerman et al., 1985; Pinkley, 1990; De Dreu and McCusker, 1997). Within our perspective, metaphors provide the basis for participants to define task characteristics. For example, a *negotiation as seduction* metaphor suggests a different task than a *negotiation as dental work* metaphor.

The second level of analysis is *scripts*. Scripts concern norms for interaction. The kind of question at stake for an analysis of scripts is, "*How are we doing the tasks of negotiating?*". Metaphors highlight aspects of the negotiation context that can enable or constrain particular patterns of interaction. In experimental situations, for example, subjects are constrained by instructions to exchange offers in a particular way. This can include specific instructions about when and how negotiators can interact (e.g., send offers back and forth in a sequential, turn-taking manner). Outside of the laboratory, the instructions for patterns of interaction are contained in metaphors. For example, a *negotiation as tango* metaphor would suggest that one person should lead during the negotiation process, whereas concepts from a *negotiation as tennis* metaphor would suggest that either person can lead at different times depending on who has earned the right to "serve."

Finally, the third level of analysis is *feelings*. Feelings in negotiation are based on performance standards. In laboratory studies, negotiators are given instructions that define outcomes associated with different levels of performance (e.g., "Try to get as many points for yourself as possible"). In real life, metaphors include concepts about what counts as effective performance (i.e., when we should be happy about negotiation results). The question underlying the use of metaphor to interpret feelings is, "How are we evaluating the result of the negotiation?" For example, a *negotiation as individual sport* metaphor suggests that feelings will depend on which negotiator ended up with a relative advantage over the other. Or, a *negotiation as family vacation* metaphor suggests that mutual advantage is a basis for feelings.

SOCIAL FUNCTIONS OF METAPHOR

A second function of metaphors is that they remove equivocality in social information and *organize social action*. Organizing concerns the mechanisms through which social actors stabilize meanings about common social conditions (Weick, 1979). Social action is said to be "organized" when social conditions exist in the life space of actors in a "sensible arrangement." Put another way, a social pattern is organized when social actors are oriented in the same way to common social conditions.

The notion of organizing dates back to Asch, who argued that "There can be no concerted action between persons unless they have cognitively structured the given conditions in somewhat similar ways" (Asch, 1959: 375). For social actors to hold common meanings their individual systems of orientation must be overlapping (Newcombe, 1959). That is, they have to be situated in the same subjective reality, i.e., looking at the situation from the same vantage point. This occurs if negotiators are using the same metaphor to define the negotiation context. Put differently, this means that negotiators are oriented in the same way to common *contexts*, and that negotiators have a similar construal of the negotiation *problem*, the *script* for solving it, and the *feelings* associated with different levels of performance.

A fundamental problem for organizing concerted social action, however, is that the information in the environment is equivocal. Equivocality is a property of social information and refers to its capacity for multiple interpretations or meanings (Weick, 1979). A well-known example of an equivocal display is Wittgenstein's duck/rabbit image. While it remains objectively the same, it can be interpreted as either a duck or a rabbit depending on how one is oriented to it.

In the context of negotiation, equivocality can come from a variety of sources. In negotiation, the "We" context is a major source of equivocality. This is because any beliefs that negotiators hold about what "we are doing" are based on assumptions about the other party. In other words, the negotiation context, as represented in the minds of negotiators as a system of "we" concepts, necessarily contains assumptions about what the other negotiators are thinking. However, it is ontologically impossible to see what another negotiator is thinking. In addition, the social world is full of a wide array of possible metaphors for negotiation. There are many contexts that might be applicable, each with its own set of problems, scripts, and feelings.

Metaphors provide negotiators with the capacity to remove equivocality about what "we are doing" in two ways. The first way for metaphors to remove equivocality is for negotiators to operate unconsciously from the same metaphor. This is more likely when a cultural group relies on a single metaphor, derived from shared experiences. The other way is for negotiators to resolve discrepancies in their beliefs about what "we are doing" through the presentation of symbols. The communication of symbols through actions can help situate negotiators in the same subjective reality, enabling concerted, organized, social action. This process is called *"co-orientation"* (Newcombe, 1959). Co-orientation to a metaphor occurs when symbols are displayed and a corresponding set of concepts are then mutually understood. Moreover, by "co-orienting" to symbols throughout negotiation, negotiators can continually cultivate a common metaphor. Communication, be it verbal or nonverbal, is an example of symbolic actions that are rooted in metaphor.

In sum, we propose that metaphors have an organizing function in negotiation. Metaphors are made up of concepts and symbols. Negotiation processes are organized when negotiators structure problems, scripts, and feelings in similar ways. This means that a common set of concepts are used for defining the negotiation context. Since concepts are ontologically subjective, and negotiation can be understood from an infinite number of metaphors, equivocality pervades negotiation. But, a stable and mutual metaphoric understanding is cultivated and reinforced in negotiation through an ongoing symbolic exchange.

METAPHORIC MODELS OF CULTURE AND NEGOTIATION

In the current formulation, cross-cultural differences amount to different ways of defining subjective realities and organizing social action in negotiation through different metaphoric mappings (and associated contexts, problems, scripts, and feelings) that have been cultivated through shared experiences. To make these differences visible, it is necessary to make *explicit* the metaphors that have been cultivated in different cultural contexts. That is, in order to compare negotiation across cultures, we need to become aware of the subsets of available metaphors and symbols that have been stored up and institutionalized through shared experience. Below, we juxtapose two metaphoric models, *"negotiation as sport"* and *"Negotiation as ie household gathering"* to describe cultural differences in negotiation for the US and Japan, respectively. In our discussion, we focus on how co-orientation to metaphoric mappings of the domain of sports versus the domain of the Japanese household entails the social construction of different problems, scripts, and feelings in negotiations in these two cultures. Table 15.1 summarizes our discussion. These are not the only metaphors that can be used to understand negotiation in these two cultures, a point to which we will return later. Yet each is based on a tremendous amount of shared experience in each cultural context, and thus offers a window into the metaphoric dynamics of negotiation in these two cultures.

SPORTS IN AMERICA

Sport plays a paramount role in the life of most Americans (Gannon and Associates, 1994). Remarking more recently on sports in America, President Bill Clinton argued "America, rightly or wrongly, is a sports-crazed country. We often see games as a metaphor for what we are as a people" (*New York Times*, April 18, 1998). Likewise, the sportswriter Thomas Boswell noted:

> These days, sports may be what Americans talk about the most. With the most knowledge. The most passion. Not so long ago, such discussions . . . were couched in specifically religious terms . . . Today, where would we reach first for material or metaphor to make

TABLE 15.1 Cultural differences for negotiation for the US and Japan, respectively

Target domain	Source domain	
Negotiation Entailments	US: Sports	Japan: Japanese ie household
Problems	To conduct a performance contest	To ensure continuity and harmony of the group
	◆ Task-oriented	◆ Relationally oriented
	◆ Conflict is normal and overt	◆ Conflict is avoided and kept covert
	◆ Discrete activity (beginning and end; events are kept separate)	◆ Continuous activity (no beginning or end; interactions in one context affect the other)
Scripts	◆ Action organized by universalistic rules	◆ Actions organized by particularistic rules
	◆ Turn-taking, reciprocity.	◆ Status and needs dictate actions
	◆ Aggressive behavior yet sportsmanship is expected	◆ Face-saving is critical; aggression is eschewed
	◆ Person is kept separate from the task	◆ Person = task (is inseparable from the task)
Feelings	◆ Outcomes are determined by skill; are explicit	◆ Outcomes are determined by roles; are implicit
	◆ Satisfaction is derived from winning	◆ Satisfaction is derived from role fulfillment

> such points to our children? Probably to sports . . . in fact, sports has become central to what remains of our American sense of community. (*Washington Post*, pp. 24–6)

Given the amount of shared experience provided by sports, this metaphor has the potential for seeing systematic patterns of cultural co-orientation in the domain of negotiation in the US.

The domain or context of sports has particular problems, scripts, and feelings that are socially agreed upon and define the activity. A sporting event is a discrete activity with a beginning and end. Each match is considered separate and unrelated. The "problem" in sports is to conduct a performance contest between opposing players based on skill. Each side in a sporting event is co-oriented to this basic problem. For example, when two heavy-weights stand eye-to-eye before a boxing match, there is a clear consensus over the "problem" to be solved by their looming social action. There is no need for one of them to ask the other "Do you have any idea what is going on here?" They step into the ring knowing that their problem is to "beat" the other side.

Sports also present a vivid image of co-orientation to scripts, or the rules that coordinate social action during the performance contest. The "scripts" in sports concern how the contest is carried out, or how the game is played. Co-orientation to scripts is necessary for the contest to occur. For example, a child playing baseball for the first time will need to learn when to hit the ball, when to run to the "bases" and when to throw the ball to other people. After "learning how to play," scripts are not something that needs to be discussed before the contest. Hitting the ball and then running to third base would be a sure way for a professional baseball player to make the evening news.

While scripts vary from sport to sport, there are numerous scripts that are common to most sports. First, sports have formal rules that are established to equalize the teams. These rules ensure that each team is given a fair chance to win by creating a clearly defined, objectively fair framework within which the competition takes place. For example, sports involve turn-taking (e.g., in boxing, exchange of blows; in baseball, batting and fielding; in football, offense and defense) in which players get equal chances to score points. Professional sports implement or change rules in order to achieve parity and enhance fair competition. For example, most professional sports hold an annual draft, in which the best new players are distributed to the inferior teams in order to give them the chance to become more competitive. Similarly, in baseball, the "expanded strike zone" rule was implemented to make pitchers more competitive when it was determined that batters had achieved an advantage.

Second, all sports involve the use of a strategy, or a calculated play about a sequence of events, to coordinate actions among players for the purpose of scoring. Strategies involve the use of logic and are based on facts and figures about pre-existing conditions. They are rarely based on feelings or intuition. Sports scripts also involve recorded action, in that points are tallied as the process ensues, and there are often no "do-overs" (i.e., going back in time). Finally, scripts in many sports serve to legitimize and enable ritualized aggression. Aggressive behavior, however, is confined to the event itself, and scripts dictate that players engage in friendly behavior outside of the event (i.e., have good sportsmanship). All of the aforementioned scripts are *universalistic* – they apply to all teams and players, regardless of position, ability, or preferences.

Sports also provide a vivid image of co-orientation to metrics of performance, which correspond to ideas about why some outcomes *feel* better than others. The "outcomes" in sports concern the meaning of actions, i.e., performance. It is understood that both sides want to win. It is not necessary to discuss whether one side *needs* or *deserves* to win more than the other. Outcomes are based solely on performance metrics. It is impossible to determine who should be happy or unhappy, i.e., who won versus lost, without them. Moreover, you are not a winner or a loser based on who you know, how hard you tried, how old you are, how long it has been since your last victory, and so on. You are a winner or a loser based on objective performance, e.g., more points. Importantly, the consequences of outcomes (i.e., winning or losing) do not need to be discussed because they produce unequivocal affective states. In individual sports, there are clear emotions associated with winners and losers: Winners are happy, losers are upset. For example, following their record-setting fourth championship defeat, there was no need to ask a member of the Buffalo Bills football team, "what are you feeling at this time?" There is a pre-existing consensus regarding how different levels of performance translate into affective states after the championship game.

Sports is a general metaphor that can be used to see culture in negotiation. To explore this, we discuss two basic types of contests – individual versus team sports.

INDIVIDUAL SPORTS AND DISTRIBUTIVE NEGOTIATION

Individual sports involve competition between individual actors. Some examples are golf, tennis, boxing, running, racing, and the like. Individual sporting events are a metaphor for distributive negotiation, a phenomenon well documented in the US (Pruitt and Carnevale, 1993).

In distributive negotiation, each side is co-oriented to the problem – to outpace the other and to demonstrate *relative advantage* over the other. Parties know that the negotiation involves zero-sum conflicting interests – one party will win and the other will lose. Co-orientation to the negotiation task from an individual sports metaphor is one way to interpret what has been called a "fixed-pie" perception (Thompson and Hastie, 1990). Negotiators do not typically begin distributive negotiation with discussion of whether interests are opposed in reality. Cultural co-orientation to the problem results in distributive negotiation when knowledge from individual sporting competitions is mapped onto the negotiation task.

There is also a "script" for distributive negotiation which follows the "script" of individual competition in many respects. Like turn-taking in sports, that script consists of reciprocal concessions. That is, parties are expected to "exchange punches" or "volleys" in the form of demands. The sports metaphor offers an explanation of the tendency for negotiators to "overbid." Starting with higher offers lets negotiators "play the game" by exchanging demands and scoring points. Negotiators use logic and strategize to obtain desired outcomes. In *The Art and Science of Negotiation*, Raiffa (1982) illustrates how negotiators need to break a problem into parts and weigh the advantages and disadvantages of different alternatives. Moreover, like sports, the distributive script also consists of recorded action and you cannot take back a concession (i.e., there are no "do-overs"). Finally, similar to ritualized aggression in sports, competitive tactics abound during negotiations (e.g., threats, warning, positional commitments). Yet like good players in sports, negotiation is viewed as a process in which substantive and relational issues should be handled separately. Parties are expected to "separate the person from the problem," and not take such behavior personally (Fisher and Ury, 1981).

In distributive negotiation, there is also co-orientation to performance metrics consistent with an individual sports metaphor. Just as we do not need to discuss what losing a championship game feels like, we do not need to discuss what making a concession feels like. We are co-oriented to concessions as a symbol of loss. Therefore, we expect that any feelings associated with concessions are negative. In this way, the sports metaphor can offer an explanation for reactive devaluation (Stillenger, Epelbaum, Keltner, and Ross, 1990). If someone makes a concession, it means that they are at a relative disadvantage and should experience the pain associated with loss. But, if they make a concession freely, or are even delighted to do so, our common understanding about what that action meant will produce suspicion. Also, agreement represents the end of the game, like a contest. When the agreement is reached, the issue is settled – one side was better than the other.

TEAM SPORTS AND INTEGRATIVE NEGOTIATION

Sports metaphors can also be used to see co-orientation in integrative negotiation. However, in this case, the sports metaphors that map knowledge from the sports domain onto the negotiation situation are team, not individual, sports. Specifically, integrative negotiation involves problems, scripts, and feelings that are similar to how we interact with team-mates.

The problem shared by team-mates is that they must work together to beat the competition and to make contributions toward this common goal. Integrative negotiation means that parties must engage in collaborative problem solving. The script for team sports involves people coordinating based on how well they contribute to meeting the group's objective. There is no discussion needed that it is in everybody's interest to pass the ball to the open player, even though, in doing so, it becomes more likely that she can score "more points" than the other players. Differences in skills are seen as opportunities to increase overall performance. Consider the Chicago Bulls during the 1990s. The team performed better as a whole when Michael Jordan did the scoring and Dennis Rodman did the rebounding. It would be less productive if each player had spent half of the game trying to be the shooter or the rebounder. This would be similar to two sisters dividing the orange in half in the famous Follet example (Pruitt and Carnevale, 1993), who were able to trade off on the peel and the pulp in order to maximize each other's interests. By "logrolling" their talent, each player contributes more to the team's output. Such logrolling is more possible when players are co-oriented to a script that enables synergy. In much the same way, collaboration in integrative negotiation is possible. While we typically think of integrative negotiation in the context of making tradeoffs on economic issues of different value, the sports metaphor lets us see how mapping knowledge from team sports co-orients negotiators to a collaborative script. Successful enactment of the relationship synergy in team sports requires accurate information about abilities, much the same way that logrolling in negotiation requires accurate information about the importance of issues.

The co-orientation to performance metrics provided by team sports also maps onto feelings in integrative negotiation. When the team wins, all the players know without discussion of who did what, etc., and that it is time to celebrate. Even though there will always be differences in objective individual measures of performance, co-orientation to performance in team sports means that success is shared by the players – i.e., it is "win–win."

In sum, sports metaphors generally provide a window on processes in distributive and integrative negotiation. Whereas there are differences in problems, scripts, and feelings that constitute the activity, they both focus on the task and substantive issues (which are kept distinct from relationships), the use of turn-taking and recorded action, and the notion that outcomes are based on skill and strategy at the table. Kinhide (1976) summarized this approach to negotiation as illustrative of an *Erabi* style (roughly "manipulative," "can do," "choosing"), wherein "a person sets his objective, develops a plan to reach that objective, and then acts to change the environment in accordance with that plan" (Cohen, 1991: 30). Thus, like American sports, negotiations are conceived of in instrumental terms and on reaching a desired solution to the task (Ting-Toomey, 1990).

Sports are a cultural metaphor for the US because there is a tremendous amount of shared experience with sporting events in this culture. "Super Bowl Sunday" is a national holiday. Most public school districts require a certain amount of physical activity in gym class every day. Given the connections between sports and negotiation processes, it could be argued that it is through contests of sport that Americans learn how to interact with one another. Through the "education of attention" (Gibson, 1979) during sports, cultural co-orientation is made possible in other domains of life. Yet this domain of experience is not necessarily shared and thus accessible as a domain to understand negotiation in other cultural contexts. Next, we discuss a metaphor of negotiation that is likely to be more applicable in the context of Japanese culture.

THE JAPANESE HOUSEHOLD (*IE*)

While sports metaphors can help to understand cultural processes in the US, it is through the organizing metaphor of the traditional Japanese household, or *ie*, from which we can view the cultural basis of problems, scripts and feelings in negotiations in Japan. The origin of the *ie* household dates back to the Meiji and feudal period of Japan (Kashima and Callan, 1994), but has persisted in modern social organization in Japan today. Like the shared experience of sports in the US, the *ie* "penetrates every nook and cranny of Japanese society" (Nakane, 1970a: 4). Lebra (1992: 16), for instance, noted that:

> No discussion of Japanese social organization would be complete without some reference to the *ie* ... Some scholars ... have gone as far to characterize Japan as an *ie*-society in the sense that the *ie* is the most basic unit and penetrates Japanese society or is replicated in many other organizations.

According to Nakane (1970b), the *ie* household is a social unit that "once established assumes its continuity regardless of changes to its members, and exists at a core of the social system as an individual unit" (p. 102). It constitutes, in essence, a well-defined social group whose members share work in an established frame of residence which controls assets (*kasan*) (Nakane, 1972; Kashima and Callan, 1994). In Japan, the *ie* has a different meaning than a typical Western notion of family in that those within the *ie* do not think of themselves as separate entities; rather there is a group consciousness (*shyuudan ishiki*) that pervades the *ie* (Nakane, 1970a).

The fundamental "problem" within the *ie* is to ensure a sense of continuity and succession over future generations. The problem is conceived of in future terms, but also reaches into the past through symbols of ancestors, such as shrines and graves (Lebra, 1992). Thus, unlike the sporting event, the problems involved in the *ie* are continuous and do not have a beginning and end. Another aspect of the *ie* is that it has mechanism for expansion, including *honke* (the first household) and *bunke* (the branch household), which are hierarchically organized and linked together through mutual obligations related to the problem of group preservation (Kashima and Callan, 1994). In this respect, the problem is merged with relationships, unlike in individual sports, where the problem (to win) is separated from the relationships involved. Like the metaphor of sports in the US, within the *ie*, there is no need to select a method to assemble consensus over "what is going on here?" All members of the *ie* family understand that they are part of an indivisible functional unit who work together to ensure the continuity of the group.

The *ie* also includes a view of scripts. The "scripts" of the *ie* are concerned with how the specific family members organize relations and share work for self-preservation. Social actions in the *ie* are coordinated through interpersonal bonds and power relationships. Activity is regulated by clear structural roles between more senior members (e.g., father or eldest son) and subordinates, and there are informal rules regarding the nature and amount of emotional involvement within the vertical structure. For instance, subordinate members of the *ie* seek acceptance and dependency from others, which is referred to as *amae* (Doi, 1973). When a person of higher status fulfills *amae*, this produces obligations (*gimu*) to repay the favors of subordinate members (*on*), all of which create a perpetual mutual involvement (Kashima and Callan, 1994). Thus, the *amae-on-gimu* system regulates interaction between members of the *ie*. As a set of coordinated actions, it provides the mechanisms through which the quality or harmony (*wa*) of the relationships are maintained in the *ie*. These informal rules are regulated by those within the *ie* structure, and are highly *particularistic*. Just as Americans are given many opportunities to be skilled in learning the formal rules of interaction in sports, Japanese are given many opportunities to gain skills in learning the informal rules which enact the coordinated scripts characteristic of the *ie*.

Finally, the *ie* organizing metaphor elucidates the cultural basis of feelings. Unlike the individual sports metaphor, differences in performance levels do not have the meaning of winning versus losing. Instead, they reflect sacrifice for the greater whole and are rewarded with loyalty. And, unlike sports, outcomes are determined not by abilities or skills that are enacted during the activity, but, rather, by ascribed characteristics of parties.

THE JAPANESE *IE* AND NEGOTIATION

The *ie* organizing metaphor can be used to examine cultural dynamics of negotiation in Japan. Interpretations of the negotiation task come from co-orientation to the conditions of survival of the group. Survival of the group requires that negotiators must incorporate another's interests in defining problems, rather than treating them as separate and opposed, as in the sports metaphor. Union activity in Japan, for instance, reflects the desire to cultivate cooperation and harmony between labor and management. Management often uses "goal alignment" techniques, whereby through information exchange, they attempt to reduce demands (e.g., for increases in wages) through increasing employees' identification with the goals of the entire organization (e.g., the company profit) (Gerhart and Milkovich, 1992). These techniques are not used as much in the US (Morishima, 1991), which is consistent with our previous analysis of the sports metaphor.

Like the household *ie*, negotiations are kept within the group or organization in Japan. For instance, there are mainly enterprise unions in Japan, which are not tied to industry, but, rather, are geared toward dealing with a particular employer (Gerhart and Milkovich, 1992). Allowing disputes to be resolved within the organization allows for more flexibility in the agreements that can be reached for the good of the group. As Nakane (1970a) noted:

> Members of a trade union, for example are too loyal to their own company to join forces
> with their brothers in other company unions ... a union movement, a confrontation,

whether they may be carried on between the managers and workers or between the faculty and students, is always carried on within an institution ... it is like domestic discord.

Just as activity is governed by status and interpersonal bonds to preserve harmony in the *ie*, behaviors (scripts) are coordinated in negotiations in a similar manner. In trying to solve the group problem, negotiators are less focused on what each brings to the table in terms of achievements, as in sports. Rather, they use ascribed status and informal context-specific rules of conduct (*shikata*) to guide the behavior of the parties in order to maximize cooperation and harmony (*wa*). Consistent with our analysis of the *ie*, Graham and his colleagues have demonstrated that variability in outcomes in dyadic negotiations in Japan is explained most by roles, not tactics, as is the case in the US (Graham, 1983). Along with this deference to verticality, however, comes a responsibility for the superior in providing continuous support and loyalty. Thus, negotiators (e.g., sellers) are able to interpret differences in outcomes which come about through deference (e.g., to buyers) as being appropriate for the reward of loyalty in future interactions.

Likewise, just as scripts are based on emotional relatedness within the Japanese *ie*, negotiators' scripts often involve appeals to the feelings and goodwill of others (e.g., the use of *amae*, *nemawashi* and *naniwabushi*), rather than to logic and rationality (March, 1990). For example, March (1990) describes the script of "*naniwabushi*" as involving an emotional appeal that takes place in three stages: the opening (*kikkake*), wherein the negotiator discusses his feelings about the relationship between the parties and his feelings; the *seme*, which details critical events that have led up to the negotiation; and the *urei*, in which the negotiator expresses great sorrow or self-pity surrounding the events. A negotiation over repayment of a loan in Japan is described as follows:

> In your approach to the finance company, you open with a statement that describes your relationship with them over the years. You tell them what a good customer you have been ... how you brought new customers to them ... This is the *kikkake*. In the *seme*, you focus on the disastrous effects the recession has had on your business ... your family now eats nothing but the Japanese equivalent of Big Macs ... you can only continue to survive if the payments are cut in half ... In the *urei*, you explain what will happen to you if your creditors do not grant this request. You will lose the automobile and therefore all your income ... So you plead "Grant my request." (March 1990: 22)

As March (1990) notes, the more emotionally moving the story, the more likely it is that it will be persuasive, as parties who do not compromise is such situations would be seen as cold-hearted. Unlike sports, the use of a victim mentality (*higaisaha ishiki*) is frequent, and not surprisingly, is not associated with the same feelings as in the sports context.

In sum, the Japanese *ie* provides a window into cultural co-orientation in negotiation. Like the *ie* household, the problems, scripts, and feelings that constitute the activity focus on relational and emotional issues (which are merged with the substantive task) (Ting-Toomey, 1990), the use of status and interpersonal bonds to guide action, and the notion that outcomes differences reflect loyalty and protection. Kinhide (1976) summarized this approach to negotiation as illustrative of an *Awase* style ("adaptive"), in which one adapts to the environment and treats the social relationship as the end in and of itself (Cohen, 1991). Thus, as in the *ie*, negotiations are conceived of in relational/emotional terms and on preserving the continuity and harmony of the group.

DISCUSSION

In this chapter, we have argued that negotiation is a socially constructed reality based on metaphoric mappings. We further argued that through apperception, metaphors create correspondences between shared domains of experience (e.g., sports, Japanese *ie*), and the negotiation environment itself, and in effect, create the subjective and social reality of negotiation. We then argued that by making dominant metaphors explicit, it is possible to see cultural processes in negotiation. Specifically, we described two metaphors, *negotiation as sport* in the US and *negotiation as ie household gathering* in Japan to illustrate our thesis that negotiations are constructed as conceptual mappings to other shared domains of experience which vary across cultures.

Our examples of metaphoric mappings were selective by necessity. For example, there are other aspects of mappings within the sports and Japanese *ie* metaphor that are informative of cultural dynamics, such as the role of audiences and third parties, conceptions of time in negotiation, the selection of negotiators, etc. An understanding of these elements in negotiation can be found through further analysis of ontological correspondences in the contrasting metaphors. For example, audiences in sporting events expect competition, whereas audiences in the Japanese *ie* expect cooperation, which can help us to understand the role of constituents in negotiations.

Furthermore, our discussion was selective in that the specific metaphors we described (sports and the *ie*) are not the only domains that are mapped to the context of negotiation in the US and Japan. Indeed, we emphasize that multiple negotiation metaphors are developed within every culture. For example, different metaphors are probably activated when individuals are negotiating with in-groups versus out-groups in collectivistic cultures (Triandis, McCusker, and Hui, 1990). Similarly, within the US, given that women have historically had less shared experience with the domain of competitive sports, both informally and professionally, it is likely that they have different "metaphors-in-use" in negotiation. A critical issue for future research, therefore, is to document the subsets of metaphors available in different cultures. In addition, we also emphasize that our conceptualization of the metaphoric construction of negotiation is dynamic, not static; that is, metaphors become activated by situational conditions and also change over time throughout social interactions. As such, we believe that it is crucial for future research to focus on the conditions under which different metaphors gain cognitive and motivational force in negotiation. Below, we discuss additional theoretical and practical implications of our metaphor perspective on negotiation.

THEORETICAL IMPLICATIONS

Theoretically speaking, a metaphoric perspective on culture and negotiation is likely to be useful in understanding and predicting cultural differences in negotiation. By documenting different metaphors-in-use, we can illuminate different levels of reality in negotiations. Metaphors can also be useful to test whether negotiation theories, which have been generally developed in the West, are applicable in other cultural contexts. For instance, many of the competitive cognitive biases that have been well-documented in the negotiation literature (fixed-pie error, self-serving biases), are likely to be constructed through dominant metaphors which highlight competition (e.g., individual sports) and are probably cultivated less in other cultural contexts.

In developing a cultural perspective on negotiation it will be important to unearth the dominant metaphors in our *science* as well. Just as humans conceptualize negotiation through metaphors, scientists also rely on the use of metaphor to develop theories (Leary, 1990; Weiner, 1991). Given that the science of negotiation has been developed in the West, it is likely that it is laden with Western metaphors (cf. Gray, 1994). Indeed, a perusal of the literature reveals symbolic evidence of underlying conceptual mappings that are reflective of battle and game metaphors (e.g., "common ground," "strategy," "matching tactics"), as well as dramaturgical metaphors (e.g., "frames," "roles") (Gelfand and Raver, 2000). To advance theorizing in this area, it would be useful to generate new metaphors in order to highlight additional components of the phenomenon that are neglected by current metaphors in the science of negotiation.

The metaphor perspective can also be useful in cross-cultural psychology (Gannon and Associates, 1994). In particular, it both complements and adds to a dimensional approach (Hofstede, 1980a). Dominant cultural metaphors, which reflect holistic accounts of shared experience, should incorporate multiple dimensions of culture (cf. Gannon and Associates, 1994). For instance, the Japanese *ie* described previously reflects the focus on vertical collectivism (Triandis and Gelfand, 1998). Likewise, individual sports in the US reflect dimensions of vertical individualism (Triandis and Gelfand, 1998). Metaphors, then, simultaneously reflect and support broad cultural themes. Yet metaphors, as dynamic, multifaceted cultural experience, may help link more distal perspectives of culture, which are captured well by a dimensional approach, to the more proximal "here and now" of the life space of the individual (i.e. individuals' cognitions), which is more predictive of behavior (Fishbein and Ajzen, 1975). We also suggest that the "here and now" of negotiating can be understood with the categories of problems, scripts, and feelings. Each is a part of every negotiation experience, and, taken together, as entailments of a surrounding metaphoric context, they provide a holistic account of negotiating.

In addition, a metaphor perspective on culture should add to basic research on subjective culture (Triandis, 1972). In recent years, researchers have begun to document and categorize the tendencies of "individualists" and "collectivists." The person, as a member of a particular cultural group, has been the basic unit of analysis. However, the nature of metaphor, as a coherent, holistic, conceptual scheme suggests an alternative view. Rather than stable traits, cultural attitudes are seen as "systems of orientation" (cf. Hong, Morris, Chui, and Benet-Martinez, 2000). This shifts the basic unit of analysis in cross-cultural research to the "here and now" of a particular social situation, rather than the person, on average, across a variety of situations. And, a metaphor view suggests that cultural attitudes are not necessarily stable across situations, but, rather, can be chosen. In effect, it might be the case that one's cultural attitude can be the product of a reasoned choice, rather than the accident of one's national heritage. In short, a metaphor perspective on culture raises interesting questions about the very nature of cultural attitudes.

PRACTICAL IMPLICATIONS: METAPHOR AND INTERCULTURAL NEGOTIATIONS

The current perspective also helps us to see why intercultural negotiations can be more difficult than intracultural negotiations (Graham, 1985). In other words, when negotiators are operating with the same metaphorical framework, as is often the case in intracultural negotiations, they co-orient to the situation, and, thus, share the same social reality. Sharing reality puts them in a better position to negotiate successfully. However, when metaphors are not shared, as is often the case in intercultural negotiations, enactment of social reality is more difficult. In short, it requires that steps must be taken to assemble consensus over problems, scripts, and feelings, or in essence, defining the constitutive rules that define the negotiation context. In this way, metaphor is a tool for *negotiating the negotiation*. A metaphor perspective then places an emphasis on problem-setting (Schön, 1993) in addition to problem-solving.

In this respect, metaphors are useful for prescriptive research on culture and negotiation. The purpose of this type of research is to prescribe methods for managing cultural dynamics in negotiation, and asks the question, "What should be done when two parties from different cultures are attempting to negotiate?" According to the current theory, cross-cultural trainers can first try to create a shared metaphor, which both parties can use to coordinate their attempts to manage their interdependence. This approach relies on perspective taking, rather than trying to change the parties themselves. As such, the most important role of cross-cultural trainers (or mediators) is the making of "generative metaphor" (Schön, 1993) and helping negotiators to restructure their cognitions to be complementary.

In addition, metaphors provide a useful tool because negotiators are not able to "see" their own culture. By using metaphors, we are in a better position to help negotiators within a culture develop an understanding of how their own culture has shaped the reality they impose on negotiation situations. As compared to a dimensional approach to cross-cultural training, this method provides a rich domain of experience within which negotiators can understand the dynamics of their culture (see Gannon, 2001, for other applications of metaphor training). Indeed, recent research within the US has shown that negotiators can benefit from receiving training which has its basis in metaphor (Loewenstein, Thompson, and Gentner, 1999).

Moreover, as described above, new metaphors can be chosen in negotiation. Since metaphors can be used to create, change, sustain, or eliminate culture as needed, the current view avoids ecological determinism (Kashima and Callan, 1994). By illuminating the functions of culture, we are able to actively "create" different cultures in negotiation. For instance, in the US, scholars and practitioners alike advocate an integrative approach to negotiation over the distributive approach. To better facilitate the use of integrative negotiation, we can encourage negotiators to apply different metaphors to enact negotiation. We can try to focus negotiators on seeing themselves as part of the same team, rather than competitors, in a sporting contest. By doing this, negotiators would be oriented to problems that are win–win in nature, scripts would relate to using each negotiator's skills and information about the situation to come up with the best strategy for both to win, and would affirm the identity that goes along with being a functional member of the same team with a common goal.

CONCLUSION

Centuries ago, Aristotle argued that "the greatest thing by far is to be a master of metaphor" (Aristotle, ca. 330 BC/1924, cited in Leary, 1990). Like Aristotle, we argue that metaphors are crucial to the understanding of cultural dynamics in negotiation. By making metaphors explicit, insights about cultural differences, and their origins, can be unearthed. Moreover, when culture can be viewed, it can also be managed. Managing culture, as metaphor, is about creating a new social reality.

NOTES

Correspondence on this chapter can be sent to either Michele J. Gelfand, Department of Psychology, University of Maryland, College Park, MD 20742
e-mail: mgelfand@psyc.umd.edu
or Christopher McCusker, School of Management and Organization, Yale University, New Haven, CT 06511
e-mail: christopher.mccusker@yale.edu
Portions of this paper were presented at the Stanford University Cultural Psychology Mini-Conference, organized by Hazel Markus in 1998. The authors express their gratitude to Paul Hanges, Yoshi Kashima, Arie Kruglanski, Peter Smith, and Harry Triandis for their very helpful comments on the content of this chapter.

1 As an example of an integrative negotiation structure, imagine a negotiation between a married couple over where to go on vacation (Pruitt, 1986). The husband insists on going to the mountains and staying in a log cabin, whereas his wife demands to go to a luxury hotel on the beach. At first glance, their interests appeared to be of a fixed-sum nature – one party's gain (going to the mountains and staying in a log cabin) is the other party's loss (going to a luxury hotel on the beach), and therefore one party will have to sacrifice his or her preferences completely in order to reach an agreement. However, with further discussion, the parties discover that there are two issues at stake in the negotiation, location and accommodations, and that they differ on the extent to which they *prioritize* these issues. Suppose that the husband reveals that his priority is the location (i.e., the mountains), while the wife reveals that her primary concern is the accommodation (i.e., the luxury hotel). By recognizing such differences in priorities, the couple can make tradeoffs that provide mutually beneficial outcomes (e.g., go to a luxury hotel in the mountains).

Part VI

CORPORATE CULTURES AND VALUES

INTRODUCTION

The last part of the book is perhaps the area that is most difficult to research, yet most important for research. The very subjective, normatively laden topics of justice, trust, and ethics are covered in these chapters. In all three cases the authors have reviewed the extant literature, used important examples to illustrate their points, and challenged us to tackle the messy research issues associated with justice, trust, and ethics across cultures.

The opening chapter by Bies and Greenberg, "Justice, Culture, and Corporate Image . . ." is a passionate discussion of the institutional and social sources of justice perceptions. Drawing on the Nike sweatshop controversy of the 1990s, Bies and Greenberg illustrate vividly how important institutionally based sources of legitimation and delegitimation can be in shaping public perceptions of fair and just behavior. They cite literature and draw upon Nike's experience to illustrate the importance of perceptions of justice to corporate profitability.

One of the most vexing issues they analyze is cultural differences in institutions, which produce legitimacy and social norms, which underpin legitimacy. Americans were outraged by some of the sweatshop practices portrayed in the Nike case while Indonesians were less outraged. Bies and Greenberg develop a compelling explanation for this discrepancy rooted in social comparison and relative deprivation theory. Their analysis forces us to ask, to what standard should corporate conduct be held? Their concerns about the Nike case in particular preview Diana Robertson's chapter (18) on business ethics more generally (later in this part). Bies and Greenberg ask, is it adequate to pursue a culturally relativistic strategy? Are there some norms that are universal, to which all companies operating in any country should adhere? Which stakeholders' views of fairness and justice should hold sway? When perceptions of corporate just or unjust behavior cross cultural lines, how do we make the right judgments and therefore the right strategic decisions about what to do? Bies and Greenberg have written a provocative chapter in which they raise the issues with passion and challenge future researchers to find the answers.

The second chapter, "Trust in Cross-Cultural Relationships," has it all. The authors, Johnson and Cullen, begin with an exhaustive review of the literature on trust and exchange, then develop a comprehensive model of trust and exchange. They next address the difficult issues that attend on cross-culture exchanges and trust building and conclude the chapter with reanalysis of data on values from 40 countries, again dovetailing nicely with some of the issues in Robertson's chapter.

Johnson and Cullen argue that any exchange relationship must start with some minimal level of trust, where trust is defined as a willingness to make oneself vulnerable to another. They identify three general bases of trust that do not depend upon the history of exchange: dispositional trust (almost a personality characteristic), instrumental calculus trust, and trust based on the institutions of society. Their discussion of trust in cross-culture exchanges focuses first on differences in the willingness to make oneself vulnerable. Some cultures have a value system that supports greater willingness to become vulnerable and therefore trust others. They also discuss differences in institutions across cultures (much as in the Peng chapter (3) and the Bies and Greenberg chapter), noting that the propensity to trust, in general, is enhanced in the presence of stable, known, and reliable institutions. The authors review significant studies that illustrate the role of national culture on trust. Finally, they discuss ways in which trust is signaled interpersonally across cultures, noting that high context cultures signal trust indirectly, while low context cultures signal trust explicitly. The opportunity for misinterpretation of intentions is clear.

The last chapter (18) in this part, by Diana Robertson, "Business Ethics across Cultures," also includes an extensive review of the literature, though Robertson argues persuasively that there is relatively little scholarship on the topic of international business ethics. Her chapter is organized around three essential questions: (1) Is there a set of universal ethical principles that can be used worldwide? (2) Should business ethics researchers search for similarities or for differences in business ethics in different countries? (3) How can we integrate international business ethics research with research on other cultures and their distinctive features? Readers will note a compelling parallel between Bies and Greenberg's call for more descriptive research with a normative foundation and Robertson's observation that the field of international business ethics suffers from insufficient integration of normative and descriptive scholarship.

What the field lacks in quantity, Robertson makes up for in quality. She reviews several approaches to international business ethics in some detail, including Donaldson and Dunfee's (1999) Integrated Social Contracts Theory and DeGeorge's (1993) work on the ethical obligations of multinationals. She also gives significant voice to non-academic efforts to affect international business ethics, including a discussion of the role of international organizations and institutions in providing guidance to multinationals. Finally, she describes several exemplar company codes of conduct, including Shell's and Coca-Cola's as company-based efforts to define international business ethics.

One of Robertson's most important points is that business ethics is defined differently in different cultures. The same behavior may be viewed as ethical in one culture and not ethical in another. Important components in a code of conduct in one country may be absent in another culture. Employee attitudes toward the importance of ethical issues may vary across cultures.

The most compelling section of this chapter is the last, in which Robertson discusses ways in which international business ethics research can be integrated with cross-cultural research in other arenas. She notes, for example, that most comparative research on business ethics reports differences but does not examine the sources of differences in national culture. Absent integration with national culture, it is difficult to know whether differences in ethical standards are functional or dysfunctional, good or bad, worthy of celebration and preservation or candidates for homogenization. She reviews the extant literature in which national culture is taken into account in business ethics and concludes that existing research represents a step in the right direction, but that much of it examines national culture at a rather superficial level. If we are truly to understand the form, substance, and centrality of business ethics conduct cross-culturally, we will have to study the interaction of business ethics and cultural values in much more depth.

Together, the three chapters in this part leave us with a compelling case for future research on issues of international business ethics in general, and trust, and procedural justice in particular. These three chapters have a strong normative flavor, perhaps the most challenging of cross-cultural management issues with which we have to contend. As all three sets of authors indicate, the research agenda is complicated but wide open. There is much yet to discover.

16

Justice, Culture, and Corporate Image: The Swoosh, the Sweatshops, and the Sway of Public Opinion

ROBERT J. BIES AND JERALD GREENBERG

> It would wreck the country's economy if wages were allowed to get too high.
>
> **(Nike CEO Phil Knight, quoted in Shaw, 1999: 39)**

> The problem is that the minimum wage does not provide for minimum subsistence.
>
> **(Asian diplomat, quoted in Gargan, 1996: 17)**

In August 1992, *Harper's* published a two-page commentary (Ballinger, 1992) about an Indonesian worker named Sadisash who was employed by Sung Hwa Corporation, a Korean manufacturing firm that subcontracted work from a large US-based corporation. Included was an image of Sadisash's pay stub, indicating that he earned only 14 cents an hour – less than the Indonesian government's standard for "minimum physical need." No one could have foreseen that this article would become the catalyst for broader media coverage and social activism that would ravage the public image of one of the world's most successful and heretofore admired corporations: Nike.

In the years that followed publication of this piece, further investigations revealed that a wide array of human rights abuses was commonplace. For example, it was alleged that Nike's Asian subcontractors also forced employees to work long hours – 10.5 hours per day for 6 consecutive days – for the equivalent of only $10 (Greenhouse, 1997). Moreover, they labored under conditions that exposed them to high levels of toxic air (e.g., in one Vietnamese factory monitored by Ernst and Young the air contained levels of the carcinogen, toluene, that were up to 177 times the amount allowed by local regulations: Greenhouse, 1997). Making matters worse, reports of physical abuse, particularly among women, also were not uncommon. In fact, in a *CBS News 48 Hours* broadcast, a worker at a factory in Vietnam that made Nike shoes said that team leaders so frequently beat employees that the phrase "to Nike" came into common usage, meaning taking out one's frustrations on a fellow worker (CBS News, 1996).

Not surprisingly, public outcries of injustice were common, leading some enraged American consumers to boycott Nike products (Brookes and Madden, 1995). The basis for their indignation was that a company that earned some $800 million on sales of $9.2 billion (in 1996) can afford to treat its employees better (Greenhouse, 1997). Adding fuel to the fire was the fact that the company routinely spends $870 million per year meticulously positioning itself as a pillar of excellence (Boje, in press) – an image that was suddenly threatened by the allegations (Glass, 1997).

As predictable as the public's cries of indignation was Nike's denial of any wrong-doing.[1] Specifically, their position has been based on three claims. First, they argue that the workers are lucky to have these jobs. In the words of a senior Nike employee, "I don't think the girls in our factories are treated badly. The wages may be small, but it's better than having no job," or the alternative, "harvesting coconut meat in the tropical sun" (Brookes and Madden, 1995: 12). Second, Nike officials claim that the problem is not the company's business, stating that "I don't think it's something you can lay at a shoe company and say 'You must accept responsibility for improving the social and living conditions of all employees'" (Brookes and Madden, 1995: 12). Finally, Nike officials indicate that they are dealing with the problems and that things are improving. To support its claim, Nike hired GoodWorks International, a firm headed by Andrew Young, the well-respected ex-mayor of Atlanta, to inspect its Asian operations. After investigating twelve of Nike's operations, Young's conclusion was that there was "no evidence or pattern of widespread or systematic abuse or mistreatment of workers" (Glass, 1997: 14).

Amidst the cries of injustice that flooded the popular press, it is curious that organizational scientists have failed to embrace the Nike case as a rallying point around which to examine matters of injustice in the workplace. We believe, however, that the allegations against Nike, and the company's reactions to these claims, can be used to illustrate several important points about the role of justice in matters of corporate impression management. By highlighting this connection in the present chapter we believe it is possible to shed light on matters of justice that organizational scientists should be studying. Accordingly, this will be one of our two major objectives in the present chapter.

Our second objective concerns the role of culture in justice and image management. The Nike case illustrates several key limitations in our understanding of cultural variables in matters of justice (Morris, Leung, Ames, and Lickel, 1999). Until now, attention to the connection between justice and culture has focused on identifying cross-cultural differences in preferences for various norms of justice (for a review, see Miles and Greenberg, 1993). We believe, however, that the events surrounding the Nike controversy illustrate additional limitations in the scope of current theory and research on organizational justice that beg to be examined. With this in mind, we will use the Nike case to illustrate ways in which current research on justice and culture may be expanded.

We begin by describing the nature of the threat that Nike faced to its corporate image. Specifically, we will argue that Nike was behaving unfairly, and that public reactions to these actions threatened the highly positive image the company enjoyed. We will then describe the ways in which Nike responded to these attacks – that is, the efforts it took to shore up its eroding public image. Although analysis of the Nike case is interesting in and of itself, its value may be seen in what it illustrates about the role of culture in justice and corporate image management. Accordingly, we will turn our attention to these matters at the end of this chapter.

Nike was Unfair

It is clear from the public's reactions that it perceived Nike as having treated its employees in an unfair and unethical manner. And, insofar as companies attempt to position themselves in the public eye as treating all stakeholders fairly and ethically, Nike's actions posed a threat to its corporate image. We will now examine the perceptions of unfairness that are likely to arise in this case and the threat to corporate image created by them.

Violations of Three Standards of Justice

There can be no doubt that the public's outcries of injustice were genuine and passionate. However, to fully understand these reactions, it is useful to apply accepted standards of justice that are well-grounded in research and theory. Specifically, we may view Nike's actions through the lenses of three established criteria of organizational justice (Greenberg, 1987; Greenberg, 1996; Cropanzano and Greenberg, 1997) – distributive justice, procedural justice, and interactional justice. As we will outline here, Nike may be seen as having violated all three forms of justice.

Distributive injustice

A state of distributive justice exists to the extent that people receive outcomes proportional to their work contributions (Homans, 1961). Typically, this is operationalized in terms of the amount of pay an individual receives relative to others who do comparable work, or an existing standard (Greenberg, 1982). Insofar as there is no evidence that any subset of Nike employees were paid more or less than others who were equally qualified, there does not appear to be any distributive injustice according to this standard. However, to the extent that employees of Nike's subcontractors were paid wages lower than minimum standards set by the government, it is clear that their pay was distributively unjust. In other words, relative to those performing comparable work outside the company, Nike's subcontractor paid its employees lower than the prevailing wage, thereby creating a distributive injustice.

Procedural injustice

Not only were the employees unfairly paid from a distributive perspective, they also were unfairly paid from a procedural perspective. That is to say, the processes used to determine the pay of Nike's employees was, itself, unfair. Procedural justice (for reviews, see Greenberg, 1987; Cropanzano and Greenberg, 1997) requires following practices that, among other things, give employees a voice in the pay decision, and that apply rules in an unbiased fashion. Clearly, Nike's subcontractor fell short of meeting procedural justice standards. Their employees had virtually no say in determining what they did, how they did it, or what they got paid. Moreover, there was a procedural impropriety in the way they were paid. Specifically, in theory, employees were to be paid an overtime wage for working in excess of 8 hours per day. However, for this to go into effect, employees were required to meet a production standard that was so high as to be unattainable. In essence, this procedure denied employees any opportunity to be paid overtime.

Interactional injustice

Beyond merely using a system that systematically forced underpayment, the employees of Nike's subcontractor also were dealt an injustice by virtue of the way they were treated by company officials. This form of justice, known as interactional justice (Bies and Moag, 1986) requires that employees be fully informed about the decisions affecting them, and that they are treated with dignity and respect (Greenberg, 1996). Failure to maintain interactional justice has been shown to lead employees to strike back at their employers, such as by stealing from them, behaving aggressively, and suing them (for a review, see Greenberg and Lind, 2000). The complete lack of voice, mistreatment, and repeated indignities to which Nike employees were subjected makes it clear that interactional injustice had occurred. What's more, because the employees were routinely abused, they were understandably reluctant to strike back at the company for mistreating them.

REPUTATIONAL CONSEQUENCES OF UNFAIRNESS FACED BY NIKE

Companies work hard at cultivating positive images of themselves. Specifically, organizations with the most positive reputations are those that are recognized: (1) by employees as being trustworthy, (2) by investors as being credible, (3) by customers as being reliable, and (4) by the community at large as being responsible (Fombrun, 1996). At the heart of these attributions is the notion of justice: It is clear that companies – like individuals (see Greenberg, 1990) – desire to position themselves as being fair in their dealings with various constituents.

To the extent that Nike was perceived as behaving unfairly toward its employees, it stood to tarnish its image of trustworthiness (by employees who could not count on the company to treat them well), credibility (by stockholders whose investments stood to be threatened), reliability (by customers who welcomed the opportunity to be associated with the company by wearing its apparel), and its responsibility (by social leaders who cast doubt on the company's actions as a global citizen). In short, by its actions, Nike was perceived to be unfair, which put its corporate image at risk.

UNFAIRNESS THREATENED NIKE'S VALUABLE CORPORATE IMAGE

To understand why the tarnishing of its image was so important, we first describe the nature of that image. Against this background we then highlight the challenges to that image that occurred.

Nike's positive corporate image

To appreciate the Nike controversy, we must understand the considerable advantage the company held in the marketplace by virtue of its positive public image (Shaw, 1999). Nike consistently scored high in *Fortune* magazine's "Most admired corporations" ratings. In fact, *Fortune* magazine put Nike's CEO, Phil Knight, on the cover of its June 23, 1997, issue, lauding him as one of the world's "greatest business leaders." Ironically, among Nike's most admired characteristics was the fact that it conformed to social and cultural expectations by adopting a corporate code of conduct that focused, in part, on labor practices overseas. Specifically, the code conveyed that Nike closely monitored the labor practices of its subcontractors around the world: Regardless of location or culture, Nike would hold its subcontractors to the highest standards.

Moreover, Nike has done an excellent job of associating itself with leaders in the world of athletics, basking in the reflection of their reputation (Shaw, 1999). For example, Nike supplied apparel to major college and university athletic teams, thereby promoting itself as a promoter of athletic excellence. And, of course, the company's well-known "Just Do It" advertising campaign with the highly regarded Michael Jordan helped the Nike "swoosh" gain recognition as a symbol of excellence worldwide.

Not surprisingly, Nike's efforts at promoting its corporate image has contributed to its financial well-being. Specifically, according to Standard and Poor's *Ratings Handbook* for 1993, investors viewed Nike as the leading company in the apparel/footwear field, having reputational capital valued at $3.9 billion (Fombrun, 1996). This figure reflects the value of Nike's brand name in the marketplace – an asset that was put at risk by the controversy surrounding it. Indeed, Nike's concerns are realistic insofar as evidence that the company's stock prices are linked to various stories about its wrongdoings (Boje, 2000).

Challenges to Nike's positive image

Against this backdrop of very favorable opinion and support, there began a trickle of attacks and threats to Nike's corporate image, which proved to be the beginning of a movement of activists to turn public sentiment against Nike. First, there was the Ballinger article that first brought Nike's practices to public awareness (Ballinger, 1992). To further heighten public awareness about Nike's practices, Ballinger placed ads in alternative weeklies in major United States cities criticizing Nike's Indonesian operations, claiming that Nike was a "corporate hypocrite" (Shaw, 1999).

About the same time, Donald Katz (1994) wrote a book about Nike, entitled *Just do it*. Although Katz initially intended to portray Nike as a role model for the "global, post-industrial enterprise," he raised a question to CEO Phil Knight as to how the self-proclaimed "company with a soul" could reconcile that image with its search for low-wage workers employed in substandard working conditions in Indonesia. Despite evidence to the contrary, Knight responded by saying, "There's no question in my mind that we're giving these people hope. This happens to be the way countries move ahead. I don't think we are doing anything wrong" (quoted in Katz, 1994: 190). Unfortunately for Nike, Knight's response gave further momentum to the adverse publicity affecting Nike.

These initial threats to Nike's corporate identity occurred at the confluence of related events that gave further legitimacy to Nike's critics. For example, there had been the NAFTA debate, during which there was made an explicit link between free trade and corporate exploitation (Shaw, 1999). Also, the Kathie Lee Gifford sweatshop controversy was about to become "high profile," and the undertow of that controversy would impact Nike (Gibbs, 1996).

Continued attacks on Nike's corporate image occurred in the media, often using provocative language. First, there was an article in *Ms.* magazine that attacked Nike as an "exploiter" of female workers (Enloe, 1995). The attacks gained further credibility and legitimacy following an article in the *New York Times*. Reporter Edward Gargan told the story of a 22-year-old worker who was fired for trying to organize workers in a Nike factory to demand an increase in their $2.10 daily wage (Gargan, 1996). Further, after being fired, the worker was locked in the Nike plant for 7 days and interrogated by Indonesian police as to his labor organizing activities.

Additional accounts appeared in the media that escalated the attacks and discrediting of the Nike corporate image. Of particular importance were eight columns critical of Nike and its overseas operations, written by Bob Herbert in the *New York Times* between June 1996 and June 1997. Each of the columns had provocative titles, such as "Brutality in Vietnam" (Herbert, 1997). The focus of each column was to point out the "contradictions" and "outright hypocrisy" of Nike's actions and advertising campaigns (Herbert, 1996).

As we noted earlier, the role of the media in discrediting Nike's corporate image was front-and-center in the CBS television journalism show, *48 Hours*. Aided by material provided by Jeff Ballinger, *48 Hours* put a "human face" on the substandard, and often abusive, working conditions of Nike's overseas operations. In addition, it introduced Vietnam as a location for several plants operated by subcontractors of Nike. This latter point would become important in the creation of "ad hoc" working groups monitoring and evaluating Nike's overseas operations, and then sharing that information with the media and other institutions critical of Nike.

Another source of legitimacy for those critical of Nike occurred when the Interfaith Center for Corporate Responsibility (ICCR) became involved. The ICCR is a coalition of Protestant, Catholic, and Jewish institutional investors with a portfolio of over $50 billion at the time. David Schiller, ICCR director of global accountability, claimed that "it is a basic human right to receive a sustainable wage" (Shaw, 1999: 31), and then ICCR introduced a resolution at the 1996 annual meeting of Nike calling for independent monitoring of Nike's overseas operations. The ICCR involvement helped transform the debate from one of "economics" to one of "justice."

Further institutional involvement occurred when Global Exchange, an institution dedicated to uncovering labor and human rights abuses, became involved in the campaign against Nike. After a visit from East Timorese human rights activist, Jose Ramon Horta, Global Exchange committed to assisting the human rights efforts in Indonesia and educating Americans about the overseas labor practices of its global business corporations, such as Nike. In addition, the considerable resources of Global Exchange would facilitate a network of international contacts and support for those critical of Nike and its overseas operations.

The Nike controversy became more accessible and "personalized" for Americans when Global Exchange arranged for the visit of Cicih Sukaresh, who was fired by a Nike subcontractor in Indonesia for organizing workers to demand the Indonesian minimum wage of $1.30 a day. Sukaresh told her story to Bob Herbert of the *New York Times*, who published it in his column entitled "Trampled Dreams" (Herbert, 1996). In addition, Global Exchange arranged for a visit for Sukaresh to Nike corporate headquarters, which is just outside of Portland, Oregon. The Sukaresh visit was a public relations nightmare for Nike, as Sukaresh was monitored closely by Nike security personnel, denied access to Nike corporate headquarters, denied water by Nike personnel, even though she was thirsty – and all of this was on television that evening. The pressure from the media and Nike critics intensified with the "personalization" of the effects of Nike's business practices.

In short, we note that Nike was taken to task for treating its employees unfairly – if not also inhumanely! These allegations called into question the image of fairness and integrity that Nike had so carefully crafted in the media. It is not unsurprising, therefore, that Nike officials, recognizing the threats to its reputation, took swift and definitive steps to shore up its eroding corporate image.

NIKE'S EFFORTS TO RESTORE ITS IMAGE

In response to efforts to delegitimate the company, Nike employed a variety of tactics. These included both strategies aimed at legitimating itself and strategies aimed at delegitimating its critics. This two-pronged approach (i.e., to defend oneself and to attack the enemy) is not without precedent. Indeed, research has shown that institutions whose legitimacy is threatened or under attack trigger legitimacy-enhancing social accounts to justify their actions (Elsbach, 1994) as well as legitimacy-enhancing structures and actions (Elsbach and Sutton, 1992; Weaver, Treviño, and Cochran, 1999). They also attempt to weaken "the enemy" by casting doubt on the legitimacy of their attackers (e.g., Dutton and Dukerich, 1991).

Legitimation through alternative and exonerating accounts

Not surprisingly, Nike failed to stand mute in response to the growing criticism and the attacks on its corporate image. In fact, the company used both enhancing and discrediting accounts to help shore up its eroding image. That is, it sought to bolster its positive image and to create a negative image of its detractors. Interestingly, it often did this in the same breath.

For example, a Nike spokesperson provided an enhancing account by claiming that the company had "taken a leadership role in trying to promote trade and act in an ethical way." At the same time, she also offered a discrediting account when criticizing the motives of Nike's critics by saying that they have "their own agendas" (Gibbs, 1996: 30).

Further, in response to criticism of their Indonesian operations, Phil Knight acknowledged that the company was "well aware" of the situation, and there was no question that "Nike could do a better job monitoring labor practices." To drive that point home, he announced that the subcontractor's plant was now under new management, the grievances of the employee had been addressed, and employees were now paid the minimum wage (Shaw, 1999). This tactic is consistent with what Elsbach (1994) has referred to as an acknowledgment – that is, a concession that something bad had happened accompanied by an explanation of why the problem was not as severe as it looks. Not taking any chances, while spinning this positive tale, Knight continued to make statements questioning the motives of institutions critical of Nike, and whose criticisms were "mean-spirited campaigns" (Shaw, 1999).

This pairing of enhancing and discrediting tactics continues to this day. For example, in recent accounts, Nike has sought to enhance its image in such ways as announcing its involvement in plans to help revitalize the economic viability of poor sections of Thailand (Lamb, 2000), training employees in its subcontracted factories in cross-cultural sensitivity (Marshall, 2000), and disclosing factory locations so that labor practices in these plants can be subject to public scrutiny (Tippit, 2000). At the same time, Nike officials have argued that anti-sweatshop protestors are "shooting themselves in the foot" by harming a company that is going out of its way to help workers (Baghwati, 2000). Another discrediting account came in the form of Knight's claim that the anti-sweatshop campaign has been instigated by the AFL–CIO in retaliation against Nike for contracting with foreign companies for its manufacturing operations (Labor's World, 2000). These examples nicely illustrate how Nike is attempting to improve its image by taking both defensive and offensive measures.

Legitimation through institutional structures and involvement

Nike's legitimation strategy was not limited to the use of accounts. The company also embedded itself in a variety of formal and informal institutional relationships designed to help bolster its image (Shaw, 1999). For example, Nike became a member of the Fashion Industry Forum, called together by then Labor Secretary Robert Reich. This forum was organized to fight sweatshops. Another example of institutional involvement was when Knight appeared alongside President Clinton during the White House announcement of the creation of the Anti-Sweatshop Task Force, of which Nike would be a member. Knight also created another institutional relationship to enhance Nike's image as being concerned with justice when he announced that Ernst and Young would monitor the company's Asian manufacturing subcontractors. It has been reported that Nike spends upwards of $10 million a year on various social campaigns designed to promote its good name and to divert attention from claims about its subcontractors' labor practices (Boje, 1999). These *institutionalizing* tactics are consistent with those taken by other companies that have faced threats to their positive image (Elsbach and Sutton, 1992).

Despite Nike's best efforts, criticism of its overseas operations mounted. In response, Nike took another direction in image management with the hiring of a consultant, former United States Ambassador and civil rights leader, Andrew Young (Shaw, 1999). Young, and his consulting firm, GoodWorks International, was asked to investigate the operations of Nike's Asian subcontractors. This legitimation strategy was intended to enhance the company's image in two ways. First, by hiring Young, Nike now had an "arm's-length outsider" to monitor conditions and evaluate the extent to which Nike was living up to its code of conduct. Second, and more importantly, it is clear that by associating itself with a civil rights leader regarded as a man of integrity and a promoter of social justice, Nike was attempting to bask in a reflected image that couldn't help but offset the threats to its reputation.

Despite these efforts, criticism against Nike grew and pressure continued to mount. This led Nike to adopt an even more high-profile institutional strategy: It signed an agreement by the Anti-Sweatshop Task Force to end sweatshops. In May 1998, with activism rising and profits falling, Knight pledged to significantly reform Nike's overseas labor practices. However, in the face of reports that Nike's abuses have continued (Campaign for Labor Rights, 1999; Manning, 1998), social activism has not abated. In fact, to the extent that Nike is perceived as having violated its own agreements to reform its ways, any reports of unfair labor practices are perceived as even more egregious than before.

Storytelling by antagonists and protagonists

If there seems to be no end to the battle between Nike and the anti-sweatshop social activists, it is because each side is continuously constructing a social reality that it "sells" to the public. Whereas activists focus on stories chronicling various labor abuses, Nike counters with claims that activists abuse the power of the internet to spread false claims about them (Boje, 1998). Both sides are engaging in what Boje (1995) has referred to as *storytelling*. In this case, Nike tells its tale in the form of press releases whereas the social activists primarily get out their story over the internet. In a recent article, Boje (1999) has likened the exchange between Nike and its detractors to the ongoing battle between the cartoon character Wile E. Coyote and his archrival, the Roadrunner. The activists see Nike as the Coyote, using trickery (in the form of public relations) and technology from the omni-present Acme Company (overseas contractors), and themselves as the Roadrunner, the hero, who keenly sidesteps detection while exposing the Coyote's treachery until he falls into his own trap.

The storytelling game is kept alive, as Boje (1999) chronicles, through several mutually used tactics. The first he dubs *micro-storytelling*, the reporting of information about specific facts. Using this technique, activists post accounts on the worldwide web designed to challenge Nike's claims that it creates a good life for its employees. At the same time, Nike counters by claiming that it has created such a good life for its subcontractors' employees that they have sufficient discretionary income to purchase luxury items.

The second tactic is *macro-storytelling*, which involves reporting information about larger-scale issues. For example, Nike describes its labor practices as promoting economic progress, promoting the economic health of the regions in which it conducts business. However, the activists claim that because Nike's actions are anti-democratic, they actually impede global economic development.

Finally, both sides rely on *spectacles*, public events that call attention to their cause. For example, activists have staged boycotts on various college campuses and in front of stores selling Nike apparel. At the same time, Nike has capitalized on such spectacles as the opening of its NikeTown stores to promote its association with high-profile celebrities, and its various social programs. By diverting attention away from the negative stories about Nike that consumers might hear, these actions are designed to create positive images in the public's mind. Indeed, research has shown that companies effectively can counter negative publicity by drawing public attention toward positive associations (Thibaut, Calder, and Sternthal, 1981).

SUMMARY

As illustrated in this section, Nike was the target of allegations of unfairness and injustice regarding "slave wages," arbitrary abuse, and violations of workers' human rights (Shaw, 1999). These allegations threatened Nike's corporate image, thereby motivating the company to engage in a variety of tactics to protect that image. By highlighting this connection between justice and corporate image management, we have accomplished our first objective. We now turn attention to our second objective – namely, to use the events of the Nike case to illustrate some limitations in the scope of current research on justice and culture.

JUSTICE AND CULTURE IN THE NIKE CASE: EXPLORING THE CONNECTIONS

Having analyzed the corporate image implications of the Nike case, we are now prepared to extend our discussion by exploring the connections between justice and culture. As part of this analysis, we will identify ways in which current research on justice and culture can be expanded.

Accounts of injustices across cultures

Accounts of Nike workers describing their working conditions in Indonesia and Vietnam (e.g., Boje, 1999; Shaw, 1999) reveal an interesting pattern. Specifically, although not all Indonesian and Vietnamese workers felt unfairly treated, there was clear evidence of overt expression of discontent among workers from both countries, which was rooted in the sense of injustice.

The sense of injustice articulated by Nike workers was rooted in violations of the three standards of justice identified previously. For example, one Indonesian worker was fired for organizing workers to demand payment of the Indonesian minimum wage, then $1.30 (Herbert, 1996). Similarly, another Indonesian worker was fired for attempting to organize workers to demand an increase in the daily wage of $2.10 at one Nike plant (Gargan, 1996). Indeed, there were other examples of collective action by Indonesian employees in response to not receiving the minimum wage (Shaw, 1999). This expression of discontent is even more compelling, given the authoritarian government of Indonesia and the clear evidence from a US State Department worldwide report that the Indonesian government sanctioned attacks on workers' rights (Shaw, 1999).

The pattern of responses to wages and working conditions was similar for Vietnamese workers. For example, angry with their abusive supervisors and sweatshop working conditions, Vietnamese workers have walked off the job in record numbers (Stewart, 1997). In one case, responding to physical abuse and beatings from their supervisors, workers at one Nike plant walked off their jobs in a strike (*CBS News*, 1996). Indeed, many Vietnamese workers readily expressed their outrage to the media regarding abusive supervisors and sweatshop working conditions (Herbert, 1997).

If we take the current approach to analyzing justice and culture, which focuses on comparative differences in cultural values, we cannot easily explain this pattern of responses: Nike workers who felt satisfied with their jobs and working conditions *and* Nike workers who engaged in acts of discontent. To elaborate, if we used the Hofstede (1980, 1991) dimensions of collectivism–individualism and power distance, both Indonesia and Vietnam would be considered collectivist and high power distance cultures. As a result, we would expect the importance of harmony, consistent with a collectivist culture, and the deference to authority, consistent with a high power distance culture, should mute the expression of discontent in the face of apparent injustice (Tyler, Boeckman, Smith, and Huo, 1997).

Although many Nike workers responded in a manner consistent with this line of reasoning, there are so many other examples of overt discontent by Nike workers (Shaw, 1999) as to suggest the need to expand the scope of current research on justice and culture. This is not to imply that the current approach has limited value, for it has been quite useful in identifying important cultural differences in justice judgments and justice-motivated behavior (e.g., for reviews, see Beugré, 1998; James, 1993; Miles and Greenberg, 1993). But the events of the Nike case suggest the need for an additional theoretical lens to make sense of the variability of responses of Nike workers to their wages and working conditions. We suggest that relative deprivation theory (for overviews, see Crosby, 1982; Tyler et al., 1997) is one such theoretical framework that can provide a more parsimonious explanation of the different pattern of responses of Nike workers.

Explaining responses in terms of relative deprivation

Relative deprivation theory emerged from one of the landmark and seminal studies on American soldiers during World War II conducted by Stouffer and his colleagues (Stouffer, Suchman, DeVinney, Star, and Williams, 1949). This research found unexpected relationships between soldiers' objective situations and their feelings of satisfaction. For example, black soldiers stationed in the south felt more satisfied with their conditions than did black soldiers in the north, even though conditions were better in the north than in the south. Why? Stouffer et al. hypothesized that black soldiers in the south compared their conditions not with the blacks in the north, but with black civilians in the south, who experienced even poorer conditions. For this reason, black soldiers in the south did not feel relatively deprived.

Another example from the Stouffer et al. study provides additional support for the concept of relative deprivation. Airmen were promoted at a more rapid pace than were the military police (MPs), yet the airmen reported greater dissatisfaction with their promotion system than did the less frequently promoted MPs. The reason is that the airmen compared their situations to their air corps peers, who were being promoted at an even more rapid rate. Conversely, the MPs were comparing their situations with other more slowly promoted military police peers, and thus reported greater satisfaction with their less rapid promotion system.

One key finding from this line of investigation, which has been corroborated by subsequent research (for a review, see Tyler et al., 1997), is that one's *subjective* satisfaction with outcomes is not a simple reaction to the *objective* qualities of those outcomes. The other key finding is that people evaluate the quality of their outcomes by comparing them with the outcomes of others or outcomes across time. Consistent with relative deprivation theory, there is evidence from Nike workers that their choice of different comparison points would distinguish those workers who expressed and acted out their discontent from those who felt satisfied and fairly treated.

From the published reports, it is clear that those Nike workers who felt fairly treated considered comparison points that allowed for a more favorable evaluation of their situation. Some of the comparison points involved distributive justice concerns, such as pay. For example, one worker felt fairly paid with the knowledge that her pay was twice the per capita income in Vietnam, where most people work on farms (Schmitt, 1999). Another worker expressed similar sentiments in comparing her situation with less favorable, lower-paying jobs of others when she stated: "If they didn't have jobs here [at the Nike plant], most of the women you see here would be planting or working part-time city jobs" (quoted in Lamb, 1999: A34). Similarly, another Vietnamese worker acknowledged that "It's a good job [with higher pay], better than most of my friends have," as the reason for the absence of discontent on his part (quoted in Lamb, 1999: A34).

Comparisons to others were not limited to outcomes; workers also made comparisons about their working conditions and treatment by supervisors, which are interactional justice concerns. For example, a Vietnamese worker expressed fairness of treatment and satisfaction by pointing out that "things were much better than before" (quoted in Schmitt, 1999: 1B) because her supervisor no longer snapped the bras of female workers as he addressed them. Whether it was temporal or social comparison processes, Nike workers were comparing their outcomes to assess the fairness of their conditions. Indeed, the reforms Nike put in place in response to public criticism resulted in improved working conditions for workers such that the claims of Nike sweatshops and mistreated workers led one worker to respond: "That's strange. Why?" (quoted in Lamb, 1999: A34).

Relative deprivation theory also can explain those workers who felt unfairly treated and expressed that discontent. For example, Indonesian workers who tried to organize others to demand a raise in the daily wage justified their actions by pointing out that their current wage was less than the minimum (Herbert, 1996; Manning, 1997). Other Indonesian workers justified their efforts at organizing workers to demand a raise in wages because they were not being paid a "living wage" (Gargan, 1996). As one Asian diplomat put it, "the minimum wage does not provide for minimum subsistence" (quoted in Shaw, 1999: 29). Finally, additional evidence of the importance of comparison standards to explain feelings of unfairness and discontent may be found in the words of one Indonesian worker who stated, "We want the same minimum wage that you have in your country" (quoted in Shaw, 1999: 46).

Again, comparisons to others were not limited to outcomes, but also comparisons about their working conditions and treatment by supervisors. For example, on March 8, 1997, which was also International Women's Day, over 50 women were ordered to run around the factory on a very hot, sunny day as punishment for failing to wear regulation shoes to work (Herbert, 1997). Twelve of the women had to go to the hospital because they collapsed. In response to this incident, a Vietnamese American businessman stated, "Vietnamese all over the country were outraged that on International Women's Day, when most companies give women workers flowers and other gifts . . . they had to spend the day in the emergency room" (quoted in Herbert, 1997: A29). Indeed, it is foreign employers in Vietnam, such as Nike, who, while bringing more jobs, create not only complaints of unfair wages, but also complaints centering on the use of corporal punishment by supervisors and unsafe working conditions (Stewart, 1997).

Implications

Given that relative deprivation theory proves useful in explaining cross-cultural aspects of justice, there are several implications for future theory-building and research on justice and culture. For example, the current approach to research on justice and culture, which focuses on comparative differences in justice judgments between cultures, is a *culture-specific perspective* (Tyler et al., 1997). By contrast, relative deprivation theory takes a *universal perspective*, suggesting greater similarity across cultures (Tyler et al., 1997). Interestingly, relative deprivation theory has been used to explain feelings of fairness and acts of discontent in a variety of different countries (see Tyler et al., 1997, for a review).

To continue this line of reasoning, future research on justice and culture should not only focus on culture-specific variables, but also include more universal variables, such as social and temporal comparison processes, as suggested by relative deprivation theory. In addition, the events of the Nike case suggest that these comparison processes may be "cued" or "primed" by social institutions such as the media (e.g., print, television), investigative groups (e.g., Vietnam Labor Watch) and human rights activists (e.g., Global Exchange). As such, future research on justice and culture should examine the influence of social institutions on individual judgments, and to what extent, across time, these social institutions, as well as the internet, may shape the construal of justice to be less culture-specific.

To punctuate this line of reasoning, our analysis suggests that there may be more similarities between cultural groups than are addressed by the current approach to research on justice and culture. We argue that good theory-building and research on culture and justice should look for both differences and similarities. As such, we agree with Brett, Tinsley, Jansesens, Barsness, and Lytle (1997) who argued, "it is equally important to search for differences as to search for similarities between cultures. Cross-cultural research is inherently comparative, and the goal for cross-cultural researchers should be twofold: to understand the range of variability *and* the uniformity of human behavior" (p. 82).

CULTURE AND CORPORATE IMAGE MANAGEMENT

Culture is not only related to justice, as we have discussed, but corporate image management as well. In this connection, Nike initially took the approach of the cultural relativists (for an overview of this approach, see Donaldson, 1992). That is, different rules apply to different cultures – or, in other words, "when in Rome, do as the Romans do." The official cultural relativism of Nike could be found in a Nike document entitled the Memorandum of Understanding, which detailed the importance of conforming to all applicable government regulations and local rules (Katz, 1994). The cultural relativism could also be heard in the words of Nike's vice president for production, Dave Taylor, who stated: "We don't set policy within factories; it is their business to run" (quoted in Katz, 1994: 191).

But, as we have illustrated in this chapter, the Nike position of cultural relativism ultimately proved to be politically unviable. In response to changing circumstances and growing social pressure, Nike incrementally adapted its strategy and ultimately improved the labor practices of its overseas operations. Indeed, while Nike has benefited economically from the globalization of business, it also has been experiencing an unforeseen consequence. Namely, it is being judged by the public in terms of broad moral guidelines (see DeGeorge, 1993) – including respect for core human values that would determine the minimum ethical standards for all companies regardless of country or culture (see Donaldson and Dunfee, 1994, 1999). Although the challenge to conform to those guidelines is made more difficult as the cultural context matters (Treviño and Nelson, 1995), the cultural context that mattered in the Nike case was not the host country, but the home country.

Indeed, as the events of the Nike controversy demonstrate, it is not only cultural differences in individual fairness judgments that matter, but also the social construal of fairness and justice by other parties who perceive themselves as stakeholders in the matters of global business corporations. And, as the Nike controversy demonstrates, these stakeholders need not only be from the "host" country, but they may also be from the corporation's "home" country.

CONCLUSION

Given that global business corporations, such as Nike, increasingly are faced with dealing with multiple audiences across different cultures, how can they present a consistent corporate image of justice? (Boje, 1999) suggests that achieving such consistency is impossible. Writing from the perspective of a postmodern ethicist examining the words and actions of Nike, Boje states it thusly:

> There is also the question of the public image or what I call *faciality*. Here Nike has a happy smiling faciality. The face of Nike comes through in its press releases, slogan, speeches, reports, and web pages. The above face looks terrific. But the faciality painted by the Activists puts a few cracks and blemishes in the perfect image of Nike . . . Activist groups seek to reframe the face of Nike and Nike seeks to reimage the face of the activists; each seeks to point out the blemishes, marks, and inconsistencies. It is a strange dialogue. In a postmodern sense it is impossible for either Nike or Activist to be consistent across time and across events as they present their public faces. Few of us ever achieve the congruence between thoughts and actions that Gandhi did. (p. 90)

Despite Boje's assessment, the Nike case has shown us that global companies can expect increasing pressure in the future from a variety of activist groups to move toward a consistent public image of justice (Useem, 2000).

Given the difficulty, if not the impossibility, of presenting a consistent public image of justice in both Western and Third World countries, and the social and reputational consequences that will follow as a result, what is a global business corporation to do? As one response, which we identified in the first section of the chapter, corporations and their critics will play an elaborate multi-party storytelling game (Boje, 1995). Thus, one direction for future research on justice and culture is to analyze and deconstruct the stories across time and culture, or what Boje (1999) describes as an intertextual weave, an indirect dialogue between a global corporation, Nike in the present case, and its critics. Looking for progress toward justice, not perfection, becomes the objective of researcher and activist alike.

In conclusion, the events of the Nike case brought to center-stage prominent issues of human rights and human dignity in the workplace. Such issues have not been the focus of much research by US-based researchers (for notable exceptions, see Bies, 2000; and Tyler and Lind, 1992). As the globalization of justice continues, the issue of human rights promises to inform the study of organizational justice in general (Treviño and Bies, 1997), and not just in the context of justice and culture. Indeed, to address clearly normative concerns such as human rights will broaden our research focus, raise new and important research questions, and contribute to the development of more complete models for understanding justice, ostensibly the goal of science.

NOTE

1 In this chapter, we neither support nor refute the claims made against Nike. Instead, we use others' claims against Nike and its refutations to illustrate our points.

17

Trust in Cross-Cultural Relationships

Jean L. Johnson and John B. Cullen

Numerous authors have cited trust as a vital lubricant for relationships. In exchange relationships, where a party's outcomes depend on the behavior and intent of the exchange partner, trust is particularly crucial. Without trust, the objectives or outcomes of the exchange are in constant and chronic jeopardy. The incentive for exchange would be absent. Without some level of trust, much exchange would not happen.

Research on trust and its role in exchange has proliferated since the 1990s. However, despite the insights offered by scholars, we do not yet have a generalizable and comprehensive model of trust in exchange. Further, the issue of trust in cross-cultural exchange has become compelling because of globalization. In this chapter we develop a comprehensive conceptual model of trust and use it to extend our understanding of trust in the complicated and intriguing arena of cross-culture exchange.

We present a model of trust in exchange based on theory from multiple disciplines. The model integrates and advances ideas from several excellent reviews (e.g., Kramer 1999) and work in the *Academy of Management Review*'s (1998) special topic forum on trust. Our model extends earlier work in three ways: (1) the model is generalizable in that it applies to an array of exchange situations, such as those involving individuals, organizations, and individuals and organizations; (2) the model is comprehensive in that it simultaneously considers trust at the inception of exchange, along with the manifestation and dynamics of trust; (3) the model reconciles and integrates both rational–economic and socio-psychological perspectives on trust.

Three major components make up our model. First, we suggest that most if not all exchange is predicated at its inception on some preliminary or initializing level of trust deriving from various bases. Some bases are general, applying almost universally across exchange encounters, while other bases apply only to a particular exchange type or situation. Second, the bases give rise to beliefs about the exchange partner's behaviors and intentions. These beliefs are the explicit manifestation of trust in exchange. Third, the model depicts interaction in the exchange relationship as greatly influencing trust. Importantly, beyond initializing trust levels, due to the interaction dynamic between the exchange participants, trust changes, sometimes strengthening, sometimes decreasing.

The model considers the dynamic nature of trust through an extensive treatment of signaling behavior in exchange.

In subsequent sections, we extend our understanding of trust to the complicated situation of cross-culture exchange. We reviewed literature in the context of the various components of the model. While there are a number of comparative studies of trust in different cultural settings, they are often limited to the US, Japan, and China. To address this shortcoming, we add to our understanding of trust with reanalyses of cross-national data on values and beliefs in over 40 societies (World Values Study Group, 1994).

AN INTEGRATIVE MODEL OF TRUST

Scholars have struggled to define trust in a way that is theoretically sound, sufficiently generalizable and yet reasonably parsimonious. This is not an endeavor to be taken lightly as evidenced by the numerous definitions in literatures ranging from psychology, to interfirm, economics, sociology, and management (Hosmer, 1995). In these disciplines, scholars have offered a variety of approaches, many of which have advanced our thinking on some fronts while frustrating our efforts on others.

Early theorists suggested that trust involves the willingness to make oneself vulnerable to the actions of another (Deutsch, 1958, 1962; Coleman, 1990; Mayer, Davis, and Schoorman, 1995). It is noteworthy that trust in absence of other, i.e., a referent, is meaningless. Trust involves at least two entities in relation to each other. For example, in an interpersonal relationship, the trust referent is the other person. As another example, a person may feel that she trusts some entity such as a product or an organization. Likewise in business relationships, trust can happen between firms.[1] Thus, trust involves some referent without stipulating the form that the referent (e.g., a person, a firm, or a product), or indeed even the focal trusting entity itself, must take. In addition, while the parties need not be in a relationship, trust cannot happen unless it is in relation to another entity. In our discussions, we focus on the trust of focal relative to the referent.

A second implication is that trust is volitional. Both focal and referent have a choice and, in some form or another, make a conscious decision of whether to trust. Trust is not automatic. Only in some situations does it occur. A third implication is that the amount of trust can vary. Focal can choose to limit the vulnerability assumed. Focal's trust of referent allows referent a range of behaviors not otherwise possible (Coleman, 1990). In limiting the assumption of vulnerability, focal constrains and limits the range of behaviors in which referent may engage in the exchange.

Casting of trust as willingness to assume vulnerability provides an excellent platform for our conceptualization (see figure 17.1). We see trust rooted in six bases, three general or universal and three situation-specific. Out of the trust bases, stem the observable manifestations of trust – beliefs about the behaviors and intentions of the referent. Below we discuss trust manifestations and the trust bases. Then we discuss another crucial source of trust, the relationship dynamic.

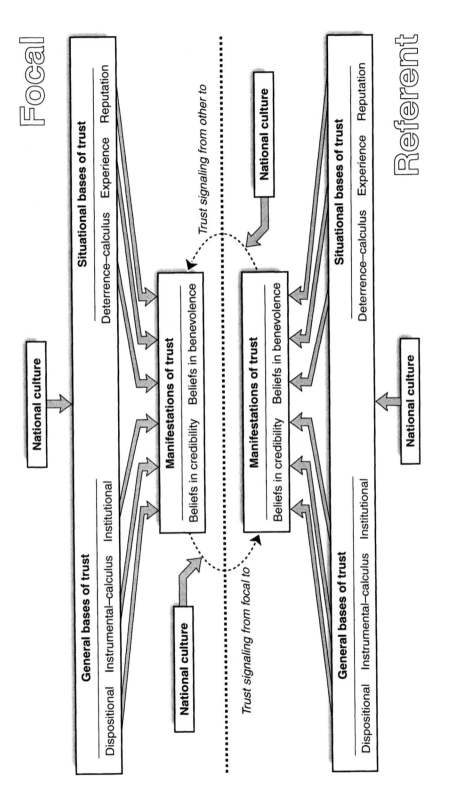

FIGURE 17.1 An integrative model of trust

Manifestations of trust

In trusting, focal assumes vulnerability of some type and magnitude (Deutsch, 1958, 1962; Coleman, 1990). Vulnerability is a psychological state generated by the expectancy of a positive or nonnegative outcome in connection with the behavior of the trust referent (Hosmer, 1995; Kramer, 1999; Rousseau, Sitkin, Burt, and Camerer, 1998). Because of focal's outcome expectations and referent's influence over those outcomes, trust can be observed, i.e., it is manifest in focal's beliefs about referent's behaviors and intentions toward focal in the exchange episode. In figure 17.1, we show the manifestations of trust at the center of the model.

The literature indicates that focal's beliefs about referent's behaviors fall into two general categories, credibility and benevolence. *Credibility* is the more objective, involving behaviors directly focused on performance of the core exchange activity (McAllister 1995). In these beliefs, focal exhibits confidence in referent's objective through beliefs that referent has and will use their capabilities, competencies, expertise, and resources to make a successful exchange that meets outcome expectations (Blau, 1964; Ganesan, 1994; McAllister, 1995; Moorman, Deshpande, and Zaltman, 1993). Focal believes that referent will behave reliably and predictably in fulfilling the outcome expectancy of focal. In contrast, *benevolence* involves beliefs about the more emotional aspects of referent's behavior. Benevolence involves focal's beliefs about referent's positive intention in the exchange (Ganesan, 1994; McAllister, 1995). It connotes the extent to which focal believes that referent has intentions of goodwill and will not jeopardize the exchange outcome, and will in fact support enhanced outcomes in the exchange even when new conditions arise.

THE BASES OF TRUST

Conventional treatments suggest that trust develops over time. However, it is unlikely that exchange would be conceived in total absence of trust. Some initial levels of trust likely exist before any interaction or exchange activities (McKnight, Cummings, and Chervany, 1998). We suggest that these exchange-initializing trust levels are rooted in factors surrounding the exchange. These factors are the bases of trust. Below we discuss general and situation-specific trust bases.

As depicted in figure 17.1, one category of the trust bases is more general in nature. These bases stand apart from any specific relationship or referent and are not connected to a particular situation, exchange episode, or incident. Instead, they come into play across a variety of exchange incidents and an array of relationships. The general bases of trust include dispositions, instrumental-calculus, and institutions.

Dispositions refer to pre-existing and relatively constant characteristics that influence how a participants in exchanges will conduct their interactions with others. They are unobservable states or traits in an individual's personality or an organization's cognitive system (Weiss and Adler, 1984). As such, they are stable behavioral tendencies and traits that result in certain consistencies in actions across an array of situations (Pervin, 1989; Sitkin and Weingart, 1995; Staw, Bell, and Clausen, 1986). Dispositions come in a variety of forms. For example at the individual level, our proclivity for intimacy affects how we act in relationships (Goto, 1996). Arguably, one of the most important dispositions is to trust (Rotter, 1967, 1980). The dispositional base of trust implies that focal or referent has a fundamental faith in the goodness of humankind and tends to exhibit trust across an array of situations and referents (Rotter, 1967, 1980). The assumption is that others are most often well behaved and intentioned. The less than flattering perspective on the disposition to trust is gullibility. Some level of a disposition to trust likely plays a role in most of our lives.

The calculus base of trust takes two distinct forms, deterrence-calculus and instrumental-calculus, both predicated on cost–benefit analysis. The instrumental-calculus is the general form. Fundamentally, instrumentalism is a rational utilitarian perspective on human nature. Instrumental-calculus-based trust involves self-optimizing through a rational utilitarian reasoning. When it comes into play, trust happens because focal finds it is easier to trust referent than not to do so. Focal trusts in order to avoid the costs and demands of not trusting. A worst case scenario of not trusting referent means that focal must constantly monitor referent's performance and must engage in relentless renegotiating. The ultimate cost in not trusting is the necessity of searching out a replacement for the exchange. This involves energy and emotional and real costs for focal. In trusting, focal eliminates these costs with full realization that betrayal and negative outcomes could result. Focal engages in a reward–cost balancing that essentially involves playing the odds (Coleman, 1990; Deutsch, 1958, 1962). Though there may be intermittent costs, over the long term, outcomes are better with trust than without it. Focal defaults to positive beliefs about the credibility and good intentions of referent because it is easier to do so. It is a case of focal trusting until there is some demonstrable reason not to do so.

Institutions, the third general basis of trust, are social patterns of activity, symbolic systems, controls, and ways of ordering reality (Friedland and Alford, 1991). They guide, empower, and constrain the conduct of individuals and organizations. Examples of institutions are regulatory or watchdog agencies, legal recourse, and special interest groups such as consumer or trade associations. Institutions provide a basis for trust for two reasons. First, institutions limit referent's ability to behave in negative ways, allowing focal to form and hold beliefs about expectations of positive outcomes. Second, when violation occurs, institutions provide mechanisms of voice and recourse for the betrayed. Trust derives from the threat of legal and social sanctions built in by institutions (McKnight, Cummings, and Chervany, 1998; Zucker, 1986), i.e., from the security blanket provided by institutional safeguards. Under the protection of this security blanket, focal forms beliefs about referent's credibility and intentions.

In contrast to the general trust bases, the situational bases of trust relate to a particular exchange episode or relationship. They include deterrence-calculus, experience, and referent reputation. These factors likely do not generalize and often do not generate trust outside of a certain specific circumstance.

In contrast to the instrumental-calculus base, which comes into play across an array of exchange situations, deterrence-calculus is situation-specific. Like the instrumental-calculus base, deterrence is predicated on instrumentality and utilitarian concerns. It is grounded in cost–benefit analysis, potential for returns, past investments, and switching costs. A crucial difference is that with deterrence the cost–benefit issues of returns, investments, and switching costs come into play exclusively for the specific exchange situation at hand. The deterrence-calculus basis of trust involves the use of artificial mechanisms put into place that, in a sense, force trust. Such bases are introduced into the exchange situation intentionally to act as safeguards against undesirable behaviors by referent (Williamson, 1983, 1993, 1996). Credible commitments and hostages are common examples of the mechanisms used as deterrents. A credible commitment is an investment made in the normal course of exchange. The exchange is arranged so that trust violation by the referent results in forfeiture of the investment, a possibility that serves to constrain referent's behavior. Use of the hostage is where referent places something of value at risk explicitly to ensure desirable conduct. A penalty clause in a contract exemplifies the hostage concept (Williamson, 1983). In some exchange relationships due to normal investments required by the partners, a natural mutual hostage situation emerges (Williamson, 1993, 1996). In any case, these mechanisms provide strong disincentives to misbehave, allowing focal to easily form beliefs about referent's behavior and intentions.

Another situational basis of trust is experience, loosely interpreted as a learning perspective on trust. Experience can serve as a basis of trust in two ways, both limited in their application to a specific exchange episode or a specific class of exchange episodes. First, experience with a particular referent, from past exchange episodes or other sources of information, provides focal with some expectation concerning how a referent will behave. This type of experience as a basis of trust is confined exclusively to exchange episodes involving the specific referent. Based on either direct or indirect experience with referent, focal can formulate beliefs about referent's credibility and good intentions in the current or next exchange episode.

In addition, focal's experience can expand to include a certain type of referents or class of exchange situations. Focal can trust after learning how a certain category of referents behaves or after understanding the role of certain referents (Kramer, 1999). For example, consumers purchasing automobiles might base their trust of a dealer on their experiences with other dealers. Because focal has information about what can be expected in the behavior and conduct by a referent in this type of exchange process, focal can form beliefs about the referent's intentions of benevolence toward them and about their credibility.

Reputation is the third situational basis of trust. It is the general estimation held by external constituents regarding a party such as a person or an organization (Rao, 1994; Weigelt and Camerer, 1988). Reputation rests on the ascription of certain characteristics to a party by consensus of the entities with which the party interacts. In the model (figure 17.1), focal along with others will, by implied consensus, ascribe a set of characteristics to referent. Thus, a party's reputation is very much in the public domain (Whetten and Godfrey, 1998). Reputation can be attached directly to individuals in their exchange activities. However, reputation can take a variety of other forms as well. For example, brand equity, the set of associations which consumers link with a brand, translates directly into a product's reputation (Keller, 1998). Likewise, a corporation's reputation translates directly into its image. Through observations of the firm's behavior, parties interacting with it refract ascribed traits and characteristics resulting in reputation (Dutton and Dukerich, 1991; Whetten and Godfrey, 1998). As a basis of trust, referent's reputation can be a major factor (Lahno, 1995). If the traits and characteristics ascribed in referent's reputation involve the right type of business conduct, honesty, forthrightness, delivery on promises, etc., focal's beliefs regarding referent's credibility and benevolence will often follow readily.

In summary, with regard to the trust bases, we reiterate that exchange most often would not begin without some trust in place. It is difficult to imagine a situation where exchange would move forward without some initial positive beliefs about the referent's credibility and benevolence. This trust derives from the bases though not all six bases need to come into play in all situations. In various exchange situations, focal's beliefs about referent's intentions and credibility will derive from different bases and combinations of bases. The bases coming into play may be either general or situational or some combination of both. Further, they can combine in ways that can become quite complex and are often unanticipated. We conjecture that in some situations, the various bases may compensate for one another. For example, focal's experience with a certain group of referents may lead to negative beliefs about a specific referent's intentions and credibility. Yet, if some mechanism is put into place to safeguard focal's interests and limit referent's undesirable behaviors (deterrence-calculus), there may be an initial level of trust sufficient to move the exchange process forward.

THE DYNAMICS OF TRUST

In the previous sections, we suggested that initial trust levels of trust, rooted in the six bases, are manifest in focal's beliefs about referent's behavior. If exchange consists of an isolated, discrete incident, the initial level of trust derived from the various bases is the end of trust as well as the beginning. The initializing trust is the only opportunity for trust, and indeed, is all the isolated exchange requires. In many situations, however, exchange extends beyond an isolated episode, occurring over time with multiple transaction episodes. In such cases, exchange involves a relationship, perhaps between two firms, an individual and a firm, or individuals in some commercial activity. In an exchange relationship, trust is far from static. Through behaviors and interactions over time, trust strengthens or weakens. Thus, the initial level of trust is simply a starting point. To explore trust over time in an exchange relationship, we first examine the conditions for trust and then the relationship interaction dynamics.

A review of the literature suggests several conditions for the evolution of trust in exchange relationships. The conditions for trust are important for initial trust levels as well as for the relationship over time. However, these conditions play out in the relationship dynamic in a more crucial way because they often have strong and pervasive dyadic implications. The conditions suggested by the literature include motivational investment, risk, and interdependence (Dwyer, Schurr, and Oh, 1987; Rousseau, Sitkin, Burt, and Camerer, 1998; Sheppard and Sherman, 1998). Though we discuss each condition separately, they are clearly interrelated and likely act in conjunction with one another to set up trust growth or decline.

Motivational investment is a crucial condition for increasing trust. To the extent that the interests of the exchange parties align, trust has the potential to increase and build to some optimal level (Dasgupta, 1988; Dwyer, Schurr, and Oh, 1987; Wicks, Berman, and Jones, 1999). The alignment of interests means that both parties see benefits and/or some enhancement of outcomes that can be gained through trusting. Essentially, there is a sense of bilateral motivation to build and increase trust, with a limiting dose of prudence attached. Both focal and referent simultaneously want a strengthening of their own beliefs in the partner's credibility and benevolence, and a complementary strengthening in the partner's belief in their credibility and benevolence. In the zone of optimal trust strengthening there is complete overlap in the motivational investment of both focal and referent. When the motivation is not mutual or bilateral, some weakening of trust is possible. Asymmetries in trust can destabilize a relationship over repeated interactions and transactions.

Risk is the second important condition for trust augmentation (Coleman, 1990). The greater the probability and magnitude of loss, the greater the required strength of trust. When outcomes are trivial, trust building is not a compelling issue for exchange relationship partners (Bhattacharya, Devinney, and Pillutla, 1998).

Interdependence is a third condition for trust. The greater the interdependence, the more compelling the pressure to trust and increase trust. That is, when the context of the relationship changes, the stakes increase which encourages trust building. Interdependence also relates to risk issues directly in that interdependence increases risk. The deeper the relationship and the greater the interdependence, the greater the risk and therefore, the greater the likelihood that trust will evolve positively or negatively beyond the initial levels (Sheppard and Sherman, 1998). However, risk can stand apart from interdependence if there are other sources for the exchange.

An additional crucial influence in the strengthening or weakening of trust is the dynamics of signaling in a relationship over multiple interaction episodes. As figure 17.1 depicts, in interactions between the exchange relationship participants, actors compose, send, receive, and decode signals about trust. To help us understand the signaling activities involved in the strengthening or weakening of trust in the exchange relationship, we draw on the theoretical perspective known as symbolic interactionism (Blummer, 1961; Couch, 1989; Mead, 1934).[2]

Symbolic interactionism suggests that people act toward things (objects, etc.) through and because of the meaning that those things have for them. The meanings of things derive out of interactions with others and further evolve from interpretive processes of how others act toward a person with regard to the things (Blummer, 1961). The central ideas in symbolic interactionism such as self-interaction, interpretation, symbols, and joint action are especially crucial in understanding trust dynamics in exchange relationships.

Self-interaction suggests that an actor engages in social interaction with him/herself. The actor notes and defines things, interprets them, determines their significance, and organizes response on that basis. In this process, interpretation can be viewed as the assignment of meaning. However, interpretation is part of a larger and even more crucial process, that of developing significant symbols. Significant symbols emerge through the process of identifying objects and actions, determining their significance, and interpreting or assigning their meaning. That is, symbols emerge through complex social arrangements, coordination and co-orientation of relevant participants. They simultaneously derive from shared experience and provide vehicles for sharing additional experiences. The role of symbols is important because mastering them means that the attention and direction of another's behavior is accomplished (Couch, 1989). Obviously, this activity has important implications in exchange relationships.

Participants use symbols to indicate lines of action to each other and interpret the indications made by the other party or parties. Focal makes indications, i.e. engages in some behavior with regard to referent. Referent notes focal's indications or lines of actions, determines their significance, and interprets them. Referent then plans his/her own line of action accordingly, again using symbols. In this joint action, lines of behavior are built up with respect to the lines of action of others. Actions are developed in the light of referent's activities, obviously with continual and pervasive adjustments (Blummer, 1961).

Beyond the initializing trust levels in the exchange relationship, trust becomes a dynamic, cyclical, and reciprocal phenomenon. It pivots on the development of appropriate signals, the suitable use of those signals, the appropriate interpretation and reading of signals received, and the generation and production of appropriate response signals in return.

In the exchange relationship dynamic, symbols provide the vehicle for trust signaling. Focal and referent attribute meanings to objects, gestures, and behaviors and use these as the basis for their beliefs regarding partner credibility and benevolence. The identification and production of significant symbols results simultaneously from self-interaction and joint activity. To be effective, both focal and referent must participate. In this co-orientation and cooperative, consensual signal production, what sort of behaviors, gestures and objects amplify into significant symbols of trust or trustworthiness? What behaviors by referent suggest to focal that referent can be trusted? What behaviors by focal might suggest to referent that focal does indeed hold strong positive beliefs about the credibility and benevolence of referent?

In a study of trust dynamics, the authors conducted 27 in-depth interviews with managers in interfirm exchange relationships. The trust signaling behaviors most frequently mentioned by the managers involved role performance, or more precisely role expansion, and incidences of exchange partners, not only delivering on promises, but also delivering more than expected in the exchange. Managers indicated that concession in negotiation could serve as trust-signaling symbols, as well as the resolution of conflict incidences in ways that result in both procedural and outcome justice. Forbearance in the wielding of power even when warranted seemed to act as a powerful symbol in trust augmentation. The existence of recourse and voice mechanisms in the relationship also represents symbols that signal trust. Partner accommodation and flexibility in times of crises or changes seemed especially important trust symbols. In addition, strong information sharing signaled trust and trustworthiness in exchange relationships. Consistent with these findings, related research indicates that trust-signaling symbols involve behaviors suggestive of openness and receptivity in communication patterns, fairness and discretion in interactions (Butler, 1991).

Despite the variety in exchange relationships and signaling behaviors, significant symbols often derive from routine activities and role performance in exchange relationships. Though apparently small, because of their frequency and consistency, these symbols accrue as powerful trust signals, constantly augmenting and reinforcing beliefs of partner credibility and benevolent intentions. Conversely, in non-routine critical incidents (e.g., crises), supportive behaviors can directly convert to symbols signaling trust in a powerful way. These critical incidences are serendipitous and unlike symbols in the day-to-day routine of the relationship, not readily evoked. However, they may be as or even more powerful. In either case, it is critical that the symbols are co-developed and accepted as significant by all in the exchange relationship.

Mastery of trust symbol production and use allows exchange partners to deliberately nurture and evoke trust. In interactions, indications embedded with trust signals are constantly being transmitted. For trust strengthening, participants must recognize a suitable occasion for trust signaling, then construct the trust message; the fitting symbol(s) needs to be embedded in the indications and lines of action. Some occasions may warrant stronger signals to produce the desired trust response. Thus, ineffective signaling may be a matter of an incorrect symbol, an inappropriately weak signal, or failure to recognize an appropriate signaling occasion. To complicate this further, symbols evolve and change constantly, and new symbols are constantly introduced (Blummer, 1961; Couch, 1989).

In the interaction process, focal uses appropriate symbols at appropriate occasions to telegraph the trust message which is interpreted by referent. In turn, referent selects symbols that embody the suitable responding signal and indicates his/her own lines of action. Simultaneously, referent's lines of action often undergo realignment and signals must be modified to accommodate new symbols or altered interpretation. With their symbol usage and lines of action, both focal and referent attempt to induce a certain preferred response from the partner, specifically the augmentation of beliefs in credibility and benevolence suggestive of an increased willingness to assume vulnerability. The line of action and indications are formulated not only in response to past signaling, but in anticipation of the partner's next line of action. This formative mutual realignment involves not only responding but also prefiguring one another's responses. The notion of reciprocity may be useful in understanding the formative dynamic in strengthening trust (Gouldner, 1960). For example, Johnson, Cullen, Sakano, and Takiuchi (1997) found some evidence of reciprocity in trust. Focal's trust generated trust on the part of referent and vice versa.

Importantly, as with all patterns in social interactions, trust is not self-supporting. It depends on recurrent affirmation through appropriate signaling (Blummer, 1961). If these sustaining and reinforcing signals are disrupted, beliefs regarding partner credibility and benevolence will not strengthen. In the extreme, failed or ineffective signaling can neutralize trust. In this case of trust absence, even the initiating trust levels may have been undermined by the lack of affirmation. Though it should not be confused with distrust which is the explicit expectation of negative outcomes, the absence of trust or trust neutrality has serious implications in exchange relationships (Lewicki, McAllister, and Bies, 1998). Absence of trust suggests low expectation or hopelessness of positive outcomes. Unless there are mitigating conditions, such as extreme dependence and no other source for making exchange, the relationship can be jeopardized.

Though little is known about trust durability and degradation in exchange relationships, some evidence suggests that time is a factor. If trust is buttressed by strong bases and by other conditions such as interdependence, or some levels of motivational investment, it may take longer periods of diminished or ineffective signaling to degrade it and the degradation may be less. In addition, the strength of trust before periods of neglect, ineffective signaling, or even betrayal mitigates the damage (Robinson, 1996).

As we noted, exchange happens between a variety of entities involving direct and often repeated interaction that can take place at fairly intimate and proximate levels. However, commercial exchange may not involve this intimacy and direct interaction. For example, when focal is a consumer purchasing a bag of potato chips, referent, who may be considered as the maker of the product or as the product's brand identity (Keller, 1998), is quite distant. Even with repeated exchange, the relationship dynamic is absent in any real sense; the ability to signal trust is constrained and minimal. Further, while focal's trusting of referent is crucial in the exchange, referent apparently does not need to trust focal. We label this situation as apparently unilateral trust.

While there is no apparent trust signaling between focal and referent in unilateral trust situations, we suggest that recurrent affirmation comes in the form of referent's continued and consistent delivery on expectations and keeping of promises. For example, when the product continually delivers on performance expectations, it is a signal of trust. Focal's belief in referent's credibility strengthens through this process. Similarly, in product failure, by moving to correct the failure and reduce focal's disappointment, referent can reinforce focal's belief in referent's credibility, as Johnson and Johnson's skillful response to the Tylenol scare demonstrated.

CULTURE

Previous chapters in this volume summarized the cross-cultural frameworks developed by Geert Hofstede and Fons Trompenaars. Some of the dimensions and descriptions of culture overlap among the various treatments and with related work (Kluckhohn and Strodtbeck, 1961; Triandis, 1995). However, each cultural dimensional classification, briefly described below, offers some unique and valuable perspective that adds to our discussion.

In his study of 53 nations, Hofstede developed cultural dimensions based on individual values and beliefs about work in organizations. Yet the basic notions can be extended to a variety of exchange situations. Hofstede's dimensions of national culture include power distance, uncertainty avoidance, masculinity, individualism versus collectivism and long-term orientation.

Power distance deals with the cultural expectation of equality among people. High power distance means that authority is accepted and that inequality is preferred. Those in leadership positions or in the upper echelons of society should have more privileges than others. Importantly, the power and privileges of the superiors should not be hidden. In contrast, low power distance suggests that class differences are not good. No group or person is inherently entitled to any more privilege than others. A boss may supervise work but is no better than anyone else and has no particular difference outside of the immediate work situation (Hofstede, 1980a; Cullen, 1999).

Uncertainty avoidance concerns cultural tendencies with regard to how people respond to what is risky or dangerous and what is different. High uncertainty avoidance means that there is only a very limited tolerance for ambiguity and that people avoid change and risk. Conformity and consensus are important in uncertainty avoidance. Because it brings uncertainty, risk, and ambiguity, conflict is not viewed favorably. Low uncertainty cultures tolerate change, ambiguity, and risk. Likewise, conflict is seen as a normal course of events and not hugely disturbing (Hofstede, 1980a; Cullen, 1999).

Masculinity addresses the tendency to emphasize and value traditional gender roles, and to tend toward strong distinctions between traditional male and female roles. Machismo is valued. Men are expected to be more assertive and dominant. Expectations about what is accepted in a man's behavior versus what is expected in a woman's behavior are relatively strong (Hofstede, 1980a; Cullen, 1999). Low masculinity cultures blur the distinction between the genders. For example, in such cultures males may be more expressive and affectionate with each other than a traditional male role might suggest.

Long-term orientation involves a cultural perspective on time that values patience and self-sacrifice. In cultures where a long-term orientation predominates thrift and saving are important. People accept that persistence over a long period is necessary to achieve goals (Chinese Culture Connection, 1987; Hofstede and Bond, 1984).

Individualism versus collectivism considers the identity of people as individuals or in relationship to a group in society (Niles, 1998). Individualistic cultures view the individual as the dominant focus. Individual achievement is valued as is responsibility for one's own actions. In individualistic cultures, people can determine their roles in and contribution to the collective. Collectivism views people not as unique individuals but in terms of group membership. Groups such as family, team, social class, and organization define the person de-emphasizing uniqueness, self-determination, and lone accomplishment (Cullen, 1999; Hofstede, 1980a; Niles, 1998; Triandis, 1995; Trompenaars, 1994; Trompenaars and Hampden-Turner, 1998).

Members of collectivist societies see themselves as part of groups and give priority to group goals (Triandis, 1995c). However, collectivist tendencies can nest in a hierarchical fashion and come into play at different levels of social activity or groups. In certain situations, the relevant group where collectivist tendencies activate is the family. In other situations, collectivism is activated at the employer firm level. In yet still other situations, the nation is the relevant group.

In his study of national culture involving approximately 15,000 managers, Trompenaars, (1994; Trompenaars and Hampden-Turner, 1998) used the five relational orientations proposed by Talcott Parsons (1951) as dimensions along which culture varies. One of the dimensions offered by Trompenaars, individualism vs. collectivism, was developed earlier by Hofstede and discussed above. Trompenaars (1994; Trompenaars and Hampden-Turner, 1998) also developed some conclusions on cultural variance in terms of orientations toward time and toward the environment. However, these seem less relevant to trust in exchange so we do not include them here.

Four other dimensions of culture used by Trompenaars include: universalism versus particularism, neutral versus emotional, specific versus diffuse, achievement versus ascription.

Universalism suggests that there are rules or appropriate and acceptable ways of doing things and we look to those rules and ways in all situations. The opposite end of the continuum is particularism: attention is on the unique situation and relationship at hand. In particularistic orientations, rules may be in place and fully recognized but exceptions can always be made for friends, family, etc. Exceptions are not only tolerated and accepted, but to no small extent, expected. The focus is on situation-to-situation judgments and the exceptional nature of circumstances as they change (Trompenaars, 1994; Trompenaars and Hampden-Turner, 1998).

The neutral versus emotional dimension of culture concerns the acceptability of expressing emotions. With a neutral orientation, interactions are objective, detached and task-focused. It emphasizes achieving objectives without the messy interference of emotions. In contrast, with an emotional orientation, all forms of emotion are appropriate in almost all situations. Expressions of anger, laughter, gesturing, and a range of emotional outbursts are considered normal and acceptable. The natural and preferred way is to find an immediate outlet for emotions (Trompenaars, 1994; Trompenaars and Hampden-Turner, 1998).

Specific versus diffuse addresses the extent to which an individual is involved in their business relationships as a person. When the tendency is for an individual to have a very limited, task and objectively focused relationship, the culture is considered to have a specific orientation. Written contracts frequently prescribe and delineate such specific relationships. In a specific-oriented culture, business is segregated from other parts of life. Parties in exchange know each other, but the knowing is very limited and for limited purposes. Conversely, in diffuse-oriented cultures, business or exchange relationships are more encompassing and involving. In diffuse-oriented cultures, the preference is for an involvement of multiple areas and levels of life simultaneously; truly private and segregated spaces in life are quite small. In doing business, the parties come to know each other personally and more thoroughly, and become acquainted with each other across a variety of life's dimensions and levels (Trompenaars, 1994; Trompenaars, and Hampden-Turner, 1998).

The dimension identified as achievement versus ascription addresses the manner by which status is accorded. In achievement-oriented cultures, status is earned by an individual's performance and accomplishments. In contrast, when a culture is ascription-oriented, various inherent characteristics or associations ascribe status. For example, the vehicles for ascription often include schools or universities attended or age. In ascription-oriented situations, titles and their frequent usage play a large part in interactions (Trompenaars, 1994; Trompenaars and Hampden-Turner, 1998).

Edward Hall (1966, 1976, 1983; Hall and Hall, 1990) isolated another aspect of cultural variance attached to language and communication in the culture, high versus low context. In low-context cultures, people state things directly and explicitly. Often these cultures rely on languages with words that have specific and exact meanings; frequently a word or term has only one meaning. In contrast, in high-context cultures, the attendant conditions surrounding a specific situation provide much of the meaning to communication. Much communication is nonverbal, indirect and implicit. It can be interpreted only in the context of the situation. In high-context cultures, languages tend to have words with multiple meanings. No meaning can be attached to these words without understanding the situation surrounding their usage (Cullen, 1999).

CULTURE'S ROLE IN THE BASES AND EVOLUTION OF TRUST

In this section, we use our general model of trust and the three frameworks developed by Hofstede, Trompenaars, and Hall to consider cross-cultural differences in trust. We examine cultural differences for trust between actors from within the same culture and for trust between actors from different cultures (across culture). Where possible, our presentation uses past empirical research and new analyses of cross-national data.

Unfortunately, the research body addressing cross-cultural trust is sparse in three areas. A review of the trust literature (see Kramer, 1999 and Ross and LaCroix, 1996, for other recent reviews) shows little empirical study of the influences of national culture on trust: (1) using more than two or three cultural dimensions from any of the accepted systems of cultural dimensions or classifications; (2) using more than two-country comparisons; and (3) emphasizing intercultural exchange. Consequently, we are forced to draw inferences based on two-country comparisons or offer selected observations and extensions based on theory and single nation research.

As noted above, the dispositional bases of trust refer to the enduring tendencies that actors bring to exchange regarding trust. These include a general trust in people regardless of the relationship and trust of more distal entities such as the government or a product. In this section, we consider evidence that some national cultures have value systems that predispose actors to trust others. That is, we examine research that shows cultural differences in the general attribution of referent as trustworthy. Trustworthiness is focal's belief that referent has internalized norms and values that lead them to behave credibly and benevolently.

The common hypothesis is that more individualistic societies, with their focus on self-interested behavior rather than what benefits the group (Earley, 1989; Triandis, 1989), have values that promote opportunism or self-interested behavior with guile (Williamson, 1996). Symbolic statements such as "let the buyer beware" seem to support this cultural value in societies such as the US. Alternatively, collectivist cultures with their strong in-group ties and long-term relationships often are presumed to have a stronger predisposition for trust, especially toward in-group members. Such logic leads some trust theorists to offer the hypothesis that people from individualistic cultures enter relationships expecting opportunism and thus have low trust expectations (Doney, Cannon, and Mullen, 1998).

However, alternative theoretical reasoning (e.g., Yamagishi 1988a, 1988b) and most, but not all (e.g., Hemesath and Pomponio, 1998), of the empirical evidence (e.g., Yamagishi, Cook, and Watabe, 1998) suggests the opposite. That is, the counter-conclusion is that people from individualistic cultures are generally more predisposed to trust than people from collectivist cultures. For example, Yamagishi (1988a, 1988b; Yamagishi and Yamagishi, 1994) found that US Americans, representing a highly individualistic culture, tended to have significantly higher basic trust levels than the Japanese, representing a highly collectivist culture. With parallel implications, Kim and Son (1998) reported similar findings for Koreans and US Americans. Interestingly, the evidence suggesting that people from individualistic cultures have a higher predisposition to trust than people from collectivist cultures is quite robust and seems to consistently hold, at least when the US is compared with Japan, Korea, and China. One hypothesis, offered as an explanation, suggests that trust for people in general (predispositional basis) is too diffuse a target for people in collectivist cultures. People from cultures that make strong distinctions between in-groups and out-groups may require a more specific trust referent. However, the evidence discussed below disputes this alternative.

Zhang (1990; see also Zhang and Bond 1993) examined the effects of the trust referent's proximity to focal on focal's general tendency to trust. He tested whether or not focal's general tendency to trust differed if referent was from an in-group or an out-group for US Americans, PRC Chinese, and Hong Kong Chinese. His results indicated that US Americans and Hong Kong Chinese did not differ from each other in their basic levels of trust for in-groups (e.g., intimates or acquaintances) or out-groups (strangers).

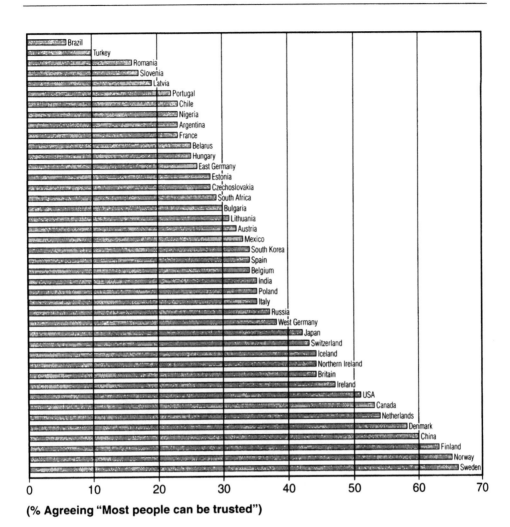

(% Agreeing "Most people can be trusted")

FIGURE 17.2 Levels of general trust in people

Subjects from the People's Republic of China, however, had a higher trust of acquaintances and strangers than Hong Kong Chinese and US Americans. Overall, this study
supports the positive relationship between individualistic cultural orientations and the
predisposition to trust.

Research by the World Values Study Group (1994; Inglehart, Basañez, and Moreno,
1998) provides perhaps the most comprehensive information, in terms of number of
countries considered, on cultural values regarding predisposition to trust. The World
Values Survey (WVS) contains interview data on 45 societies (not all of which are nation
states) and is based on national random or quota sampling of adults 18 and over with a
total *n* of nearly 90,000. Data were gathered by local professional survey research
companies or survey research institutions (Inglehart, 1994). Detailed information on the

research procedures is available in Inglehart (1994; Inglehart, Basañez, and Moreno, 1998) and will not be repeated here.

To provide additional information of cross-cultural differences in trust dispositions we reanalyzed the WVS data focusing on questions related to trust. As an indicator of general predisposition to trust, the WVS asked respondents whether they agreed to the statement: "Generally speaking, would you say that most people can be trusted or that you can't be too careful in dealing with people?" The dichotomous response categories were: "Most people can be trusted" and "Can't be too careful." Figure 17.2 shows the percentage of respondents in each society responding that "Most people can be trusted."

Nordic countries had the highest predisposition to trust. Consistent with most previous research and arguments by Yamagishi and his colleagues, the US ranked ahead of the more collectivist countries of Japan and South Korea. However, China had levels of general trust similar to the Nordic countries.

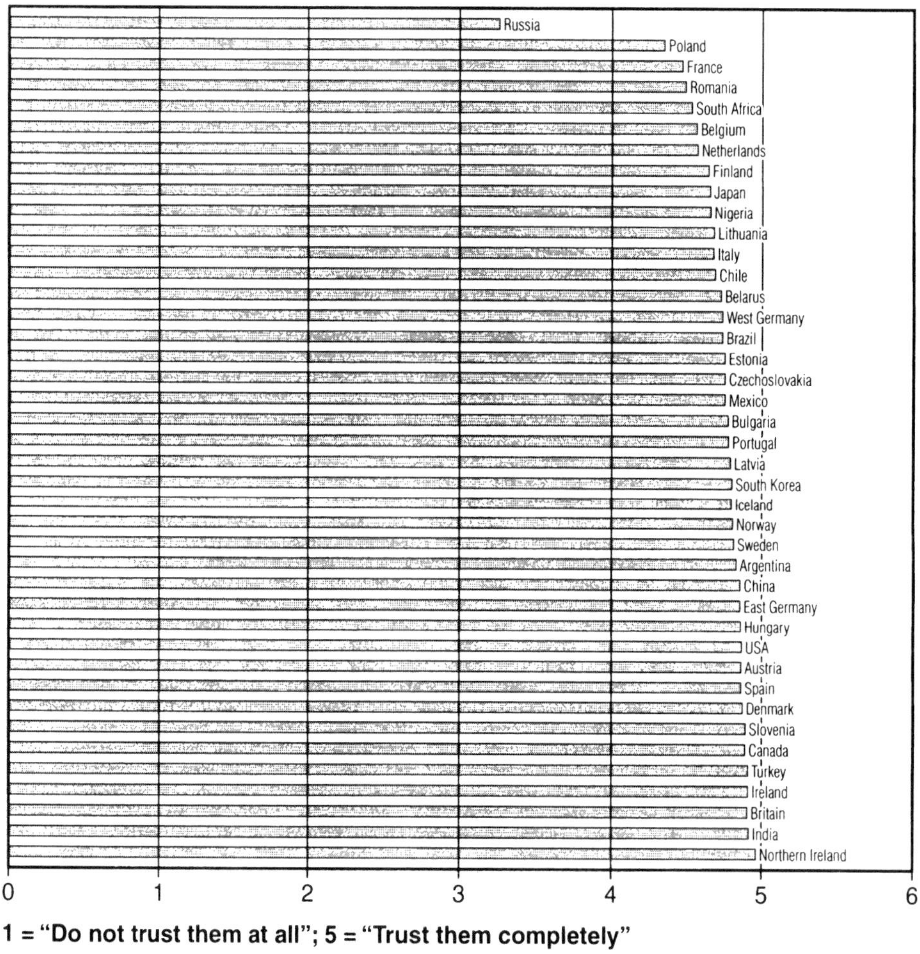

1 = "Do not trust them at all"; 5 = "Trust them completely"

FIGURE 17.3 Trust of family

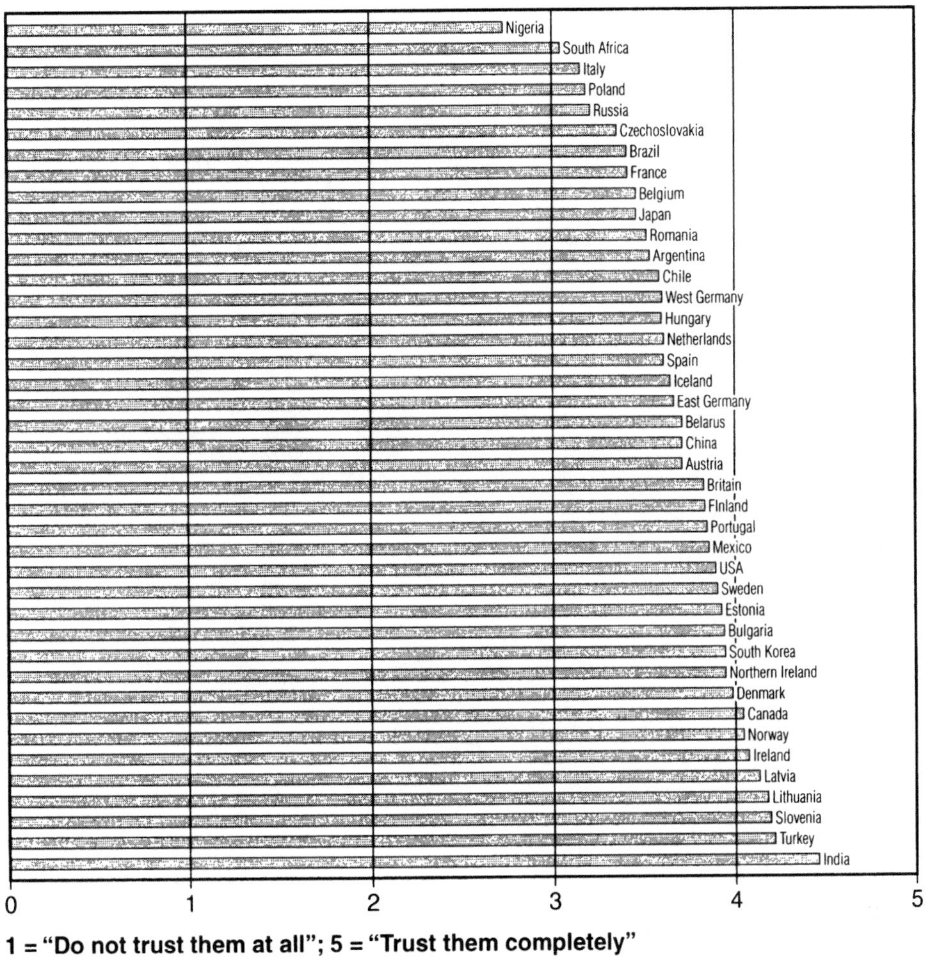

Nigeria
South Africa
Italy
Poland
Russia
Czechoslovakia
Brazil
France
Belgium
Japan
Romania
Argentina
Chile
West Germany
Hungary
Netherlands
Spain
Iceland
East Germany
Belarus
China
Austria
Britain
Finland
Portugal
Mexico
USA
Sweden
Estonia
Bulgaria
South Korea
Northern Ireland
Denmark
Canada
Norway
Ireland
Latvia
Lithuania
Slovenia
Turkey
India

0   1   2   3   4   5

1 = "Do not trust them at all"; 5 = "Trust them completely"

FIGURE 17.4 Trust of people from own country

Following the initial logic of the Zhang (1990) study, we also reasoned that general tendencies to trust might vary by culture depending on the trust referent, specifically whether the trust referent was in-group or out-group. Consequently, using a larger number of countries, we wanted to verify Zhang's counterintuitive findings that trust predisposition, even with a specific referent, may be lower in collectivist cultures.

Figures 17.3 and 17.4 show trust levels from the WVS data for "trust of family members" and "trust of countrymen" (*sic*), respectively. Similar to Zhang's (1990) findings, the WVS data also counter the stereotype of more collectivist cultures having higher levels of in-group trust. For example, respondents from the US ranked their trust of family above that of people from China, Japan, and South Korea and their trust of people from their own country above Japan and China.

In summary, past research and the WVS indicate that the prototypical individualist

TABLE 17.1 Correlations among levels of trust and dimensions of culture

	General trust	Trust of family	Trust of countrymen	Power distance	Uncertainty avoidance	Hofstede's individualism	Masculinity	Long-term orientation	High context	Universalism	Trompenaars' individualism
Trust of family	0.068										
Trust of countrymen	0.201	0.506									
Power distance	0.513	0.202	0.108								
Uncertainty avoidance	0.688	0.368	0.415	0.389							
Hofstede's individualism	-0.501	0.090	0.025	-0.661	-0.340						
Masculinity	0.343	-0.040	0.262	0.056	0.198	0.043					
Long-term orientation	0.181	0.279	0.240	0.768	0.393	-0.880	-0.309				
High context	0.610	0.183	0.373	0.839	0.813	-0.724	0.149	0.813			
Universalism	-0.409	-0.350	-0.138	-0.833	-0.548	0.796	-0.194	-0.841	-0.843		
Trompenaars' individualism	-0.180	-0.323	-0.389	0.421	0.017	-0.294	-0.058	0.409	0.322	-0.172	
Achievement	-0.396	-0.159	-0.332	-0.133	-0.485	0.549	-0.246	-0.827	-0.213	0.401	-0.080

culture (the US) has higher levels of trust than the prototypical collectivist cultures of Japan, China, and Korea (opposite to stereotypical image of collectivist cultures being more trusting). As the figures show, this finding is true whether the trust referent is people in general, family members, people from the same country, or in-group members or out-group members.

Beyond individualism/collectivism, however, we have little systematic evidence on whether any of the other nine cultural dimensions influence dispositionally based trust. To shed some light on this issue, we examined country-level correlations of selected cultural dimensions with the trust measures from the WVS discussed previously. Table 17.1 shows these correlations with pairwise deletion of missing data.

In developing the correlations in table 17.1, we used the same country-level trust data from the WVS as those reported in the figures. In table 17.1, information on power distance, uncertainty avoidance, masculinity, and individualism and long-term orientation dimension came from Hofstede (1991). Data on long-term orientation was available for the fewest countries. A simple classification of high context (coded 1) low context (coded 0) was derived from the work of Hall (1976). For the Trompenaars dimensions, we used selected rankings from his 1994 book to assign scores to countries on achievement orientation, universalism, and individualism. When Trompenaars had more than one indicator for a cultural dimension he chose not to combine the questions into one index. Thus, some countries have different ranking depending on the question used, and not all countries have data on the same questions. To optimize WVS information, we chose to examine the cultural dimensions using Trompenaars' indicators that had the greatest overlap with our sample of countries from the WVS. The number of countries used to estimate correlations ranged from 9 to 41.

Table 17.1 indicates that general predisposition to trust is higher in countries with high uncertainty avoidance. That is, people in cultures more oriented to needs for stability and change, as well as lack of conflict, seem more predisposed to trust in general. Table 17.1 also shows that high power distance correlates with the predisposition to trust. In cultures where people prefer to have explicit vertical alignment of power in place, they apparently have more of a tendency to trust. In addition, high context language correlates with predispositions to trust. In cultures where communication is not explicit and clearcut, but instead relies on the attendant conditions, people tend to be more trusting in general. Finally, the data indicate that, when trusting involves a specific referent as opposed to the general predisposition, cultural differences do not seem to play a significant role, at least as referent-focused trust is measured here.

The correlations in table 17.1 provide further information on the controversy of the collectivism–trust predisposition hypothesis. In contrast to the US–Japan comparison discussed above, the WVS data suggest that the traditional hypothesis of a relationship between collectivism and a propensity to trust does have some general support. Individualism correlates negatively with the three measures of trust. This finding is stronger for Hofstede's measure of individualism than for the measure derived from the Trompenaars study. Thus, these data and previous findings suggest that, while the general hypothesis regarding the greater propensity to trust among collectivist cultures seems true, it may not apply to the US and Japanese.

The uncertainty avoidance and high-context cultural dimensions produced the most consistent relationships with the predisposition to trust. The positive correlations of uncertainty avoidance and high context with the three forms of trust (trust in general, of family members, and of members of the same national culture) hold even when individualism is partialed out. Thus, given these data and earlier findings regarding unexpectedly high levels of trust in some societies, we suspect that the collectivism/individualism continuum may not be the best cultural source of differences in trust dispositions. Taken overall, the evidence suggests to us that researchers should look to the dimensions of uncertainty avoidance and high/low context to understand cultural influences on the predisposition basis of trust rather than to individualism–collectivism.

Further, in our discussion of the bases of trust, we suggested that they work in tandem, reinforce one another, and generally relate in complex ways. Theory suggests that this may be especially relevant in understanding instrumental-calculus and institutional bases of trust cross-culturally. Although our model of trust suggests that instrumental-calculus should figure into any actor's trust of a referent, there is little cross-cultural evidence to suggest whether or not utilitarian rationality varies by culture. However, we suspect that the distinction between the form and content of the reasoning may be relevant in understanding possible cultural differences. By form of reasoning we mean that actors use the same format or logic to reach the decision to trust (i.e., the benefits of trust offset the costs of betrayal). By content of reasoning we mean that actors, even when using the same form of logic, consider different contextual factors to reach the decision to trust. Moreover, these contextual factors may be quite different in different cultural settings. For example, a guarantee of product delivery on time may lead one company to trust another. However, the context of that certainty may come from law, tradition, trading group sanctions, etc. Thus, content involves the role of institutional bases of trust in different cultures. Government, law, family, educational system, and patterns of relationships based on age, gender, caste, etc. form the institutional framework of a society.

We believe, and the evidence seems to support the proposition that social institutions generally arise to facilitate trust. That is, social institutions help reduce the uncertainty of interactions and lead to stable patterns of interaction in all forms (Luhmann, 1979). There is no requirement that societies use the same social institutions, but there must exist a functional equivalence (Merton, 1968) to provide base levels of trust. Rational actors then consider these institutions as factors in their calculations of whether or not and how much to trust (Coleman, 1990). Thus different characteristics of social institutions in various cultures result in different content used for utilitarian rational reasoning, which provides the bases of trust in various cultures. The work of Yamagishi and his colleagues illustrates this process through theoretical argument and extensive empirical research from cross-cultural experiments and survey research.

Yamagishi argues that Japanese trust rests on a mutual assurance based on institutionalized long-standing business and personal relationships. However, US Americans often begin with the assumption of trust. Their assurance rests on the further assumption that, if violated, the formal social institutions such as the legal and political systems will enforce trust. For example, the United States, on a per capita basis, jails more corporate executives and penalizes more corporations financially than all other Western nations in combination (Carroll and Gannon, 1997).

The distinction between internal sanctions based on long-standing business or personal relationships and formal sanctions helps to explain how both social institutional systems, though different, can lead to trust in relationships. Consider a recent experiment by

Yamagishi and his colleagues (Yamagishi, Cook, and Watabe, 1998). The experiment showed that Japanese and US Americans had no differences in their formation of committed relationships, once the level of general trust and the degree of social uncertainty were controlled. Yamagishi concludes that committed social relationships based on mutual monitoring and sanctioning seemed to reduce uncertainty in Japan. His theoretical reasoning apparently builds on the observations of Japan by the anthropologist Ruth Benedict (1946). She noted that collectivist societies build social institutions that emphasize mutual monitoring and control through shame while societies such as the US have social institutions (legal and religion) that emphasize individual responsibility and guilt. Thus, the rational actor in Japanese society need not view referent as trustworthy in order to trust. Instead, the pattern of mutually committed personal relationships is so powerful that focal can be assured and form beliefs regarding referent's behaviors and intent without the assumption of the referent's trustworthiness. Different substantively, yet functionally equivalent, the rational actor in the US can begin with the assumption of trust and rely on social institutions with controls such as the sanctity of contract to safeguard against violations of initial trust.

The recent experiment by Hayashi, Ostrom, Walker, and Yamagishi (1999) further illustrates this stream of reasoning. As with much of the Yamagishi research, the Hayashi et al. (1999) experiment uses the classic prisoner's dilemma game to examine mutual cooperation under conditions that require trust. The structure of the two-person prisoner's dilemma provides a payoff for mutual cooperation (the win–win strategy) that is greater than mutual defection (the lose–lose strategy). However, the largest payoff goes to the partner who defects when the other partner cooperates (the win–lose strategy). Thus, the "dominating strategy" for the two-person prisoner's dilemma is mutual defection or deficit equilibrium (Kollock, 1998). The dominating strategy is the one that leads to the most "rational" outcome for the individual regardless if all are hurt by this strategy. Hence, prisoner's dilemma is a useful game for pitting Western individual rationality against collectivist decision-making norms (or the Japanese version of these norms).

Specifically, Hayashi et al. (1999) replicated an earlier study of the Japanese (Watabe et al., 1996), except with data from US Americans to provide a cross-cultural comparison. The important manipulation in the study was whether partner 2 would know the results of partner 1's decision before making his or her decision. Without any knowledge of their partner's move, 38 percent of the US subjects cooperated while only 12 percent of the Japanese subjects cooperated. Hayashi et al. (1999) attributed this finding to the generally higher levels of US propensity to trust. When the Japanese subjects made their decisions with the knowledge that their partners would learn of their choice, 83 percent choose cooperation as compared to 56 percent of the US Americans. Why is there this radical shift in trust in conditions that Hayashi et al. consider "logically similar" since there is no real control over a partner's behavior? Apparently, understanding that the partner will know one's behavior taps into the structural expectations of cooperation in Japanese society. These researchers suggest that communication of one's behavior creates an illusion of control based on the strong Japanese social institution of assured mutual cooperation.

In conclusion, the enormous amount of research by Yamagishi and colleagues since the 1990s demonstrates that the instrumental-calculus basis for trust probably combines and works in tandem with institutionalized beliefs regarding referent's behaviors and intentions. Such beliefs arise from long-standing personal and business relationships. Taken together, this body of evidence suggests that we can expect similar findings in other collectivist cultures regarding the role of long-standing relationships as a source of trust through the limits and constraints they place on undesirable behaviors of referent.

Although less extensive, research on the particularistic ties of *guanxi* or "connections" in Chinese societies indicates that long-standing personal and family relationships play a significant role as a basis of trust in that culture. These deeply embedded and important mutual commitment networks act as institutional checks and balances on the behaviors of trust referents, providing focal with assurances so that trust happens. Work by Earley (1993) showed the salience in China of provincial origin and kinship as a basis of *guanxi*. Tsui and Farh (1997) found that *guanxi* contacts were more important in work relationships than were other demographic similarities. Similarly, Farh, Tsui, Xiz, and Cheng (1998) found effects of *guanxi* on trust in both vertical superior/subordinate dyads and business associations among Chinese executives. These findings were supported in both Taiwan and the PRC. The effects for *guanxi* were stronger in business relationships than in other relationships. The bases of *guanxi* were relatives, former classmates, and same place of birth. *Guanxi* may be important for the choice of a relationship partner (Farh, et al., 1998) thus suggesting that relationship patterns factor into the calculus of deciding whether to take the risk of trusting (Kiong and Kee, 1998).

Other evidence on the effects of long-standing relationships on trust comes from more macro-level research studying inter-firm relationships. Lane and Bachmann (1997) found that the trade associations in Germany lead to more trust between firms because they foster the development of long-standing systematic technical norms and business standards practices. In contrast, British trade associations are more fragmented, develop less standardized relationships and, in turn, have lower trust in inter-firm relationships.

In addition, there is almost no research on which we can draw to consider the cross-cultural differences in the situational bases of trust. However, we believe that many of the arguments developed above for cultural differences in instrumental-calculus also apply to specific trust situations. Yamagishi argues that Japanese society is built on stable and mutually committed relationships. These patterns of relationships provide assurance through checks and constraints on behaviors. This security blanket provides assurance of benevolence and performance that is a functional equivalent to trustworthiness of a partner. Deterrence-calculus based trust focuses on the presence of credible commitment and hostages. Cultures with strong networked relationships, which involve demonstrated past commitments, have in many ways an institutionalized system of credible commitments. That is, the Japanese, and perhaps other collectivist societies, use deterrence-calculus in a relatively more routine way than individualistic societies to constrain the undesirable behaviors of referent and allow for trust by focal.

Although reputation can be important in exchange transactions in low-context cultures (Frombrun, 1996), we believe that reputation may be even more important as a basis of trust in high-context cultures. For example, people in all cultures make unsecured transactions on the basis of reputation. Consider a transaction with a professional or technician such as a physician or electrician. In this situation, reputation provides information beyond formal credentials on the expected performance. However, in a high-context culture the attendant information and conditions associated with an interaction is a larger component of the information available. If one accepts that reputation is largely part of the attendant conditions of the exchange, then it may play a larger role as a basis of trust in high-context cultures.

In high power distance societies we expect that experience may be a more important situational basis of trust. In this particular application, we see experience with particular roles, and thus role based trust, as key. When focal has some experience or has learned what to expect from a certain group of referents, i.e. a certain role, focal can more readily act on beliefs about the referents' credibility and benevolence. Since high power distance societies recognize positional authority by roles (e.g., father, boss), past experience with particular roles brings mutual expectations. If the focal holds a position of lower status than the referent, then the expectation is often that superior owes the subordinate benevolence in return for loyalty (Hofstede, 1991).

We expect three situational bases of trust to behave differently in higher uncertainty avoidance societies than in lower uncertainty avoidance cultures. When a society has norms and values that support order and predictability, mechanisms such as penalty clauses in contracts that deter a violation of trust (deterrence-calculus) are attractive and harmonious with the culture. Experience with a particular referent or a role in general can also reduce uncertainty. That is, an expectation of future behavior based on past behavior is, at least in terms of probability, more certain than the risks of a virgin exchange. Reputation also adds to the information stores of the focal from the high uncertainty avoidance culture. More information in turn reduces uncertainty and increases the expectation or belief in the referent's credibility or benevolence.

In particularistic cultures, we expect the deterrence-calculus base of trust to come into play in a stronger way. Particularistic tendencies mean that rules and standards of conduct would not guide referent's exchange behavior. There would probably be a tendency toward exceptions in actions and behaviors in the conduct of exchange. Given the expectation and acceptance of exceptions in conduct, focal's beliefs of referent's credibility may be compromised. This suggests that focal may feel the need to secure the exchange with mechanisms such as hostages or credible commitments.

In our integrative model of trust, we developed several complex ideas regarding the dynamics of trust. However, most of the supporting literature for our model comes from US authors and, we presume, reflects their perspective on US culture. When one considers that most of the comparative research uses one-shot prisoner's dilemma games or cross-sectional surveys, it is not surprising that we know little of trust dynamics within different cultures. Even in the US, few studies of trust have addressed trust dynamics as conceptualized in our model and thus, we know very little about trust signaling in the US American culture.

A related issue to the evolution of trust within different cultures involves the evolution of trust across cultures though inter-cultural exchanges. Here we believe the issues of encoding and decoding symbolic signals of trust become crucial. Again, this is an area of limited research on trust, but is an area that might be informed by the cross-cultural negotiation and communication research (see Gelfand and McCusker, this volume). We will now use some of this literature to illustrate how our model might apply in different cultural situations and interactions.

Cross-cultural encoding and decoding are basic components of all communication. They are also points in the communication process that lead to a miscommunication or a breakdown in cross-cultural communication. Language, verbal, and nonverbal communication patterns differ by culture and affect the ability of the sender and receiver to properly interpret a message (Gudykunst and Ting-Toomey, 1988). Given that many of these same verbal and nonverbal communications serve as trust signaling symbols in the cross-cultural exchange relationship, it is easy to see how trust dynamics could go awry. Fox (1997) even speculated that completely valid cross-cultural communication between people from disparate cultural backgrounds may be impossible.

Communication factors, such as discreetness, openness, and receptivity, have been cited as trust signals. Negotiation researchers see these signals as motivating conditions for successful negotiations (Ross and LaCroix, 1996). The assumption that such behaviors or communications signal trust is far from a viable assumption in across-culture situations. Part of the formative social interactions involving trust augmentation is the production of trust signals as well as their appropriate interpretation and use. This means that participants in a relationship must mutually develop and agree on what behavior, activity, or gesture in the relationship serves as a trust signal. When viewed through the lens of cultural differences, the production of effective across-culture trust signals may be even more problematic than their appropriate use.

The negotiation literature is filled with warnings and examples of what can go wrong with misunderstood signals in cross-cultural settings. For example, Graham and Herberger (1983) caution US negotiators to avoid the "John Wayne" style of independence, aggression, and directness as inappropriate for less individualistic negotiation partners. From the US perspective, being direct may be seen as an effective trust signal. In other cultures, it may signal a lack of trust or even distrust. There is no agreement and co-orientation with regard to the interpretation and production of the trust signal. Graham's (1985) classic study of negotiation differences by cultural groups found wide variance in the verbal tactics used and the type of first offers made. Many negotiation tactics that are acceptable in one culture might be considered a "dirty trick" in another culture (Adler, 1991). For example, Volkema (1998) studied perceptions of negotiation tactics for Mexicans and US Americans and found that Mexicans perceived fewer of the tactics as "ethical." Thus, in cross-cultural interactions behaviors that assume the role of significant symbols can signal unintended and sometimes destructive messages regarding trust.

Anthropological fieldwork by Lindsley (1999) provides some direct insights on the difficulties of cross-cultural signal coding and decoding regarding trust. Lindsley (1999) identified core symbols in US–Mexican interactions in border *maquiladora*. An important symbol for the Mexicans, especially those who were from the region, emphasized stability. These symbols were expressed through concepts such as "never moving" and considering "employees as fixed expenses." Fieldwork suggested that stability is particularly rooted in the family. This was reflected in perceptions of the US family with comments like Americans "have a divorce every four years." It was also reflected in the *maquiladora* through the rotation of US managers, which Mexican managers viewed as instability that had a negative effect on communication. In contrast, communication of local managers with local workers, where communication was based on lifelong knowledge and an integration of family and organizational identities, was very effective.

Signaling trust by Mexican managers was accomplished by demonstrating mutual obligation where the subordinate shows obedience and loyalty and the superior shows concern for interests of the subordinates. Lindsley (1999) concluded that trust is related to feelings of knowing and being emotionally close to the other; it builds through signs of concern for other and mutual protection of face. Signals by US managers that countered these processes and diminished trust with their Mexican colleagues and subordinates included: "saying you don't understand," "showing stress," "telling someone what to do," "telling people they are wrong," "hurting people's feelings," "confronting," and direct communication. This research recounts an example of how variance on just one cultural dimension, diffuseness (the Mexican culture) versus specificity (the US culture), can interfere with the production and use of trust-signaling symbols.

Given the great potential for misreading, either through a lack of signal production or misuse of signals in cross-cultural relationships, what does lead to successful outcomes? Research seems to suggest that the motivation to overcome the difficulties of producing, encoding, and decoding of trust signals eventually leads to trust (Porter, 1997). That is, when actors invest effort and time to communicate and are flexible to adjust to cultural differences, the behaviors involved in doing so seem to signal and strengthen trust. For example, in strategic alliance research, Aulakh, Kotabe, and Sahay (1996) found that, from the perspective of the US Americans, the expectation of a continued relationship, perceptions of partner and self-flexibility, information exchange, and social control as a monitoring mechanism enhanced trust in US joint ventures with Asian, European, and South American partners. Social control occurs through repeated interactions and the development of shared culture of the joint venture. Essentially, when partners worked hard to overcome the cultural barriers to trust, that alone was seen as a powerful trust building signal by the US Americans. Similarly, more extensive two-way communication also enhanced trust of partners in cross-border alliances representing companies from 28 countries in the international construction industry (Sarkar, Cavusgil, and Evirgen, 1997).

Research on non-equity strategic alliances by Johnson, Cullen, Sakano, and Takenouchi (1996) found that focal's cultural sensitivity led to partner trust for both US and Japanese partners. They also reported that focal trust leads to partner trust for both cultures, suggesting the existence of a trust cycle. Similarly, most experts who study business negotiations believe that trust builds through mutual feedback in a "trust cycle" (Butler, 1995; Zand, 1972). Partners often feel vulnerable in the initial stages of a relationship (Neale and Bazerman, 1992) and often begin the relationship suspicious of each other's motives. This early vulnerability and suspicion make partners tentative in their involvement in the relationship and reluctant to reveal true motives. Increased interaction reduces signaling errors and increases trust. Perhaps focal's most reliable and universally appropriate signals of trust are behaviors that show focal's trust of referent.

Negotiation researchers also posit that unreliability, unfairness, and opportunistic behavior by partners set a relationship on a path toward dissolution, called the distrust cycle (Zand, 1972). A few studies do suggest that the nature of the distrust cycle might be affected by culture (e.g., Parks and Vu, 1994). Those from cultural groups with higher levels of initial trust in prisoner's dilemma games, which is usually correlated with higher levels of dispositional trust, show less severe declines in trust in repeated plays of the game.

CONCLUSION

In concluding the cross-cultural application of our model, it is clear that there are a number of areas with extensive research support, particularly information on cross-cultural differences in the bases of trust. In contrast, other components of our trust model have little or no accompanying and supporting body of research. Thus, when we move to considerations of the relationship dynamic and trust signaling, our conclusions are necessarily much more speculative. However, we see the utility of this application as mapping out areas for future research.

In summary, this chapter presented an integrative model of trust emphasizing general and situational bases of trust and manifestations of trust. To test part of the model, we used national surveys of perceived trust in the cultural frameworks developed by Hofstede, Trompenaars and Hall. We then used the integrative model to examine related aspects of culture, such as cross-cultural negotiating. This model requires additional testing, but it does provide a framework for understanding the elusive but critical issue of trust, both within one culture and across cultures.

NOTES

1 We note that caution should be used in attributing individual behaviors, motivations, and psychological states to macro-level entities such as firms. Having said that, our perspective is that trust can happen at the collective (e.g., a firm) in the sense that a trusting climate, either intraorganizationally or interorganizationally exists. Obviously, individual managers are integral in the development, perpetuation, and enactment of such trusting climates.

2 Symbolic interactionism is a complex and sometimes controversial theoretical and methodological perspective. It is not our intent here to fully elucidate or extend any particular set of notions subsumed in symbolic interactionism. We are not necessarily proponents of naturalistic inquiry nor are we critics of it. We do not wish to suggest any particular alliance with any of the schools of thought within symbolic interactionism (e.g., the "Iowa school" or the "Chicago school"). Our goal is to use the theory as a vehicle for explaining and understanding trust-signaling phenomena in exchange relationships. We review the theory's fundamental concepts only to the extent that it serves to develop the necessary theoretical platform for extending our understanding of how trust increases.

18

Business Ethics across Cultures

DIANA C. ROBERTSON

Two Asian MBA students at a US business school are accused of a violation of the school's honor code. Despite overwhelming evidence against them, the two students refuse to admit to the transgression. US student members of the school's honor council are frustrated by this reluctance to admit guilt and feel that the penalties should be harsher because of the students' denial. The Asian students, on the other hand, are more interested in saving face. Their perspective leads them to think that denial is more honorable, and hence more ethical, than confession.

Whose ethics prevail in this situation? And, more importantly, whose ethics *should* prevail? If the Asian students choose future employment with US firms, will they and should they adhere to US ethical standards? If they work for Asian firms, will they and should they follow the norms of Asian business ethics? If they work for a US multinational firm in their home country, will they and *could* they somehow seek to combine the ethics of the two cultures?

Such questions fall under the domain of research on business ethics, and more specifically, under that of international business ethics. The study of business ethics is concerned with what is right and wrong, and thus is an inquiry into what we ought and ought not to do in the conduct of business (DeGeorge, 1999). It is an application of moral values to complex problems. Business ethics is interested both in the rules that govern business activities and in the values embedded in the practice of business.

The field of business ethics is relatively young, having grown and become more prominent since the 1970s. During that time, increasing numbers of business schools have offered both elective and required courses in ethics, and a body of research has been established with several journals devoted to the topic. As Stark noted in 1993, signs of the "ethics boom" abound. At that time, 90 percent of US business schools offered some course or module in ethics, and three academic journals featured articles exclusively on the topic. More recently, an indicator of the expansion of interest in the topic of business ethics is the growing number of websites (predominantly US) devoted to the subject.

By contrast, the more specialized field of international business ethics is less fully formed. Examination of business ethics journals reveals a relative dearth of articles on international issues. Nearly all the data are generated in the United States. Similarly, international business journals, such as the *Journal of International Business Studies* and the *Columbia Journal of World Business*, publish relatively few articles on business ethics. One can even question whether a field of international business ethics exists. The fact that the question can be raised suggests that there remains a great deal of work to be done in this area.

At the same time, however, there does appear to be increasing recognition among business ethicists of the importance of including international topics in their research. For example, a special issue of *Business Ethics Quarterly* in 1997 addressed the growing interconnectedness of ethical matters between international and domestic business. Similarly, a special issue of the *Journal of Business Ethics* in 1999 focused on the subject of international marketing ethics. Articles in the *Journal of Business Ethics* in 1999 included topics as far ranging as employee attitudes in Croatia (Goic), ethics sensitivity and awareness in organizations in Kuwait (Al-Kazemi and Zajac), ethical behavior in South Africa (Van Zyl and Lazenby), and contemporary views of business ethics in China (Harvey).

As the study of international business ethics develops, more fundamental underlying questions need to be addressed. Most importantly, what do we mean by international business ethics? A broad definition of international business ethics includes cross-national research in which comparisons are made between ethics in two or more countries. This definition suggests that the focus of international business ethics research must be comparative. Additionally, should there even be a field of international business ethics? If so, what is its mission? Do scholars today hold a coherent vision of the future of the field? If we could look ahead thirty years to a field of international business ethics encompassing business school courses and journals, what would we want to see included and excluded, and what would we want to see as the focus?

Answers to some of the most intriguing and key questions in business ethics (considered nationally, but not internationally) are not yet known. Do people behave ethically because of their individual upbringing or do certain situations bring about ethical (and unethical) behavior? Why do some people consistently tell the truth in the workplace, whereas others will bend the truth to their own advantage? Why are some people tempted by the potential monetary rewards associated with the use of inside information? Why do some people appear comfortable with unethical behavior that harms the firm, such as cheating on expense accounts, but would not dream of cheating a fellow employee?

In *international* business ethics, similar questions abound. Why is the study of business ethics in some countries focused on macro issues such as the compatibility of ethics and capitalism, and in other countries on micro issues such as the behavior of employees in a firm? Or, why do cultures differ in what they consider to be an ethical issue? For example, why is sexual harassment in the workplace considered an important ethical issue in the United States? By extension, why do some people in the US consider a schoolboy's insistence on a kiss from his classmate to be sexual harassment and to constitute an ethical issue? In other cultures, the stolen kiss is considered a natural part of growing up.

In teaching international business ethics to MBA students, I find that the most commonly recurring and difficult questions center on the issue of bribery. Some students have encountered instances of bribery. Additionally, bribery scandals attract media attention, and all the students have read about bribery. For example, in 1995, IBM offered $10 million to officials of Argentina's state-owned Banco Nacion to secure a $350 million contract to computerize the bank's 525 branches. In 1999, the repercussions of this incident were still in the headlines. Nor are the scandals confined to countries outside the US. In 1998, civic boosters of Salt Lake City, Utah, gave members of the International Olympic Committee gifts that included scholarships, free medical care, and help with a lucrative property deal. Occurrences such as these raise a series of questions. When, and in which cultures, is gift-giving a natural part of conducting business, and when does a gift become a bribe? Is it ethical to bribe government or corporate officials in some cultures? If so, which ones and under what conditions? This thorny and complicated issue of bribery is one that business ethics scholars have discussed and researched a great deal, yet questions still remain.

The overall objective of this chapter is to examine to what extent scholars in the field of international business ethics are asking and answering the questions that will provide the greatest contribution to the field. The following sections contain both overarching and secondary questions that international business ethics could most usefully address. The focus will be on evaluating how far researchers have come in answering the questions, on the methods used to address the questions, and on what future work needs to be undertaken in the field of international business ethics. The questions singled out for their importance to the field are:

1 Is there a set of universal business ethics principles that can be used worldwide?
2 Should business ethics researchers search for similarities or for differences in business ethics in different countries?
3 How can we integrate international business ethics research with research on other cultures and their distinctive features?

IS THERE A SET OF UNIVERSAL BUSINESS ETHICS PRINCIPLES THAT CAN BE USED WORLDWIDE?

This is perhaps the most important and essential question in the study of international business ethics and one that has received attention from business ethics scholars, as well as organizations and corporations. The question encompasses a vast amount of ethical territory. Those in favor of universal ethical principles, universalists or absolutists, seek a set of universal ethical principles to underlie all business activity. Examples of such principles are, "Treat people with respect," or "Do no harm." Relativists, on the other hand, believe that ethical principles cannot be applied universally, but instead must be tailored to the particular country or culture in which the business is conducted. They contend that each culture can make the best determination for itself of what is and is not ethical.

Universalists are concerned that relativism's lack of universal principles renders any practice acceptable as long as it is acceptable in its own culture, and therefore never allows for the possibility of reform of a practice that is not acceptable in other cultures. An extreme form of relativism can condone slavery, torture, or even murder in a specific culture. Relativists, on the other hand, assert that the imposition of universal ethical principles on all cultures (supported by universalists) can be interpreted as a form of "ethical imperialism." Relativists are of the opinion that those formulating and stating the principles put themselves in an all-knowing, god-like position, believing that they can determine what is best for everyone.

Additionally, the question can be phrased to ask not only if there *is* a set of universal ethical principles, but also if there *ought to be* such a set of principles. Could there be one ethic? Could there be one culture? And *should* there be one ethic and one culture? A further question stems from these. Is there a global context for business, and more particularly for business ethics? Or will the context always be at least somewhat dependent on local cultures? Can businesspeople think in terms of a global context?

It may be useful to look to other fields of study for clues as to how to begin to answer such questions. Trompenaars (1994) has not investigated ethics per se across cultures, but has studied values in cultures and has identified seven cultural dimensions, some of which directly relate to ethical issues. One of Trompenaars' cultural dimensions is universalism versus particularism. In a universalist culture "what is good and right can be defined and always applies," whereas in a particularist culture, greater attention is paid to the obligations of relationships and to special circumstances (p. 8). Trompenaars' categorization suggests that interest in universal principles in business ethics is culture-bound – that only cultures that are universalist recognize the value of universal ethical principles.

In fact, all research is bound by the culture in which it is conducted and the background and biases of those conducting the research. Trompenaars' dimension suggests the irony that the search for universalism is not appropriate in all cultures, thus seemingly dooming the notion of universal ethical principles. It is necessary to keep this caveat in mind as we explore the research on international business ethics, especially because so much of it has been conducted from a Western perspective, and specifically, from an American perspective. Ideally, if a set of global ethical principles were to be formulated, these principles would emerge from a consensus of all countries of the world, not just Western and First World countries. However, if only Western countries believe in the search for universal principles, it is unlikely that all nations will participate in the fashioning and adoption of global ethical principles.

In order to examine the research on universal ethical principles, first it is important to understand the distinction between normative business ethics research and descriptive (or empirical) business ethics research (Goodpaster, 1984; DeGeorge, 1999).

Normative and descriptive business ethics research

Normative research is concerned with *what ought to be*, whereas descriptive or empirical research is concerned with *what is*. Normative research has typically been in the domain of the philosopher, and empirical research usually in that of the social scientist.

A healthy tension or an uneasy peace (depending on your point of view) exists between the normative and descriptive camps, and there is little collaborative research between them (Victor and Stephens, 1994). In 1994, an entire issue of *Business Ethics Quarterly* was devoted to the controversy surrounding the desirability of attempts to integrate normative and descriptive theories. Victor and Stephens make a strong case for such integration, arguing that normative research that ignores descriptive research is "unreal philosophy" – philosophical principles formulated with no basis in fact. Take the example of deceptive practices of salespeople who sell their products overseas. If a salesperson promises a delivery date that cannot possibly be met, this lack of truthtelling cannot be evaluated without understanding the context and the effect of the deceit on others.

The reverse is also true. Victor and Stephens characterize descriptive research without a normative foundation as "amoral social science." Descriptive research that aims to assess the incidence of false promises about expected delivery dates can only do so through a normative assessment of what is wrong with false promises. Donaldson (1994), however, expresses concern that descriptive research that shows *what is* will become confused with *what ought to be*. If descriptive research demonstrates that it is common practice among salespeople to promise delivery dates that they know are unrealistic, that does not mean that the practice is ethical. Donaldson's misgivings center on the hazard of the interpretation of empirical results of prevailing ethical norms as the representation of ethical standards, thus leading to an "ethics of consensus."

Other researchers hold that a significant theory of the relationship of business to societal and ethical issues cannot be attained until integration between normative and empirical research is achieved (Kahn, 1990; Frederick, 1994; Jones and Wicks, 1999; Swanson, 1999). Weaver and Trevino (1994) outlined three conceptions of the relationship between normative and empirical business ethics: parallel, symbiotic, and integrative. The parallel view stipulates that the normative and empirical domains remain separate. The symbiotic perspective states that the two areas rely on each other for guidance in setting agendas or applying results. Only the integrative perspective fully merges normative and empirical business ethics. However, as the authors pointed out, integrative is the most difficult to achieve, requiring social scientists and philosophers not only to work closely with each other, but also to become fully involved in each other's fields.

Despite the ongoing debate about both the desirability and feasibility of integrating normative and descriptive perspectives, there is some agreement that each area of research has made a contribution to the field. Furthermore, it is assumed that each area will continue to do so in the future, rather than one specialty tending to dominate the field to the exclusion of the other. This is especially important in research on international business ethics because both perspectives make a valuable contribution.

The response from academic research

In international business ethics, the contribution of normative research has been the search for, and the identification of, principles by which international companies should conduct their business abroad. In effect, normative researchers are answering the question about the existence of universal business ethics principles by saying, "Yes, it is possible to formulate such principles and it is our objective to do so." Thus, the search for global ethical principles lies clearly in the normative domain. In fact, it is tempting to characterize normative ethics as more interested in universal principles than is descriptive ethics. However, this is overly simplistic. It is true that normative theorists search for universal truths. It is also true that the nature of the endeavor in which empirical researchers build information about different cultures necessarily reveals differences in ethical attitudes and behavior. However, as some research in international business ethics shows, the two can be mutually dependent.

The most prominent example of such dependence is the work of Donaldson and

Dunfee (1994, 1999), who have developed and applied Integrative Social Contracts Theory (ISCT) to situations involving two or more conflicting sets of ethical norms. In their 1999 book, the authors devoted considerable discussion to the question of what happens "when ethics travel." Through the use of an extensive example of bribery, the authors demonstrated the usefulness of ISCT in analyzing and addressing ethical conflicts. Fundamental to ISCT are the concepts of hypernorms and moral free space. Hypernorms are universal principles considered to be so fundamental that they serve as higher-order norms by which lower-order norms are judged and "include, for example, fundamental human rights or basic prescriptions common to most major religions. The values they represent are by definition acceptable to all cultures and organizations" (Donaldson and Dunfee, 1999: 221).

Hypernorms constitute key limits on moral free space. Moral free space is described as the "freedom of individuals to form or join communities and to act jointly to establish moral rules applicable to the members of the community" (1999: 38). Hypernorms can be characterized as "universal limits on community consent" (1999: 49). An individual faced with an ethical issue must delve into tricky ethical territory by identifying and juxtaposing hypernorms and norms formed by local communities. Thus, ISCT is useful in analyzing situations in which the norms of two different cultures collide. Multinational corporations operating abroad often face a conflict between host and home country norms of business ethics. In the example of bribery, it can appear that the norms of a host culture support the practice. However, as Donaldson and Dunfee pointed out, bribery can also violate a community norm that specifies the duties of the agent receiving the bribe. A company employee who pockets a bribe in a competitive bidding situation violates a duty to his or her employer. Ethical analysis is further complicated by the fact that bribery also in some instances may violate a hypernorm.

Donaldson and Dunfee cautioned against the notion of "photocopying" home country values or ethics and exporting them to the host country. Such replication of successful home country programs is disrespectful to the host country's culture and violates the concept of moral free space. A solution in one culture cannot be applied in another without taking into account the moral rules of the culture's community. Donaldson and Dunfee used the analogy that one does not speak to each of one's friends in the exact same way. Ethical cultures are different, just as friends are different, and these differences need to be acknowledged and understood. "Being true to one's own ethics often means not only sticking by one's own sense of right and wrong, but respecting the right of other cultures to shape their own cultural and economic values" (1999: 232).

In his earlier work, Donaldson (1989) espoused the notion of a fundamental international right and outlined ten specific international rights. Included in these are "the right to freedom of physical movement, the right to ownership of property, the right to freedom from torture, and the right to a free trial" (p. 81). As Donaldson pointed out, rights have correlative duties that need to be exercised by multinational corporations. Going beyond the minimum includes a duty to help protect individuals from the deprivation of their rights, and finally, a duty to aid the deprived. Through a series of examples, Donaldson illustrated methods for multinational managers to find compromises when home and host country ethical standards collide.

Donaldson developed a method called an "ethical algorithm" to aid managerial decision-making regarding ethical (or unethical) behavior on the part of multinational corporations in host countries. Donaldson outlined two basic rules for determining the permissibility of an activity common in the host country, but not permitted in the home country. The first rule states that if the difference is based solely on economic conditions, the practice is permissible only if the members of the home country would, under similar economic conditions, regard the practice as permissible. For example, in the export of pesticides to other countries, there are instances in which a product that is banned in a developed country is still acceptable to an underdeveloped one. Possible harmful side effects from the pesticide do not present the same perceived threat in a country where the threat of starvation from lack of crop production is more imminent. Hypothetically, if one can imagine a First World country in similar economic conditions, the country might well welcome the use of the pesticide.

The second rule identified by Donaldson states that when the conflict is not based on economic differences, a practice will be permissible only if it is required to conduct business successfully in the host country, and if the practice does not violate a fundamental international right. If it is necessary for a multinational petroleum company to exclude women in Saudi Arabia from its hiring process, then one must next ask the question of whether this practice violates a fundamental international right. While Western cultures consider discrimination against women to be unacceptable, the debate may still continue as to whether this is a fundamental *international* right.

Similarly, DeGeorge has written extensively on the ethical obligations of multinational companies. DeGeorge (1993) identified three types of ethical conflicts: (1) pressures on individuals to violate personal norms: (2) inconsistent cultural norms: and (3) host versus home country interests and values. His work focused on norm conflicts between host country and home country, and he has developed a series of guidelines to assist multinational firms that are operating in less-developed countries.

The first of DeGeorge's guidelines is that "multinationals should do no intentional direct harm" (p. 46), and the second is that "multinationals should produce more good than harm for the host country" (p. 47). Of course, part of the challenge of normative research is to determine the definition of "good" and "harm." DeGeorge acknowledged that his guidelines are not exhaustive, but that they do "illustrate the ethical considerations that a firm must take into account if it is to act ethically and with integrity" (p. 55). An instance of potential application of DeGeorge's analysis of host versus home country interests is the Monsanto Company's decision not to commercialize the terminator gene, an experimental biotechnology opposed by rural advocates because it would make seeds sterile (Kilman, 1999). In poor nations such as India, farmers depend heavily on the seed they save from their harvests. In this instance, Monsanto appears to have weighed the potential good of the commercialization of the gene (bringing advanced biotechnology to less developed countries) against the potential harm (loss of crops for farmers in those countries).

DeGeorge applied his ethical guidelines to the 1984 poisonous gas leak from a Union Carbide pesticide plant in Bhopal, India. This tragedy killed about 3,500 people and injured at least another 200,000 in the poor, overcrowded shantytown that had grown up around the plant. The catastrophe left a shocked world wondering how such a thing could have happened and who should be held responsible. DeGeorge illustrated how following his guidelines could have prevented the Bhopal disaster. Ultimately, DeGeorge concluded that: "The hope for ethics in international business lies ultimately in the development of adequate international background institutions and in the willingness of multinationals to recognize their ethical obligations and act in accordance with them" (DeGeorge, 1993: 56). The realization of this hope depends upon sufficient agreement among the various countries and cultures of the world in order to develop these international background institutions. DeGeorge did not make clear how such agreement could be achieved and did not specify which countries (if not all) would be involved in the development of the institutions.

One of the ways that DeGeorge proposed that we resolve ethical issues is through the use of a concept he terms "ethical displacement." Ethical displacement assumes that various ethical problems cannot always be solved at the level on which they occur. Instead, they need to be resolved at a higher level. For example, an individual confronted with a request for a bribe may need to look to someone in a supervisory or managerial position in the individual's firm to deal with the issue. Again, this suggests that ethical issues are not easily resolvable. In fact, DeGeorge stated explicitly that there is no simple formula to follow in making ethical decisions. Dunfee and Donaldson were very clear on this point as well. Hypernorms, by themselves, do not lead to the answers to complex ethical issues. DeGeorge challenged managers to make use of "moral imagination" in their search for solutions to difficult ethical issues in business.

The response from international organizations

In addition to this academic interest in the normative ethical principles of international business, a number of organizations have devised sets of international ethical principles applicable to all companies in their business conduct abroad. Prominent among these are the Caux Round Table (CRT) Principles for Business. In order to address global issues of common concern, senior business leaders from Europe, North America, and Japan launched the Caux Round Table in 1986. Initially, the organization focused on the tensions arising from trade imbalances. Later, in 1994, CRT initiated a broad statement of ethical principles based on the premise that the world business community should play a key role in improving not only economic conditions, but also social conditions.

The CRT principles embody general statements, such as "respect for rules" and "respect for the environment," as well as a more specific set of stakeholder principles. These stakeholder principles include a responsibility to "provide our customers with the highest-quality products and services consistent with our requirements," and the responsibility to "provide jobs and compensation that improve workers' living conditions." Listed as stakeholders are customers, employees, owners/investors, suppliers, competitors, and communities. This is an extensive list, particularly in that competitors are considered to be stakeholders. CRT responsibilities to competitors include a broad set of responsibilities such as to "foster open markets for trade and investment," as well as more specific responsibilities to "refuse to acquire commercial information by dishonest or unethical means, such as industrial espionage." Very few corporate codes of ethics contain a statement of responsibility to competitors as stakeholders. Furthermore, at a time when firms in many countries are just beginning to formulate codes of ethics, it is encouraging to see the comprehensiveness of the Caux Round Table principles.

Similarly, in 1997, the Conference Board launched an initiative to address the topic of global business ethics principles (Berenbeim, 1999). The Conference Board is a non-profit, non-advocacy organization whose purpose is to improve the business enterprise system and to enhance the contribution of business to society. A working group comprised of both academics and businesspeople is engaged in the process of "promoting a better understanding of the practical issues in formulating and implementing global business ethics principles" (p. 4). The initial report stated that current trends favor the corporate articulation of global business ethics codes. These trends include growing North American and European participation in world markets and an accompanying responsibility to Asian, African, and Latin American countries, and greater emphasis on corporate and individual responsibility for conduct and financial performance.

Of the 61 members of the working party, 51 are US-based, with nine from Europe and one from Japan. This point is not made to single out the Conference Board, but instead to illustrate the difficulties of adequate representation of all nations in any group charged with formulating worldwide principles. The Conference Board has worked to counter this American bias by convening working group meetings in Asia, Europe, and South America. Furthermore, a survey on corporate ethics initiatives, especially codes of ethics, was sent to companies worldwide. Of the responding companies, about 53 percent were outside the US. Frederick (1991) made a similar point that international accords are not truly representative of the views of all nations, but that the perspectives of developed nations tend to dominate. It is likely that even agreements which include the representation of nations around the globe, such as that of the United Nations, are reached because less developed and less powerful nations feel compelled to agree with the views of the more powerful developed countries.

Frederick (1991) examined six international accords containing ethical guidelines for multinational corporations. Not all apply specifically to multinational corporations, but those that do include the Organization for Economic Cooperation and Development (OECD) Guidelines for Multinational Enterprises issued in 1976 and the International Labor Office Tripartite Declaration of Principles Concerning Multinational Enterprises and Social Policy issued in 1977. By analysis of these six accords, Frederick was able to derive a "set of explicitly normative guides for the policies, decisions, and operations of multinational corporations" (p. 166). These normative guides include recommendations that multinationals should respect the right of employees to join trade unions and to bargain collectively, and that multinationals should respect host-country job standards and upgrade the local labor force through training. Frederick acknowledged the difficulties involved in implementing such codes of conduct. Nevertheless, he concluded that the existence of these sets of guidelines shows the emergence of a transcultural corporate ethic.

More recently, in 1997, the OECD Convention on Combating Bribery of Foreign Public Officials in International Business Transactions was signed by all 29 OECD member countries[1] as well as five non-member countries (Argentina, Brazil, Bulgaria, Chile, and the Slovak Republic). The OECD is an organization of countries committed to a market economy and a pluralistic democracy. It was formed to provide governments a setting in which to develop economic and social policy. The OECD's convention on bribery facilitates a coordinated move toward adopting national legislation making it a crime to bribe foreign public officials. It offers a definition of bribery, a system of monitoring compliance, and a requirement that member countries impose sanctions on offenders. Earlier guidelines (issued by the OECD in 1976) restricting multinational companies from interfering in the political affairs of host countries are believed to have had impact, particularly on US and European multinational firms (Haegg, 1983).

The response from multinational corporations

Holland (1997) maintained that we are beginning to see a global "market for morality" emerging. Developments in more homogeneous access to markets, technology, and information lead managers of global firms to seek greater homogeneity in their approach to business ethics issues. Furthermore, Holland argued that as more companies extend their operations into other countries, they quickly become enmeshed in a "tangle of local, national, international and corporate standards." Increasing global consensus about a core of global ethical principles could provide a useful set of standards for firms to follow as they navigate their way through this "tangle." One clear benefit of such consensus is that no individual firm would have to initiate its own set of principles, and no one firm would need to position itself as a pioneer on the ethics front.

A number of large multinational companies have issued codes of ethics or codes of conduct that outline company expectations of employee behavior throughout the world. These codes range from general statements of principles, such as Johnson and Johnson's Credo, or Procter and Gamble's Core Values and Principles, to manual-like documents containing guidelines on how to handle specific incidents in ethics in international business. Johnson and Johnson's Credo contains statements about the firm's responsibility to stakeholders, including customers, employees, and communities. It makes assertions such as, "We must provide competent management, and their actions must be just and ethical." Procter and Gamble's principles relating to customers are at a similar level of generality and include, "We develop superior understanding of consumers and their needs."

On the other hand, the Shell Group, in conjunction with its General Business Principles (1997), provides a "management primer" on dealing with bribery and corruption to managers worldwide. This document clearly defines what constitutes a bribe, versus a gift or a facilitating payment, and also outlines the most prevalent forms of corruption. The primer warns against both active bribery ("offering or seeking money, pledges or benefits in exchange for favours") and passive bribery ("accepting gifts, money, pledges or benefits in exchange for which the person who accepts misuses his position by favouring the giver"). The document makes clear the unethical nature of bribery. "Bribes generally involve payments to someone to pervert the course of business by taking improper or illegal action." It also states that bribes "are neither legally nor morally acceptable." Shell is equally clear about the consequences of not following corporate guidelines. In 1997, there were 23 cases in which Shell employees were found to have solicited or accepted bribes. All were fired.

Most codes of ethics fall between the two extremes of those encompassing general principles and those that address employee behavior expected in specific situations. Two such examples are the codes of the Coca-Cola Company and that of the Marubeni Corporation.

The Coca-Cola Company's Code of Business Conduct (1998) "applies to the Company's business worldwide and to all Company employees." The code is distributed to employees together with a letter from the CEO, emphasizing the importance of ethical conduct in maintaining the company's "time-honored reputation." This letter acknowledges that the code cannot possibly address every situation pertaining to ethics, but urges employees to discuss decisions about ethical issues with their supervisor and, if necessary, with "the designated representative of the General Counsel assigned to your area." (This advice sounds a great deal as if it is following DeGeorge's concept of ethical displacement.) The Coca-Cola code covers topics including conflicts of interest; dealing with government officials, government employees, company customers, and suppliers; and political contributions. The code also outlines the company's system for monitoring compliance and applying disciplinary action.

Marubeni Corporation, one of Japan's leading general trading firms, asks all employees in its offices in 82 countries to sign a document stating that they will abide by the company's code of conduct (1998). Marubeni's code is especially strict on some issues such as political contributions, which are forbidden. Employees agree "to refrain from providing money, gifts or other types of economic gain to public officials or those of similar position." The Marubeni code contains provisions on obeying the law, respecting human rights, avoiding conflicts of interest, protecting the company's assets, promoting free competition and fair business transactions, maintaining ethical standards in the use of gifts and entertaining, and properly using company proprietary information and trade secrets. For example, the code asks employees to pledge "to be aware of the obligations of international citizenship and to obey all domestic, foreign, national and international laws, regulations and norms." The code is considered by some to be a direct response to the company's involvement in the Lockheed scandal in the early 1970s. At that time, Lockheed asked Marubeni to help win orders for jets. Lockheed offered a bribe to Japan's Prime Minister Tanaka with the expectation that he would promote more Lockheed planes in Japan. Public disclosure of the payments received by Tanaka produced outrage among the Japanese people and ultimately led to Tanaka's resignation.

Codes of ethics or codes of conduct that address employee behavior worldwide are a recent phenomenon. Perhaps it is too soon to attempt to evaluate their effectiveness overall, although some companies, such as Shell, monitor the internal effectiveness of their own code. The trend has been for more companies to adopt such codes. Additionally, many firms outside the US and Europe are adopting codes of ethics that do not extend to overseas operations, but do provide comprehensive guidelines for domestic operations. Two such examples are Samsung, a Korean information and telecommunications conglomerate, and Banco de Crédito del Perú, a bank in Peru. Samsung's code includes internal policy issues relating to opportunity and promotion and competition across departments. External policy aims to prevent bribery both from and to clients and to protect proprietary information. Banco de Crédito del Perú's code is especially concerned with preventing activities of bank employees, officers, and directors that may lead to fraudulent operations, money-laundering activities, and leaking of confidential information.

It will be interesting to see if this trend continues and if any controversy over corporate codes develops. To date, there has been little questioning among business ethics researchers of the right of the companies to expect (indeed, in many cases, to demand) that employees follow corporate ethics. Despite the fact that such company ethics may potentially collide with one's personal ethics, one's future employment may depend on compliance with company ethics. Furthermore, employees asked to sign that they will abide by a code may feel an increased burden of responsibility if the firm is accused of any wrongdoing.

This section has demonstrated that a great deal of work in international business ethics has focused on devising universal or global ethical principles. Most of these principles are formulated at a high level of abstraction. Some have been criticized for being so general that they are meaningless. For example, what does it mean to "Do no harm"? In some situations harm inevitably will result, and it is a question of determining the greater and the lesser harm. For instance, a multinational textile firm employs women in Latin America to assemble clothes for more than 14 hours a day. One must weigh the harm incurred by the long working hours against the harm of these women not being employed. On the other hand, without the articulation of universal ethical principles, international business ethics can offer only disjointed case-by-case analysis of situations. Such analysis provides little guidance to those individuals actually confronting ethical issues.

SHOULD BUSINESS ETHICS RESEARCHERS SEARCH FOR SIMILARITIES OR FOR DIFFERENCES IN BUSINESS ETHICS IN · DIFFERENT COUNTRIES?

This second question is very much related to the question of universalism. Should the objective of research be to document differences or to search for similarities? If the search is for similarities, is this an empirical search or a normative one? That is, are we looking for evidence of similar cultural ethical beliefs, or do we believe that there *should be* universal ethical truths to which all people in all cultures should adhere? For the most part, descriptive or empirical research in international business ethics has been engaged in the search for differences. By its very nature, research that reports similarities commands less attention. Before looking at the nature of this empirical research, the arguments for convergence and divergence will be examined.

Convergence or divergence?

Carroll and Gannon (1997) presented a series of arguments to support the position that there will be increasing convergence, as well as a set of arguments that there will be increasing divergence, in the behaviors, ethical and otherwise, of managers around the world. (It should be noted that their discussion is confined to managers, and did not extend to all employees.) Their perspective started with the assumption that there are "differences in the ethicality of managerial decisions in various societies" (p. 173). Given these differences, the authors were interested in predicting whether these differences will become more pronounced, stay the same, or become less pronounced.

Carroll and Gannon's reasoning to support future convergence of managerial behavior was based upon:

> a growing body of international law governing business relationships among countries, a growing convergence in human resource management systems, and a growing convergence in certain factors influencing organizational cultures such as business strategies employed. (p. 177)

As businesses increasingly operate in more countries around the globe, many firms are searching for ways to ensure a more predictable approach to managerial decision-making through worldwide-standardized policies and procedures. Media and technology make it possible for individuals throughout the world to share experiences. Companies have shifted their thinking to a more international focus, increasingly recognizing that truly globalized firms require a new dimension in corporate decision-making (Danley, 1994). Levitt (1983) extolled the virtues of a "clarified global focus" and the economic benefits of large-scale production of standardized items.

On the other hand, Adler and Ghadar (1990) presented an argument for divergence. They contended that international corporate evolution increases (rather than decreases) the demands for cultural sensitivity. The more that firms market their products internationally, the more they need to understand differences in target markets based on cultural differences. Instead of companies moving toward mass customization to serve overseas markets, firms need to differentiate their products according to cultural considerations in the target markets. Desai and Rittenburg (1997) addressed the issue of divergence, specifically looking at ethics. The authors cited ethical differences across countries as one part of a growing complexity of information inputs and processes in multinational firms' strategic and operational decision-making. They concluded that it will be nearly impossible to achieve global consensus on ethics in the near future.

In 1992, Vogel maintained that business ethics had not yet globalized, and went on to provide a number of reasons why this was true. The reasons he gave have changed little since then. Vogel argued that the prominence of business ethics in the US can be explained by the "distinctive institutional, legal, social and cultural context of the American business system" (p. 30). Vogel maintained that the US is distinctive in three ways in its approach to the topic of business ethics: (1) the role of the individual and individual rights tends to be emphasized in the US as the most important source of ethical values; (2) business ethics tends to be more legalistic and rules-oriented in the US, which is borne out by the emphasis on codes of ethics and the need to codify the guidelines as to what constitutes ethical behavior; and (3) individuals in the US are more likely to consider their own ethical rules to be applicable across cultures. Van Luijk (1990) agreed that business ethics in the US is distinctive to a culture in which individualism is revered and people tend to make ethical decisions based on an individual value system. By contrast, in Germany, there is a greater emphasis on consensual ethics or "communicative" ethics, with the *group* forming the basis of the value system and that of ethical norms and decision-making.

If Vogel was correct about the distinctiveness of the context of US business, it is not just a matter of time before the topic of business ethics diffuses to other countries. On the contrary, other countries may have natural barriers to the adoption of business ethics in the form of their own distinctive institutional, legal, social, political, and cultural contexts of their business systems. Russia is a prominent example. A combination of political history (oppressive and corrupt political regimes) and economic factors (recent move toward a market economy) has created uncertainty about appropriate business behavior, particularly ethical behavior. Years of autocratic rule have left people cynical, distrustful, and unsure of how to engage in cooperative ethical business conduct (Taylor, Kazakov, and Thompson, 1997).

A summary of the Carroll and Gannon arguments suggests that important differences continue to exist, but that at the same time, there are attempts in law and in business practice to impose universal standards. A similar phenomenon is happening in business ethics, that is, that international organizations such as the Caux Round Table are devising a universal set of ethical principles, even though considerable country differences in approach to ethical issues remain. For example, in the computer software industry countries have taken different stances on the practice of software piracy. Donaldson (1996) reported piracy rates of 35 percent in the US, 57 percent in Germany, 80 percent in Italy and Japan, and estimated the rate in most Asian countries to be nearly 100 percent. Donaldson attributed these differences to culture and to ethical attitudes in a culture, but argued that an international standard is needed. If software piracy is permitted internationally, software companies will be reluctant to invest in the development of new products. Thus, *divergence* of country perspectives exists, and Donaldson is advocating *convergence* of country standards, specifically the adoption of the "highest" or strictest standard.

Descriptive international business ethics research

Four types of descriptive or empirical international business ethics research are dominant: (1) research focusing on corporations in different countries and their approach to ethical issues, particularly corporate ethics initiatives, such as codes of ethics; (2) research examining *attitudes* of managers or business students in different countries about ethical issues; (3) research investigating the *behavior* and perceptions of behavior of businesspeople and public officials in different countries; and (4) research providing information about how different countries and different cultures view the field of business ethics. The last of these will be discussed later in the chapter when attention turns to the importance of culture in shaping ethical attitudes and behavior.

Corporate ethics initiatives

One area in which cross-national differences have been documented is that of corporate codes of ethics (Langlois and Schlegelmilch, 1990; Robertson and Schlegelmilch, 1993; Schlegelmilch and Robertson, 1995). This research explored the content of corporate codes of ethics in different countries as a means of demonstrating differences in how ethical issues are viewed. (Of course, what is considered an ethical issue in different countries constitutes the most fundamental question.) Given the existence of cultural differences, one would not expect unanimity across countries about which issues will be emphasized in corporate codes of ethics. Indeed, this proves to be the case.

Langlois and Schlegelmilch (1990) found significant differences between the US and Europe with regard to employee conduct, supplier and contractor relations, and political interests. US codes were more likely to contain extensive reference to employee interests, whereas European codes were more likely to include guidelines on political interests. Similarly, American managers were more likely than British, German, and Austrian managers to perceive personnel issues, including fairness and discrimination, as ethical issues to be included in corporate codes (Schlegelmilch and Robertson, 1995).

Managerial and student attitudes about business ethics

A further stream of empirical research has examined the attitudes of managers or business students toward business ethics issues and has documented that differences do exist from country to country. The work of Becker and Fritzsche (1987a, 1987b) is representative of such cross-national managerial studies. Their survey compared attitudes to ethics codes and statements about ethics among managers from France, Germany, and the US. They found that the French respondents were more optimistic about the positive effect of ethics codes than were the German and American respondents (1987a). (In contrast, Vogel in 1992 reported skepticism in France about the effectiveness of ethics codes.) Additionally, American managers were most solidly in agreement with the statement that "Sound ethics is good business," and expressed the strongest disagreement with the statement, "Let the buyer beware." Overall, the authors concluded that the French respondents can be characterized as optimistic about ethics codes and business ethics, the German respondents as pessimistic, and the American respondents as realistic. In a similar study, the authors found that managers in France, Germany, and the US approached ethics vignettes differently (Becker and Fritzsche, 1987b). For example, French and German managers were more likely to pay a bribe than were their US counterparts.

Although Becker and Fritzsche's work focused on the US and European countries, other studies have compared Asian and American managers. For example, McDonald and Zepp (1988) contrasted Hong Kong managers' and Western managers' views on which activities in business are considered most unethical and on how ethical issues in business should best be addressed. The researchers presented survey respondents with a decision to report unsafe products to outside authorities (known as "whistle blowing" in the US), even if it might jeopardize the firm's position. The results indicated that 50 percent of Hong Kong managers (compared to 23 percent of American managers) felt no obligation to report. Also, Hong Kong managers believed that additional government regulation would improve ethical practices in Asian business (82 percent), in sharp contrast to American respondents who preferred to see ethical issues handled by the American corporations themselves.

Azevedo, Paul, and Von Glinow (1994) presented a summary of 14 studies of both managerial and business school student attitudes to ethical issues. Among the student attitude studies were a comparison of US and Taiwanese students, in which US students had higher ethical standards on issues of misrepresentation (White and Rhodeback, 1992). Comparisons of American and Israeli students (Prebe and Reichel, 1988) and American, Australian, and Israeli students (Small, 1992) revealed few differences in attitudes toward ethical issues. Of the 14 studies included, greater country differences were found among managers than among students. One can only speculate as to why this would be the case. Perhaps the business school student experience is more comparable around the world than is the managerial experience. Or, perhaps, because a sample of managers tends to include a wider age range than a sample of students, student ethical attitudes are more homogeneous.

All but two of the studies reviewed by Azevedo, Paul, and Von Glinow compared the US to other countries, rather than comparing two or more countries outside the US. It should be noted, however, that more recent articles in the *Journal of Business Ethics* include a comparison of business school students in Malaysia and New Zealand (Goodwin and Goodwin, 1999), a comparison of management practices of firms in Australia and Sri Lanka (Batten, Hettihewa, and Mellor, 1999), and a comparison of Korean and Japanese managers (Lee and Yoshihara, 1997). A further study published in *Business Ethics: A European Review* analyzed student attitudes in 14 countries, including Chile, Mexico, Colombia, Slovenia, the Czech Republic, and Romania (Grubisic and Goic, 1998). Students in Central European countries were found to be more "individualistic" in viewing work as a means of satisfying their own needs than were students in developed Western and Latin American countries.

This discussion has reviewed examples of international research that explore corporate ethics initiatives and managerial and business school student attitudes to business ethics. The review is not meant to provide a comprehensive overview of that research, as there are many more such studies not included. Instead, the aim is to call attention to the *type* of research that has been conducted. Most of these studies tend to document country differences, but rarely do they tie their conclusions to the values or political and legal systems of the cultures under study. This point will be developed later in the discussion of the importance of understanding a culture in relation to its business ethics attitudes and practice.

Perceptions of behavior

Transparency International (TI) is an organization that monitors unethical practice in countries around the world and rank-orders these countries according to their level of corruption. The mission of the organization is to curb corruption by mobilizing a global coalition. TI focuses on the abuse of public office for private gain, such as the bribing of public officials, taking kickbacks in public procurement, or embezzling public funds. The TI Corruption Perceptions Index first published in 1995 collapses data from a number of sources. It measures perceptions about the level of corruption within countries on the part of samples of businesspeople, risk analysts, investigative journalists, country experts, and the general public. Most of the sources sample country residents, who rely on their own internal viewpoint (as opposed to an expatriate's external viewpoint) to assess the meaning and degree of corruption in their own cultural context. Based on these perceptions, 85 countries are assigned a corruption perception score from 1 to 10 and are rank-ordered according to their score (table 18.1). In the 1999 rankings, Denmark received a perfect score of 10 and was ranked number one (meaning that it has the least perceived corruption); Finland, Sweden, and New Zealand closely followed it. The countries perceived to be the most corrupt are Cameroon, Nigeria, Indonesia, Azerbaijan, and Uzbekistan. The US was ranked number 18 and Japan number 25.

What do we do with cultural differences when we find them?

Do we acknowledge (and perhaps even celebrate) cultural differences in business ethics, or do we try to ignore them, or find ways to show that they are not really differences at all? Minow (1990) speaks of the key question of when to acknowledge and when to ignore differences. Minow discusses the fundamental "dilemma of difference" by asking, "when does treating people differently emphasize their differences and stigmatize or hinder

TABLE 18.1 Transparency international: the corruption perceptions index

Country rank	Country	1999 CPI score	Country rank	Country	1999 CPI score
1	Denmark	10.0		Lithuania	3.8
2	Finland	9.8		South Korea	3.8
3	Sweden	9.4	53	Slovak Republic	3.7
	New Zealand	9.4	54	Philippines	3.6
5	Canada	9.2		Turkey	3.6
	Iceland	9.2	56	Mozambique	3.5
7	Singapore	9.1		Zambia	3.5
8	Netherlands	9.0	58	Belarus	3.4
9	Norway	8.9		China	3.4
	Switzerland	8.9		Latvia	3.4
11	Luxembourg	8.8		Mexico	3.4
12	Australia	8.7		Senegal	3.4
13	United Kingdom	8.6	63	Bulgaria	3.3
14	Germany	8.0		Egypt	3.3
15	Hong Kong	7.7		Ghana	3.3
	Ireland	7.7		Macedonia	3.3
17	Austria	7.6		Romania	3.3
18	USA	7.5	68	Guatemala	3.2
19	Chile	6.9		Thailand	3.2
20	Israel	6.8	70	Nicaragua	3.1
21	Portugal	6.7	71	Argentina	3.0
22	France	6.6	72	Colombia	2.9
	Spain	6.6		India	2.9
24	Botswana	6.1	74	Croatia	2.7
25	Japan	6.0	75	Ivory Coast	2.6
	Slovenia	6.0		Moldova	2.6
27	Estonia	5.7		Ukraine	2.6
28	Taiwan	5.6		Venezuela	2.6
29	Belgium	5.3		Vietnam	2.6
	Namibia	5.3	80	Armenia	2.5
31	Hungary	5.2		Bolivia	2.5
32	Costa Rica	5.1	82	Ecuador	2.4
	Malaysia	5.1		Russia	2.4
34	South Africa	5.0	84	Albania	2.3
	Tunisia	5.0		Georgia	2.3
36	Greece	4.9		Kazakhstan	2.3
	Mauritius	4.9	87	Kyrgyz Republic	2.2
38	Italy	4.7		Pakistan	2.2
39	Czech Republic	4.6		Uganda	2.2
40	Peru	4.5	90	Kenya	2.0
41	Jordan	4.4		Paraguay	2.0
	Uruguay	4.4		Yugoslavia	2.0
43	Mongolia	4.3	93	Tanzania	1.9
44	Poland	4.2	94	Honduras	1.8
45	Brazil	4.1		Uzbekistan	1.8
	Malawi	4.1	96	Azerbaijan	1.7
	Morocco	4.1		Indonesia	1.7
	Zimbabwe	4.1	98	Nigeria	1.6
49	El Salvador	3.9	99	Cameroon	1.5
50	Jamaica	3.8			

them on that basis? and when does treating people the same become insensitive to their difference and likely to stigmatize and hinder them on *that* basis?" (emphasis in original) (p. 20). Although Minow focused on differences such as race, gender, and physical ability within the same culture, her questions are applicable to cultural differences as well.

Transparency International's search for differences is based on the single universal ethical principle of anti-corruption. Comparison of practice from country to country invites an evaluative dimension against some universal standard. In this case, a search for differences is in fact relying on a value judgment about corruption that relates back to the question of universal principles and answers: Yes, there is a universal ethical principle of anti-corruption. Thus, it cannot be assumed that the search for differences necessarily is motivated by interest in preserving those differences.

How can we integrate international business ethics research with research on cultures and their distinctive features?

Recall the opening scenario describing the differing views of the Asian and the US business school students regarding a violation of the school's honor code. On the surface, it appears that the critical question in the incident described was whether it is more ethical to admit to a transgression or not. Instead, deeply held cultural beliefs influence individual perspectives about what is and is not ethical. It is important for international business ethics researchers to learn how attitudes to ethical issues vary in different countries. It is equally, or more important, to learn how the contexts of the different countries give rise to different ways of thinking about ethical issues.

As has been discussed, there is a great deal written on the question of whether one has to bribe in order to do business in certain cultures. The answer to such a question is of great practical assistance to a businessperson confronted with a request for a bribe. However, from a research point of view, it is interesting to ask more fundamental questions about the dimensions of the culture that support or do not support bribery, even particular forms of bribery. Suppose that two countries display different levels of tolerance of bribery. Country "A" looks the other way at all forms of bribery, even significant bribery of public officials. Country "B" only condones "grease" or "facilitating payments" considered necessary to get a telephone installed or a shipment through customs. What features of the two cultures support these distinctions? Knowledge of legal, political, and economic differences will increase understanding of the origins of the different approaches to ethical issues. Perhaps Country "A" pays its public officials very little and counts on bribery to provide supplemental income. Or perhaps the tax structure of Country "A" is conducive to bribery. Note that understanding of these country differences is not offered as *justification* of the practice, only as *explanation*.

An anthropologist's view of business ethics should prove valuable in promoting an understanding of business ethics issues in different cultures. Social scientists who conduct research on business ethics tend to be psychologists and sociologists. However, the anthropological point of view has an important contribution to make as well. Anthropologists define culture broadly as the way that human beings understand the world (Ronen, 1986). Culture develops over time and consists of shared understandings. Without an appreciation of culture, it is more difficult to interpret practices such as the use of child labor in India, or the responsibility of a US multinational firm selling glue that is used as a stimulant by street children in Honduras. An inviting avenue for investigation of country contexts is the conduct of empirical research on the cultures of different countries along the lines of Hofstede (1984) and Trompenaars (1994). Both Hofstede and Trompenaars outlined dimensions of cultures and identified specific countries exhibiting those dimensions.

Hofstede's cultural dimensions (1984) are the following: individualism–collectivism (the extent to which individuals define themselves as individuals or members of a group), power distance (the degree of acceptance by the less powerful of an unequal distribution of power), uncertainty avoidance (the extent to which individuals feel threatened by and try to avoid ambiguous situations), and masculinity–femininity (the extent to which society's dominant values emphasize assertiveness and materialism or relationships with people and quality of life).

A promising area of research is the use of such cultural dimensions to study ethical issues in business. For example, Trevino and Nelson (1999) examined two of the cultural dimensions of Hofstede (1984) and their implications for ethical or unethical behavior. They discussed hiring practices in collectivist and individualistic societies, pointing out that in a collectivist society, such as Taiwan or Columbia, nepotism is an accepted hiring practice. Those in a collectivist society argue that knowing the family of the applicant is considered an important qualification for hiring. Similarly, a close-knit group of families in Mexico City and Monterrey has dominated the boards of directors of most major Mexican corporations (Smith, 1999). In an individualistic culture like the US, such practices may be seen as taking unfair advantage of family connections. In addition to cultural dimensions, economic factors play a part. Additionally, nepotism is more likely to be acceptable in countries in which family businesses and privately held companies dominate.

Trevino and Nelson also explored possible ethical implications of power distance, the extent to which people accept a hierarchical distribution of power in their organizations and in their society. In cultures with a large power distance, such as the Philippines or Venezuela, it is easier for employees to concur that the boss has power simply by virtue of being the boss, and employees are less likely to question authority. If the boss asks an employee to lie to a client, for example, the employee is likely to think that it is more unethical to disobey the boss than it would be to engage in the practice of deceiving the client.

Vitell, Nwachukwu, and Barnes (1993) used Hofstede's work to formulate a series of propositions about how business practitioners in different cultures would respond to issues of corporate ethics. The authors looked at all four of Hofstede's dimensions of culture. They proposed that managers in countries that are high on the individualism dimension (such as Canada and Australia) will be less likely to take into consideration either formal or informal professional, industry, and organizational norms when forming their own ethical norms. Instead, managers will rely on their own personal norms, most likely formed through early family, educational, and religious experiences. Managers in countries high on individualism also will be likely to consider themselves more important stakeholders than owners/stockholders or other employees (Vitell, Nwachukwu, and Barnes, 1993). An additional hypothesis could be formulated – that this individualism may lead managers to make more independent decisions about ethical issues and to consider themselves "above the law" (or in this case "above the ethics of the organization") than would be true in collectivist cultures, such as Pakistan or Peru.

In countries with a large power distance, such as Singapore or France, business practitioners will be more likely both to take their ethical cues from their superiors (versus their peers) and to rely on professional, industry, and organizational formal norms (versus informal work group norms) when forming their own ethical norms (Vitell, Nwachukwu, and Barnes, 1993). If this were the case, one could hypothesize also that relatively few instances of corporate whistle blowing would occur, in which an employee exposes the unethical practices of the firm and often the unethical behavior of the employee's superiors in the corporate hierarchy.

In countries with high uncertainty avoidance, such as Greece or Portugal, managers are more likely to be intolerant of any deviations from group or organizational norms. Additionally, they are: (1) more likely to consider organizational norms as they form their own personal norms; (2) less likely to perceive ethical problems; (3) more likely to perceive the negative consequences of "questionable" actions; and (4) more likely to consider the owners/stockholders and other employees as more important stakeholders than themselves.

Societies that are characterized as masculine, such as Austria or Italy, are more likely to encourage individuals (especially males) to engage in ambitious, competitive behavior and to strive for material success. Businesspeople in countries that are high on the masculinity dimension also will be less likely to perceive ethical problems and will be less influenced by professional, industry, and organizational codes of ethics for employees (Vitell, Nwachukwu, and Barnes, 1993). One could hypothesize also that in these cultures the cutting of ethical corners or the taking of ethical shortcuts might be condoned as long as the end result of "success" was achieved. Incentive systems that allot rewards based on individual performance, such as bonus systems, would be expected to lead to more unethical behavior than would be true in a feminine culture like the Netherlands or Sweden. Future research is needed to confirm or disconfirm these hypotheses.

Doney, Cannon, and Mullen (1998) investigated the influence of national culture on the development of trust, generating a series of propositions concerning the ways in which trust is formed and the transfer of trust, using all four of Hofstede's dimensions. For example, they posited that individuals who trust others (trustors) in high power distance cultures are more likely to form trust via calculative and capability processes, relative to counterparts in low power distance cultures. A calculative process is one in which an individual considers the costs and benefits of another party either cheating or cooperating in a relationship. The trustor infers that it would (or would not) be in the other party's best interest to cheat. Capability processes refer to a trustor's willingness to trust based on an assessment of a person's skills and competencies, and thus the ability to meet obligations, as well as the trustor's expectations. In low power distance cultures, people hold an egalitarian view of others and are less likely to emphasize inequalities in ability and expertise.

To illustrate this point, take the hypothetical example of a purchasing agent in Malaysia, a high power distance culture. This purchasing agent works for a large insurance company and chooses among office equipment vendors. The purchasing agent forms a relationship of trust with a particular office equipment salesperson. In a calculative scenario, the trust is formed because the purchasing agent has enough leverage through the size of the potential purchase to believe that the salesperson will not try to cheat. The salesperson relies both on the expectation of this particular sale and of repeat business.

Or, in a capability scenario, the purchasing agent trusts the salesperson because the purchasing agent perceives the salesperson to be extremely competent.

One of Trompenaars' (1994) seven dimensions of culture, universalism versus particularism, has already been discussed. The other six are: individualism versus collectivism; neutral versus emotional; specific versus diffuse; achievement versus ascription; attitudes to time (focus on the past, present, or future); and attitudes toward the environment (nature). As is true of Hofstede's work, Trompenaars' cultural dimensions can be readily applied to business ethics issues. In cultures that are highly achievement-oriented such as that of the US, differentiation among job candidates on merit-based credentials is considered to be sound human resource management, whereas differentiation on ascribed attributes such as age, gender, and ethnicity is considered to be discrimination. But in an ascription-based culture, such as Egypt, one would hypothesize that discrimination is likely to be viewed differently.

Another prominent framework for studying dimensions of cultures is provided by Kluckhohn and Strodtbeck's (1961) value orientations. Their six value orientations contrast societies in terms of their views concerning individual nature (good, good and evil, or evil); relationships with the world (dominance, harmony, or subjugation); relationships with other people (individualist or collectivist); primary type of activity (doing, controlling, or being); and, according to their orientation in time (past, present, or future), and space (private, public, or mixed). Such values have obvious links to business ethics issues. For example, a culture that is future-oriented would be hypothesized to place more emphasis on responsibility to the environment and its preservation for future generations, than will a culture that is more oriented to the present or to the past.

The work of Gannon and Associates (1994) constitutes an approach to culture that also has applicability to the field of international business ethics. Gannon examined the culture of 17 countries through an in-depth use of metaphor. Metaphors are used to describe the overall country culture and include "the Italian opera," "French wine," "the Russian ballet," "the Turkish coffeehouse," and "the Chinese family altar." Although a country's culture is captured in a single metaphor, each metaphor is developed to include an additional three to six characteristics of the metaphor. For example, the metaphor for Italy is opera, and its dimensions are pageantry and spectacle, voice, exteriority, and the interaction between the chorus and the lead singers. Through exploration of these cultural dimensions, understanding of the seeming contradictions in all societies is enhanced. Such detailed exploration of the characteristics of a culture also would aid in the understanding of ethical beliefs in that culture.

Ethical beliefs and behavior are culturally embedded. An important avenue of research is that of deeper understanding of how different cultures lead to different ethical perspectives. The concern is that much of the cross-cultural empirical work documents country differences at a surface level, but needs to delve more deeply into the culture to understand the context from which ethical differences stem. Essential questions about the nature of business ethics are expected to vary from culture to culture. For example, who "owns" ethics in a culture? In other words, whose responsibility is ethics? Is ethical behavior the sole responsibility of the individual, the corporation, the society, or a more global enterprise? Cultural answers to these questions will increase understanding of ethical and unethical behavior, as well as answering questions such as why companies in a culture feel the need to codify (or not to codify) principles of business ethics.

How do ethical norms become established in cultures and what is needed to change them?

The current state of business ethics and international business ethics research does not address the question of how ethical norms develop and change. Analyzing how ethical norms are integrated with other parts of the culture will lead to greater understanding of how norms evolve and become solidified. For example, Trompenaars' dimension of universalism and particularism refers to the tendency of a culture to focus more on rules (universalism) than on relationships (particularism). Trompenaars poses the following hypothetical situation:

> You are riding in a car driven by a close friend. He hits a pedestrian. You know he was going at least 35 miles per hour in an area of the city where the maximum allowed speed is 20 miles per hour. There are no witnesses. His lawyer says that if you testify under oath that he was only driving 20 miles per hour it may save him from serious consequences. What right has your friend to expect you to protect him? (Trompenaars, 1994: 34)

Trompenaars found that in universalist cultures, such as the US, most respondents feel little or no obligation to testify on behalf of their friend. However, in particularist cultures, such as South Korea or Russia, where the relationship to the friend is the most important consideration, respondents were willing to lie in their testimony to protect their friend. In the US, perjuring yourself to protect your friend is considered to be unethical, but in a particularist culture, refusing to demonstrate your loyalty and not lying for your friend is considered to be the more unethical offense.

One can examine an ethical concept such as moral approbation and its relationship to cultural dimensions (Jones and Ryan, 1997). Moral approbation is defined as "the desire for moral approval from oneself or others" (p. 664). Jones and Ryan argued that moral approbation is an important factor as an actor confronts a situation in which a decision about an ethical (or unethical) course of action is required. However, one can also speculate about the cultures in which moral approbation will have the greatest meaning. According to Trompenaars, one would expect it to have less meaning in cultures where relationships are not very important. By extension, firms can also seek moral approbation. Reputational effects and consumer perceptions of the firm's ethical stance may be more important in cultures where relationships are important.

It would be interesting to take further examples of ethical concepts, many of which have been developed in the US and to examine their appropriateness in other cultures. Equally important would be the study of ethical concepts developed in other cultures.

Stages of development in business ethics in different countries

An earlier section of this chapter stated that one form of empirical research in international business ethics is research that provides information about how different countries and different cultures view the field of business ethics. Illustrations of three specific countries focus on what is known about business ethics in each country. The three countries, Japan, Denmark, and Nigeria, have been chosen because they represent different stages of development in the topic of business ethics. Recall also that of the 99 countries surveyed, Transparency International ranked Denmark the least corrupt

JAPAN

There has been a great deal of documentation on the shape of the field of business ethics in some developed countries such as Japan (Badaracco, 1993; Carpenter, 1991; Taka, 1994, 1997). DeGeorge (1994) named Japan as one of four countries outside the US and Europe in which the field of business ethics has "taken hold." (The others are Australia, Brazil, and Hong Kong.) Taka (1997) explained that the majority of Japanese business ethicists prefer a definition of business ethics as a discipline that is concerned with the relationships between corporate activities and the realization of fairness both inside and outside corporations. The focus is thus on corporations. More wide-reaching societal issues, as well as governmental and family issues, are considered to be outside the discipline of business ethics.

Furthermore, Japanese understanding of business ethics can be achieved only with a parallel understanding of the social and religious dimensions of the culture (Taka, 1994). Japanese norms of appropriate moral behavior are influenced by both traditional and modern religions, and tend to emphasize the importance of group responsibility and morality, as well as individual morality. The individual's relationship to the group is of critical importance, as Japan is a collectivist society. An ethical principle such as loyalty to the firm takes on a different meaning in Japan than it does in a highly individualistic country. In the United States, MBA students typically hold an expectation of staying in their first job after graduation for a short time. They tend to view their future careers in individual terms. In contrast, Japanese students expect to remain loyal to the firm, perhaps even for a lifetime, and think about their careers in relation to the firm that employs them (although less so than was true in the past).

Differences in perspectives on business ethics between the US and Japan are reflected in managerial attitudes. For example, American managers tend to rely on their own individual ethics in making business decisions, whereas Japanese managers are more likely to follow company policy (Nakano, 1997). Nakano concluded that Japanese managers are also more likely than their American counterparts to be cultural relativists and to make ethical decisions that "depend on the situation." Carpenter (1991) found that US and Japanese managers who were engaged in cross-national business negotiations had differing perceptions about trust and confidence issues. Japanese managers viewed American behavior, such as inattention to local business customs and aggressive social behavior in the course of negotiations, as designed to take advantage of the Japanese side. These views were firmly rooted in Japanese values about how a business negotiation *should* take place. Similarly, American managers felt that the Japanese engaged in "wrongful behavior," including a refusal to be open and clear in the negotiating process.

As corporate life in Japan changes, the perception of ethical issues is changing as well. Some companies for the first time are facing the prospect of employee layoffs. Issues concerning the rights and treatment of women in the workplace also are emerging. Although these are issues that Western firms have addressed for some time, it is clear that Japanese, not Western, solutions will be needed.

country. Japan was ranked number 25, and Nigeria was one of the two most corrupt countries (ranked number 98). (See boxes for further information on business ethics in Japan, Denmark, and Nigeria.)

DENMARK

Recent research has informed us of the state of business ethics in Denmark (Pruzan, 1998). Pruzan identified five major themes around which interest in the topic is focused: the "political consumer" (the consumer who is deeply concerned about the environment and corporate social responsibility), ethical investing, corporate social responsibility, social and ethical accounting, and values-based management. Pruzan also outlined the interest in business ethics at the Copenhagen Business School, where courses on power and ethics have been offered since 1992 at the undergraduate, masters, and Ph.D. levels of study.

Certainly, it is difficult to find scandals associated with business in Denmark. The topic of the social responsibility of business has received a great deal of attention, resulting in heightened public awareness and action throughout the 1990s. For example, in 1996, Carlsberg made a decision not to carry out plans to build a brewery in Burma, following intense lobbying by human rights activists who protested against Burma's human rights record. Similarly, Cheminova, a well-known producer of Danish pesticides, had been involved in the production and sale of toxic products used by unprotected, untrained workers in Costa Rica. When this practice was disclosed in 1997, senior management at Cheminova stopped all further sale of the product until it could be provided in a safer form (Pruzan, 1998).

Broberg (1996) discussed a "Scandinavian" viewpoint on corporate social responsibility that is concerned with issues such as corporate governance and government regulation. Looking at Sweden, Finland, and Denmark, he concluded that there is a great deal of interest in questions such as the representation of non-shareholder interests on the board of directors, and how corporate management can use its power for the benefit of society as a whole. For example, when Scandinavian companies lay off employees, they spend large sums of money in counseling and training those employees, as well as in providing severance payments.

Using a series of vignettes similar to those of a Fritzsche and Becker (1984) study, university business students in Denmark were found not to be significantly more ethical than students in the US or New Zealand (Lysonski and Gaidis, 1991). Nor were they more ethical than the American managers surveyed in the original study. Given the high ranking of Denmark by Transparency International and other information about the importance of corporate social responsibility in Denmark, these results are surprising. Perhaps if such a survey were conducted today, it would yield different results. Or, perhaps it is corporate responsibility, and issues concerning the relationship of business to society, that have captured the attention of the Danish people, rather than individual ethical behavior in business.

NIGERIA

Nigeria is the largest trading partner of the US in sub-Saharan Africa and is of interest to the study of international business ethics for a number of reasons. Recall that Nigeria received a very low ranking by Transparency International, ranked number 98 out of 99 countries. Additionally, Nigeria has a poor human rights record, as well as an unstable economic and political system. Finally, the Shell Group's involvement in Nigeria has called attention to issues of multinational firms' ethical responsibilities in developing countries. Shell has been criticized for making no effort to avert the execution of nine environmental activists by the Nigerian government in 1995. The activists had protested against Shell for its alleged environmental damage to their homeland. Critics point to Shell's lack of public condemnations of the government as indicative of support for the brutal military regime. As the most prominent oil company operating in Nigeria, Shell found itself the target of international outrage. Shell maintained throughout the controversy that companies should not use their economic influence to "prop up" or bring down governments.

Studies of Nigeria have documented various types of cross-border fraud (Anonymous, 1997). The fraudulent proposals aimed primarily at US businesspeople include money transfer and government contract scams, real estate scams, crude oil scams, fraudulent orders for US products, and a host of other forms of impersonation and hoaxes. At the same time, it is important not to stereotype the entire Nigerian business community because of highly publicized fraud.

Tsalikis and Nwachukwu (1991) compared US and Nigerian business school student views of bribery and extortion in international commerce. Through a series of vignettes, this survey looked at how American students evaluated a bribe by an American businessperson to a US government official, a foreign businessperson to a US government official, and an American businessperson to a foreign government official. Similarly, their Nigerian sample looked at a bribe of a Nigerian businessperson to a Nigerian government official, a foreign businessperson to a Nigerian government official, and a Nigerian businessperson to a foreign government official. Their results indicated that Nigerian students do indeed see bribery as a fact of life (much more so than the American students do), but that they do not appreciate foreigners bribing their own Nigerian government officials. In other words, respondents believe that it is acceptable for Nigerians to bribe Nigerians, but not acceptable for others to do so. The authors concluded that the familiar adage espousing relativism, "When in Rome, do as the Romans do" should be modified to "When in Rome, the Romans don't want you to do as the Romans do" (p. 97).

Research on Japanese business ethics has developed to the point of beginning to link ethical attitudes and behavior to underlying dimensions of the culture. We also know a great deal about ethics in European countries through the work of the European Business Ethics Network and their published conference proceedings, as well as from work published in *Business ethics: A European review*. These studies suggest that interest in business ethics is coming into its own in Denmark, as well as in other European countries. However, we do not know as much about business ethics in less developed countries, such as Nigeria. This can be explained by the "uphill battle" that business ethics faces in becoming part of the culture in developing countries (Rossouw, 1994). Unfortunately, this difficulty leaves a huge gap in our knowledge about business ethics. Developing countries are likely to be the ones affected by the ethical guidelines of multinationals, yet comparatively little is known about how business ethics issues are viewed in those countries.

If business ethics is to a certain extent a diffusion process, who is likely to adopt ethical standards and who is not?

If we think of diffusion processes, we can look at the intriguing question not only of who is likely to adopt defined standards of business ethics, but also who is unlikely ever to adopt them. Let us take business school courses on ethics as an example. Such courses have their origins in the US, but are increasingly being adopted in other countries. Mahoney (1990) documented the existence of numerous and growing business ethics courses in the UK and continental Europe. Even the schools that do not offer a formal course on business ethics are likely to include the topic in other courses. This is especially true in European business schools, which tend to include more social sciences courses in general than do US business schools.

Additionally, there are business ethics initiatives taking place in universities around the world. For example, the MBA program (ESEADE) of the Universidad Francisco Marroquín in Guatemala conducted a survey to determine the feasibility of offering business ethics seminars to senior managers of mid-size and large companies (1998). (Transparency International ranked Guatemala number 68 in its Corruption Perceptions Index.) The university interviewed 77 senior managers face to face. The researchers began by asking a series of questions about the interviewees' perceptions of the importance of ethics, and then asked about potential interest in attending a seminar on the topic. The results indicated a strong interest in the topic, with 86 percent of the managers rating ethics as "very important." Managers were asked to name the aspects that a person should have in order to contribute to a firm's success. Among the six most important factors named, three are related to ethics: responsibility, work ethic, and honesty.

Studies such as this one in Guatemala indicate that there is interest in business ethics courses worldwide, both on the part of academic institutions and on the part of businesspeople. If it is true that business school MBA programs universally are adopting business ethics courses, then future research is needed to document the ways in which this adoption process has been tailored to individual countries.

THE CONTRIBUTION OF RESEARCH ON INTERNATIONAL BUSINESS ETHICS

If business ethicists believe that ethics is an integral part of day-to-day business decision-making processes, then international business ethics should not be considered a field entirely separate from international management. The following section examines the potential contribution of business ethics research to international management understanding.

As we have seen, international business ethics research tends to formulate principles at a reasonably high level of abstraction. However, at the same time, scholars have illustrated the use of the principles with highly concrete examples. Much as businesspeople might find it desirable, there is no such thing as a guidebook on how to do business overseas. Nor should there be. Ethical issues are idiosyncratic and complex. A request for a bribe from a customs official in Brazil might not be considered identical to a request for a bribe from a government official in Indonesia. Business ethics research has provided a means both for analysis and for application of ethics principles to each of these situations, but it cannot provide a step-by-step formula for resolving each one.

The normative contribution is important at both a morality level and a strategic level, two perspectives that sometimes become intertwined and potentially confused. As Lohr and Steinmann (1998) pointed out, we must not lose sight of the moral dimension when we discuss the strategy perspective, which aims at economic organization only. For the most part, normative researchers are not formulating economic strategy for corporations operating abroad. Instead, they are outlining the moral stance that corporations should take. However, it is now commonplace to argue that "Good ethics is good business." If corporate leaders believe this to be the case, they may act ethically or responsibly for strategic purposes, rather than for moral reasons. Research is needed that considers both a strategic and an ethical perspective, as well as the interaction between the two.

Normative research (such as that of DeGeorge, 1993; Donaldson, 1989; and Donaldson and Dunfee, 1994, 1999) has done an excellent job of calling attention to the concept of international human rights, and especially to the responsibilities of companies on this topic. This research has also presented clearly and cogently the debate between universalist and relativist perspectives of business ethics.

As mentioned, the mission of a field of international business ethics is not to provide a recipe for managers to use in handling ethical issues in other countries. However, there are several contributions to international management research from both normative and empirical research in the field. The normative contribution includes:

1 Identification of the norms by which firms *should* abide in their international business conduct.
2 Increased awareness on the part of managers of ethical responsibilities in other countries.
3 Ability to convince managers that extreme relativism is not an appropriate method for resolving ethical issues abroad. Among others, Freeman and Gilbert (1988) and Bowie (1997, 1999) have argued eloquently against a relativist perspective.
4 Aid to companies in providing guidelines for their employees as they operate abroad. Both academic research and the initiatives of organizations such as the Caux Round Table are useful in this respect.

The empirical contribution has been to lay the foundation of knowledge about the treatment of business ethics in other cultures. It is important for business ethicists to gain understanding of how the subject is treated in cultures other than their own. It is equally important for businesspeople to explore perspectives other than their own, both as to what constitutes an ethical issue as well as the appropriate responses to those ethical issues that arise in business.

The nature of empirical research necessarily means that knowledge is built in stages. Studies of practice in different countries at different points in time constitute the pieces that can be fitted together to form an overall picture of the practice of international business ethics. At this point, there are only a few studies that address certain key issues. There is little empirical research that demonstrates how actual ethical *practice* differs from country to country, in terms of what managers report that they do when confronted with an ethical issue. There is little research relating the economic, legal, religious, or political dimensions of a culture to perspectives on what is considered ethical and unethical within that culture. Finally, there is little if any hypothesis testing in the empirical research on international business ethics.

An overarching hypothesis that "Culture matters" appears to underpin much of the empirical cross-cultural or cross-national research. This can be illustrated with the following hypothetical example. Suppose that the overall expectation is that Turkish business school students are likely to see ethical issues differently than do US business school students. But how can this overall hypothesis be tied to specific cultural differences? Perhaps American business school students are more likely to see employee privacy, such as the privacy of employee e-mail, as an ethical issue than are Turkish students because the US is a highly individualistic culture, concerned with protecting the rights of individuals and individual employees. Turkey, on the other hand, falls more toward the collectivism end of the individualism–collectivism continuum. A specific hypothesis could be devised to test this expectation.

Furthermore, specific hypotheses could be formulated that would tie into the laws of different cultures. In cultures in which the law is highly developed to protect corporate interests, one would expect a different set of ethical issues than those in cultures in which the law is more protective of individual interests. For example, US legal protection of worker safety and individual property rights is far-reaching, whereas China's worker safety standards are often more lenient, and property rights are limited. Furthermore, in China, moral laws and codes generally are not believed to be necessary to ensure a moral society. Instead, personal and social moral standards of conduct are strong (Steidlmeier, 1997). A similar point can be made for cultures in which a particular religion is dominant. How would this religious emphasis be expected to manifest itself in attitudes toward issues of international business ethics? Clearly, an extensive empirical research agenda exists on topics of international business ethics. Understanding the ways in which business ethics issues are related to important features of a given culture will increase the international businessperson's ability to navigate the territory of business ethics issues in other cultures.

The contribution of empirical research includes:

1 Understanding of business ethics in other cultures (at this point in time, primarily in developed rather that in developing countries).
2 Analysis of the relationship between a culture and business ethics within that culture.

International management research also has a great deal to offer to international business ethics research. The contribution of the work of cross-national researchers such as

Hofstede has already been discussed. Additionally, theories generated in the field of international management have potential application to business ethics. As has been discussed, much of the empirical work in international business ethics has not engaged in hypothesis testing, nor has it been theory-driven.

FUTURE DIRECTIONS

Stark's (1993) article, "What's the Matter with Business Ethics?" pointed out the gap between theory and practice in business ethics. Stark criticized academic research for its inability to provide useful guidance to managerial decision-making about ethical issues. One wonders if Stark will be tempted at some point to write a follow-up article entitled, "What's the Matter with International Business Ethics?" Many of the same criticisms apply, with the added urgency that some of the most difficult ethical issues occur in the international arena. Similarly, Dean (1998) argued that the field of business ethics must contain a service component if it is to be regarded as the *profession* of business ethics. Dean questioned whether business ethics qualifies as a profession on this basis. He asked if business ethics is guiding behavior in the world of business and, more importantly, whom the field of business ethics is serving. By extension, international business ethics can only be considered a profession based on its concrete benefit to real-world problems.

As this chapter has discussed, studies in the nascent field of international business ethics are moving toward enhancing managerial ability to handle issues of business ethics globally. Normative research provides a means of addressing international business ethics issues. Empirical research documents the study of business ethics in various countries and provides information on managerial attitudes. Empirical studies that relate cultural dimensions and business ethics attitudes have the potential ability to explain why managers and employees make the decisions that they do regarding business ethics issues.

In addition to practical applications, the field of international business ethics (if it is to be a field), needs to continue to build theory. Linkage with theory in other fields such as cultural anthropology and international management has also been recommended in this chapter. Three areas to be mined in the next decade of research on international business ethics are: (1) model building and testing to assist in decision-making about business ethics issues; (2) the study and explanation of actual ethical (and unethical) behavior, rather than attitudes or hypothetical or intended behavior; and (3) research that is inclusive of all nations and cultures, regardless of their stage of economic development.

Model-building and testing

A promising avenue of research is the construction of models that can aid in decision-making about international business ethics issues. For example, Buller, Kohls, and Anderson (1997) developed a model for addressing cross-cultural ethical conflicts based on theories of conflict resolution (figure 18.1). Their model is a decision-tree analysis, employing a series of three questions for the decision-maker to ask about the particular ethical issue encountered. The first question asks: "Is the situation high in moral significance?" The second question is: "Does the manager have a high level of influence

| **Critical questions** | Is this situation high in moral significance? | Do I have a high level of influence over the outcome of the situation? | Is there a high level of urgency to resolve the situation? |

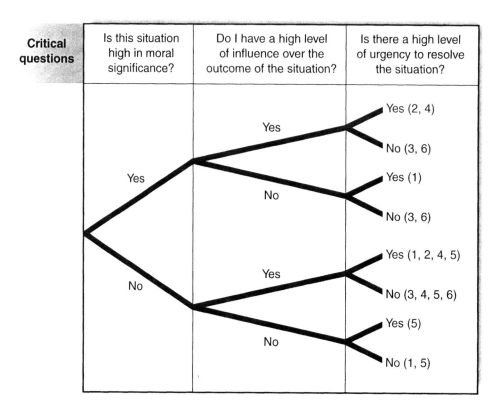

FIGURE 18.1 Model for determining strategies for resolving cross-cultural conflicts
Note: Numbers in parentheses are strategies that are feasible and arguably defensible. Strategies are as follows: 1 = avoiding; 2 = forcing; 3 = education; 4 = negotiation; 5 = accommodation; 6 = collaboration.
Source: Buller et al. (1997)

over the outcome of the ethical situation?" Finally, the decision-maker asks: "Is there a high level of urgency to resolve the situation?" The model then suggests that each of the eight possible outcomes warrants the use of a particular method of conflict resolution. Additionally, the authors presented a series of recommendations about the use of conflict-resolution techniques. For example, if all strategies are possible, collaborative problem solving should be used whenever possible, especially when the issues at stake are highly significant to both parties.

Stajkovic and Luthans (1997) based their model on social cognitive theory. National culture serves as the foundation for generating and shaping institutional, organizational, and personal factors, which in turn influence ethical standards in business and business conduct across cultures. Legislation, particularly ethics legislation, is included as an institutional factor. Codes of ethics are identified as organizational factors, and personal factors encompass values and beliefs, moral development, and "self-regulation."

These two models are very different in their orientations. That of Buller, Kohls, and

Anderson is meant to aid the decision-maker, whereas the Stajkovic and Luthans model is meant to increase understanding of the basis of ethical standards and behavior in a culture. Nevertheless, both build on existing theory in their model construction and point to the need for using existing theory, as well as generating new theory, in the field of international business ethics.

Study of behavior

Another area in need of greater development is the study of actual ethical (and unethical) behavior. Methodologically, it is no doubt easier to study attitudes than to document behavior. Respondents to surveys may be reluctant to confess to their own unethical behavior and may overstate their ethical behavior. However, this is a constraint that can be overcome (often through inventive methodology), as studies in fields such as criminology have demonstrated.

Links between corporate strategy and ethics can be investigated through the study of senior executive behavior in decision-making and implementation of strategy. For example, in the 1980s, Merck & Company made a series of decisions to develop and distribute the drug, Mectizan, to combat river blindness in less developed countries. These decisions were made despite the expectation that the drug would never make a profit. On the other hand, firms have been known to dump products overseas because they do not meet safety standards in the home country. Examination of what firms have actually done will enhance understanding of the relationship between ethics and corporate goals.

CONCLUSION

It is tempting for international business ethics researchers, especially American researchers, to pack up US studies and take them abroad. For example, we know a great deal about corporate ethics practices in the US (Weaver, Trevino, and Cochran, 1999). A natural extension of this research is to ask what forms of corporate ethics practices (e.g., codes of ethics, ethics offices, ethics hotlines) have been adopted in other countries. Certainly, this is useful information to have. However, this research must be conducted from the point of view of the country under study and the perspective of what corporate ethics practices mean within that country's culture, rather than strictly as a comparison to what is happening in the US. Furthermore, ethical issues can be expected to vary according to the stage of a country's economic and political development. The fact that formal corporate ethics practices may not exist in a country's firms should not lead to the conclusion that these firms are less ethical than US firms.

International business ethics research is at a critical point in its development. As this chapter demonstrates, substantial work has been done over the past few decades, but much work remains to be done. It is important to take stock of future directions to ensure that the field has relevance for businesspeople, advances knowledge, and holds a coherent view of business ethics in all nations, not only in developed nations.

NOTE

1 OECD member countries are Australia, Austria, Belgium, Canada, Czech Republic, Denmark, Finland, France, Germany, Greece, Hungary, Iceland, Ireland, Italy, Japan, Korea, Luxembourg, Mexico, Netherlands, New Zealand, Norway, Poland, Portugal, Spain, Sweden, Switzerland, Turkey, United Kingdom, and the United States.

References

Abegglen, J. C. and Stalk, G. (1985). *Kaisha: The Japanese corporation*. New York: Basic Books.

Abrams, D., Ando, K., and Hinkle, S. (1998). Psychological attachment to groups. Cross-cultural differences in organizational identification and subjective norms as predictors of workers' turnover intentions. *Personality and Social Psychology Bulletin*, 24, 1027–39.

Academy of Management Review (1998). Special topic forum on trust in and between organizations, 23(3), 387–620.

Acuff, F. L. (1997). *How to negotiate anything with anyone anywhere around the world*. New York: AMACOM.

Adams, J. (1976). The potential for personal growth arising from intercultural experiences. In J. Adams, J. Hayes and B. Hopson (eds), *Transition: Understanding and managing personal change* (pp. 65–83). London: Robertson.

Adams, S. (1965). Inequity in social exchange. In L. Berkowitz (ed.), *Advances in experimental social psychology*, Vol. 2. New York: Academic Press.

Adelman, M. B. (1988). Cross-cultural adjustment: A theoretical perspective on social support. *International Journal of Intercultural Relations*, 12, 183–204.

Adler, N. J. (1981). Re-entry: Managing cross-cultural transitions. *Group and Organization Studies*, 6, 341–56.

Adler, N. J. (1983). Cross-cultural management research: The ostrich and the trend. *Academy of Management Review*, 8, 226–32.

Adler, N. J. (1986). *International dimensions of organizational behavior*. Boston: PWS-Kent: 127–133.

Adler, N. J. (1987). Pacific basin managers: A gaijin, not a woman. *Human Resource Management*, 26, 169–91.

Adler, N. J. (1991). *International dimensions of organizational behavior*, 2nd edn. Boston: PWS-Kent.

Adler, N. J. (1996). Global women political leaders: An invisible history, an increasingly important future *Leadership Quarterly*, 7(1), 133–61.

Adler, N. J. (1997a). Global leaders: A dialogue with future history. *International Management*, 1(2), 21–33.

Adler, N. J. (1997b). Global leadership: Women leaders. *Management International Review*, 37 (special issue 1), 135–43.

Adler, N. J. (1997c). *International dimensions of organizational behavior*, 3rd edn. Boston: Kent.

Adler, N. J. (1998a). Did you hear? Global leadership in charity's world. *Journal of Management Inquiry*, 7(2), 21–33.

Adler, N. J. (1998b). Societal leadership: The wisdom of peace. In S. Srivastva (ed.) *Executive wisdom and organizational change* (pp. 243–337). San Francisco: Jossey-Bass.

Adler, N. J. (1999a). Global leaders: Women of influence. In G. Powell (ed.), *Handbook of gender in organizations* (pp. 239–61). Thousand Oaks, CA: Sage.

Adler, N. J. (1999b). Global entrepreneurs: Women, myths, and history. *Global Focus*, 1(4), 125–34.

Adler, N. J. (1999c). Twenty-first century leadership: Reality beyond the myths. In A. M. Rugman (series ed.) and R. Wright (volume ed.), *Research in global strategic management*, Vol. 7: *International entrepreneurship: Globalization of emerging business* (pp. 173–90). Greenwich, CT: JAI Press.

Adler, N. J. (in press). *International dimensions of organizational behavior*, 4th edn. Cincinnati, OH: South Western Press.

Adler, N. J. and Bartholomew, S. (1992). Managing globally competent people. *Academy of Management Executive*, 6(3), 52–65.

Adler, N. J., Brahm, R., and Graham, J. L. (1992). Strategy implementation: A comparison of face-to-face negotiations in the People's Republic of China and the United States. *Strategic Management Journal*, 13, 449–66.

Adler, N. J., Brody, L. W., and Osland, J. S. (2000). The women's global leadership forum: Enhancing one company's global leadership capability. *Human Resource Management*, 39(2–3), 209–25.

Adler, N. J., Brody, L. W., and Osland, J. S. (2001, in press). Advances in global leadership: The women's global leadership forum. In W. H. Mobley (ed.), *Advances in global research*, vol. 2. Greenwich, CT: JAI Press.

Adler, N. J. and Ghadar, F. (1990a). International strategy from the perspective of people and culture: The North American context. In A. M. Rugman (ed.), *Research in global strategic management: International business research for the twenty-first century; Canada's new research agenda*, Vol. 1 (pp. 179–205).

Adler N. J. and Ghadar, F. (1990b). Strategic human resource management: a global perspective. In R. Pieper (ed.), *Human resource management: An international comparison* (pp. 235–60). New York: de Gruyter.

Adler, N. J., Graham, J. L., and Gehrke, T. S. (1987). Business negotiations in Canada, Mexico, and the U.S. *Journal of Business Research*, 15(4), 411–29.

Adler, P. S. (1975). The transitional experience: An alternative view of culture shock. *Journal of Humanistic Psychology*, 15, 13–23.

Adler, P. S. (1987). Culture shock and the cross-cultural learning experience. In L. F. Luce (ed.), *Toward internationalism: Readings in cross-cultural communication* (pp. 24–35). Cambridge, MA: Newbury House.

Ah Chong, L. M. and Thomas, D. C. (1997). Leadership perceptions in cross-cultural context: Pakeha and Pacific islanders in New Zealand. *Leadership Quarterly*, 8, 275–94.

Ajzen, I. (1991). The theory of planned behavior. *Organizational Behavior and Human Decision Processes*, 50, 179–211.

Al-Kazemi, Ali and Zajac, G. (1999). Ethics sensitivity and awareness within organizations in Kuwait: An empirical exploration of espoused theory and theory-in-use. *Journal of Business Ethics*, 20(4).

Al-Zahrani, S. S. A. and Kaplowitz, S. A. (1993). Attributional biases in individualistic and collectivist cultures: A comparision of Americans and Saudis. *Social Psychology Quarterly*, 56, 223–33.

Albert, R. D. (1983). The intercultural sensitizer or culture assimilator: A cognitive approach. In D. Landis and R. W. Brislin (eds). *Handbook of Intercultural training*, Vol. 2 (pp. 186–217). New York: Pergamon.

Alderfer, C. P. (1972). *Existence, relatedness, and growth*. New York: Free Press.

Aldrich, H. (1979). *Organizations and environments*. Englewood Cliffs, NJ: Prentice-Hall.

Allen, R. (1983). Collective invention. *Journal of Economic Behavior and Organization*, 4, 1–24.

Allen, T. J. and Cohen, S. (1969). Information flow in research and development laboratories. *Administrative Science Quarterly*, 14, 12–19.

Allport, G. W. (1937). *Personality: A psychological interpretation*. New York: Henry Holt.

Allport, G. W. (1939). Attitudes. In C. Murchison (ed.), *Handbook of social psychology*. Worcester, MA: Clark University Press.

Almeida, P. (1996). Knowledge sourcing by foreign multinationals: Patent citation analysis in the U.S. semiconductor industry. *Strategic Management Journal*, special issue on "Knowledge and the firm," 7, 155–65.

Almeida, P. and Kogut, B. (1997). The exploration of technological diversity and geographic localization of innovation. *Small Business Economics*, 9, 21.

Almeida, P. and Kogut, B. (1999). The localization of knowledge and the mobility of engineers in regional networks. *Management Science*, 45, 905–17.

Almeida, P., Grant, R., and Song, J. (1998). The role of international corporations in cross-border knowledge transfer in the semiconductor industry. In M. A. Hitt, J. E. R. Costa and R. D. Nixon (eds), *Managing strategically in an interconnected world*. Chichester: John Wiley & Sons.

Almeida, P. and Rosenkopf, L. (2000). *Firm size and the mechanisms of external learning: Increasing opportunity and diminishing usefulness*. Working paper, McDonough School of Business, Georgetown University.

Altocchi, J. and Altocchi, L. (1995). Polyfaceted psychological acculturation in Cook Islanders. *Journal of Cross-Cultural Psychology*, 26, 426–40.

Amir, Y. (1969). Contact hypothesis in ethnic relations. *Psychological Bulletin*, 71, 319–42.

Amir, Y. (1976). The role of intergroup contact in change of prejudice and ethnic relations. In P. H. Katz (ed.), *Towards the elimination of racism* (pp. 245–308). New York: Pergamon.

Anand, R. P. (1981). *Cultural factors in international relations* (pp. 63–76). New Delhi: Abinhav.

Anderson, E. (1990). Two firms, one frontier: On assessing joint venture performance. *Sloan Management Review*, 31(2), 19–30.

Anderson, E. and Weitz, B. (1989). Determinants of continuity in conventional industrial channel dyads. *Marketing Science*, 8(4): 310–23.

Anderson, J. C. and Narus, J. A. (1984). A model of the distributor's perspective of distributor–manufacturer working relationships. *Journal of Marketing*, 48 (fall), 62–74.

Anderson J. C. and Narus, J. A. (1990). A model of distributor firm and manufacturer firm working partnerships. *Journal of Marketing*, 54 (January), 42–58.

Andrews, T. (1999). Crossverging managerial practice in post-crisis Thailand. Unpublished manuscript, presented to the Centre of Southeast Asian Studies, October 28.

Anonymous (1997). Doing business in Nigeria: Distinguishing between the profitable and the questionable. *Business America*, 118(12), 30–2.

Appleyard, M. (1996). How does knowledge flow? Interfirm patterns in the semiconductor industry. *Strategic Management Journal*, 17 (special issue), 137–54.

Argyle, M. (1982). Intercultural communication. In S. Bochner (ed.), *Cultures in contact: Studies in cross-cultural interaction* (pp. 61–79). Oxford: Pergamon.

Argyle, M., Furnham, A., and Graham, J. A. (1981). *Social situations*. Cambridge: Cambridge University Press.

Argyle, M. and Kendon, A. (1967). The experimental analysis of social performance. In L. Berkowitz (ed.), *Advances in experimental social psychology* (Vol. 3). New York, NY: Academic Press.

Aristotle (1924). Rhetoric (W. R. Roberts, trans.). In W. D. Ross (ed.), *The works of Aristotle*, Vol. 11 (pp. 1354–420). Oxford: Clarendon Press (Original work written ca. 330 BC).

Armstrong, J. S. and Collopy, F. (1996). Competitive orientation: Effects of objectives and information on managerial decisions and profitability. *Journal of Marketing Research*, 33, 188–99.

Arthur Andersen, Inc. (1999). *Network '99: "Hot topics" summary report*. Chicago: Arthur Andersen Human Capital Services.

Arthur, W. and Bennett, W. (1995). The international assignee: The relative importance of factors perceived to contribute to success. *Personnel Psychology*, 48, 99–114.

Arthur, W. and Bennett, W. (1997). A comparative test of alternative models of international assignee job performance. *New Approaches to Employee Management*, 4, 141–72.

Aryee, S. and Stone, R. J. (1996). Work experiences, work adjustment and psychological well-being of expatriate employees in Hong Kong. *The International Journal of Human Resource Management*, 7, 150–64.

Asante, M. K. and Gudykunst, W. B. (eds) (1989). *Handbook of international and intercultural communication*. Newbury Park: Sage.

Asch, S. (1959). A perspective on social psychology. In S. Koch (ed.), *Psychology: A study of a science* Vol. 3, pp. 363–83.

Ashford, S. J. (1986). Feedback-seeking in individual adaptation: A resource perspective. *Academy of Management Journal*, 29(3), 465–87. Greenwich, CT: JAI Press.

Ashford, S. J. (1989). Self-assessments in organizations: A literature review and integrative model. In L. L. Cummings and B. M. Staw (eds), *Research in Organizational Behavior*, 11, 133–74.

Ashford, S. J. and Cummings, L. L. (1983). Feedback as an individual resource: Personal strategies of creating information. *Organizational Behavior and Human Performance*, 32, 370–98.

Ashford, S. J. and Northcraft, G. B. (1992). Conveying more (or less) than we realize: The role of impression management in feedback-seeking. *Organizational Behavior and Human Decision Processes*, 53, 310–34.

Ashford, S. J. and Tsui, A. S. (1991). Self-regulation for managerial effectiveness: The role of active feedback seeking. *Academy of Management Journal*, 34(2), 251–80.

Ashkanasy, N., Wilderom, C., and Peterson, M. F. (eds) (2000). *Handbook of organizational climate and culture*. Thousand Oaks, CA: Sage.

Ashmore, R., Del Boca, F., and Wohlers, A. (1986). Gender stereotypes. In R. D. Ashmore and F. D. Del Boca (eds), *The social psychology of female–male relations: A critical analysis of central concepts*. Orlando, FL: Academic Press.

Aspinwall, L. G. and Taylor, S. E. (1993). Effects of social comparison direction, threat, and self-esteem on affect, self-evaluation, and expected success. *Journal of Personality and Social Psychology*, 64(5), 708–22.

Astley W. G. and Van De Ven (1983). Central perspectives and debates in organization theory. *Administrative Science Quarterly*, 28, 245–73.

Attewell, P. (1994). Information technology and the productivity paradox. In D. H. Harris (ed.), *Organizational linkages: Understanding the productivity paradox* (pp. 13–53). Washington: National Academy Press.

Atwater, L. E. and Yammarino, F. J. (1997). Self–other rating agreement: A review and model. *Research in Personnel and Human Resources Management*, 15, 121–74.

Au, K., Peng, M. W., and Wang, D. (2000). Interlocking directorates, firm strategies, and performance in Hong Kong: Towards a research agenda. *Asia Pacific Journal of Management*, 17, 29–47.

Aulakh, P., Kotabe, M., and Sahay, A. (1996). Trust and performance in cross-border marketing partnerships: A behavioral approach. *Journal of International Business Studies*, 27 (special issue), 1005–32.

Awadzi, W. K. (1987). Determinants of joint venture performance: A study of international joint ventures in the United States. Ph.D. dissertation, Louisiana State University.

Aycan, Z. (1997). Acculturation of expatriate managers: A process model of adjustment and performance. In Z. Aycan (ed.), *Expatriate management: Theory and research*, Vol. 4 (pp. 1–41). Greenwich, CT: JAI Press.

Ayman, R. and Chemers, M. M. (1983). Relationship of supervisory behavior ratings to work group effectiveness and subordinate satisfaction among Iranian managers. *Journal of Applied Psychology*, 68, 338–41.

Azevedo, A., Paul, K., and Von Glinow, M. (1994). An integrative framework for cross-cultural research on business ethics. Paper presented to the Sixth Annual Conference of the Society for the Advancement of Socio-Economics, Paris.

Badaracco, J. (1991). *Knowledge links: How firms compete through strategic alliances.* Boston: Harvard Business School Press.

Badaracco, J. L., Jr (1993). The IBM–Fujitsu conundrum. In M. Hoffman, J. Brown Kamm, and R. E. Frederick (eds), *Emerging global business ethics* (pp. 79–88). Westport, CT: Greenwood Publishing Group.

Badawy, M. K. (1979). Managerial attitudes and need orientations of Mideastern executives: An empirical cross-cultural analysis. *Academy of Management Proceedings*, 39, 293–7.

Bagwhati, J. (2000, May 2). Nike wrongfoots the student activists. *Financial Times*, p. 11.

Bailey, J. R., Chen, C. C., and Dou, S.-G. (1997). Conceptions of self and performance-related feedback in the US, Japan and China. *Journal of International Business Studies*, 28(3), 605–25.

Baker, J. C. and Ivancevich, J. M. (1971). The assignment of American executives abroad: Systematic, haphazard or chaotic? *California Management Review*, 13, 39–44.

Baliga, G. M. and Baker, J. C. (1985). Multinational corporate policies for expatriate managers: Selection, training, evaluation. *SAM Advanced Management Journal*, 50, 31–8.

Baligh, H. H. (1994). Components of culture: Nature, interconnections, and relevance to the decisions on the organization structure. *Management Science*, 40, 14–27.

Ball, J. (1996). Identity formation in Confucian-heritage societies: Implications for theory, research and practice. Paper presented at the 26th International Congress of Psychology, August, Montreal, Canada.

Ballinger, J. (1992, August). The new free-trade heel. *Harper's*, pp. 46–7.

Bandura, A. (1977). *Social learning theory.* Englewood Cliffs, NJ: Prentice-Hall.

Bandura, A. (1986). *Social foundation of thought and action: A social cognitive theory.* Englewood Cliffs, NJ: Prentice-Hall.

Bandura, A. (1991). Social cognitive theory of self-regulation. *Organizational Behavior and Human Decision Processes*, 50, 248–85.

Bandura, A. (1996a). Reflections on human agency. In J. Georgas, M. Manthuli, E. Besevekis, and A. Kokkei (eds), *Contemporary psychology in Europe: Theory, research, and applications* (pp. 194–210). Goettingen, Germany: Hogrefe and Huber.

Bandura, A. (1996b). *Self-efficacy: The exercise of control.* New York: Freeman.

Barber, B. (1995). All economies are "embedded." *Social Research*, 62, 387–413.

Barham, K. (1991). Developing the international manager. In P. Reid (ed.), *Global management: Culture, context, competence.* Ashridge College, Ashridge.

Barkema, H. G. and Vermeulen, F. (1997). What differences in the cultural backgrounds of partners are detrimental for international joint ventures? *Journal of International Business Studies*, 28, 845–64.

Barna, L. M. (1983). The stress factor in intercultural relations. In D. Landis and R. W. Brislin (eds), *Handbook of intercultural training*, Vol. 2 (pp. 19–49). New York: Pergamon.

Barna, L. M. (1988). Stumbling blocks in intercultural communication. In L. A. Samovar and R. E. Porter (eds), *Intercultural communication: A reader*, 5th edn (pp. 322–30). Belmont: Wadsworth.

Barney, J. (1991). Firm resources and sustained competitive advantage. *Journal of Management*, 17, 99–120.

Bartholomew, S. (1997). National systems of biotechnology innovation: Complex interdependence in the global system. *Journal of International Business Studies*, 28(2), 241–66.

Bartlett, C. A. (1979). Multinational structural evolution: The changing decision environment in international divisions. Doctoral dissertation, Harvard Business School.

Bartlett, C. A. and Ghoshal, S. (1986). Tap your subsidiaries for global reach. *Harvard Business Review* (November–December), 87–94.

Bartlett, C. A. and Ghoshal, S. (1989a). *Managing across borders: The transnational solution.* Boston: Harvard Business School Press.

Bartlett, C. A. and Ghoshal, S. (1989b). Managing across borders: New organizational responses. *Sloan Management Review,* 29(1), 43–53.

Bartlett, C. A. and Ghoshal, S. (1995). *Transnational management.* Chicago, IL: Irwin.

Bartlett, C. A. and Ghoshal, S. (1998). *Managing across borders: The transnational solution,* 2nd edn. Boston, MA: Harvard Business School.

Barr, S. H. and Conlon, E. J. (1994). Effects of distribution of feedback in work groups. *Academy of Management Journal,* 37(3), 641–55.

Bass, B. M. (1985). *Leadership and performance beyond expectations.* New York: Free Press.

Bass, B. M. (1990). *Bass and Stogdill's handbook of leadership,* 3rd edn. New York: Free Press.

Bass, B. M. (1997). Does the transactional–transformational leadership paradigm transcend national boundaries? *American Psychologist,* 52, 130–9.

Bass, B. M. and Avolio, B. J. (1993). Transformational leadership: A response to critiques. In M. M. Chemers and R. Ayman (eds), *Leadership theories and research: Perspectives and directions.* New York: Academic Press.

Bass, B. M., Burger, P. C., Doktor, R., and Barrett, G. V. (1979). *Assessment of managers: An international comparison.* New York: Free Press.

Batten, J., Hettihewa, S., and Mellor, R. (1999). Factors affecting management: Comparing a developed and a developing economy. *Journal of Business Ethics,* 19(1), 51–9.

Baughn, C. (1995). Personal and organizational factors associated with effective repatriation. In J. Selmer (ed.), *Expatriate management: New ideas for international business* (pp. 215–30). Westport: Quorum Books.

Baumeister, R. F. and Tice, D. M. (1985). Self-esteem and responses to success and failure: Subsequent performance and intrinsic motivation. *Journal of Personality,* 53, 450–67.

Baumgarten, K. (1995). Training and development of international staff. In A. Harzing, and J. van Ruysseveldt (eds), *International human resource management: An integrated approach* (pp. 205–28). London: Sage.

Bayes, J. (ed.) (1991). Women and public administration: International perspectives. *Women and Politics,* 11(4), 111–31.

Bazerman, M. H. and Carroll, J. S. (1987). Negotiator cognition. In B. M. Staw and L. L. Cummings (eds), *Research in organizational behavior,* Vol. 9 (pp. 247–88). Greenwich, CT: JAI Press.

Bazerman, M. H., Curhan, J. R., Moore, D. A., and Valley, K. L. (2000). Negotiation. *Annual Review of Psychology,* 51, 279–314.

Bazerman, M. H., Magliozzi, T., and Neale, M. A. (1985). Inegrative bargaining in a competitive market. *Organizational Behavior and Human Decision Processes,* 35, 294–313.

Bazerman, M. H. and Neale, M. A. (1983). Heuristics in negotiation. Limitations to effective dispute resolution. In M. H. Bazerman and R. J. Lewicki (eds), *Negotiating in organizations.* Beverley Hills: Sage.

Beamish, P. W. (1984). Joint venture performance in developing countries. Ph.D. dissertation, University of Western Ontario.

Beamish, P. W. (1985). The characteristics of joint ventures in developed and developing countries. *Columbia Journal of World Business,* 20(3), 13–19.

Beamish, P. W. (1988). *Multinational joint ventures in developing countries.* London: Routledge.

Beamish, P. W. (1993). The characteristics of joint ventures in the People's Republic of China. *Journal of International Marketing,* 1(2), 29–49.

Beamish, P. W. (1994). Joint ventures in LDCs: Partner selection and performance. *Management International Review,* 34, 60–75.

Beamish, P. W. and Banks, J. C. (1987). Equity joint ventures and the theory of the multinational enterprise. *Journal of International Business Studies,* 18(2), 1–16.

Becker, H. and Fritzsche, D. J. (1987a). Business ethics: A cross-cultural comparison of managers' attitudes. *Journal of Business Ethics*, 6(4), 289–95.

Becker, H. and Fritzsche, D. J. (1987b). A Comparison of the Ethical Behavior of American, French and German Managers. *Columbia Journal of World Business*, 22(4), 87–95.

Befus, C. P. (1988). A multilevel treatment approach for culture shock experienced by sojourners. *International Journal of Intercultural Relations*, 12, 381–400.

Behrman, J. (1970). *National interest and the multinational enterprise*. New York, NY: Prentice-Hall.

Benedict, R. (1946). *The chrysanthemum and the sword*. Boston, MA: Houghton-Mifflin.

Bennett, J. M. (1993a). Cultural marginality: Identity issues in intercultural training. In R. Michael Paige (ed.), *Education for intercultural experience*. Yarmouth, Maine: Intercultural Press.

Bennett, J. M. (1999). Turning frogs into interculturalists: A student-centered developmental approach to teaching intercultural competence. Paper presented at the Cross-Cultural Colloquium, June 11. Los Angeles: UCLA (as published by Janet M. Bennett and Milton J. Bennett, The Intercultural Communication Institute, Portland, Oregon).

Bennett, M. J. (1986). Towards ethnorelativism: A developmental model of intercultural sensitivity. In R. M. Paige (ed.), *Cross-cultural orientation: New conceptualizations and applications* (27–69). Lanham: University Press of America.

Bennett, M. J. (1993a). Towards a developmental model of intercultural sensitivity. In R. M. Paige (ed.), *Education for intercultural experience*. Yarmouth, Maine: Intercultural Press.

Bennett, M. J. (1993b). Towards ethnorelativism: a developmental model of intercultural sensitivity. In R. M. Paige (ed.), *Education for intercultural experience* (pp. 21–71). Yarmouth, ME: Intercultural Press.

Bennis, W. (1992). "On the leading edge of change" *Executive Excellence*, 9(4), 5–9.

Benson, P. G. (1978). Measuring cross-cultural adjustment: The problem of criteria. *International Journal of Intercultural Relations*, 2, 21–37.

Berenbeim, R. E. (1999). The Conference Board Research Report 1243–99–RR. *Global corporate ethics practices: A developing consensus*.

Berger, P. L. and Luckmann, T. 1964. *The social construction of reality*. New York: Doubleday.

Berman, J. J., Murphy-Berman, V., and Singh, P. (1985). Cross-cultural similarities and differences in perceptions of fairness. *Journal of Cross-Cultural Psychology*, 16(1), 55–67.

Berry, J. W. (1991). Cultural variations in field dependence–independence. In S. Wapner and J. Demick (eds), *Field dependence–independence: Cognitive style across the life span* (pp. 289–308). Hillsdale, NJ: Erlbaum.

Berry, J. W. (1997). An ecocultural approach to the study of cross-cultural I/O Psychology. In P. C. Earley and M. Erez (eds), *New perspectives on international industrial/organizational psychology*. San Francisco: Jossey-Bass.

Berscheid, E. and Walster, E. H. (1969). *Interpersonal attraction*. Reading, MA: Addison-Wesley.

Bettenhausen, K. L. (1991). Five years of groups research: what we have learned and what needs to be addressed. *Journal of Management*, 17(2), 345–81.

Beugré, C. D. (1998). *Managing fairness in organizations*. Westport, CT: Quorum.

Bhagat, R. S., Kedia, B. L., Crawford, S. E., and Kaplan, M. R. (1990). Cross-cultural issues in organizational psychology: Emergent trends and directions for research in the 1990s. *International Review of Industrial and Organizational Psychology*, 5, 59–99.

Bhagat, R. S., and McQuaid, S. J. (1982). Role of subjective culture in organizations: A review and directions for future research. *Journal of Applied Psychology*, 67(5), 653–85.

Bhagat, R. S. and Prien, K. O. (1996). Cross-cultural training in organizational contexts. In D. Landis and R. S. Bhagat (eds), *Handbook of intercultural training*, 2nd edn (pp. 216–30). Thousand Oaks: Sage.

Bhattacharya, R., Devinney, T. M., and Pillutla, M. M. (1998). A formal model of trust based on outcomes. *Academy of Management Review*, 23, 459–72.

Bhawuk, D. P. (1990). Cross-cultural orientation programs. In R. W. Brislin (ed.), *Applied cross-cultural psychology* (pp. 325–46). Newbury Park: Sage.

Bhawuk, D. P. (1998). The role of culture theory in cross-cultural training. A multimethod study of culture specific, culture general, and culture theory-based assimilators. *Journal of Cross-Cultural Psychology*, 29, 630–55.

Bies, R. J. (2000). Interactional (in)justice: The sacred and the profane. In J. Greenberg and R. Cropanzano (eds), *Advances in organizational justice*. Stanford, CA: Stanford University Press.

Bies, R. J. and Moag, J. S. (1986). Interactional justice: Communication criteria of fairness. In R. J. Lewicki, B. H. Sheppard, and M. H. Bazerman (eds), *Research on negotiation in organizations* (pp. 43–55). Greenwich, CT: JAI Press.

Bigoness, W. J. and Blakely, G. L. (1996). A cross-national study of managerial values. *Journal of International Business Studies*, 4, 739–53.

Bird, A. and Dunbar, R. (1991). Getting the job done over there: Improving expatriate productivity. *National Productivity Review*, 10, 145–56.

Bird, A., Heinbuch, S., Dunbar, R., and McNulty, M. (1993). A conceptual model of the effects of area studies training programs and a preliminary investigation of the model's hypothesized relationships. *International Journal of Intercultural Relations*, 17, 415–36.

Birdseye, M. G. and Hill, J. S. (1995). Individual, organizational/work and environmental influences on expatriate turnover tendencies: An empirical study. *Journal of International Business Studies*, 26, 787–813.

Björkman, I. and Gertsen, M. (1993). Selecting and training Scandinavian expatriates: Determinants of corporate practice. *Scandinavian Journal of Management*, 9(2), 145–64.

Black, J. S. (1988). Work role transitions: A study of American expatriate managers in Japan. *Journal of International Business Studies*, 19, 277–94.

Black, J. S. (1990). The relationship of personal characteristics with the adjustment of Japanese expatriate managers. *Management International Review*, 30, 119–34.

Black, J. S. (1992). Coming home: The relationship of expatriations with repatriation adjustment and job performance. *Human Relations*, 45, 177–92.

Black, J. S. and Gregersen, H. B. (1990). Expectations, satisfaction, and intention to leave of American expatriate managers in Japan. *International Journal of Intercultural Relations*, 14, 485–503.

Black, J. S. and Gregersen, H. B. (1991). Antecedents to cross-cultural adjustment for expatriates in Pacific Rim assignments. *Human Relations*, 44, 497–515.

Black, J. S., Gregersen, H. B., and Mendenhall, M. E. (1992). *Global assignments: Successfully expatriating and repatriating international managers*. San Francisco: Jossey-Bass.

Black, J. S., Gregersen, H. B., Mendenhall, M. E., and Stroh, L. K. (1999). *Globalizing people through international assignments*. New York: Addison-Wesley Longman.

Black, J. S. and Mendenhall, M. E. (1990). Cross-cultural training effectiveness: A review and a theoretical framework for future research. *Academy of Management Review*, 15, 113–36.

Black, J. S. and Mendenhall, M. E. (1991). The U-curve adjustment hypothesis revisited: A review and theoretical framework. *Journal of International Business Studies*, 22, 225–47.

Black, J. S., Mendenhall, M. E., and Oddou, G. R. (1991). Toward a comprehensive model of international adjustment: An integration of multiple theoretical perspectives. *Academy of Management Review*, 16, 291–317.

Black, J. S. and Porter, L. W. (1991). Managerial behaviors and job performance: A successful manager in Los Angeles may not succeed in Hong Kong. *Journal of International Business Studies*, 22, 99–113.

Black, J. S. and Stephens, G. K. (1989). The influence of the spouse on American expatriate adjustment and intent to stay in Pacific Rim overseas assignments. *Journal of Management*, 15, 529–44.

Blackler, F. (1993). Knowledge and the theory of organizations: Organizations as activity systems and the reframing of management. *Journal of Management Studies*, 30, 863–84.

Blackman, C. (1997). *Negotiating China: Case studies and strategies*. St Leonards, NSW, Australia: Allen & Unwin.

Blau, P. 1964. *Exchange and power in social life*. New York, NY: Wiley and Sons.

Blinder, A. S. (1999). Eight steps to a new financial order. *Foreign Affairs*. September–October.

Blocklyn, P. L. (1989). Developing the international executive. *Personnel*, 66, 44–7.

Blodgett, L. L. (1987). A resource-based study of bargaining power in U.S.–foreign equity joint ventures. Ph.D. dissertation, University of Michigan.

Blodgett, L. L. (1991). Partner contributions as predictors of equity share in international ventures. *Journal of International Business Studies*, 22, 63–78.

Blodgett, L. L. (1992). Factors in the instability of international joint ventures: An event history analysis. *Strategic Management Journal*, 13, 475–81.

Blumenthal, J. F. (1988). Strategic and organizational conditions for joint venture formation and success. Ph.D. dissertation, University of Southern California.

Blummer, H. (1961). *Symbolic interactionism: Perspective and method*. Englewood Cliffs, NJ: Prentice-Hall.

Blunt, P. (1976). Management motivation in Kenya: Some initial impressions. *Eastern African Research and Development*, 6(1), 11–21.

Blunt, P., and Jones, M. L. (1992). *Managing African organizations*. Berlin: Walter de Gruyter.

Bochner, S. (ed.) (1981). *The mediating person: Bridges between cultures*. Cambridge: Schenkman.

Bochner, S. (1982). *Cultures in contact: Studies in cross-cultural interaction*. New York: Pergamon.

Bochner, S., Lin, A., and McLeod, B. M. (1980). Anticipated role conflict of returning overseas students. *Journal of Social Psychology*, 110, 265–72.

Boddewyn, J. (1999). The domain of international management. *Journal of International Management*, 5, 3–14.

Boddewyn, J. and Brewer, T. (1994). International-business political behavior: New theoretical directions. *Academy of Management Review*, 19, 119–43.

Boisot, M. and Child, J. (1996). From fiefs to clans and network capitalism: Expanding China's emerging economic order. *Administrative Science Quarterly*, 41, 600–28.

Boje, D. M. (1995). Stories of the storytelling organization: A postmodern analysis of Disney as Tamara-land. *Academy of Management Journal*, 38, 997–1035.

Boje, D. M. (1998). *How critical theory and critical pedagogy can unmask Nike's labor practices*. Paper presented at the annual meeting of the Academy of Management, San Diego, CA, August.

Boje, D. M. (1999). Is Nike Roadrunner or Wile E. Coyote? A postmodern organization analysis of double logic. *Journal of Business and Entrepreneurship*, 2, 77–109.

Boje, D. M. (2000, January 14). *Nike stories and stock reports*. Posted on the World Wide Web at http://cvac.nmsu.edu/~dboje/nikestockstories.html

Bonache, J. and Brewster C. (2001, forthcoming). Knowledge transfer and the management of expatriation. *Thunderbird International Business Review*.

Bonache, J. and Fernandez, Z. (1997). Expatriate compensation and its link to the subsidiary strategic role: A theoretical analysis. *International Journal of Human Resource Management*, 8, 457–75.

Bond, M. H. (1987). Chinese values and the search for culture-free dimensions of culture. *Journal of Cross-Cultural Psychology*, 18, 143–64.

Bond, M. H. (1988). Finding universal dimensions of individual variation in multicultural studies of values: The Rokeach and Chinese value surveys. *Journal of Personality and Social Psychology*, 55, 1009–15.

Bond, M. H. (1997). Two decades of chasing the dragon. In M. H. Bond (ed.), *Working at the interface of cultures* (pp. 179–90). London and New York: Routledge.

Bond, M. H. and Kwang, L. (1986). The social psychology of Chinese people. In M. H. Bond (ed.), *The psychology of the Chinese people* (pp. 213–66). New York: Oxford University Press.

Bond, M. H., Leung, K., and Wan, C. K. (1982). How does cultural collectivism operate? The impact of task and maintenance contributions on reward distributions. *Journal of Cross-Cultural Psychology*, 13(2), 186–200.

Bond, M. H. and Venus, C. K. (1991). Resistance to group or personal insults in an ingroup or outgroup context. *International Journal of Psychology*, 26(1), 83–94.

Bond, M. H., Wan, K. C., Leung, K., and Giacalone, R. A. (1985). How are responses to verbal insult related to cultural collectivism and power distance. *Journal of Cross-Cultural Psychology*, 16(1), 111–27.

Bond, R. and Smith, P. B. (1996). Culture and conformity: A meta-analysis of studies using Asch's line judgment task. *Psychological Bulletin*, 119, 111–37.

Bontempo, R., Lobel, S. A., and Triandis, H. C. (1989). Compliance and value internalization among Brazilian and U.S. students. Unpublished manuscript.

Bontempo, R. and Rivero, J. C. (1992). Cultural variation in cognition: The role of self-concept in the attitude–behavior link. Paper presented at the American Academy of Management meeting in Las Vegas, Nevada, August.

Borg, M. and Harzing, A. W. (1996). Karriereprade und Effektivität internationaler Führungskräfte. In K. Macharzina and J. Wolf (eds), *Handbuch internationales führungskräfte-management* (pp. 279–97). Stuttgart: Raabe.

Bouquet, C. and Hébert, L. (1999). *The governance structure of Japanese subsidiaries in Europe.* Working paper, Richard Ivey School of Business.

Bowie, N. E. (1997). Relativism, cultural and moral. In Patricia H. Werhane and R. Edward Freeman (eds), *Encyclopedic dictionary of business ethics* (pp. 551–5). Malden, MA: Blackwell Publishers Inc.

Bowie, N. E. (1999). *Business ethics: A Kantian perspective.* Malden, MA: Blackwell Publishers Inc.

Boxall, P. (1995). Building the theory of comparative HRM. *Human Resource Management Journal*, 5(5), 5–17.

Boyacilliger, N. (1990). Role of expatriates in the management of interdependence, complexity and risk of MNEs. *Journal of International Business Studies*, 21, 357–78.

Brandt, V. S. (1974). Skiing cross-culturally. *Current Anthropology*, 15, 64–6.

Brayfield, A. H. and Crockett, W. H. (1955). Employee attitudes and employee performance. *Psychological Bulletin*, 52: 396–424.

Brett, J. M. and Okumura, T. (1998). Inter- and intracultural negotiations: U.S. and Japanese negotiators. *Academy of Management Journal*, 41, 495–510.

Brett, J. M., Tinsley, C. H., Janssens, M., Barsness, Z. I., and Lytle, A. L. (1997). New approaches to the study of culture in industrial/organizational psychology. In P. C. Earley and M. Erez (eds), *New perspectives in international industrial/organizational psychology* (pp. 75–129). San Francisco: New Lexington.

Brewer, M. (1993). Social identity, distinctiveness, and in-group homogeneity. *Social Cognition*, 11(1), 150–64.

Brewer, M. and Gardner, W. (1996). Who is this "we"? Levels of collective identity and self-representations. *Journal of Personality and Social Psychology*, 71, 83–93.

Brewster, C. (1991). *The management of expatriates.* London: Kogan Page.

Brewster C. (1995). Effective expatriate training. In J. Selmer (ed.), *Expatriate management: New ideas for international business* (pp. 57–71). Westport, CT: Quorum Books.

Brewster, C. J. (1999). Different paradigms in strategic HRM: Quest raised by comparative research. In P. Wright, L. Dyer, J. Boudreau and G. Milkovich (eds), *Research in personnel and HRM.* Greenwich, CT: JAI Press.

Brewster, C. and Harris H. (eds) (1999). *International HRM: Contemporary issues in Europe.* London: Routledge.

Brewster C. and Holt, L. H. (2000). Human resource management: The northern Europe contribution. In *HRM in northern Europe*. Oxford: Blackwell.

Brewster, C. and Larsen, H. H. (2000). Human resource management: The Northern Europe contribution. In C. Brewster and H. H. Larsen (eds), *HRM in northern Europe*. Oxford: Blackwell.

Brewster, C., Morley, M., and Mayshofer, W. (2000). *New challenges for human resource management*. London: Macmillan.

Brewster, C. and Pickard, J. (1994). Evaluating expatriate training. *International Studies of Management and Organization*, 24, 18–35.

Brewster, C. and Scullion, H. (1997). Expatriate HRM: A review and an agenda. *Human Resource Management Journal*, 7, 32–41.

Briody, E. K., and Chrisman, J. B. (1991). Cultural adaptation on overseas assignments. *Human Organization*, 50, 264–82.

Brislin, R. (1981). *Cross-cultural encounters: Face-to-face interaction*. New York: Pergamon.

Brislin, R. (1993). *Understanding culture's influence on behavior*. Fort Worth, Texas: Harcourt-Brace.

Brislin, R., Landis, D., and Brandt, M. E. (1983). Conceptualizations of intercultural behavior and training. In D. Landis and R. W. Brislin (eds), *Handbook of intercultural training*, Vol. 1 (pp. 1–35). New York: Pergamon.

Brislin, R. and Yoshida, T. (1994). *Intercultural communication training: An introduction*. Thousand Oaks: Sage.

Broberg, M. P. (1996). Corporate social responsibility in the European communities: The Scandinavian viewpoint. *Journal of Business Ethics*, 15(6), 615–22.

Brockner, J. and Chen, Ya-Ru (1996). The moderating roles of self-esteem and self-construal in reaction to a threat to the self: Evidence from the People's Republic of China and the United States. *Journal of Personality and Social Psychology*, 71, 603–15.

Brod, H. and Kaufman, M. (eds) (1994). *Theorizing masculinities*. Thousand Oaks, CA: Sage.

Brooke, M. Z. and Remmers, H. L. (1970). *The strategy of multinational enterprise*. London: Longman.

Brookes, B. and Madden, P. (1995). *The globe-trotting sports shoe*. London: Christian Aid. Downloaded from the world wide web at
http://www.saigon.com/nike/christian-aid.htm

Brouthers, K. and Bamossy, G. (1997). The role of key stakeholders in international joint venture negotiations: Case studies from Eastern Europe. *Journal of International Business Studies*, 28, 285–308.

Broverman, I., Broverman, D., Clarkson, F., Rosenkrantz, P., and Vogel, S. (1972). Sex role stereotypes and clinical judgements of mental health. *Journal of Consulting and Clinical Psychology*, 34, 1–7.

Brown, R. (1987). How to choose the best expatriates. *Personnel Management*, June, 67.

Bruner, J. (1990). *Acts of meaning*. Cambridge: Cambridge University Press.

Brynjolfsson, E. (1993). The productivity paradox of information technology. *Communications of the ACM*, 36(12), 67–77.

Brynjolfsson, E. and Hitt, L. M. (1998). Beyond the productivity paradox. *Communications of the ACM*, 41(8), 49–55.

Buck, T., Filatotchev, I., and Wright, M. (1998). Agents, stakeholders, and corporate governance in Russian firms. *Journal of Management Studies*, 35, 81–104.

Buckley, P. and Casson, M. (1988). A theory of cooperation in international business. In F. Contractor and P. Lorange (eds), *Cooperative strategies in international business* (pp. 31–53). Toronto, ON: Lexington Books.

Buera, A. and Gluek, W. (1979). Need satisfaction of Libyan managers. *Management International Review*, 19(1): 113–23.

Buller, P. F., Kohls, J. J., and Anderson, K. (1997). A model for addressing cross-cultural ethical conflicts. *Business and Society*, 36(2), 169–93.

Burawoy, M. and Krotov, P. (1992). The Soviet transition from socialism to capitalism: Worker control and economic bargaining. *American Sociological Review*, 57, 16–38.

Burgess, R. L. and Huston, T. L. (1983). Social exchange in developing relationships: an overview. In R. L. Burgess and T. L. Huston (eds), *Social exchange in developing relationships* (pp. 3–28). New York, NY: Academic Press.

Burke, P. J., and Reitzes, D. C. (1981). The link between identity and role performance. *Social Psychology Quarterly*, 44: 83–92.

Burke, P. J. and Reitzes, D. C. (1991). An identity theory approach to commitment. *Social Psychology Quarterly*, 54, 239–51.

Burke, P. J. and Tully, J. (1977). The measurement of role/identity. *Social Forces*, 55, 880–97.

Burns, J. M. (1978). *Leadership.* New York: Harper and Row.

Burton, K. (1994). *The business culture in Spain.* Boston: Butterworth-Heinemann.

Business Week (1999a). Recovery without reform. August 9, 28–31.

Business Week (1999b). Size does matter in Asia's cyber race. May 17, 58–60.

Butler, J. K., Jr (1991). Toward understanding and measuring conditions of trust: Evolution of a conditions of trust inventory. *Journal of Management*, 17(3), 643–63.

Butler, J. K., Jr (1995). Behavior, trust, and goal achievement in a win–win negotiating role play. *Group and Organization Management*, 20, 486–501.

Buzzell, R. D. and Gale, B. T. (1987). *The PIMS principles: Linking strategy to performance.* New York: Free Press.

Caligiuri, P. and Lazarova, M. (2001). Strategic repatriation policies to enhance global leadership. In M. Mendenhall, T. Kuhlmann, and G. Stahl (eds), *Developing global business leaders: Policies, processes, and innovations* (pp. 243–56). Westport, CT: Quorum Books.

Camp, R. (1989). *Entrepreneurs and politics in Mexico.* New York: Oxford University Press.

Campaign for Labor Rights (1999, December). *Cruel treatment working for Nike in Indonesia.* Washington, DC: Author.

Campbell, C. G., Graham, J. L., Jolibert, A., and Meissner, H. G. (1988). Marketing negotiations in France, Germany, U.K. and the U.S. *Journal of Marketing*, 52(2), 49–62.

Campbell, D. T. (1958). Common fate, similarity, and other indices of the status of aggregates of persons as social entities. *Behavioral Science*, 3, 14–25.

Campbell, J. (1968). *Hero with a thousand faces.* Princeton: Princeton University Press.

Campbell, J. P. (1990). Modeling the performance prediction problem in industrial and organizational psychology. In M. D. Dunnette and L. M. Hough (eds), *Handbook of industrial and organizational psychology*, 2nd edn. (pp. 687–732). Palo Alto: Consulting Psychologists Press.

Campion, M. A., Medsker, G. J., and Higgs, A. C. (1993). Relations between work group characteristics and effectiveness: Implications for designing effective work groups. *Personnel Psychology*, 46, 823–50.

Carnevale, P. J. (1995). Property, culture, and negotiations. In R. M. Kramer and D. M. Messick (eds), *Negotiation as a social process: New trends in theory and research* (pp. 309–23). Thousand Oaks, CA: Sage.

Carnevale, P. J. and Pruitt, D. G. (1992). Negotiation and mediation. *Annual Review of Psychology*, 43, 531–82.

Carpenter, J. W. (1991). Ethical dissimilarities in Japanese–American business. In K. Paul (ed.), *Contemporary issues in business society in the United States and abroad* (pp. 259–97). England: Edwin Mellen Press.

Carroll, G. (1993). A sociological view on why firms differ. *Strategic Management Journal*, 14, 237–49.

Carroll, S. J. and Gannon, M. J. (1997). *Ethical dimensions of international management.* Thousand Oaks, CA: Sage Publications.

Casimir, G. and Keats, D. M. (1996). The effects of work environment and in-group membership on the leadership preferences of Anglo-Australians and Chinese Australians. *Journal of Cross-Cultural Psychology*, 27, 436–57.

Casmir, R. (1992). Third-culture building: A paradigm shift for international and intercultural communication. *Communication Yearbook*, 16, 407–28.

Caudill, W. and Scarr, H. (1962). Japanese value orientations and culture change. *Ethnology*, 1, 53–91.

Caux Round Table Principles for Business (1994). Washington, DC: Caux Round Table Secretariat.

Caves, E. (1982). *Multinational enterprise and economic analysis*. Cambridge, England: Cambridge University Press.

CBS News (1996, October 7). *Transcript from CBS News 48 Hours, "Boycott Nike."* Downloaded from the world wide web at
http://wwwlsaigon.com/nike/48hrfmt.htm

Chandler, A. D., Jr (1962). *Strategy and structure: Chapters in the history of the American industrial enterprise.* Cambridge, MA: MIT Press.

Chandler, A. D., Jr (1990). *Scale and scope: The dynamics of industrial capitalism.* Cambridge, MA: Harvard University Press.

Chang, S. (1995). International expansion strategy of Japanese firms: Capability building through sequential entry. *Academy of Management Journal*, 38(2), 383–407.

Channon, D. F. (1973). *The strategy and structure of British enterprise.* Boston: Division of Research, Graduate School of Business Administration, Harvard University.

Chatman, J. A. and Barsade, S. G. (1995). Personality, organizational culture, and cooperation: Evidence from a business simulation. *Administrative Science Quarterly*, 40, 423–43.

Chen, C. C. (1995). New trends in reward allocation preferences: A Sino-U.S. comparison. *Academy of Management Journal*, 38(2), 408–28.

Chen, C. C., Chen, X.-P., and Meindl, J. R. (in preparation). How can cooperation be fostered? The cultural effects of individualism–collectivism.

Chen, C. C., Meindl, J. R., and Hunt, R. G. (1997). Testing the effects of vertical and horizontal collectivism: A study of reward allocation preferences in China. *Journal of Cross-Cultural Psychology*, 28(1), 44–70.

Chen, Y., Brockner, J., and Katz, T. (submitted). Individual-primacy and collective-primacy as bases for in-group bias: Evidence from the United States and the People's Republic of China.

Chertkoff, J. M. and Esser, J. K. (1976). A review of experiments in explicit bargaining. *Journal of Experimental Social Psychology*, 12, 464–86.

Chew, I. K. H. and Putti, J. (1995). Relationship on work-related values of Singaporean and Japanese managers in Singapore. *Human Relations*, 48(10), 1149–70.

Chick, G. (1997). Cultural complexity: The concept and its measurement. *Cross-Cultural Research*, 31, 275–307.

Child, J. (1972). Organizational structure, environment, and performance: The role of strategic choice. *Sociology*, 6, 1–22.

Child, J. (1977). *Organizations: A guide to problems and practice.* New York, NY: Harper and Row.

Child, J. (1981). Culture, contingency, and capitalism in the cross-national study of organizations. In L. L. Cummings and B. M. Staw (eds), *Research in organizational behavior*, Vol, 3 (pp. 303–56). Greenwich, CT: JAI Press.

Child, J. (1994). *Management in China during the age of reform.* Cambridge: Cambridge University Press.

Child, J. (1997). Strategic choice in the analysis of action, structure, organizations, and environment: Retrospect and prospect. *Organization Studies*, 18, 43–76.

Child, J., Yanni Yan and Yuan Lu (1997). Ownership and control in Sino-foreign joint ventures. In P. W. Beamish and J. P. Killing (eds), *Cooperative strategies: Asian Pacific perspectives*, Vol. 3 (pp. 181–225). San Francisco, CA: New Lexington Press.

Chinese Culture Connection, The (1987). Chinese values and the search for culture-free dimensions of culture. *Journal of Cross-cultural Psychology*, 18, 143–64.

Chodorow, N. (1978) *The reproduction of mothering.* Berkeley: University of California Press.

Choi, I., Nisbett, R. E., and Norenzayan, A. (1999). Causal attribution across cultures: Variation and universality. *Psychological Bulletin*, 125, 47–63.

Choi, Y.-E. (1996). The self in different context: Behavioral analysis. Paper presented at the International Congress of Psychology, Montreal, August.

Chung, K. H., Lee, H. C., and Jung, K. H. (1997). *Korean management: Global strategy and cultural transformation*. Berlin: Walter de Gruyter.

Church, A. T. (1982). Sojourner adjustment. *Psychological Bulletin*, 91, 540–72.

Clark, C. (1961). *Growthmanship: A study in the mythology of investment*. London: Institute of Economic Affairs.

Clark, M., Ouellette, R., Powell, M. C., and Milberg, S. (1987). Recipient's mood, relationship type, and helping. *Journal of Personality and Social Psychology*, 53, 94–103.

Cleveland, J. N., Gunnigle, P., Heray, N., Morley, M., and Murphy, K. (1999). US multinationals and human resource management: Evidence on HR practices in European subsidiaries. Paper presented at the Second Irish Academy of Management Conference, University of Limerick, September 9–10.

Coase, R. H. (1937). The nature of the firm. *Economica*, 4, 386–405.

The Coca-Cola Company (1998) (revision from 1989). *Code of Business Conduct*. Atlanta, Georgia.

Cohen, R. (1987). Problems in intercultural communication in Egyptian–American diplomatic relations. *International Journal of Intercultural Relations*, 11, 29–47.

Cohen, R. (1991). *Negotiating across cultures*. Washington, DC: United States Institute of Peace Press.

Cohen, W. and Levinthal, D. (1990). Absorptive capacity: A new perspective on learning and innovation. *Administrative Science Quarterly*, 35, 128–52.

Coleman, J. S. (1990). *Foundations of social theory*. Cambridge, MA: Harvard University Press.

Collier, M. J. and Thomas, M. (1988). Cultural identity: An interpretative perspective. In Y. Y. Kim and W. B. Gudykunst (eds), *Theories in intercultural communication* (pp. 99–120). Newbury Park: Sage.

Collin, S.-O. (1998). Why are these islands of conscious power found in the ocean of ownership?: Institutional and governance hypotheses explaining the existence of business groups in Sweden. *Journal of Management Studies*, 35, 719–46.

Condon, R. and Yousef, F. (1975). *An introduction to intercultural communication*. New York: Bobbs-Merrill.

The Conference Board (1996). *Managing expatriates return: A research report*. (Report Number 1148–96–RR). New York: The Conference Board, Inc.

Conlon, E. J. and Barr, S. H. (1989). A framework for understanding group feedback. *Advances in group processes*, Vol. 6 (pp. 627–48). Greenwich, CT: JAI Press.

Contractor, F. and Lorange, P. (1988). Why should firms cooperate? The strategy and economic basis for cooperative ventures. In F. Contractor and P. Lorange (eds), *Cooperative strategies in international business*. New York: Lexington

Cook, K. S. (1977). Exchange and power in networks of international relations. *The Sociological Quarterly*, 18 (winter), 62–82.

Cook, K. S. and Whitmeyer, J. M. (1992). Two approaches to social structure: Exchange theory and network analysis. *Annual Review of Sociology*, 18, 109–27.

Costa, P. T. and McCrae, R. R. (1992). *Revised NEO-Personality Inventory (NEO-PI-R) and NEO Five Factor Inventory (NEO-FFI) professional manual*. Odessa: Psychological Assessment Resources, Inc.

Couch, C. J. (1989). *Social processes and relationships: A formal approach*. New York: General Hall.

Coviello, N. and Munro, H. (1997) Network relationships and the internationalization process of small software firms. *Scandinavian International Business Review*, 6(4), 361–86.

Cox, T. H. (1993). *Cultural diversity in organizations*. San Francisco: Berrett Koehler.

Cox, T. H., Lobel, S. A., and McLeod, P. L. (1991). Effects of ethnic group cultural differences on cooperative versus competitive behavior on a group task. *Academy of Management Journal*, 34, 827–47.

Coyle, W. (1988). *On the move: Minimizing the stress and maximizing the benefit of relocation*. Sydney: Hampden.

Crant, J. M. and Bateman, T. S. (1993). Assignment of credit and blame for performance outcomes. *Academy of Management Journal*, 36(1), 7–27.

Cropanzano, R. and Greenberg, J. (1997). Progress in organizational justice: Tunneling through the maze. In C. L. Cooper and I. T. Robertson (eds), *International review of industrial and organizational psychology*, Vol. 12 (pp. 317–72). London: Wiley.

Cropanzano, R., James, K., and Citera, M. (1993). A goal hierarchy model of personality, motivation, and leadership. In L. L. Cummings and B. M. Staw (eds), *Research in Organizational Behaviour*, 15, 267–322. Greenwich, CT: JAI Press.

Crosby, F. (1982). *Relative deprivation and working women*. New York: Oxford University Press.

Cross, J. (1965). A theory of bargaining process. *American Economic Review*, 40, 67–94.

Crozier, M. (1964). *The bureaucratic phenomenon*. Chicago: University of Chicago Press.

Cui, G. and Awa, N. E. (1992). Measuring intercultural effectiveness: An integrative approach. *International Journal of Intercultural Relations*, 16, 311–28.

Cullen, J. B. (1999). *Multinational management: A strategic approach*. Cincinnati, OH: Southwestern University Press.

Cupach, W. R. and Imahori, T. T. (1993). Identity management theory: Communication competence in intercultural episodes and relationships. In R. L. Wiseman and J. Koester (eds), *Intercultural communication competence* (pp. 112–31). Newbury Park: Sage.

Cushner, K. and Landis, D. (1996). The intercultural sensitizer. In D. Landis and R. S. Bhagat (eds), *Handbook of intercultural training*, 2nd edn (pp. 185–201). Thousand Oaks, CA: Sage.

Cyert, R. and Goodman, P. (1997). Creating effective university–industry alliances: An organizational learning perspective. *Organizational Dynamics*, 25(4), 45–57.

Dacin, M. T., Ventresca, M., and Beal, B. (in press). The embeddedness of organizations: Dialogues and directions. *Journal of Management*.

Daft, R. and Lengl, R. (1986). Organizational information requirements, media richness and structure design. *Management Science*, 32(5), 554–71.

Dale, R. (1999). Asian eonomies could be drifting into part II of crisis. *International Herald Tribune*, October 15.

D'Andrade, R. (1984). Cultural meaning systems. In R. A. Shweder and R. A. LeVine (eds), *Culture theory: Essays on mind, self and emotion*. Cambridge: Cambridge University Press.

Dang, T. (1977). Ownership, control and performance of the multinational corporation: A study of U.S. wholly-owned subsidiaries and joint ventures in the Philippines and Taiwan. Ph.D. dissertation, University of California, Los Angeles.

Daniel, S. J. and Reitsperger, W. D. (1994). Strategic control-systems for quality: An empirical comparison of the Japanese and United States electronics industry. *Journal of International Business Studies*, 25(2), 275–94.

Daniels, J. D., Pitts, R. A., and Tretter, M. J. (1984). Strategy and structure of U.S. multinationals: An exploratory study. *Academy of Management Journal*, 27(2), 292–307.

Daniels, J. D., Pitts, R. A. and Tretter, M. J (1985). Organizing for dual strategies of product diversity and international expansion. *Strategic Management Journal*, 6, 223–37.

Danley, J. R. (1994). *The role of the modern corporation in a free society*. Notre Dame: University of Notre Dame Press.

Dasgupta, P. (1988). Trust as a commodity. In D. Gambetta (ed.), *Trust: Making and breaking cooperative relations* (pp. 49–72). Oxford, England: Blackwell.

Daun, A. (1991). Individualism and collectivity among Swedes. *Ethnos*, 56, 165–72.

D'Aveni, R. (1994). *Hypercompetition: Managing the dynamics of strategic maneuvering*. New York: Free Press.

David, K. H. (1971). Culture shock and the development of self-awareness. *Journal of Contemporary Psychotherapy*, 4, 44–8.

David, K. H. (1972). Intercultural adjustment and applications of reinforcement theory to problems of culture shock. *Trends*, 4, 1–64.

David, K. H. (1976). The use of social learning theory in preventing intercultural adjustment problems. In P. B. Pedersen, W. J. Lonner and J. G. Draguns (eds), *Counseling across cultures* (pp. 123–38). Honolulu: University of Hawaii Press.

Davidson, A. R., Jaccard, J. J., Triandis, H. C., Morales, M. L., and Diaz-Guerrero, R. (1976). Cross-cultural model testing: Toward a solution of the etic–emic dilemma. *International Journal of Psychology*, 11, 1–13.

Davidson, W. H. and Haspeslagh P. (1982). Shaping a global product organization. *Harvard Business Review*, 60(4), 125–32.

Davis, G., Diekmann, K., and Tinsley, C. (1994). The decline and fall of the conglomerate firm in the 1990s: The deinstitutionalization of an organizational form. *American Sociological Review*, 59, 547–70.

Davis, H. J. and Rasool, S. A. (1988). A reconsideration of England's values research in cross-cultural management. In R. Farmer and E. McGoun (eds), *Advances in international comparative management* (pp. 109–25). Greenwich, CT: JAI Press.

Davis, J. (1996). From informal to formal markets: A case study of Bulgarian food markets during transition. *Comparative Economic Studies*, 38, 37–51.

Davis, J., Patterson, J., and Grazin, I. (1996). The collapse and reemergence of networks within and between republics of the former Soviet Union. *International Business Review*, 5, 1–21.

Davis, L. and North, D. C. (1971). *Institutional change and American economic growth*. Cambridge and New York: Cambridge University Press.

Debrus, C. (1995). Die Betreuung von Mitarbeitern während des Auslandseinsatzes: Aus der Praxis der Henkel KGaA. In T. M. Kühlmann (ed.), *Mitarbeiterentsendung ins Ausland, Auswahl, Vorbereitung, Betreuung und Wiedereingliederung* (pp. 161–75). Göttingen: Verlag für Angewandte Psychologie.

De Cieri, H. and Dowling, P. J. (1999). Strategic human resource management in multinational enterprises. In P. M. Wright, L. D. Dyer, J. W. Boudreau, and G. T. Milkovich (eds), *Strategic human resource management in the twenty-first century*, Vol. 4: *Research in personnel and human resource management*. Stamford, CT: JAI Press.

De Cieri, H., Dowling, P. J., and Taylor, K. F. (1991). The psychological impact of expatriate relocation on partners. *International Journal of Human Resource Management*, 377–414.

De Dreu, C. K. W. and McCusker, C. (1997). Gain–loss frames and cooperation in two-person social dilemmas: A transformational analysis. *Journal of Personality and Social Psychology*, 72(5), 1093–106.

Dean, P. (1998). *Examining the profession and the practice of business ethics*. Working Group on Global Business Ethics Principles, Conference Board.

DeGeorge, R. T. (1993). *Competing with integrity in international business*. New York: Oxford University Press.

DeGeorge, R. T. (1994). International business ethics. *Business Ethics Quarterly*, 4(1), 1–9.

DeGeorge, R. T. (1999). *Business ethics*. Upper Saddle River, NJ: Prentice-Hall.

Delios, A. and Beamish, P. W. (1999). Ownership strategy of Japanese firms: Transactional, institutional and experience influences. *Strategic Management Journal*, 20(10), 915–33.

Deller, J. (1997). Expatriate selection: Possibilities and limitations of using personality scales. In Z. Aycan (ed.), *Expatriate management: Theory and research*, Vol. 4 (pp. 93–116). Greenwich, CT: JAI Press.

Deloitte, Haskins and Sells International (1989). *Teaming up for the nineties: Can you survive without a partner?* New York, NY: Deloitte, Haskins and Sells.

DeNisi, A., Cafferty, T. P., and Meglino, B. M. (1984). A cognitive view of the performance appraisal process: A model and research propositions. *Organizational Behavior and Human Performance*, 33, 360–96.

DeNisi, A., and Williams, K. J. (1990). Cognitive approaches to performance appraisal. In G. R. Ferris and K. M. Rowland (eds), *Performance evaluation, goal setting, and feedback* (pp. 47–93). Greenwich, CT: JAI Press.

Denison, E. L. (1980). The contributions of capitalism to economic growth. *American Economic Review*, 70, 220–4.

Den Hartog, D. N., House, R. J., Hanges, P. J., Dorfman, P. W., Ruiz-Quintanilla, S. A., and 170 co-authors (1999). Emics and etics of culturally-endorsed implicit leadership theories: Are attributes of charismatic/transformational leadership universally endorsed? *Leadership Quarterly*.

Den Hartog, D. N. and Verburg, R. M. (1997). Charisma and rhetoric: Communicative techniques of international business leaders. *Leadership Quarterly*, 8, 355–91.

Desai, A. B. and Rittenburg, T. (1997). Global ethics: An integrative framework for MNE's. *Journal of Business Ethics*, 16(8), 791–800.

Deshpande, S. P. and Viswesvaran, C. (1992). Is cross-cultural training of expatriate managers effective? A meta analysis. *International Journal of Intercultural Relations*, 16, 295–310.

Deutsch, M. (1958). Trust and suspicion. *Journal of Conflict Resolution*, 2, 265–79.

Deutsch, M. (1962). Cooperation and trust: Some theoretical notes. In M. R. Jones (ed.), *Nebraska Symposium on Motivation* (pp. 275–319). Lincoln, NE: University of Nebraska Press.

Deutsch, M. (1973). *The resolution of conflict: Constructive and destructive processes*. New Haven, CT: Yale University Press.

Deutsch, M. and Krauss, R. M. (1962). Studies of interpersonal bargaining. *Journal of Conflict Resolution*, 6, 52–76.

DeVos, G. A. (1968). Achievement and innovation in culture and personality. In E. Norbeck, D. Price-Williams, and W. M. McCords (eds), *The study of personality: An interdisciplinary approach*. New York: Holt, Rinehart, and Winston.

DeVos, G. A. and Mizushima, K. (1973). Delinquency and social change in modern Japan. In G. A. DeVos (ed.), *Socialization for achievement: Essays on the cultural psychology of the Japanese*. Berkeley: University of California Press.

Dhawan, N., Roseman, I. J., Naidu, R., K., Thapa, K., and Rettek, S. I., (1995). Self-concepts across two cultures: India and the United States. *Journal of Cross-Cultural Psychology*, 26, 606–21.

Diaz-Guerrero, R. (1979). The development of coping style. *Human Development*, 22, 320–31.

Diener, E., Diener, M., and Diener, C. (1995). Factors predicting the subjective well-being of nations. *Journal of Personality and Social Psychology*, 69, 851–64.

DiMaggio, P. (1997). Culture and cognition. *Annual Review of Sociology*, 23, 263–87.

DiMaggio, P. and Powell, W. (1983). The iron cage revisited: Institutional isomorphism and collective rationality in organizational fields. *American Sociological Review*, 48, 147–60.

DiMaggio, P. and Powell, W. (1991). Introduction. In W. Powell and P. DiMaggio (eds), *The new institutionalism in organizational analysis*. Chicago: University of Chicago Press.

Ding, D. Z. (1997). Control, conflict, and performance: A study of U.S.–Chinese joint ventures. *Journal of International Marketing*, 5(3), 31–45.

Dinges, N. G. (1983). Intercultural competence. In D. Landis, and R. W. Brislin (eds), *Handbook of intercultural training*, Vol. 1 (pp. 176–202). New York: Pergamon.

Dinges, N. G. and Baldwin, K. D. (1996). Intercultural competence. In D. Landis and R. S. Bhagat (eds), *Handbook of intercultural training*, 2nd edn (pp. 106–23). Thousand Oaks: Sage.

Doi, L. T. (1973). *The anatomy of dependence*. Tokyo: Kodansha International.

Donaldson, T. (1989). *The ethics of international business*. New York: Oxford University Press.

Donaldson, T. (1992a). The language of international corporate ethics. *Business Ethics*, 2, 279–81.

Donaldson, T. (1992b). When in Rome . . . do what? International business and cultural relativism. In P. Minus (ed.), *The ethics of business in a global economy* (pp. 67–78). Boston: Kluwer.

Donaldson, T. (1994). When integration fails. *Business Ethics Quarterly*, 4(2), 157–70.

Donaldson, T. (1996). Values in tension: Ethics away from home. *Harvard Business Review*, 74(5), 48–56.

Donaldson, T. and Dunfee, T. W. (1994). Towards a unified conception of business ethics: Integrative social contracts theory. *Academy of Management Review*, 19, 252–84.

Donaldson, T. and Dunfee, T. W. (1999). *Ties that bind: A social contracts approach to business ethics.* Boston: Harvard Business School Press.

Doney, P. M., Cannon, J. P., and Mullen, M. R. (1998). Understanding the influence of national culture on the development of trust. *Academy of Management Review*, 23(3), 601–20.

Dore, R. (1987). *Taking Japan seriously.* Stanford, CA: Stanford University Press.

Dorfman, P. W. (1996) International and cross-cultural leadership. In B. J. Punnett and O. Shenkar (eds), *Handbook for international management research* (pp. 267–349). Cambridge, MA: Blackwell.

Dorfman, P. W., Howell, J. P., Hibino, S., Lee, J. K., Tate, U., and Bautista, A. (1997). Leadership in Western and Asian countries: Commonalities and differences in effective leadership processes across cultures. *Leadership Quarterly*, 8, 233–74.

Dougherty, D. (1992). Interpretive barriers to successful product innovation in large firms. *Organization Science*, 3, 179–202.

Dowling, P. and Schuler, R. (1990). *International dimensions of human resource management.* Boston: PWS-Kent.

Dowling, P. J., Schuler, R. S., and Welch, D (1994). *International dimensions of human resource management.* Belmont, CA: Wadsworth.

Dowling, P. J., Welch, D. E., and Schuler, R. S. (1999). *International human resource management: Managing people in a multinational context*, 3rd edn. Cincinnati, OH: South-Western Publishing Company.

Doz, Y. and Prahalad, C. K. (1986). Controlled variety: A challenge for human resource management in the MNC. *Human Resource Management*, 25 (spring), 55–71.

Due, J., Madsen, J. S., and Jensen, C. S. (1991). The social dimension: convergence or diversification of IR in the single European market. *Industrial Relations Journal*, 22(2), 85–102.

Duhaime, I. M. and Schwenk, C. (1985). Conjectures on cognitive simplification in acquisition and divestment decision making. *Academy of Management Review*, 10, 287–95.

Dunbar, E. (1992). Adjustment and satisfaction of expatriate U.S. personnel. *International Journal of Intercultural Relations*, 16, 1–16.

Dunning, J. H. (1980). Towards an eclectic theory of international production: Some empirical tests. *Journal of International Business Studies*, 11, 9–31.

Dunning, J. H. (1993). *Multinational enterprises and the global economy.* Wokingham: Addison-Wesley.

Durkheim, E. (orig. 1893; tr. 1984). *The division of labor in society.* London: Macmillan.

Dussauge, P., Garrette, B., and Mitchell, W. (1998). Acquiring partners; capabilities: Outcomes of scale and link alliances between competitors. In M. A. Hitt, J. E. R. Costa, and R. D. Nixon (eds), *Managing strategically in an interconnected world.* Chichester: John Wiley & Sons.

Dutton, J. E. and Dukerich, J. M. (1991). Keeping an eye on the mirror: Image and identity in organizational adaptation. *Academy of Management Journal*, 34(3), 517–54.

Dwyer, F. R., Schurr, P. H., and Oh, S. (1987). Developing buyer–seller relations. *Journal of Marketing*, 51 (April), 11–28.

Dwyer, P., Johnston, M., and Lowry, K. (1996). Out of the typing pool into career limbo. *Business Week*, April 15, 92–4.

Dyal, J. A. and Dyal, R. Y. (1981). Acculturation, stress and coping: Some implications for research and education. *International Journal of Intercultural Relations*, 5, 301–28.

Dyas, G. P. and Thanheiser, H. T. (1976). *The emerging European enterprise: Strategy and structure in French and German industry.* London: Macmillan.

Dyer, J. (1996). Does governance matter? Keiretsu alliances and asset specificity as sources of Japanese competitive advantage. *Organization Science*, 7(6), 649–66.

Dyer, J. (1997). Effective interfirm collaboration: How firms minimize transaction costs and maximize transaction value. *Strategic Management Journal*, 18, 535–56.

Dyer, J. and Singh, H. (1998). The relational view: Cooperative strategy and sources of interorganizational competitive advantage. *Academy of Management Review*, 23, 660–79.

Eagly, A. H. and Johnson, B. T. (1990). Gender and leadership style: A meta-analysis. *Psychological Bulletin*, 108(2), 233–56.

Earley, P. C. (1986). Supervisors and shop stewards as sources of contextual information in goal setting: A comparison of the United States with England. *Journal of Applied Psychology*, 71(1), 111–17.

Earley, P. C. (1987). Intercultural training for managers: A comparison of documentary and interpersonal methods. *Academy of Management Journal*, 30, 685–98.

Earley, P. C. (1989). Social loafing and collectivism: A comparison of the United States and the People's Republic of China. *Administrative Science Quarterly*, 34(4), 565–81.

Earley, P. C. (1993). East meets West meets Mideast: Further explorations of collectivistic and individualistic work groups. *Academy of Management Journal*, 36(2), 319–48.

Earley, P.C. (1994). Self or group? Cultural effects of training on self-efficacy and performance. *Administrative Science Quarterly*, 39, 89–117.

Earley, P. C. (1997a). *Face, harmony, and social structure: An analysis of organizational behavior across cultures*. New York: Oxford University Press.

Earley, P. C. (1997b). Doing an about-face: Social motivation and cross-cultural currents. In P. C. Earley and M. Erez (eds), *New perspectives on international industrial/organizational psychology* (pp. 243–55). San Francisco: New Lexington Press.

Earley, P. C. (1999). Playing follow the leader: Status-determining traits in relation to collective efficacy across cultures. *Organizational Behavior and Human Decision Processes*, 80, 1–21.

Earley, P. C. and Erez, M. (1997). Introduction. In P. C. Earley and M. Erez (eds), *New perspectives in international industrial/organizational psychology* (pp. 1–10). San Francisco: New Lexington Press.

Earley, P. C. and Gibson, C. B. (1998). Taking stock in our progress of individualism and collectivism: 100 years of solidarity and community. *Journal of Management*, 24, 265–304.

Earley, P. C., Gibson, C. B., and Chen, C. C. (1999). How did I do versus how did we do? Intercultural contrasts of performance feedback search and self efficacy. *Journal of Cross-Cultural Psychology*, 30, 596–621.

Earley, P. C. and Mosakowski, E. (1996). Experimental international management research. In B. J. Punnett and O. Shenkar (eds), *Handbook of International Management Research* (pp. 83–114). London: Blackwell Publishers.

Earley, P. C. and Mosakowski, E. (2000). Creating hybrid team cultures: An empirical test of international team functioning. *Academy of Management Journal*, 43, 26–49.

Earley, P. C. and Singh, H. (1995). International and intercultural research: What's next? *Academy of Management Journal*, 38(2), 327–40.

Earley, P. C. and Stubblebine, P. (1989). Intercultural assessment of performance feedback. *Group and Organization Studies*, 14(2), 161–81.

Economist, The (1993). Musical chairs, July 17.

Economist, The (1998). Emerging market indicators, April 11.

Eden, D. (1975). Intrinsic and extrinsic rewards and motives: Replication and extension with kibbutz workers. *Journal of Applied Social Psychology*, 5, 348–61.

Edgerton, R. B. (1985). *Rules, exceptions, and social order*. Berkeley: University of California Press.

Edström, A. and Galbraith, J. (1977a). Alternative policies for international transfers of managers. *Management International Review*, 17, 11–22.

Edström, A. and Galbraith, J. (1977b). Transfer of managers as a coordination and control strategy in multinational organizations. *Administrative Science Quarterly*, 22, 248–63

Edström, A. and Lorange, P. (1984). Matching strategy and human resources in multinational corporations. *Journal of International Business Studies*, 15, 125–37.

Edwards, P. K., Ferner, A., and Sisson, K. (1993). *People and the process of management in the multinational company: A review and some illustrations.* IRRU, Warwick, Warwick papers in industrial relations.

Edwards, R. (1979). *Contested terrain: The transformation of the workplace in the twentieth century.* New York: Basic Books.

Egelhoff, W. G. (1982). Strategy and structure in multinational corporations: An information-processing approach. *Administrative Science Quarterly*, 27(3), 435–58.

Egelhoff, W. G. (1988a). Strategy and structure in multinational corporations: A revision of the Stopford and Wells model. *Strategic Management Journal*, 9, 1–14.

Egelhoff, W. G. (1988b). *Organizing the multinational enterprise: An information-processing perspective.* Cambridge, MA: Ballinger Publishing Company.

Egelhoff, W. G. (1991). Information-processing theory and the multinational enterprise. *Journal of International Business Studies*, 22(3), 341–68.

Eisenhardt, K. M. (1989). Building theories from case study research. *Academy of Management Review*, 14, 532–50.

Elenkov, D. S. (1995). Russian aerospace MNCs in global competition. *Columbia Journal of World Business*, 30, 66–78.

Elenkov, D. S. (1998). Can American management concepts work in Russia? A cross-cultural comparative study. *California Management Review*, 40(4), 133–57.

El-Hayek, T. and Keats, D. M. (1999). Leader characteristics and motivations in Lebanese- and Anglo-Australians. In J. Lasry, J. Adair, and K. Dion (eds), *Latest contributions to cross-cultural psychology* (pp. 257–68). Lisse NL: Swets and Zeitlinger.

Elizur, D., Borg, I., Hunt, R., and Beck, I. M. (1991). The structure of work values: A cross-cultural comparison. *Journal of Organizational Behavior*, 12, 21–38.

Elron, E. (1997). Top management teams within multinational corporations: Effects of cultural heterogeneity. *Leadership Quarterly*, 8, 393–412.

Elron, E., Shamir, B., and Ben-Ari, E. (1998). *Why don't they fight each other? Cultural diversity and operational unity in multinational forces.* Working paper, Hebrew University, Jerusalem.

Elsbach, K. D. (1994). Managing organizational legitimacy in the California cattle industry: The construction and effectiveness of verbal accounts. *Administrative Science Quarterly*, 39, 57–88.

Elsbach, K. D. and Sutton, R. I. (1992). Acquiring organizational legitimacy through illegitimate actions: A marriage of institutional and impression management theories. *Academy of Management Journal*, 35, 699–738.

Encaoua, D. and Jacquemin, A. (1982). Organizational efficiency and monopoly power: The case of French industrial groups. *European Economic Review*, 19, 25–51.

Engelhard, J. and Hein, S. (1996). Erfolgsfaktoren des Auslandseinsatzes von Führungskräften. In K. Macharzina and J. Wolf (eds), *Handbuch internationales führungskräfte-management* (pp. 83–111). Stuttgart: Raabe.

England, G. W. (1975). *The manager and his values: An international perspective from the United States, Japan, Korea, India, and Australia.* Cambridge, MA: Ballinger.

England, G. W. and Koike, R. (1970). Personal values systems of Japanese managers. *Journal of Cross-Cultural Psychology*, 1, 21–40.

England, G. W. and Quintanilla, A. R. (1989). Major work meaning patterns in the national labor forces on Germany, Japan, and the United States. In S. B. Prasad (ed.), *Advances in international comparative management* (pp. 77–94). Greenwich, CT: JAI Press.

Engle, E. M. and Lord, R. G. (1997). Implicit theories, self-schemas, and leader–member exchange. *Academy of Management Journal*, 40(4), 988–1010.

Enloe, C. (1995). The globetrotting sneaker. *Ms.*, March–April, p. 36.

Enright, M. J. (1993). The determinants of geographic concentration in industry. Working paper, Harvard Business School.

Erez, M. (1986). The congruence of goal-setting strategies with socio-cultural values and its effects on performance. *Journal of Management*, 12, 83–90.

Erez, M. (1990). Toward a model of cross-cultural industrial and organizational psychology. In H. C. Triandis, M. D. Dunnette, and L. M. Hough (eds), *Handbook of industrial and organizational psychology*, 2nd edn, Vol. 4 (pp. 559–608). Palo Alto, CA: Consulting Psychology Press.

Erez, M. (1992). Interpersonal-communication systems in organizations, and their relationships to cultural values, productivity and innovation: The case of Japanese corporations. *Applied Psychology, an International Review*, 41(1), 43–64.

Erez, M. (1994). Toward a model of cross-cultural industrial and organizational psychology. In H. C. Triandis, M. D. Dunnette, and L. Hough (eds), *Handbook of industrial and organizational psychology*, 2nd edn, Vol. 4 (pp. 559–607). Palo Alto, CA: Consulting Psychology Press.

Erez, M. (1997). A culture based model of work motivation. In P. C. Earley and M. Erez (eds), *New perspectives on international industrial and organizational psychology* (pp. 193–242). San Francisco, CA: Lexington Press.

Erez, M. and Earley, P. C. (1987). Comparative analysis of goal-setting strategies across cultures. *Journal of Applied Psychology*, 72(4), 658–65.

Erez, M. and Earley, P. C. (1993). *Culture, self-identity, and work*. New York: Oxford University Press.

Erez, M. and Somech, A. (1996). Is group productivity loss the rule or the exception? Effects of culture and group-based motivation. *Academy of Management Journal*, 39(6), 1513–37.

Evans, P. (1996). Economic and security dimensions of the emerging order in the Asia Pacific. In D. Wurfel and B. Burton (eds), *Southeast Asia in the new world order: The political economy of a dynamic region* (pp. 3–16). Basingstoke: Macmillan.

Evans, P. and Doz, Y. (1992). Dualities: A paradigm for human resource and organisational development in complex multinationals. In V. Pucik, N. Tichy, and C. Barnett (eds), *Globalising management: Creating and leading the competitive organization*. New York: Wiley.

Evans, P., Doz, Y., and Laurent, A. (eds) (1989). *Human resource management in international firms: Change, globalization, innovation*. London: Macmillan.

Evans, P. and Genadry, N. (1999). A duality-based prospective for strategic human resource management. In P. M. Wright, L. D. Dyer, J. W. Boudreau, and G. T. Milkovich (eds), *Strategic human resource management in the twenty-first century*, Vol. 4: *Research in personnel and human resource management*. Stamford, CT: JAI Press.

Evans, P., Lank, E., and Farquhar, A. (1990). Managing human resources in the international firm: Lessons from practice. In P. Evans, J. Doz, and A. Laurent (eds), *Human resource management in international firms* (pp. 113–43). London: Macmillan.

Fagenson, E. A. and Jackson, J. J. (1994). The status of women managers in the United States. In N. J. Adler and D. N. Izraeli (eds), *Competitive frontiers: Women managers in a global economy* (pp. 388–404). Cambridge, MA: Blackwell.

Fagre, N. and Wells, L. T. (1982). Bargaining power of multinationals and host governments. *Journal of International Business Studies*, 13(2), 9–24.

Farh, J. L., Earley, P. C., and Lin, S.-C. (1997). Impetus for action: A cultural analysis of justice and organizational citizenship behavior in a Chinese society. *Administrative Science Quarterly*, 42, 421–44.

Farh, J. L., Tsui, A. S., Xiz, K., and Cheng, B. (1998). The influence of relational demography and guanxi: The Chinese case. *Organizational Science*, 9(4), 471–88.

Faure, G. O. and Rubin, J. Z. (1993). *Culture and negotiation*. Newbury Park: Sage Publications.

Feather, N. T. (1994). Attitudes toward high achievers and reactions to their fall: Theory and research concerning tall poppies. In M. Zanna (ed.), *Advances in experimental social psychology*, Vol. 25 (pp. 1–73). New York: Academic Press.

Feldman, D. C. and Thomas, D. C. (1992). Career management issues facing expatriates. *Journal of International Business Studies*, 23, 271–94.

Feldman, D. C. and Tompson, H. B. (1993). Expatriation, repatriation, and domestic geographical relocation: An empirical investigation of adjustment to new job assignments. *Journal of International Business Studies*, 24, 507–29.

Feldman, J. M. (1981). Beyond attribution theory: Cognitive processes in performance appraisal. *Journal of Applied Psychology*, 66, 127–48.

Ferraro, G. P. (1990). *The cultural dimension of international business*. New Jersey: Prentice-Hall.

Fiedler, F. E., Mitchell, T., and Triandis, H. C. (1971) The culture assimilator: An approach to cross-cultural training. *Journal of Applied Psychology*, 55, 95–102.

Financial Times (1998). Clinton calls for chaebol reform, November 23.

Fiol, M. and Lyles, M. (1985). Organizational learning. *Academy of Management Review*, 10(4), 803–14.

Fiorina, C. (1998) Anytime you have a fiercely competitive business. *Nortel World*, November, p. 8.

Fishbein, M. and Ajzen, I. (1975). *Belief, attitude, intention and behavior: An introduction to theory and research*. Reading, MA: Addison-Wesley.

Fisher, A. B. (1992). When will women get to the top? *Fortune*, September 21, pp. 44–56.

Fisher, H. (1999). *The first sex: The natural talents of women and how they are changing the world*. New York: Random House.

Fisher, R. (1980). *International negotiation: A cross-cultural perspective*. Yarmouth: Intercultural Press, Inc.

Fisher, R. and Ury, W. (1981). *Getting to yes: Negotiating agreements without giving in*. New York: Penguin.

Fiske, A. P. (1991). *Structures of social life: The four elementary forms of human relations: communal sharing, authority ranking, equality matching, market pricing*. New York: Free Press

Fiske, A. P. (1992). The four elementary forms of sociality: Framework for a unified theory of social relations. *Psychological Review*, 99, 689–723.

Fladmoe-Lindquist, K. and Jacque, L. (1995). Control modes in international service operations: The propensity to franchise. *Management Science*, 41(7), 1238–49.

Foa, E. B. and Foa, U. G. (1976). Resource theory of social exchange. In J. W. Thibaut, T. T. Spence, and R. C. Carson (eds), *Contemporary topics in social psychology*. Morristown: General Learning.

Foa, U. and Foa, E. (1974). *Societal structures of the mind*. Springfield, IL: Thomas.

Fombrun, C. J. (1996). *Reputation: Realizing value from the corporate image*. Boston: Harvard Business School.

Fondas, N. (1997). The origins of feminization. *Academy of Management Review*, 22, 257–82.

Fontaine, G. (1996). Roles of social support systems in overseas relocation: Implications for intercultural training. *International Journal of Intercultural Relations*, 10, 361–78.

Forsgren, M., Holm, U., and Johanson, J. (1995) Division headquarters go abroad: A step in the internationalisation of the multinational corporation. *Journal of Management Studies*, 32(4), 473–91.

Forsgren, M. and Pahlberg, C. (1992). Subsidiary influence and autonomy in international firms. *Scandinavian International Business Review*, 1(3), 41–52.

Forster, N. (1997). The persistent myth of high expatriate failure rates: A reappraisal. *The International Journal of Human Resource Management*, 8, 414–33.

Fox, C. (1997). The authenticity of intercultural communication. *International Journal of Intercultural Relations*, 21(1), 85–103.

Franke, R. H. (1974). An empirical appraisal of the achievement motivation model applied to nations. Unpublished doctoral dissertation, University of Rochester, Rochester, NY (Dissertation Abstracts, 34(4): 1959–B), p. 31.

Franke, R. H. (1979). Investment for economic growth? Paper presented at the annual meeting of the American Association for the Advancement of Science, Houston, TX (6 pp.).

Franke, R. H. (1980). Worker productivity at Hawthorne. *American Sociological Review*, 45, 1006–27.

Franke, R. H. (1987). Technological revolution and productivity decline: Computer introduction in the financial industry. *Technological Forecasting and Social Change*, 31, 143–54.

Franke, R. H. (1992a). Table supplements to Franke (1992b) in symposium presentation on cultures of performance, annual meeting of the Academy of Management, Las Vegas, NV.

Franke, R. H. (1992b). The relationship between cultural and economic performance. In H. E. Glass and M. A. Hovde (eds), *Handbook of business strategy*, 1992–3 Yearbook (ch. 7, pp. 1–21).

Franke, R. H. (1997). Industrial democracy and convergence in economic performance: Comparative analysis of industrial nations in the 1970s and 1980s. *Research in the Sociology of Work*, 6, 95–108.

Franke, R. H. (1999). Transformation of the second world from plan to market: Economic effects of culture, convergence, and investment. *International Journal of Business*, 4(1), 39–52.

Franke, R. H., Hofstede, G., and Bond, M. H. (1991). Cultural roots of economic performance: A research note. *Strategic Management Journal*, 12, 165–73.

Franke, R. H., Mento, A. J., and Brooks, W. W. (1985). Corporate culture across cultures. Paper presented at the annual meeting of the Academy of Management, San Diego, CA. (An abridged 18-page and an unabridged 37-page version.)

Franke, R. H. and Sagafi-nejad, T. (1999). Democracy, freedom, and performance. Paper presented at the annual meeting of the Strategic Management Society, Berlin.

Franko, L. G. (1971). *Joint venture survival in multinational corporations*. New York: Praeger.

Franko, L. G. (1973). Who manages multinational enterprises? *Columbia Journal of World Business*, 8(2), 30–42.

Frazier, G. L. and Rody, R. C. (1991). The use of influence strategies in interfirm relationships in industrial product channels. *Journal of Marketing*, 55 (January), 52–69.

Frederick, W. C. (1991). The moral authority of transnational corporate codes. *Journal of Business Ethics*, 10(3), 165–77.

Frederick, W. C. (1994). The virtual reality of fact vs. value: A symposium commentary. *Business Ethics Quarterly*, 4(2), 171–73.

Freeman, M. A. (submitted). Demographic correlates of individualism and collectivism: A study of social values in Sri Lanka.

Freeman, R. E. and Gilbert, D. R., Jr (1988). *Corporate strategy and the search for ethics*. Englewood Cliffs, NJ: Prentice-Hall.

French, J. R. P., Israel, J., and As, D. (1960). An experiment in a Norwegian factory: Interpersonal dimension in decision-making. *Human Relations*, 13, 3–19.

French, J. R. P., Kay, E, and Meyer, H. H. (1966). Participation and the appraisal system. *Human Relations*, 19, 3–20.

Friday, R. A. (1989). Contrasts in discussion behaviors of German and American managers. *International Journal of Intercultural Relations*, 7, 53–67.

Friedkin, N. E. (1993). Structural bases of interpersonal influence in groups: A longitudinal case study. *American Sociological Review*, 58(6), 861–72.

Friedland, R. and Alford, R. R. (1991). Bringing society back in: Symbols, practices, and institutional contradictions. In P. J. Dimaggio and W. W. Powell (eds), *The new institutionalism in organizational analysis* (pp. 232–63). Chicago: Chicago University Press.

Friedman, W. G. and Beguin, J. (1971). *Joint international business ventures in developing countries*. New York: Columbia University Press.

Fritzsche, D. J. and Becker, H. (1984). Linking management behavior to ethical philosophy: An empirical investigation. *Academy of Management Journal*, 27(1), 166–75.

Frombrun, C. (1996). *Reputation*. Boston: Harvard University Press.

Frye, T. (1997). Governing the Russian equities market. *Post-Soviet Affairs*, 13, 366–95.

Fukuyama, F. (1996). *Trust: The social virtues and the creation of prosperity*. New York: Free Press.

Furnham, A. (1988). The adjustment of sojourners. In Y. Y. Kim and W. B. Gudykunst (eds), *Cross-cultural adaptation: Current approaches* (pp. 42–61). Newbury Park: Sage.

Furnham, A. and Bochner, S. (1982). Social difficulty in a foreign culture: An empirical analysis of culture shock. In S. Bochner (ed.), *Cultures in contact* (pp. 161–98). New York: Pergamon.

Furnham, A. and Bochner, S. (1986). *Culture shock: Psychological reactions to unfamiliar environments.* New York: Methuen.

Gabarro, J. J. (1987). The development of working relationships. In J. Lorsch (ed.), *Handbook of organizational behavior* (pp. 172–89). Englewood Cliffs, NJ: Prentice-Hall.

Gabrenya, W. K., Jr, Latane, B., and Wang, Y. (1981). *Social loafing among Chinese overseas and US students.* Paper presented at the Second Asian Conference of the International Association for Cross-Cultural Psychology, Taipei, Taiwan, ROC, August.

Gabrenya, W. K., Latane, B., and Wang, Y. (1983). Social loafing in cross-cultural perspective. *Journal of Cross-Cultural Psychology*, 14, 368–84.

Gabrenya, W. K., Latane, B., and Wang, Y. (1985). Social loafing on an optimizing task: Cross-cultural differences among Chinese and Americans. *Journal of Cross-Cultural Psychology*, 16, 223–42.

Gabrieldis, C., Stephan, W., Ybarra, O., Dos Santos-Pearson, V., and Villareal, L. (1997). Preferred styles of conflict resolution. *Journal of Cross-Cultural Psychology*, 28, 661–72.

Gaines, S. O., Jr, Marelich, W. D., Bledsoe, K. L., Steers, W. N., Henderson, M. C., Granrose, C. S., Barajas, L., Hicks, D., Lyde, M., Rios, D. I., Garcia, B. F., Farris, K. R., and Page, M. S. (1997). Links between race/ethnicity and cultural values as mediated by racial/ethnic identity and moderated by gender. *Journal of Personality and Social Psychology*, 72, 1460–76.

Galbraith, J. R. (1973). *Designing complex organizations.* Reading, MA: Addison-Wesley.

Galbraith, J. R. (1987). Organization design. In J. Lorsch (ed.), *Handbook of organization behavior* (pp. 343–57). Englewood Cliffs, NJ: Prentice-Hall.

Ganesan, S. (1994). Determinants of long-term orientation in buyer–seller relationships. *Journal of Marketing*, 22(2), 1–19.

Gannon, M. J. (2001). *Working across cultures: Applications and exercises.* Thousand Oaks, CA: Sage.

Gannon, M. J. and Associates (1994). *Understanding global cultures: Metaphorical journeys through 17 countries.* Thousand Oaks, CA: Sage.

Gannon, M. J. and Carroll, S. (1997). *Ethical dimensions in international management.* Beverly Hills: Sage.

Gannon, M. J., Flood, P. C., and Paauwe, J. (1999). Managing human resources in the third era: Economic perspectives. *Business Horizons*, 42(3), 41–7.

Gargan, E. (1996). An Indonesian asset is also a liability. *New York Times*, March 16, p. 17.

Gatignon, H. and Anderson, E. (1986). Modes of foreign entry: A transaction cost analysis. *Journal of International Business Studies*, 17, 1–27.

Gebrielidis, C., Stephan, W., Ybarra, O., Dos Santos-Pearson, V., and Villareal, L. (1977). Preferred styles of conflict resolution. *Journal of Cross-Cultural Psychology*, 28, 661–77.

Gedajlovic, E. and Shapiro, D. (1998). Management and ownership effects: Evidence from five countries. *Strategic Management Journal*, 19, 533–52.

Geen, R. G. and Gange, J. J. (1977). Drive theory of social facilitation: Twelve years of theory and research. *Psychological Bulletin*, 84, 1267–88.

Geertz, C. (1973). *The interpretation of cultures.* New York: Basic Books.

Gelfand, M. J. and Christakopoulou, S. (1999). Culture and negotiator cognition: Judgment accuracy and negotiation processes in individualistic and collectivistic cultures. *Organizational Behavior and Human Decision Processes*, 79, 248–69.

Gelfand, M. J. and Dyer, N. (2000). A cultural perspective on negotiation: Progress, pitfalls, and prospects. *Applied Psychology: An International Review*, 41(1), 62–99.

Gelfand, M. J. and Raver, J. L. (2000). Metaphors in the science of negotiation. Paper presented at the International Association for Cross-Cultural Psychology, Pultusk, Poland, July.

Gelfand, M. J. and Realo, A. (1999). Individualism–collectivism and accountability in intergroup negotiations. *Journal of Applied Psychology*, 84, 721–36.

Gentner, D. (1983). Structure-mapping: A theoretical framework. *Cognitive Science*, 7, 155–70.

George, J. M. (1992). Extrinsic and intrinsic origins of perceived social loafing in organizations. *Academy of Management Journal*, 35, 191–202.

Gerganov, E. N., Dilova, M. L., Petkova, K. G., and Paspalanova, E. P. (1996). Culture-specific approach to the study of individualism/collectivism. *European Journal of Social Psychology*, 26, 277–97.

Gerhart, B. and Milkovich, G. T. (1992). Employee compensation: Research and practice. In M. Dunnette and L. Hough (eds), *Handbook of industrial and organizational psychology*, 2nd edn, Vol. 3 (pp. 481–569). Palo Alto, CA: Consulting Psychologists Press, Inc.

Geringer, J. M. (1986). Criteria for selecting partners for joint ventures in industrialized market economies. Ph.D. dissertation, University of Washington.

Geringer, J. M. and Hébert, L. (1989). Control and performance of international joint ventures. *Journal of International Business Studies*, 20(2), 235–54.

Geringer, J. M. and Hébert, L. (1991). Measuring joint venture performance. *Journal of International Business Studies*, 22(2), 249–63.

Gerlach, M. (1992). *Alliance capitalism: The social organization of Japanese business*. Berkeley: University of California Press.

Gersick, C. J. G. (1988). Time and transition in work teams: Toward a new model of group development. *Academy of Management Journal*, 31, 9–41.

Gertsen, M. C. (1990). Intercultural competence and expatriates. *International Journal of Human Resource Management*, 3, 341–62.

Ghemawat, P. and Khanna, T. (1998). The nature of diversified business groups: A research agenda and two case studies. *Journal of Industrial Economics*, 46, 35–61.

Ghoshal, S. (1987). Global strategy: An organizing framework. *Strategic Management Journal*, 8, 425–40.

Ghoshal, S. and Bartlett, C. A. (1990). The multinational corporation as an interorganizational network. *Academy of Management Review*, 15, 603–25.

Ghoshal, S., Korine, H., and Szulanski, G. (1994). Interunit communication in multinational corporations. *Management Science*, 40, 96–110.

Ghoshal, S. and Nohria, N. (1989). Internal differentiation within multinational corporations. *Strategic Management Journal*, 10(4), 323–37.

Gibbons, F. X. and Gerrard, M. (1991). Downward comparison and coping with threat. In J. M. Suls and T. A. Wills (eds), *Social comparison: Contemporary theory and research* (pp. 317–45). Hillsdale, NJ: Erlbaum Associates.

Gibbs, N. (1996). Cause celeb. *Time*, June 17, pp. 28–30.

Gibbs, R. W., Jr (1990). Psycholinguistic studies on the conceptual basis of idiomaticity. *Cognitive Linguistics*, 1, 417–62.

Gibson, C. B. (1995). An investigation of gender differences in leadership across four countries. *Journal of International Business Studies*, 26(2), 255–79.

Gibson, C. B. (1997). Do you hear what I hear? A framework for reconciling intercultural communication difficulties arising from cognitive styles and cultural values. In P. C. Earley and M. Erez (eds), *New perspectives on international industrial/organizational psychology* (pp. 335–62). San Francisco, CA: Lexington Press.

Gibson, C. B. (1999). Do they do what they believe they can? Group efficacy and group effectiveness across tasks and cultures *Academy of Management Journal*, 42.

Gibson, C. B., Randel, A., and Earley, P. C. (in press). Work team efficacy: An assessment of group confidence estimation methods. *Group and Organization Management*.

Gibson, C. B. and Zellmer-Bruhn (1999). Working Paper, University of Southern California.

Gibson, J. J. (1979). *The ecological approach to visual perception.* Boston: Houghton Mifflin.

Gilligan, C. (1982). *In a different voice: Psychological theory and women's development.* Cambridge, MA: Harvard University Press.

Ginsberg, A. and Buchholz, A. (1990). Converting to for-profit status: Corporate responsiveness to radical change. *Academy of Management Journal*, 33, 445–77.

Gire, J. T. and Carment, D. W. (1987). Chinese culture connection: Chinese values and the search for culture-free dimensions of culture. *Journal of Cross-Cultural Psychology*, 18, 143–64.

Glass, S. (1997). The young and the feckless. *The New Republic*, September 15, pp. 14–17.

Glenn, E. S., Witmeyer, D., and Stevenson, K. A. (1977). Cultural styles of persuasion. *International Journal of Intercultural Relations*, 1, 52–66.

Glennon, L. M. (1979). *Women and dualism.* New York: Longman.

Goic, S. (1999). Employees' attitudes towards employee ownership and financial participation in Croatia: Experiences and cases. *Journal of Business Ethics*, 21(2–3), 145–55.

Goldman, A. (1992). Intercultural training of Japanese for U.S.–Japanese interorganizational communication. *International Journal of Intercultural Relations*, 16, 195–215.

Gomez-Mejia, L. and Balkin, D. B. (1987). The determinants of managerial satisfaction with expatriation and repatriation process. *Journal of Management Development*, 6, 7–17.

Gooderham, P. N., Nordhaug, O., and Ringdal, K. (1999). Institutional determinants of organizational practices: Human resource management in European firms. *Administrative Science Quarterly*, 44(3), 507–31.

Goodpaster, K. E. (1984). *Ethics in management.* Boston: Harvard Business School Press.

Goodwin, J. and Goodwin, D. (1999). Ethical judgments across cultures: A comparison between business students from Malaysia and New Zealand. *Journal of Business Ethics*, 18(3), 267–81.

Goto, S. (1996). To trust or not to trust: Situational and dispositional determinants. *Social Behavior and Personality*, 24(2), 119–32.

Gouldner, A. W. (1960). The norm of reciprocity: A preliminary statement. *American Sociological Review*, 25 (April), 161–78.

Govier, T. (1994a). Is it a jungle out there? Trust, distrust, and the construction of social reality. *Dialogue*, 33, 237–52.

Govier, T. (1994b). An epistemology of trust. *International Journal of Moral Social Studies*, 8, 155–74.

Grabher, G. and Stark, D. (eds) (1997). *Restructuring networks in post-socialism.* Oxford: Oxford University Press.

Grace, N. M. (1995). *The feminized male character in twentieth-century literature.* Lewiston, NY: Edwin Millen Press.

Graen, G. B. and Wakabayashi, M. (1994). Cross-cultural leadership making: Bridging American and Japanese diversity for team advantage. In H. C. Triandis, M. D. Dunnette, and L. Hough (eds), *Handbook of industrial and organizational psychology*, 2nd edn, Vol. 4 (pp. 415–46). Palo Alto, CA: Consulting Psychologists Press.

Graham, J. L. (1983). Brazilian, Japanese, and American business negotiations. *Journal of International Business Studies*, 5, 47–52.

Graham, J. L. (1984). Comparison of Japan and U.S. business negotiation. *International Journal of Research in Marketing*, 1, 51–68.

Graham, J. L. (1985). The influence of culture on the process of business negotiations: An exploratory study. *Journal of International Business Studies*, 16(2), 81–96.

Graham, J. L. and Herberger, R. A., Jr (1983). Negotiators abroad: Don't shoot from the hip. *Harvard Business Review*, 61, 160–8.

Graham, J. L., Evenko, L. I., and Rajan, M. N. (1993). An empirical comparison of Soviet and American business negotiations. *International Journal of Business Studies*, 23, 387–418.

Graham, J. W. and Organ, D. W. (1993). Commitment and the covenantal organization. *Journal of Managerial Issues*, 5, 482–502.

Granovetter, M. (1985). Economic action and social structure: The problem of embeddedness. *American Journal of Sociology*, 91, 481–510.

Granovetter, M. (1994). Business groups. In N. Smelser and R. Swedberg (eds), *Handbook of economic sociology* (pp. 453–75). Princeton, NJ: Princeton University Press.

Granrose, C. S. (1997). Cross-cultural socialization of Asian employees in U.S. organizations. In C. S. Granrose and S. Oskamp (eds), *Cross-cultural work groups* (pp. 186–211). Thousand Oaks, CA: Sage Publications.

Granrose, C. S. and Oskamp, S. (1997). *Cross-cultural work groups*. Thousand Oaks, CA: Sage Publications.

Grant, R. M. (1995). *Contemporary strategy analysis*. Cambridge, MA: Blackwell.

Grant, R. M. (1996a). Prospering in dynamically-competitive environments: Organizational capability as knowledge integration. *Organization Science*, 7, 375–87.

Grant, R. M. (1996b). Toward a knowledge-based theory of the firm. *Strategic Management Journal*, 17 (winter, special issue), 109–22.

Grant, R. M. and Baden-Fuller, C. (1995). A knowledge-based theory of inter-firm collaboration. *Academy of Management*, Best Papers Proceedings.

Gray, B. (1994). The gender-based foundations of negotiation theory. In R. J. Lewicki, B. H. Sheppard, and R. J. Bies (eds), *Research on negotiation in organizations*, Vol. 4 (pp. 3–36). Greenwich, CT: JAI Press.

Gray, B. and Aimin Yan (1992). A negotiations model of joint venture formation, structure and performance: Implications for global management. In S. B. Prasad (ed.), *Advances in international comparative management*, Vol. 7 (pp. 41–75). Greenwich, CT: JAI Press.

Gray, H. P. (1996). Culture and economic performance: Policy as an intervening variable. *Journal of Comparative Economics*, 23, 278–91.

Greenberg, J. (1982). Approaching equity and avoiding inequity in groups and organizations. In J. Greenberg and R. L. Cohen (eds), *Equity and justice in social behavior* (pp. 389–435). New York: Academic Press.

Greenberg, J. (1987). A taxonomy of organizational justice theories. *Academy of Management Review*, 12, 9–22.

Greenberg, J. (1990). Looking fair vs. being fair: Managing impressions of organizational justice. In L. L. Cummings and B. M. Staw (eds), *Research in organizational behavior*, Vol. 12 (pp. 111–57). Greenwich, CT: JAI Press.

Greenberg, J. (1996). *The quest for justice on the job: Essays and experiments*. Thousand Oaks, CA: Sage.

Greenberg, J. and Lind, E. A. (2000). The pursuit of organizational justice: From conceptualization to implication to application. In C. L. Cooper and E. A. Locke (eds), *Industrial and organizational psychology: Linking theory with practice* (pp. 72–108). Oxford: Blackwell.

Greenhouse, S. (1997). Nike shoe plant in Vietnam is called unsafe for workers. *New York Times*, November 8, p. 1.

Gregersen, H. B. and Black, J. S. (1992). Antecedents to commitment to a parent company and a foreign operation. *Academy of Management Journal*, 35, 65–90.

Gregersen, H. B., Black, J. S., and Hite, J. (1995). Expatriate performance appraisal in U.S. multinational firms. *Journal of International Business Studies*, 27, 711–38.

Gregersen, H. B., Morrison, A. J., and Black, J. S. (1998). Developing leaders for the global frontier. *Sloan Management Review*, 40, 21–32.

Grove, C. L. and Torbiörn, I. (1985). A new conceptualization of intercultural adjustment and the goals of training. *International Journal of Intercultural Relations*, 9, 205–33.

Grubisic, D. and Goic, S. (1998). Student attitudes towards business ethics in countries in transition. *Business Ethics: A European Review*, 7(3), 163–77.

Gruenfeld D. H., Thomas-Hunt M. C., and Kim P. H. (1998). Cognitive flexibility, communication strategy, and integrative complexity in groups: Public versus private reactions to majority and minority status. *Journal of Experimental Social Psychology*, 34, 202–26.

Gu, B. H. (1990). Beijing municipal bureau chiefs performance-appraisal plan and implementation. *Chinese Law and Government*, 23(4), 74–84.

Gudykunst, W. B. (ed.) (1993). *Communication in Japan and the United States*. Albany, NY: State University of New York Press.

Gudykunst, W. B., Gunzley, R. M., and Hammer, M. R. (1996). Designing intercultural training. In D. Landis and R. S. Bhagat (eds), *Handbook of intercultural training*, 2nd edn (pp. 61–80). Thousand Oaks, CA: Sage.

Gudykunst, W. B. and Hammer, M. (1983). Basic training design: Approaches to intercultural training. In D. Landis and R.W. Brislin (eds), *Handbook of intercultural training*, Vol. 1. Elmsford, NY: Pergamon.

Gudykunst, W. B. and Kim, Y. Y. (1992). *Communicating with strangers: An approach to intercultural communication*, 2nd edn. New York: McGraw-Hill.

Gudykunst, W. B., Matsumoto, Y., Ting-Toomey, S., Nishida, T., and Karimi, H. (1994). Measuring self-construals across cultures: A derived etic analysis. Paper presented at the International Communication Association Convention in Sydney, Australia, July.

Gudykunst, W. B., Ting-Toomey, S., and Chua, E. (1988). *Culture and interpersonal communication*. Newbury Park, CA: Sage.

Gulati, R. (1995a). Does familiarity breed trust? The implications of repeated ties for contractual choice in alliances. *Academy of Management Journal*, 38(2), 85–112.

Gulati, R. (1995b). Social structure and alliance formation patterns: A longitudinal analysis. *Administrative Science Quarterly*, 40, 619–52.

Gulati, R. (1998). Alliances and networks. *Strategic Management Journal*, 19(4), 293–317.

Gullander, S. (1976). Joint venture and corporate strategy. *Columbia Journal of World Business*, (spring), 104–14.

Guth, W. D. and Tagiuri, R. (1965). Personal values and corporate strategy. *Harvard Business Review*, 123–32.

Guthrie, G. M. (1975). A behavioral analysis of culture learning. In R. W. Brislin, S. Bochner, and W. J. Lonner (eds), *Cross-cultural perspectives on learning* (pp. 95–115). New York: Wiley.

Guthrie, G. M. (1981). What you need is continuity. In S. Bochner (ed.), *The mediating person: Bridges between cultures* (pp. 96–112). Cambridge: Schenkman.

Guzzo, R. and Waters, J. A. (1982). The expression of the affect and the performance of decision-making groups. *Journal of Applied Psychology*, 67, 67–74.

Guzzo, R. (1986). Group decision making and group effectiveness in organizations. In P. S. Goodman (ed.), *Designing effective work groups*. San Francisco, CA: Jossey-Bass.

Guzzo, R., Yost, P. R., Campbell, R. J., and Shea, G. P. (1993). Potency in groups: Articulating a construct. *British Journal of Social Psychology*, 32, 87–106.

Habib, M. and Victor, B. (1991). Strategy, structure, and performance of US manufacturing and service MNCs. *Strategic Management Journal*, 12, 589–606.

Hackman, J. R. (1976). Groups in organizations. In M. D. Dunnette (ed.), *Handbook of industrial and organizational psychology*. Chicago, IL: Rand-McNally Press.

Hackman, J. R. (1987). The design of work teams. In Jay Lorsch (ed.), *Handbook of organizational behavior* (pp. 89–136). New York: Prentice-Hall.

Hackman, J. R. (1990). Introduction. In J. R. Hackman (ed.), *Groups that work (and those that don't)*. San Francisco: Jossey-Bass.

Hackman, J. R., Oldham, G. R., Janson, K., and Purdy, K. (1975). A new strategy for job enrichment. *California Management Review*, 17, 57–71.

Haegg, C. (1983). Sources of international business ethics. *Management International Review*, 23(4), 73–8.

Haire, M., Ghiselli, E. E., and Porter, L. W. (1961). *Managerial thinking: An international study*, 2nd edn 1966. New York: Wiley.

Hall, E. T. (1966). *The hidden dimension*. New York: Doubleday.

Hall, E. T. (1976). *Beyond culture*. New York: Doubleday.

Hall, E. T. (1983). *The dance of life*. New York: Doubleday.

Hall, E. T. (1992). *An anthropology of everyday life: An autobiography*. New York: Anchor.

Hall, E. T. and Hall, M. R. (1990). *Understanding cultural differences*. Yarmouth, ME: Intercultural Press.

Hallén, L., Johanson, J., and Seyed-Mohamed, N. (1991). Interfirm adaptation in business relationships. *Journal of Marketing*, 55 (April), 29–37.

Hambrick, D. C., Cho, T. S., Chen, M. J. (1996). The influence of top management team heterogeneity on firms' competitive moves. *Administrative Science Quarterly*, 41, 659–84.

Hambrick, D. C., Davison, S. C., Snell, S. A., and Snow, C. C. (1998). When groups consist of multiple nationalities: Towards a new understanding of the implications. *Organization Studies*, 19, 181–205.

Hambrick, D. C., Macmillan, I. A., and Day, D. L. (1982). Strategic attributes and performance in the BCG matrix: A PIMS based analysis of industrial product business. *Academy of Management Journal*, September, 510–31.

Hambrick, D. C. and Mason, P. A. (1984). Upper echelons: The organization as a reflection of its top managers. *Academy of Management Review*, 9, 193–206.

Hamel, G. (1991). Competition for competence and inter-partner learning within international strategic alliances. *Strategic Management Journal*, 12 (special issue), 83–103.

Hamel, G., Doz, Y., and Prahalad, C. K. (1989). Collaborate with your competitors – and win. *Harvard Business Review*, 67(1), 133–9.

Hamill, J. (1983). The labour relations practices of foreign-owned and indigenous firms. *Employee Relations*, 5(1), 14–17.

Hamill, J. (1989). Expatriate policies in British multinationals. *Journal of General Management*, 14, 18–33.

Hamilton, G. and Biggart, N. W. (1988). Market, culture, and authority: A comparative analysis of management and organization in East Asia. *American Journal of Sociology*, 94, S52–S94.

Hamilton, G. and Feenstra, R. (1995). Varieties of hierarchies and markets: An introduction. *Industrial and Corporate Change*, 4, 51–91.

Hammer, M. R. (1989). Intercultural communication competence. In M. K. Asante and W. B. Gudykunst (eds), *Handbook of international and intercultural communication* (pp. 247–60). Newbury Park: Sage.

Hammer, M. R. (1999). A measure of intercultural sensitivity: The intercultural development inventory. In S. M. Fowler and M. G. Mumford (eds.), *The intercultural sourcebook: Cross-cultural training methods*, Vol. 2 (pp. 61–72). Yarmouth, ME: The Intercultural Press.

Hammer, M. R. and Champy, J. (1993). *Reengineering the corporation*. New York: HarperBusiness.

Hammer, M. R., Hart, W., and Rogan, R. (1998). Can you go home again? An analysis of the repatriation of corporate managers and spouses. *Management International Review*, 38, 67–86.

Hammer, M. R., Nishida, H., and Wiseman, R. L. (1996). The influence of situational prototypes on dimensions of intercultural communication competence. *Journal of Cross-Cultural Psychology*, 27, 267–82.

Hampden-Turner, C. (1990). *Charting the corporate mind: From dilemma to strategy*. Oxford: Blackwell.

Hampden-Turner, C. (1993). The structure of entrapment: Dilemmas standing in the way of women managers and strategies to resolve these. Paper presented at the Global Business Network Meeting, New York, December 9–10.

Hampden-Turner, C. and Trompenaars, A. (1993). *The seven cultures of capitalism*. New York: Doubleday.

Harari, E. and Zeira, Y. (1974). Morale problems in non-American multinational corporations in the United States. *Management International Review*, 14, 43–57.

Harpaz, I. (1990). The importance of work goals: An international perspective. *Journal of International Business Studies*, 21(1), 75–93.

Harriman, A. (1996). *Women/men/management*. Westport, CT: Praeger.

Harrison, L. E. and Huntington, S. P. (eds) (2000). *Culture matters: How values shape human progress*. New York: Basic Books.

Harris, H. and Brewster, C. (1999). The coffee machine system: How international resourcing really works. *International Journal of Human Resource Management*.

Harris, P. R. and Moran, R. T. (1991). *Managing cultural differences*, 3rd edn. Houston: Gulf.

Harvey, B. (1999). Graceful merchants: A contemporary view of Chinese business ethics. *Journal of Business Ethics*, 20(1), 85–92.

Harvey, M. G. (1982). The other side of foreign assignments: Dealing with the repatriation dilemma. *Columbia Journal of World Business*, 1, 53–9.

Harvey, M. G. (1985). The executive family: An overlooked variable in international assignments. *Columbia Journal of World Business*, 20(1), 84–93.

Harvey, M. G. (1989). Repatriation of corporate executives: An empirical study. *Journal of International Business Studies*, spring, 131–44.

Harvey, M. G. (1993). Empirical evidence of recurring international compensation problems. *Journal of International Business Studies*, 24(4), 785.

Harvey, M. G. (1997). Focusing the international personnel performance appraisal process. *Human Resource Development Quarterly*, 8, 627–58.

Harzing A.-W. (1995). The persistent myth of high expatriate failure rates. *International Journal of Human Resource Management*, 6(2), 457–74.

Hawrysh, B. M. and Zaichkowsky, J. L. (1989). Cultural approaches to negotiations: Understanding the Japanese. *European Journal of Marketing*, 25, 40–54.

Hayashi, C. (1992). Quantitative social research: Belief systems, the way of thinking, and sentiments of five nations. *Behaviormetrika*, 19, 127–70.

Hayashi, K., Harnett, D. L., and Cummings, L. L. (1973). Personality and behavior in negotiations: An American–Japanese empirical comparison. Working paper. Fujinomiya, Japan: Institute for International Studies and Training.

Hayashi, N., Ostrom, E., Walker, J., and Yamagishi, T. (1999). Reciprocity, trust, and the sense of control. *Rationality and Society*, 11(1), 27–46.

Hébert, L. (1994). Division of control, relationship dynamics and joint venture performance. Ph.D. Dissertation, University of Western Ontario.

Hébert, L. (1997). Does control matter? A path model of the control–performance relationship in IJVs. *Management International*, 1(1), 33–47.

Heckhausen, H. (1971). Trainingskurse zur erhohung der leistungsmotivation und der unternehmerischen aktivitat in einem entwicklungsland: Eine nachtragliche analyze des erzelten motivwandels. *Zeitschrift fur Entwicklungspsychologie und Pädagogish Psychologie*, 3, 253–68.

Hedley, B. (1977). Strategy and the business portfolio. *Long Range Planning*, February, pp. 7–16.

Hedlund, G. (1986). The hypermodern MNC: A heterarchy? *Human Resource Management*, 9, 9–35.

Hedlund, G. and Nonaka, I. (1993). Models of knowledge management in the West and Japan. In P. Lorange, B. Chakravarathy, J. Roos, and A. Van de Ven (eds), *Implementing strategic processes: Change, learning and co-operation*. Oxford: Basil Blackwell.

Heenan, D. and Perlmutter, H. (1979). *Multinational organization development*. Reading, MA: Addison-Wesley.

Heine, S. J. (1998). Self-enhancement and self-improvement: Two ways to motivate the self. Paper presented to the cultural psychology conference at Stanford University, August.

Heine, S. J. and Lehman, D. R. (1997). The cultural construction of self-enhancement: An examination of group-serving biases. *Journal of Personality and Social Psychology*, 72, 1268–83.

Helgesen, S. (1990). *The female advantage: Women's ways of leadership*. New York: Doubleday.

Heller, F. A. and Wilpert, B. (1981). *Competence and power in managerial decision making*. Chichester: Wiley.

Helmolt, K. and Müller, B. D. (1993). Zur vermittlung interkultureller koompetenzen. In B. D. Müller (ed.), *Interkulturelle wirtschaftskommunikation* (pp. 509–48). Munich: Iudicum.

Hemesath, M. and Pomponio, X. (1998). Cooperation and culture: Students from China and the United States in a prisoner's dilemma. *Cross-Cultural Research*, 32(2), 171–84.

Hennart, J.-F. (1988). A transaction costs theory of equity joint venture. *Strategic Management Journal*, 9(4): 361–74.

Herbert, B. (1996). Trampled dreams. *The New York Times*, July 12, p. A27.

Herbert, B. (1997). Brutality in Vietnam. *The New York Times*, March 28, p. A29.

Herold, D. M. and Fedor, D. B. (1998). Individuals' interaction with their feedback environment: The role of domain-specific individual differences. *Research in personnel and human resource management*, 16, 215–54. Greenwich, CT: JAI Press.

Herrigel, G. (1993). Large firms, small firms, and the governance of flexible specialization: The case of Baden Württemberg and socialized risk. In B. Kogut (ed.), *Country competitiveness*. New York: Oxford University Press.

Hetts, J. J., Sakuma, M., and Pelham, B. W. (submitted). Two roads to self-adoration: Implicit and explicit self-evaluation and culture.

Hill, C. (1983). Conglomerate performance over the economic cycle. *Journal of Industrial Economics*, 32, 197–211.

Hill, C. (1990). Cooperation, opportunism and the invisible hand: Implications for transaction cost theory. *Academy of Management Review*, 15(3), 500–13.

Hill, C. (1995). National institutional structures, transaction cost economizing, and competitive advantage: The case of Japan. *Organization Science*, 6, 119–31.

Hill, R. C. (1988). Joint venture strategy formulation and implementation: A contingency approach. Ph.D. Dissertation, Texas A and M University.

Hiltrop, J. M. and Janssens, M. (1990). Expatriation: Challenges and recommendations. *European Management Journal*, 8, 19–26.

Hirschman, A. O. (1982). Rival interpretations of market society: Civilising, destructive or feeble? *Journal of Economic Literature*, 20, 1463–84.

Hitt, M., Ireland, D. R., and Hoskisson, R. (1995). *Strategic management: Competitiveness and globalization*. St Paul, MN: West Publishing Company.

Ho, D. Y.-F. (1976). On the concept of face. *American Journal of Sociology*, 81, 867–90.

Hoffer, E. (1951). *The true believer: Thoughts on the nature of mass movements*. New York: Harper and Row.

Hofstede, G. (1980a). *Culture's consequences: International differences in work-related values*. Beverly Hills, CA: Sage.

Hofstede, G. (1980b). Motivation, leadership, and organization: Do American theories apply abroad? *Organizational Dynamics*, 9, 42–63.

Hofstede, G. (1983). Dimensions of national cultures in fifty cultures and three regions. In J. R. Deregowski, S. Dziurawiec, and R. C. Annis (eds), *Expiscations in cross-cultural psychology* (pp. 335–55). Lisse, Netherlands: Swets and Zeitlinger.

Hofstede, G. (1984). *Culture's consequences: International differences in work-related values*. Beverly Hills, CA: Sage.

Hofstede, G. (1985). The interaction between national and organizational value systems. *Journal of Management Studies*, 22; 347–57.

Hofstede, G. (1986). Editorial: The usefulness of the "organizational culture" concept. *Journal of Management Studies*, 23, 253–7.

Hofstede, G. (1993). Cultural constraints in management theory. *Academy of Management Executive*, 7(1), 81–93.

Hofstede, G. (1997). *Cultures and organizations: Software of the mind*, 1st edn 1991. New York: McGraw-Hill.

Hofstede, G. (1998a). A case for comparing apples with oranges: International differences in values. *International Journal of Comparative Sociology*, 39, 16–31.

Hofstede, G. (1998b). Identifying organizational subcultures: An empirical approach. *Journal of Management Studies*, 35, 1–12.

Hofstede, G. (1999). The universal and the specific in 21st-century global management. *Organizational Dynamics*, 27 (summer), 34–43.

Hofstede, G. and Bond, M. H. (1984). Hofstede's cultural dimensions: An independent validation using Rokeach's Value Survey. *Journal of Cross-Cultural Psychology*, 15, 417–33.

Hofstede, G. and Bond, M. H. (1988). The Confucian connection: From cultural roots to economic growth. *Organizational Dynamics*, 16(4), 4–21.

Hofstede, G., Neuijen, B., Ohayv, D. D., and Sanders, G. (1990). Measuring organizational cultures: A qualitative and quantitative study across twenty cases. *Administrative Science Quarterly*, 35, 286–316.

Holland, R. C. (1997). What are the prospects for a global code of business ethics? Working Paper. SEI Center for Advanced Studies in Management, Wharton School, University of Pennsylvania.

Hollingsworth, J. R. and Boyer, R. (1997). Coordination of economic actors and social systems of production. In J. R. Hollingsworth and R. Boyer (eds), *Contemporary capitalism*. Cambridge: Cambridge University Press.

Holmes, T. H. and Rahe, R. H. (1967). The social readjustment rating scale. *Journal of Psychosomatic Research*, 11, 213–18.

Holt, D. (1997). A comparative study of values among Chinese and U.S. entrepreneurs. *Journal of Business Venturing*, 12, 483–505.

Holt, J. and Keats, D. M. (1992). Work cognitions in multicultural interaction. *Journal of Cross-Cultural Psychology*, 23(4), 421–43.

Holtgraves, T. (1997). Styles of language use: Individual and cultural variability in conversational indirectness. *Journal of Personality and Social Psychology*, 73, 624–37.

Homans, G. C. (1961). *Social behavior: Its elementary forms*. New York: Harcourt, Brace and World.

Hong, Y. Y., Morris, M. W., Chiu, C. Y., and Benet-Martinez, V. (2000). Multicultural minds: A dynamic constructionist approach to culture and cognition. *American Psychologist*, 55(7), 709–20.

Hoopes, D. S. (1979). Intercultural communication concepts and the psychology of intercultural experience. In M. D. Pusch (ed.), *Multicultural education: A cross-cultural training approach* (pp. 10–38). La Grange Park: Intercultural Networks.

Hopkins, M. E., Lo, L., Peterson, R. E., and Seo, K. K. (1977). Japanese and American managers. *Journal of Applied Psychology*, 96, 71.

Hoppe, M. H. (1990). A comparative study of country elites: International differences in work-related values and learning and their implications for management training and development. Unpublished dissertation, University of North Carolina, Chapel Hill.

Hoppe, M. H. (1998). Validating the masculinity/femininity dimensions from 19 countries. In G. Hofstede and Associates (eds), *The taboo dimension of national cultures* (pp. 29–43). Thosand Oaks, CA, London, and New Delhi: Sage.

Horsch, J. (1995). *Auslandseinsatz von Stammhaus-Mitarbeitern*. Frankfurt am Main: Peter Lang.

Hoskisson, R. and Hitt, M. (1990). Antecedents and performance outcomes of diversification. *Journal of Management*, 16, 461–509.

Hosmer, L. T. (1995). Trust: The connecting link between organizational theory and philosophical ethics. *Academy of Management Review*, 20(2), 370–403.

Hossain, S. and Davis, H. A. (1989). Some thoughts on international personnel management as an emerging field. In A. Nedd, G. R. Ferris, and K. M. Rowland (eds), *Research in personnel and human resources management: International human resources management*. London: Greenwich.

House, R. J. (1977). A 1976 theory of charismatic leadership. In J. G. Larsen and J. G. Hunt (eds), *Leadership: The cutting edge* (pp. 189–204). Carbondale, IL: Southern Universities Press.

House, R. J. (1987). The "all things in moderation" leader: A review of *The behavioral science of leadership*. *Academy of Management Review*, 12, 164–9.

House, R. J., Hanges, P., Ruiz-Quintanilla, S. A., Dorfman, P. W., Javidan, M., Dickson, M., Gupta, V., and 170 co-authors (1999). Cultural influences on leadership and organizations: Project GLOBE. In W. F. Mobley, M. J. Gessner, and V. Arnold (eds), *Advances in global leadership*, Vol. 1 (pp. 171–233). Stamford, CT: JAI Press.

House, R., Rousseau, D. M., and Thomas-Hunt, M. (1995). The meso-paradigm: A framework for the integration of micro and macro organizational behavior. In L. L. Cummings and B. W. Staw (eds), *Research in organizational behavior*, Vol. 17 (pp. 71–114). Greenwich, CT: JAI Press.

House, R. J., Wright, N. S., and Aditya, R. N. (1997). Cross-cultural research on organizational leadership: A critical analysis and a proposed theory. In P. C. Earley and M. Erez (eds), *New perspectives on international industrial/organizational psychology* (pp. 535–625). San Francisco, CA: New Lexington.

Hu, H. C. (1944). The Chinese concepts of face. *American Anthropologist*, 46, 45–64.

Hubbard, R. and Palia, D. (1999). A re-examination of the conglomerate merger wave in the 1960s: An internal capital markets view. *Journal of Finance*, 54, 1131–52.

Hughes, E. C. (1971). *The sociological eye: Selected papers*. Chicago: Aldine-Atherton, Inc.

Hui, C. H. (1988). Measurement of individualism-collectivism. *Journal of Research on Personality*, 22, 17–36.

Hui, C. H. and Graen, G. (1997). Guanxi and professional leadership in contemporary Sino-American joint ventures in mainland China. *Leadership Quarterly*, 8, 451–65.

Hui, C. H. and Triandis, H. C. (1986). Individualism–collectivism: A study of cross-cultural researchers. *Journal of Cross-Cultural Psychology*, 20, 296–309.

Hui, H. C., Triandis, H. C., and Yee, C. (1991). Cultural differences in reward allocation: Is collectivism the explanation? *British Journal of Social Psychology*, 30, 145–57.

Hui, C. H., Yee, C., and Eastman, K. L. (1995). The relationship between individualism–collectivism and job satisfaction. *Applied Psychology: An International Review*, 44, 276–82.

Hunt, J. G. and Peterson, M. F. (1997). Two scholars' views of some nooks and crannies in cross-cultural leadership research. *Leadership Quarterly*, 8, 343–54.

Huntington, S. (1996). *The clash of civilizations and the remaking of the world order*. New York: Simon and Schuster.

Huo, Y. P. and Steers, R. M. (1993). Cultural influences on the design of incentive systems: The case of East Asia. *Asia Pacific Journal of Management*, 10(1), 71–85.

Huo, Y. P. and Von Glinow, M. A. (1995). On transplanting human-resource practices to China: A culture-driven approach. *International Journal of Manpower*, 16(9), 3.

Ibarra, H. (1992). Homophily and differential returns: Sex differences in network structure and access in an advertising firm. *Administrative Science Quarterly*, 37, 422–47.

Ilgen, D. R., Barnes-Farrell, J. L., and McKellin, D. B. (1993). Performance appraisal process research in the 1980s: What has it contributed to appraisals in use? *Organizational Behavior and Human Decision Processes*, 54, 321–68.

Ilgen, D. R., Fisher, C. D., and Taylor, M. S. (1979). Consequences of individual feedback on behaviour in organizations. *Journal of Applied Psychology*, 64(4), 349–71.

Inglehart, R. (1994). *Codebook for the 1981–1984 and 1990–1993 World Values Survey*. Ann Arbor: Institute for Social Research.

Inglehart, R., Basañez, M., and Moreno, A. (1998). *Human values and beliefs: A cross-cultural sourcebook.* Ann Arbor: University of Michigan Press.

Inkeles, A. (1977). Understanding and misunderstanding individual modernity. *Journal of Cross-Cultural Psychology,* 8, 135–76.

Inkeles, A. and Smith, D. H. (1974). *Becoming modern: Individual change in six developing countries.* Cambridge, MA: Harvard University Press.

Inkpen, A. (1992). Learning and collaboration: An examination of North American–Japanese joint ventures. Ph.D. dissertation, The University of Western Ontario.

Inkpen, A. (1998). Learning and knowledge acquisition through international strategic alliances. *Academy of Management Executive,* 12(4), 69–80.

International Labor Office (1997). *Breaking through the glass ceiling: Women in management.* Geneva: International Labor Office.

Itami, H. (1987). *Mobilizing invisible assets.* Cambridge, MA: Harvard University Press.

Ivancevich, J. M. (1969). Selection of American managers for overseas assignments. *Personnel Journal,* 48, 189–93.

Iwawaki, S. and Lynn, R. (1972). Measuring achievement motivation in Japan and Great Britain. *Journal of Cross-Cultural Psychology,* 3, 219–20.

Iwao, S. (1993). *The Japanese woman: Traditional image and changing reality.* New York: Free Press.

Iyengar, S. S. (1998). Rethinking the value of choice: A cultural perspective on intrinsic motivation. Paper presented to the Culture and Psychology conference, Stanford University, August.

Iyengar, S. S. and Lepper, M. R. (1999). Rethinking the value of choice: A cultural perspective on intrinsic motivation. *Journal of Personality and Social Psychology,* 76, 349–66.

Iyengar, S. S., Lepper, M. R., and Ross, L. (in press). Independence from whom? Interdependence with whom? Cultural perspectives on in-groups versus out-groups. In D. Miller and D. Prentice (eds), *Cultural divides: Understanding and overcoming group conflict.* New York: Sage.

Jackson, S. E. (1981). Measurement of commitment to role identities. *Journal of Personality and Social Psychology,* 40, 138–46.

Jackson, S. E. and Associates (1992). *Diversity in the workplace: Human resources initiatives.* New York: Guilford Press.

Jackson, S. E., Brett, J. F., Sessa, V. I., Cooper, D. M., Julin, J. A., and Peyronnin, K. (1991). Some differences make a difference: Individual dissimilarity and group heterogeneity as correlates of recruitment, promotions, and turnover. *Journal of Applied Psychology,* 76, 675–89.

Jackson, S. E., May, K. E., and Whitney, K. (1995). Understanding the dynamics of diversity in decision-making teams. In R. A. Guzzo, E. Salas, and Associates (eds), *Team effectiveness and decision making in organizations* (pp. 204–61). San Francisco, CA: Jossey-Bass Publishers.

Jaeger, A. M. and Kanungo, R. N. (1990). *Management in developing countries.* London: Routledge.

Jaggi, B. (1979). Need importance of Indian managers. *Management International Review,* 19(1), 107–13.

James, K. (1993). The social context of organizational justice: Cultural, intergroup, and structural effects on justice behaviors and perceptions. In R. Cropanzano (ed.), *Justice in the workplace: Approaching fairness in human resource management* (pp. 21–50). Hillsdale, NJ: Lawrence Erlbaum Associates.

James, W. (1890). *The principles of psychology.* New York: Holt.

Janger, A. R. (1980). *Organization of international joint venture.* New York: Conference Board.

Janosik, R. (1987). Rethinking the culture–negotiation. *Negotiation Journal,* 3, 385–95.

Janssens, M. (1995). Intercultural interaction: A burden on international managers? *Journal of Organizational Behavior,* 16(2), 155–68.

Jarillo, J.-C. (1988). On strategic networks. *Strategic Management Journal,* 9(1), 31–41.

Jehn, K. (1995). A multimethod examination of the benefits and detriments of intragroup conflict. *Administrative Science Quarterly,* 40, 256–82.

Jehn, K., Chadwick, C., and Thatcher, S. M. B. (1997). To agree or not to agree: The effects of value congruence, individual demographic dissimilarity, and conflict on workgroup outcomes. *International Journal of Conflict Management*, 8, 287–305.

Jehn, K., Northcraft, G., and Neale, M. (1997). *Opening Pandora's box: A field study of diversity, conflict, and performance in work groups*. Working paper, Wharton School, University of Pennsylvania.

Jemison, D. B. and Sitkin, S. B. (1986). Corporate acquisitions: A process perspective. *Academy of Management Review*, 11, 145–63.

Jensen, M. C. and Meckling, W. H. (1976). Theory of the firm: Managerial behavior, agency costs, and ownership structure. *Journal of Financial Economics*, 3, 305–60.

Jewkes, J., Sawyers, D., and Stillerman, R. (1958). *The sources of invention*. London: Macmillan.

Johanson, J. and Mattsson, L.-G. (1987). Interorganizational relations in industrial systems: A network approach compared with the transaction-cost approach. *International Studies of Management and Organization*, 17(1), 34–48.

Johnston, J. (1991). An empirical study of repatriation of managers in UK multinationals. *Human Resource Management Journal*, 1(4), 102–8.

Johnson, J. (1997). Russia's emerging financial–industrial groups. *Post-Soviet Affairs*, 13, 333–65.

Johnson, J. L., Cullen, J. B., Sakano, T., and Takenouchi, H. (1996). Setting the stage for trust and strategic integration in Japanese–U.S. cooperative alliances. *Journal of International Business Studies*, 27(5), 981–1004.

Johnson, J. P. and Lenartowicz, T. (1998). Culture, freedom, and economic growth: Do cultural values explain economic growth. *Journal of World Business*, 33, 332–56.

Jones, M. L. (1988). Managerial thinking: An African perspective. *Journal of Management Studies*, 25(5), 481–505.

Jones, T. M. and Ryan, L. V. (1997). The link between ethical judgment and action in organizations: A moral approbation approach. *Organization Science*, 8(6), 663–80.

Jones, T. M. and Wicks, A. C. (1999). Convergent stakeholder theory. *Academy of Management Review*, 24(2), 206–21.

Kabanoff, B. (1997). Organizational justice across cultures. In P. C. Earley and M. Erez (eds), *New perspectives on international industrial and organizational psychology* (pp. 676–712). San Francisco, CA: Lexington Press.

Kagitcibasi, C. (1990). Family and socialization in cross-cultural perspective: A model of change. *Nebraska symposium on motivation*, 1989, 37, 135–200. Lincoln, Nebraska: University of Nebraska Press.

Kagitcibasi, C. (1997). Individualism and collectivism. In J. W. Berry, M. H. Segall, and C. Kagitcibasi (eds), *Handbook of cross-cultural psychology*, 2nd edn (pp.1–50). Boston: Allyn and Bacon.

Kahn, W. A. (1990). Toward an agenda for business ethics research. *Academy of Management Review*, 15(2), 311–28.

Kanfer, R. and Ackerman, P. L. (1996). A self-regulatory skills perspective to reducing cognitive interference. In I. G. Sarason and B. R. Sarason (eds), *Cognitive interference theories: Methods and findings*. New York: Erlbaum.

Kanter, R. M. (1977). *Men and women of the corporation*. New York: Basic Books.

Kanter, R. M. (1994). Comments on Nancy A. Nichols' *Reach for the top*: Women and the changing facts of work life. Boston: Harvard Business School Press, as cited in the book review by John R. Hook in *The Academy of Management Executive*, 8(2), 87–9.

Kanungo, R. N. and Wright, R. W. (1983). A cross-cultural comparative study of managerial job attitudes. *Journal of International Business Studies*, fall, 115–28.

Kao, J. (1993). The worldwide web of Chinese business. *Harvard Business Review*, March–April, 24–36.

Karagozoglu, N. and Lindell, M. (1998). Internationalization of small and medium-sized technology-based firms: an explanatory study. *Journal of Small Business Management*, 36(1), 44–59.

Karl, K. A., O'Leary-Kelly, A. M., and Martocchio, J. J. (1993). The impact of feedback and self-efficacy on performance in training. *Journal of Organizational Behaviour*, 14, 379–94.

Kashima, E. S. and Kashima, Y. (1998). Culture and language: The case of cultural dimensions and personal pronoun use. *Journal of Cross-Cultural Psychology*, 29, 461–86.

Kashima, Y. (1994). Cultural metaphors of the mind and the organization. In A. M. Bouvy and F. J. R. van de Vijver (eds), *Journeys into cross-cultural psychology* (pp. 351–63). Amsterdam: Swets and Zeitlinger.

Kashima, Y. and Callan, V. J. (1994). The Japanese work group. In H. C. Triandis, M. Dunnette, and L. M. Hough (eds), *Handbook of industrial and organizational psychology*, 2nd edn, Vol. 4. Palo Alto: Consulting Psychologists Press.

Kashima, Y., Siegel, M., Tanaka, K., and Kashima, E. S. (1992). Do people believe behaviors are consistent with attitudes? Toward a cultural psychology of attribution processes. *British Journal of Social Psychology*, 331, 111–24.

Kasprzyk, D., Montano, D. E., and Fishbein, M. (1998). Application of an integrated behavioral model to predict condom use: A prospective study among high HIV risk groups. *Journal of Applied Social Psychology*, 28, 1557–83.

Katz, D. (1994). *Just do it: The Nike spirit in the corporate world*. New York: Random House.

Kealey, D. J. (1989). A study of cross-cultural effectiveness: Theoretical issues, practical applications. *International Journal of Intercultural Relations*, 13, 387–428.

Kealey, D. J. (1996). The challenge of international personnel selection. In D. Landis and R. S. Bhagat (eds), *Handbook of intercultural training*, 2nd edn (pp. 80–105). Thousand Oaks: Sage.

Kealey, D. J. and Protheroe, D. R. (1996). The effectiveness of cross-cultural training for expatriates: An assessment of the literature on the issue. *International Journal of Intercultural Relations*, 20, 141–65.

Kealey, D. J. and Ruben, B. D. (1983). Cross-cultural personnel selection: Criteria, issues and methods. In D. Landis and R. W. Brislin (eds), *Handbook of intercultural training*, Vol. 1 (pp. 155–75). New York: Pergamon.

Keck, S. L. (1997). Top management team structure: Differential effects by environmental context. *Organization Science*, 8: 143–56.

Keesing, R. M. (1981). Theories of culture. In R. W. Casson (ed.), *Language, culture and cognition: Anthropological perspectives* (pp. 42–66). New York: Macmillan.

Keister, L. (1998). Engineering growth: Business group structure and firm performance in China's transition economy. *American Journal of Sociology*, 104, 404–40.

Keller, K. L. (1998). *Strategic brand management: Building, measuring, and managing brand equity*. Upper Saddle River, NJ: Prentice-Hall.

Kelley, H. H. (1973). The process of causal attributions. *American Psychologist*, 28, 107–29.

Kelley, H. H. and Thibaut, J. W. (1978). *Interpersonal relations: A theory of interdependence*. New York: Wiley and Sons.

Kelley, L. and Worthley, R. 1981: The role of culture in comparative management: A cross-cultural perspective. *Academy of Management Journal*, 24, 164–73.

Kendall, D. W. (1981). Repatriation: An ending and a beginning. *Business Horizons*, 6, 21–5.

Kerlinger, G. (1951). Decision making in Japan. *Social Forces*, 30, 36–41.

Kerr, S. and Jermier, J. M. (1978). Substitutes for leadership: Their meaning and measurement. *Organizational Behavior and Human Performance*, 22, 375–403.

Khanna, T. and Palepu, K. (1997). Why focused strategies may be wrong for emerging markets. *Harvard Business Review*, July–August, 41–51.

Khanna, T. and Palepu, K. (1999). Policy shocks, market intermediaries, and corporate strategy: The evolution of business groups in Chile and India. *Journal of Economics and Management Strategy*, 8, 270–310.

Khanna, T. and Palepu, K. (in press). Is group affiliation profitable in emerging markets? An analysis of diversified Indian business groups. *Journal of Finance*.

Kidder, L. (1992). Requirements for being "Japanese": Stories of returnees. *International Journal of Intercultural Relations*, 16, 383–94.

Killing, J. P. (1982). How to make a global joint venture work. *Harvard Business Review* (May–June), 120–7.

Killing, J. P. (1983). *Strategies for joint venture success*. New York: Praeger.

Killing, J. P. (1988). Understanding alliances: The role of task and organizational complexity. In F. Contractor and P. Lorange (eds), *Cooperative strategies in international business* (pp. 55–68). Toronto, ON: Lexington Books.

Kilman, S. (1999). Monsanto won't commercialize terminator gene. *Wall Street Journal*, October 5.

Kim, K. I., Park, H. J., and Suzuki, N. (1990). Reward allocations in the U.S., Japan, and Korea: A comparison of individualistic and collectivistic cultures. *Academy of Management Journal*, 33(1), 188–98.

Kim P. H. (1997). When what you know can hurt you: A study of experiential effects on group discussion and performance. *Organizational Behavior and Human Decision Processes*, 69, 165–77.

Kim, U. (1994). Introduction. In Kim, U., Triandis, H. C., Kagitcibasi, C., Choi, S.-C., and Yoon, G. (eds), *Individualism and collectivism: Theory, method and applications*. Newbury Park, CA: Sage

Kim, U., Triandis, H. C., Kagitcibasi, C., Choi, S.-C., and Yoon, G. (1994). *Individualism and collectivism: Theory, method and applications*. Newbury Park, CA: Sage

Kim, Y. (1988). *Communication and cross-cultural adaptation: An integrative theory*. Clevedon: Multilingual Matters.

Kim, Y. (1989). Intercultural adaptation. In M. K. Asante and W. B. Gudykunst (eds), *Handbook of International and Intercultural Communication* (pp. 275–94). Newbury Park: Sage.

Kim, Y. and Ruben, B. D. (1988). Intercultural transformation: A systems theory. In Y. Kim and W. B. Gudykunst (eds), *Theories in intercultural communication* (pp. 299–321). Newbury Park: Sage.

Kim, Y. and Son, J. (1998). Trust, cooperation and social risk: A cross-cultural comparison. *Korea Journal*, 38 (spring), 131–53.

Kimura, H. (1980). Soviet and Japanese negotiating behavior: The spring 1977 fisheries talks. *Orbis*, 24, 43–67.

Kinhide, M. (1976). The cultural premises of Japanese diplomacy. In Japan Center for International Exchange (ed.), *The silent power*. Tokyo: Simul Press.

Kiong, T. C. and Kee, Y. P. (1998). Guanxi bases, Xinyong and Chinese business networks. *British Journal of Sociology*, 49(1), 75–96.

Kirchmeyer, C. and Cohen, A. (1992). Multicultural groups: Their performance and reactions. *Group and Organization Management*, 17, 153–70.

Kitayama, S. (1993). Culture, self, and emotion: The nature and functions of "good moods/feelings" in Japan and the United States. Mimeo. Also lecture given at East–West Center, Honolulu, Hawaii on October 21.

Kitayama, S. (1996). The mutual constitution of culture and self: Implications for emotion. Paper presented to the meetings of the American Psychological Society, June.

Kitayama, S. (1999). Cultural affordances and the collective construction of the self. Paper presented to the symposium on "Individualism and Collectivism: Recent Theoretical and Empirical Findings" Nicosia, Cyprus, March.

Kitayama, S., Markus, H. R., Matsumoto, H., and Norasakkunkit, V. (1997). Individual and collective processes in the construction of the self: self-enhancement in the United States and self-criticism in Japan. *Journal of Personality and Social Psychology*, 72, 1245–67.

Klimoski, R. and Mohammed, S. (1994). Team mental model: Construct or metaphor? *Journal of Management*, 20, 403–37.

Klineberg, O. (1982). Contact between ethnic groups: a historical perspective of some aspects of theory and research. In S. Bochner (ed.), *Cultures in contact: Studies in cross-cultural interaction* (pp. 45–76). New York: Pergamon.

Kluckhohn, F. and Strodtbeck, F. L. (1961). *Variations in value orientations*. New York: Harper and Row.

Kluger, A. N. and DeNisi, A. (1996). The effects of feedback intervention on performance. A historical review, a meta-analysis, and a preliminary feedback intervention theory. *Psychological Bulletin*, 119(2), 254–84.

Kobayashi, N. (1982). The present and future of Japanese multinational enterprises: A comparative analysis of Japanese and US–European multinational management. *International Studies of Management and Organization*, 12(1), 38–59.

Kobrin, S. J. (1988). Expatriate reduction and strategic control in American multinational corporations. *Human Resource Management*, 27(1), 63–75.

Kobrin, S. J. (1994). Is there a relationship between a geocentric mind-set and multinational strategy? *Journal of International Business Studies*, 3, 493–512.

Koch, M., Nam, S. H., and Steers, R. M. (1995). Human resource management in South Korea. In L. Moore and D. Jennings (eds), *Human resource management on the Pacific rim* (pp. 217–42). Berlin: Walter de Gruyter.

Kochan, T., Batt, R., and Dyer, R. (1992). International human resource studies: A framework for future research. In D. Lewin et al. (eds), *Research frontiers in industrial relations and human resources*. Madison: Industrial Relations Research Association.

Kogut, B. (1988a). A study of life cycle of joint ventures. In F. Contractor and P. Lorange (eds), *Cooperative strategies in international business* (pp. 169–85). Toronto, ON: Lexington Books.

Kogut, B. (1988b). Joint venture: Theoretical and empirical perspectives. *Strategic Management Journal*, 9, 319–32.

Kogut, B. (1992). Country capabilities and permeability of borders. *Strategic Management Journal*, 12, 33–48.

Kogut, B. (1993). Introduction. In B. Kogut (ed.), *Country competitiveness: Technology and the organizing of work*. New York: Oxford University Press.

Kogut, B. and Singh, H. (1988). The effect of national culture on the choice of entry mode. *Journal of International Business Studies*, 19, 411–32.

Kogut, B. and Zander, U. (1993). Knowledge of the firm and the evolutionary theory of the multinational corporation. *Journal of International Business Studies*, 4, 625–45.

Kogut, B. and Zander, U. (1996). What firms do? Coordination, identity and learning. *Organization Science*, 7, 502–18.

Kohlberg, L. (1981). *Essays on moral development*. New York: Harper and Row.

Kohn, M. K. (1969). *Class and conformity*. Homewood, IL: Dorsey Press.

Kollock, P. (1998). Social dilemmas: the anatomy of cooperation. *Annual Review of Sociology*, 24(2), 183–214.

Kopp, R. (1994). International human resource policies and practices in Japanese, European, and United States multinationals. *Human Resource Management*, 33(4), 581–99.

Korn Ferry International (n.d.). *Developing leadership for the 21st century*. www.kornferry.com/offeur.htm

Kramer, R. M. (1999). Trust and distrust in organizations: Emerging perspectives, enduring questions. *Annual Review of Psychology*, 50, 569–98.

Kramer, R. M. and Messick, D. M. (eds) (1995). *Negotiation as a social process: New trends in theory and research*. Thousand Oaks, CA: Sage.

Kraut, A. I. and Ronen, S. (1975). Validity of job facet importance: A multinational, multicriteria study. *Journal of Applied Psychology*, 60, 671–7.

Krus, D. J. and Rysberg, J. A. (1976). Industrial managers and nAch: Comparable and compatible? *Journal of Cross-Cultural Psychology*, 7, 491–6.

Kühlmann, T. M. (1995a). Die Auslandsentsendung von fach- und führungskräften: Eine einführung in die schwerpunkte und ergebnisse der forschung. In T. M. Kühlmann (ed.), *Mitarbeiterentsendung ins Ausland* (pp. 1–30). Göttingen: Verlag für Angewandte Psychologie.

Kühlmann, T. M. (1995b). Vom "kulturschock" zum "kulturlernen": Ansätze zur vorbereitung auf den Auslandseinsatz. *Zeitschrift für Berufs- und Wirtschaftspädagogik*, 91, 142–54.

Kühlmann, T. M. (2001). The German approach to developing global leaders via expatriation. In M. Mendenhall, T. Kühlmann, and G. Stahl (eds), *Developing global business leaders: Policies, processes, and innovations* (pp. 57–72). Westport, CT: Quorum Books.

Kühlmann, T. M. and Stahl, G. K. (1998). Diagnose interkultureller kompetenz: Entwicklung und evaluierung eines Assessment Centers. In C. Barmeyer und J. Bolten (eds), *Interkulturelle personalorganisation* (pp. 213–23). Berlin: Verlag Wissenschaft and Praxis.

Kumar, S. and Seth, A. (1998). The design of co-ordination and control mechanisms for managing joint venture-parent relationships. *Strategic Management Journal*, 19(6), 579–99.

Kumar, B. and Steinmann, H. (1988). Führungskonflikte im Deutsch-Japanischen management. *Journal of Labour Problems*, 26, 59–76.

Kume, T. (1985). Managerial attitudes toward decision-making: North America and Japan. In W. P. Gudykunst, L. P. Stewart, and S. Ting-Toomey (eds), *Communication, culture and organizational processes* (pp. 231–57). Beverly Hills, CA: Sage.

Kunda, G. (1992). *Engineering culture: Control and commitment in a high-tech corporation*. Philadelphia: Temple University Press.

Labor's World (editorial) (2000). *Wall Street Journal*, May 3, p. A26.

Lahno, B. (1995). Trust, reputation, and exit, in exchange relationships. *Journal of Conflict Resolution*, 39(3), 495–510.

Lakoff, G. L. (1987). *Women, fire, and dangerous things: What categories reveal aout the mind*. Chicago: University of Chicago Press.

Lakoff, G. L. (1993). The contemporary theory of metaphor. In A. Ortony (ed.), *Metaphor and thought*, 2nd edn (pp. 202–51). Cambridge: Cambridge University Press.

Lakoff, G. and Johnson, M. (1980). *Metaphors we live by*. Chicago: University of Chicago Press.

Lamb, D. (1999). Job opportunity or exploitation? *Los Angeles Times*, April 18, p. C1.

Lamb, D. (2000). Economic program revitalizing Thailand's countryside. *Los Angeles Times*, February 27, p. A34.

Landau, S. F. (1984). Trends in violence and aggression: A cross-cultural analysis. *International Journal of Comparative Sociology*, 24, 132–58.

Landauer, T. K. (1995). *The trouble with computers: Usefulness, usability, and productivity*. Cambridge, MA: MIT Press.

Landis, D. and Wasilewski, J. H. (1999). Reflections on 22 years of the International Journal of Intercultural Relations and 23 years in other areas of intercultural practice. *International Journal of Intercultural Relations*, 23(4), 535–74.

Lane, C. and Bachmann, R. (1997). Co-operation in inter-firm relations in Britain and Germany: The role of social institutions. *British Journal of Sociology*, 48(2), 226–54.

Lane, P., Lyles, M., and Salk, J. (1998). Relative absorptive capacity, trust and interorganizational learning in international joint ventures. In M. A. Hitt, R. E. R. Costa, and R. D. Nixon (eds), *Managing strategically in an interconnected world*. Chichester: John Wiley & Sons.

Langlois, C. C. and Schlegelmilch, B. B. (1990). Do corporate codes of ethics reflect national character? Evidence from Europe and the United States. *Journal of International Business Studies*, 21(4), 519–39.

Larson, A. L. (1988). Cooperative alliances: A study of entrepreneurship. DBA dissertation, Harvard University.

Latane, B., Williams, K. D., and Harkins, S. G. (1979). Many hands make light the work: The causes and consequences of social loafing. *Journal of Personality and Social Psychology*, 37, 822–32.

Latham, G. P., Erez, M., and Locke, E. A. (1988). Resolving scientific disputes by the joint design of crucial experiments by the antagonists: Application to the Erez–Latham dispute regarding participation in goal setting. *Journal of Applied Psychology*, 73, 753–72.

Latham, G. P. and Yukl, G. A. (1975). Effects of assigned and participative goal setting on performance and job satisfaction. *Journal of Applied Psychology*, 60, 299–302.

Lau, D. C. and Murnighan, J. K. (1998). Demographic diversity and faultlines: The compositional dynamics of organizational groups. *Academy of Management Review*, 23, 325–40.

Laurent, A. (1986). The cross-cultural puzzle of international human resource management. *Human Resource Management*, 25, 91–102.

Lawler, E. E. (1992). *The ultimate advantage: Creating the high involvement organization.* San Francisco: Jossey-Bass.

Lawler, J. J. and Bae, J. (1998). Overt employment discrimination by multinational firms: Cultural and economic influences in a developing country. *Industrial Relations*, 37, 126–51.

Lawrence, B. S. (1997). Perspective: The blackbox of organizational demography. *Organization Science*, 8, 1–22.

Lawrence, P. and Lorsch, J. (1969). *Organization and environment.* Homewood, IL: Irwin.

Lay, C., Fairlie, P., Jackson, S., Ricci, T., Eisenberg, J., Sato, T., Teeaeaer, A., and Melamud, A. (1998). Domain-specific allocentrism-idiocentrism: A measure of family connectedness. *Journal of Cross-Cultural Psychology*, 29, 434–60.

Lazarus, R. S. (1980). The stress and coping paradigm. In C. Eisdorfer, D. Cohen, and A. Kleinman (eds), *Theoretical bases for psychopathology* (pp. 177–214). New York: Spectrum.

Lazarus, R. S. and Folkman, S. (1984). *Stress, appraisal, and coping.* New York: Springer.

Lazarus, R. S. and Launier, R. (1978). Stress-related transactions between person and environment. In L. A. Pervin and M. Lewis (eds), *Perspectives in interactional psychology* (pp. 287–327). New York: Plenum.

Leary, D. E. (ed.) (1990). *Metaphors in the history of psychology.* Cambridge: Cambridge University Press.

Lebra, T. S. (1992). Introduction. In T. Lebra (ed.), *Japanese social organization.* Hawaii: University of Hawaii Press.

Lecraw, D. J. (1984). Bargaining power, ownership, and profitability of transnational corporations in developing countries. *Journal of International Business Studies*, 15(1), 27–43.

Lee, B. (1993). The legal and political realities for women managers: The barriers, the opportunities and the horizon ahead. In E. A. Fagenson (ed.), *Women in management: Trends, issues and challenges in managerial diversity* (pp. 246–73). Newbury Park, CA: Sage.

Lee, C. and Beamish, P. W. (1995). Characteristics and performance of Korean joint ventures in LDCs. *Journal of International Business Studies*, 26(3): 637–54.

Lee, C.-Y. and Yoshihara, H. (1997). Business ethics of Korean and Japanese managers. *Journal of Business Ethics*, 16(1), 7–21.

Lee, F. (1997). When the going gets tough, do the tough ask for help? Help seeking and power motivation in organizations. *Organizational behavior and human decision processes*, 72(3), 336–63.

Lee, Y.-T. and Seligman, M. E. P. (1997). Are Americans more optimistic than the Chinese? *Personality and Social Psychology Bulletin*, 23, 32–40.

Leung, K. (1997). Negotiation and reward allocations across cultures In P. C. Earley and M. Erez (eds), *New perspectives on international industrial and organizational psychology* (pp. 640–75). San Francisco, CA: Lexington Press.

Leung, K. and Bond, M. H. (1984). The impact of cultural collectivism on reward allocation. *Journal of Personality and Social Psychology*, 47(4), 793–804.

Leung, K., Su, S. K., and Morris, M. W. (submitted). When is criticism not constructive? Social interpretations of negative supervisory feedback in two cultures.

Leviatan, U. and Rosner, M. (1980). *Work and organization in kibbutz industry.* Norwood, PA: Norwood Publications.

Levinson, N. and Asahi, M. (1995). Cross-national alliances and interorganizational learning. *Organizational Dynamics*, 24(20), 50–62.

Levinthal, D. (1992). Wisdom from Wharton: R&D as investment in learning. *Chief Executive*, 81, 62–5.

Levinthal, D. A. and Fichman, M. (1988). Dynamics of inter-organizational attachments: Auditor–client relationships. *Administrative Science Quarterly*, 33, 345–69.

Levitt, T. (1983). The globalization of markets. *Harvard Business Review*, 61(3), 92–102.

Lewicki, R. J., McAllister, D. J., and Bies, R. J. (1998). Trust and distrust: New relationships and realities. *Academy of Management Review*, 23(3), 438–58.

Lewin, K. (1935). *A dynamic theory of personality*. New York: McGraw-Hill.

Lewin, K. (1951). *Field theory and social science*. New York: Harper.

Lewin, K., Lippitt, R., and White, R. K. (1939). Patterns of aggressive behavior in experimentally created climates. *Journal of Social Psychology*, 10, 271–99.

Li, M. C. (1992). The patterns of in-group favoritism in a collectivist and individualistic society. *International Journal of Psychology*, 27, 558.

Lickel, B., Hamilton, D. S., Wieczorkowska, G., Lewis, A., Sherman, S. J., and Uhles, A. N. (1998). Varieties of groups and the perception of group entitativity. University of California, Santa Barbara, Unpublished paper.

Lin, J. L., Yu, C.-M. J., and Seetoo, D.-H. W. (1997). Motivations, partners' contributions and control of international joint ventures. In P. W. Beamish and J. P. Killing (eds), *Cooperative strategies: Asian Pacific perspectives* (pp. 115–34). San Francisco, CA: New Lexington Press.

Lin, Z. (1997). Ambiguity with a purpose: The shadow of power in communication. In P. C. Earley and M. Erez (eds), *New perspectives on international industrial/organizational psychology* (pp. 363–76). San Francisco, CA: New Lexington Press.

Lincoln, J. R. and Kalleberg, A. L. (1990). *Culture, control, and commitment: A study of work organization and work attitudes in the United States and Japan*. Cambridge: Cambridge University Press.

Lind, E. A. and Tyler, T. R. (1988). *The social psychology of procedural justice*. New York: Plenum.

Lindsley, D. H., Brass, D. J., and Thomas, J. B. (1989). Efficacy–performance spirals: A multilevel perspective. *Academy of Management Review*, 20(3), 645–78.

Lindsley, S. L. (1999). Communication and "the Mexican way": Stability and trust as core symbols in maquiladoras. *Western Journal of Communication*, 63(1), 1–31.

Lipman-Blumen, J. (1983). Emerging patterns of female leadership in formal organizations. In M. Horner, C. C. Nadelson, and M. T. Notman (eds), *The challenge of change* (pp. 61–91). New York: Plenum Press.

Lippman, S. and Rumelt, R. P. (1982). Uncertain imitability: An analysis of interfirm differences in profitability under competition. *Bell Journal of Economics*, 13, 418–38.

Littler, C. and Salaman, G. (1984). *Class at work: The design, allocation and control of jobs*. London: Batsford.

Locke, E. A. (1976). The nature and causes of job satisfaction. In M. D. Dunnette (ed.), *Handbook of industrial and organizational psychology*. Chicago: Rand McNally.

Locke, E. A. (1991). The motivation sequence, the motivation hub, and the motivation core. *Organizational Behavior and Human Decision Processes*, 50, 288–99.

Locke, E. A. and Latham, G. P. (1990). *A theory of goal setting and task performance*. Englewood Cliffs, NJ: Prentice-Hall.

Locke, E. A., Latham, G. P., and Erez, M. (1988). The determinants of goal commitment. *Academy of Management Journal*, 13(1); 23–39.

Locke, E. A. and Schweiger, D. M. (1979). Participation in decision-making: One more look. In B. M. Staw (ed.), *Research in organizational behavior*, Vol. 1. Greenwich, CT: JAI Press.

Lodahl, T. and Kejner, M. (1965). The definition and measurement of job involvement. *Journal of Applied Psychology*, 49, 24–33.

Loewenstein, J., Thompson, L., and Gentner, D. (1999). Analogical encoding facilitates knowledge transfer in negotiation. *Psychonomic Bulletin & Review*, 6, 586–97.

Lohr, A. and Steinmann, H. (1998). The ethical dimension of cross-cultural business activities. In H. Lange et al. (eds), *Working across cultures* (pp. 7–31). The Netherlands: Kluwer Academic Publishers.

London, M. (1995). *Self and interpersonal insight*. New York: Oxford University Press.

Lorange, P., Roos, J., and Bronn, P. S. (1992). Building successful strategic alliances. *Long Range Planning*, 25(6), 10–18.

Lord, R. G., Bining, J. F., Rush, M. C., and Thomas, J. C. (1978). The effect of performance cues and leader behavior in questionnaire ratings of leadership behavior. *Organizational Behavior and Human Performance*, 21, 27–39.

Lord, R. G. and Maher, K. J. (1991). *Leadership and information processing: Linking perceptions and performance*. Boston: Unwin-Hyman.

Lorenz, E. H. (1988). Neither friends nor strangers: Informal networks of subcontracting in French industry. In D. Gambetta (ed.), *Trust: Making and breaking cooperative relations* (pp. 194–210). New York: Blackwell.

Lü, J. and Hébert, L. (1999). Foreign control and survival: The case of Japanese ventures in Asia. Working paper, R. Ivey School of Business, The University of Western Ontario.

Luhmann, N. (1979). *Trust and power*. New York: Wiley.

Luo, Y. and Peng, M. W. (1999). Learning to compete in a transition economy: Experience, environment, and performance. *Journal of International Business Studies*, 30(2): 269–96.

Lusch, R. F. (1976). Sources of power: their impact on intrachannel conflict. *Journal of Marketing Research*. 13 (November), 382–90.

Luthans, F. and Kreitner, R. (1985). *Organizational behavior modification*. Glenview, IL: Scott, Foresman.

Lynch, R. P. (1989). *The practical guide to joint ventures and alliances*. New York: Wiley and Sons.

Lysgaard, S. (1955). Adjustment in a foreign society: Norwegian Fulbright grantees visiting the United States. *International Science Bulletin*, 7, 45–51.

Lysonski, S. and Gaidis, W. (1991). A cross-cultural comparison of the ethics of business students. *Journal of Business Ethics*, 10(2), 141–50.

Lytle, A. L., Brett, J. M., Barsness, Z. I., Tinsley, C. H., and Janssens, M. (1995). A paradigm for confirmatory cross-cultural research in organizational behavior. In L. L. Cummings and B. M. Staw (eds), *Research in organizational behavior*, Vol. 17 (pp. 167–214). Greenwich, CT: JAI Press.

Ma, H. K. (1988). The Chinese perspective on moral judgment and development. *International Journal of Psychology*, 23, 201–27.

Ma, V. and Schoeneman, T. J. (1995). Individualism versus collectivism: A comparision of Kenyan and American self-concept. Paper presented to the meeting of the Western Psychological Association, Los Angeles, CA, March.

Maccoby, E. and Jacklin, C. (1974). *The psychology of sex differences*. Stanford, CA: Stanford University Press.

Madhok, A. (1997). Cost, value and foreign market entry mode: The transaction and the firm. *Strategic Management Journal*, 18(1), 39–61.

Maehr, M. L. (1977). Sociocultural origins of achievement motivation. *International Journal of Intercultural Relations*, 1, 81–104.

Maehr, M. L. and Nichols, J. G. (1980). Culture and achievement motivation: A second look. In N. Warren (ed.), *Studies in cross-cultural psychology*, Vol. 3 (pp. 221–67). New York: Academic Press.

Mahoney, J. (1990). *Teaching business ethics in the UK, Europe and the USA: A comparative study*. London: Athlone Press.

Maitland, I., Bryson, J., and Van de Ven, A. H. (1985). Sociologists, economists and opportunism. *Academy of Management Review*, 10(1), 59–65.

Makino, S. and Beamish, P. W. (1998). Performance and survival of joint ventures with non-conventional ownership structures. *Journal of International Business Studies*, 29(4), 797–818.

Makino, S. and Delios, A. (1996). Local knowledge transfer and performance: Implications for alliance formation in Asia. *Journal of International Business Studies*, 27(5), 905–27.

Malinowski, B. (1927). *The father in primitive psychology*. New York: Norton.

Mann, L. (1980). Cross cultural studies of small groups. In H. C. Triandis and R. W. Brislin (eds), *Handbook of cross-cultural psychology*, Vol. 5 (pp. 155–209). Boston: Allyn and Bacon.

Manning, J. (1997). Nike plants balk at $2.36 a day. *Portland Oregonian*, April 3, p. A1.

Manning, J. (1998). Nike sued over its Asian factories. *The Oregonian*, April 21, p. 1.

Mansell, M. (1981). Transcultural experience and expressive response. *Communication Education*, 30, 93–108.

Mansfield, E. (1988). Industrial innovation in Japan and the United States. *Science*, 1769–74.

March, R. M. (1990). *The Japanese negotiator: Subtlety and strategy beyond Western logic*. New York: Kodansha International.

March, J. G. and Simon, H. A. (1968). *Organizations*. New York: Wiley.

Marginson, P. (1994). Multinational Britain: Employment and work in an internationalized economy. *Human Resource Management Journal*, 4(4), 63–80.

Marginson, P., Armstrong, P., Edwards, P., Purcell, J., and Hubbard, N. (1993). The control of industrial relations in large companies: An initial analysis of the second company level industrial relations survey. *Warwick Papers in Industrial Relations*, 45, December.

Markus, H. R. and Kitayama, S. (1991). Culture and the self: Implications for cognition, emotion, and motivation. *Psychological Review*, 98(2), 224–53.

Markus, H. R., Kitayama, S., and Heiman, R. J. (1997). Culture and "basic" psychological principles. In E. T. Higgins and A. W. Kruglanski (eds), *Social psychology: Handbook of basic principles* (pp. 857–913). New York: Guilford Press.

Marsden, P. V. (1990). Network data and measurement. *Annual Review of Sociology*, 16, 435–63.

Marshall, J. (1984). *Women managers: Travellers in a male world*. New York: Wiley.

Marshall, R. (1997). Variances in levels of individualism across two cultures and three social classes. *Journal of Cross-Cultural Psychology*, 28, 490–5.

Marshall, S. (2000). Executive action: Cultural sensitivity on the assembly line. *Asian Wall Street Journal*, February 28, p. 7.

Martella, D. and Maass, A. (submitted). Unemployment and life satisfaction: The moderating role of time structure and collectivism.

Martin, J. N. (1984). The intercultural reentry: Conceptualization and directions for future research. *International Journal of Intercultural Relations*, 8, 115–34.

Martin, J. N. (1994). Intercultural communication: A unifying concept for international education. In G. Althen (ed.), *Learning across cultures* (pp. 109–43). NAFSA.

Martin, J. N., Bradford, L., and Rohrlich, B. (1995). Comparing predeparture expectations and post-sojourn reports: A longitudinal study of U.S. students abroad. *International Journal of Intercultural Relations*, 19(1), 87–110.

Martinez, R. and Dacin, M. T. (1999). Efficiency motives and normative forces: Combining transaction costs and institutional logic. *Journal of Management*, 25, 75–96.

Marubeni Corporation (1998). *Code of conduct*. Tokyo.

Marx, E. (1996). *International human resource practices in Britain and Germany*. London: Anglo–German Foundation for the Study of Industrial Society.

Maslow, A. H. (1954). *Motivation and personality*. New York: Harper.

Matlay, H. (1997). *The globalization tendencies of firms operating in the small business sector of the British economy: An overview*. Oxford: Second Foundation.

Matsui, T., Kakuyama, T., and Onglatco, M. L. (1987). Effects of goals and feedback on performance in groups. *Journal of Applied Psychology*, 72, 407–15.

Matsui, T. and Terai, I. (1979). A cross-cultural study of the validity of expectancy theory of work motivation. *Journal of Applied Psychology*, 60(2), 263–5.

Matsumoto, D., Weissman, M. D., Preston, K., Brown, B. P., and Kupperbusch, C. (1997). Context-dependent measurement of individualism and collectivism on the individual level. The individualism–collectivism interpersonal assessment inventory. *Journal of Cross-Cultural Psychology*, 28, 743–67.

Matsusaka, J. (1993). Takeover motives during the conglomerate merger wave. *RAND Journal of Economics*, 24, 357–79.

Maurice, M., Sellier, F., and Silvestre, J. (1986). *The social foundations of industrial power*. Cambridge, MA: MIT Press.

Mayer, R. G., Davis, J. H., and Schoorman, H. D. (1995). An integrative model of organizational trust. *Academy of Management Review*, 20(3), 709–34.

Mayrhofer, W. and Brewster, C. (1996). In praise of ethnocentricity: Expatriate policies in European multinationals. *International Executive*, 38(6), 749–78.

Maznevski, M. L. (1994). Understanding our differences: Performance in decision-making groups with diverse members. *Human Relations*, 47(5), 531–52.

McAllister, D. J. (1995). Affect- and cognition-based trust as foundations for interpersonal cooperation in organizations. *Academy of Management Journal*, 38(1), 24–59.

McCall, M. (1994). Identifying leadership potential in future international executives: Developing a concept. *Consulting Psychology Journal*, 46(1), 49–62.

McCarthy, D. J., Puffer, S. M., and Shekshnia, S. V. (1993). The resurgence of an entrepreneurial class in Russia. *Journal of Management Inquiry*, 2(2), 125–37.

McClelland, D. C. (1961). *The achieving society*. Princeton, NJ: Van Nostrand.

McClelland, D. C. and Winter, D. G. (1969). *Motivating economic achievement*. New York: Free Press.

McCusker, C. R. (1994). Individualism–collectivism and relationships in distributive negotiation: An experimental analysis. Unpublished doctoral thesis, University of Illinois, Department of Psychology.

McCusker, C. R. (2001). A holistic account of negotiating. Working paper. Yale School of Management.

McDonald, G. and Zepp, R. (1988). Ethical perceptions of Hong Kong and Chinese business managers. *Journal of Business Ethics*, 7(11), 835–45.

McFarland, C. and Buehler, R. (1995). Collective self-esteem as a moderator of the frog-pond effect in reactions to performance feedback. *Journal of Personality and Social Psychology*, 68(6), 1055–70.

McGrath, J. E. (1984). *Groups: Interaction and performance*. New Jersey: Prentice-Hall.

McGrath, R., MacMillan, I., Yang, E., and Tsai, W. (1992). Does culture endure, or is it malleable? Issues for entrepreneurial economic development. *Journal of Business Venturing*, 7, 441–58.

McKnight, D. H., Cummings, L. L., and Chervany, N. L. (1998). Initial trust formation in new organizational relationships. *Academy of Management Review*, 23(3), 473–91.

McPherson, J. M., Popielarz, P. A., and Drobnic, S. (1992). Social networks and organizational dynamics. *American Sociological Review*, 57(2), 153–70.

Mead, G. H. (1934). *Mind, self and society*. Chicago: University of Chicago Press.

Mead, R. (1998). *International management: Cross-cultural dimensions*. Oxford: Blackwell.

Mead, R., Jones, C. J., and Chansarkar, B. (1997). The managerial elite in Thailand: their long- and short-term career aspirations. *International Journal of Management*, 14(3), 387–94.

Meindl, J. R., Ehrlich, S. B., and Dukerich, J. M. (1985). The romance of leadership. *Administrative Science Quarterly*, 30, 78–102.

Mendenhall, M. (1999). On the need for paradigmatic integration in international human resource management. *Management International Review*, 39(3), 65–88.

Mendenhall, M. (2001). New perspectives on expatriate adjustment and its relationship to global leadership development. In Mendenhall, M., Kuhlmann, T., and Stahl, G. (eds), *Developing global business leaders: Policies, processes, and innovations* (pp. 1–18). Westport, CT: Quorum Books.

Mendenhall, M., Dunbar, E., and Oddou, G. (1987). Expatriate selection, training, and career-pathing: A review and critique. *Human Resource Management*, 26, 331–45.

Mendenhall, M., Kuhlmann, T. M., and Stahl, G. K. (2000). *Developing global business leaders: Policies, processes and innovations.* Westport, CT: Quorum Books.

Mendenhall, M. and Macomber, J. (1997). Rethinking the strategic management of expatriates from a nonlinear dynamics perspective. In Aycan, Z. (ed.), *Expatriate Management: Theory and Research*, Vol. 4 (pp. 41–61). Greenwich, CT: JAI Press.

Mendenhall, M., Macomber, J., Gregersen, H., and Cutright, M. (1998). Nonlinear dynamics: A new perspective on international human resource management research and practice in the 21st century. *Human Resource Management Review*, 8(1), 5–22.

Mendenhall, M. E. and Oddou, G. R. (1985). The dimensions of expatriate acculturation: A review. *Academy of Management Review*, 10, 39–47.

Mendenhall, M. E. and Oddou, G. R. (eds) (1990). *International human resource management.* Boston: PWS-Kent.

Mendenhall, M. and Stahl, G. K. (2000). Expatriate training and development: Where do we go from here? *Human Resource Management Journal*, 39(2–3), 251–65.

Merton, R. K. (1968). *Social theory and social structure.* New York: Free Press.

Meschi, P. (1997). Longevity and cultural differences of international joint ventures: Toward time based cultural management. *Human Relations*, 50, 211–29.

Messick, D. M. and Mackie, D. M. (1989). Intergroup relations. *Annual Review of Psychology*, 40, 45–81.

Meyer, J. and Rowan, B. (1977). Institutionalized organizations: Formal structure as myth and ceremony. *American Journal of Sociology*, 83, 340–63.

Miles, J. and Greenberg, J. (1993). Cross-national differences in preferences for distributive justice norms: The challenge of establishing fair resource allocations in the European community. In J. B. Shaw, P. S. Kirkbride, and K. M. Rowland (eds), *Research in personnel and human resources management* (supplement 3, pp. 133–56). Greenwich, CT: JAI Press.

Miles, R. E. and Snow, C. C. (1984). Fit, failure and the hall of fame. *California Management Review*, 16(3), 10–28.

Milgrom, P. and Roberts, J. (1992). *Economics, organization and management.* Englewood Cliffs, NJ: Prentice-Hall.

Milkman, R. (1992). The impact of foreign investment on US industrial relations: The case of California's Japanese-owned plants. *Economic and Industrial Democracy*, 13(2), 151–81.

Miller, D. J., Giacobbe-Miller, J. K., and Zhang, W. (1998). A comparative study of Chinese and U.S. distributive justice values, goals, and allocative behaviors. In J. L. Cheng and R. B. Peterson (eds), *Advances in international comparative management* (pp. 185–206). Greenwich, CT: JAI Press.

Miller, E. L. (1973). The international selection decision: A study of some dimensions of managerial behavior in the selection decision process. *Academy of Management Journal*, 14, 239–52.

Miller, J. G. (1984). Culture and the development of everyday social explanation. *Journal of Personality and Social Psychology*, 46, 961–78.

Miller, J. G. (1994). Cultural diversity in the morality of caring: Individually-oriented versus duty-oriented interpersonal codes. *Cross-Cultural Research*, 28, 3–39.

Miller, J. G. (1997). Theoretical issues in cultural psychology. In J. W. Berry, Y. H. Poortinga, and J. Pandy (eds), *Handbook of Cross-Cultural Psychology*, 2nd edn, Vol. 1 (pp. 85–128). Needham Heights, MA: Allyn and Bacon.

Milliman, J., Nason, S., Gallagher, E., Hou, P., von Glinow, M. A., and Lowe, K. B. (1998). The impact of national culture on human resource management practices: The case of performance appraisal. In J. L. Cheng and R. B. Peterson (eds), *Advances in international comparative management* (pp. 157–83). Greenwich, CT: JAI Press.

Milliman, J., Nason, S., von Glinow, M. A., Hou, P., Lowe, K. B., and Kim, N. (1995). In search of "best" strategic pay practices: An exploratory study of Japan, Korea, Taiwan, and the United States. In S. B. Prasad (ed.), *Advances in international comparative management* (pp. 227–52). Greenwich, CT: JAI Press.

Milliman, J., von Glinow, M. A., and Nathan, M. (1991). Organizational lifecycles and strategic international human resource management in multinational companies: Implications for congruence theory. *Academy of Management Review*, 16(2), 318–39.

Mills, J. and Clark, M. S. (1982). Exchange and communal relationships. In L. Wheeler (ed.), *Review of personality and social psychology*, Vol. 3 (pp. 121–44). Beverly Hills, CA: Sage.

Minow, M. (1990). *Making all the difference: Inclusion, exclusion, and American law.* Ithaca, NY: Cornell University Press.

Minturn, L. and Lambert, W. W. (1964). *Mothers of six cultures.* New York: Wiley.

Mintzberg, H. (1973). *The nature of managerial work.* New York: Harper and Row.

Misumi, J. (1984). Decision-making in Japanese groups and organizations. In B. Wilpert and A. Sorge (eds), *International perspectives on organizational democracy.* New York: Wiley.

Misumi, J. (1985). *The behavioral science of leadership: An interdisciplinary Japanese research program.* Ann Arbor, MI: University of Michigan Press.

Misumi, J. and Haraoka, K. (1960). An experimental study of group decision (III). *Japanese Journal of Educational Psychology*, 1, 136–53.

Misumi, J. and Peterson, M. F. (1985). The performance-maintenance (PM) theory of leadership: Review of a Japanese research program. *Administrative Science Quarterly*, 30, 196–223.

Misumi, J. and Shinohara, H. (1967). A study of effects of group decision on accident prevention. *Japanese Journal of Educational Social Psychology*, 6, 123–34.

Mitchell, T. R. (1997). Matching motivational strategies with organizational contexts. In L. Cummings and B. Staw (eds), *Research in organizational behavior*, Vol. 19 (pp. 57–149). Greenwich, CT: JAI Press.

Mitroff, I. (1987). *Business not as usual.* San Francisco: Jossey-Bass.

Mitroff, I. I. and Linstone, H. A. (1993). *The unbounded mind: breaking the chains of traditional business thinking.* Oxford: Oxford University Press.

Mjoen, H. and Tallman, S. (1997). Control and performance in international joint ventures. *Organization Science*, 8, 257–74.

Mody, A. (1993). Learning through alliances. *Journal of Economic Behavior and Organization*, 20, 151–70.

Moghaddam, F. M. (1997). Change and continuity in organizations: Assessing intergroup relations. In C. S. Granrose and S. Oskamp (eds), *Cross-cultural work groups* (pp. 36–60). Thousand Oaks, CA: Sage Publications.

Montgomery, C. (1994). Corporate diversification. *Journal of Economic Perspective*, 8, 167–78.

Moorman, C., Deshpande, R., and Zaltman, G. (1993). Factors affecting trust in market research relationships. *Journal of Marketing*, 57(1), 81–101.

Morck, R., Shleifer, A., and Vishny, R. (1990). Do managerial objectives drive bad acquisitions? *Journal of Finance*, 45, 31–48.

Morgan, G. (1986). *Images of organization.* Newbury Park, CA: Sage

Morris, M. W., Leung, K., Ames, D., and Lickel, B. (1999). Views from inside and outside: Integrating emic and etic insights about culture and justice judgment. *Academy of Management Review*, 24, 781–96.

Morris, M. W. and Peng, K. (1994). Culture and cause: American and Chinese attributions for social and physical events. *Journal of Personality and Social Psychology*, 67, 949–71.

Morrison, E. W. and Bies, R. J. (1991). Impression management in the feedback-seeking process:

A literature review and research agenda. *Academy of Management Review*, 16(3), 522–41.

Moscovici, S. (1976). *Social influence and social change*. London: Academic Press.

Moskowitz, D. S., Suh, E. J., and Desaulniers, J. (1994). Situational influences on gender differences in agency and communion. *Journal of Personality and Social Psychology*, 66, 753–61.

MOW International Research Team (1987). *The meaning of working*. London: Academic Press.

Mowday, R. T. (1996). Equity theory predictions of behavior in organizations. In R. M. Steers, L. W. Porter, and G. A. Bigley (eds), *Motivation and leadership at work* (pp. 53–83). New York: McGraw-Hill.

Mowday, R. T., Porter, L. W., and Steers, R. M. (1982). *Employee-organization linkages: The psychology of employee commitment, absenteeism, and turnover*. New York: Academic Press.

Mowery, D., Oxley, J., and Silverman, B. (1996). Strategic alliances and interfirm knowledge transfer. *Strategic Management Journal*, 17 (special issue), 77–91.

Mueller, W. F. (1966). The origins of the basic inventions underlying DuPont's major process and product innovations, 1920–50. In R. Nelson (ed.), *The rate and direction of inventive activity*. Princeton: National Bureau of Economic Research.

Murdock, M. (1990). *The heroine's journey*. Boston: Shambhala.

Murphy-Berman, V. J., Berman, P., Singh, P., Pachuri, A., and Kumar, P. (1984). Factors affecting allocation to needy and meritorious recipients: A cross-cultural comparison. *Journal of Personality and Social Psychology*, 46, 1267–72.

Murray, H. A. (1938). *Explorations in personality*. New York: Oxford University Press.

Na, E. and Loftus, E. F. (1998). Attitudes toward law and prisoners, conservative authoritarianism, atribution, and internal–external control: Korean and American law students and undergraduates. *Journal of Cross-Cultural Psychology*, 29, 595–615.

Nakane, C. (1970a). *Japanese society*. Berkeley, CA: University of California Press.

Nakane, C. (1970b). *Kazokuno kozo (The structure of family)*. Tokyo: Tokyo University Press.

Nakane, C. (1972). *Human relations in Japan*. Japan: Ministry of Foreign Affairs.

Nakano, C. (1997). A survey study on Japanese managers' views of business ethics. *Journal of Business Ethics*, 16, 1737–51.

Nam, S. H. (1991). Cultural and managerial attributions for group performance. Unpublished doctoral dissertation, Lundquist College of Business, University of Oregon.

Nam, S. H. (1995). Culture, control, and commitment in international joint ventures. *International Journal of Human Resource Management*, 6, 553–67.

Nandakumar, P. (1985). Towards effective performance-appraisal systems. *Indian Journal of Social Work*, 46(1), 119–23.

Napier, N. K., and Taylor, S. (1995). *Western women working in Japan: Breaking corporate barriers*. Westport, CT: Quorum Books.

Nathan, J. H., Marsella, A. J., Horvath, A. M., and Coolidge, F. L. (submitted). The concepts of individual, self, and group in Japanese national, Japanese–American, and European–American samples: A semantic differential analysis.

Natlandsmyr, J. H. and Rognes, J. (1995). Culture, behavior, and negotiation outcomes: A comparison and cross-cultural study of Mexican and Norwegian negotiators. *International Journal of Conflict Management*, 6, 5–29.

Naumann, E. (1992). A conceptual model of expatriate turnover. *Journal of International Business Studies*, (3), 499–531.

Naumann, E. (1993). Organizational predictors of expatriate job satisfaction. *Journal of International Business Studies*, 24, 61–80.

Neale, M. A. and Bazerman, M. H. (1992). Negotiator cognition and rationality: A behavioral decision theory perspective. *Organizational Behavior and Human Decision Processes*, 39, 228–41.

Nedd, A., Ferris, G. R., and Rowland, K. M. (1989). *Research in personnel and human resources management*. London: Greenwich.

Nelson, R. (1991). Why do firms differ and how does it matter? *Strategic Management Journal*, 12 (winter), 61–74.

Nemeth, C. J. (1986). Differential contributions of majority and minority influence. *Psychological Review*, 91, 23–32.

Newcombe, T. M. (1959). Individual systems of orientation. In S. Koch (ed.), *Psychology, a study of science: Formulations of the person and the social context*, Vol. 3 (pp. 384–422). New York: McGraw-Hill.

Newman, J., Bhatt, B., and Gutteridge, T. (1978). Determinants of expatriate effectiveness: A theoretical and empirical vacuum. *Academy of Management Review*, 4, 655–61.

Newman, K. L. and Nollen, S. D. (1996). Culture and congruence: The fit between management practices and national culture. *Journal of International Business Studies*, 27(4), 753–79.

Newman, K. L. and Nollen, S. D. (1998). *Managing radical organizational change*. Thousand Oaks, CA: Sage.

Newman, L. S. (1993). How individualists interpret behavior: Idiocentrism and spontaneous trait inference. *Social Cognition*, 11, 243–69.

Nicholson, J. D., Stepina, L. P., and Hochwarter, W. (1990). Psychological aspects of expatriate effectiveness. *Research in Personnel and Human Resource Management*, supplement 2, 127–45.

Nicholson, N. and Imaizumi, A. (1993). The adjustment of Japanese expatriates to living and working in Britain. *British Journal of Management*, 4, 119–34.

Niles, F. S. (1998). Individualism–collectivism revisited. *Cross-Cultural Research*, 32(4), 315–41.

Niles, S. (1998). Achievement goals and means: A cultural comparison. *Journal of Cross-Cultural Psychology*, 29(5), 656–67.

Nisbett, R. and Ross, L. (1980). *Human inference: Strategies and shortcomings of social judgment*. Englewood Cliffs, NJ: Prentice-Hall.

Nisbett, R. and Cohen, D. (1996). *Culture of honor*. Boulder, CO: Westview Press.

Nohria, N. and Ghoshal, S. (1994). Differentiated fit and shared values: Alternatives for managing headquarters–subsidiary relations. *Strategic Management Journal*, 15, 491–502.

Nonaka, I. (1994). A dynamic theory of organizational knowledge creation. *Organization Science*, 5, 14–37.

Noricks, J. S., Agler, L. H., Bartholomew, M., Howard-Smith, S., Martin, D., Pyles, S., and Shapiro, W. (1987). Age, abstract things and the American concept of person. *American Anthropologist*, 89, 667–75.

North, D. (1981). *Structure and change in economic history*. New York: Norton.

North, D. (1990). *Institutions, institutional change, and economic performance*. Cambridge, MA: Harvard University Press.

Northcraft, G. B. and Ashford, S. J. (1990). The preservation of self in everyday life: The effects of performance expectations and feedback context on feedback inquiry. *Organizational Behavior and Human Decision Processes*, 47, 42–64.

Nutterbrock, L. and Freudiger, P. (1991). Identity salience and motherhood: A test of Stryker's theory. *Social Psychology Quarterly*, 54(2), 146–57.

Oberg, K. (1960). Cultural shock. Adjustment to new cultural environments. *Practical Anthropology*, 7, 177–82.

Ochs, E. (1988). *Culture and language development: Language acquisition and language socialization in a Samoan village*. Cambridge: Cambridge University Press.

Odaka, K. (1986). *Japanese management: A forward looking analysis*. Tokyo: Japan Productivity Organization.

OECD (1976). *Guidelines for multinational enterprises*. Paris: Organization for Economic Cooperation and Development.

OECD (1997). *Globalization and small and medium sized enterprizes (SMEs): Synthesis report and country studies*. Paris: Organization for Economic Cooperation and Development.

Oettingen, G. (1997). Culture and future thought. *Culture and Psychology*, 3(3), 353–81.

Ohmae, K. (1989). The global logic of strategic alliances. *Harvard Business Review* (March–April), 143–54.

Ohbuchi, K. and Takahashi, Y. (1994). Cultural styles of conflict management in Japanese and Americans: Passivity, covertness, and effectiveness of strategies. *Journal of Applied Social Psychology*, 24, 1345–66.

Oishi, S., Schimmack, U., Diener, E., and Suh, E. (in press). The measurement of values and individualism–collectivism. *Personality and Social Psychology Bulletin*, 24, 1177–89.

Oliner, S. D. and Sichel, D. E. (1994). Computers and output growth revisited: How big is the puzzle? *Brookings Papers on Economic Activity*, 1988(2), 273–333.

Oliver, C. (1991). Strategic responses to institutional processes. *Academy of Management Review*, 16, 145–79.

Oliver, C. (1997). Sustainable competitive advantage: Combining institutional and resource-based views. *Strategic Management Journal*, 18, 679–713.

Olson, M. (1971). *The logic of collective action*. Cambridge, MA: Harvard University Press.

Ones, D. S. and Viswesvaran, C. (1997). Personality determinants in the prediction of aspects of expatriate job success. *New Approaches to Employee Management*, 4, 63–92.

Onglatco, M. L. U. (1988). *Japanese quality control circles: Features, effects, and problems*. Tokyo: Asian Productivity Center.

O'Reilly, C. A. (1991). Organizational behavior: Where we've been, where we're going. *Annual Review of Psychology*, 42, 427–58.

O'Reilly, C. A., III, Caldwell, D. F., and Barnett, W. P. (1989). Work group demography, social integration, and turnover. *Administrative Science Quarterly*, 34, 21–37.

Organ, D. W. (1990). The motivational basis of organizational citizenship behavior. In L. L. Cummings and B. Staw (eds), *Research in Organizational Behavior*, 12, 43–72. Greenwich, CT: JAI Press.

Orpen, C. (1978). Relationship between job satisfaction and job performance among Western and tribal black employees. *Journal of Applied Psychology*, 63, 263–5.

Ortony, A. (ed.) (1993). *Metaphor and thought*, 2nd edn. Cambridge: Cambridge University Press.

Osland, J. (1990). The hero's adventure: The overseas experience of expatriate businesspeople. Unpublished doctoral dissertation. Case Western Reserve University.

Osland, J. (1995). *The adventure of working abroad: Hero tales from the global frontier*. San Francisco, CA: Jossey-Bass. Jossey-Bass Management series.

Osland, J. (2001). The quest for transformation: The process of global leadership development. In M. Mendenhall, T. M. Kühlmann, and G. K. Stahl (eds), *Developing global business leaders: Policies, processes, and innovations* (pp. 137–56). Westport, CT: Quorum Books.

Osland, J. and Bird, A. (in press). Beyond sophisticated stereotyping: A contextual model of cultural sensemaking. *Academy of Management Executive*.

Osland, J. S., Snyder, M. M., and Hunter, L. (1998). A comparative study of managerial styles among female executives in Nicaragua and Costa Rica. *International Studies of Management and Organization*, 28(2), 54–73.

Ouchi, W. G. (1977). The relationship between organizational structure and organizational control. *Administrative Science Quarterly*, 22, 92–112.

Ouchi, W. G. (1979). A conceptual framework for the design of organizational control mechanisms. *Management Science*, 25, 833–48.

Ouchi, W. G. (1980). Markets, bureaucracies and clans. *Administrative Science Quarterly*, 25, 129–41.

Oxley, J. (1997). Appropriability hazards and governance in strategic alliance: A transaction cost approach. *Journal of Law, Economics and Organization*, 13, 387–409.

Oyserman, D., Sakamoto, I., and Lauffer, A. (1998). Cultural accommodation: Hybridity and the framing of social obligation. *Journal of Personality and Social Psychology*, 74, 1606–18.

Ozawa, K., Crosby, M., and Crosby, F. (1996). Individualism and resistance to affirmative action:

A comparison of Japanese and American samples. *Journal of Applied Social Psychology*, 26, 1138–52.

Palmer, D., Jennings, P., and Zhou, X. (1993). Late adoption of multidivisional form by large U.S. corporations: Institutional, political, and economic accounts. *Administrative Science Quarterly*, 38, 100–31.

Park, S. H. and Russo, M. V. (1996). When competition eclipses co-operation: An event history analysis of joint venture failure. *Management Science*, 42(6), 875–90.

Park, S. H. and Ungson, G. R. (1997). The effect of national culture, organisational complementarity, and economic motivation on joint venture dissolution. *Academy of Management Journal*, 40(2), 279–307.

Parker, B. and McEvoy, G. M. (1993). Initial examination of a model of intercultural adjustment. *International Journal of Intercultural Relations*, 17: 355–79.

Parkhe, A. (1992). Interfirm strategic alliances: Empirical test of a game-theoretic model. Ph.D. dissertation, Temple University.

Parkhe, A. (1993). Interfirm diversity, organizational learning and longevity in global strategic alliances. *Journal of International Business Studies*, 22, 579–601.

Parks, C. D. and Vu, A. D. (1994). Social dilemma behavior of individuals from highly individualist and collectivist cultures. *Journal of Conflict Resolution*, 38(4), 708–18.

Parsons, T. (1951). *The social system*. New York: Free Press.

Paulus, P. B. (1984). *Basic group processes*. New York: Springer-Verlag.

Pavan, R. J. (1972). The strategy and structure of Italian enterprise. Doctoral dissertation, Harvard Graduate School of Business.

Pearson, V. M. S. and Stephan, W. G. (1998). Preferences for styles of negotiation: A comparison of Brazil and the U.S. Training Section. *International Journal of Intercultural Relations*, 22(1), 67–83.

Pedersen, P. (1995). *The five stages of culture shock*. Westport, CT: Greenwood Press.

Pelled, L. H. (1996). Demographic diversity, conflict, and work group outcomes: An intervening process theory. *Organization Science*, 7, 615–31.

Pelled, L. H., Eisenhardt, K. M., and Xin, K. R. (1999). Exploring the black box: An analysis of work group diversity, conflict, and performance. *Administrative Science Quarterly*, 44, 1–28.

Pelled, L. H. and Xin, K. R. (1997). Birds of a feather: Leader–member demographic similarity and organizational attachment in Mexico. *Leadership Quarterly*, 8, 433–50.

Pellico, M. T. and Stroh, L. K. (1997). Spousal assistance programs: An integral component of the international assignment. In Z. Aycan (ed.), *Expatriate management: Theory and research*, Vol. 4 (pp. 227–44). London: JAI Press.

Peltonen, T. and Neovvius, M. (1998). Repatriation and career systems: Finnish public and private sector repatriates in their career lines. In Brewster and Harris (eds), *International HRM: Contemporary issues in Europe*. London: Routledge.

Peng, M. W. (1997). Firm growth in transitional economies: Three longitudinal cases from China, 1989–96. *Organization Studies*, 18(3), 385–413.

Peng, M. W. (2000). *Business strategies in transition economies*. Thousand Oaks, CA: Sage.

Peng, M. W. (2001). How do new entrepreneurs create wealth in transition economies? *Academy of Management Executive* (in press).

Peng, M. W., Buck, T., and Filatotchev, I. (1999). Post-privatization restructuring and firm performance: Theory and evidence from Russia. Paper presented at the annual meeting of the Academy of Management, Chicago, August.

Peng, M. W. and Heath, P. (1996). The growth of the firm in planned economies in transition: Institutions, organizations, and strategic choice. *Academy of Management Review*, 21(2), 492–528.

Peng, M. W. and Lee, S. H. (2000). What determines the scope of the firm? Institutional insights and extensions from emerging economies. Paper presented at the Academy of International Business conference, Phoenix, AZ.

Peng, M. W. and Luo, Y. (2000). Managerial ties and firm performance in a transition economy: The nature of a micro–macro link. *Academy of Management Journal*, 43(3), 486–501.

Peng, M. W., Luo, Y., and Sun, L. (1999). Firm growth via mergers and acquisitions in China. In L. Kelley and Y. Luo (eds), *China 2000: Emerging business issues* (pp. 73–100). Thousand Oaks, CA: Sage.

Peng, T. K. and Peterson, M. F. (1998). Contingent and noncontingent social rewards and punishments from leaders: Do U.S. and Japanese subordinates make comparable distinctions? *International Business Review*, 7, 69–87.

Pennings, J. M. (1993). Executive reward systems: A cross-national comparison. *Journal of Management Studies*, 30(2), 261–80.

Penrose, E. T. (1959). *The theory of growth of the firm*. London: Basil Blackwell.

Pepitone, A. and Triandis, H. C. (1987). On the universality of social psychological theories. *Journal of Cross-Cultural Psychology*, 18, 471–98.

Perlmutter, H. (1969). The tortuous evolution of the multinational corporation. *Columbia Journal of World Business*, 1, 9–18.

Perrow, C. (1986). *Complex organizations. A critical essay*, 3rd edn. Glenway, IL: Scott, Foresman and Co.

Pervin, L. A. (1989). Persons, situations, interactions: The history of a controversy and a discussion of theoretical models. *Academy of Management Review*, 14(3), 350–60.

Peteraf, M. A. (1993). The cornerstones of competitive advantage. A resource-based view. *Strategic Management Journal*, 14, 179–91.

Peters, N. B. (1997). Patterns of acculturative stress and acculturation attitudes among South African Indians. *OnLine Journal of Psychology*, 2, 80–99.

Peterson, M. F. (1988). The Japanese PM theory of leadership: What's in it for the US? *Organizational Dynamics*, 16, 22–38.

Peterson, M. F. (1998). Embedded organizational events: Units of process in organizational science. *Organization Science*, 9, 16–33.

Peterson, M. F., Brannen, M. Y., and Smith, P. B. (1994). Japanese and U.S. leadership: Issues in current research. In S. B. Prasad (ed.), *Advances in international and comparative management*, Vol. 9 (pp. 57–82). Greenwich, CT: JAI.

Peterson, M. F., Elliott, J. R., Bliese, P. D., and Radford, M. H. B. (1996). Profile analysis of sources of meaning reported by U.S. and Japanese local government managers. In P. Bamberger, M. Erez, and S. Bacharach (eds), *Research in the sociology of organizations* (pp. 91–147). Greenwich, CT: JAI.

Peterson, M. F. and Hunt, J. G. (1997). International perspectives on international leadership. *Leadership Quarterly*, 8, 203–32.

Peterson, M. F., Maiya, K., and Herreid, C. (1994). Adapting Japanese PM leadership field research for use in Western organisations. *Applied Psychology: An International Review*, 43, 49–74.

Peterson, M. F., Peng, T. K., and Smith, P. B. (1999). Using expatriate supervisors to promote cross-border management practice transfer: The experience of a Japanese electronics company. In J. Liker, M. Fruin, and P. Adler (eds), *Remade in America: Transplanting and transforming Japanese production systems* (pp. 294–327). New York: Oxford University Press.

Peterson, M. F., Radford, M. H. B., Savage, G., and Hama, Y. (1994). Event management and evaluated department performance in U.S. and Japanese local governments. In A.-M. Bouvy, F. van de Vijver, P. Boski, and P. Schmitz (eds), *Journeys in cross-cultural psychology* (pp. 374–85). Amsterdam: Swets and Zeitlinger.

Peterson, M. F. and Smith, P. B. (2000). Meanings, organization and culture: Using sources of meaning to make sense of organizational events. In N. Ashkanasy, C. Wilderom, and M. F. Peterson (eds), *Handbook of organization culture* (pp. 101–16). Thousand Oaks, CA: Sage.

Peterson, M. F., Smith, P. B., and Tayeb, M. H. (1993). Development and use of English versions of Japanese PM leadership measures in electronics plants. *Journal of Organizational Behavior*, 14, 251–67.

Peterson, R. B. and Schwind, H. F. (1975). Personnel problems in international companies and joint ventures in Japan. *Academy of Management Proceedings*, 35, 282–4.

Pfeffer, J. (1983). Organizational demography. In L. L. Cummigns and B. M. Staw (eds), *Research in Organization Behavior*. Vol. 5 (pp. 299–357). Greenwich, CT: JAI Press.

Pfeffer, J. and Salancik, G. R. (1978). *The external control of organizations: A resource dependence perspective*. New York: Harper and Row.

Phalet, K. and Hagendoorn, L. (1996). Personality adjustment to acculturative transitions: The Turkish experience. *International Journal of Psychology*, 31, 131–44.

Pickard, J. and Brewster, C. (1995). Repatriation: Closing the circle. *International HR Journal*, 4(2), 45–9.

Pinder, C. C. and Das, H. (1979). Hidden costs and benefits of employee transfers. *Human Resource Planning*, 2, 135–45.

Pinkley, R. L. (1990). Dimensions of conflict frame: Disputants' interpretations of conflict. *Journal of Applied Psychology*, 75, 117–26.

Piore, M. and Sabel, C. (1984). *The second industrial divide: Possibilities for prosperity*. New York: Basic Books.

Podsiadlowski, A. and Spiess, E. (1996). Zur Evaluation eines interkulturellen trainings in einem deutschen grossunternehmen. *Zeitschrift für Personalforschung*, 10, 48–66.

Polanyi, M. (1962). *Personal knowledge: Towards a post-critical philosophy*. Chicago, IL: University of Chicago Press

Polyani, M. (1966). *The tacit dimension*. New York: Anchor Day Books.

Porter, G. (1997). Trust in teams: Member perceptions and the added concern of cross-cultural interpretations. In M. M. Beyerlien, D. A. Johnson, and S. T. Beyerlien (eds), *Advances in interdisciplinary studies of work teams*, Vol. 4 (pp. 45–77). Greenwich, CT: JAI Press.

Porter, L. W. and Lawler, E. E. (1968). *Managerial attitudes and performance*. Homewood, IL: Irwin.

Porter, M. E. (1980). *Competitive strategy: Techniques for analyzing industries and competitors*. New York: Free Press.

Porter, M. E. (1986). *Competition in global industries*. Boston: Harvard Business School Press.

Porter, M. E. (1990a). The competitive advantage of nations. *Harvard Business Review*, March–April, 73–93.

Porter, M. E. (1990b). *The competitive advantage of nations*. New York: Free Press.

Porter, M. E. and Fuller, M. B. (1986). Coalitions and global strategy. In M. E. Porter (ed.), *Competition in global industries* (pp. 315–44). Boston, MA: Harvard Business School Press.

Powell, G. (ed.) (1999). *Handbook of gender in organizations*. Thousand Oaks, CA: Sage.

Powell, W. (1996). Commentary on the nature of institutional embeddedness. *Advances in Strategic Management*, 13, 293–300.

Powell, W. and Brantley, P. (1992). Competitive co-operation in biotechnology: Learning through networks? In N. Nohria and R. Eccles (eds), *Networks and organizations* (pp. 366–94). Boston: Harvard Business School Press.

Powell, W., Koput, K., and Smith-Doerr, L. (1996). Interorganizational collaboration and the locus of innovation: Networks of learning in biotechnology. *Administrative Science Quarterly*, 41, 116–45.

Powell, W. and Smith-Doerr, L. (1994). Networks and economic life. In N. Smelser and R. Swedberg (eds), *Handbook of economic sociology* (pp. 368–402). Princeton, NJ: Princeton University Press.

Prahalad, C. K. and Bettis, R. A. (1986). The dominant logic: A new linkage between diversity and performance. *Strategic Management Journal*, 7, 485–502.

Prahalad, C. K. and Doz, Y. (1987). *The multinational mission: Balancing global demands and global vision*. New York: Free Press.

Prebe, J. F. and Reichel, A. (1988). Attitudes towards business ethics of future managers in the U.S. and Israel. *Journal of Business Ethics*, 7(12), 941–9.

Price Waterhouse (1997). *International assignments: European policy and practice.*

Provan, K. G. and Skinner, S. J. (1989). Interorganizational dependence and control as predictors of opportunism in dealer–supplier relations. *Academy of Management Journal*, 32(1), 202–12.

Pruitt, D. G. (1981). *Negotiation behavior.* New York: Academy Press.

Pruitt, D. G. (1986). Achieving integrative agreements in negotiation. In R. White (ed.), *Psychology and the prevention of nuclear war* (pp. 35–50). New York: New York University Press.

Pruitt, D. G. and Carnevale, P. J. (1993). *Negotiation in social conflict.* Buckingham: Open University Press.

Pruitt, D. G. and Rubin, J. Z. (1986). *Social conflict: Escalation, stalemate, and settlement.* New York: McGraw-Hill.

Prussia, G. E. and Kinicki, A. J. (1996). A motivational investigation of group effectiveness using social-cognitive theory. *Journal of Applied Psychology*, 81, 187–98.

Pruzan, P. (1998). Theory and practice of business ethics in Denmark. In L. Zsolnai (ed.), *The European difference: Business ethics in the community of European management schools* (pp. 1–15). Boston, MA: Kluwer Academic Publishers.

Pucik, V. (1984). White collar human resource management in large Japanese manufacturing firms. *Human Resource Management*, 23, 257–76.

Pucik, V. (1992). Globalization and human resource management. In V. Pucik, N. Tichy, and C Barnett (eds), *Globalizing management.* New York: John Wiley and Sons.

Puffer, S. (1994). Understanding the bear: A portrait of Russian business leaders. *Academy of Management Executive*, 8, 41–54.

Punnett, B. J. and Ricks, D. A. (1992). *International business.* Boston: PWS-Kent Publishing Co.

Punnett, B. J. and Shenkar, O. (eds) (1996). *Handbook for international management research.* London: Blackwell.

Pusch, M. D. (1994). Cross-cultural training. In G. Althen (ed.), *Learning across cultures* (pp. 109–43). NAFSA.

Putnam, L. L. and Poole, M. (1987). Conflict and negotiation. In F. Jablin, L. Putnam, K. Roberts, and L. Porter (eds), *Handbook of organizational communication: An interdisciplinary perspective* (pp. 549–99). Newbury Park, CA: Sage.

Pye, L. (1982). *Chinese commercial negotiating style.* Cambridge, MA: Oelgeschlager, Gunn, and Hain.

Pyke, F., Becattini, G., and Sengenberger, W. (1990). *Industrial divide and inter-firm co-operation in Italy.* Geneva: International Institute of Labor Studies.

Quinn, R. E. (1988). *Beyond rational management: Mastering the paradoxes and competing demands of high performance.* San Francisco: Jossey-Bass.

Radford, M. H. B., Mann, L., Ohta, Y., and Nakane, Y. (1991). Differences between Australian and Japanese students' reported use of decision processes. *International Journal of Psychology*, 26, 35–52.

Radhakrishnan, P. and Chan, D. K. S. (1997). Cultural differences in the relation between self-discrepancy and life satisfaction. *International Journal of Psychology*, 32(6), 387–98.

Rafii, F. (1978). Joint ventures and transfer of technology to Iran: The impact of foreign control. DBA dissertation, Harvard University.

Ragins, B. R., Townsend, B., and Mattis, M. (1998). Gender gap in the executive suite: CEOs and female executives report on breaking the glass ceiling. *Academy of Management Executive*, 12(1), 28–42.

Rahim, A. (1983). A model for developing key expatriate executives. *Personnel Journal*, 62, 312–17.

Raiffa, H. (1982). *The art and science of negotiation.* Cambridge, MA: Belknap.

Ralston, D. A., Gustafson, D., Cheung, F., and Terpstra, R. (1992). Eastern values: A comparison of U.S., Hong Kong, and PRC managers. *Journal of Applied Psychology*, 77, 664–71.

Ralston, D. A., Gustafson, D. J., Cheung, F. M., and Terpstra, R. H. (1993). Differences in managerial values: A study of U.S., Hong Kong, and PRC managers. *Journal of International Business Studies*, 249–75.

Ralston, D. A., Holt, D., Terpstra, R., and Yu, K. C. (1997). The impact of national culture and economic ideology on managerial work values: A study of the United States, Russia, Japan, and China. *Journal of International Business Studies*, 28, 177–207.

Ramamoorthy, N. and Carroll, S. J. (1998). Individualism/collectivism orientations and reactions toward alternative human resource management practices. *Human Relations*, 51(5), 571–88.

Rao, A. and Hashimoto, K. (1996). Intercultural influence: A study of Japanese expatriate managers in Canada. *Journal of International Business Studies*, 27, 443–66.

Rao, A., Hashimoto, K., and Rao, A. (1997). Universal and culture-specific aspects of managerial influence: A study of Japanese managers. *Leadership Quarterly*, 8, 295–312.

Rao, H. (1994). The social construction of reputation: Certification contests, legitimization, and the survival of organizations in the American automobile industry: 1895–1912. *Strategic Management Journal*, 15(1), 29–44.

Ratiu, I. (1983). Thinking internationally: A comparison of how international executives learn. *International Studies of Management and Organization*, 13, 139–50.

Ravlin, E. C., Thomas, D. C., and Ilsev, A. (in press). Beliefs about values, status, and legitimacy in multicultural groups: Influences on intra-group conflict. In P. C. Earley and H. Singh (eds), *Innovations in international and cross-cultural management*. Thousand Oaks, CA: Sage Publications.

Read, R. (1993). Politics and policies of national economic growth. Unpublished dissertation, Stanford University, Stanford, CA.

Realo, A., Allik, J., and Vadi, M. (1997). The hierarchical structure of collectivism. *Journal of Research on Personality*, 31, 93–116.

Redding, S. G. (1990). *The spirit of Chinese capitalism*. New York: de Gruyter.

Reddy, M. J. (1993). The conduit metaphor: A case of frame conflict in our language about language. In A. Ortony (ed.), *Metaphor and thought*, 2nd edn (pp. 164–201). Cambridge: Cambridge University Press.

Reddy, R. and Gibbons, J. L. (1995) Socio-economic contexts and adolescent identity development in India. Paper presented at the meetings of the Society for Cross-Cultural Research, February.

Reed, R. and DeFilippi, R. (1990). Causal ambiguity, barriers to imitation, and sustainable competitive advantage. *Academy of Management Review*, 15, 88–102.

Reitz, H. J. (1975). The relative importance of five categories of needs among industrial workers in eight countries. *Academy of Management Proceedings*, 270–73.

Reitz, H. J. and Jewell, L. N. (1979). Sex, locus of control, and job involvement: A six-country investigation. *Academy of Management Journal*, 22, 72–80.

Reykowski, J. (1994). Collectivism and individualism as dimensions of social change. In U. Kim, H. C. Triandis, C. Kagitcibasi, S.-C. Choi, and G. Yoon (eds), *Individualism and collectivism: Theory, method, and applications* (pp. 276–92). Newbury Park: CA: Sage.

Reynolds, C. (1986). Compensation of overseas personnel. In J. J. Famularo (ed.), *Handbook of human resources administration*. New York: McGraw-Hill.

Rhee, E., Uleman, J. S., and Lee, H. K. (1996). Variations in collectivism and individualism by in-group and culture: Confirmatory factor analyses. *Journal of Personality and Social Psychology*, 71, 1037–54.

Roberts, K. R. and Boyacigiller, N. A. (1984). Cross-national organizational research: The grasp of the blind men. In B. Staw and L. Cummings (eds), *Research in organizational behavior* (pp. 423–75). Greenwich, CT: JAI Press.

Robertson, D. C. and Schlegelmilch, B. B. (1993). Corporate institutionalization of ethics in the United States and Great Britain. *Journal of Business Ethics*, 12(4), 301–12.

Robinson, S. L. (1996). Trust and breach of the psychological contract. *Administrative Science Quarterly*, 41(4), 574–99.

Roesch, S. C., Carlo, G., Knight, G. P., Koller, S. H., and Dos Santos, R. P. (submitted). Between- or within-culture variation? Nationality as a moderator of the relations between individual differences and resource allocation preferences.

Roethlisberger, F. and Dickson, W. J. (1967, 1939). *Management and the worker*. Boston: Harvard University Press.

Rohner, R. (1987). Culture theory. *Journal of Cross-Cultural Psychology*, 18, 8–51.

Rokeach, M. (1973). *The nature of human values*. New York: Free Press.

Rona-Tas, A. (1994). The first shall be last? Entrepreneurship and communist cadres in the transition from socialism. *American Journal of Sociology*, 100, 40–69.

Ronen, S. (1986). *Comparative and multinational management*. New York: John Wiley and Sons.

Ronen, S. (1989). Training the international assignee. In I. L. Goldstein (ed.), *Training and development in organizations* (pp. 417–53). San Francisco: Jossey-Bass.

Ronen, S. and Shenkar, O. (1985). Clustering countries on attitudinal dimensions: A review and synthesis. *Academy of Management Review*, 3, 435–54.

Rosener, J. (1990). Ways women lead. *Harvard Business Review*, 68(6), 119–25.

Roskies, E., Iida-Miranda, M. L., and Stroebel, M. G. (1977). Life changes as predictors of illness in immigrants. In C. D. Spielberger and I. G. Saranson (eds), *Stress and anxiety*, Vol. 4 (pp. 3–21). New York: Wiley.

Ross, W. and LaCroix, J. (1996). Multiple meanings of trust in negotiation theory and research: A literature review and integrative model. *International Journal of Conflict Management*, 7(4), 314–60.

Rossouw, Gedeon J. (1994). Business ethics in developing countries. *Business Ethics Quarterly*, 4(1), 43–51.

Rotter, J. B. (1967). A new scale for the measurement of interpersonal trust. *Journal of Personality*, 35(4), 651–65.

Rotter, J. B. (1980). Interpersonal trust, trustworthiness, and gullibility. *American Psychologist*, 35(1), 443–52.

Rousseau, D. M., Sitkin, S. B., Burt, R. S., and Camerer, C. (1998). Not so different after all: A cross-discipline view of trust. *Academy of Management Review*, 23(3), 393–404.

Rozenzweig, P. M. and Nohria, N. (1994). Influence on human resource management practices in multinational corporations. *Journal of International Business Studies*, 25(2), 229–52.

Ruben, B. D. and Kealey, D. (1979). Behavioral assessment of communication competency and the prediction of cross-cultural adaptation. *International Journal of Intercultural Relations*, 3, 15–47.

Rubin, J. Z. and Brown, B. R. (1975). *The social psychology of bargaining and negotiation*. New York: Academic Press.

Rumelt, R. P. (1974). *Strategy, structure, and economic performance*. Boston: Division of Research, Graduate School of Business Administration, Harvard University.

Rumelt, R. P., Schendel, D., and Teece, D. (eds) (1994). *Fundamental issues in strategy: A research agenda*. Boston: Harvard Business School Press.

Runyon, K. E. (1973). Some interactions between personality variables and management styles. *Journal of Applied Psychology*, 57, 288–94.

Sagie, A. (1997). Leader direction and employee participation in decision-making: Contradictory or compatible practices? *Applied Psychology: An International Review*, 46, 387–415.

Sagie, A., Elizur, D., and Yamauchi, H. (1996). The structure and strength of achievement motivation: A cross-cultural comparison. *Journal of Organizational Behavior*, 17, 431–44.

Salacuse, J. W. (1991). *Making global deals: Negotiating in the international marketplace*. Boston: Houghton Mifflin.

Salili, F. (1979). Determinants of achievement motivation for women in developing countries. *Journal of Vocational Behavior*, 14, 297–305.

Salili, F. and Hau, K.-T. (1994). The effect of teachers' evaluative feedback on Chinese students' perception of ability: A cultural and situational analysis. *Educational Studies*, 20(2), 223–36.

Salili, F., Hwang, C.-E., and Choi, N. F. (1989). Teachers' evaluative behavior: The relationship between teachers' comments and perceived ability in Hong Kong. *Journal of Cross-Cultural Psychology*, 20(2), 115–32.

Salk, J. (1992). Shared management joint ventures: Their development patterns, challenges and possibilities. Unpublished doctoral dissertation, Sloan School of Management, MIT, Cambridge, MA.

Samovar, L. A. and Porter, R. E. (eds) (1991). *Intercultural communication: A reader*, 6th edn. Belmont: Wadsworth.

Sanger, D. E. (1993). Performance related pay in Japan. *International Herald Tribune*, October 5, p. 20.

Sarkar, M., Cavusgil, S. T., and Evirgen, C. (1997). A commitment–trust mediated framework of international collaborative venture performance. In P. W. Beamish and J. P. Killing (eds), *Cooperative strategies: North American perspectives* (pp. 255–85). San Francisco: New Lexington Press.

Sastry, J. and Ross, C. E. (1998). Asian ethnicity and the sense of personal control. *Social Psychology Quarterly*, 61, 101–20.

Saxenian, A. (1994). *Regional advantage*. Cambridge, MA: Harvard University Press.

Saywell, T. (1999). Motive power: China's state firms bank on incentives to keep bosses operating at their peak. *Far Eastern Economic Review*, July 8, 67–8.

Schaan, J.-L. (1983). Parent control and joint venture success: The case of Mexico. Ph.D. dissertation, University of Western Ontario.

Schecter, J. L. (1998). *Russian negotiating behavior: Continuity and transition*. Washington DC: US Institute of Peace Press.

Schein, V. (1975). The relationship between sex role stereotypes and requisite management characteristics. *Journal of Applied Psychology*, 60(3), 340–4.

Schein, V., Muller, R., and Jacobson, C. (1989). The relationship between structured and requisite management characteristics among college students. *Sex-Roles*, 20(1–2), 103–10.

Scherm, E. (1995). *Internationales Personalmanagement*. Munich; Vienna.

Schlegelmilch, B. B., and Robertson, D. C. (1995). The influence of country and industry on ethical perceptions of senior executives in the U.S. and Europe. *Journal of International Business Studies*, 26(4), 859–81.

Schmitt, J. (1999). Nike's image problem: After global outcry, company makes some strides to improve. *USA Today*, October 4, p. 1B.

Schneider, S. C. (1988). National vs. corporate culture: Implications for human resource management. *Human Resource Management*, 27, 231–46.

Schneider, S. C. and Barsoux, J. L. (1997). *Managing across cultures*. London: Prentice-Hall.

Schneider, S. C., Wittenberg-Cox, A., and Hansen, L. (1991). *Honeywell Europe*, INSEAD.

Schollhammer, H. (1975). Current research in international and comparative management issues. *Management International Review*, 15(2–3), 29–40.

Schön, D. A. (1993). Generative metaphor: A perspective on problem-setting in social policy. In *Metaphor and thought*, 2nd edn (pp. 137–63). Cambridge: Cambridge University Press.

Schröder, A. (1995). Die Betreuung von Mitarbeitern während des Auslandseinsatzes: Wissenschaftliche Grundlagen. In T. M. Kühlmann (ed.), *Mitarbeiterentsendung ins Ausland: Auswahl Vorbereitung und Wiedereingliederung* (pp. 144–60). Göttingen: Verlag für Angewandte Psychologie.

Schuler, R. S., Dowling, P. J., and De Cieri, H. (1993). An integrative framework of strategic international human resource management. *International Journal of Human Resource Management*, 4(4), 717–64.

Schwartz, S. H. (1990). Individualism–collectivism: Critique and proposed refinements. *Journal of Cross-Cultural Psychology*, 21, 139–57.

Schwartz, S. H. (1992). Universals in the content and structure of values: Theoretical advances and empirical tests in 20 countries. In M. Zanna (ed.), *Advances in experimental social psychology*, Vol. 25 (pp. 1–66). New York: Academic Press.

Schwartz, S. H. (1994). Beyond individualism and collectivism: New cultural dimensions of values. In U. Kim, H. C. Triandis, C. Kagitcibasi, S.-C. Choi, and G. Yoon (eds), *Individualism and collectivism: Theory, method, and applications* (pp. 85–122). Newbury Park, CA: Sage.

Schwartz, S. H. and Bardi, A. (submitted). Value hierarchies across cultures: Taking a similarities perspective.

Schwartz, T., White, G. M., and Lutz, C. (eds) (1992). *New directions in psychological anthropology*. New York: Cambridge University Press.

Scott, W. R. (1987). The adolescence of institutional theory. *Administrative Science Quarterly*, 32, 493–511.

Scott, W. R. (1995). *Institutions and organizations*. Thousand Oaks, CA: Sage.

Scullion, H. (1994): Staffing policies and strategic control in British multinationals. *International Studies of Management and Organization*, 24(3), 86–104.

Scullion, H. and Brewster, C. (1997). A review and agenda for expatriate HRM. *Human Resource Management Journal*, 7(3), 32–41.

Seagrave, S. (1995). *Lords of the rim*. London: Bantam.

Searle, J. R. (1995). *The social construction of social reality*. New York: Free Press.

Sedaitis, J. (1998). The alliances of spin-offs versus start-ups: Social ties in the genesis of post-Soviet alliances. *Organization Science*, 9, 368–87.

Seelye, H. N. (1988). *Teaching culture: Strategies for intercultural communication*. Lincolnwood: NTC.

Seelye, H. N. and Wasilewski, J. (1979). Toward a taxonomy of coping strategies used in multicultural settings. Paper presented at the Meeting of the Society for Intercultural Education, Training, and Research, March, Mexico City.

Seidler, V. J. (1994). *Unreasonable men: Masculinity and social theory*. London: Routledge.

Selmer, J. (1997). *Vikings and dragons: Swedish management in Southeast Asia*. Kowloon, Hong Kong: David C. Lam Institute for East–West Studies, Hong Kong Baptist University.

Selmer, J. (in press). The Chinese connection? Adjustment of western vs. ethnic Chinese expatriate managers in China. *Journal of Business Research*.

Selmer, J. and Shiu, L. S. C. (1999). Coming home? Adjustment of Hong Kong Chinese expatriate business managers assigned to the People's Republic of China. *International Journal of Intercultural Relations*, 23(3), 447–66.

Selznick, P. (1996). Institutionalism "old" and "new." *Administrative Science Quarterly*, 41, 270–7.

Shaffer, M. A. and Harrison, D. A. (1998). Expatriates' psychological withdrawal from international assignments: Work, nonwork, and family influences. *Personnel Psychology*, 51, 87–118.

Shamir, B. (1990). Calculations, values, and identities: The sources of collectivistic work motivation. *Human Relations*, 43, 313–32.

Shamir, B., Arthur, M. B., and House, R. J. (1994). The rhetoric of charismatic leadership: A theoretical extension, a case study and implications for research. *Leadership Quarterly*, 5, 25–42.

Shane, S. A. (1992). Why do some societies invent more than others? *Journal of Business Venturing*, 7, 29–46.

Shane, S. A. (1995). Uncertainty avoidance and the preference for innovation championing roles. *Journal of International Business Studies*, 26, 47–68.

Shaw, B. B., Deck, J. E., Ferris, G. R., and Rowland, K. M. (1990). *Research in personnel and human resource management*. Greenwich, CT; London.

Shaw, R. (1999). *Reclaiming America: Nike, clean air, and the new national activism*. Berkeley, CA: University of California Press.

The Shell Group (1997, revised from 1976). *The Shell General Business Principles*. London, England.

Shenkar, O. and Li, J. (1999). Knowledge search in international cooperative ventures. *Organization*

Science, 10, 134–43.

Shenkar, O. and Ronen, S. (1987). Structure and importance of work goals among managers in the People's Republic of China. *Academy of Management Journal*, 30, 564–76.

Shenkar, O. and von Glinow, M. A. (1994). Paradoxes of organizational theory and research: Using the case of China to illustrate national contingency. *Management Science*, 40, 56–71.

Sheppard, B. H. and Sherman, D. M. (1998). The grammars of trust: A model and general implications. *Academy of Management Review*, 23(3), 422–37.

Shetty, Y. K. (1971). International manager: A role profile. *Management International Review*, 11, 19–31.

Shin, Y. K. and Kim, H. G. (1994). Individualism and collectivism in Korean industry. In G. Yoon and S. C. Choi (eds), *Psychology of the Korean people: Collectivism and individualism* (pp. 189–208). Seoul: Dang-A.

Shleifer, A. and Vishny, R. (1994). Politicians and firms. *Quarterly Journal of Economics*, November, 995–1025.

Shweder, R. A. and LeVine, R. A. (1984). *Culture theory: Essays on mind, self and emotion*. New York: Cambridge University Press.

Sieveking, N., Anchor, K., and Marston, R. C. (1981). Selecting and preparing expatriate employees. *Personnel Journal*, 60, 197–202.

Simon, H. A. (1962). The architecture of complexity. *Proceedings of the American Philosophical Society*, 106(6), 467–83.

Simonin, B. (1999). Ambiguity and the process of knowledge transfer in strategic alliances. *Strategic Management Journal*, 20, 595–623.

Sinangil, H. K. and Ones, D. S. (1997). Empirical investigations of the host country perspective in expatriate management. In Z. Aycan (ed.), *Expatriate management: Theory and research*, Vol. 4 (pp. 173–205). Greenwich, CT: JAI Press.

Sinclair, J. (1980). Discourse in relation to language structure and semiotics. In S. Greenbaum, G. Leech, and J. Svartvik (eds), *Studies in English linguistics for Randolph Quirk* (pp. 110–24). London: Longman.

Singelis, T. M. (1994). The measurement of independent and interdependent self-construals. *Personality and Social Psychology Bulletin*, 20, 580–91.

Singelis, T. M. and Sharkey, W. F. (1995). Culture, self-construal, and embarrassability. *Journal of Cross-Cultural Psychology*, 26, 622–44.

Singelis, T. M., Triandis, H. C., Bhawuk, D. S., and Gelfand, M. (1995). Horizontal and vertical dimensions of individualism and collectivism: A theoretical and measurement refinement. *Cross-Cultural Research*, 29, 240–75.

Singh, R. (1981). Prediction of performance from motivation and ability: An appraisal of the cultural difference hypothesis. In J. Pandey (ed.), *Perspectives on experimental social psychology in India* (pp. 21–53). New Delhi: Concept.

Sinha, J. B. P. (1980). *The nurturant task leader*. New Delhi: Concept.

Sinha, J. B. P. (1994). Cultural embeddedness and the developmental role of industrial organizations in India. In H. C. Triandis, M. D. Dunette, and C. M. Hough (eds), *Handbook of industrial and organizational psychology*, 2nd edn, Vol. 4. Palo Alto, CA: Consulting Psychology Press.

Sinha, J. B. P. (1996). *The cultural context of leadership and power*. New Delhi: Sage.

Sinha, J. B. P. (1997). A cultural perspective on organizational behavior in India. In P. C. Earley and M. Erez (eds), *New perspectives on international industrial/organizational psychology* (pp. 727–64). San Francisco, CA: Lexington Press.

Sirota, D. and Greenwood, M. J. (1971). Understanding your overseas workforce. *Harvard Business Review*, 14(1), 53–60.

Sitkin, S. B. and Wiengart, L. (1995). Determinants of risky decision-making behavior: A test of the mediating role of risk perceptions and propensity. *Academy of Management Journal*, 38(6), 1573–92.

Skoyles, J. (1998) The Greek revolution. Homepage
http://www,users.globalnet.co.uk/^skoyles/index.htm

Slocum, J. W. (1971). A comparative study of the satisfaction of American and Mexican operatives. *Academy of Management Journal*, 14, 89–97.

Small, M. W. (1992). Attitudes towards business ethics held by western Australian students: A comparative study. *Journal of Business Ethics*, 11(10), 745–52.

Smith, G. (1999). Crack open Mexico's crony-packed boards. *Business Week*, March 29.

Smith, K. G., Smith, K. A, Olian, J. D., Sims, H. P., Jr, and others (1994). Top management team demography and process: The role of social integration and communication. *Administrative Science Quarterly*, 39, 412–38.

Smith, P. B. and Bond, M. H. (1994). *Social psychology across cultures*. Boston: Allyn and Bacon.

Smith, P. B., Dugan, S., and Trompenaars, F. (1996). National culture and managerial values: A dimensional analysis across 43 nations. *Journal of Cross-Cultural Psychology*, 27, 231–64.

Smith, P. B., Kruzela, P., Groblewska, B., Halasova, D., Pop, D., Czegledi, R., and Tsvetanova, S. (2000). Effective ways of handling work events in Central and Eastern Europe. *Social Science Information*.

Smith, P. B., Misumi, J., Tayeb, M. H., Peterson, M. F., and Bond, M. H. (1989). On the generality of leadership style measures across cultures. *Journal of Occupational Psychology*, 62, 97–109.

Smith, P. B. and Peterson, M. F. (1988). *Leadership, organizations and culture: An event management model*. London: Sage.

Smith, P. B., Peterson, M. F., and Misumi, J. (1994). Event management and work team effectiveness in Japan, Britain and USA. *Journal of Occupational and Organizational Psychology*, 67, 33–43.

Smith, P. B., Peterson, M. F., Misumi, J., and Bond, M. H. (1992). A cross-cultural test of Japanese PM leadership theory. *Applied Psychology: An International Review*, 41, 5–19.

Smith, P. B., Peterson, M. F., and 13 co-authors (1994). Organizational event management in 14 countries: A comparison with Hofstede's dimensions. In A.-M. Bouvy, F. van de Vijver, P. Boski, and P. Schmitz (eds), *Journeys into cross-cultural psychology* (pp. 364–73). Lisse, NL: Swets and Zeitlinger.

Smith, P. B. and Peterson, M. F. (1995). Beyond value comparisons: Sources used to give meaning to management work events in 29 countries. Paper presented at Academy of Management Meeting, Vancouver, BC, August.

Smith, P. B., Peterson, M. F., and Wang, Z. M. (1996). The manager as mediator of alternative meanings. *Journal of International Business Studies*, 27, 115–37.

Smith, P. B. and Schwartz, S. H. (1997). Values. In J. W. Berry, M. H. Segal, and C. Kagitcibasi (eds.), *Handbook of cross-cultural psychology*, Vol. 3: *Social behavior and applications* (pp. 77–118). Boston: Allyn and Bacon.

Smith, P. B., Wang, Z. M., and Leung, K. (1997). Leadership, decision-making and cultural context. Event management within Chinese joint ventures. *Leadership Quarterly*, 8, 413–31.

Smith, R. F. (1989). *Negotiating with the Soviets*. Bloomington: Indiana University Press.

Sohn, J. H. (1994). Social knowledge as a control system: A proposition and evidence from the Japanese FDI behavior. *Journal of International Business Studies*, 25(2), 295–324.

Solow, R. M. (1957). Technical change and the aggregate function. *Review of Economics and Statistics*, 39, 312–20.

Solow, R. M. (1958). Technical progress and the production function: A reply. *Review of Economics and Statistics*, 40, 411–13.

Solow, R. M. (1987). We'd better watch out. *New York Times Book Review*, July 12, p. 36.

Soulsby, A. and Clark, E. (1996). The emergence of post-communist management in the Czech Republic. *Organization Studies*, 17, 227–47.

Soutar, G. and Savery, L. (1991). Who should decide? Key areas for participation. *Leadership and*

Organizational Development Journal, 12(5), 8–11.

Spender, J. C. (1996). Making knowledge the basis of a dynamic theory of the firm. *Strategic Management Journal*, 17 (winter special issue), 45–62.

Spitzberg, B. (1989). Issues in the development of a theory of interpersonal competence in the intercultural context. *International Journal of Intercultural Relations*, 13, 241–68.

Spitzberg, B. (1991). Intercultural communication competence. In L. A. Samovar and R. E. Porter (eds), *Intercultural communication: A reader*, 6th edn (pp. 353–65). Belmont: Wadsworth.

Spradley, J. P. and Phillips, M. (1972). Culture and stress: A quantitative analysis. *American Anthropologist*, 74, 518–29.

Spreitzer, G. M., McCall, M., and Mahoney, J. D. (1997). Early identification of international executive potential. *Journal of Applied Psychology*, 82(1), 6–29.

Stahl, G. K. (1998). *Internationaler einsatz von führungskräften*. Munich: Oldenbourg.

Stahl, G. K. (1999). Deutsche führungskräfte im Auslandseinsatz: Probleme und problemlöseerfolg in Japan und den USA. *Die Betriebswirtschaft*, 59, 687–703.

Stahl, G. K. (2001). Using behavioral assessment techniques as tools for international management development: An exploratory study. In M. Mendenhall, T. Kühlmann, and G. Stahl (eds), *Developing global business leaders: Policies, processes, and innovations* (pp. 197–210). Westport, CT: Quorum Books.

Stajkovic, A. D. and Luthans, F. (1997). Business ethics across cultures: A social cognitive model. *Journal of World Business*, 32(1), 17–34.

Stark, A. (1993). What's the matter with business ethics? *Harvard Business Review*, 71(3), 38–48.

Stark, D. (1996). Recombinant property in East European capitalism. *American Journal of Sociology*, 101, 993–1027.

Staw, B. M., Bell, N. E., and Clausen, J. A. (1986). The dispositional approach to job attitudes: A lifetime longitudinal test. *Administrative Science Quarterly*, 31(1), 56–77.

Steers, R. M. (1989). The cultural imperative in HRM research. In G. R. Ferris and K. M. Rowland (eds), *Research in personnel and human resources management*, supplement 1 (pp. 23–32). Greenwich, CT: JAI Press.

Steers, R. M. (1999). *Made in Korea: Chung Ju Yung and the rise of Hyundai*. New York: Routledge.

Steers, R. M., Bischoff, S. J., and Higgins, L. H. (1992). Cross-cultural management research: The fish and the fisherman. *Journal of Management Inquiry*, 1, 321–30.

Steers, R. M., Porter, L. W., and Bigley, G. (1996). *Motivation and leadership at work*. New York: McGraw-Hill.

Steers, R., Shin, Y., and Ungson, G. (1989). *The chaebol: Korea's new industrial might*. New York: Harper Business, Ballinger Division.

Steidlmeier, P. (1997). Business ethics and politics in China. *Business Ethics Quarterly*, 7(3), 131–43.

Stening, B. W. (1979). Problems in cross-cultural contact: A literature review. *International Journal of Intercultural Relations*, 3, 269–313.

Stephan, W. G., Stephan, C. W., and de Vargas, M. C. (1996). Emotional expression in Costa Rica and United States. *Journal of Cross-Cultural Psychology*, 27, 147–60.

Stephens, D., Kedia, B., and Ezell, D. (1979). Managerial need structures in U.S. and Peruvian industries. *Management International Review*, 19, 27–39.

Stephens, G. and Black, J. S. (1991). The impact of spouse's career-orientation on managers during international transfers. *Journal of Management Studies*, 28, 417–28.

Stewart, I. (1997). Vietnam's fed-up workers striking for rights. Associated Press, *San Francisco Chronicle*, June 23, p. A10.

Steyrer, J. and Mende, M. (1994). Transformational leadership: The local market success of Austrian branch bank managers and training applications. Paper presented at International Congress of Applied Psychology, Madrid.

Stillenger, C., Epelbaum, M., Keltner, D., and Ross, L. (1990). The "reactive devaluation" barrier to conflict resolution. Unpublished manuscript, Stanford University, Palo Alto.

Stoecker, R. (1991). Evaluating and rethinking the case study. *Sociological Review*, 88–112.

Stoner, J. A., Aram, J. D., and Rubin, J. (1972). Factors associated with effective performance in overseas work assignments. *Personnel Psychology*, 25, 303–18.

Stopford, J. M. and Wells, L. T., Jr (1972). *Managing the multinational enterprise*. New York: Basic Books.

Stouffer, S. A., Suchman, E. A., DeVinney, L. C., Star, S. A., and Williams, R. M., Jr (1949). *The American soldier*, Vol. 1: *Adjustments during army life*. Princeton, NJ: Princeton University Press.

Strazar, M. D. (1981). The San Francisco peace treaty: Cross-cultural elements in the interaction between the Americans and the Japanese. In R. P. Anand (ed.), *Cultural factors in international relations* (pp. 63–76). New Delhi: Abinhav.

Stroh, L. K., Dennis, L. E., and Cramer, T. C. (1994). Predictors of expatriate adjustment. *International Journal of Organizational Analysis*, 2(2), 176–92.

Stroh, L. K., Gregersen, H. B., and Black, J. S. (1998). Closing the gap: Expectations versus reality among repatriates. *Journal of World Business*, 33, 111–24.

Stryker, S. (1980). *Symbolic interactionism: A social structural version*. Menlo Park, CA: Benjamin/Cummings.

Stryker, S. (1987). Identity theory: Developments and extensions. In K. Yardley and T. Honess (eds), *Self and identity: Psychosocial perspectives* (pp. 89–103). London: Wiley.

Stryker, S. (2000). Symbolic interaction theory. *Encyclopedia of Psychology*. Washington, DC and New York: American Psychological Association and Oxford University Press.

Stryker, S. and Serpe, R. C. (1982). Commitment, identity salience, and role behavior: Theory and research examples. In W. Ickes and E. Knowles (eds), *Personality, roles, and social behavior* (pp. 199–218). New York: Springer-Verlag.

Suh, E., Diener, E., Oishi, S., and Triandis, H. C. (1998). The shifting basis of life satisfaction judgments across cultures: Emotions versus norms. *Journal of Personality and Social Psychology*, 74, 482–93.

Sun, H. and Bond, M. H. (1999). The structure of upward and downward tactics of influence in Chinese organizations. In J. Lasry, J. Adair and K. Dion (eds), *Latest contributions to cross-cultural psychology* (pp. 286–302). Lisse, NL: Swets and Zeitlinger.

Sundaram, A. K. and Black, J. S. (1992). The environment and internal organization of multinational enterprises. *Academy of Management Review*, 17, 729–57.

Sunday Times (1993). Wages of death delight Japanese, December 11, pp. 1, 21.

Sussman, N. M. (1986). Re-entry research and training: Methods and implications. *International Journal of Intercultural Relations*, 10, 235–54.

Suutari, V. and Brewster, C. (1998). The adaptation of expatriates in Europe: Evidence from Finnish multinationals. *Personnel Review*, 27(2), 89–103.

Swaak, R. A. (1995). Expatriate failures: Too many, too much cost, too little planning. *Compensation and Benefits Review*, 27, 47–55.

Swann, W. B., Jr and Reed, S. J. (1981). Self-verification processes: How we sustain our self-conceptions. *Journal of Experimental Social Psychology*, 17, 351–72.

Swann, W. B., Jr, Stein-Seoussi, A., and Giesler, R. B. (1992). Why people self-verify. *Journal of Personality and Social Psychology*, 62(3), 392–401.

Swanson, D. L. (1999). Toward an integrative theory of business and society: A research strategy for corporate social performance. *Academy of Management Review*, 24(3), 506–21.

Szalay, L. B. (1993). *The subjective worlds of Russians and Americans: A guide for mutual understanding*. Chevy Chase, MD: Institute of Comparative Social and Cultural Studies.

Szulanski, G. (1996). Exploring internal stickiness: Impediments to the transfer of best practice within the firm. *Strategic Management Journal* (winter special issue), 17, 27–44.

Tahvanainen, M. (1998). *Expatriate performance management: The case of Nokia telecommunications*. Published dissertation. Helsinki School of Economics and Business Administration.

Tajfel, H. H. and Turner, J. C. (1979). An integrative theory of intergroup conflict. In W. G. Austin and S. Worchel (eds), *The social psychology of intergroup relations* (pp. 33–47). Monterey, CA: Brooks/Cole.

Tajfel, H. and Turner, J. C. (1986). The social identity theory of intergroup behaviour. In S. Worchel and W. G. Austin (eds), *Psychology of intergroup relations* (pp. 7–24). Chicago: Nelson-Hall.

Tajfel, H. (1982). Social psychology of intergroup relations. *Annual Review of Psychology*, 33, 1–39.

Taka, I. (1994). Business ethics: A Japanese view. *Business Ethics Quarterly*, 4(1), 53–78.

Taka, I. (1997). Moralogy as business ethics. *Journal of Business Ethics*, 16(5), 507–19.

Takeuchi, R. and Hannon, J. M. (1996). The antecedents of adjustment for Japanese expatriates in the United States. Paper presented to the annual meeting of the Academy of International Business, Banff, Canada.

Tallman, S. (1991). Strategic management models and resource-based strategies among MNEs in a host market. *Strategic Management Journal*, 12, 69–83.

Tallman, S. and Fladmoe-Lindquist, K. (1994). A resource-based model of the multinational firm. Paper presented in the Strategic Management Society Conference, Paris, France.

Tan, J. J. and Litschert, R. (1994). Environment–strategy relationship and its performance implications: An empirical study of the Chinese electronics industry. *Strategic Management Journal*, 15, 1–20.

Tan, J. J. and Peng, M. W. (1999). Culture, nation, and entrepreneurial strategic orientations: Implications for an emerging economy. Working paper. Columbus: Fisher College of Business, The Ohio State University.

Tannenbaum, A. S. (1980). Organizational psychology. In H. C. Triandis and R. W. Brislin (eds), *Handbook of cross-cultural psychology*, Vol 5 (pp. 281–334). Boston: Allyn and Bacon.

Taylor, M. S., Tracy, K. B., Renard, M. K., Harrison, J. K., and Carroll, S. J. (1995). Due process in performance appraisal: A quasi-experiment in procedural justice. *Administrative Science Quarterly*, 40, 495–523.

Taylor, S., Beechler, S., and Napier N. (1996). Toward an integrative model of strategic international human resource management. *Academy of Management Review*, 21(4), 959–65.

Taylor, T. C., Kazakov, A. Y., and Thompson, C. M. (1997). Business ethics and civil society in Russia. *International Studies of Management and Organization*, 27(1), 5–18.

Teece, D. (1992). Competition, cooperation and innovation: Organizational arrangements for regimes of rapid technological progress. *Journal of Economic Behavior and Organization*, 18(1), 1–26.

Thatcher, S. M. B., Jehn, K. A., and Chadwick, C. (1998). What makes a difference? The impact of individual demographic differences, group diversity, and conflict on individual performance. Wharton School, University of Pennsylvania, working paper.

Thelen, H. A. (1959). Work-emotionality theory of the group as organism. In S. Koch (ed.), *Psychology a study of a science: Formulations of the person and the social context*, Vol. 3 (pp. 544–611). New York: McGraw-Hill.

Thibaut, A. M., Calder, B. J., and Sternthal, B. (1981). Using information processing theory to design marketing strategies. *Journal of Marketing Research*, 18, 73–9.

Thibaut, J. W. and Kelley, H. H. (1959). *The social psychology of groups*. New York: Wiley.

Thoits, P. A. (1983). Multiple identities and psychological well-being. *American Sociological Review*, 49, 174–87.

Thoits, P. A. and Virshup, L. K. (1997). Me's and we's: Forms and functions of social identities. In R. D. Ashmore and L. Jussim, *Self and identity: Fundamental issues*, Vol. 1 (pp. 106–33). Oxford: Oxford University Press.

Thomas, A. (1994). Können interkulturelle begegnungen vorurteile verstärken? In A. Thomas (ed.), *Psychologie und multikulturelle gesellschaft: Problemanalysen und problemlösungen* (pp. 227–38). Göttingen: Verlag für Angewandte Psychologie.

Thomas, A. (1995). Die vorbereitung von mitarbeitern für den Auslandseinsatz: Wissenschaftliche grundlagen. In T. M. Kühlmann (ed.), *Mitarbeiterentsendung ins Ausland* (pp. 85–118). Göttingen: Verlag für Angewandte Psychologie.

Thomas, D. A. and Ely, R. J. (1996). Making differences matter: A new paradigm for managing diversity. *Harvard Business Review*, September–October, 79–90.

Thomas, D. C. (1998). The expatriate experience: A critical review and synthesis. In J. L. Cheng, and R. B. Peterson (eds), *Advances in international comparative management*, Vol. 12 (pp. 237–73). Greenwich, CT: JAI Press.

Thomas, L. G. and Waring, G. (1999). Competing capitalisms: Capital investment in American, German, and Japanese firms. *Strategic Management Journal*, 20, 729–48.

Thompson, J. D. (1967). *Organizations in action*. New York: McGraw-Hill.

Thompson, L. (1990). Negotiation behavior and outcomes: Empirical evidence and theoretical issues. *Psychological Bulletin*, 108(3), 515–32.

Thompson, L. and Hastie, R. (1990). Social perception in negotiation. *Organizational Behavior and Human Decision Processes*, 47, 98–123.

Thompson, L., Peterson, E., and Dray, L. (1995). Social context in negotiation: An information-processing perspective. In R. M. Kramer and D. M. Messick (eds), *Negotiation as a social process: New trends in theory and research* (pp. 5–36). Thousand Oaks, CA: Sage.

Tillman, A. U. (1990). The influence of control and conflict on performance of Japanese–Thai joint ventures. DBA dissertation, Nova University.

Ting-Toomey, S. (1988). A face–negotiation theory. In Y. Kim and W. Gudykunst (eds), *Theory in intercultural communication*. Newbury Park, CA: Sage.

Ting-Toomey, S. (1990). Toward a theory of conflict and culture. In W. Gudykunst, L. Stewart, and S. Ting-Toomey (eds), *Communication, culture, and organizational processes* (pp. 71–86). Beverly Hills, CA: Sage.

Ting-Toomey, S. and CoCroft, B. (1994). Face and facework: Theoretical and research issues. In S. Ting-Toomey (ed.), *The challenge of facework: Cross-cultural and interpersonal issues*. SUNY series in human communication processes. Albany, NY: State University of New York Press.

Tinsley, C. (1998). Models of conflict resolution in Japanese, German, and American cultures. *Journal of Applied Psychology*, 83, 316–23.

Tippit, S. (2000). *Nike posts labor data on Web*. Los Angeles, CA: Reuters English News Service, June 1.

Tjosvold, D., Hui, C., and Law, K. S. (1997). The leadership relationship in Hong Kong: Power interdependence and controversy. In K. Leung, U. Kim, S. Yamaguchi, and Y. Kashima (eds), *Progress in Asian Social Psychology*, 1, 295–310.

Tomlinson, J. W. C. (1970). *The joint venture process in international business: India and Pakistan*. Cambridge, MA: MIT Press.

Torbiörn, I. (1982). *Living abroad: Personal adjustment and personnel policy in the over-seas setting*. New York: Wiley.

Torbiörn, I. (1985). The structure of managerial roles in cross-cultural settings. *International Studies of Management and Organizations*, 15, 52–74.

Torbiörn, I. (1987). Culture barriers as a social psychological construct: An empirical validation. In Y. Y. Kim and W. B. Gudykunst (eds), *Cross-cultural adaptation: Current approaches* (pp. 168–90). Newbury Park, CA: Sage.

Tornblom, K. Y., Jonsson, D., and Foa, U. G. (1985). Nationality, resource class, and preferences among three allocation rules: Sweden vs. USA. *International Journal of Intercultural Relations*, 9, 51–77.

Toyne, B. (1989). International exchange: A foundation for theory building in international business. *Journal of International Business Studies*, 20(2), 1–18.

Trafimow, D. and Finlay, K. (1996). The importance of subjective norms for a minority of people:

Between-subjects and within-subjects analyses. *Personality and Social Psychology Bulletin*, 22, 820–8.

Trafimow, D., Triandis, H. C., and Goto, S. (1991). Some tests of the distinction between the private and collective self. *Journal of Personality and Social Psychology*, 60, 649–55.

Transparency International Corruption Perceptions Index (1999).

Treviño, L. K. and Bies, R. J. (1997). Through the looking glass: A normative manifesto for organizational behavior. In C. L. Cooper and S. E. Jackson (eds), *Creating tomorrow's organizations: A handbook for future research in organizational behavior* (pp. 439–52). London: John Wiley and Sons.

Treviño, L. K. and Nelson, K. A. (1995). *Managing business ethics: Straight talk about how to do it right*, 2nd edn 1999. New York: John Wiley and Sons.

Triandis, H. C. (1971). *Attitude and attitude change*. New York: Wiley.

Triandis, H. C. (1972). *The analysis of subjective culture*. New York: Wiley.

Triandis, H. C. (1975). Cultural training, cognitive complexity, and interpersonal attitudes. In R. W. Brislin, S. Bochner, and W. J. Lonner (eds), *Cross-cultural perspectives on learning* (pp. 39–78). Beverly Hills, CA: Sage.

Triandis, H. C. (1980a). *Handbook of cross-cultural psychology*. Boston: Allyn and Bacon.

Triandis, H. C. (1980b). Values, attitudes, and interpersonal behavior. In H. E. Howe and M. M. Page (eds), *Nebraska symposium on motivation, 1979* (pp. 195–260). Lincoln, Nebraska: University of Nebraska Press.

Triandis, H. C. (1988). Collectivism vs. individualism: A reconceptualization of a basic concept in cross-cultural social psychology. In G. K. Verma and C. Bagrey (eds), *Cross-cultural studies of personality, attitudes and cognition*. London: Macmillan.

Triandis, H. C. (1989). The self and social behavior in differing cultural contexts. *Psychological Review*, 98, 506–20.

Triandis, H. C. (1990a). Cross-cultural industrial and organizational psychology. In H. C. Triandis, M. D. Dunnette, and L. M. Hough (eds), *Handbook of industrial and organizational psychology*, 2nd edn, Vol. 4 (pp. 103–72). Palo Alto, CA: Consulting Psychologists.

Triandis, H. C. (1990b). Cross-cultural studies of individualism and collectivism. In J. Berman (ed.), *Nebraska symposium on motivation, 1989* (pp. 41–133). Lincoln, Nebraska: University of Nebraska Press.

Triandis, H. C. (1993). Collectivism and individualism as cultural syndromes. *Cross-Cultural Research*, 27, 155–80.

Triandis, H. C. (1994a). *Culture and social behavior*. New York: McGraw-Hill.

Triandis, H. C. (1994b). Culture: Theoretical and methodological issues. In H. C. Triandis, M. D. Dunnette, and L. Hough (eds), *Handbook of industrial and organizational psychology*, 2nd edn, Vol. 4. Palo Alto: Consulting Psychologists Press.

Triandis, H.C. (1995a). *Individualism and collectivism*. Boulder, CO: Westview.

Triandis, H. C. (1995b). Motivation and achievement in collectivist and individualist cultures. In M. L. Maehr and P. R. Pintrich (eds), *Advances in motivation and achievement: Culture, motivation, and achievement*, Vol. 9 (pp. 1–30). Greenwich, CT: JAI Press.

Triandis, H. C. (1995c). A theoretical framework for the study of diversity. In M. M. Chemers, S. Oskamp, and M. A. Costanzo (eds), *Diversity in organizations: New perspectives for a changing workplace* (pp. 11–36). Thousand Oaks: Sage.

Triandis, H. C. (1996). The psychological measurement of cultural syndromes. *American Psychologist*, 51, 407–15.

Triandis, H. C. and Bhawuk, D. P. S. (1997). Culture theory and the meaning of relatedness. In P. C. Earley and M. Erez (eds), *New perspectives on international industrial/organizational psychology* (pp. 13–52). San Francisco, CA: New Lexington Press.

Triandis, H. C., Bontempo, R., Leung, K., and Hui, H. C. (1990). A method for determining cultural, demographic, and personal constructs. *Journal of Cross-Cultural Psychology*, 21, 302–18.

Triandis, H. C., Bontempo, R., Betancourt, H., Bond, M., Leung, K., Brenes, A., Georgas, J., Hui,

C. H., Marin, G., Setiadi, B., Sinha, J. B. P., Verma, J., Spangenberg, J., Touzard, H., and de Montmollin, G. (1986). The measurement of etic aspects of individualism and collectivism across cultures. *Australian Journal of Psychology*, 38, 257–67.

Triandis, H. C., Bontempto, R., Villareal, M. J., Asai, M., and Lucca, N. (1988). Individualism and collectivism: Cross-cultural perspectives on self-in-group relationships. *Journal of Personality and Social Psychology*, 54, 323–38.

Triandis, H. C., Brislin, R., and Hui, C. H. (1988). Cross-cultural training across the individualism–collectivism divide. *International Journal of Intercultural Relations*, 12, 269–89.

Triandis, H. C., Carnevale, P., Gelfand, M., Robert, C., Wasti, A., Probst, T., Kashima, E., Dragonas, T., Chan, D., Chen, X. P., Kim, U., Kim, K., de Dreu, C., van de Vliert, E., Iwao, S., Ohbuchi, K. C.-I., and Schmitz, P. (2001). Culture, personality and deception. *International Journal of Cross-Cultural Management*, 1, in press.

Triandis, H. C., Chan, D.-K., Bhawuk, D. P. S., Iwao, S., and Sinha, J. B. P. (1995). Multimethod probes of allocentrism and idiocentrism. *International Journal of Psychology*, 30, 461–80.

Triandis, H. C., Chen, X. P., and Chan, D.-K. (1998). Scenarios for the measurement of collectivism and individualism. *Journal of Cross-Cultural Psychology*, 29, 275–89.

Triandis, H. C. and Gelfand, M. (1998). Converging measurement of horizontal and vertical individualism and collectivism. *Journal of Personality and Social Psychology*, 74, 118–28.

Triandis, H. C., Leung, K., Villareal, M., and Clack, F. L. (1985). Allocentric vs. idiocentric tendencies: Convergent and discriminant validation. *Journal of Research in Personality*, 19, 395–415.

Triandis, H. C., Marin, G., Lisansky, J., and Betancourt, H. (1984). Simpatia as a cultural script of Hispanics. *Journal of Personality and Social Psychology*, 47, 1363–74.

Triandis, H. C., McCusker, C., and Hui, C. H. (1990). Multimethod probes of individualism and collectivism. *Journal of Personality and Social Psychology*, 59(5), 1006–20.

Triandis, H. C. and Singelis, T. M. (1998). Training to recognize individual differences in collectivism and individualism within culture. *International Journal of Intercultural Relations*, 22, 35–48.

Triandis, H. C. and Vassiliou, V. A. (1972). Interpersonal influence and employee selection in two cultures. *Journal of Applied Psychology*, 56, 140–5.

Trice, H. M. and Beyer, J. M. (1993). *The cultures of work organizations*. Englewood Cliffs, NJ: Prentice-Hall.

Trilling, L. (1972). *Sincerity and authenticity*. London: Oxford University Press.

Trompenaars, F. (1994). *Riding the waves of culture: Understanding cultural diversity in business*. London: Nicholas Brealey Publishing.

Trompenaars, F. and Hampden-Turner, C. (1998). *Riding the waves of culture: Understanding diversity in global business*, 2nd edn. Chicago: Irwin.

Trubinsky, P., Ting-Toomey, S., and Lin, S. (1991). The influence of individualism–collectivism and self-monitoring on conflict styles. *International Journal of Intercultural Relations*, 15, 65–84.

Tsalikis, J. and Nwachukwu, O. (1991). A comparison of Nigerian to American views of bribery and extortion in international commerce. *Journal of Business Ethics*, 10(2), 85–98.

Tse, D., Lee, K.-H., Vertinsky, I., and Wehrung, D. (1988). Does culture matter? A cross-cultural study of executives' choice, decisiveness, and risk adjustment in international marketing. *Journal of Marketing*, 52(4), 81–95.

Tsui, A. S. (1998). The influence of relational demography and guanxi in Chinese organisations. Paper presented at the 24th International Congress of Applied Psychology, San Francisco.

Tsui, A. and Ashford, S. (1994). Adaptive self-regulation: A process view of managerial effectiveness. *Journal of Management*, 20, 93–121.

Tsui, A. S., Egan, T. D., and O'Reilly, C. A., III (1992). Being different: Relational demography and organizational commitment. *Administrative Science Quarterly*, 37, 549–79.

Tsui, A. S. and Farh, J. L. (1997). Where Guanxi matters: relational demography and Guanxi in the Chinese context. *Work and Occupations*, 24, 56–79.

Tung, R. L. (1981). Selection and training of personnel for overseas assignments. *Columbia Journal of World Business*, 16(1), 68–78.

Tung, R. L. (1982). Selection and training procedures of U.S., European and Japanese multi-nationals. *California Management Review*, 25, 57–71.

Tung, R. L. (1987). Expatriate assignments: Enhancing success and minimizing failure. *Academy of Management Executive*, 1(2), 117–25.

Tung, R. L. (1988). Career issues in international assignments. *Academy of Management Executive*, 2, 241–4.

Tung, R. L. (1991a). Handshakes across the sea: Cross-cultural negotiating for business success. *Organizational Dynamics*, 19(3), 30–40.

Tung, R. L. (1991b). Motivation in Chinese industrial enterprises. In R. M. Steers and L. W. Porter (eds), *Motivation and work behavior* (pp. 342–51). New York: McGraw-Hill.

Tung, R. (1997a). International and intranational diversity. In C. S. Granrose and S. Oskamp (eds), *Cross-cultural work groups* (pp. 163–85). Thousand Oaks, CA: Sage Publications.

Tung, R. L. (1997b). A study of the expatriation/repatriation process. In *Exploring international assignees' viewpoints* (pp. 2–12). Arthur Andersen, Inc.

Tung, R. L. (1998). American expatriates abroad: From neophytes to cosmopolitans. *Journal of World Business*, 33, 125–44.

Tung, R. L. and Arthur Andersen, Inc. (1997). *Exploring international assignees' viewpoints: A study of the expatriation/repatriation process.* Chicago, IL: Arthur Andersen Human Capital Services.

Tung, R. L. and Miller, E. L. (1990). Managing in the twenty-first century: The need for global orientation. *Management International Review*, 30, 5–18.

Turner, J. C. (1985). Social categorization and the self-concept: A social-cognitive theory of group behavior. In E. J. Lawler (ed.), *Advances in group processes: Theory and research*, Vol. 2. Greenwich, CT: JAI Press.

Turner, J. C., Hogg, M. A., Oakes, P. J., Reicher, S. D., and Wetherell, M. (1987). *Rediscovering the social group: A self-categorization theory.* Oxford: Blackwell.

Tushman, M. and Anderson, P. (1986). Technological discontinuities and organizational environments. *Administrative Science Quarterly*, 31, 439–65.

Tyler, T. R., Boeckmann, R. J., Smith, H. J., and Huo, Y. J. (1997). *Social justice in a diverse society.* Boulder, CO: Westview Press.

Tyler, T. R. and Lind, E. A. (1992). A relational model of authority in groups. In M. P. Zanna (ed.), *Advances in experimental social psychology*, Vol. 25 (pp. 115–91). San Diego, CA: Academic Press.

Ungson, G. R., Steers, R. M., and Park, S. H. (1997). *Korean enterprise: The quest for globalization.* Cambridge: Harvard Business School Press.

United Nations (1981). *Statistical yearbook: 1981.* New York: United Nations.

Universidad Francisco Marroquín (1998). *Diagnóstico de oportunidad de seminarios acerca del tema etica (Study to Explore Opportunities to Offer Seminars about Ethics)*, MBA Program (ESEADE), July.

Useem, J. (2000). There's something happening here. *Fortune*, May 15, pp. 232–44.

Van de Ven, A. H. and Walker, G. (1984). The dynamics of inter-organizational coordination. *Administrative Science Quarterly*, 29, 598–621.

Van Dyne, L., Graham, J. W., and Dienesch, R. M. (1994). Organizational citizenship behavior: Construct redefinition, measurement, and validation. *Academy of Management Journal*, 37, 765–802.

Van Luijk, H. J. L. (1990). Recent developments in European business ethics. *Journal of Business Ethics*, 9(7), 537–44.

Van Zandt, H. F. (1970). How to negotiate in Japan. *Harvard Business Review*, 45–56.

Van Zyl, E. and Lazenby, K. (1999). Ethical behaviour in the South African organizational context: Essential and workable. *Journal of Business Ethics*, 21(9), 15–22.

Vance, C. M., McClaine, S. R., Boje, D. M., and Stage, H. D. (1992). An examination of the transferability of traditional performance appraisal principles across cultural boundaries. *Management International Review*, 32(4), 313–26.

Vance, C. M. and Smith-Ring, P. (1994). Preparing the host country workforce for expatriate managers: The neglected other side of the coin. *Human Resource Development Quarterly*, 5, 337–52.

Verma, J. (1992). Allocentrism and relational orientation. In S. Iwawaki, Y. Kashima, and K. Leung (eds), *Innovations in cross-cultural psychology* (pp. 152–63). Amsterdam/Lisse, The Netherlands: Swets and Zeitlinger.

Verma, J. and Triandis, H. C. (1998). The measurement of collectivism in India. Paper presented at the meetings of the International Association of Cross-Cultural Psychology, Bellingham, WA, August.

Victor, B. and Stephens, C. U. (1994). A synthesis of normative philosophy and empirical social science. *Business Ethics Quarterly*, 4(2), 145–55.

Vijver, F. V. and Leung, K. (1997). *Methods and data analysis for cross-cultural research*. Thousand Oaks, CA: Sage.

Vitell, S. J., Nwachukwu, S. L., and Barnes, J. H. (1993). The effects of culture on ethical decision-making: An application of Hofstede's typology. *Journal of Business Ethics*, 12(10), 753–60.

Vogel, D. (1992). The globalization of business ethics: Why America remains distinctive. *California Management Review*, 35(1), 30–49.

Vogel, E. F. (1963). *Japan's new middle class*. Berkeley: University of California Press.

Volkema, R. J. (1998). A comparison of perceptions of ethical negotiation behavior in Mexico and the United States. *International Journal of Conflict Management*, 9(3), 218–33.

Von Hippel, E. (1988). *Sources of innovation*. New York: Oxford University Press.

Vroom, V. H. (1964). *Work and motivation*. New York: Wiley.

Wagner, J. A., III (1992). Individualism–collectivism and free riding: A study of main and moderator effects. Paper presented at the Las Vegas, Nevada, meetings of the Academy of Management, August.

Wagner, J. A., III (1995). Studies of individualism–collectivism: Effects on cooperation in groups. *Academy of Management Journal*, 38, 152–70.

Wagner, J. A., III, Leana, C. R., Locke, E. A., and Schweiger, D. M. (1997). Cognitive and motivational frameworks in U.S. research on participation: A meta-analysis of primary effects. *Journal of Organizational Behavior*, 18(1), 49–65.

Wagner, J. A., III and Moch, M. K. (1986). Individualism–collectivism: Concept and measurement. *Group and Organizational Studies*, 11, 280–304.

Waldinger, R., Aldrich, H., and Ward, R. (1990). *Ethnic entrepreneurs*. Thousand Oaks, CA: Sage.

Walsh, J. P. (1988). Selectivity and selective perception: An investigation of managers' beliefs structures and information processing. *Academy of Management Journal*, 31, 873–96.

Walton, S. J. (1992). Stress management training for overseas effectiveness. *International Journal of Intercultural Relations*, 16, 507–26.

Walton, R. E. and McKersie, R. (1965). *A behavioral theory of labor negotiations: An analysis of a social interaction system*. New York: McGraw-Hill.

Ward, C. (1996). Acculturation. In D. Landis and R. S. Bhagat (eds), *Handbook of intercultural training*, 2nd edn (pp. 124–47). Thousand Oaks: Sage.

Ward, C. and Chang, W. C. (1997). "Cultural fit": A new perspective on personality and sojourner adjustment. *International Journal of Intercultural Relations*, 21, 525–33.

Ward, C. and Kennedy, A. (1992). Locus of control, mood disturbance, and social difficulty during cross-cultural transitions. *International Journal of Intercultural Relations*, 16, 175–94.

Ward, C. and Kennedy, A. (1999). The measurement of sociocultural adaptation. *International Journal of Intercultural Relations*, 23(4), 659–77.

Ward, C., Okura, Y., Kennedy, A., and Kojima, T. (1998). The U-curve on trial: A longitudinal study of psychological and sociocultural adjustment during cross-cultural transition. *International Journal of Intercultural Relations*, 22(3), 277–91.

Warkentin, M. E., Sayeed, L., and Hightower, R. (1997). Virtual teams versus face-to-face teams: An exploratory study of a Web-based conference system. *Decision Sciences*, 28: 975–96.

Wasti, S. A. (1999). Organizational commitment in a collectivist culture: The case of Turkey. Unpublished Ph.D. dissertation. University of Illinois, Urbana-Champaign.

Watabe, M., Terai, S., Hayashi, N., and Yamagishi, T. (1996). Cooperation in the one-shot prisoner's dilemma based on expectations of reciprocity. *Japanese Journal of Experimental Social Psychology*, 36, 183–98.

Watson, W. E., Kumar, K., and Michaelson, L. K. (1993). Cultural diversity's impact on interaction process and performance: Comparing homogeneous and diverse task groups. *Academy of Management Journal*, 36, 590–602.

Weaver, G. R. (1986). Understanding and coping with cross-cultural adjustment stress. In R. M. Paige (ed.), *Cross-cultural orientation: New conceptualizations and applications* (pp. 111–45). Lanham: University Press of America.

Weaver, G. R. and Treviño, L. K. (1994). Normative and empirical business ethics: Separation, marriage of convenience, or marriage of necessity? *Business Ethics Quarterly*, 4(2), 129–43.

Weaver, G. R., Treviño, L. K., and Cochran, P. L. (1999). Corporate ethics programs as control systems: Influences of executive commitment and environmental factors. *Academy of Management Journal*, 42, 41–57.

Weaver, G. R., Treviño, L. K., and Cochran, P. L. (1999). Corporate ethics practices in the mid-1990's: An empirical study of the *Fortune* 1000. *Journal of Business Ethics*, 18(3, part I), 283–94.

Weber, M. (1924; 1947). *The theory of social and economic organization* (trans. T. Parsons). New York: Free Press.

Weber, M. (1958). *The Protestant ethic and the spirit of capitalism* (trans. Talcott Parsons). New York: Scribner.

Weber, W. and Festing, M. (1991). Entwicklungstendenzen im internationalen personalmanagement: Personalführung im wandel. *Gables Magazine*, 2.

Weick, K. (1979). *The social psychology of organizing*. New York: McGraw-Hill.

Weigelt, K. and Camerer, C. (1988). Reputation and corporate strategy: A review of recent theory and applications. *Strategic Management Journal*, 9(5), 443–54.

Weiner, B. (1980). *Human motivation*. New York: Holt, Rinehart and Winston.

Weiner, B. (1991). Metaphors in motivation and attribution. *American Psychologist*, 46(9), 921–30.

Weiss, H. M. and Adler, S. (1984). Personality and organizational behavior. In B. M. Staw and L. L. Cummings (eds), *Research in organizational behavior*, Vol. 6 (pp. 1–50). Greenwich, CT: JAI Press.

Weiss, S. E. (1993). Analysis of complex negotiations in international business: The RBC perspective. *Organizational Science*, 4(2), 269–300.

Weissman, D. and Furnham, A. (1987). The expectations and experiences of a sojourning temporary resident abroad: A preliminary study. *Human Relations*, 40, 313–26.

Weisz, J. R., Rothbaum, F. M., and Blackburn, T. C. (1984). Standing out and standing in: The psychology of control in America and Japan. *American Psychologist*, 39, 955–69.

Welch, D. (1994) Determinants of international human resource management approaches and activities: A suggested framework. *Journal of Management Studies*, 31, 139–63.

Weldon, E. (1984). Deindividuation, interpersonal affect, and productivity in laboratory task groups. *Journal of Applied Social Psychology*, 14, 469–85.

Weldon, E. and Jehn, K. A. (1995). Examining cross-cultural differences in conflict management behavior: A strategy for future research. *International Journal of Conflict Management*, 6, 387–403.

Wellington, S. W. (1996). *Women in corporate leadership: Progress and prospects*. New York City: Catalyst.

Welsh, D. H. B., Luthans, F., and Sommer, S. M. (1993). Managing Russian factory workers: The impact of U.S.-based behavioral and participative techniques. *Academy of Management Journal*, 36(1), 58–79.

Wernerfelt, B. (1984): A resource-based view of the firm. *Strategic Management Journal*, 5, 171–80.

West, M. W. (1959). Thinking ahead: The jointly-owned subsidiary. *Harvard Business Review*, (July–August), 31–2.

Wexley, K. N. and Klimosky, R. (1994). Performance appraisal: An update. In G. R. Ferris and K. M. Rowland (eds), *Performance evaluation, goal setting, and feedback* (pp. 1–45). Greenwich, CT: JAI Press.

Whetten, D. A. and Godfrey, P. C. (1998). *Identity in organizations: Building theory through conversations*. Thousand Oaks, CA: Sage.

White, L. P. and Rhodeback, M. J. (1992). Ethical dilemmas in organization development: A cross-cultural analysis. *Journal of Business Ethics*, 11(9), 663–70.

Whitley, R. (1992). Societies, firms and markets: The social structuring of business systems. In R. Whitley (ed.), *European business systems: Firms and markets in their national contexts*. London: Sage.

Whitley, R., Henderson, J., Czaban, L., and Lengyel, G. (1996). Trust and contractual relations in an emerging capitalist economy. *Organization Studies*, 17, 397–420.

Wilkinson, I. F. (1979). Power and satisfaction in channels of distribution. *Journal of Retailing*, 55 (summer), 79–94.

Williams, J. and Bennett, S. (1975). The definition of sex stereotypes via the adjective check list. *Sex Roles*, 1, 327–37.

Williamson, O. E. (1975). *Markets and hierarchies: Analysis and antitrust implications*. New York: Free Press.

Williamson, O. E. (1979). Transaction cost economics: The governance of contractual relations. *Journal of Law and Economics*, 22, 3–61.

Williamson, O. E. (1983). Credible commitments: Using hostages to support exchange. *American Economic Review*, 73(4), 519–40.

Williamson, O. E. (1985). *The economic institutions of capitalism: Firms, markets, relational contracting*. New York: Free Press.

Williamson, O. E. (1991). Strategizing, economizing, and economic organization. *Strategic Management Journal*, 12 (winter), 75–94.

Williamson, O. E. (1993). Calculativeness, trust, and economic organization. *Journal of Law and Economics*, 36 (April), 453–86.

Williamson, O. E. (1996). *The mechanisms of governance*. New York: Free Press.

Williamson, O. E. and Ouchi, W. G. (1981). The markets and hierarchies program of research: Origins, implications, prospects. In A. Van de Ven and W. F. Joyce (eds), *Perspectives on organizational design and behavior* (pp. 347–70). New York: Wiley and Sons.

Wilson, M. S. and Dalton, M. A. (1998). *International success: Selecting, developing, and supporting expatriate managers*. Greensboro, NC: Center for Creative Leadership.

Winch, G. and Schneider, E. (1993). Managing the knowledge-based organization: The case of architectural practice. *Journal of Management Studies*, 30(6), 923–37.

Wirth, E. (1992). *Mitarbeiter im Auslandseinsatz*. Weisbaden: Gabler.

Wiseman, R. L. and Koester, J. (eds) (1993). *Intercultural communication competence*. Newbury Park: Sage.

Wolf, J. (1999). *Strategien und strukturen Deutscher nationaler und internationaler unternehmen*. Habilitationsschrift, Universität Hohenheim.

Wolf, J. and Egelhoff, W. G. (1999). A reexamination of strategy and structure in multinational corporations. Working Paper, Universität Hohenheim.

Womack, J., Jones, D., and Roos, D. (1990). *The machine that changed the world*. New York: Rawson Associates.

Wood, J. V., Giordano-Beech, M., Taylor, K. L., Michela, J. L., and Gaus, V. (1994). Strategies of social comparison among people with low self-esteem: Self-protection and self-enhancement. *Journal of Personality and Social Psychology*, 67(4), 713–31.

Woodcock, C. P. and Geringer, J. M. (1990). Parent strategy, ownership structure, cultural congruity and joint venture performance. *Proceedings of the ASAC Conference*, Whistler, BC.

Woodell, V. (1989). Individualism and collectivism: The effect of race and family structure. Mimeo, unpublished students' paper, Detroit, MI.

World Bank (1980). *World development report*. Washington: World Bank.

World Bank (1996). *World development report*. Washington: World Bank.

World Values Study Group (1994). *World values survey, 1981–1984 and 1990–1993* (Computer file), ICPSR version. Ann Arbor: Institute for Social Research.

Wright. E. O. (1978). *Class, crisis, and the state*. London: Verso Editions/NLB.

Wright, P. and McMahan, G. (1992). Theoretical perspectives for strategic human resource management. *Journal of Management*, 18(2), 295–320.

Yamada, A. and Singelis, T. (1999). Biculturalism and self-construal. *International Journal of Intercultural Relations*, 23, 697–709.

Yamagishi, T. (1988a). Exit from the group as an individualistic solution to the public good problem in the United States and Japan. *Journal of Experimental Social Psychology*, 24, 530–71.

Yamagishi, T. (1988b). The provision of a sanctioning system in the United States and Japan. *Social Psychology Quarterly*, 51, 265–71.

Yamagishi, T., Cook, K. S., and Watabe, M. (1998). Uncertainty, trust, and commitment formation in the United States and Japan. *American Journal of Sociology*, 104 (July).

Yamigishi, T. and Yamagishi, M. (1994). Trust and commitment in the United States and Japan. *Motivation and Emotion*, 18(2), 129–66.

Yamaguchi, S. (1994). Empirical evidence on collectivism among the Japanese. In U. Kim, H. C. Triandis, C. Kagitcibasi, S.-C. Choi, and G. Yoon (eds), *Individualism and collectivism: Theory, method, and applications* (pp. 175–88). Newbury Park, CA: Sage.

Yamaguchi, S. (1998). The meaning of amal. Paper presented at the Congress of the International Association of Cross-Cultural Psychology, Bellingham, WA, August.

Yamaguchi, S., Kuhlman, D. M., and Sugimori, S. (1995). Personality correlates of allocentric tendencies in individualist and collectivist cultures. *Journal of Cross-Cultural Psychology*, 26, 658–72.

Yan, A. and Gray, B. (1994). Bargaining power, management control, and performance in U.S.–China joint ventures: A comparative case study. *Academy of Management Journal*, 37, 1478–517.

Yeager, M. A. (1999). *Women in business*, Vols 1, 2, and 3. Cheltenham: Elgar Reference Collection.

Yeh, R.-S. and Lawrence, J. J. (1995). Individualism and Confucian dynamism: A note on Hofstede's cultural root to economic growth. *Journal of International Business Studies*, 26, 655–69.

Yeung, A. and Ready, A. (1995). Developing leadership capabilities of global corporations: A comparative study in eight nations. *Human Resource Management*, 34(4), 529–47.

Yin, R. K. (1994). *Case study research: Design and methods* (rev. edn). Newbury Park, CA: Sage.

Yoshikawa, M. J. (1987). Cross-cultural adaptation and perceptual development. In Y. Y. Kim and W. B. Gudykunst (eds), *Cross-cultural adaptation: Current approaches* (pp. 140–8). Newbury Park: Sage.

Yu, A.-B. and Yang, K.-S. (1994). The nature of achievement motivation in collectivist societies. In U. Kim, H. C. Triandis, C. Kagitcibasi, S.-C. Choi, and G. Yoon (eds), *Individualism and collectivism: Theory, method, and applications* (pp. 239–50). Thousand Oaks, CA: Sage.

Yuchtman, E. (1972). Reward distribution and work-role attractiveness in the Kibbutz: Reflections on equity theory. *American Sociological Review*, 37, 581–95.

Yukl, G. A. (1994). *Leadership in organizations*, 3rd edn. Englewood Cliffs, NJ: Prentice-Hall.

Yun, C. K. (1973). Role conflicts of expatriate managers: A construct. *Management International*

Review, 13, 105–13.

Zaharna, R. S. (1989). Self-shock: The double-binding challenge of identity. *International Journal of Intercultural Relations*, 13, 501–22.

Zaheer, A., McEvily, B., and Perrone, V. (1998). Does trust matter? Exploring the effects of interorganizational and interpersonal trust on performance. *Organization Science*, 9(2), 141–59.

Zand, D. E. (1972). Trust and managerial problem solving. *Administrative Science Quarterly*, 17(2), 229–39.

Zander, A. W. and Medow, H. (1963). Individual and group aspiration. *Human Relations*, 16, 89–105.

Zander, U. and Kogut, B. (1995). Knowledge and the speed of the transfer and imitation of organizational capabilities: An empirical test. *Organization Science*, 6(1), 76–92.

Zartman, I. W. (1993). A skeptic's view. In G. O. Faure and J. Z. Rubin (eds), *Culture and Negotiation* (pp. 17–21). Newbury Park: Sage.

Zeira, Y. (1975). Overlooked personnel problems of multinational corporations. *Columbia Journal of World Business*, 10, 96–103.

Zeira, Y. and Banai, M. (1984). Present and desired methods of selecting expatriate managers for international assignments. *Personnel Review*, 13, 29–35.

Zeira, Y. and Banai, M. (1985). Selection of expatriate managers in MNCs: The host-environment point of view. *International Studies of Management and Organization*, 15, 33–51.

Zeira, Y. and Harari, E. (1979). Host-country organizations and expatriate managers in Europe. *California Management Review*, 21, 40–50.

Zeitling, L. R. (1996). How much woe when we go: A quantitative method for predicting culture shock. *International Journal of Stress Management*, 3, 85–98.

Zhang, J. (1990). Target-based interpersonal trust: A model and cross-cultural comparison. M.A. thesis, Chinese University of Hong Kong.

Zhang, J. and Bond, M. H. (1993). Target-based interpersonal trust: Cross-cultural comparison and the cognitive model. *Acta Psychologica Sinica*, 25, 164–72.

Zhang, W.-B. (1999). *Confucianism and modernization: Industrialization and democratization of the Confucian regions*. New York: St Martin's.

Zucker, L. G. (1986). Production of trust: Institutional sources of economic structure, 1840–1920. In B. M. Staw and L. L. Cummings (eds), *Research in Organizational Behavior*, 8 (pp. 53–111). Greenwich, CT: JAI Press.

Index

Printed in the United Kingdom by
Lightning Source UK Ltd., Milton Keynes
138799UK00001B/28/P